The Gordon Highlanders
1919–1945

THE LIFE OF A REGIMENT
VOLUME V

The Gordon Highlanders
in the
Second World War

Wilfrid Miles

The Naval & Military Press Ltd

Published by

The Naval & Military Press Ltd
in association with the
Gordon Highlanders Museum

Unit 5 Riverside, Brambleside,
Uckfield, East Sussex,
TN22 1QQ England

Tel: +44 (0) 1825 749494
www.naval-military-press.com
www.nmarchive.com

First published as
The Life of a Regiment, Volume V
© The Gordon Highlanders
This edition first published 2019
for the Regiment by The Naval & Military Press

Cover illustration:
Men of the 5/7th Gordon Highlanders
occupy a defensive position 17 June 1944.

In reprinting in facsimile from the original, any imperfections are inevitably reproduced and the quality may fall short of modern type and cartographic standards.

Dorothy Wilding

His Royal Highness The Duke of Gloucester, K.G., K.T., K.P.,
Colonel-in-Chief of the Regiment.

MESSAGE

from

HIS ROYAL HIGHNESS

THE DUKE OF GLOUCESTER
K.G., K.T., K.P.

Colonel-in-Chief, The Gordon Highlanders

THE EARLY DAYS of the Second World War brought widespread reverses to our Armed Forces, of which this Regiment bore a heavy share in the grievous loss of three Battalions.

I had, however, the stirring experience of seeing how the Regiment reformed and closed its ranks; how under resolute leadership the men of The Gordon Highlanders whether in the bitterly fought campaigns in AFRICA, SICILY, ITALY, BURMA and NORTH–WEST EUROPE or in the the face of disaster and unbelievable privations in captivity in MALAYA and GERMANY, served to turn defeat into victory with all the courage, endurance and stubborn spirit summed up in the single word of the Regimental Motto—

'BYDAND'

I therefore welcome the publication of this record of their achievements, the fifth volume of *The Life of a Regiment*.

Henry.

FOREWORD

by

THE EARL OF CAITHNESS
Colonel of the Regiment

THE AUTHOR'S PREFACE so ably indicates the contents of this volume of the Life of our Regiment that I would not do more than add that, covering as it does the years of the Second World War, it may well be regarded as one of the most important.

The stirring events of these and the preceding years Captain Wilfrid Miles has faithfully recorded for us, at the same time giving, wherever possible, pictured glimpses of the Regiment's domestic life. Every page bears witness to the care with which he has set about this formidable task and makes this volume a notable addition to our History.

The story shows how officers and men of The Gordon Highlanders have faced the fortunes of peace and war from 1919 to 1945.

In the fifteen years since then more history, as yet unwritten, has been made by men of the same indomitable spirit as that which shines in the pages of this book. It is to be hoped that in due course their deeds also may be as carefully chronicled as those in this fifth volume of *The Life of a Regiment*.

CAITHNESS

May 1961   Colonel, The Gordon Highlanders

CONTENTS

	PAGE
Message from H.R.H. the Duke of Gloucester, Colonel-in-Chief of The Gordon Highlanders	v
Foreword by the Earl of Caithness, Colonel of the Regiment	vi
Author's Preface	ix

BETWEEN TWO WARS
1919-39

Aftermath—Overseas Service 1920-34—The Regiment at Home 1921-34—Overseas Service 1934-39—The Regiment at Home 1935-39   3

THE SECOND WORLD WAR
1939-45

France and Belgium, 1939-40

    The Twilight War—Dyle to Dunkirk—Saar Front—Somme to St. Valery   33

Malaya and Singapore, 1939-42

    Defence Problems—Retreat in Malaya—Johore—Singapore Tragedy   87

The Regiment at Home   113

Victory in North Africa, 1942-43

    El Alamein to Enfidaville

        Egypt—El Alamein—Advance to El Agheila—Buerat—Tripoli—Tunisia Mareth—Mareth to Sfax—Enfidaville   130

    Algiers to Tunis   173

Tunisia—Pantelleria—Tunisia   182

Conquest of Sicily, 1943

    A New Venture—The Landing—Advance Inland—Vizzini: Sferro—The Route to Messina   187

CONTENTS

	PAGE
Italy 1943-45	
Farewell to Africa—Anzio—Florence and the Apennines	219
Victory in North-West Europe, 1944-45	
Preparation—The Triangle and Colombelles—Odon Battlefront—East of the Orne—South from Caumont: Estry—Pursuit to the Seine—St. Valéry: Le Havre—Into Holland—Battles of the Maas—Nijmegen Salient—Ardennes—Rhineland Battle—Passage of the Rhine—The Drive Through Germany	248
India 1942-44	
R.A.C. and Royal Artillery—Kohima and After	367
Victory in Burma 1945	
Operations on the Irrawaddy—Towards Rangoon—The Lost Batteries	379
India 1945	408
Epilogue	410
Index	411

MAPS AND SKETCHES

	PAGE
France and Belgium, 1939-40 (Dunkirk inset)	36
Saar Front, May 1940	60
South of the Somme, June 1940 (St. Valéry inset)	66
Abbeville, 4th-5th June, 1940	in text 69
Malaya	in text 88
Southern Johore, 25th-31st January, 1941	94
Singapore (with inset)	102
El Alamein, 23rd October, 1942	132
El Alamein: Highland Division, 23rd October, 1942	134
El Alamein–El Agheila	146
El Agheila–Tripoli	152
Tripoli–Gabes	160
Gabes–Enfidaville	168
Tunisia (North)	174
Tunisia, March-May 1943	176
Sicily Landings, 10th July, 1943	in text 192
Eastern Sicily, July-August 1943	196
Operations round Sferro, July-August 1943	204
Tunisia–Pantelleria–Sicily–Italy	in text 221
Anzio, January-May 1944	in text 223
Anzio Salient 3rd-4th February, 1944	in text 226
Apennines (Arrow Route), September-November 1944 (Florence inset)	238
Monte Grande	in text 244
Normandy, June-August 1944 (Cherbourg inset)	254
The Triangle and Colombelles, June-July 1944	258
Odon Battlefront, June-July 1944	268
Caumont	in text 279
Estry	in text 281
Approach to the Seine, August 1944	in text 291
Seine Crossing, 27th-28th August 1944	294
The Maas (South), September-December 1944, January 1945	308

MAPS AND SKETCHES

	PAGE
The Maas (North), October-December 1944	310
Ardennes, January 1945 (Brussels-Marche inset)	in text 322
Rhineland Battle, February 1945	326
Goch	in text 335
Schloss Calbeck	in text 341
Rhine Crossing, 23rd-30th March, 1945	344
Rees	in text 347
Germany, April-May 1945	354
Elbe Crossing, 29th-30th April, 1945	in text 356
Kohima	in text 374
Burma	380
Irrawaddy west of Mandalay	in text 382
Irrawaddy–Myingyan–Taungtha	388
Pyawbwe–Pegu	398

PLATES

H.R.H. The Duke of Gloucester, Colonel-in-Chief of the Regiment *frontispiece*

Between pages 112 *and* 113

General Wavell with men of the 2nd Gordons, Singapore

100th (Gordon Highlanders) Anti-Tank Regt. R.A. demonstrate 6-pdr. to the Colonel-in-Chief

The Prime Minister inspects the 5th/7th Gordons in Egypt

General Montgomery chats to Pipe-Major Anderson, 1st Gordons

The Battle of Sferro, from the painting by I. G. M. Eadie

6th Gordons near Marradi

General Sir Ian Hamilton celebrates his 91st birthday with officers of the Regiment

5th/7th Gordons in Kaatsheuvel

5th/7th Gordons enter Germany

Buffaloes cross the Rhine

2nd Gordons on the floodbank of the Rhine

2nd Gordons in the woods beyond the Elbe

General Sir Claude Auchinleck reviews the 116th Regt. (Gordon Highlanders) R.A.C.

A tank of the 116th Regt. comes out of action near Taungtha

AUTHOR'S PREFACE

If there are nine and sixty ways—all of them right—of constructing tribal lays then the same may well be true of regimental histories which are, indeed, tribal lays of a sort; yet some kind of pattern must be preserved. To cover in one volume more than a quarter of a century in the life of the Gordon Highlanders means to crowd infinite riches into little room, for the period embraces the Second World War. The space devoted to the years of peace, 'between the wars', is less than I would have liked it to be, but the Gordon Highlander is, first and foremost, a fighting man, and something must be sacrificed in order to see as much as possible of him in action. And even in action there are so many changes of scene, so many turns and twists of fortune, that a plain tale must suffice.

Memories grow dim, but I have made no attempt to provide an outline history of the Second World War. It seems better to look upon events from the standpoint of the particular Battalion concerned; and I can only hope that enough has been said of the issues involved in each theatre of war where Gordon Highlanders were engaged.

Twenty years of peace had brought certain changes of equipment and tactics, so that in 1939 the soldier took the field under conditions which differed from those of 1914. The Army was beginning—but only beginning—to wear a 'new look', and, owing to our unpreparedness, much tribulation ensued before we were able to face our powerful adversaries on anything like equal terms.

The potency of air power and the development of armoured forces transformed the battlefield. On the ground elaborate trench systems had had their day: mobility and increased fire power, largely controlled by radio communication, were essential to success. As always victory depended upon the proper co-ordination of all arms and services.

And as the war progressed more respect was paid to the intelligence and understanding of the fighting man. Higher commanders took pains to ensure that the soldier appreciated the nature of the operation in which he was about to engage. Junior leaders and their men had much less reason than heretofore to advance under the impression that

'We go to gain a little patch of ground,
That hath in it no profit but the name.'

The infantry battalion, more mobile and with increased fire power, demanded of all ranks a higher standard of technical accomplishment. As a member of a rifle company a Gordon Highlander's weapons were still the rifle and bayonet, the grenade and the light automatic; but he might be an anti-tank gunner or a mortar man, or, trained in observer's duties and map reading, serve in the intelligence section. If a signaller he became a radio operator. Again, he might be the expert driver of a tracked or half-tracked vehicle, for the battle transport—the trucks and jeeps and carriers which brought forward the weapons and ammunition which could not be manhandled—was an essential part of the battalion's fighting power.

A war of movement meant that the infantryman was often carried long distances on wheels or tracks. Sometimes he rode into battle on a tank. Yet he still had to be capable of long marches, and his load, even in battle order, was always considerable. Physical fitness still ranked very high among the soldierly virtues. Gas was not used by either side, but the minefield constituted a new and ever constant hazard. Digging was never 'out', for slit trenches were needed almost everywhere as a protection against air attack and concentrations of artillery and mortar fire. Thanks to the advancement of medical science the wounded were tended in ways never before possible: for instance, blood transfusions, often performed upon the very fringe of the battlefield, saved many lives. The spiritual needs of the soldier were never forgotten and increased attention was paid to his morale and well-being when he was 'out of the line'.

The conditions under which the Gordon Highlander campaigned throughout the seasons in the cultivated lands of western Europe naturally differed in many respects from the hazards and hardships he endured further from home. Like his fathers before him he was called upon to fight the King's enemies in divers strange and uncomfortable regions of the earth; and Malaya, Africa, Sicily, Italy, India and Burma each saw the methods of modern warfare adapted to a different climate and terrain.

The hundred and fiftieth anniversary of the birth of the Gordon Highlanders (the old 92nd) was marked by a message from their Colonel-in-Chief conveying the congratulations and good wishes of His Royal Highness. No formal celebration was possible on 24th June, 1944, but it was perhaps appropriate that six battalions of the Regiment were at this time engaged in a struggle against the forces of aggression, the purpose for which the Gordons had been raised in 1794.

Many Gordon Highlanders fought their war apart from the Regiment, with other units and in various appointments and commands.

Major (later Lieut.-Colonel) Ivan Lyon, who escaped from Singapore after the surrender, went to Australia, and in September 1943 he led a raid upon Japanese shipping at Singapore. The attacks were made in three canoes, each containing two men, from forward bases in the islands south of the anchorage, explosive charges being fixed secretly to many vessels. The tonnage of Japanese shipping damaged or destroyed amounted to nearly 40,000, and the whole expedition returned to Australia without mishap, having traversed 4,000 miles of enemy dominated waters. In September 1944 an attempt under the same leadership to repeat the exploit ended in disaster: the alarm was given and our men, obliged to disperse, were hunted down among the islands by the Japanese. Lieut.-Colonel Lyon and others were killed, some were captured, and the fate of the rest is uncertain. Two authors, Ronald McKie and Brian Connell, have told in detail the story of these ventures.

Lieutenant S. W. Chant, as a Commando officer, took part in the raid upon St. Nazaire in March 1942. He was in H.M. destroyer *Campbeltown* which, filled with explosive, was used to destroy the lock gates of Forme Ecluse. Chant led the demolition squad who leapt ashore and blew up the dock pumping station: he received several wounds and became a prisoner of war.

War diaries are generally regarded as dull reading, but in those of the Gordon Highlanders a sentence, or even a phrase, often reveals the temper or state of a Battalion in words which cannot be bettered. The letters to the Colonel of the Regiment from commanding officers—most battalion commanders were good correspondents—are of considerable value. Certain short battalion histories, notably *6th Gordons 1939-1945* compiled by Major J. C. Williamson, M.C., and *Gordon Highlanders in North Africa and Sicily* by Felix Barker (5th/7th Battalion), have been a great help. On some points reference has been made to the Rev. P. D. Thomson's *The Gordon Highlanders* (1933 edition) and the Regimental magazine *The Tiger and Sphinx* has been drawn upon with advantage as occasion required.

My thanks are due to the Regimental History Committee, presided over by the Colonel of the Regiment, Lord Caithness, for the facilities they have afforded me and for their guidance in various matters. Captain R. Fogg-Elliot, as secretary, responded nobly to all my demands.

Many officers of the Gordons have been good enough to supply valuable comment and criticism by drawing upon their own knowledge and experience. I am very grateful to them.

Mr. D. W. King, O.B.E., Librarian at the War Office, and his staff have lent their aid freely and cheerfully in clearing up some points.

Mrs. George Shield, a good friend of the Regiment, assumed responsibility for the Index, undertaking this important task as a labour of love.

In preparing the maps and sketches the expert assistance of Colonel T. M. M. Penney, of the Historical Section (Military Branch) at the Cabinet Office, has been invaluable. To him my humble and hearty thanks. My rough originals were copied for reproduction by Scottish Studios & Engravers Ltd., Glasgow.

No attempt has been made to summarise the distinguished services of the London Scottish and of the linked regiments in the Commonwealth. In case this should be regarded as a regrettable omission mention must be made of the work of their own accomplished historians.

The London Scottish, long associated with the Gordon Highlanders, have appeared in the Army List as a Territorial battalion of the Regiment since 1936. They are well served by their history *The London Scottish in the Second World War 1939-45* by Brigadier C. N. Barclay.

The history of the Toronto Scottish, 1939-45, is by Major D. W. Grant and published under the title *Carry On!* Also from Toronto comes '*Dileas*': *The 48th Highlanders of Canada 1929-1956* by Captain Kim Beattie. This is a continuation of his earlier work. The Capetown Highlanders (at that time the Duke of Connaught and Strathearn's Own) provided, with the First City (Grahamstown) Regiment, an amalgamated service unit whose story in the Second World War was published for the author, Major L. G. Murray M.C., by *The Cape Times Ltd*. Although the 5th Australian Battalion (Victorian Scottish) did not take the field, the 2/5th Battalion has an impressive record of service in the Middle East and in New Guinea.

W. M.

BETWEEN TWO WARS
1919-39

Aftermath

At the conclusion of the First World War when the nation began to adjust itself to peace conditions, the Army reverted to something very like its pre-war pattern. In the Gordon Highlanders, as in most British infantry regiments, the paramount purpose was to reconstitute the Regular battalions who had dwindled to cadres as demobilization proceeded. One battalion was required for service overseas. The other, at home, trained and equipped for modern war, would also be called upon to furnish the drafts needed to keep the sister battalion up to establishment.

The backwash of the war, however, made considerable demands upon our armed forces. An Army of Occupation remained in Germany. In many other regions abroad peace and order had yet to be established, and some of our troops were sent on special missions to ensure that the conditions of the Armistice and of the subsequent Peace Treaties were observed.

The 1st Gordon Highlanders were 'reconstructed' at Cromarty, where the cadre had arrived from Germany in May 1919, under the command of Lieut.-Colonel C. J. Simpson. Being ear-marked for foreign service as soon as ready, the Battalion had first call upon the Regular soldiers rejoining from hospitals, convalescent establishments, and prisoners of war camps. Numbers were made up by enlistments for two, three or four years. Demobilization freed many Regular officers who had been commanding brigades or battalions or had held staff appointments, and these returned to regimental duty in their permanent rank.

In September 1919 the Battalion strength was 700, of whom a large number were trained men well versed in the customs of the Regiment. Before the end of the month the 1st Gordons moved to Duddingston, near Edinburgh, for 'strike duty', but the feared civil disturbance came to little and at the end of October the Battalion were sent to Ireland. Here, while stationed at Athlone and Limerick, the strength increased to the unwieldy number of 1,389.

January 1920 saw a move to Catterick, and on the way came the opportunity to shake hands with the 2nd Battalion who, at that time, were at Collinstown Camp near Dublin. The two Battalions had met on previous occasions in their history: at Deolali 1898, in South Africa 1900, and in France 1917.

Less than three months later the 1st Gordons were put under orders to join the 'Army of the Black Sea'.

The cadre of the 2nd Gordon Highlanders had arrived at Aberdeen from Italy in March 1919, Lieut.-Colonel A. D. Greenhill Gardyne assuming command. In July at Phoenix Park, Dublin, the Battalion was reformed on the 3rd (Special Reserve) Battalion, the receiving and training unit who had supplied drafts to all battalions of the Gordon Highlanders throughout the war. As demobilization of the Army proceeded a large number of men—most of them due or nearly due for discharge—had accumulated in the 3rd Battalion and the 2nd Gordons, on taking over, found that their strength was 48 officers and 1,844 other ranks.

Nearly all these men were awaiting demobilization, but as fast as a contingent departed to civil life fresh arrivals were taken on the strength, some of them remaining with the Battalion for only a few days, some for little more than a day. The orderly room and the quartermaster's office worked almost day and night until the ebb and flow began to subside. About 150 men volunteered for the North Russia Relief Force, others re-engaged or re-enlisted, and gradually the 2nd Battalion assumed its proper shape. When, in the autumn, a move was made to Collinstown Camp, Dublin, nearly all the transients had disappeared.

At this time the state of tension in Ireland was increasing, and outbreaks of lawlessness were soon to develop into savage guerilla war. The 2nd Gordons were called upon to provide many guards and piquets under almost active service conditions, but so far there had been no attack upon our troops. An attempt to intercept a Gordon despatch rider cycling into Dublin resulted in the discomfiture of his assailant, and no other 'incident' occurred.

At Collinstown the 2nd Gordons found it possible to revive many of the diversions of a home service battalion in peace time. The band and pipers played in camp and at mess. In August the Battalion won the Irish Army Athletic Championship for which no less than twenty-four units competed. Football was started in earnest.

Towards the end of 1919 came the reunion with the 1st Battalion, who were on their way from Athlone to Catterick. Lieut.-Colonel Simpson and some of his officers dined with the 2nd Gordons, and a football match resulted in the defeat of the hosts.

Before Christmas the 2nd Gordons were warned for service in Silesia. Under the terms of the Peace Treaty a plebiscite was to be held in this province to decide whether it should become Polish or German, and the presence of Allied troops was needed to ensure that the voting should be conducted in proper fashion. As a preliminary the 2nd Gordons were moved to Lichfield in January 1920, all ranks quitting Ireland without regret.

And then, after an advance party had actually reached Cologne on their way to Silesia, the move was cancelled. The Gordons were to return to Scotland instead. In March they arrived at Maryhill Barracks, Glasgow, and here, in May, their commanding officer, Lieut.-Colonel A. D. Greenhill Gardyne took leave of them, invalided from the Service after thirty-two years in the Regiment. His successor was Lieut.-Colonel P. W. Brown, who had been in command of the Depôt.

At Glasgow the 2nd Gordons had the opportunity they wanted to set them on the road to a proper standard of efficiency. All ranks were beginning to know each other; there was a general smartening up in drill and dress; musketry courses were fired; and company training, after the experiences of the war, took on a more up-to-date character. In August the Battalion found the Royal Guard at Ballater.

The aftermath of the war saw the disappearance of the 1st Garrison Battalion Gordon Highlanders, formed in October 1916 of men who were unfit for active service and officered, for the most part, by other than Gordon Highlanders. The Battalion had been sent to India and were stationed at Rawalpindi from April 1919 until January 1920, being then brought home and disbanded.

After demobilization in 1919 a reconstitution of our Territorial forces was considered by the Government. Obviously the old volunteer spirit was too valuable an asset to be disregarded, and in 1920 a new Territorial Army, mainly on the lines of the old Territorial Force, came into being. There was one notable difference. Men who joined the Territorial Army undertook to serve wherever required in the event of war. The establishment was fixed at 345,000, but only half this number was expected to be recruited in peace time.

In the Gordon Highlanders recruiting for the Territorial battalions started in February 1920 and went fairly well from the outset. The 5th Battalion, who drew upon the counties of Aberdeen and part of Kincardine, were 250 strong by the end of the year, and the 6th Battalion, with headquarters at Keith, recruited about 170 men, half of them from Banffshire. The 4th (City of Aberdeen) Battalion did rather better, but the difficulties of the 7th (Deeside) Battalion were manifest. With headquarters at Banchory they had only part of Kincardineshire from which to recruit.

Overseas Service
1920-34

It was in March 1920, after they had been less than three months at Catterick, that the 1st Gordon Highlanders received orders to join the Army of the Black Sea.

About a year previously the Greek invasion of Asia Minor had brought about a resurgence of Turkish national feeling which found expression in military action under the leadership of Mustafa Kemal, later known to fame as Kemal Ataturk. The Allies had not yet concluded a peace treaty with the Sultan's Government and, as the Nationalist movement threatened to spread westward from Anatolia, Allied troops—British, French and Italian—occupied Constantinople in March 1920.

The 1st Gordons embarked at Southampton on 25th March and reached Constantinople on 9th April. After taking part in a demonstration march through the city, they left next day for Tuzla, which was regarded as 'a desolate spot', on the Ismid peninsula. They were brigaded with Indian troops.

About Ismid, at the head of the Gulf of Ismid, the Nationalist troops of Kemal were confronted by a line of defences upon which our troops were still working. West of this line the disarming of the Turkish Government forces in accordance with the terms of the Armistice was in progress. Bands of Nationalists who approached the defences from the east were dispersed or persuaded to retire by a show of force, but the utmost vigilance was required to prevent sabotage on the Ismid-Tuzla railway.

On 9th May a Gordon Highlander detachment of mounted infantry (forty-two other ranks under Lieutenant J. M. Stewart) was formed. They were sent to Derindje.

In the middle of June the Kemalists, while protesting that they had no desire to attack our troops, moved against Ismid. Our air force, the guns of our warships and our artillery promptly came into action, and the Turks made no attempt to close. Sent up from Tuzla, the Gordons arrived at Ismid on 15th June, and two companies under Major A. Craufurd were despatched to extricate a company of the 24th Punjabis out on a forward position of the Ismid defences. This was done. The companies had an exhausting climb in great heat and came under machine-gun fire, one Gordon private being reported missing.

The Battalion took over a portion of the Ismid defences and started to improve and extend them. On 22nd July a four days reconnaissance was carried out, a bloodless affair which involved searching a number of villages for concealed arms and ammunition. A brigade reconnaissance in which the Gordons took part occupied the first fortnight of August.

On 2nd September D Company under Major S. R. McClintock conducted an operation against brigands on the south side of the Gulf of Ismid. Also under Major McClintock's command were four rifle companies of half-trained Greek soldiery. The Greeks possessed only one officer who could read and write and were difficult people to control in rugged scrub-covered country. The Highlanders lost three men wounded—one of them died of wounds—and won special praise from the brigade commander. ' The way in which the 1st Gordons carried out their task reflected the greatest credit on their training and the leadership of the company officers.'

Next day, while crossing the Gulf by lighter one private fell overboard and was saved by the gallant exertions of Private G. Waddell, who was afterwards awarded the bronze medal and certificate of the Royal Humane Society.

Meanwhile, on 3rd September, the remainder of the Battalion had departed upon a reconnaissance into Anatolia as far as Armasha. This operation occupied a week, and at the end of the month the Gordons returned to Tuzla.

The mounted infantry platoon was still in being and at the end of the year moved to Biyuk Dere, joining the Thracian Mounted Infantry.

By 17th November the Gordons had moved to Haidar Pasha whence a steam ferry provided easy access to the capital. The Jocks were much impressed by Constantinople, the skill of the local pickpockets compelling the reluctant admiration of certain Aberdonians. Haidar Pasha was voted ' a good station '. Boating and bathing and all the usual sports could be enjoyed ; and the Y.M.C.A. was much appreciated as ' very different from the old bun-and-sermon institution '.

Four Vickers guns were drawn in January 1921, these weapons to become part of normal equipment ; and two Stokes guns (light mortars) were added later.

In March Lieut.-Colonel C. Ogston, who had served in Russia with a British military mission, succeeded Lieut.-Colonel Simpson in command.

The Gordons continued to excel at most forms of sport and athletics. In March they carried off the Command Football Cup presented by the Commander-in-Chief, Sir Charles Harington. In April they won the Army of the Black Sea Boxing Competition, and were supreme at the Army Acquatic Sports and the Army Athletic Meeting. On 1st October, the Highland Games were held at Haidar Pasha on the usual peace-time scale, for the first time since 1914.

There were some alarms. In July three companies were employed in digging and wiring a defensive line in Asia Minor opposite Constantinople. Also to be remembered is the August night when the Gordons were rushed to the help of the people of Scutari where a great fire devoured more than a thousand of the old wooden houses in the city.

In the summer of 1921 the advance of the Greek Army in Anatolia had resulted in the capture of Eski Shehr and, although a stalemate ensued thereafter, the threat of a Kemalist advance on Constantinople was removed. Thus it became possible to reduce the British forces in Turkey, and on 20th November the 1st Gordons embarked for Malta. Sir Charles Harington came on board to say farewell. In a letter to the commanding officer he wrote:

> I hope you will accept for yourself and convey to all ranks my grateful thanks for all you have done to uphold the honour of the British Army in Constantinople. I have watched with great pleasure the standard of your Battalion rising daily towards your well-known pre-War level. That level can only be reached by real hard work on the part of the officers, W.O.'s and N.C.O.'s and by the loyal support of the men which you enjoy. I congratulate you on your achievement and on the many trophies which you have won in this command.

The Gordons had a stormy passage in an unseaworthy vessel which was obliged to seek shelter at Mudros before completing the voyage. They arrived at Malta on 27th November and took over St. Andrew's Barracks, 'fairly new as barracks go'. At the beginning of February 1922 they were joined by the married families from home, and it did not take long to settle down to garrison routine.

In Malta facilities for field training are limited, but the 1st Gordons soon showed a steady improvement in signalling and musketry. Plenty of time was left for athletics, cricket, swimming, water polo and both codes of football. Competition was keen, for many rivals were to be found among other units of the garrison to say nothing of the Royal Navy. At the Malta Command Boxing Tournament in March the Gordons supplied the winners at all weights.

But the Battalion had not seen the last of Turkey. At the end of July 1922 they received a warning order to prepare again for service in that troubled region and on 17th September they marched out, at a few hours notice, to embark for Chanak.

The new crisis was the result of Mustafa Kemal's rise in power and prestige. In August 1922 he had utterly routed the Greeks in Anatolia and Smyrna went up in flames. Greek divisions still held

Adrianople and Turkish Thrace, and the danger that now threatened was a Kemalist advance which would bring war into Europe. At the end of 1921 a neutral zone had been demarcated round Constantinople, the Bosphorus and the Dardanelles and the Allies had prevented the Greek forces from entering it. This zone had now to be denied to the Turks, and British forces were hurried to the scene.

Chanak, on the Asiatic side of the Dardanelles, was held by the Allies as a bridgehead, and at Chanak the 1st Gordons disembarked. In this region Kemal had sufficient forces to create a delicate situation. Open hostilities were to be avoided if possible and the Gordons found that, as the Turkish troops were inclined to acts of provocation, only a judicious blend of firmness and restraint could prevent a clash of arms.

The arrival of more reinforcements soon meant a change of scene for the Battalion who, in November 1922, made the sea passage to Rodosto in eastern Thrace. Rodosto is remembered for its plague of black flies.

The Greeks, by agreement, were now retreating in eastern Thrace followed up by the Turks who were inclined to push their advance more quickly than had been stipulated. It was the task of the Gordons to act as a buffer between the two forces and so keep the peace. One Gordon patrol, while 'holding the ring', was fired on by the Turks and promptly returned the fire. Under cover of a white flag the Turks apologised: the Gordons had been mistaken for Greeks, but when they showed fight the error was obvious.

By December 1922 the Gordons' task was finished and the Battalion sailed for the Bosphorus to go into billets near Haidar Pasha and begin a peace-time routine which lasted for several months. In April 1923 Lieut.-Colonel H. P. Burn succeeded Lieut.-Colonel Ogston.

The only time of tension came in May, and was caused by a Greco-Turkish crisis at the Lausanne conference which delayed the signing of the Peace Treaty. So the Gordons had little to worry about. They became champions at a British Forces in Turkey Sports Meeting and did well in sailing and rowing races, even against the sailors. Towards the end of July the bandmaster brought out the instruments from Malta and the band was reconstituted.

On 25th August the Gordons bade a final farewell to Turkey where, during their two tours of service, they had lost one lance-corporal and ten privates. A memorial to these men is in the Crimean cemetery at Scutari.

The Battalion landed at Malta on the 30th and returned to St. Andrew's Barracks. Garrison duties and training included some ceremonial occasions. Lord Plumer, Governor and Commander-in-Chief, inspected the Gordons before he left for home in June 1934, and the Battalion mounted a guard of honour for the arrival of Lord Plumer's successor, General Sir Walter Congreve, V.C. In September they did very well at the Malta Command Rifle Meeting.

As November ended came a call to reinforce our troops in Cairo where political and civil disturbances had culminated in the murder of the Sirdar, Sir Lee Stack. On 2nd December the Gordons embarked for Egypt in H.M. aircraft-carrier *Eagle*. The Regiment has always been great friends of the Royal Navy and they settled down to ship discipline so well and cheerfully as to call for a special word of appreciation from the Commander-in-Chief Mediterranean Fleet. On their part the Gordons were not slow to thank their naval hosts.

Arriving at Port Said on 5th December, the Battalion went by train to 'a wired and uncomfortable camp' at Abbassieh where they joined the Cairo Brigade. It soon became clear, however, that no active operations would ensue; and the Jocks were able to visit the Sphinx and the Pyramids, and, always ready for a new experience, to ride cheerfully and uncomfortably on camel-back.

It was only a matter of a few weeks before the Battalion resumed their regular tour of service overseas. They were now for India. Some of them spent Hogmanay 'in a shed at Port Said', and on New Year's Day 1925 the Gordons left for Bombay.

Their first station in India was Secunderabad, but two companies went to Belgaum where they were frequently employed in tactical demonstrations at the Senior Officers School. In February the Gordons won the Poona District Boxing Tournament.

The commanding officer, Lieut.-Colonel Burn, shot his first tiger while on shikar in the Central Provinces, and added five to the bag before returning from leave.

The pipers of the Gordons won much goodwill by instructing the pipers of certain Indian irregulars whose flattering efforts to adopt some semblance of Highland garb had startling results.

At this time 50 per cent. of the Battalion were Aberdeen or Aberdeenshire men and 83 per cent. were Scots. The Commander in-Chief, General Sir Claude Jacob, visited the Gordons at normal training in July and had nothing but good to say of them.

In January 1926 Major I. Picton-Warlow, from the 2nd Battalion, was appointed to command in succession to Lieut.-Colonel Burn. During this year the Gordons formed a polo team which entered local competitions, being the only infantry team to do so. In their first season they could not hope to achieve much, but some enjoyable games were played.

Certain changes in dress were made in order to bring the Battalion into line with the 2nd Gordons at home. Regimental buttons were worn by all ranks from October 1926 and sporrans were taken into wear in the following February. White spats were to make their appearance later, after the move to Delhi.

This came in November 1927. Delhi—'New Delhi' with its Viceroy's palace, legislative buildings, government offices and imposing houses all laid out in the modern manner—was, of course, a very special station. Except in the hot weather, spent by the Government in Simla, the garrison were much occupied by ceremonial parades and guard duties. The Viceroy's Guard, in particular, called for the very highest standard of drill and turn out, and in these particulars the Gordons were never found wanting.

Less ornamental duties were heavy. Times of political tension, Hindu and Moslem festivals, strikes, all were liable to develop into civil disturbances which could not be permitted in or near the capital. On these occasions the Gordons had to be ready to reinforce their company in Delhi Fort and to provide a 'moveable column' for despatch to any district where trouble was anticipated. It was difficult to find the men for all these demands, especially in the hot weather when large parties were sent in rotation to the hill station of Kailana. Fortunately the Gordons had no serious clash with the civil population during their service in Delhi.

In 1928 the Battalion was attached to the 8th (Bareilly) Brigade for collective training, and thus met the 2nd Gurkhas, old comrades of the Tirah campaign. On 29th November the Gordons entertained the Gurkhas to the great pleasure of all concerned.

In February 1929 a Highland Brigade Gathering was held. It lasted a week and saw the Gordons triumph over the 2nd Seaforth, the 2nd H.L.I. and the 1st Black Watch by a very narrow margin.

Lieut.-Colonel F. Bell succeeded Lieut.-Colonel Picton-Warlow in command in January 1930. At the end of November the Gordons left Delhi for Landi Kotal in the Khyber Pass. All ranks were in fine fettle. They considered themselves 'fit to take part in anything that may come along'.

Life on the North-West Frontier was much as the 1st Gordons had known it thirty years before. The defences—small forts and blockhouses—had, however, been modernised and the precautions against rifle thefts made more elaborate. Duties were rather heavy, for many guards and piquets were required, and the state of vigilance could never be relaxed. No one was shot during the Battalion's stay on the Frontier and no rifles were lost.

In March 1932 a very fit Battalion moved to Peshawar, where there were more facilities for sport, and officers could turn out with the Peshawar Vale Hunt. In April came a touch of ceremonial with the visit of the Viceroy. The Gordons entertained him to dinner.

The Battalion left India early in 1934 after Lieut.-Colonel Bell had been succeeded by Lieut.-Colonel J. M. Hamilton in January. Palestine was the destination, and at Haifa the Highlanders received a warm welcome. In May they were inspected by the High Commissioner, General Sir Arthur Wauchope. These were the days of the British mandate, and internal security duties were important and exacting; but there seemed ample time for other affairs. 'Navy Week' at Haifa, in July 1934, was a great success; warships of many nations paid 'goodwill visits'; and a Spanish training ship produced a Galician piper who aroused much interest.

Battalion exercises now took on a new aspect. With the help of hired transport—including taxi cabs—the Gordons turned out as motorised infantry.

The Battalion had been serving abroad since 1919, and were now due for Home. From Haifa they went to Egypt to embark, and on 5th January 1935 arrived at Gibraltar. Here a special call was made for the reunion with the 2nd Battalion, who were just beginning their tour of service overseas; but the visit was a very short one, and the 1st Gordons landed in England about a week later.

The Regiment at Home
1921-34

By 1921 the 2nd Gordons at Maryhill Barracks, Glasgow, considered themselves back to peace-time soldiering. In April, however, came a sudden emergency. The great coal strike seemed to threaten more serious trouble and the Government proclaimed a 'state of national emergency'. Certain classes of the Army Reserve were called up and further, rather drastic, measures were taken. Since the Territorial Army could not be used in aid of the civil power, a special Defence Force was recruited from volunteers, many of whom took their discharge from the Territorial Army in order to be available. Officers of the Defence Force were given temporary Regular commissions.

Glasgow, where Communist influence was traceable, seemed a likely centre of trouble, so troops of all arms, with bluejackets and marines, were brought into the city. The Gordons provided extra guards, in-lying piquets and patrols during the period of tension which lasted some weeks. By June life had returned to normal.

In July the Battalion were sent to Ireland, where, after nearly eighteen months of agonising guerilla warfare, the Sinn Fein rebellion was nearing collapse. Soon after the Gordons reached the Curragh the Government initiated a truce which, after considerable negotiation, resulted in 'partition' and the establishment of Eire, the Irish Republic.

The Gordons were involved in only one 'incident' and that a trifling affair. An attempt was made to ambush the train in which a baggage party was travelling, but an exchange of fire resulted only in the wounding of two civilians. The Regiment, indeed, may be considered fortunate in that both 1st and 2nd Battalions escaped service in Ireland during the 'troubles'.

On 13th July General Sir Nevil Macready, Bt., himself an old Gordon Highlander, inspected the 2nd Battalion, who were soon dispersed in small detachments about the countryside. The truce was generally well observed, and none of these parties had anything unpleasant to report.

After the Treaty was ratified by the Free State Parliament later in 1921 the 2nd Gordons returned to Maryhill Barracks whence a draft of 163 were despatched to join the 1st Battalion in Malta.

Before the end of the year the 2nd Battalion moved northwards to Fort George, and here Lieut.-Colonel Brown was invalided from the Service. Lieut.-Colonel J. L. G. Burnett assumed command on 31st December.

In the spring of 1922 the last of those non-commissioned officers and men who were serving on special engagements took their discharge, leaving the Battalion with none but normally enlisted Regular soldiers, but reduced in strength to 341 other ranks.

Some improvements in dress were now possible. The white shell jacket having gone for good, sergeants wore the red sash with service dress. Claymores made their appearance again. Collar badges ('tigers' in white metal) were issued to the rank and file: officers continued to wear the sphinx collar badge in service dress. Sporrans did not come in before December 1924, and white spats and regimental buttons not until July 1925.

At Fort George anything more advanced than battalion training was out of the question, but in 1924 the Gordons did very well in the skill-at-arms competitions at the Royal Tournament, Olympia. In June a training march which was also calculated to attract recruits took the Battalion to Aberdeen and back by way of Nairn, Forres, Elgin and Keith. They started in the rain, but hot weather soon made the tented camps more comfortable and the whole exercise, which took nineteen days, was voted a great success.

At the Scottish Command Highland Games in August the 2nd Gordons won the cup for piping and dancing, and the pipers and drummers went south afterwards to take part in the Searchlight Tattoo at Wembley Exhibition.

Winter at Fort George proved rather trying: the weather was severe and the reconstruction of the barracks was in progress. Nevertheless the standard of musketry improved, and another very creditable draft were despatched to the 1st Battalion. The pipes and drums did a good recruiting tour of the feeing markets.

In March 1925 the Battalion scored several skill-at-arms successes at the Scottish Command Bronze Medal Tournament held in Edinburgh. The training march, which started from Fort George on 26th May, took in parts of the Regimental area not visited in 1924. This time the route was Dufftown, Ballater, Aboyne Castle, Banchory and Crathes to Aberdeen, and back by Ellon, Peterhead, Strichen, Fraserburgh, Banff, Portsoy, Buckie and Auldearn. The bad weather was more than balanced by the hospitality everywhere received.

One company moved to Edinburgh to take over the Castle duties for June, and the Battalion provided the King's Guard at Ballater. As in the previous year, the pipes and drums performed at Wembley Tattoo. In October came a move to Bordon in the Aldershot Command.

THE REGIMENT AT HOME, 1921-34

On 31st, December 1925, there were 525 Scots in the Battalion, 114 English and 13 Irish. It should be remembered that men of Scottish descent recruited in England were recorded as English.

The Gordons came to like Bordon. Training in the Aldershot Command was, of course, fairly strenuous, but sports and games flourished. The season 1925-6 was only the second year of the Battalion Rugby team, but they reached the third round of the Army Cup.

In June 1926 the Gordons marched to Bisley to spend a fortnight under canvas in very hot weather, acting as markers at the Army Rifle Association meeting. During the summer, polo, which had not been played in the Battalion since 1914, was started again.

The commanding officer, who had succeeded as Sir James Burnett of Leys, 13th baronet, in the previous January, completed his tenure in December. His successor was Lieut.-Colonel J. Forbes-Robertson, V.C., from The Border Regiment.

In 1927 the pipes and drums played at the Royal Tournament in London, taking into wear feather bonnets, doublets and plaids. At this time the pipes and drums numbered forty-eight of all ranks and the band forty-three. Soon afterwards the time-honoured titles of 'pipe-major' and 'drum-major' received official recognition, replacing the prosaic styles of 'sergeant-piper' and 'sergeant-drummer'.

The Battalion boxers, encouraged by Captain C. M. Usher, were showing great improvement. Boy Garland, a bantam weight, won the Army Boxing Championship of 1927 and then repeated his success at the Imperial Services meeting. Finally he became A.B.A. champion.

At the end of 1927, after a draft of 112 had been sent to the 1st Battalion, the strength was 624 all ranks.

The Gordons were now reorganising in accordance with a new establishment, a Headquarter Wing being formed to include all 'specialists'. In the spring of 1928 an anti-tank section of one officer and eighteen other ranks was organised, but no weapons were yet available. The machine-gun platoon was expanded to company strength and replaced D (rifle) Company.

After the autumn manoeuvres of 1928 the 2nd Gordons moved to Northern Ireland. The anti-tank section had now become a platoon but left Bordon still unequipped: indeed departure from the Aldershot Command seemed to portend a goodbye to soldiering on the most up-to-date scale.

And Ballykinlar Camp with its 'huts and rats and mud' was not a cheerful prospect, despite its proximity to the oft-sung mountains of Mourne. The persistently wet weather sadly interfered with training—notably manoeuvres near Loch Neagh—and most forms of outdoor activity. Yet a high standard of musketry was attained and point-to-point meetings attracted riders and spectators. The year 1930, with the economy axe at work, opened with disquieting rumours of disbandment or amalgamation; but also with whispers of mechanization.

At this time the Battalion mustered 547 of all ranks and of these 99 were 'foreigners'.

The wet summer of 1930 is described as 'heart breaking'. Undoubtedly the band, which performed at the Antwerp Exhibition in July, had the best of it. All enjoyed the sea passage out and home in H.M. cruiser *Frobisher*.

Lieut.-Colonel S. R. McClintock succeeded Lieut.-Colonel Forbes-Robertson, V.C., in December 1930.

Summer training at Bohill in 1931 was carried out in surprisingly good weather, but at the beginning of the New Year the Gordons, very thankfully departed for Aldershot. They were met at the station and played into Malplaquet Barracks by the bands, in full dress, of four different units, an unexpected compliment which was very much appreciated.

The Battalion settled down very well at Aldershot. All ranks worked hard and played hard. When musketry courses and company training had been completed preparations began for the Tattoo at which the Gordons, in scarlet and feather bonnets, were seen at their very best. The pipes and drums were massed with those of three other Scottish units.

In July the Battalion combined with the 2nd Camerons to hold a Highland 'at home' with piping, dancing and games. The band and drums fulfilled an engagement in Copenhagen in September, making many friends among the Danes.

The summer had been fine and hot and the weather held for brigade and divisional training which included operations against a mechanised enemy. By this time the Gordons were as strong as any battalion on the home establishment; and the recruits received from the Depôt were in every way up to the exacting standard of the Regiment.

In the spring of 1933 a contingent of the London Scottish spent a week-end with the Battalion who saw to it that these London members of the regimental family spent a profitable and enjoyable time. The year ran its usual course at Aldershot: the Tattoo, the Horse Show, the Command Rifle Meeting, Bisley, and then, after brigade training, manoeuvres which ended with some strenuous days on Salisbury Plain.

In January 1934 the 2nd Gordons recovered their drums which had been left in Ostend, on account of transport difficulties, after the Battalion had landed at Zeebrugge in October 1914. The

THE REGIMENT AT HOME, 1921-34

drums had been found by the Germans before the end of the First World War and removed to Berlin; now, through the efforts of Sir Ian Hamilton, who wrote direct to President Hindenburg 'as soldier to soldier', they were restored to the Battalion. Sir Ian and Lieut.-Colonel McClintock went to Berlin and received the drums from the Germans with due ceremony and mutual expressions of goodwill. Hitler had become Chancellor by this time, but Hindenburg, still the figurehead, represented the old German Army. The arrival of the drums at Aldershot was greeted in appropriate fashion.

More than fifteen years had passed since Germany had acknowledged defeat, and such a gesture as the restoration of the drums seemed to betoken a period of settled peace. That peace-time conditions prevailed in the British Army was shown by the slowness of promotion in the Gordons. At this time the senior subaltern of the 2nd Battalion had twelve and a half years service.

Two companies of the London Scottish spent Easter with the 2nd Gordons, whose tour of home service was drawing to an end. They packed up as soon as divisional training was over and were played out of barracks by the pipes and drums of the 2nd Camerons and the band of the 1st Royal West Kent Regiment. Sir Ian Hamilton was there to see them off when they sailed for Gibraltar in October 1934. Lieut.-Colonel McClintock also said goodbye. His successor was Lieut.-Colonel G. T. Burney, son of an officer well remembered in the Regiment.

In attracting the type of recruit who could be turned into a disciplined young soldier with a proper pride in himself and in his Regiment the Depôt relied to a considerable extent upon the half-yearly feeing markets held in the small towns of the three shires: Aberdeen, Banff and Kincardine. On these occasions the pipers always had their appeal.

The officers commanding the Depôt during the early post-war years were, first, Lieut.-Colonel P. W. Brown and then Lieut.-Colonel H. P. Burn, followed by Major W. Neish.

The daily round was enlivened by the visits of the 2nd Battalion on their training marches of 1924 and 1925, and by the appearance of the London Scottish, who marched from Aberdeen to Perth in August 1925. In that year, when General Ritchie, G.O.C.-in-C. Scottish Command, inspected the Depôt he saw 130 recruits on parade, most of them Aberdonians, and only a very few from south of the Border.

Both the Depôt and the 4th Gordons provided guards of honour in September when the King and Queen visited Aberdeen to open an extension of the art gallery.

Plans were now being made for a new Depôt to be built just beyond the Bridge of Don on the Ellon road. The prospect of more and better accommodation than the old Castlehill Barracks could provide was hailed with satisfaction; but it proved to be a distant prospect.

In March 1926 Major W. Neish was succeeded in command by Major F. Bell, who was followed in May 1928 by Major C. M. Usher.

The gradual mechanization of the army being now in view, a lecture was given to all ranks at the beginning of 1930. To many of those present this was their first introduction—albeit only in theory—to a considerable variety of vehicles. Some gathered that 'although in the next war we shall probably be carried about, it was likely to be extremely uncomfortable'.

The winter of 1930-31 was severe and there was much sickness, but recruiting continued to be satisfactory. In May 1931 Major Usher was succeeded by Major R. D. Robertson. Now, for reasons of economy, it appeared that the building of the new barracks at the Bridge of Don would be long delayed.

In March 1934 Major W. J. Graham assumed command of the Depôt.

The Territorial battalions of the Regiment put in some steady spade work between 1920 and 1924, and some changes were made.

The 5th and the 7th Battalions became one, being numbered first 5th and subsequently 5th/7th Gordon Highlanders. With headquarters and one company at Bucksburn, the 5th/7th had other company headquarters at Ellon, Banchory and Stonehaven, and widely scattered detachments over eastern Aberdeenshire and Kincardine.

The 4th Gordons (City of Aberdeen), 5th/7th Gordons, 4th/5th Black Watch and 6th/7th Black Watch now constituted the 153rd Brigade of the Highland Division. The 6th Gordons, with headquarters at Keith, belonged to the 152nd Brigade.

There were some changes in command. In December 1923 Lieut.-Colonel C. D. Peterkin had taken over the 4th Gordons from Lieut.-Colonel L. Mackinnon, who had been in command since February 1920. Lieut.-Colonel R. Bruce, 7th Gordons, retired in June 1924 and Lieut.-Colonel J. Milne then had the amalgamated 5th/7th Battalion.

In 1924 the strength of the 4th Gordons was 17 officers and 535 other ranks, and that of the 5th/7th Battalion 16 officers and 572. Both battalions went into camp at Montrose for their fortnight's annual training.

The 6th Gordons, well over 500 strong, had a good muster in camp at Nairn, although the wet spring prevented the attendance of many farm workers who were kept busy on the land.

By 1925 the 5th/7th Battalion began to get up-to-date with the formation of a Headquarters Company. The recruiting efforts of all three Battalions never slackened, and the commanding officers much appreciated the support of the employers of labour who encouraged their men to become Gordon Highlanders, and made it as easy as possible for them to attend drills and the annual camp.

The 4th and the 5th/7th Battalions were in camp at Dreghorn, on the lower slopes of the Pentlands, in 1925. This was a favourite spot for, although the hill country made field training a rather strenuous pursuit, the attractions of Edinburgh were near at hand. The 6th Battalion camp was at Grantown-on-Spey.

Although the 6th Gordons found that wastage occurred through men leaving the district—some to emigrate—their numbers were up to establishment in the autumn of 1926. The 5th/7th Battalion increased steadily in strength from year to year, and this despite the fact that 'some young men show a tendency to pack up when they get married'.

The 6th Gordons lost Lieut.-Colonel Sir G. W. Abercromby, Bt., who had commanded them for seven years, in June 1927. He was succeeded by Lieut.-Colonel R. Steuart-Menzies. In February 1928 Lieut.-Colonel C. D. Peterkin, who had served in the Battalion for nineteen years, relinquished command of the 4th Gordons, and was succeeded by Lieut.-Colonel J. H. McI. Gordon. In the following June Lieut.-Colonel Milne of the 5th/7th Gordons gave way to Lieut.-Colonel R. Adam.

The 4th Gordons mustered 83 per cent. of their strength for camp at Blairadam, near Kinross, in 1929. The weather was ideal and the Chief of the Imperial General Staff, Field-Marshal Sir George Milne—himself an Aberdonian—paid the Battalion a visit. Despite the official pre-occupation with economy it was 'planned to get the band into scarlet'. In the previous year the pipes and drums were proudly described as 'back to pre-war review order'.

All three Battalions were showing a steady improvement in their standard of efficiency; and at this time the 6th Gordons took special pride in their transport, which was still dependent upon the horse.

Despite bad weather the attendance at the 1930 camp of the 4th Gordons was better than ever. In the afternoons the camp was open to visitors, and entertaining them was said to have been a greater test of stamina for all ranks than any soldierly exercise.

In June 1931 Lieut.-Colonel A. S. Fortune, who had served continuously in the 6th Gordons since the early days of the First World War, succeeded Lieut.-Colonel Steuart-Menzies in command.

After several years of successful camps it came as a great shock to learn that, as a measure of Government economy, the camps for 1932 were to be cancelled. The prospect of no camp—no week or fortnight of soldiering with pay and allowances—was discouraging in the extreme; but the three Battalions strove to make the best of things.

The 4th Gordons took their men out by bus to Scotstown Moor for night operations, and held a voluntary camp, with no pay or allowances, at Montrose which was attended by 300 men. The 5th/7th held week-end camps, and their machine gunners attended for voluntary training at Glenmuick. At Lessendrum, near Huntly, eight officers and 75 other ranks of the 6th Gordons—non-commissioned officers, signallers, range takers and selected privates—went under canvas for a week of instruction.

In 1932 the 6th Gordons won many shooting trophies, and at the end of the year could report that their ranks were filled: in fact they were 'twenty-two over establishment and other men wanted to join'.

Lieut.-Colonel G. P. Geddes had followed Lieut.-Colonel Adam in command of the 5th/7th Gordons in June 1932, and in February 1933 Lieut.-Colonel R. L. J. Henderson succeeded Lieut.-Colonel Gordon in the 4th Battalion.

In 1933 the 4th Gordons received the privilege of marching through the city of Aberdeen with bayonets fixed.

During the summer of this year the three Battalions went to camp again under the usual conditions, the 4th Gordons to Gailes, the 5th/7th and the 6th to Aberdour in Fife. While here many of the 5th/7th managed a visit to the Fleet at Rosyth. Next year the 6th Gordons broke new ground by going to camp at Barry, whilst the 4th and the 5th/7th returned to Dreghorn.

While in camp the 4th Gordons were inspected at Holyrood by King George V, who was accompanied by Queen Mary. His Majesty had expressed a wish to see a Territorial battalion on parade, so this was a great occasion. To mount the commanding officer, second-in-command and adjutant chargers were lent by those very good friends of the Gordons, the Royal Scots Greys.

In 1924 *The Tiger and Sphinx*, journal of the Gordon Highlanders, was brought to life again after a lapse of twenty-six years. Edited from the Depôt, the journal depended mainly upon contributions, including illustrations, from each Battalion, Regular and Territorial; and news was frequently received from the affiliated Regiments in the Dominions.

The link with the 48th Highlanders of Canada, whose home is in Toronto, was already recognised officially, and Sir Ian Hamilton became Honorary Colonel of the Regiment. In 1930 the 5th Australian Infantry (Victorian Scottish) entered the family with Sir Ian as Honorary Colonel, but the tie with the Victorian Scottish is really of older standing. The formal alliance with the Capetown Highlanders (Duke of Connaught and Strathearn's Own) was announced in 1932, and here again the connection is really of much earlier date.

In 1932 'The Cock o' the North' was adopted as the Regimental March. The tune is associated with the Dukes of Gordon, whose family raised the old 92nd, so it most appropriately replaced 'Highland Laddie' which, so far as is known, has no particular association with the Regiment.

The Gordon Highlanders Regimental Association, whose object is to keep in touch with ex-members of the Regiment with an eye to their welfare in civil life, dates from April 1930. The Association welded together the older, smaller associations in Glasgow, Edinburgh, London and other places; and the Gordon Highlanders Club in Aberdeen, opened with due ceremony in August 1923, housed a 'central office'.

Lieut.-Colonel Forbes-Robertson, V.C., had most to do with setting these wheels in motion. He applied himself to the matter soon after he assumed command of the 2nd Gordons, Sir Ian Hamilton, Colonel of the Regiment, being ever ready with his advice and support.

Overseas Service
1934-39

The 2nd Gordon Highlanders had arrived at Gibraltar in October 1934. They took over 'rather scattered quarters which seemed to extend the whole length of the Rock ", and found themselves much occupied with guard duties and garrison fatigues.

On 5th January 1935 occurred the meeting with their brethren of the 1st Battalion, who were on their way home from Palestine. The 1st Gordons had been allowed to make a special call at Gibraltar, and the two Battalions paraded together and were inspected by Sir Charles Harington, the Governor and Commander-in-Chief. Sir Ian Hamilton, Colonel of the Regiment, made a special journey from England in order to be present.

The 2nd Gordons found that Gibraltar improved on acquaintance. In sports and games the other units of the garrison and the Royal Navy provided plenty of competition and some of the Gordon officers turned out with the Royal Calpe Hunt. In due season football gave way to rowing and swimming, and hunting to polo. On several occasions the Fleet took parties of the Gordons to sea.

The Silver Jubilee of King George V was celebrated by the trooping of the colour on 6th May 1935, and at night a searchlight tattoo was followed by fireworks. In May, too, the band and pipers of the Gordons paid a visit to Madrid, where they received a warm welcome and were a great success.

Both at garrison rifle meetings and in garrison athletics the Battalion did very well. In September they won the subalterns' polo cup. They continued to be great friends of the Royal Navy, and when the 4th Destroyer Flotilla left for home passages were provided for a number of Gordon Highlanders who were due for leave.

In June 1936 the Battalion was suddenly transported to Egypt, embarking in H.M. battle cruiser *Repulse*. At Malta they were transferred to the cruisers *Exeter* and *Shropshire* and landed at Alexandria. They stayed six weeks in Egypt and rather expected to go on to Palestine, where the Arab 'strike' was worrying the British authorities. Instead, the *Repulse* brought them back to the Rock.

The Spanish Civil War was now causing some inconvenience, if not anxiety, at Gibraltar, and no excursions into Spanish territory were permitted. Our polo ground was in Spain.

The Gordons had a great send-off from Gibraltar when they left for Singapore in March 1937. All ranks looked forward to service in the Far East—a new experience for nearly all of them—

and their first impressions when they took over the comfortable Selerang barracks at Changi on the island of Singapore were entirely favourable.[1]

At this time the defence of Singapore was considered a matter of great importance; indeed, the security of the naval base was reckoned as second in priority to the defence of the United Kingdom. The potential aggressor in the Far East could only be Japan, but the course of events in Europe pointed to danger nearer home. In 1936 Germany had reoccupied the Rhineland.

Meanwhile the 2nd Gordons took their part in the celebration parades which marked the Coronation of King George VI and His Majesty's birthday. A grand military tattoo at Farrar Park in August 1937 owed much of its success to the pipes and drums of the Gordons, whose Highland dancing was a great attraction.

The training of the Battalion made all ranks familiar with boat work, for they practised night landings on Singapore Island, mostly from native craft. In this and other exercises they saw much of the 1/2nd Punjab Regiment, whose own dancing and piping interested the Gordons very much.

Musketry took the Battalion to the neat Singinting camp about ten miles from Port Dickson in Negri Sembilan, one of the Federated Malay States. Here they used the range of the Malay Regiment, and were made very welcome. Parties of the Gordons paid informal visits to many places in Malaya, including the island of Penang, and were everywhere well received. For the St. Andrew's Day celebrations in 1938 the pipers were in demand 'all over Malaya and even in Sumatra'.

Training was still chiefly a matter of reconnaissance and the manning of the Singapore defences with the practice of opposed landings both on the island and on the coast of Johore. Later a platoon of the Gordons entered into permanent occupation of Pengerang on the south-eastern tip of Johore where expenditure on coast defences had been approved.

The 2nd Gordons were gradually being brought up to date with transport and other equipment, and among other novelties the Boys anti-tank rifle was received. The companies were reformed on the new three-section, three platoon basis, the pipers providing personnel for a mortar platoon and the drummers that for an antiaircraft section. Also, a pioneer platoon was formed.

In December 1938 came a change of command, Lieut.-Colonel G. T. Burney being succeeded by Lieut.-Colonel W. J. Graham.

And now the 2nd Gordons looked forward to another change of scene, for in the next trooping season they were due to depart for India, where Mhow was reported to be a very pleasant station.

[1] See maps pp. 88 and 102.

The Regiment at Home
1935-39

The 1st Gordons, who arrived from overseas in January 1935, found that their first Home station was Edinburgh. Here they were welcomed by their old friends, the Royal Scots Greys, and settled down to a not uneventful year.

In May the Silver Jubilee of King George V was the occasion of a special parade, and the Gordons provided a guard of honour for the Duke of Kent when His Royal Highness visited Edinburgh. The Battalion were 'at home' to the public on 17th August, and the band and pipers, who had been to the Brussels Exhibition to play during 'British Week', were present at the opening of the new Depôt of the Gordon Highlanders on 14th September. Battalion training this year was on more realistic lines than had been customary in the past when tactical exercises had tended to be formal and conventional in character. Football and cricket flourished and a Rugby team was started.

King George V died on 20th January 1936, and the 1st Gordons supplied a guard of honour for the proclamation of King Edward VIII at Holyrood and at Mercat Cross, Stonehaven. In May the Battalion moved out to camp at Stobs for three months strenuous training; but Stobs was not regarded with great favour for 'there was not much level ground for games'. The Gordons provided the King's Guard at Ballater this year. The band departed on a tour of South Africa.

In March 1937 the Duke of Gloucester presented the 1st Gordons with new colours. The old colours had been received in 1899 at the hands of a former Royal Colonel-in-Chief, the Prince of Wales, afterwards King Edward VII.

This was the year of the Coronation of King George VI. Among the troops drawn from many Regiments, British Commonwealth and Empire, who were called to London for the ceremony on 12th May was a detachment of the 1st Gordons, who bore themselves with proper pride. Asked what 'mob' he belonged to one private made the crushing retort: 'I dinna belong to any mob. I'm a Gordon Highlander.'

In Edinburgh the Battalion were visited by officers and men from the Coronation contingents, the guests including a party of the affiliated Regiment, the 48th Highlanders of Canada, Toronto.

The King and Queen visited Edinburgh in July, and with the

THE REGIMENT AT HOME, 1935-39

departure of Their Majesties, came an end to ceremonial occasions and a return to uninterrupted work.

On 8th August a composite company commanded by Major G. E. Malcolm, left Edinburgh for a recruiting march through Aberdeenshire. The column, fully mechanised, was able to cover 600 miles in five days, and provided valuable experience for the drivers and a great opportunity to meet old friends who excelled themselves in Highland hospitality.

The Battalion were gradually assuming an up-to-date look. Transport now included twenty trucks, six 30-cwt. lorries, and seven motor cycles. In September a short exercise was carried out at Stobs with the Gordons 'completely mechanised', made up with vehicles to the latest establishment of an infantry battalion. Two-seater Austin cars carried the company commanders.

In January 1938 Lieut.-Colonel J. M. Hamilton completed his tenure of command, and was followed by Lieut.-Colonel C. M. Usher who in his earlier days, as an outstanding Rugby forward, had been capped sixteen times for Scotland.

A move to Aldershot was made in the early spring, but before leaving Edinburgh the Gordons were becoming familiar with the Bren gun and anti-tank rifle and a mortar platoon was training hard.

At Aldershot the Gordons found themselves with the 2nd Hampshire Regiment—afterwards replaced by the 1st Loyals—and the 2nd North Staffordshire in the 2nd Brigade, commanded by Brigadier L. Carr, himself a Gordon Highlander. In June, however, he was succeeded by Brigadier C. E. Hudson, V.C. The 2nd Brigade were in the 1st Division, commanded by Major-General Hon. H. R. L. G. Alexander, later to become Field-Marshal Earl Alexander of Tunis.

The Gordons were now part of the spearhead which, as the British Expeditionary Force, was intended to take the field, fully trained and equipped, without delay should occasion arise. But on their arrival at Aldershot the Battalion had some way to make up before they reached the required standard of efficiency. Facilities for musketry had been limited at their Edinburgh station; now they could get all the practice they needed on the range. They soon received ten Bren-gun carriers and a carrier platoon was formed. Another sign of the times was that the Royal Air Force gave A Company the experience of being air-borne. In April the Gordons took part in a tank-infantry exercise for the benefit of the King and Queen, who had come to see the Army at work.

Yet life at Aldershot was not all work and no play, for the Searchlight Tattoo was held in June; and the Battalion games and a Highland gathering of the 1st Gordons and 1st Argyll & Sutherland Highlanders were notable events. When winter came several Gordon officers appeared in the hunting field.

In September 1938, however, war seemed very near. The whole nation had waited to hear if Hitler's designs on Czechoslovakia could be, or would be, thwarted by Great Britain and France. Then the Prime Minister, Mr. Neville Chamberlain, returned from Munich with his assurance of 'peace for our time'. The phrase has been given many interpretations: Mr. Churchill described the result of this parley with Hitler as 'a defeat without a war'. At any rate the two Western Powers, negotiating from weakness, had obtained a little more time to arm against the aggressor.

At Munich proposals had been discussed for an international commission to delimit, with or without plebiscites, certain areas of Czechoslovakia for German occupation in addition to the Sudeten territory. These proposals affected the 1st Gordons in so far that the Battalion were put at short notice to move to Czechoslovakia as part of an international force for plebiscite supervision duties. No move was made, for the fate of the Czechs was determined otherwise.

There is little to record of the 1st Gordons during the year that followed. They suffered, as all units of the British Expeditionary Force suffered, from the nation's reluctance to re-arm. No large-scale training of the divisions had been held for some years; and our Field Army still lacked the weapons, equipment and organization needed for modern war.

A strong detachment from the Depôt represented the Regiment at the Silver Jubilee Thanksgiving Service held by the Aberdeen City Council in May 1935.

In September came the long awaited move from the old Castlehill Barracks to the new Depôt so long a-building beyond the Bridge of Don. The central figure at the ceremonial opening on 14th September was the 11th Marquess of Huntly, whose tartan the Gordons wear. He was surrounded by a distinguished company, among them Sir Ian Hamilton, Colonel of the Regiment, the Marquess of Aberdeen, Lieutenant of the County, the Lord Provost of Aberdeen, and Lieut.-Colonel Hamilton commanding the 1st Battalion of the Gordons.

Recruiting declined somewhat in 1936, but in the spring of 1937 the 1st Gordons had been well enough supplied with new blood to rank as one of the strongest infantry battalions on the Home establishment. Major A. M. B. Norman succeeded Major W. J. Graham in command of the Depôt in April 1937. In

August the visit of a mechanised company of the 1st Battalion created much interest and had a good effect upon recruiting.

The Territorial Battalions continued in well doing and were attracting more men. In May 1935 at the Silver Jubilee celebrations the Lord Provost of Aberdeen took the salute of the 4th Gordons when they marched past 400 strong.

Fortunately the War Office were now able to be more generous —or one might say more reasonable—in the matter of pay and allowances, so that each Territorial battalion could look forward to a well-attended camp. The 4th and the 5th/7th Gordons, and three other battalions of the Highland Division were in camp together at Barry. The 6th Battalion were at Tain.

In August the death of Lieut.-Colonel R. L. J. Henderson deprived the 4th Gordons of a popular commanding officer. At his funeral the firing party was provided by the Depôt. Lieut.-Colonel W. Philip, who had served in the Battalion since he enrolled as a private, succeeded to the command. It was he who took the 4th Gordons to France after war came.

The 4th Gordons tried an innovation in the shape of war games for officers during 1936. The machine-gunners, now sixty strong, were doing very well with the Vickers gun. Ceremonial occasions included a parade of 300 of all ranks for the proclamation of King Edward VIII and, in May, a combined march-past and church parade of all Territorial Army units in Aberdeen.

The annual camp for the 4th and the 5th/7th Battalions was at Dunfermline in 1936, but they were not there at the same time. The 5th/7th Gordons observe with satisfaction that 'training was not interrupted by the weather nor by generals', but the 4th were not so fortunate, at least as regards the weather. The 6th Gordons had a record attendance at Tain.

There were two changes of command in June of this year: Lieut.-Colonel A. D. Buchanan-Smith succeeded Lieut.-Colonel G. P. Geddes in the 5th/7th and Lieut.-Colonel J. L. Ledingham followed Lieut.-Colonel A. S. Fortune in the 6th Battalion. These new commanding officers took their battalions overseas when the Highland Division reinforced the British Expeditionary Force in France.

To attract recruits the 4th Battalion introduced weekly 'guest nights' so that visitors might see squads engaged in various forms of training, and examine arms and equipment.

Coronation year saw three officers and 25 other ranks of each Battalion in London for duty on the day of the ceremony.

In 1937 the company headquarters of the 6th Gordons at Buckie was burnt down, causing much trouble and inconvenience, not the least worry being that there were no funds for rebuilding the place.

The 4th and 5th/7th Gordons both went to camp at Dreghorn where they were quite close to the 1st Battalion in Edinburgh. Tactical demonstrations by detachments of Regulars proved very instructive, and distinguished visitors included the Chief of the Imperial General Staff. The 6th Gordons were at Craigluscar, and marched through Edinburgh, where they spent a week-end with the 1st Battalion at Redford Barracks. Also, they had a visit from the mechanised company of the 1st Gordons.

The European crisis of 1938 brought a considerable influx of recruits, the 4th Gordons being able to report that they were up to establishment, while the 5th/7th showed a surplus. Camp at Cambuslang proved very popular with the 4th Gordons, who were able to visit the Glasgow Exhibition. For the 5th/7th Battalion the great event was a mechanised route march with the men in platoon trucks, the whole Battalion moving on wheels for three days. The 6th Gordons were in camp at Barry.

In the autumn of 1938 the 4th Gordons, now five per cent. over establishment, were selected to be the machine-gun battalion of the Highland Division. One of the first results of this rather drastic change was the arrival of so much new equipment that new premises were needed in which to store it. All ranks quickly became keen on the Vickers gun.

The place of the 4th Gordons in the 153rd Brigade was taken by the 6th Battalion from the 152nd Brigade, and the brigades of the Highland Division were reorganised on the modern three-battalion basis. The 153rd Brigade which had always been known as the Black Watch and Gordon Brigade, now consisted of the 4th Black Watch, 5th/7th Gordons and 6th Gordons.

The year preceding the outbreak of the Second World War was one of strenuous preparation, for the implications of Munich were soon seen in their true perspective. There was so much to be done. War industries required to be established and developed so that our expanding armed forces could be furnished with modern weapons and equipment. The Army, with inadequate resources, was called upon to receive and to turn into trained soldiers the great numbers of men who were directed from civilian life. In May 1939 the Compulsory Training Act was passed by Parliament; but earlier, in March—after the Germans had entered Czechoslovakia—the Government had decided upon a big voluntary effort. The Territorial Army was to be brought not only up to establishment, but doubled.

While the 1st Gordon Highlanders at Aldershot pursued their accustomed round with the knowledge that should war come they would embark for France with the Expeditionary Force, and the 2nd Gordons sat in garrison at Singapore, the Territorial battalions of the Regiment turned to their recruiting task.

In Aberdeen the 4th (Machine-Gun) Battalion held week-end camps and welcomed a steady influx of recruits. The 4th, who were already over establishment, aimed to form another machine-gun battalion, and Lieut.-Colonel J. H. McI. Gordon was appointed to command it—the 8th Gordon Highlanders. For the first few months the 8th existed as a part of the parent Battalion, and it was not until mobilization on 1st September, 1939, that they attained full independence.

The districts from which the 5th/7th Gordons drew their recruits were Buchan, Mar and Mearns, with the addition, authorised during the winter of 1937, of Fraserburgh. The Shetlands had always been included in the 7th Battalion area, but no attempt had been made to draw upon the islands since the end of the First World War. Now, in the spring of 1939, the assistant adjutant of the 5th/7th paid the Shetlands a visit, and in a very short time recruited 100 men. The 5th/7th beat up for recruits in Skene, Dunecht, Newmachar, Kingswells, Fintray, Fetterangus, and New Pitsligo, and many old 5th Battalion men rejoined. The 5th/7th Gordons were the first battalion in Scotland to reach a double establishment, and the commanding officer received from the War Office a mild reproof for having exceeded the requisite number.

When the 5th/7th went into camp in the summer at Dreghorn they were 1,200 strong, and at the end of August orders were received to divide the Battalion into two. Thenceforward the 5th Battalion consisted of the men from Buchan and Formartine, and the 7th Battalion, under the command of Lieut.-Colonel J. N. Reid, of those from Mar and Mearns. Thus the amalgamation of the 5th and the 7th Gordons, carried out in 1934, was reversed.

The 6th Gordons aimed at having 1,000 men each week at the annual camp at Dreghorn. A demonstration company known as the 'circus' was formed to display the Bren gun and the mortar, the new drill in 'threes', and physical drill. Accompanied by the pipes and drums in full dress the circus visited Portgordon, Cornhill, Aberchirder, Rothiemay, Rhynie, Inverurie, Fyvie and Newmills. 'Local celebrities' backed the call for recruits and the young men came in. It was not long before a new unit, the 9th Gordon Highlanders, sprang from the surplus of the 6th Battalion, and the 9th found their commanding officer in Lieut.-Colonel W. T. Murray Bissett.

His Royal Highness the Duke of Gloucester had become Colonel-in-Chief of the Gordon Highlanders on 12th March, 1937, the first member of the Royal Family to hold the appointment since the Prince of Wales, who afterwards ascended the throne as King Edward VII.

Sir Ian Hamilton relinquished the Colonelcy of the Regiment, a life appointment in those days, on 1st June, 1939. On the previous 16th January he had reached the age of 86 years, and he felt that his powers were no longer equal to his duty as he saw it. He was no 'arm chair' Colonel. No journey had been too long, no undertaking too arduous for him if it were on behalf of his Regiment. His love for the Gordon Highlanders and his pride in them will long be remembered.

His successor was Major-General Sir James Burnett of Leys, 13th baronet, whose distinguished record of service embraced the South African War, 1899-1902, and the First World War. Since vacating command of the 2nd Gordon Highlanders in 1926 he had commanded the 14th Brigade of the Shanghai Defence Force, 1927, the 153rd Brigade of the 51st (Highland) Division, 1928, and the 8th Brigade, 1930. From 1931 to 1935 he had been G.O.C. the Highland Division.

THE SECOND WORLD WAR
1939-45

Withdrawal to Escaut—Ypres-Comines Canal—Dunkirk 1940—Somme 1940—St. Valéry-en-Caux—**Odon**—La Vie Crossing—Lower Maas—Venlo Pocket—Rhineland—**Reichswald**—Cleve—**Goch**—**Rhine**—**North-West Europe 1940, '44-'45**—El Alamein—Advance on Tripoli—**Mareth**—Medjez Plain—**North Africa 1942-43**—Landing in Sicily—**Sferro**—Sicily 1943—**Anzio**—Rome—Italy 1944-45.

FRANCE AND BELGIUM
1939-40

The Twilight War

Meanwhile the march of events in Europe was bringing war ever nearer to Britain. In April 1939 Italy had invaded Albania. In May Germany and Italy formed an offensive-defensive alliance; and in August Germany signed a 'non-aggression' pact with Russia. Hitler's next move was to announce that Danzig had been incorporated in the German *Reich*. His intentions against Poland were only too clear, and both Great Britain and France stood pledged to defend Poland against aggression.

These were the last uneasy days of peace. On 1st September was issued the order for general mobilization: the German armies had invaded Poland. There could be no hope that Hitler would withdraw them when he received our ultimatum, and on 3rd September, timing British action with that of France, the Prime Minister announced to the House of Commons that we were at war with Germany.

Recollections of the previous struggle were still too fresh in men's minds for anyone to anticipate a quick and easy victory. In 1914 the nation was caught up in a great wave of enthusiasm, and the chief anxiety of the optimists was that the fight might be over before they could get to the front. Now, twenty-five years later, a realistic mood prevailed: all were aware that another European war threatened catastrophe of which the outcome could not be foreseen.

At Aldershot, however, the scene resembled in some respects that of a quarter of a century before. On 4th September the 1st Gordon Highlanders received from the Depôt 199 reservists, next day a second party arrived, and a number of officers joined. Yet, compared with 1914, an infantry battalion, with Bren light machine-guns, mortars and anti-tank rifles, wore a different appearance. Ten Bren-gun carriers formed an extra platoon. The horse had disappeared, and the maintenance of mechanised transport demanded new skills and a new routine. All the officers were motorists.

The British Expeditionary Force was for France and, as in 1914, its numbers were not impressive when compared with the armies of our Ally; but the quality of its officers and men was undoubted, and it would grow as fresh divisions joined it as soon as they were trained and equipped, or could be spared from the defence of the Homeland.

Having made their final preparations during a succession of air raid alarms which were no more than alarms, the 1st Gordons began to move on 20th September when the transport left for Southampton. The remainder of the Battalion followed two days later and, after an uneventful crossing, reached Cherbourg on the morning of the 23rd.

The journey to the forward area took a week by road and rail; and here the commanding officer may be gratefully remembered for his forethought in buying straw so that the troops might have some degree of comfort in their trucks during the long and tedious train journey of twenty-four hours which took them from la Hutte, eight miles north of le Mans, to Arras.

Arras was reached on the 30th, and here the Gordons suffered a minor catastrophe. Before beginning the two hours' march to Neuville opportunity was taken for a grand brew-up of tea which proved undrinkable. Salt had been added instead of sugar.

By this time General Gamelin, Supreme Commander of the Allied Forces in France, had decided to stand upon the defensive. The Allies were not yet ready to do more, nor were their defensive preparations complete. Farther to the East events moved swiftly: after the fall of Warsaw on 27th September Germany and Russia proceeded with the partition of Poland. Hitler could now concentrate upon mounting his great offensive in the West.

At Neuville the 1st Gordons were concerned with a more personal matter. To ease the supply situation they were ordered to live on the country—by purchase of course—and all ranks fared pretty well under this arrangement, which did not last long.

On 5th October the Battalion left by road and rail for the area south-east of Lille, where the 1st Division were settling in. The British Expeditionary Force had been allotted part of the field defences, still far from complete, which fringed the Belgian border from the western end of the Maginot Line to the sea.

After five days at Sainghin-en-Melantois, where the inhabitants proved kind and helpful and the amenities included a church service, baths, and a cinema, the Gordons moved to Templeuve-en-Pevéle, and got down to a routine of hard work in very wet weather. A range was improvised for mortar practice: the main task was to prepare Templeuve for all-round defence.

As the Gordons were in the reserve brigade of the 1st Division their endeavours were often impeded by divisional working parties engaged in repairing roads or drawing stores. There seemed to be as much digging to do as there had been in the old war, but the work was rather more complicated: anti-tank ditches, and emplacements for anti-tank guns were needed, while not everyone took kindly to mixing concrete.

The British soldier is used to hardship and monotony, but only those who were in France and Belgium at the time can appreciate the depressing conditions of the winter of 1939-40. Heavy rains were followed by frost and snow, thaw and frost again. To keep the new defences in repair often seemed a hopeless task. All effort was hampered by the bitter weather and life was rendered more harassing by the black-out regulations which restricted movement after dark.

Attack from the air was always to be expected, and an officer of the Gordons who made a flight over the area discovered how difficult it was to conceal trenches and emplacements from air observation, though new cement work, covered with straw against frost, certainly presented a hay-stack effect.

Lord Gort, the Commander-in-Chief, and the Divisional commander, Major-General Hon. H. R. L. G. Alexander, paid the Gordons a visit on 28th October. Next day three companies were moved to Cysoing, a large village eight miles south-east of Lille and only three from the Belgian border.

Work on the defences of Cysoing and Templeuve continued. Air alarms were frequent and some air activity was seen. The Duke of Gloucester, Colonel-in-Chief of the Gordons, visited the Battalion in November and found all ranks in good heart, making the best of a dreary existence on the threshold of a neutral country.

Belgium still clung to the vain hope that her neutrality would be respected by Germany if she were careful not to take any defensive measures which might provoke the aggressor. Nevertheless she agreed that, if she were attacked, French and British forces should come to her aid: the Allies would enter Belgium and take up defensive positions, the French on the Meuse from Givet to Namur and north of Namur, the British on the line of the river Dyle, east of Brussels. This plan, after much discussion, was definitely adopted by General Gamelin in November 1939. It was known to the the British as ' Plan D '.

Before the end of November the whole of the 1st Gordons were concentrated at Cysoing. On 5th December they lined the streets to greet the King, Lieut.-Colonel Usher being among those presented to His Majesty.

On 17th December the commanding officer assembled the Battalion to impart some unwelcome news. The kilt was no

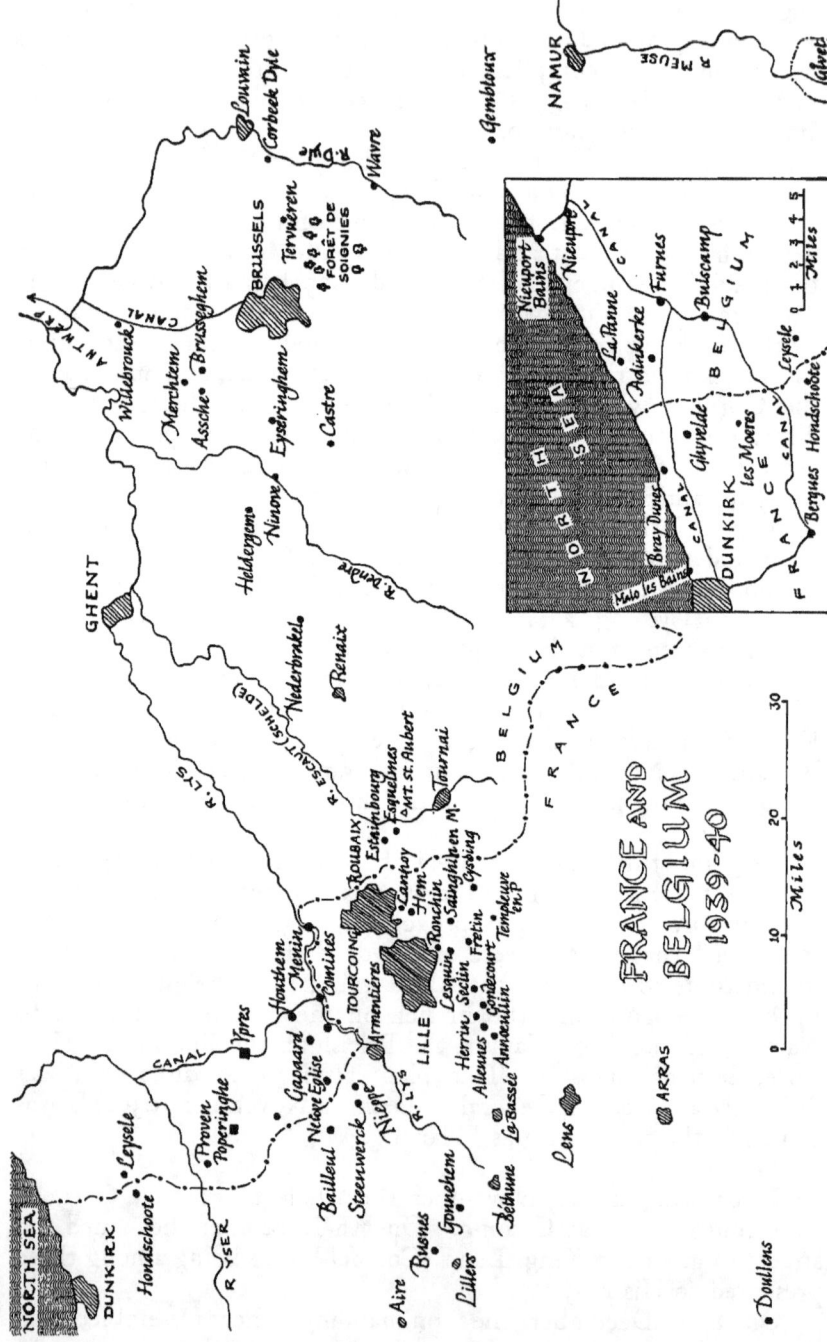

longer to be worn: in future Highlanders would wear the battle-dress common to the rest of the Army. This was, however, to be a temporary measure, for the Adjutant-General had given a written assurance that the kilt should come into its own again as soon as the war was over.

Christmas festivities included a battalion dance and a children's party with Highland dancing. The New Year celebrations, with a special dinner for all ranks, was, of course, an event. Once a week the pipes and drums played Retreat in the village square, and the weekly concerts and cinema shows were well organised and highly popular. Leave to the United Kingdom was opened, and a party left for home every week.

One extra duty was thrust upon the Gordons: the provision of patrols to check smuggling across the Franco-Belgian frontier and the entry into France of 'unauthorised persons'. This work, which demanded some knowledge of the niceties of French law, was really the business of customs officers and police; but the French authorities could not cope with it unaided.

The Gordons were not the only British troops who sometimes wondered when the war would begin. In the middle of January 1940, however, when the Allies had good reason to fear the imminence of a big German offensive in the West, all leave was cancelled and all routine movements stopped. The British, under Plan D, stood ready to move into their battle positions in Belgium. This was a false alarm, but an exercise called 'Pack' showed that the 1st Gordons, at least, could move with the minimum of delay. The only hitch was that the transport, with the temperature well below freezing point, found great difficulty in starting up.

On 9th February the Battalion marched eighteen miles to line part of the route along which M. le Brun, President of the French Republic, drove on a tour of inspection.

Soon afterwards the Gordons lost their commanding officer, Lieut.-Colonel C. M. Usher being promoted colonel and appointed Area Commandant St. Malo. He left on 22nd February and was given a great send-off. With the pipers leading the way, his car was pulled along the cobbled streets to the station by a team of sergeants: altogether a fitting tribute to an officer who had given twenty-nine years' devoted service to the Regiment. Major H. Wright succeeded to the command.

On the last day of the month the Gordons were paid a very graceful compliment by our French allies. By special invitation a detachment of forty with six pipers, under Captain J. de B. Stansfeld, was sent to Caudry where General Picard, commanding a mechanised cavalry division, presented honours and awards to his officers and men. The Highlanders formed part of the guard of honour, and the hospitality of the French 4th Dragoons was something to be remembered.

Here one must spare a thought for the 2nd Brigade Anti-Tank Company which had been formed at Roclincourt, near Arras, in October 1939, and had moved up to the Lille area later in that month. Each battalion in the brigade contributed a platoon to this company, so the unit was one-third Gordons, their platoon being commanded by 2nd-Lieutenant J. I. R. Dunlop. The company commander was Major L. G. Murray of the 1st Gordons.

A side-light on our unpreparedness for war is shown by the fact that at first the company possessed neither guns nor vehicles. The guns—25-mm. Hotchkiss, three to a platoon—certainly arrived before many days, but transport came later, so that, for a time, carriers had to be borrowed from the battalions. The succeeding months were mainly devoted by the company to practice on a range near Calais.

The 4th Gordon Highlanders, Aberdeen's own battalion, received their mobilization orders in their home city. Two of the earliest ploys were a thorough medical inspection and the despatch of the enthusiastic youngsters who were under nineteen to the newly-raised 8th Battalion, who also took those adjudged unfit for service overseas. Training was carried out at Blackdog and at Westburn Park.

Although they had become a machine-gun battalion the 4th Gordons still belonged to the 51st (Highland) Division, but they were soon to start upon a separate career. On 25th September they were warned for service overseas in the near future, and preparations to move were made. On the 30th a notice in battalion orders gave the names of three Aberdeen ladies to whom wives and families of the men could apply if in any difficulty after the Battalion had left. Aberdeen takes care of her own.

The move to Aldershot began at the beginning of October, and at their new station the Gordons received large drafts to bring them up to war establishment. For the most part these were composed of reservists with machine-gun experience, but they also included twenty drivers from the R.A.S.C. who were particularly welcome seeing that the Battalion were short of trained drivers. Of the new arrivals, well over 300 in all, ninety-one were Gordons; most of the others came from English regiments.

Among the officer postings was Lieutenant (later Captain) E. J. D. Snowball, a Regular officer of the Argyll & Sutherland Highlanders, who became adjutant before the start of active operations and continued so after the return from Dunkirk. His services are well remembered.

Later in the month Major-General V. M. Fortune, commanding the Highland Division, came to say goodbye. The Battalion had passed from the 51st to become ' G.H.Q. troops '.

As a machine-gun battalion—four companies each of twelve Vickers guns—they could expect to be ' employed in depth on counter-preparation tasks ', usually under divisional command; and there were many who could not understand why the divisional command should not be that of the 51st. None wanted to leave his friends and compatriots, but there was consolation in the thought that of all Gordon Territorial units the 4th Battalion would be the first in the field.

They were, indeed, to be the first battalion of the Territorial Army to join the British Expeditionary Force, and were so informed by the Chief of the Imperial General Staff, General Sir Edmund Ironside, when he visited Aldershot. The Regular divisions already in France needed their proper complement of machine-gun battalions.

So it was that, after only eight weeks of specialised training, the 4th Gordons went overseas. On 27th October they left Aldershot for Southampton to embark for Cherbourg. They reached the French port early next morning, and by 4th November had taken over good billets at Vermelles, in the mining country between Lens and Béthune. They came under the command of the 4th Division (II Corps) and were allotted a fortnight for overhauling guns and vehicles before starting a strenuous training programme. Instructors were provided from other units, and the Gordons received a visit of encouragement from Lieut.-General Sir A. Brooke, the Corps commander.

Early in December, when winter had set in, the Battalion moved up to Roubaix. On the 6th a detachment attended a parade which was inspected by the King, His Majesty being accompanied by the Duke of Gloucester, Colonel-in-Chief of the Gordon Highlanders, and Lord Gort. About this time a present of footballs from the Aberdeen and Queen's Park Clubs was gratefully received.

Christmas Day and the New Year were celebrated in appropriate fashion and in very wintry weather. Snow persisted, so parties of Gordons were required to clear it from the streets of Roubaix.

On 8th February, 1940 Lieut.-Colonel W. Philip left the Battalion, and was succeeded in command by Lieut.-Colonel R. A. G. Taylor, a Royal Scots Fusilier. Before this, leave to the United Kingdom had been opened.

During the next two months the 4th Gordons were engaged in hard and profitable training. They took part in a number of divisional schemes lasting several days and carried out battalion exercises both by day and night. In addition to these activities machine-gun positions were sited and built in a divisional reserve line.

The 51st (Highland) Division was one of the first of the Territorial divisions to join the British Expeditionary Force in France. This was only to be expected, and not only by reason of the high reputation won by the 51st in the First World War: the same soldierly spirit had endured in the Highlands throughout the intervening years, and the new generation who in 1939 filled the ranks of the Highland Division could be counted upon to tread worthily in the steps of their fathers.

The 5th Gordons mobilized at Bucksburn, where billets were good but training was handicapped by lack of equipment for modern war. On 9th September the Battalion was inspected by the Colonel of the Regiment, Major-General Sir James Burnett of Leys, and this was the last occasion on which the colours appeared upon parade. Ninety-eight other ranks who were under age or otherwise unfit for service overseas were transferred to the 7th Battalion at Banchory.

At Keith the 6th Gordons experienced the same difficulties in their preparation for active service, but deficiencies in equipment were steadily made good.

At the beginning of October the Highland Division moved south. The 5th Gordons left Bucksburn for Farnborough on the 7th and on the same day the 6th Battalion were given a great send-off from Keith. Both 5th and 6th went into unfinished barracks at Cove, where the workmen were still busy and no great degree of comfort was to be expected. Here the 5th Gordons welcomed a draft of sixty-eight from the Depôt (now called Infantry Training Centre) and 139 men joined from the 7th Battalion. The 6th Gordons received 104 other ranks from the Cameronians I.T.C. and 124 from the 9th Gordons. In both 5th and 6th Battalions transport vehicles were made up to war establishment.

In December a move was made into Maida and Corunna Barracks at Aldershot. The Gordons—that is to say the whole Division—were now in hard training, and the advent of what proved to be an exceptionally hard winter made soldiering a tough business, a foretaste of what was to come.

On 5th January Brigadier G. B. Rowan Hamilton relinquished command of the 153rd Brigade, being medically unfit, and was succeeded by Brigadier G. T. Burney, a Gordon Highlander with a distinguished record as a regimental officer.

The King and Queen inspected the Highland Division on 18th January and next day, a day of bitter cold, the Gordons enjoyed a ceremonial occasion of their own.

The 1st Canadian Division, who had recently arrived at Aldershot, contained the 48th Highlanders of Canada, the allied Regiment of the Gordons, and the 75th Toronto Scottish, whose affiliation to the London Scottish made them, also, 'relations'. On 9th January the two Canadian battalions and the 5th and 6th Gordons paraded under Brigadier Burney. They were inspected by Sir James Burnett of Leys, who took the salute as Gordon and Canadian Highlanders marched past to the massed pipes and drums of the 153rd Brigade.

This marked the last occasion on which the 5th and 6th Gordons were seen in the kilt.

At the end of January 1940 the Highland Division crossed to France by a shorter sea-route than had been used by our forces at the beginning of the war. Then the risk of sea and air attack in the narrow waters of the Channel had led to the choice of Cherbourg as the port of disembarkation for troops, stores and heavy vehicles being sent to Brest, St. Nazaire and Nantes, and La Pallice. Now, as the Germans had shown little disposition to interfere with our convoys, troops were sent to Le Havre.

After a peaceful daylight passage the 5th Gordons landed on 30th January. Next day the 6th Gordons arrived. The Division assembled north of the Seine in the country between Le Havre an Rouen, the two battalions of Gordons occupying the area St. Aubin-Louvretot-Touffreville.

In France the weather seemed even worse than it had been in England. Frost and snow and flood-water wrought such havoc to the British communications that the forward movement of the Division was delayed for two days. However, by 10th February the Highlanders were concentrated in the Lillers-Béthune area, the 5th Gordons being at Gonnehem and the 6th near Busnes.

The weather did not improve and outside activities were severely restricted. The 5th Gordons record floods and almost continuous rain; the 6th emphasise the extreme cold and the snow which followed. One comfort was the provision of hot baths.

While at Gonnehem the 5th Gordons provided a very smart guard of honour for the French General Fagalde, who was on a visit to Divisional headquarters at Béthune.

At the beginning of March the Division moved up nearer to the Belgian frontier, south and south-west of Lille, the 5th Gordons going to Gondecourt and Herrin, the 6th to Allennes-les-Marais and Annoeullin near by. Training continued, interrupted at times by work on field defences.

Higher authority had decided that it would be good for the Territorial divisions in France to exchange one battalion per brigade for a Regular battalion. The Regulars coming in were expected to introduce a little professional polish which the outgoing Territorials would acquire when brigaded with Regulars.

In the Highland Division this business was very well arranged. The 153rd Brigade lost the 6th Gordons to the 2nd Brigade of the 1st Division and received the 1st Gordons.

The exchange was carried out with a touch of ceremony and expressions of comradeship characteristic of the British Army. The Corps commander, Lieut.-General Sir J. Dill, sent the 1st Gordons a message commending them for their good work at Aldershot and in France. At a special parade on 6th March Major-General Alexander and Brigadier Hudson bade the Battalion farewell. Next day the 1st Gordons were played out of Cysoing by the band of the North Staffordshire, who also provided a company to line the route near the starting-point. The Brigadier and many of the Loyals were there to see the Gordons go, and the inhabitants of Cysoing waved and shouted goodbye.

At Fretin, on the road to Seclin, the 1st Battalion met the 6th Battalion, who were on their way to take their place in the 2nd Brigade, and half-an-hour was allowed for an informal mingling of Regulars and Territorials and the exchange of news. The commander of the 153rd Brigade, Brigadier Burney, moved among them. He was there to wish the 6th Battalion God-speed and to welcome the 1st Gordons. Himself a Gordon, he seemed inclined to apologise for wearing a red hat, which he called his 'bull teaser', instead of a glengarry.

When the 1st Gordons entered the area of the Highland Division General Fortune was there to receive them, and on reaching Seclin the pipes and drums of the 5th Gordons were ready to play them to their billets at Allennes-les-Marais.

The 6th Gordons had bidden farewell to the 153rd Brigade in somewhat similar fashion, and when the Battalion reached Cysoing all ranks were made welcome and soon settled down as a battalion in a Regular brigade. On arrival, however, they lost their commanding officer, Lieut.-Colonel Ledingham being appointed town-major of Roubaix. Lieut.-Colonel P. T. Pirie, another Gordon Highlander, arrived on 24th March to assume command.

Hard training, including some brigade exercises, kept the 6th Gordons busy, and detachments were sent to fire on the ranges at Dannes, on the coast between Calais and Boulogne. Working parties for the defences were also in demand and, being now near the Belgian frontier, the Battalion had to take their share of customs and police duties in the form of providing control posts and patrols.

At the end of April the 2nd Brigade moved back to the Amiens reserve training area, the Gordons being billeted at Pas-en-Artois.

The 2nd Brigade Anti-Tank Company had sent its 1st Gordons platoon to the 153rd Brigade company on 6th March, receiving in exchange the 6th Gordons platoon under 2nd-Lieutenant R. Fraser. More range practice was carried out at Calais during March and April before the company moved to the reserve training area with the 2nd Brigade.

Although gratified to find themselves among Highland men and in a brigade which included their own 5th Battalion and was commanded by a Gordon Highlander, the 1st Gordons found that they had taken on rather onerous responsibilities. The Brigade called upon them for trained signallers and men for intelligence and transport duties; and soon the 1st Division were asking that two officers and six senior non-commissioned officers be sent back to assist the 6th Gordons in their training. The departure of two companies to help in digging a trench which was to carry a signal cable to General Headquarters situated between Doullens and Arras left a very depleted battalion. Fortunately the two companies were only away for ten days; and in spite of all these demands a number of men were sent to Dannes for mortar, anti-tank rifle and grenade practice.

In two respects the 1st Gordons found that their Territorial brethren were better provided for than they were themselves.

They had brought out to France in the previous September the transport which they had been using for two years : the Highland Division had been equipped with new vehicles at mobilization. It was therefore difficult for the Regulars to equal the standard of maintenance and performance set by the Territorials. All that could be done was done by the 1st Gordons; and their drivers proved superior in a series of night-driving tests.

Again, the units of the Highland Division had all come overseas with their full establishment of pipe bands. Embarking as they did with little thought for anything but the grim business of war the 1st Gordons were not equipped on this peace-time scale. However, by sending home to the Depôt for additional sets of pipes and drums the 1st Battalion were soon able to perform with credit when the massed pipe bands of the Brigade played Retreat.

At the end of March the Highland Division moved northwestward to extend the British occupation of the frontier region by relieving the French in the sector Armentières-Bailleul.

The 5th Gordons left Gondecourt with regret, for the inhabitants of this pleasant village were friendly and hospitable folk and the *maire*—said to be a Communist—had been helpful in many ways. Having marched fifteen miles to Nieppe, the Battalion took over from the French 48th Regiment four concrete blockhouses and certain entrenchments; and also the customs and control duties on the frontier. It was, also, the turn of the 5th Gordons to send two companies to work on the cable trench near Arras.

While the Battalion was at Nieppe a French resident gave a silver cup for competition between the football teams of the various British units and a French civilian team. The 5th Gordons, always keen on the game, had the satisfaction of beating the French in the final.

There was plenty of work for all on the defences which were unfinished, and weak by any standard. The 1st Gordons, after they had settled in at Steenwerck, discovered that the elaborate maps and fire plans handed over by the French represented, for the most part, *projets*. Certain defences, however, did exist. One company took possession of a number of concrete bunkers built as emplacements for the French 25-mm. anti-tank gun, the weapon with which all British anti-tank gunners had been equipped. But the guns used by us were of an older pattern and could not be introduced into the bunkers.

Occupied in improving the field works and manning in their turn the control posts on the frontier, the 1st Gordons found themselves busy enough, with few men to spare for their own training. They could do little to assist their Territorial friends. Moreover, the order was given that the demands of agriculture had precedence over training, which is to say that no field movements that involved damage to growing crops could be permitted. For the moment, at least, the ploughshare was more important than the sword.

At Steenwerck the Duke of Gloucester again visited the 1st Gordons, His Royal Highness walking round some of the billets without fuss or ceremony. Also at Steenwerck was revived an old practice which had its origin in the late seventeenth century during the campaigns in the Low Countries.

The town possessed quite a number of inviting shops and estaminets, and Highland men are proverbially adept at making friends wherever they may be. To cut short their revelry by night and to warn all men that they must be in their billets by the prescribed hour of ten o'clock, the drummers of the 1st Gordons marched through the town beating Tattoo.

About the middle of April when the long cold winter had passed the Highland Division received orders to move south and take over a sector of the defences in front of the Maginot Line between the rivers Moselle and Saar. Since December 1939 the British Expeditionary Force had been sending brigades in rotation for a fifteen days tour of duty on the Saar front where they were, at least, in contact with the enemy; but the 51st were the first—and only—complete division to go.

All ranks welcomed the prospect, for monotonous duty behind the frontier of a neutral country—a state of affairs which General Fortune had called 'unnatural'—was to no one's taste. Now there seemed some prospect of getting to grips with the Germans.

Already, on 9th April, Germany had struck her first blow in the West by invading Norway and Denmark. Denmark, in no condition to defend herself, was quickly over-run. Allied troops were hastily despatched to the assistance of Norway where a campaign, conducted against a better trained and better equipped enemy who also possessed superiority in the air, held a doubtful chance of success. At the beginning of May the British forces began to evacuate central Norway, though the Allies were still planning to capture Narvik in the north.

It was known that German armies were massing beyond the frontiers of Holland and Belgium, and in France the Allies awaited the onslaught of the aggressor. They had not long to wait. What the journalists called the 'phony war' and Winston Churchill the 'twilight war' was ended.

Dyle to Dunkirk

In the early morning of 10th May heavy air attacks were made against the Allied airfields. The invasion of Holland and Belgium had begun. Promptly British General Headquarters issued orders to operate Plan D : the advance into Belgium to occupy the line of the river Dyle.

As the 2nd Brigade were in the reserve training area, their first move was back to their billets in the neighbourhood of Lille, all infantry being carried in motor transport. The 6th Gordons, who record that the roads were much congested with traffic which was under attack by German bombers, reached Cysoing at 4 p.m. without mishap.

At 6 p.m. on 11th May the move into Belgium began, the 2nd Brigade forming a column of 330 vehicles which occupied thirty-three miles of road space. The route was Tournai-Renaix-Ninove to the outskirts of Brussels, where the Gordons 'debussed'—the usual term for alighting from any form of wheeled transport—and marched about five miles to a rest camp reached on the early morning of 12th May.

Lieut.-Colonel Pirie and his second-in-command Major Bradshaw, were both on leave when the Battalion left Pas-en-Artois for Cysoing, the commanding officer being actually in England. Thanks to the Royal Air Force he was flown out in time to lead his people across the Belgian frontier.

The Gordons marched forward to the Dyle on Sunday, 12th May, starting at 10.30 a.m. It was a fine morning and many inhabitants were seen out for a walk, apparently little disturbed by the German invasion. There were about fifteen miles to go, and the Battalion moved with intervals between companies as a precaution against air attack. The *Luftwaffe*, however, were seeking other targets on this day.

In the evening the Gordons took over their allotted front on the Dyle, south of Corbeek, in the sector which had been held by the 3rd Brigade until the 2nd Brigade should arrive. Two rifle companies were in front with two in support about half a mile in rear. The carrier platoon took up outpost positions a mile east of the river.

The Dyle is a quiet stream flowing in a shallow valley which here varies from 500 to 1,200 yards in width. In places there was flood water, but not so extensive as the Gordons had been led to expect. The wooded slopes of the valley, higher on the eastern side, afforded opportunities for the infiltration of a thinly held line. The railway, which follows the eastern bank, might be accounted some obstacle to the rapid advance of armoured forces.

The Gordons found that the Belgians had wired the forward posts and had constructed a well-camouflaged blockhouse. They were the centre battalion of the Brigade, with the 1st Loyals on their right and the 2nd North Staffordshire on their left. The anti-tank company covered the bridges at Neeryssche and Corbeek and the high ground on the left of the Brigade. Sappers were already preparing the Dyle bridges for demolition while a long procession of refugees moved across them.

After a quiet night the Gordons spent 13th May in improving their defences. The Louvain-Brussels road was packed with refugees and Belgian military transport, all making for the capital. Fires could be seen in Louvain, which was under heavy attack from the air. Enemy aircraft did not trouble the Gordons much, but the anti-tank company claimed one hit on a German bomber.

On 14th May the *Luftwaffe* were busy, both in attack and in reconnaissance. Some aircraft flew low and machine-gunned our anti-tank positions without doing any harm. About noon all the Brigade carriers were ordered back across the Dyle, and soon the light tanks and the armoured cars of our cavalry followed suit. Later, the Gordons saw parties of German infantry on the eastern slopes beyond the river, but the enemy made no attempt to cross. Our guns had opened harassing fire, and in the evening the Dyle bridges were blown.

The Germans attacked Louvain on this day, but could make little impression on the 3rd Division who held the left of the British sector.

On other parts of the Allied front battle had been joined in earnest, the success of the German offensive proving but a prelude to the disasters which followed. The defences of Holland were overcome so rapidly that on 14th May the Dutch Army were forced to capitulate. The Belgians, who aimed to defend the line of the Albert canal from Antwerp to the Meuse, could not hold it, and were withdrawing to positions on the British left, with their right north of Louvain. But perhaps the gravest news came from the south. Advancing through the Ardennes, hill and forest country which the French had considered an impossible route for armour, the enemy had struck hard at the French Ninth Army and forced it back over the Meuse. By 13th May he had established bridge-heads over the river at Dinant and near Sedan; and his armoured divisions had already arrived on the eastern bank. With only a short delay they began to cross. Nearer the British the advanced troops of the French First Army, in the Gembloux gap between the Meuse and the Dyle, were conducting a fighting withdrawal.

The full significance of these events could hardly be known to the 6th Gordons, who sat in their positions along the Dyle, awaiting with confidence a German attack from across the river.

The 4th Gordons at Roubaix remained attached to the 4th Division, in reserve, and were not called upon to move on 10th May. After a series of air-raid alarms during the night—these continued all next day—the companies moved their machine-guns to defend the nearby airfields at Ronchin and Lesquin against possible enemy airborne landings. On the 12th A Company reported a German bomber shot down, its four occupants being in Belgian uniform; a platoon of B Company rescued the pilot of a British aircraft which had crashed.

It was on the afternoon of 14th May that the 4th Gordons marched into Belgium, the 4th Division having now begun to move up. Refugees crowded the roads, especially east of Tournai, and in the evening B Company brought their machine guns into action against an attack by German bombers. It was a hot, exhausting day and the Gordons were glad to reach Brusseghem, about six miles north-west of Brussels, soon after 8 p.m.

There was fighting along the Dyle on 15th May. The Germans, who seemed to have closed up to the river during the night, opened artillery and mortar fire along the whole British front. Our guns replied. In the late afternoon the enemy attacked the North Staffordshire but were driven off. The Gordons were not troubled until the evening, when a party of Germans almost blundered upon a post commanded by Lieutenant Victor Reid and were dispersed by fire. Although there were a few alarms and some confused firing in the course of the night, the Gordons saw no more of the enemy and, as yet, had not lost a man.

Actually, the German pressure on the British during the 15th had been on the northern flank, where Louvain was again the scene of sharp fighting, and to the south near Wavre. At the end of the day our front was still intact, but the First French Army, next on the right, had been forced back. To this movement the British were obliged to conform.

On this day Major Murray's anti-tank company were ordered out of action, and in the evening began to withdraw to a position at Tervueren in the Forest of Soignies, halfway between the Dyle and Brussels.

The 6th Gordons, still in the line on the Dyle, were pounded by the German artillery and mortars on 16th May. They were also under air attack and one mortar detachment of the Battalion was destroyed by a direct hit. In the evening the 2nd Brigade were ordered to withdraw—unwelcome news to men who had held their own with ease and knew little of what was happening elsewhere. They sensed that something was very wrong when verbal orders were received to dump blankets, packs and officers' valises, because no transport was available to carry them.

At night the Gordons found little difficulty in getting away, although shells were falling on the high ground west of the river. There were some casualties. Before he could get his platoon out, 2nd-Lieutenant I. S. Farquharson, a very promising young officer, was mortally wounded by a sniper; and two men were killed and five wounded.

The whole Brigade reached the Tervueren position by dawn of the 17th, being guided into it by the anti-tank company. Tervueren railway station was in flames, having been heavily bombed from the air.

Lord Gort, the Commander-in-Chief, had arranged with the French to withdraw in three stages from the line of the Dyle to the river Escaut (Schelde), where it was hoped that a protracted resistance might be made. Thus there was no rest for the 6th Gordons on 17th May. The withdrawal of the 2nd Brigade continued through Brussels, a platoon of the anti-tank company, with one section of the Gordon carriers attached, acting as rearguard. Major Murray made dispositions to cover the main approaches to the city, and remained until the Brigade and the cavalry had passed through.

Brussels presented an amazing sight, for many of the inhabitants seemed either unaware of, or indifferent to, the German menace. Tramcars were still running, and some of our stragglers secured a tram-ride into Brussels. The Brigade crossed the Charleroi canal west of the city and, being now in divisional reserve, were able to take a short rest. The troops had marched fifteen miles under a blazing sun, and many had had no sleep for two days.

At dusk on the 17th all were on the move again, the march becoming more and more impeded by crowds of fleeing civilians, mixed with transport of all kinds. There seemed to be little attempt at traffic control, and the frequent jams and delays tried the tempers of everyone. Fortunately no enemy aircraft appeared.

In the early morning of the 18th the Brigade reached the Castre-Eyseringham road. Only a few hours rest was permitted here. When the retreat was resumed the anti-tank platoons acted as rearguard, but made no contact with the enemy. By 5 p.m. all troops were behind the river Dendre.

The position of the 6th Gordons was about five miles southwest of Ninove, and with three companies 'up' they held about 1,500 yards of the river line. The weather was still hot and oppressive and rations were running short. The congestion of traffic had caused much intermixture of units, and there were many stragglers who had lost their companies through no fault of their own. Perhaps it was as well that the Germans did not follow up. The Dendre bridges were blown in the evening.

Next day, 19th May, the retreat took on a rather different aspect. The distance to be traversed between the Dendre and the Escaut was too great for tired marching men, so transport had to be provided. There would have been enough lorries to carry the whole Brigade but for the loss of a number of vehicles by the attack of enemy bombers. The 6th Gordons, after withdrawing from the river line under air attack, found that one of their companies would have to march.

Some men were picked up by vehicles of other units, but Lieutenant Hutcheon obtained seventy volunteers who were prepared to foot it. Then a better way was found. Abandoned bicycles were easy to acquire, and soon every man had a mount. This party rejoined the Battalion at the end of the day after a nerve-racking ride amid lorries, cars, guns, troops and refugees, for the whole of the 1st Division were using one road, with brigades and battalions mixed in great confusion. Enemy aircraft made some attacks;

had the *Luftwaffe* given the column its serious attention nothing short of disaster would have ensued.

The route was by Nederbrakel to Renaix, and thence to the northern outskirts of Tournai, part of the way lying across the path of a German advance from the east. Yet no contact with the enemy was made and eventually the battalions of the 1st Division were deployed along the Escaut. The 6th Gordons were allotted a narrow front at Esquelmes.

While, in this fashion, the 6th Gordons and the 2nd Brigade Anti-Tank Company reached the Escaut position, the 4th Gordons had been in close contact with the enemy.

On May 16th the 4th Division, reserve to the II Corps on the British left, had deployed along the canal south of Willebroeck in the area north of Brussels. Belgian troops were on their left. Next day the Gordons left Brusseghem for a position south of Assche to cover with their machine guns the general withdrawal to the river Dendre. They were part of a rearguard which included the 5th Inniskilling Dragoon Guards and the 15th/19th Hussars, and supported an intermediate defence line some six miles east of the river. This line was to be held until noon of the 18th.

The 4th Division began to withdraw to the Dendre on the evening of 17th May, the Belgians doing likewise. Soon after 9 o'clock next morning the 4th Gordons were in action but the enemy did not press on. At noon, the appointed time, the Battalion—all but one company—managed to withdraw across the river to Heldergem, although some of the bridges had already been blown or were under attack.

The morning had proved rather a trying one, for the Gordon companies were dispersed over a very wide front and, as they had no radio sets, all messages had to be sent by despatch rider. In maintaining communication the cavalry, who kept in wireless touch with the commander of the rearguard, were a great help in passing orders and information; and both the Dragoon Guards and the Hussars lent valuable assistance when the time for withdrawal came.

The remaining company of the Gordons were not so fortunate. They had been detached to join a northern flank guard which was expected to get in touch with Belgian troops between Assche and Merchtem; but the Belgians had already retreated. Our troops clashed with the advancing Germans in this vicinity during the early hours of the 18th and found it very difficult to disengage. Some detachments never received orders to withdraw and fought on as long as possible although outnumbered and surrounded. The chief sufferers were the 15th/19th Hussars. The 14th Anti-Tank

Regiment lost seven guns; the 4th Gordons reported Major J. F. Wallace, 2nd-Lieutenants J. A. Wood and F. D. Morgan and sixty-five other ranks missing.

The retirement of the 4th Division from the Dendre to the Escaut began on the night of 18th May, the 4th Gordons moving back to Renaix during a bombing attack which took heavy toll of the unhappy refugees on the roads. To cover the withdrawal, the machine guns of the Gordons occupied positions at Renaix, where they came under command of the 1st Division, until the next afternoon. Then they were able to pull out across the river, and go into billets around Estaimbourg. On this day Captain W. A. Holmes and one private who had been cut off during the withdrawal managed to rejoin.

On 20th May, when our forces were standing on the line of the Escaut, the two battalions of the Gordon Highlanders, the 4th and the 6th, lay barely two miles apart, the 4th at Estaimbourg and the 6th at Esquelmes in the line held by the 2nd Brigade in the centre of the 1st Division. On the flanks of the 6th Gordons the Brigade anti-tank company had one platoon supporting the North Staffordshire and one supporting the Loyals.

Although the Escaut forms some sort of military obstacle the water was low, and the numerous woods and coppices in the meadow lands on either side of its winding course were by no means favourable to the defence. Also, the sector held by the 2nd Brigade was dominated by Mont St. Aubert, partly tree-clad, which rises to a height of nearly 500 feet.

The Germans had not yet closed up to the river, and the 20th was a quiet day, giving some opportunity to improve the defences. At dusk the 6th Gordons were moved back into reserve, about a mile in rear.

On the morning of 21st May the enemy opened a heavy artillery and mortar bombardment and made several attempts to cross the river. In the 2nd Brigade the North Staffordshire on the left were engaged and suffered some loss but they gave no ground. A platoon of the Gordons and a company of sappers were put to work on a reserve line.

Meanwhile the enemy successes in the south had placed Lord Gort's forces in great jeopardy. Sweeping through the remnants of the French Ninth Army the German armoured divisions had driven swiftly forward from the Meuse, heading north-westward through Cambrai and across the old battlefields of the Somme. By 20th May—despite one check at Arras where British troops were still opposing the advance—they had arrived on the Somme at

Amiens and Abbeville and were approaching the coast near Etaples. The British lines of communication, which ran back to the Normandy ports and to Brittany, were severed; and there was little hope of closing the huge gap which yawned between the main French armies and the French First Army, the British and the Belgians in the north.

The French High Command—General Weygand succeeded Gamelin as Supreme Commander on 20th May—was no longer able to control events, and the British Expeditionary Force, facing east, was now threatened with attack from the west. There could be no more talk of a protracted resistance on the Escaut: the Belgians were to withdraw behind the Lys, and the British to the old frontier defences they had worked upon during the winter, with the French First Army on their right.

Lord Gort had already reported to the War Office that retreat to the coast about Dunkirk might become inevitable.

The 6th Gordons were heavily shelled on the morning of the 22nd. Captain Duncan Annand, commanding D Company, was severely wounded when walking round his company positions, and was killed by a mortar bomb while being taken to a casualty clearing station. One private was killed and three were wounded on this day.

Withdrawal began after darkness had fallen, the Gordons moving at midnight. A ten-mile march brought them to the frontier defences at Hem, south of Roubaix, where they occupied the right of the Brigade position.

The 4th Gordons arrived nearby. They put half their machine guns into blockhouses in front of Lannoy, the other two companies being kept in reserve.

The withdrawal of the Division from the Escaut had not been followed up by the Germans, and the 23rd was a day of rather uncanny calm, apart from some desultory shelling. Our patrols were active, and next day the North Staffordshire and the Loyals both reported encounters with German motor-cyclists. Hostile shelling grew heavier, and the inhabitants of Roubaix and of the surrounding district began to leave their homes. The Gordons used their transport to take some of these poor people back to Lille, and parties of the Battalion collected stray cattle and drove them into specially selected areas. The troops were on half-rations now, but did very well by drawing upon the stocks of the deserted shops.

On the 25th the enemy began a systematic bombardment of the forward posts. There were patrol clashes, and in one of these the 6th Gordons lost Lieutenant Harry Shand, wounded and captured, although another patrol made a gallant effort to rescue him. The Battalion also had one man killed, one missing, and five wounded on this day.

Enemy aircraft were active on the morrow and sounds of fighting were heard away to the west, but, in the view of the 2nd Brigade, 'the Germans were not worrying about us very much'. There was a little excitement on the 27th when a party of Germans approached the 6th Gordons, and Captain Baucher's company managed to account for a number of them. Then came orders for a rapid withdrawal to the Lys, north-west of Armentières. All realised the meaning of such a move.

Lord Gort had already taken measures to form a defensive front facing west, using such units and detachments as were at hand. This 'Canal Line' ran southward from Gravelines on the coast to St. Omer, and thence to Aire, Béthune and la Bassée.

The Germans captured Boulogne on the 25th and Calais next day, then brought heavy pressure to bear upon the Canal Line which they penetrated at some points. About Ypres, on the north-eastern side of the salient held by the Allies, a gap had developed between the British left and the Belgian right. This gap our 5th and 50th Divisions had been sent to fill; but on the 28th the Belgian Army capitulated. The Belgians had reached the limit of their endurance, but even before they collapsed it was obvious that only the speedy retreat of the British into the Dunkirk perimeter could save them from a like disaster.

The 6th Gordons left Hem about midnight on 27th/28th May, orders having been changed: the 2nd Brigade—less the North Staffordshire who were detached in order to deliver a local counter-attack—were now to go straight through to the coast at Bray Dunes. The anti-tank company had already got their guns out of the blockhouses and started off. The German artillery were firing on the deserted positions, but the Gordons, for their part, suffered no loss.

After marching through the night, at times in heavy rain, they reached Neuve Eglise in the early morning and paused to rest. The roads were crowded with troops, transport of all descriptions, and refugees, all moving, with frequent halts and traffic jams, north-westward towards the coast.

Neuve Eglise was thronged with troops and soon came under shell fire, while bombs from German aircraft exploded in the streets. The stretcher bearers of the Gordons strove very gallantly to tend the many wounded, a dangerous and difficult task. A number of Belgian cavalry horses stampeded into the square, and these terrified animals had to be rounded up before the trucks conveying the wounded could be got away. The Gordons, more fortunate than others, departed from Neuve Eglise with a loss of only three killed and eight wounded.

Now on to Poperinghe where, before evening, Gordons and Loyals took up a defensive position. The anti-tank company had already arrived from Hem, after being nine hours on the road.

Poperinghe was bombed by the *Luftwaffe*. A report that German armour was approaching from the west proved to be false, but put the anti-tank company on the alert when all they wanted was a little rest.

At night came orders to dump everything which could not be carried by the men, and to put all vehicles out of action. After this depressing task had been done the 6th Gordons got on the move again, 'a very hard march' continuing well into next day. Enemy bombing attacks were persistent. The ditches were filled with French transport vehicles which had been turned off the road, but, even so, the traffic jams were so frequent that the Brigadier abandoned his car and set out on foot for Bray Dunes. Later, on 29th May, after marching for several miles in single file along the side of a railway track, the Gordons arrived at Bray Dunes and, with the Loyals, were ordered to occupy the French frontier defences near the sea.

Major Murray, with his anti-tank company, had left Poperinghe a little earlier than the 6th Gordons. Despite the traffic chaos, and the exhaustion of his drivers who fell asleep at every involuntary halt, he reached Proven about 4 a.m. on the 29th. Here he decided to leave the main road and trust to the byways where progress proved to be easier. He brought his company into deserted Hondschoote, where fires were burning and the ground was covered with the wrecked and abandoned equipment of an army in retreat. Further on the French had to be dissuaded from blowing a bridge over the Bergues-Furnes canal until the company had crossed. But a lot of derelict transport had first to be dragged clear with the help of stray farm horses, while close at hand a large ammunition dump burned fiercely with frequent explosions. Threading their course through crowds of French stragglers, the company entered Bray Dunes at three in the afternoon of the 29th.

On 30th May the 6th Gordons were manning the defences near the extreme left of the Dunkirk perimeter, C Company taking over bridge and traffic control duties from the Loyals. The anti-tank company had their guns in position from Ghyvelde to the sea, one gun being mounted for anti-aircraft defence. Bray Dunes was a mass of transport and humanity, British troops marching to the beaches, 'detachments of French marching in various directions', and many French and Belgian civilians, lost and bewildered.

The night had been quiet, but aircraft attacks continued at intervals throughout the day, while the German artillery conducted a steady bombardment. The 6th Gordons had little to do but await attack; and they were glad of the respite, for since 13th May they had covered about 145 miles, mostly on foot. In the afternoon, however, a report that Bergues was in danger of capture resulted in the Brigade sending off as reinforcement the Loyals and the anti-tank company. The company mustered every available man, leaving their guns unguarded, and the whole force, after being hurried away in trucks, found the Bergues garrison in no need of help. Ten men sent back to look after the anti-tank guns found one missing and only four still serviceable, but these went into action on the Adinkerke road and railway when the company returned to Bray Dunes next day.

On this day, the 31st, the 6th Gordons lost one man killed but were not attacked. The hostile shelling and bombing were mainly directed upon the beaches, and in Bray Dunes it was possible to restore some sort of order. Organised French units were now to be seen, and the Zouaves who took over the defence of the extreme left of the perimeter were 'fine fellows, ready to fight'. Then at 10 p.m. came the order to withdraw and march at once to the mole in Dunkirk harbour. The Brigade were to embark for England.

An hour later the movement began. Under cover of the friendly dark the 6th Gordons gained the beach and marched towards the town. Though they were under shell-fire for almost the whole way, the Gordons only had one man wounded, and he was able to keep going with the aid of a stick. At dawn the German bombers attacked, but the Battalion, now marshalled along the mole side by side with French troops in two dense columns, suffered no harm. As all could see, the anti-aircraft fire of the Navy prevented the bombers from coming in to strike.

The Gordons were embarked in destroyers and sailed about 6 a.m. on 1st June. Again the *Luftwaffe* attacked, and two aircraft were shot down by the guns of H.M. destroyer *Codrington* to everyone's great comfort and satisfaction. Without further incident the Gordons were brought safely to Dover, where a warm welcome awaited them.

The last of the 2nd Brigade to leave Dunkirk were the anti-tank company. On June 1st Major Murray destroyed his guns—likewise a British light tank which had been picked up in Bergues, repaired, and adopted. The company then boarded a carrier and nine trucks and started for Dunkirk. They had to run the gauntlet of the German bombardment, and one salvo destroyed the bridge at Ghyvelde just after the little column had passed safely over. About 10 a.m. the company reached the harbour. Later in the day they embarked in a passenger steamer and, although under heavy air attack for a time, reached Folkestone safely in the evening.

The 4th Gordons, who had put their machine-guns into the defences east of Lannoy, were ordered into divisional reserve on the night of 22nd May. On the next night they were moved to Marcq-en-Baroeuil, between the northern suburbs of Lille and the south-western edge of Tourcoing. On the 24th B Company were sent to obstruct the airfield at Canteleux, east of Lille, for fear that it might be used by the *Luftwaffe*.

The Gordons could see considerable activity in the air, but, for the moment, they seemed to have no part in the war. On the afternoon of the 25th, however, they were transferred from the 1st Division to the 4th Division, who were holding part of the eastern front further to the north. The Battalion had orders to take up positions on the canal between Comines and Ypres, so moved to Gapaard in the evening and started to dig in.

Next morning they found themselves under the command of the 5th Division, supporting the 13th Brigade and the 143rd Brigade.

The 27th May is to be remembered for the staunch defence of the canal by the 5th Division, who were attacked by three German divisions. An enemy break-through in this quarter might well have meant complete disaster to our II Corps, if not to Lord Gort's whole Command.

Heavy bombardments by the German artillery and mortars and almost continuous bombing attacks tried the defenders to the utmost. On the right, near Comines, the 143rd Brigade were forced back; the 13th Brigade near Houthem also had to give ground. The machine-gun support of the Gordons never faltered, and as the day wore on it seemed that the whole front of the 5th Division was covered only by the fire of the Battalion. At night, however, very gallant counter-attacks drove the Germans back and made the line secure.

Fighting died down on 28th May, the day of the Belgian surrender, and when the order came to withdraw to the river Yser it was possible to disengage without much difficulty. All documents and nearly all trucks and motor cycles were destroyed before the 4th Gordons moved at 9.30 p.m. Next day saw them in support of the 143rd Brigade on the Yser with Battalion headquarters back at Leysele. There was little respite from bombing attacks during the 29th, and after darkness fell the Gordons and what was left of the 5th Division made their way back into the Dunkirk perimeter. This move was a complicated affair, the Gordon companies moving independently. They were not reunited until the morning of the 30th, when most of the Battalion moved from the Moeres area to a position near Adinkerke.

The Gordons had now left the 5th for the 50th Division, whose 151st Brigade held a front between Moeres and Bulscamp, supported by a composite company—termed D Company and commanded by Captain S. A. Wilson-Brown—of the Battalion. The guns covered the Dunkirk-Furnes canal, east of Moeres.

Enemy aircraft bombed and machine-gunned the beaches throughout the day, but paid little attention to the troops holding this part of the perimeter.

Early next morning D Company came under heavy mortar fire which did considerable damage. By the evening only four guns were left in action. Waves of hostile aircraft came over at frequent intervals, still making for the beaches, and although bombardment was heavy along the perimeter it was noticeable that the Germans made little effort to close.

On the night of 31st May the 4th Gordons, with the exception of D Company, moved to Malo les Bains, where they were allotted an area in a field about half-a-mile from the beach. This proved to be an uncomfortable spot, for shells were bursting all round, so the Gordons moved nearer to the sea before digging themselves in. Meanwhile D Company had withdrawn the four remaining guns and came back to join the Battalion.

Attacks from the air were heavier and more persistent on 1st June. At 12.30 p.m. the commanding officer, Lieut.-Colonel Taylor, was called to a conference at Brigade headquarters, where instructions for a last stand—if such should be necessary—were given. At 2 p.m. orders were changed: the Gordons would embark at Dunkirk for home.

At 8 p.m. the Battalion moved along the beaches to the outskirts of Dunkirk. Two hours later they joined the troops who were moving out along the mole. Their slow progress towards the ships was made under a heavy bombardment which, by great good fortune, left untouched the long column of men. At midnight, with shells still falling near, the 4th Gordons were embarking on two destroyers. At 1.30 a.m. on June 2nd they left Dunkirk and, surviving the manifold risks of the sea passage, arrived safely at Dover in the early morning.

Later the tale of losses for the whole campaign showed nine other ranks killed and twenty-nine wounded, and four officers and 171 others missing.

One cannot recall the evacuation from Dunkirk without a salute to the Royal Air Force, the Merchant Navy, and the ' little ships', and to the skill, courage and efficiency of the Royal Navy on whom, in the last resort, all depended. The Gordon Highlanders—4th Battalion, 6th Battalion, and the Gordon platoon of the 2nd Brigade Anti-Tank Company—were deeply conscious of the debt they owed to those who had ensured their good deliverance.

The Gordons returned to England in the shadow of defeat, after a lost campaign. More fortunate than many of their comrades, as they would be the first to admit, they had borne themselves proudly in battle, and had accepted hardship and frustration with characteristic fortitude. After Dunkirk the name of the Regiment stood as high as ever.

Saar Front

When the 51st (Highland) Division moved to the Saar late in April they bade farewell to Lord Gort's Command. They were never to rejoin it.

The 154th Brigade, first to go, took over the sector which had been held by a British brigade for months past. Brigadier Burney, commanding the 153rd, left for Metz with his three battalion commanders on 21st April. Next day the 5th Gordons moved by rail, detraining at Moyeuve Grande and marching ten miles to Bousse and Blettange. The 1st Gordons started south on the same day by the same route. Their billets were at Haute Guenange and Basse Guenange, east of the Moselle. Late on the 29th a sixteen miles march brought the Battalion to Veckring, where the remainder of the night and all next day were spent in very comfortable French barracks.

At Veckring the 1st Gordons found themselves actually 'in' the Maginot Line, for the village lay between two of the great forts, massive structures of concrete, low sited, powerfully armed, their subterranean galleries, installations and magazines immune from almost any kind of bombardment. The chain of these great works stretched from the Swiss border to the vicinity of Longwy, where ended the frontier common to France and Germany.

The Maginot Line had cost France too many francs; and its garrison, perhaps, absorbed too many good troops at the expense of the field armies. In so far as it fostered a purely defensive mentality its influence was bad. Also, as the Allies were well aware, the Maginot Line could be outflanked on the north by a German thrust through neutral Belgium.

But the Highland Division were concerned with the forward defences which extended eastward beyond the line of forts for nearly seven miles towards the German frontier.

In the outpost line, called the *Ligne de Contact*, small detachments bickered with German patrols. Some sectors, but not that taken over by the 153rd Brigade, possessed a *Ligne de Soutien*—a support line. Under weight of an enemy attack withdrawal would be made to the *Ligne de Recueil*, which lay about four miles in rear of the outpost positions and was intended to be a 'line of resistance'. In rear again were defences, appropriately called *brisants*, designed to break up any hostile penetration which approached the line of forts.

Behind the forts a beginning—only a beginning—had been made on the construction of a *Ligne d'Arrêt Corps d'Armée* which was intended as an additional insurance against an enemy breakthrough.

On their way south the Highlanders had passed through towns and villages where life went on as usual, and in Metz itself at this time it was still possible to dine and dance. East of the Maginot Line the countryside presented a different picture. The rich land of Lorraine was bright with the promise of spring, the orchards were in bloom and the beechwoods green with new growth; but there was no sign of normal life. Farm houses were deserted, byres dark and empty, no cattle drank from the streams, shuttered houses confronted the village streets where only military traffic passed. The inhabitants, with their livestock and all their most cherished possessions, had been moved westward to clear the ground for battle.

The 1st Gordons who were to take over the *Ligne de Contact* in the Brigade sector, sent forward reconnaissance parties wearing French helmets so that enemy observers should not suspect an international relief. The night of 30th April was spent by the company and platoon commanders with their opposite numbers of the battalion they were about to relieve. These Frenchmen were Bretons of the 34th Infantry Regiment, 'a very cheerful lot of officers and men' who did not seem disposed to take the war too seriously.

The Battalion had moved out of Veckring on 30th April to bivouac in the Forêt Dominale de Kalenhofen, a large and noble extent of woodland in keeping with its impressive name. The *Ligne de Contact* was taken over, without trouble or interference by the enemy, on the night of 1st May. All four companies were up, and each occupied three platoon posts: six in Grössenwald, three in the smaller woods named Wölschler and Petit Wölschler, and three in Heydwald. On the right of the 1st Gordons were the 154th Brigade. A French division were on the left.

Jutting out from Heydwald and forming an awkward salient was a small wood called Bois Carré. The Gordons found that the

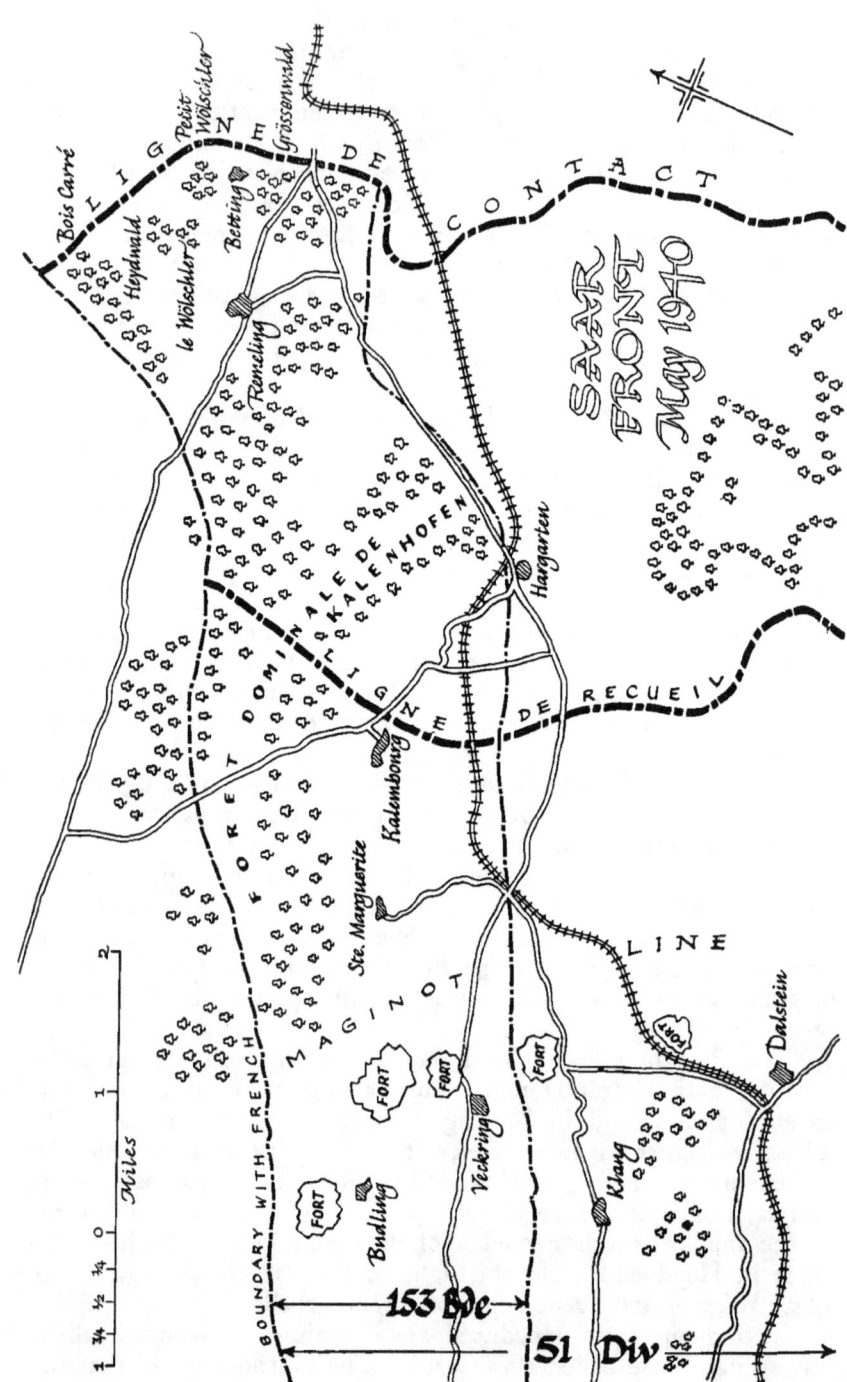

French were in the habit of occupying Bois Carré by day and leaving it to the Germans at night; and this arrangement was allowed to stand, seeing that the wood was only of value as an observation post. The village of Betting, north of Grössenwald and in advance of the general line, was another matter. Betting was isolated and exposed, difficult to support or reinforce; but 2nd-Lieutenant P. B. Hay's platoon sat in the village undisturbed for six days.

The Gordons looked with a doubtful eye upon the existing defences, for the casual efficiency of the French is sometimes apt to appear more casual than efficient. Digging and wiring parties, therefore, went to work.

The 2nd May was a quiet day, but there was air and artillery activity on the 3rd. At night, and on the two succeeding nights, patrols approached the posts held by C Company. On each occasion the Germans were driven off by fire. This appears to be the first time that German troops introduced themselves to the 1st Gordons.

The Battalion was relieved by the 4th Black Watch on 7th May, and withdrew from the *Ligne de Contact* to the village of Budling in the Maginot Line.

Meanwhile the 5th Gordons were coming forward. On the morning of 4th May, they had arrived at Budling, where they were fêted by the out-going French battalion, but found the field defences, the *brisants*, in need of considerable improvement. On the night of 7th May the 5th Battalion moved up and relieved the Black Watch in the *Ligne de Receuil*, which lay just in front of the villages of Kalembourg and Ste. Marguerite. There were no alarms, but German aircraft were seen to be active over the whole front.

At 7 a.m. on 10th May the 5th Gordons received the *mise en garde* signal: 'man battle stations at once!' The German invasion of the Low Countries had begun and enemy armoured forces were about to make their fatal thrust through the Ardennes to shatter the French Ninth Army. The sound of heavy artillery fire farther north could be heard, and bombs were falling on Metz.

The Battalion were ready in battle positions by 10.30 a.m., but the day was a quiet one. At night the enemy shelled some of our forward batteries for an hour, and the Gordons caught a little of the bombardment; but they suffered no loss.

They were due to take over the *Ligne de Contact* from the Black Watch on the 13th, and all excitement had died down when, on the afternoon of the 12th, a party of eleven officers and about 120 men went forward to prepare for the relief. One officer and his opposite number of the Black Watch went out towards Betting, but they were stopped by machine-gun fire which barred the approaches to the village. The enemy seemed determined to 'bite off' Betting where the Black Watch platoon who occupied it were soon hotly engaged.

An hour after the 1st Gordons received the 'stand to arms' signal they were ordered to occupy the *brisants*, the covering positions in the woods and villages in the approaches to the forts. On the evening of the 12th they started to move into the *Ligne de Receuil* to replace the 5th Battalion, who were about to go forward. The 1st Gordons had noticed that the enemy aircraft 'were spotting for their guns without much hindrance'.

The night was quiet, but at 4 a.m. on 13th May a heavy artillery and mortar bombardment fell on the Brigade front, which was still held by the Black Watch. Our artillery replied. Half-an-hour later the hostile barrage lifted and German infantry attacked in the growing light. This effort made little impression against the fire of a stout defence, but the enemy tried again at seven o'clock and again at nine, gaining a little ground on the southern edge of Grössenwald. The post in Petit Wölschler was over-run, and here 2nd-Lieutenant D. A. Innes and seven men of the 5th Gordons were captured. Innes, who was wounded, died in a German hospital six days later. Other losses of the 5th Gordons on this day amounted to three killed and one wounded.

At Betting the isolated platoon of the Black Watch held on grimly all day, although some of the buildings were in flames. In the evening a Brigade patrol—kept in hand for any special enterprise—was sent forward to the rescue. Lieutenant Rhodes of the 1st Gordons commanded this patrol. By skilful and determined leadership he broke through to the village and, thus reinforced, the little garrison were able to fight their way back, bringing in a German officer prisoner. For this, and for other good work while in command of the Brigade patrol, Rhodes won the Military Cross, being the first officer in the Highland Division to do so.

On being relieved by the 1st Gordons on the night of 12th May the 5th Battalion had moved forward to bivouac behind the *Ligne de Contact*. During the 13th, with the sound of battle in their ears, they advanced again, lying up in the woods south of Remeling ready to relieve the Black Watch at night.

They started soon after darkness fell. While their commanding officer, Lieut.-Colonel A. D. Buchanan-Smith, watched them pass he was, as he wrote later, 'struck by their serious faces and their confidence in their officers. I wonder', he mused, 'how many will ever again possess those boyish faces.' He was never to know. Colonel Buchanan-Smith had been fighting against illness for many weeks; after watching the men he had trained for battle go forth to their first ordeal he had to leave them for a hospital bed. So the

5th Gordons entered the fight under the command of Major R. N. Christie, who had come to them as adjutant in the autumn of 1936.

The relief passed off well, except for the loss of 2nd-Lieutenant Scott-Raeburn, who was killed while guiding C Company into their positions in the Wölschler.

One of the posts in Grössenwald had been flattened by artillery fire and no attempt was made to re-establish it. About dawn on the morning of 14th May the German guns opened again, the heaviest bombardment falling in the area of Captain W. H. Lawrie's D Company in Heydwald. Few men were hit, but the damage to the defences was considerable and the telephone cable to Battalion headquarters was cut. When, after an hour and a half, the shelling ceased no infantry attack followed, and the Gordons breakfasted in peace. The Battalion, as was said at the time, were 'all sitting tight and feeling cheerful'.

There was much to do in repairing the defences, and German snipers in Bois Carré required to be discouraged by Bren-gun fire. 2nd-Lieutenant Morrison, the Battalion intelligence officer, wished to set up the usual observation post in Bois Carré, and the first step was to clear the wood of Germans. This was done, a number of the enemy being killed in the process, and the observation post duly established; but it was shelled persistently for over two hours and had to be abandoned in the late afternoon. The bombardment was the prelude to an infantry attack which the fire of D Company repulsed.

A lively night ensued, with German patrols active, and sudden bursts of artillery fire along the whole front. Forward communications were damaged, and it was obvious that the German gunners had registered on the exits to Remeling village, occupied by Headquarters Company.

Just before dawn of 15th May the hostile artillery again concentrated on Heydwald, and at six o'clock, when the barrage lifted, an infantry attack came in. The fire of the Gordons, well supported by our artillery, drove the Germans back with considerable loss, and the enemy then opened a heavy bombardment which lasted three hours.

Captain Lawrie, commanding D Company, had no news of his two forward posts on the edge of Heydwald. The telephone line was cut, and no runner appeared with a message. A patrol sent forward to gain contact was driven back by machine-gun fire from a point between these two posts. Lawrie reported his troubles by runner to the Battalion: his two forward posts cut off and he himself with only twenty-eight men holding the shattered defences of his one remaining position. This message brought a reply in the shape of a fighting patrol under Lieutenant H. McR. Gall. Gall took his men forward through the wood and met heavy fire from the enemy, who was now in possession of the posts. There was nothing to do but to disengage.

At 4 p.m. Major Christie was told by the Brigade that he might bring D Company back if he thought it necessary. Orders to withdraw at once were sent by runner to Lawrie who arrived with his twenty-eight men at Battalion headquarters outside Remeling at about six in the evening. The losses of D Company on this day were two officers and sixty men missing and six men wounded. Of the officers, 2nd-Lieutenant N. Duncan was never heard of again, and 2nd-Lieutenant M. S. Langham became a prisoner of war. Gall, who had skilfully covered the withdrawal of the remnant of D Company, was awarded the Military Cross.

General Condé, commanding the French Third Army, had already determined upon a general retirement, for the French on both flanks of the Highland Division had been heavily engaged and needed some respite. There were orders and counter-orders, but General Fortune was at length authorised to pull back to the *Ligne de Receuil*, held in the 153rd Brigade sector by the 1st Gordons.

The 5th Gordons began their retirement at a quarter past eight that evening. C Company, covered by machine guns of the 1st Kensington, slipped away from the Wölschler, and were followed by A and B Companies from Grössenwald. Remeling was held till midnight, when the carrier platoon came through. There were no casualties.

On the morning of 16th May the Battalion assembled at Brigade headquarters, now at Veckring, and then took over the Dalstein and Klang 'gaps' in the Maginot Line. Here they remained until 20th May, seeing nothing of the enemy except his aircraft, but roused out on several occasions to hunt for mythical parachutists.

Meanwhile the 1st Gordons held the new front line, the *Ligne de Receuil*. They saw the 5th Battalion pass through this position on the night of the 15th, and kept their own patrols active. Next day Germans were located in Hargarten, whence a machine gun opened fire, B Company losing two non-commissioned officers and a private in this vicinity. Our artillery shelled the village next day, but the Gordon patrols gained no further contact with the enemy.

On 20th May, when Weygand succeeded Gamelin and the Germans had reached the Somme at Amiens and Abbeville, the French decided to relieve the Highland Division on the Saar front. The 5th Gordons, indeed, moved that same evening, after Major J. Clark from the 1st Battalion had arrived to take command. Two night marches and one night's run in R.A.S.C. transport saw the arrival of the Battalion in the Etain area on the edge of the Argonne forest.

The 1st Battalion moved out of the *Ligne de Receuil* on the night of 22nd May, withdrawing very nicely through the three miles of country to the Maginot Line while the sappers finished their demolitions. Near Veckring Brigadier Burney saw them pass. Following a night march in heavy rain the 1st Gordons travelled in motor transport to rejoin the Brigade. They had lost one man killed, twelve wounded, and one missing since their arrival on the Saar front.

By this time the whole of the Highland Division had been drawn into reserve.

Somme to St. Valéry

Cut off from Lord Gort's Command by the German breakthrough, the Highland Division remained, perforce, at the disposal of our Ally. A rather hurried decision to send the Highlanders to the help of the French Second Army, fighting on the southern flank of the break-through, brought both the 1st and the 5th Gordons to a hide near Varennes. Then orders were changed. The French considered it of paramount importance to restore the situation on the Somme : the Division must be transferred with all speed to this battle-front.

Now, as a staff officer said, ' everything became mixed up for a time '. The vehicles were to go by road, the marching troops by rail, and this complicated series of movements through a part of France which was about to fall into the grip of the invader proved a harassing business for all concerned.

The rail parties were obliged to follow a roundabout route. They travelled through Vitry-le-François, Troyes, Orléans, Blois, Amboise, Tours, le Mans, to Rouen. Here the two portions of the 5th Gordons were reunited and set forth in French buses to a rendezvous in the Forêt de Hellet, south-west of the river Bresle. They arrived on 28th May. Near by were the 1st Gordons.

The vehicles of the two battalions formed part of the huge column moving westward by road. From Varennes the route was by Vitry-le-François to Sezanne, thence northward of Paris through Gisors to the rendezvous south-west of the Bresle. The distance of nearly 300 miles was covered in four stages, partly by night but mostly by day.

Railway arrangements had worked well, for only minor setbacks and delays were suffered by the troop trains. On the roads British staff work with French co-operation had ensured a smooth passage, and here credit must be given to the high standard of

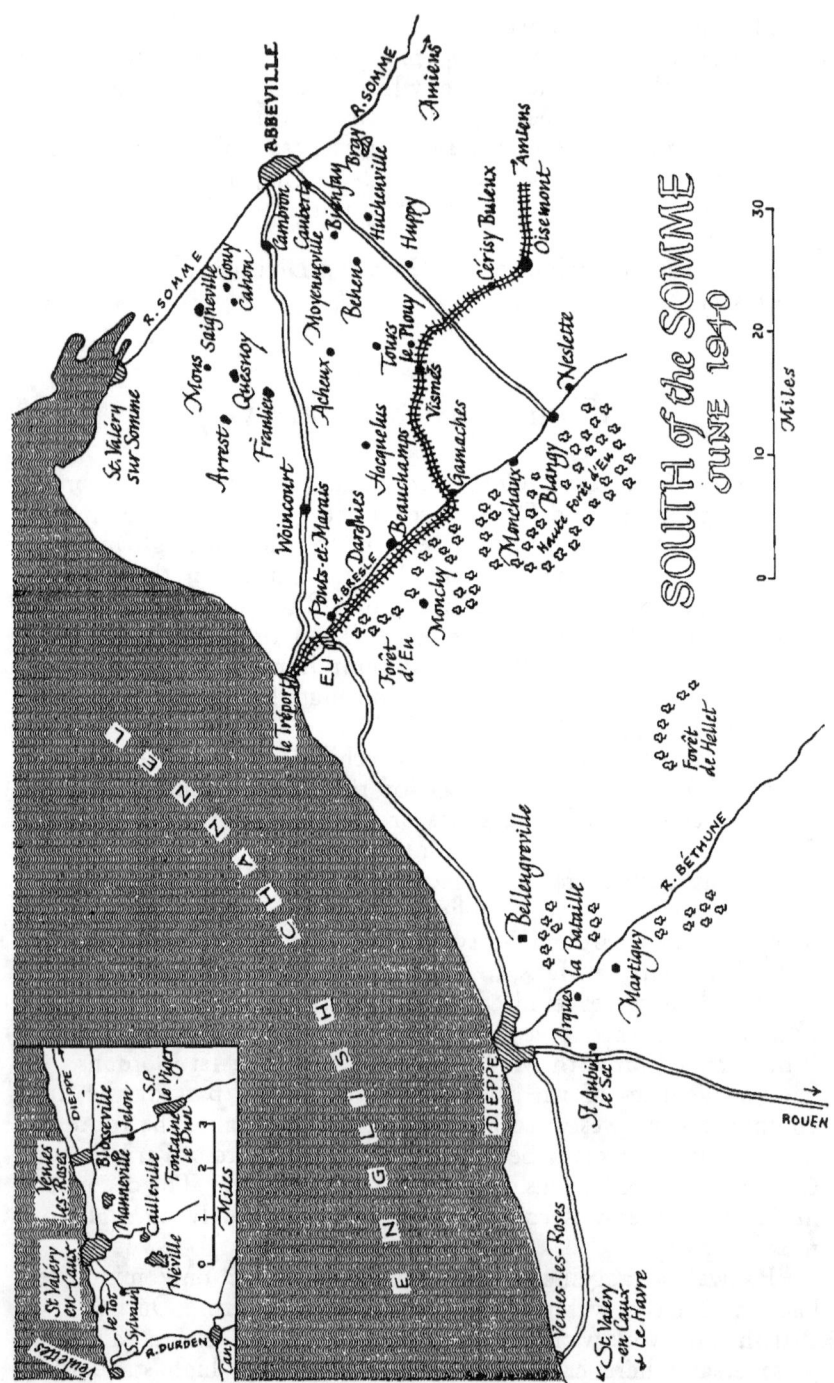

driving and march discipline in the Highland Division. Very few vehicles came to grief.

By 30th May the 1st and 5th Battalions of the Gordons were ready for further action. The news from the north was bad: Boulogne and Calais lost, the Belgian resistance at an end, the evacuation from Dunkirk begun. What was to do here in Normandy?

The 1st Gordons, ordered forward across the river Bresle to Tours, passed through a deserted countryside. The inhabitants had fled in haste, leaving their homes and shops unsecured, their cows unmilked, and all manner of livestock straying at will. German tanks had already been reported east of Tours, so the Gordons were called upon to block the approaches to the village and be ready to defend it.

Meanwhile the 5th Battalion had also crossed the Bresle, and by the evening of 31st May were in Vismes-au-Mont and le Plouy. On their way forward they had seen German dive-bombers attacking some of the neighbouring villages, and hailed the destruction of four of the enemy by British fighters.

The German advance to the lower Somme was a threat to our base ports in Normandy. Already the troops employed on the lines of communication in this region and the men in the base depôts had been organised in fighting formations; Dieppe was cleared of stores and arrangements made to block the harbour; and the supplies accumulated at Le Havre were being reduced to a minimum.

On the Somme the Germans had established a bridge-head at St. Valéry and another, more formidable, at Abbeville. Four times, on 27th May and the three succeeding days, the French had attacked at Abbeville, all with little avail; and in this fighting our 1st Armoured Division, hurriedly despatched to France, had been engaged. Now the Highland Division were to take part in a fresh effort under the command of the French IX Corps, the left wing of the French Tenth Army. The Highlanders took over their part of the Allied front on the last day of May.

The country south of the lower Somme is dotted with villages and little towns, copses and extensive woods; and at this time standing crops covered the fields. In places bluffs overlook the canalised river, but in general the ground slopes down in irregular spurs from the north-eastern banks of the Bresle. The Highland Division occupied a string of defensive localities extending from Bray to the sea. In the centre was the 153rd Brigade.

The 1st Gordons came forward after dark on 1st June to relieve the 1st Black Watch (154th Brigade) in front of Acheux. All went well. At six o'clock next morning Lieut.-Colonel Wright went up to visit his forward companies. When he returned to his headquarters at 2 p.m. he was informed that the Black Watch were coming in again, as the Gordons were required for the attack to be delivered on 4th June. So in the evening the Battalion were withdrawn to the woods in front of Quesnoy.

Having been placed under the command of the 152nd Brigade, the 5th Gordons relieved the 4th Seaforths on the night of 2nd June. Three companies occupied Moyenneville while D Company and Battalion headquarters went to the neighbouring village of Behen. The taking over was not accomplished without loss. During the afternoon Captain W. Diack, commanding C Company, who had gone forward to view the ground, was killed by mortar fire, together with his servant and a Seaforth guide. The Headquarters Company had casualties from shell fire in the evening.

Moyenneville was very near the German machine-gun posts on the south-western face of the Abbeville bridgehead, and suffered accordingly. About midnight a bombardment opened on the village and continued until noon of 3rd June. One section of A Company were completely wiped out. To set against this, a platoon of the same company suspected enemy activity in a group of haystacks to their right front and fired them by means of tracer bullets. Thus were revealed and disposed of several light machine-guns and two German observation posts. In this hot corner of the battle-field the Gordons had to endure spasmodic mortar bombardment and the attention of dive-bombers which, although trying to the nerves, did little harm.

Much depended upon the Allied attack planned for 4th June. Control of the Somme crossings was, in the French view, essential for the defence of Paris; and as the Germans were being steadily reinforced, this seemed the last chance of driving them back over the river at Abbeville.

The French armour (the newly arrived 2nd Armoured Division) were to attack along the slopes of Mont de Caubert, while their 31st Division, who only came forward from the Bresle on the evening of 3rd June, would advance from the line Bienfay-Moyenneville to secure the high ground west of Rouvroy. To cover the right flank our 152nd Brigade had the task of capturing Caubert and the woods to the south of the village; on the left the 153rd Brigade were to attack south-eastward and capture Grand Bois on the spur overlooking Cambron. Brigadier Burney entrusted this operation to the 1st Gordons.

The 1st Gordons were holding a line among the woods of Cahon. A Company, on the extreme left, had their left flank on

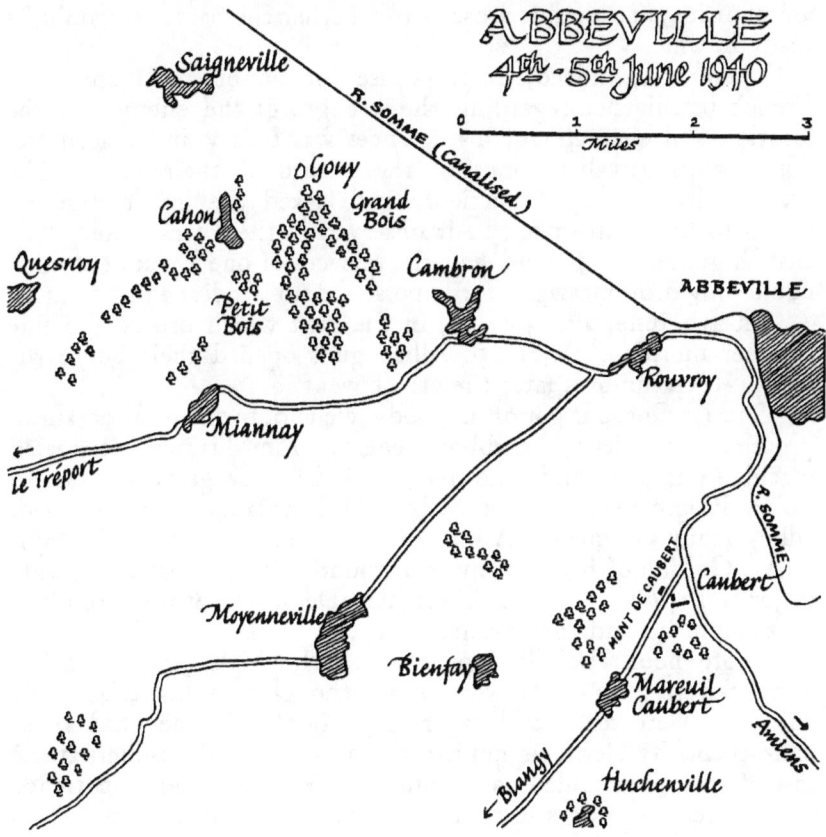

the Somme; B and C Companies, who were to attack, extended the front towards Petit Bois. D Company were held in reserve. June 3rd was spent in careful preparation, for Lieut.-Colonel Wright was determined that his men, who had never yet had a chance to get at the Germans and were eager to attack instead of remaining on the defensive, should make the most of this opportunity. Artillery and machine-gun support was carefully planned, the progress of the advance to be signalled to the batteries by red Véry lights fired from the right of C Company. All ranks knew what was required of them, and were keen and confident.

To start their attack the French 31st Division were to pass through the 5th Gordons at Moyenneville. On the afternoon of 3rd June French officers arrived to make a rather sketchy reconnaissance. They gave the impression of being depressed and lacking in confidence. Their division had only just arrived behind the battle-front, and all were tired men. In rear, throughout the late afternoon and evening, the French artillery were dumping ammunition, and doubts arose as to whether the batteries would be ready in time.

There was, indeed, ample cause for doubt and depression. French intelligence regarding the strength of the enemy and the location and character of his defences was scanty and inaccurate. The troops had little idea of the nature of their tasks. The artillery had deployed hurriedly and lacked the information on which to base a fire plan. Air observation there was none. The British gunners, it is true, had the services of one Lysander which could only drop messages, for it possessed no wireless equipment.

On 4th June, at 3.30 a.m., in the mist which preceded a fine summer morning, about 250 Allied guns opened their bombardment. Ten minutes later the attack went in.

The 1st Gordons got off in good style and, in the semi-darkness, proceeded to clear a stubborn enemy from his well-concealed machine-gun posts amid the trees and thick undergrowth of Grand Bois. Progress was never easy, but the Highlanders forged ahead, killing many Germans. A burst of machine-gun fire killed Major D. W. Gordon of B Company and wounded his company sergeant-major and two runners, but Lieutenant Denniston Sword promptly took command and the advance went on.

Before noon the Gordons reached the high ground on the south-eastern edge of the wood and, although they had taken their objective, were ready and eager to go further. They had killed more than fifty Germans and had taken a number of prisoners at the cost of some forty killed and wounded. With growing impatience they waited for orders to resume the advance, but no such orders came. At last, in the evening they were told to withdraw, giving up all they had won. Theirs had been the sole success of the day, and the failure of the main attack had left the Battalion with their right flank exposed in a position judged to be untenable.

All ranks came back bitterly disappointed at such an ending to a day which had opened so well. They had done what had been asked of them, and were ready and anxious to do more; yet all had been in vain.

The main attack had never prospered from the start. The story of the gallant but abortive efforts to reach Caubert belongs to the 4th Camerons. The 2nd Seaforth cleared the way for the advance of the French heavy tanks which, late in arriving, foundered in an unsuspected minefield or were shot up by the German artillery as they approached the slopes of Mont Caubert. The 4th Seaforth, who were to follow the tanks, strove mightily but in vain. In this fashion the battalions of the 152nd Brigade spent themselves to no purpose as they tried to help forward the French armour.

Further to the left, the French 31st Division began to pass through the 5th Gordons at Moyenneville about 3.30 a.m., the fire of the Highlanders covering the advance. A little more than an hour later some of the Frenchmen began to drift back again. They had seen many of the tanks destroyed or put out of action, and they themselves had made little impression upon the German machine-gunners so well concealed in the woods. The Gordons sent forward 2nd-Lieutenant Thom's platoon to engage the enemy in a small wood to the north-east of their line, and a few French tanks turned towards the same objective; but nothing was achieved by this ill-coordinated effort.

A few prisoners had been brought in, but by 8 a.m. it seemed obvious to the Gordons that the attack had failed. German observers must have seen the French retreating through Moyenneville, for the hostile artillery now concentrated on the village.

Later, a company of the Gordons were ordered to the assistance of the 4th Camerons near Huchenville, beyond the Blangy-Abbeville road. D Company, who by some mischance had not eaten that morning, were sent; and on their way they were attacked by dive-bombers. Beyond Huchenville they moved into a wood to cover the withdrawal of the Camerons, and were almost immediately engaged, for the Germans were advancing. The fire of the Highlanders drove them back.

As the day wore on the Battalion awaited the coming of the French troops who were due to relieve them at Behen and Moyenneville. When the French commander arrived he considered the position too exposed, and refused to bring his troops up. Lieut.-Colonel Clark thereupon referred to the Brigade, and was told to move out as already ordered. In the end the relief was carried out and the 5th Gordons marched across to Huchenville; but the take-over was an untidy business and A Company, who were unable to get away before midnight, did not rejoin the Battalion until the early hours of the next morning. Their transport was shelled on the way.

On 5th June the Germans launched a powerful offensive along a front of fifty miles. Their attack from the lower Somme was directed against Rouen and the lower Seine; and its success sealed the fate of the Highland Division.

Shortly after dawn, about four o'clock, heavy rifle fire was heard by the 1st Gordons. Soon it was reported that the 154th Brigade, facing the Somme on the left, were under attack and that the right flank had been driven in. C Company, who had suffered most in the action of the previous day, and were now in reserve, moved to the point of danger. At the same time Captain Stewart Aylmer began to pull the left of A Company out of the Somme valley near Gouy.

On the 154th Brigade front Saigneville had been surrounded and captured, and the enemy was pressing on regardless of loss to Mons, Arrest and Franleu. In and around these villages the 7th and 8th Argyll and Sutherland Highlanders, vastly outnumbered, maintained the unequal struggle until overwhelmed. Looking eastward, the Gordons saw Germans advancing in force from Grand Bois.

The Battalion were certainly in grave danger, for the enemy had driven forward nearly two miles on either flank. Withdraw they must, and Lieutenant Basil Brooke's carrier platoon covered the movement by fighting a delaying action with boldness and skill. The carriers were sadly overmatched, and all but one of them were lost or put out of action.

Lieut.-Colonel Wright had decided to retire to the le Tréport-Abbeville road, but to extract the Battalion was no easy matter. He left his second-in-command, Major C. D. M. Hutchins, to bring back C Company, the remains of the carrier platoon, and Battalion headquarters. Captain Donald Alexander of C Company had been wounded by mortar fire, and Lance-Corporal Groves and Private Knight tried to carry him away. Captain Alexander feared that their care of him would delay the withdrawal, and gave them one last order: to leave him. He died in German hands.

Mr. Leal, the regimental sergeant-major, who travelled in a reserve ammunition truck, took a wrong turning and ran straight into a German anti-tank gun. Both he and his driver were killed.

Meanwhile the commanding officer had gone forward in person to conduct the withdrawal of A, B and D Companies. Thanks to Gordon discipline and a skilful use of ground, these companies got away with very little loss, and by 11 a.m. the whole Battalion were on the le Tréport-Abbeville road.

Contact with the Brigade was now restored, and Brigadier Burney sent up a machine-gun platoon of the 1st Kensington to keep down the enfilade fire which was worrying the Gordons' right flank. Soon a further withdrawal was ordered, but only for a short distance. The four rifle companies of the Battalion were then extended for 3,000 yards, each company holding a 'tank proof' wood.

The new position was unsatisfactory in the extreme, for the Germans had reached the le Tréport-Abbeville road in considerable force, and the left flank of the Gordons was threatened by other hostile forces now well beyond Franleu. When the situation had been made clear by a personal visit of Brigadier and commanding officer to General Fortune himself, approval was given for another withdrawal that night. Before dawn of 6th June, the 1st Gordons were occupying the high ground near the river Bresle, north-west of Gamaches.

The 5th Gordons spent the morning of 5th June in Huchenville, under shell fire but not directly involved in the German advance. In the early hours of the morning, however, B Company had been sent forward a mile to Mareuil-Caubert, where a company of the 4th Camerons held a forward position. The Gordons were to relieve the Camerons, but the latter had obtained Brigade permission to stay until darkness fell rather than withdraw in daylight over open ground. So Gordons and Camerons together defended Mareuil-Caubert against the full fury of the German attack. No reinforcement could reach them, and they were soon surrounded; but they fought on grimly for twenty hours before the survivors gave in.

Battalion headquarters had received orders to withdraw down the Blangy road at noon; but before moving Lieut.-Colonel Clark tried, without success, to get a message through to his ill-fated B Company. By early afternoon the Gordons were in Huppy, where they became the target for repeated attacks by dive-bombers and at night they were withdrawn to the railway south-east of the Blangy road. Here they found themselves in the centre of the Brigade front, with the 2nd Seaforth on the right at Cérisy-Buleux and the 4th Camerons on the left.

On the night of June 5th the front of the Highland Division extended from Oisemont north-westward to the vicinity of Woincourt whence, facing roughly north, it ran back to the coast. By hard fighting and at considerable cost the Highlanders and certain French forces with them had, for the moment, stemmed the German onslaught. But everyone was very tired, and the troops were too thin on the ground. General Fortune asked that his front should be shortened, but there were no reinforcements in sight; and his request that a retirement be made to the Bresle line received no immediate reply.

The 1st Gordons in their position north-west of Gamaches spent the early morning of 6th June in preparing for a renewal of the struggle, with Bren guns and anti-tank rifles well dug in. When the Germans advanced—infantry on foot with light automatics, machine guns and mortars in close support and motorised infantry following—the fire of the Highlanders brought them to a halt. Thenceforward the Battalion were under artillery bombardment and mortar and machine-gun fire, but they were able to cover, in some measure, parties of the 4th Black Watch coming back from Dargnies and Hocquelus towards Beauchamps.

The 5th Gordons on the railway north-west of Oisemont were vouchsafed a quiet morning on 6th June, and many of them got some much needed sleep. In the early afternoon a heavy attack developed on the left against the 4th Camerons, who were pushed back from some of their forward posts. A carrier section of the Gordons under Lieutenant D. Ritchie and a platoon of A Company commanded by 2nd-Lieutenant Gall joined in a counter-attack which restored the situation. Later the enemy advanced to attack Cérisy-Buleux, passing across the front of the Gordons whose fire, partly in enfilade, killed many Germans. Unfortunately it was not possible to kill enough, and as evening drew on the Battalion saw increasing numbers of the enemy on their front. In small parties he was pushing closer and closer in.

At 7 p.m. General Fortune was able to order the retirement to the line of the Bresle which, according to the French, was to be held 'at all costs'. The 5th Gordons withdrew at 9.30 p.m., when the foremost Germans were within fifty yards. Covered by the fire of Ritchie's carriers — Ritchie was awarded the Military Cross for his good work—the Battalion slipped away in the darkness lit by the flames of burning Oisemont. A march of four miles brought them to the Bresle at Neslette, the bridge being blown by the sappers half an hour after the Highlanders had crossed. They tumbled into lorries and were carried to the Forêt d'Eu where, in the early hours of the 7th, they were welcomed back to the 153rd Brigade by the Brigadier.

It was nearly 10 p.m. when the 1st Gordons began to make their way down to the river at Gamaches. Here also the enemy was pressing hard. Captain Aylmer had reconnoitred the crossing, and his A Company were to provide covering fire if the need arose. Then Lieut.-Colonel Wright was informed that the Germans had broken through on his left, and might reach the bridge first. This was a false alarm, but the commanding officer was able to ensure that the 75th Field Regiment—gunners from Aberdeen—would cover the crossing from positions south of the bridge.

Actually the Gordons reached the further bank without being bothered by the enemy, but they were only just in time. The moon was rising, and in her revealing light German bombers swooped down to attack the Bresle crossings. The Gordons, in their new position, were then dealing with a very welcome hot meal.

The Bresle river line seemed a good defensive position. So, at least, it appeared to the 1st Gordons as they looked down upon the wrecked bridge at Gamaches and the flooded fields which divided them from the enemy on the morning of 7th June. But the whole of the Highland Division sadly needed a respite from action, as General Fortune was well aware.

In position near the coast were the 6th Royal Scots Fusiliers, a pioneer battalion attached to the Division; next were A Brigade, part of the forces improvised from the troops on the lines of communication; from Beauchamps to Gamaches the remnants of the 154th Brigade held the front; and from Gamaches to Monchaux lay the 153rd Brigade. The 152nd Brigade had been drawn into reserve, French troops of the IX Corps taking over the sector from Monchaux to Blangy.

German troops, their strength unknown, had already penetrated the weak left flank by crossing the Bresle at Ponts-et-Marais and Eu, to reach the Forest of Eu. A Brigade were doing their best to round up these intruders, and found it no easy task; but a report that German tanks were in the forest proved to be false.

Although a brisk exchange of artillery fire continued all day on the 7th, there was no close action on the Highland Division front. The 5th Gordons, now in divisional reserve, received a welcome reinforcement of 130 men who had been sent up from Rouen, and a new B Company was formed with Captain Shankley in command.

On June 8th the 5th Gordons were roused by reports that there were Germans in Monchy. Patrols went out in all directions but found no enemy: hours of much needed rest had been sacrificed in vain. The 1st Gordons passed another day of vigilance but were not engaged.

The fate of the Highland Division was now being shaped by events further south, where the French were in great trouble. German armoured forces had not only turned the Bresle line, but had driven in between the main body of the Tenth Army and the IX Corps, which was left to its own devices. General Fortune was now under the virtually independent command of General Ihler, whose corps also included the French 31st and 40th Divisions and two cavalry divisions—partly horsed—all very weak in numbers.

General Fortune was still in communication with London, and the British Government were anxious to save the Highland Division from disaster; but they emphasised the fact that the Division must support the French to the utmost. There could be no thought of deserting our Ally. The situation became more involved when, at a conference held in the afternoon at IX Corps headquarters General Fortune was told that the whole of the corps would fall back slowly to Rouen and withdraw across the Seine.

It was much too late to do anything of the sort, for the Germans were already approaching Rouen. But, at any rate, it was recognised that a retirement from the Bresle could not be delayed any longer; and for the whole of the IX Corps the only line of retreat was through the coastal region in the direction of Le Havre. So it was approved that the first movement of the Highland Division must be to the Béthune river, south-east of Dieppe.

On the night of 8th June, every available R.A.S.C. vehicle was used as a troop-carrier. The 1st Gordons found that sufficient transport had been provided to carry two companies at a time, so that by using a shuttle service each man would have to march only half the distance to be covered. The process of thinning out the front positions began at 9 p.m., and at half-past ten the first two companies were on their way. By 8 a.m. on 9th June the whole Battalion had arrived on the southern edge of the Forest of Eu, some fourteen miles west of the Bresle. After breakfast a few hours sleep was possible; then came an order to occupy a position some two miles to the west where the 1st Lothians and Border Horse (the divisional cavalry regiment) had been bickering with the advancing Germans. The Gordons, however, saw nothing of the enemy, and waited for orders to continue the retreat.

The 5th Gordons, who had now been placed under 154th Brigade command, were not so fortunate as their comrades of the 1st Battalion. Orders had reached Lieut.-Colonel Clark so late that no transport was available, and there was nothing for it but to march fourteen miles in the darkness. To say that the Battalion set out cheerfully would be to claim too much. Bren guns, ammunition, anti-tank rifles, entrenching tools and the rest of the gear weighed heavily after the first mile or so, and the grim jest was not so frequent as the muttered curse. Yet, despite these afflictions of the spirit and the weariness of the flesh, the Battalion, still in good shape, arrived at Bellengreville soon after daylight on 9th June.

On this day the Germans entered Rouen and, having driven the French Tenth Army across the Seine, began to sweep in overwhelming force northward in the direction of the coast. The commander of the IX Corps now gave his formal consent to the retirement on Le Havre.

General Fortune already had some troops on the line of the Béthune river, and Dieppe had been evacuated on the previous day. At night Dieppe harbour was blocked. The Royal Navy were arranging to embark the Highland Division from Le Havre, so to reach Le Havre was now the pressing need.

The port was weakly defended, and General Fortune therefore organized, at Arques-la-Bataille, 'Arkforce', which was to reinforce the troops at Le Havre and cover the retreat of the remainder of the Division. Arkforce was composed of A Brigade, the remnants of the 7th and 8th Argyll and Sutherland Highlanders, the 4th Black Watch, and various artillery, engineer, and pioneer units. There were no Gordons in it.

While Arkforce moved westward during the night of the 9th the 1st Gordons and the 5th Gordons made their way back to the Béthune river. Both Battalions had another experience of roads congested with troops and transport, the frequent checks so exasperating to tired men who endeavoured to keep moving as they fought against sleep. By the morning of 10th June the 1st Gordons were resting in woods west of the Béthune, while the 5th held part of the river line.

The 5th Gordons dug in with all four rifle companies up, between Martigny and Arques-la-Bataille. Their positions were in the river valley with steep slopes rising in rear. A little before noon of this hot, sultry day the enemy was seen to be moving down the slopes beyond the river. He was at once engaged by our artillery and mortars, and the advance came to a standstill. Opposite D Company, on the outskirts of Arques, the Germans were bolder and lost the more heavily in consequence. Lieut.-Colonel Clark afterwards told the Brigadier that he had never seen troops in close order so badly caught by concentrated Bren-gun fire.

All this was very well, but later in the afternoon a vicious artillery bombardment opened on the Gordons, who suffered considerable loss. The road back from the river was uphill and much exposed, so that the removal of the wounded was a hazardous business; and here Lance-Corporal Borthwick did gallant work by taking his truck to and fro under fire between the river line and the dressing station.

Meanwhile General Fortune had received news of the gravest import. Arkforce had started in time to get through to Le Havre and eventually embarked from the port; but the road to Le Havre was now closed. The Germans held the crossings of the river Durdent from Cany northwards to the coast at Veulettes. Then followed a report that British destroyers which were off the coast had been engaged by German guns firing from the cliffs near St. Valéry-en-Caux.

The Navy were now ready to evacuate troops from the neighbourhood of St. Valéry, and General Fortune informed the War Office that he might ask for the remnants of his division to be taken off from this locality. With the consent of General Ihler, commander of the IX Corps, he made his plans. He would form a defensive perimeter at St. Valéry and keep the Germans at bay while the embarkation proceeded. At best the operation would be a difficult one, for St. Valéry is only a small fishing port situated at a break in the cliffs, the tiny harbour with its narrow entrance sufficient only for local needs in times of peace.

So the last move of the Highland Division was to bring them to St. Valéry.

Later, on 10th June, Brigadier Burney called his battalion commanders to a conference. Only then were these officers informed of the truly desperate state of affairs. Stores and kit were to be destroyed at once, so that every available vehicle could be used to carry the troops and their weapons.

The 5th Gordons were told that they must hold the Béthune line until 10 p.m. At nine o'clock they were ordered to hold on for an extra hour. When they finally departed to take their place in the perimeter covering St. Valéry only enough transport was available to carry three companies; the remainder of the Battalion marched until they were picked up by R.A.S.C. lorries at St. Aubins-le-Sec.

In the afternoon the 1st Gordons had been warned that they might have to reinforce their brethren of the 5th on the Béthune river. Then a different task was given them. Lieut.-Colonel Wright was hastily summoned to see General Fortune and told that his Battalion must move at once to clear the Germans from Cany on the river Durdent.

The Gordons lay in the woods behind Arques. Cany was twenty miles away. Transport was promised but failed to arrive, but the Battalion, as always, rose to the occasion. In rather ruthless fashion—there was no time for elaborate explanations—enough vehicles of various types were commandeered to carry everyone; and then began a nightmare journey along the coast road to St. Valéry, where an assembly point had been named.

Traffic congestion was worse than ever. The roads leading westward and south-westward were a welter of British transport, French transport—much of it horse drawn—marching men, staff cars, motor cycles and stragglers. Efforts to restore some sort of order out of near chaos were almost hopeless: there was certainly no hope of keeping the Gordon convoy together. Despite fierce argument some trucks were forced to take to side-roads, others were repeatedly held up. For the Gordons, to whom time was all important, this was, perhaps the most exasperating experience they had ever known. Lieut.-Colonel Wright eventually reached the assembly point outside St. Valéry with two and a half companies, no mortars, and no signal equipment. Yet he could not delay, and he set off for Cany at once.

Only two miles had been covered when General Fortune arrived in person to stop the column. There was no point now in trying to reach Cany. The 1st Gordons were placed under command of the 152nd Brigade and assigned a place in the St. Valéry perimeter, which they occupied in the early morning of 11th June.

The 5th Gordons, likewise caught in the congestion of traffic, had moved slowly back towards St. Valéry during the night. Before day broke they had reached their allotted position.

When the Highland Division began to dig in around St. Valéry in the early hours of 11th June, they were sadly reduced in numbers and in fire power, with ammunition and rations running short. The ground was open, with some growing crops; and though narrow sunken roads linked the farms and villages, there was little to hamper the movement of hostile armour.

On the eastern side of the perimeter the 5th Gordons were near the villages of St. Pierre-le-Viger and Ielon, with the 4th Seaforth on their left. On their right were the 1st Black Watch, whose line extended southward almost to Fontaine-le-Dun. Then, to the west, came a gap which French troops, facing south, were expected to fill.

The 1st Gordons, on the western face, were not in touch with the 2nd Seaforth, who held le Tot and a line of posts extending to the sea. The 4th Camerons, on the left of the Gordons, faced almost due south.

More and more troops were coming in, and many of those who had lost their units during the retreat from the Béthune river managed to rejoin. Isolated parties of Frenchmen who refused to be parted from their transport were still on their way. The gap between the 1st Gordons and the 2nd Seaforth was filled, inadequately enough, by the arrival of a company of the 7th Norfolk, a pioneer battalion attached to the Division.

Lieut.-Colonel Wright, whose headquarters were at a farm on the outskirts of Néville, had three rifle companies disposed in a chain of posts, with one company in reserve. The 1st Gordons were now, more or less, united again, but they were without their mortars and their signal equipment. The only means of communication within the Battalion was by runner.

The companies worked on their defences throughout the morning. Apart from aircraft which took an increasing interest in these activities, the Germans made no sign. About noon, however, groups of hostile infantry appeared away to the south, where signal lights and the movement of armoured cars were seen.

While his men prepared for battle the commanding officer received from General Fortune this heartening message which had been sent to all battalion commanders:

The Navy will probably make an effort to take us off by boat, perhaps tonight, perhaps in two nights. I wish all ranks to realise that this can only be achieved by the full co-operation of everyone. Men may have to walk five or six miles. The utmost discipline must prevail.

Men will board the boats with equipment and carrying arms. Vehicles will be rendered useless without giving away that this is being done. Carriers should be retained as the final rearguard. Routes back to the nearest highway should be reconnoitred and officers detailed as guides. Finally, if the enemy should attack before the whole force is evacuated, all ranks must realise that it is up to them to defeat them. He may attack with tanks, and we have quite a number of anti-tank guns behind. If the infantry can stop the enemy's infantry, that is all that is required, while anti-tank guns and rifles inflict casualties on armoured fighting vehicles.

This was good news indeed. The Navy would begin to take them off that night; and if the Germans attacked they were to be held at bay until the time came to go. All ranks of the Gordons were prepared to do that.

At three o'clock in the afternoon a powerful force of German tanks, deployed for battle, moved obliquely across the front of the Gordons, heading for the thinly held line of Norfolk pioneers. Gordons from the left and Seaforths from the right opened fire with every weapon they possessed, but light machine-guns, light anti-tank guns, and anti-tank rifles could make little impression on the German armour. Spraying fire from their heavy machine-guns, the tanks held on their course, over-ran the unfortunate pioneers, and headed for St. Valéry.

Strange to say, no German infantry followed in support of the armour and, so far as the Gordons were concerned, the battle died down. C Company, in reserve, and Battalion headquarters lost some men killed or wounded by the enemy machine guns: the three forward companies had taken no hurt at all.

The German tanks drove on to break through the Seaforth in the woods near le Tot and seize the high ground near the coast. When, in the early evening, they attempted to enter St. Valéry, they were foiled by the stout resistance of the troops, who held an inner line of defence. Here 2nd-Lieutenant P. B. Hay, now transport officer of the 1st Gordons, fought gallantly for several hours. He kept his little command together, rallied men who had lost their leaders, and returned a contemptuous reply to a demand for surrender.

The 5th Gordons, facing eastward with the little village of Ielon in front of them, found that their defensive preparations were hampered by large parties of French troops, leaderless and in considerable disorder, who passed through on their way to St. Valéry. There seemed no fight left in these people, but there were very many of their compatriots who were made of sterner stuff, and bore themselves well that day.

On D Company's front Captain Lawrie had established a strong forward post consisting of one platoon with one machine-gun platoon of the 7th Northumberland Fusiliers. These worthies accounted themselves fortunate, for they occupied a farmhouse where they discovered chickens and eggs to supplement what was left of their rations.

Half-way through the afternoon another untidy column of French came past. Tired and almost panic-stricken, frantically urging on the jaded horses which drew their heavily loaded wagons, these men shouted excited warnings to the Highlanders and Fusiliers. The Boche were coming! Our men greeted these weaker vessels with appropriate retort and a certain grim amusement.

No Germans appeared, but the movements of the retreating French seemed to have attracted the attention of dive-bombers which flew into attack. Then the hostile artillery began to shell the Gordons.

At 5 p.m. the commanding officer went back to Brigade headquarters at Blosseville for a conference. About this time German tanks were seen moving across D Company's front towards Ielon, and the forward post opened fire. Soon afterwards, General Fortune's directive concerning embarkation was received. All seemed to promise well.

General Fortune had done everything possible to prevent the sacrifice of his Division. He had sent to the Commander-in-Chief Portsmouth an estimate of his requirements and the numbers, British and French, which he hoped would be able to embark. Later in the evening of 11th June he reported to Portsmouth and to the War Office that, in his opinion, the coming night offered the last chance to get away.

The Royal Navy had collected the necessary shipping in readiness to carry out what would, in any case, be a very hazardous operation. Hostile fire from the shore, combined with air attack, had compelled the ships to stand well away from the coast during the daylight hours of 11th June; but they would come in as darkness fell.

Although General Ihler did not believe that embarkation was possible, General Fortune proceeded with his plans. About 9.30 p.m. he issued verbal orders to withdraw from the outer defences: embarkation was to begin an hour later with the troops already in St. Valéry.

Then, as darkness gathered in falling rain over the land, the fate of the Highland Division was decided by the elements. The coast became shrouded in fog and the ships could not come in. There would be no embarkation that night. The last chance had gone.

No orders had reached the 1st Gordons when, at 10 p.m., the German machine guns and mortars opened intense fire upon the orchards where C Company and Battalion headquarters lay.

About twenty minutes later this fire ceased. Then the troop of Royal Horse Artillery who had been supporting the Gordons withdrew. The subaltern who had been forward observation officer informed the commanding officer that his battery expected to embark about midnight, and he understood that all troops were to withdraw before that time.

Lieut.-Colonel Wright had received no orders to move. At the moment he was concerned with the fate of his forward companies, and had sent out runners to get into touch. Not one of them got through. The enemy, covered by his deluge of fire on C Company and Battalion headquarters, had cut in behind the forward companies who were now isolated, and probably surrounded.

At 2.15 a.m. on the 12th Major Victor Campbell, brigade-major of the 152nd Brigade, drove up in his car with orders for the Gordons—and the 2nd Seaforth—to withdraw to St. Valéry. Lieut.-Colonel Wright collected C Company and the remnants of Headquarters Company. Before moving off he sent forward a patrol in another attempt to reach the other companies. This patrol reported that the Germans, in great force, barred the way. One last effort was made by Lieutenant J. I. R. Dunlop, commander of the 1st Gordons platoon in the 153rd Brigade Anti-Tank Company, who were now all casualties. Dunlop, with an orderly, covered 400 yards before he was shot in the ankle. He managed to hobble back to Battalion headquarters, and the commanding officer was then convinced that his three companies must be left to their fate.

C Company acted as advanced guard as the remnants of the Battalion made their way back. The medical officer and his stretcher bearers were left in charge of some fifty badly wounded Gordons who could not be moved.

Captain F. J. Colville, leading C Company, ran into a German tank patrol a mile and a half outside St. Valéry. Colville was killed in the fight which ensued, and Pierre Boudet, the gallant French interpreter who had been with the Gordons since their early days in France, was severely wounded. Major C. D. M. Hutchins, bringing on Headquarters Company, heard the firing and swerved to the right. The night was very dark, and no one knew where the Germans were, but he was fortunate enough—if fortunate he could be called—to bring his people into the town. Lieut.-Colonel Wright and his small party were some distance behind, and had no idea of what had happened to C Company. They walked straight into the arms of the Germans and were captured.

The 5th Gordons had made their preparations for withdrawal when orders should come. D Company's forward platoon were moved back to a position near Brigade headquarters at Blosseville there to cover the retreat. The platoon reached this position about 9 p.m. and began to dig in. Throughout the night they were shelled and also shot at with tracer bullets from their left flank. They saw nothing of the rest of the Battalion.

Half an hour after midnight a despatch rider brought orders to Lieut.-Colonel Clark: he was to fall back on St. Valéry. To verify this message 2nd-Lieutenant Hughes was sent to Blosseville, but he found that Brigade headquarters had already left. The commanding officer, very much in doubt as to what was happening in St. Valéry, set off to see for himself, after giving orders to the Battalion to withdraw.

At St. Valéry Lieut.-Colonel Clark found that no ships had come in, and was told that the French had already surrendered. The town had been fitfully bombarded all night, many buildings were ablaze, and in the streets riderless French cavalry horses and stray mules added to the confusion. Bursts of machine-gun fire swept the harbour. On the cliffs to east and west above the town the Germans waited. To Lieut.-Colonel Clark there seemed no point in bringing his men into stricken St. Valéry, so he sent a message to stop them.

The 5th Gordons had begun to withdraw at 4.30 a.m. on 12th June, covered by their carriers. Fighting seemed to be going on all round them. B Company ran into strong German forces, were surrounded, and lost. The other companies were halted outside St. Valéry at Manneville.

And now they were called upon for a final effort. In the desperate hope of holding on for another day, General Fortune had decided to drive the Germans from their commanding positions on the cliffs outside the town. Captain Shankley, on a motor cycle, arrived at Manneville with a verbal message from the Brigadier: the 5th Gordons would advance and capture the high ground near by.

Hungry, soaked to the skin, weary beyond belief, A and D Companies started, with the carriers in support, almost at the moment when the German armour was beginning to close in on the town. D Company had no chance at all: they were over-run by the tanks. A Company went grimly on, and then French troops appeared before them, masking their fire. The Frenchmen were waving white handkerchiefs, some had white rags tied to their rifles, and in this confusion A Company were surrounded by their enemies.

At the same time, Battalion headquarters and C Company, occupying a reserve position in a sunken road, saw in the cornfields between them and the Germans, other French troops bent on surrender. The Gordons had no opportunity to strike a last blow before the order came to cease fire. It was, indeed, the end.

All that were left of the 5th Gordons stood fast and laid down their arms, while the German tanks moved up to them. The Highlanders were then marshalled on the cliffs they had set out to capture so short a time before.

The platoon at Blosseville had waited in vain for the Battalion to fall back through their position. Their comrades, the machine-gunners, had been ordered back to St. Valéry. As dawn broke on 12th June, the platoon opened fire on Germans who could be seen on their front and then in small parties slipped away.

A, B and D Companies of the 1st Gordons had held on to their post in the perimeter near Néville. Defiant to the last, surrounded by the enemy, and well knowing that further resistance was useless, they made their surrender.

There is no need to dwell upon the manner in which the tragedy of St. Valéry-en-Caux came to an end: how the French commander made formal surrender at 8 a.m. on 12th June, and how General Fortune, although under French command, delayed his capitulation until he was convinced that continued resistance would be of no advantage to the Allied cause. It was more than two hours later when he ordered the men of the Highland Division to lay down their arms. At great risk and some loss, the Royal Navy had managed to embark a few thousand British and French from the beaches at Veules-les-Roses. No more could be done on the night of 11th June—and nothing thereafter.

The fate of the Highland Division, caught in the web of circumstance, can always be remembered by Scotland not only with sorrow but with pride. Officers and men had fought the good fight: it was not theirs to determine how they should finish their course.

Still dazed and unable to realise that for most of them this was to be the end of their active war service, the prisoners of war—among them the survivors of the 1st and 5th Gordon Highlanders—started on the long and weary march which took them through northern France and Belgium and Holland to Germany, there to spend nearly five years in captivity. They could not foresee that another Highland Division would be born, and that new units of the Highland regiments—two battalions of Gordon Highlanders together again in the same brigade—would go forth to turn defeat into victory and bear their full part in the triumphs that were to come.

One must spare another thought for the Gordon Highlanders who became prisoners of war; but first let us recall the wonderful example of fortitude and service set by General Fortune.

He worked tirelessly to ameliorate the conditions in the camps, arguing daily with the Germans until, often through desperation, they yielded to his requests. He was offered the opportunity of going to the camp reserved for generals: he preferred to stay with his own officers. He was the first to suffer reprisals when escapes were made and when attempts to escape were discovered. And in the end his health suffered through over-strain in setting an example of physical fitness, so that all might be the better able to withstand the hardships of those long marches which he knew must come when Germany was invaded. For his faith in victory never faltered.

Fortunately the Gordons possessed admirable warrant officers and non-commissioned officers who kept the men together, enforced discipline, and insisted upon a smart turn-out—all of which helped to maintain morale and preserve the spirit of the Regiment. Casualties during the years of captivity were remarkably few. One or two Gordons were shot by the Germans on some pretext; less than a dozen died from privation during the first winter. The majority of the men being agricultural workers, were put to work on farms where, as regards food, they fared comparatively well.

In November 1940 five officers were permitted to go from the camp at Laufen to attend the funeral of Brigadier Burney, who had died in hospital at Munich. A small party went over to Freising in the following August to bury Captain D. Crichton of the 1st Gordons, whose death was unexpected. Captain E. Altham, medical officer of the 1st Gordons, died at Lamsdorff from typhus.

Two notable attempts to escape were made by officers of the 1st Gordons. Lieutenant Peter de Winton, who was sent to a punishment camp in Poland with 500 young officers, made his first effort when the prisoners were moved back to Germany. He and three others managed to wall themselves up in a dungeon with a supply of food, afterwards emerging from their hiding place to wander about the country. They were able to find work on farms. De Winton eventually reached Warsaw, where he spent two years with the Polish resistance, learning Polish and Russian. He escaped forced labour by wearing his arm in a sling, but in the end he was picked up by the Germans.

Captain H. L. Christie, adjutant of the 1st Battalion, escaped in a refuse tip which, working on a wire pulley, ran down to a light railway. He reached the Swiss frontier, but, in making a dash for safety, was caught by two German sentries and their dog.

Several men escaped and managed to get home. Private Mitchell of the 1st Gordons got away in July 1940 while the column was on the march to Germany, worked on farms in Belgium and Holland, and was then smuggled into Amsterdam. When capture seemed unavoidable he gave himself up and was put to work in the cook-house of the local prison. A year later he was mistaken for a German and ordered for service on the Russian front. He had great difficulty in establishing his identity as a British soldier, but in 1942 he appeared at the Warburg prisoners-of-war camp in a very sorry condition.

MALAYA AND SINGAPORE
1939-42

Defence Problems

After war came to Europe the question of the security of Singapore was reviewed by the British Government. In the event of hostilities extending to the Far East responsibility for the defence of the naval base must fall upon the garrison, supported by air power until the arrival from Home of a battle-fleet strong enough to safeguard our communications with Australia and New Zealand.

War with Japan could not be regarded as imminent, and might be avoided altogether. She was still pre-occupied with her China campaign, although her ambitions were well known to the Western Powers. In any case her policy would, undoubtedly, be influenced by the progress of the war in the West.

In September 1939 the garrison of Singapore consisted of three British battalions—one of them the 2nd Gordon Highlanders —one Indian, and one newly raised Malay battalion. There was a battalion of Indian troops in Penang island, and the 12th Indian Brigade, coming from India, were earmarked for Johore. No Regular troops were available for the defence of central and northern Malaya. Our air forces were quite inadequate.

The bad news from Europe in the spring and summer of 1940 —Dunkirk, St. Valéry, Italy's intervention, the collapse of France —had instant repercussions in the Far East. The Tripartite Pact was signed by Germany, Italy and Japan; and in September Japanese troops occupied the northern part of French Indo-China.

The 2nd Gordon Highlanders at Changi had proceeded with their training. Field firing was carried out at Kuala Lumpur, in Selangor State on the mainland; the men were kept fit by frequent route-marches; the pioneer platoon received instruction by the Royal Engineers.

In June 1940 the Gordons were told that their carriers must not do more than 150 miles per month, worn-out tracks being difficult to replace. This order was one small indication of the shortage of equipment which hampered our expanding forces at home and abroad.

As was to be expected, the Battalion chafed at what they considered their 'peace-time' routine, and wondered when their

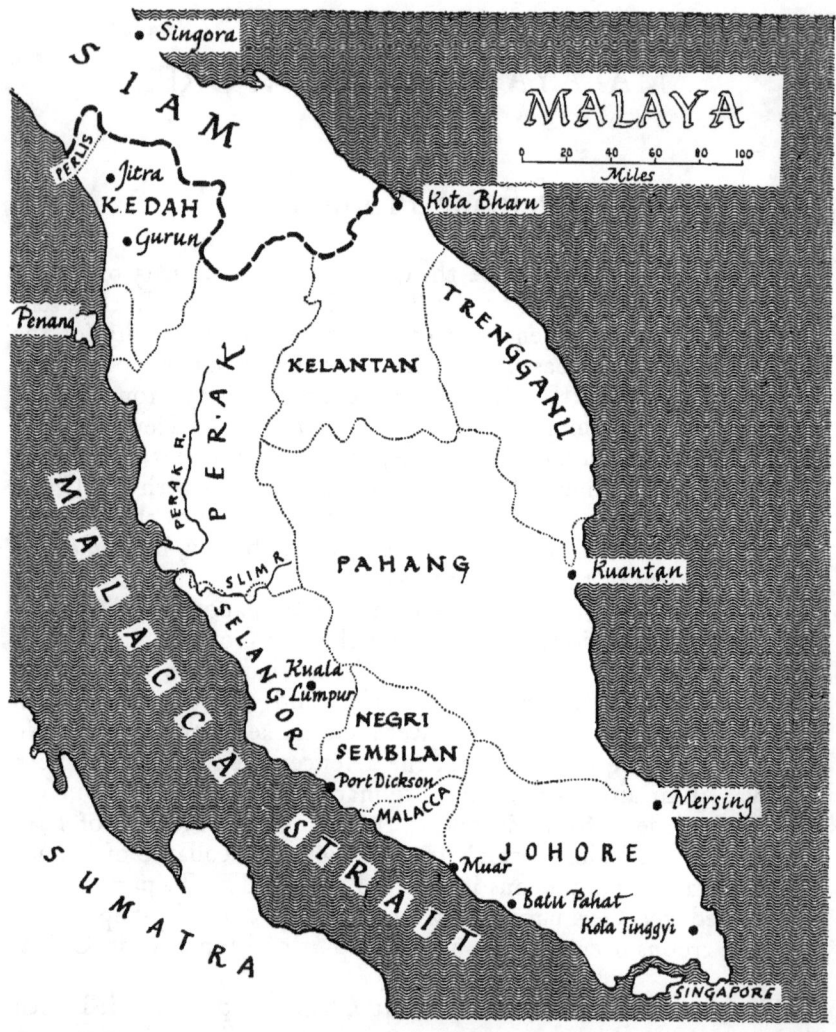

chance of active service would come. Aware that, in the normal course, the next station of the Gordons would be in India, the commanding officer would have welcomed the move. His battalion had been on garrison duty ever since they had started their overseas tour in 1934, and he felt that if they could join a divisional formation in India better training facilities would increase their chance of 'getting into the fighting'. Once arrived in India, the Gordons were unlikely to remain there inactive until the end of the war.

Lieut.-Colonel Graham's views had been invited by higher authority, but later in 1940 the decision was made that no British infantry battalion would be moved from Singapore : parties of officers and men were to be sent home and replaced by new drafts. During October 1940 the Gordons were obliged to despatch no less than eight officers and 135 other ranks; and they had then to absorb the new arrivals. Company training began at Mersing and Muar in Johore, and also at Port Dickson.

In September the Singapore garrison had been reorganised, the Gordons being posted to the 2nd Malaya Brigade, of which Lieut.-Colonel Graham assumed command for a time. Captain J. M. Lawrance of the Gordons became brigade-major.

The Chiefs of Staff in London and nearly all the Service authorities concerned were of opinion that the defence of Singapore involved the defence of the whole of Malaya. Yet to put Singapore, the Straits Settlements, and the Federated and Unfederated Malay States on a common war footing presented a number of administrative difficulties; furthermore, defence measures conflicted with the production of rubber and tin, both of great value to our war effort. And everything depended upon the arrival of the necessary troops and aircraft, though it was not easy to see how these reinforcements could be provided.

During the year which followed Dunkirk, Britain, the Commonwealth and Empire stood alone. The defence of the United Kingdom from air attack and possible invasion; the protection of our sea communications; the re-equipment of our Army at home and the supply and reinforcement of our forces in North Africa: all these were priorities. There was little to spare for the Far East; and we were not yet at war with Japan.

However, between October 1940 and September 1941, the Gordons saw a steady stream of reinforcements disembark at Singapore: five infantry brigades from India and two from Australia. Unfortunately the Indian battalions contained too many untrained recruits and were short of experienced Indian officers and non-commissioned officers, and of British officers who knew their men and spoke their language. Owing to its enforced rapid expansion the Indian Army could neither overcome these defects nor ensure that the troops were fully equipped for modern war.

As for air reinforcements, the Service Chiefs in Malaya had wanted 566 first-line aircraft, but only a quarter of this number were available when invasion came.

The Singapore garrison continued to practise defence measures: manning exercises, tests of signal communications, and blackouts. In Johore Strait the Gordons got accustomed to shooting from and at small craft. One exercise consisted of the defence of the

Tekong Besar batteries, held by the 9th Coast Regiment, R.A., against a force of 'saboteurs' consisting of one company of the Gordons. The Battalion gave tank-hunting and carrier demonstrations for the benefit of the Brigade, and their reputation in the Singapore garrison as an efficient and well-trained unit was deservedly high.

Tension in the Far East was increasing. Much seemed to depend upon negotiations between Japan and the United States. America did not want war, yet could not countenance the steady southward progress of Japan, who had set her sights high. She aimed at the elimination of Western influence in South-East Asia, and saw herself in control of the Pacific and of what she grandiloquently called 'The Great East Asia Co-Prosperity Sphere'.

Negotiations in Washington were broken off in July 1941 when the Japanese occupied southern Indo-China, thus securing a naval base within 750 miles of Singapore and airfields no more than 300 miles from the northern frontier of Malaya. Britain and the U.S.A. replied by 'freezing' all Japanese assets under their control. These measures, which deprived the potential aggressor of vital raw materials, created a new and dangerous situation; but Japan, although planning for war, was not yet ready to strike. Conversations with the Americans were resumed.

In Malaya and Singapore defence preparations were accelerated. Lieut.-General A. E. Percival, who had been commanding the British land forces since April 1941, had set two weak Indian divisions to defend northern Malaya, with one brigade in reserve. The 8th Australian Division were allotted to the defence of Johore, and another Indian brigade were available as general reserve.

The 1st and 2nd Malaya Brigades remained as the permanent garrison of Singapore island. From Changi the 2nd Gordons now sent a whole company to man the defences of Pengerang which, heretofore, had been held by one platoon.

On 29th November came a warning from the Chiefs of Staff that war might be very near: a sudden attack from Japan might have Siam as one of the objectives. In Singapore this was the signal for all troops to return to barracks. No one was unduly worried. The St. Andrew's Eve Ball in the sergeants' mess of the Gordons proved a great success.

Then on Monday, 1st December, the Gordons were ordered to occupy their war station at Pengerang. They left Selerang barracks next day.

Pengerang possessed a battery of two 6-inch guns, besides secondary armament. Its observation post served the fixed defences on Tekong island and other batteries, for Bukit Pengerang, the most southerly hill on the mainland, dominated the Singapore coastal region from the north-east. The beach defences were strong on the southern and eastern sides of the peninsula, which had been converted almost into an island by the cutting of an anti-tank ditch running from the sea to the Santi river.

While the Gordons were crossing the Strait to Pengerang there appeared in the Eastern channel a striking demonstration of British naval might. The battleship *Prince of Wales* and the battle-cruiser *Repulse*, escorted by four destroyers, were moving slowly towards their anchorage at the naval base. To the Gordons the *Repulse* was an old friend, for in 1936 she had carried them from Gibraltar to Malta and, later, back to Gibraltar from Egypt.

The arrival of these two powerful ships had a heartening effect on everyone. They had been sent in the hope that their appearance might give the Japanese pause if it were their intention to attempt a sea-borne invasion of Malaya and Singapore.

Retreat in Malaya

On the night of 7th December, 1941, and in the early hours of the following day Japan struck without warning: at Pearl Harbour, where the U.S. Pacific Fleet suffered crippling losses; in the Philippines; and at Hong Kong. And Japanese forces invaded Malaya.

The aggressor always possesses the initiative. It was our policy not to violate Siamese neutrality until we were certain that Japan was about to do so. Unfortunately our air reconnaissance failed to establish the enemy's intentions before we were forestalled at Singora and the airfields in southern Siam. So the Japanese invaded Malaya across its northern frontier; and at the same time they landed at Kota Bharu, in the north-eastern state of Kelantan.

Nearly seven weeks were to elapse before the Gordons got to grips with the Japanese, but their first glimpse of war came in the early hours of 8th December. About 3.30 a.m. seventeen Japanese bombers flew in to attack Singapore. The town was a blaze of lights, but a blackout would have made little difference, for the tropical moon rode high. To Colonel Graham and Major Stitt, who watched from their vantage point on Bukit Pengerang, it appeared that the main targets were the naval base and the Tengah and Seletar airfields. Our anti-aircraft batteries could be seen to reply vigorously amid the flash and thunder of bombs, but the enemy escaped without loss.

On 8th December Fortress Command ordered the flooding of the anti-tank ditch at Pengerang. Next day Colonel Graham, who had been appointed to command the troops in Penang island, left the Battalion. He was succeeded by Major J. H. Stitt.

The campaign in Malaya, which was to determine the fate of the Gordons at Singapore, took its tragic course. Overmatched in the air, our improvised divisions were opposed by a better equipped, better trained enemy who could not be checked on the frontier. Our northern airfields were soon lost. Then, on 10th December, came news of a disaster which at first was impossible to believe. The *Prince of Wales* and the *Repulse*, returning from an abortive attempt to launch a surprise attack upon Japanese convoys approaching Siam, had been sunk by air attack with the loss of Admiral Sir Tom Phillips and 840 officers and men. The Japanese were fast obtaining mastery of the air. Now they were masters of the sea.

From northern Malaya the tale of disaster grew as the Japanese pressed on down the west coast. The state of Perlis was lost; at the actions of Jitra and Gurun the fate of Kedah was decided; Penang island was evacuated by sea on the night of 17th December; by the 23rd our forces were back behind the Perak river. On the east coast the withdrawal from Kelantan was completed.

Now developed the struggle to defend the airfields of central Malaya. It was almost impossible to reinforce the fighting front, seeing that Johore and Singapore itself were open to attack by seaborne forces.

To the Gordon Highlanders at Pengerang it would perhaps have been a relief if attack had come. Throughout December they strengthened their defences by laying fields of anti-tank and anti-personnel mines. Native labour was employed to clear fields of fire by cutting down vegetation. Two accidents occurred with the mines, explosions killing two privates and wounding 2nd-Lieutenant D. I. Campbell and two others. After this all unlaid mines of anti-personnel type were ordered to be thrown into the sea. They had lain in store too long.

The carriers of the Gordons, which could hardly be usefully employed at Pengerang, were attached to the 2/17th Dogras in 2nd Malaya Brigade reserve.

Time was found for platoon and company training beyond the defended perimeter, and small patrols were sent out northward. At various points along the coast listening posts were set up, manned by a considerably augmented intelligence section. A small fleet of *tongkangs*, commanded at first by Captain K. M. Burnett and then by Regimental Sergeant-Major A. W. Milne, kept these posts provisioned. One platoon was detached to guard a R.A.F. radio-location station.

Early in January 1942 the disaster at Slim river sealed the fate of central Malaya. On the east coast Kuantan and its airfield were given up. A visit from General Wavell, recently appointed Supreme Commander South-West Pacific, guided the course of events. He ordered the evacuation of Selangor, Negri Sembilan, and Malacca, all resources to be concentrated upon the defence of Johore State, which formed the outer bastion of Singapore island. Now the well-trained brigades of the 8th Australian Division would come into action; an Indian brigade which had arrived in Singapore on 3rd January was available, and more reinforcements were expected.

So the retreat into Johore began, while the Japanese continued their advance down the west coast. They had intensified their air attacks upon Singapore, with the object of destroying the inadequate defences of the airfields. On 13th January a second convoy, escaping the attentions of Japanese aircraft, brought a brigade of the British 18th Division into Singapore. The ships also brought fifty-one Hurricane fighters.

The war was coming nearer to the 2nd Gordons, but so far their opportunities had been limited to the rounding up of a party of Japanese fishermen found to possess a box for housing carrier pigeons, and a fruitless search for the pilot of a Buffalo fighter seen to come down in the sea. On the 15th they were called upon to supervise the evacuation from Pengerang of the Malay population who were conveyed to Singapore island—a pitiful business, for these poor bewildered people were very reluctant to leave their homes.

On 21st January the Battalion handed over Pengerang to the 1st Mysore Infantry and crossed to Singapore to join the Fortress reserve, a move which seemed to promise more active employment. They went into camp at Bidadari.

By this time Japanese air attacks on Singapore town, the airfields and the docks had grown heavier; indiscriminate bombing of the more populous areas killed or injured over 2,000 people during the last fortnight in January.

Johore

Fighting in Johore had begun on 15th January, and when General Wavell again appeared five days later the battle was definitely going against us. Wavell could only counsel a determined resistance and the strengthening of the defences on the northern shore of Singapore island. By the 23rd the last remaining airfields in Johore had been put out of action, and on the 25th General Percival ordered a gradual withdrawal from Johore to Singapore.

At last the 2nd Gordon Highlanders were to be given their chance: and, like the 4th and 6th Gordons in Belgium, and the

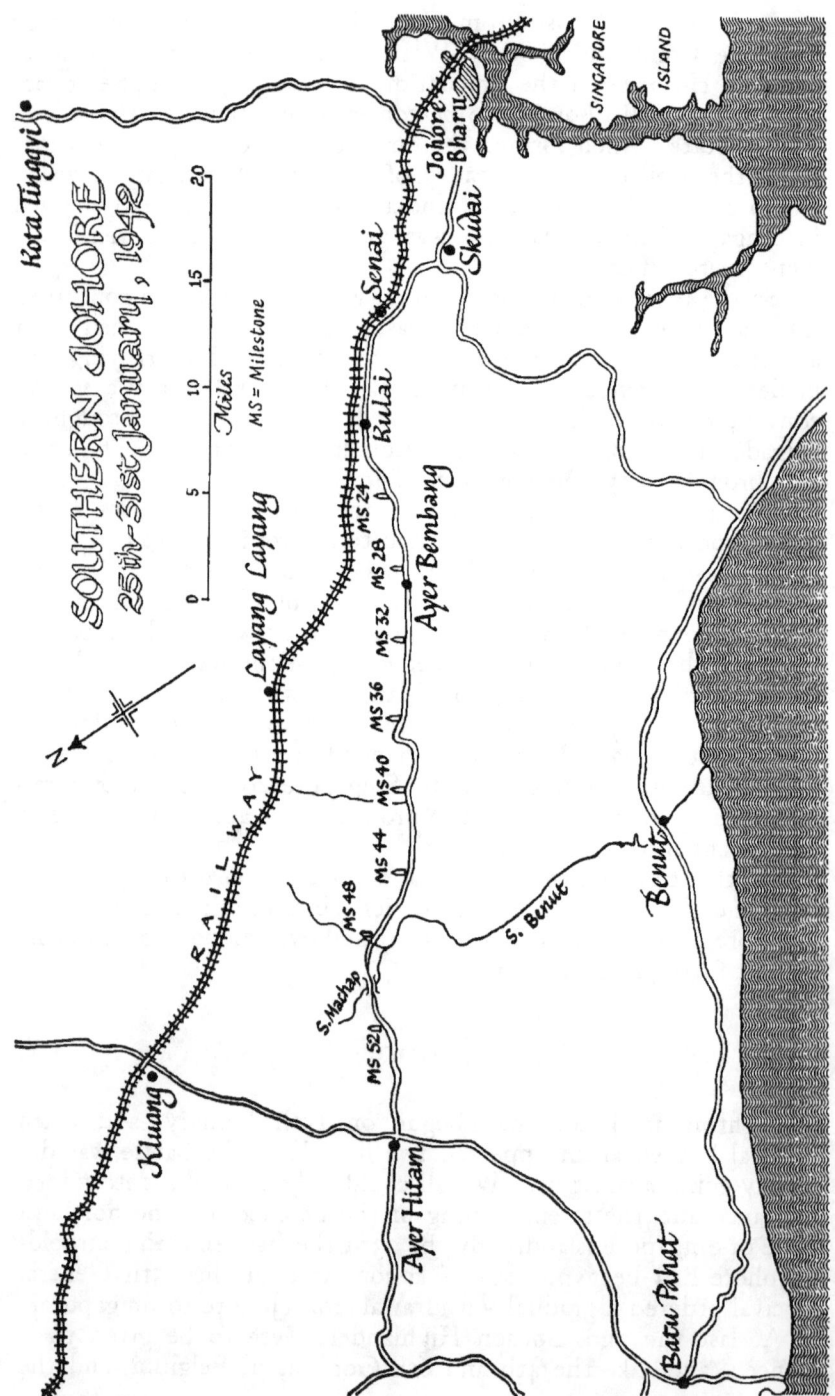

1st and 5th Battalions south of the Somme, they were fated to enter a losing battle.

On 25th January our forces were on the line Mersing—Kluang —Batu Pahat, but the enemy seemed on the point of breaking through on the western coast road. General Percival's orders were for a retirement by stages along the roads which converged upon Johore Bharu and the causeway leading to Singapore island. The Gordons were needed to reinforce Brigadier D. S. Maxwell's 27th Australian Brigade on the main trunk road leading south-east from Ayer Hitam.

Lieut.-Colonel Stitt crossed into Johore on the 25th and reported to Brigadier Maxwell. The Battalion followed in motor transport, being ordered to travel as lightly equipped as possible, without entrenching tools. After a four hours journey the Gordons arrived on the trunk road at the $45\frac{1}{2}$ milestone about 5.30 p.m.

The commanding officer was at Sungei Benut, some distance further forward. The Brigadier had informed him that the Japanese bomber swere a constant worry, troops who were not well dug in being sure to suffer heavy casualties; also, a clash with Japanese tanks was to be expected.

This was fine hearing for a Battalion who had not only been ordered to leave their tools behind, but had also handed over their tank-hunting equipment before leaving Pengerang. All that could be done was to send the regimental quartermaster-sergeant back to Singapore with orders to collect ' by any means ' all the entrenching tools he could discover. By four o'clock on the following morning he had reappeared with twenty-five picks, fifty shovels and a few native implements called *changkuls*. All these were put to immediate use.

The position taken up by the Gordons was near milestone 50. On the right of the road were B Company and D Company, who occupied part of a rubber plantation with sparse jungle growth fringing the edge of the swamp which lay in front. Rubber usually provides good cover from air observation but restricts the field of fire except along the lanes between the regular lines of trees. Targets were apt to be fleeting, and against the active Japanese enemy the utmost vigilance was needed to guard against surprise. However, a frontal attack against the forward companies would have to come in over the open swamp.

About 500 yards further back on the left of the road A Company lay among the stunted bushes of wild rhododendrons interspersed with *lalang*, a coarse grass rather like elephant grass, growing to the height of four feet or more. Here also was a good field of fire, over the swamps which bordered the Sungei Machap.

Battalion headquarters, together with C Company who formed the reserve, were another 500 yards in rear on the right of the road. The Gordons were supported by a battery of Australian 25-pdrs., and a troop of Australian anti-tank guns commanded the road at various points. Lieut.-Colonel Stitt also had a call on two companies of Australian infantry.

In such fashion then, and in country strange to them, the Gordons prepared for their first action; for they were, at last, in the forefront of the battle. Through them, as they settled down in their positions, withdrew the Australian 2/26th and 2/27th Battalions and the 2nd Loyals whom they were replacing in the 27th Australian Brigade. When all these troops had passed, the road bridge over the Sungei Machap was blown.

About 9 a.m. on 26th January Japanese aircraft came over on reconnaissance, and some dived low to use their bombs and machine guns rather at random. Two hours later about thirty Japanese were seen advancing down the road, with others following in groups. The enemy paused at the broken bridge and Platoon Sergeant-Major Ogilvie promptly engaged him with mortar fire, the first shell being a direct hit. The Japanese then deployed along the edge of the swamp to the right of the road, coming under the fire of B Company. This stopped them, but they were also trying to work round the right flank, a movement which was checked by strong patrols sent out from Major Duke's D Company and from Captain Elsmie's C Company in reserve.

About two in the afternoon, when a shortage of drinking water had begun to cause the Gordons great discomfort, the hostile aircraft came over again, skimming the tree tops to bomb and machine gun the whole position. There were no British aircraft to be seen: the Battalion were now going through their first experience of an ordeal only too familiar to our troops in Malaya.

Soon the Japanese infantry, now well supported by the fire of mortars and machine guns, attacked B Company in considerable force. The Gordons soon found that the deafening roar of the mortars was out of all proportion to the small damage inflicted by their bombs; but snipers in trees, now encountered for the first time, proved themselves a nuisance.

The scrub had caught fire near the forward anti-tank gun, and the Australian detachment had been forced to retreat from the flames. They made a spirited but unsuccessful attempt to get their gun away, and then, as the fire spread, two platoons of Captain Farquhar's A Company were brought back across the road out of harm's way, their movement attracting heavy fire.

B Company were so heavily engaged that Major Innes was obliged to give up his forward posts and about 200 yards of ground.

D Company then had to look to their open flank. Telephone communication with Battalion headquarters had been cut, so the three companies simply fought on until the Japanese effort spent itself. Away on the left the fire in the scrub died down, so that the platoons of A Company were able to re-occupy their old positions; and much vegetation had been burnt, vastly improving the field of fire.

The lull in the fighting was short. Soon a large enemy column was seen advancing down the sides of the road, a good target for the Australian 25-pdrs. which made the most of it. Nevertheless the Japanese made desperate efforts to get forward, and for a full hour the Gordons had to deal with flanking movements and sudden attempts to penetrate their front. When, at half-past six, the Battalion received orders to retire as soon as darkness fell all ranks could pride themselves on the fact that in their first encounter with the Japanese they had held them in check for a whole day and inflicted upon them considerable loss. The casualties of the Gordons amounted to fifty-eight killed, wounded and missing, among them 2nd-Lieutenant J. A. P. Russell who was killed.

The Battalion came back through the 2/26th Battalion near milestone 44½, and were directed to occupy a support position in a rubber plantation about two miles further on. In front of the Gordons was a troop of Australian 25-pdrs., and D Company were detailed as escort to the guns.

By dawn the companies were again ready for the fray, having replenished their supply of ammunition which had run very short. The Australians in front repelled a number of attacks on the 27th but the Gordons were disturbed only by the visits of hostile aircraft. In the evening a very welcome hot meal came up, the first since the Battalion's hurried departure from Singapore.

D Company had dug in on the right flank of the Australian guns, and were in touch with the 2/26th Battalion in front. The only incident, but that a very distressing one, occurred early in the afternoon when Major Duke and Captain Moir-Byres were guests at an Australian tea party. A sudden attack by dive-bombers wounded Captain Moir-Byres and also Captain Robett, the Australian troop commander, who died later.

D Company rejoined the Battalion about nine o'clock at night when another withdrawal was in progress. The 2/26th who had disengaged with some difficulty, now took up a position north-east of the trunk road on a minor road leading to the railway. The Australians thus covered the right flank of the Gordons, who became front battalion again.

The 28th January was another tough day. The Gordons maintained a standing patrol at the bend of the road in front of their defences, so received ample warning when, about 7 a.m., some thirty Japanese approached on bicycles. A section on the left of the road opened fire on this party and dealt very faithfully with it.

Then were heard the loud shouts and yells which so often preceded a Japanese attack in force, and the mortars of the Gordons opened to some purpose. They were answered by heavy fire from the enemy mortars and one of our detachments received a direct hit.

Throughout the morning the Japanese persisted in their efforts to advance down the road, and the section which had been posted on the left of the road was obliged to give ground. Then B Company, the forward company with their left on the road, bore the brunt of the attack. At one point the Japanese managed to cross the road and gain the protection of a thick patch of cover; but the Gordons dislodged them with bullet and grenade. The left of C Company, further away in the rubber on the right, were able to enfilade an enemy advance on their left front. Meanwhile, the mortar fire of the Gordons checked every attempt of the Japanese to advance along the road.

A patrol under Platoon Sergeant-Major Strachan discovered an enemy group in the jungle on the left of the road, so when these troops began to advance against the left of D Company, who were in rear of B Company, they were disposed of very nicely by fire at short range. The Gordons were well aware of the value of good patrol work in fighting the Japanese.

From overhead came the roar of enemy aircraft, but the bombs they dropped fell some distance in rear of the Battalion.

Meanwhile the enemy had started a wide out-flanking movement on the right beyond C Company and over-lapping the 2/26th Battalion on the road leading to the railway. Soon the 2/30th, holding the usual perimeter position near milestone 40, were assailed on their right and even in their rear. Answering a call for assistance, Lieut.-Colonel Stitt despatched A Company to reinforce the 2/30th, but the Australians had settled the issue with the bayonet before the Highlanders could join in. The Japanese covered their retreat by using smoke bombs—thought at the moment to contain gas—and the crisis was over.

In the late afternoon the Japanese mortars were supported by the fire of an infantry gun which paid particular attention to B and C Companies. Though many were killed or wounded the Gordons, who had repelled infantry attacks and endured mortar fire all day, were not to be shifted by this bombardment.

The Brigade had been told to hold on for 48 hours, but orders were now received to withdraw when darkness came. With the approach of night the Japanese fire died down, and Gordons and Australians were able to disengage without much trouble.

The Gordons were committed to a long march through the darkness. They had no transport, so weapons, ammunition and equipment were carried by hand. One devoted private bore an anti-tank rifle and a thousand rounds of ammunition. Tired and heavy laden, plodding on after a day of hard fighting in fierce heat, all ranks were sustained by the conviction that, whatever the future might bring, they had the measure of the Japanese.

The early hours of the 29th saw the 2/26th Battalion at milestone 31, the Gordons further back near Ayer Bembang, and the 2/30th round another road junction at milestone 27. The Gordons' position had been reconnoitred on the previous evening by Captain Farquhar, and when the Battalion arrived about 2 a.m. a meal was ready for them. It was very welcome.

The task of the Gordons on the 29th was to deal with any Japanese advance which should lap round the flanks of the 2/26th Battalion in front. Patrols were sent forward to watch for signs of enemy movement, but the Australians were able to do all that was necessary without assistance. Nevertheless the mortars of the Gordons found some targets during the day and fired about 400 rounds. One direct hit sent portions of a machine gun and of several Japanese hurtling through the air.

Later D Company became escort for an Australian battery, and at dusk the next stage of the retirement began without interference from the enemy.

At 7 p.m. the Gordons marched into the village of Senai, now a smouldering heap of ruins, climbed aboard the transport which awaited them, and were carried to a camp about five miles from Johore Bharu. Before reaching Senai they had bidden farewell to the 27th Australian Brigade. Brigadier Maxwell told Lieut.-Colonel Stitt how proud he was to have had Gordon Highlanders under his command; and he congratulated all ranks on their courage and endurance.

General Percival had decided that the last stage of the withdrawal from Johore to Singapore island should take place on the night of 30th/31st January, plans having been made for holding a bridgehead and for the demolition of the causeway.

Apart from the disaster to the 22nd Indian Brigade near Layang Layang all went well. Despite the brilliant moon there was no interference from hostile aircraft, and the fifty anti-aircraft guns allotted to the defence of the causeway did not fire a round. Our troops retired down the road along the west coast of Johore, the Ayer Hitam road, and the railway. The battalions of the 22nd Australian Brigade, coming down from the east coast through Kota Tinggyi, occupied the right sector of the bridgehead with the 2nd Gordons on their left. An inner line was held by the 2nd

Argyll and Sutherland Highlanders, now only 250 strong after being in the thick of it since the beginning of the campaign.

The causeway was 1,100 yards long and 70 yards wide. It comprised a steel road-and-railway bridge with a lock system at its northern end. British and Indian engineers, assisted by the Royal Navy, had prepared the demolition.

The Gordons had moved into their sector of the bridgehead on the morning of 30th January, the companies holding positions in depth along the road from Skudai, the foremost company being about five miles west of Johore Bharu. If attacked in force two companies would be withdrawn, covered by artillery fire from Singapore island; the remainder of the Battalion would hold on, whatever happened, until only themselves and the Argyll remained in Johore.

This was a day of waiting while long columns of vehicles drove past on their way to Singapore. There was nothing to do but wait, except for A Company who were given a baffling task. They received orders from the 22nd Australian Brigade to check each vehicle as it passed through. The intention was to prevent the infiltration of Japanese who might be using captured transport, but Captain Farquhar and Company Sergeant-Major Milton found it impossible to halt any part of the fast moving column. No driver paid the slightest heed when signalled to stop.

Darkness fell and still troops and vehicles flowed through. Explosions were heard as sappers carried out the last demolitions in Johore. Not until five o'clock on the morning of the 31st did the last of the procession appear, and then a party of Indian Sappers and Miners informed the Gordons that no organised body of troops remained behind.

Now the outer bridgehead could be given up. The Australian battalions were on the move. When they were clear the 2nd Gordons marched down to the causeway in broad daylight and crossed to the island. The two remaining pipers of the Argyll played Australians and Gordons out of Johore, and at 8.15 a.m. the Argyll crossed to the music of their own pipes.

A few minutes later the causeway was blown, leaving a water gap less than seventy yards wide and only four feet deep at low tide.

The Gordons had no great distance to march after they reached the island. They were tired men, and welcomed a rest in the woods near Mandai before climbing into the transport which took them to Ladysmith Camp. Here they found themselves alongside the 1st Manchester Regiment, old comrades in the 2nd Malaya Brigade to whom the Highlanders had now returned.

One day was spent in Ladysmith Camp and then the Battalion moved in vehicles provided by the 2/17th Dogras to Birdwood

Camp on the Changi road almost opposite to their old home: Selarang barracks, now turned into a hospital.

Singapore Tragedy

General Wavell had paid another visit to Singapore on 30th January. Although only one airfield could now be used—R.A.F. operations being conducted mainly from Sumatra—he still expected Singapore to be held. He considered that more should have been done to prepare the northern shore for defence against landings, but difficulties existed here. The many small rivers and creeks were bordered mainly by mangrove swamps, and at high tide the ground between these swamps became islands. Civilian labour was scarce, and unreliable in action, for the enemy air raids had had their effect.

The town of Singapore, normally containing some half a million inhabitants, had doubled in population owing to the influx of refugees from the mainland. North of the town, towards the centre of the island, extended a large residential district interspersed with orchards, market gardens and plantations, with some rubber; but there was much derelict land covered with secondary jungle. The roads were good.

The pipe-line which brought water from the mainland was, of course, out of action; but the supply provided by the catchment area and reservoirs among the hills in the centre of the island could be made to suffice.

The first week of February was an anxious one in Singapore, for at any time the Japanese might launch their assault. All knew that the R.A.F. had been withdrawn, except for the devoted Hurricane pilots who were still using Kallang airfield. The naval base was being evacuated. Heavy air attacks interfered with work at the docks, where troops and airmen replaced the civilians, who could not endure the ordeal. In the early morning of 5th February the last of the ships bringing in the British 18th Division was sunk by air attack, and, although the loss of life was small, anti-tank guns and other equipment remained in the wreck.

General Percival had planned an all round coastal defence for which his 70,000 combatant troops were none too many; and some were battle-weary, some untrained reinforcements, some untried local volunteers. The sector allotted to the 2nd Malaya Brigade extended from a point opposite Pulan Ubin island, round Changi, thence south-westward. The Gordons were on the left.

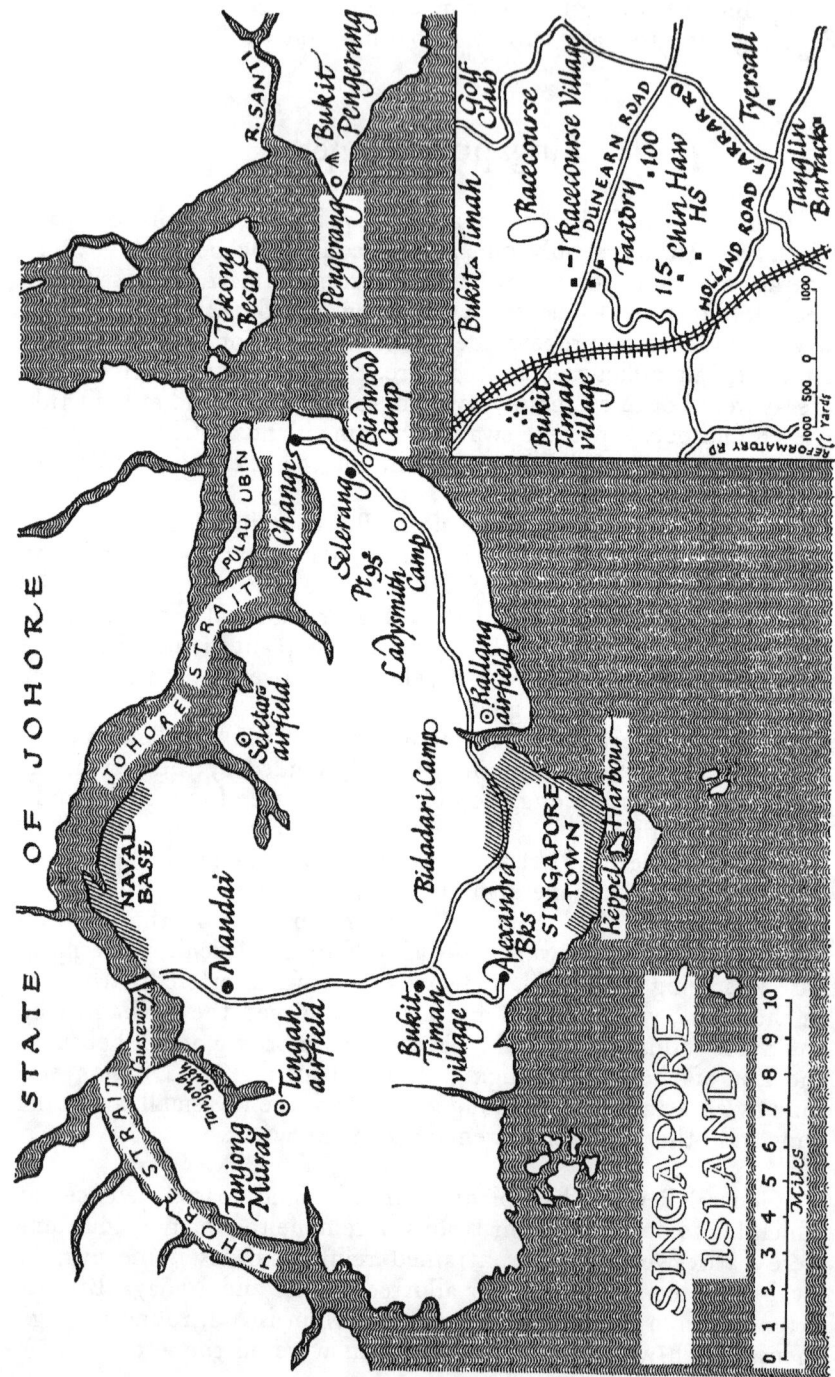

On the 5th 2nd-Lieutenant P. B. Leckie was sent with one platoon to form a standing patrol on Pulau Ubin, where Japanese landings were considered possible. For two days the platoon remained on the island, subject to the intermittent attention of dive-bombers, and were then withdrawn after a reported landing of Japanese on the western end.

D Company of the Gordons were set to clearing a mangrove swamp west of Changi spit, a loathsome job, during which the men were plagued by red ants. Each high tide, compelling a pause in the operations, was hailed with great relief.

Enemy aircraft dropped over a hundred bombs on Changi during 7th February, and Birdwood Camp, which escaped lightly on this occasion, did not fare so well next day. The adjutant Captain G. R. Roper-Caldbeck, and Q.M.S. J. Peterkin had narrow escapes, and eight Gordons were killed. The quartermaster's stores and the orderly room were completely destroyed, together with all Battalion records and secret documents. At night the Gordons were moved from Birdwood Camp to Point 95, about three miles further west, and here they were well concealed in a rubber plantation, isolated from any building or main road. On the following day Birdwood Camp was again the enemy's target, and suffered considerable damage, D Company, who were still detached from the Battalion, having five men slightly wounded.

The invasion of Singapore island had already begun. Air attacks and artillery bombardment increased in volume from 5th February onwards, and the reply of the British guns was limited by lack of observation and the need to conserve ammunition. On the night of the 8th the Japanese crossed the Strait in assault boats and attacked the 22nd Australian Brigade between Tanjong Murai and Tanjong Buloh on the north-west coast. Many boats were sunk, but the enemy came in regardless of loss and the Australians, fighting fiercely, were not numerous enough to hold him. During the morning of the 9th much ground was lost, and by the end of the day Tengah airfield was reached by the invaders. They had succeeded in landing two divisions, and were engaged in bringing over reserves with transport and tanks. Our troops were drawing back from the causeway area, after the Japanese had landed near by.

The Gordons were still kept in reserve. About one o'clock on the morning of the 10th, however, 2nd-Lieutenant J. F. Sandison, with two platoons, was sent on a special mission : he was to cross to Pulau Ubin and ascertain if the island were now occupied by the enemy. Arrived at Changi pier, the platoons came under fire from the coast defences who mistook them for Japanese. For an uncomfortable hour and a half movement, either forward or back, proved impossible and the attempt was given up. Twenty-four hours later the platoons were able to reach the island. They returned to report it free of Japanese.

General Wavell now paid his last visit to Singapore, flying in from Java on 10th February. He urged vigorous counter-attacks with all the forces available, and insisted that the garrison must fight on, prolonging its resistance to the bitter end.

The day had but added to the tale of disaster. After fierce fighting counter-attacks had failed to regain control of the causeway area. On the western side the efforts of hastily assembled reserves had ended in confusion; and the Japanese, now in great strength with about sixty tanks, captured Bukit Timah village, with its large stores of food and ammunition, during the night.

Shortly before dawn of 11th February the 2nd Gordons, after two days spent in listening to the noise of battle, received orders to move westward. While the Battalion were preparing to leave Point 95, enemy aircraft bombed the area, but caused only one casualty. Tyersall Park was reached without incident save for a collision between the commanding officer's car and an Australian lorry. Lieut.-Colonel Stitt was now informed that he was in reserve to the Australians.

At Tyersall Park an Indian base hospital formed a very obvious target from the air. On this day the Japanese attacked it viciously one stick of bombs falling upon the hutted camp which burnt so fiercely that many of the patients were trapped in the flames. Men of the Gordons promptly rushed to the harrowing scene and, at great risk to themselves, rescued a number of the wounded.

For the Battalion 11th February was a day of waiting with what patience officers and men could command. Only to Lieutenant W. de Mier, commanding the carrier platoon, and his sergeant did a chance of action come.

The carriers had escorted the Battalion to Tyersall, but one of them had been put out of commission in the bombing attack; and four of Lieutenant de Mier's men were missing. They had volunteered to drive away the ambulances abandoned by their Indian drivers. Orders were now received for a reconnaissance to be made up to the western slopes of Bukit Timah, and de Mier set off with three carriers. When they reached the Chin Haw High School de Mier left the carriers and proceeded on foot with Sergeant H. Smith. Each carried a tommy gun and two grenades. To locate our forward troops proved very difficult, and in one house there was ample evidence that some headquarters had been abandoned in a hurry. Finding two motor-cycles, the subaltern and the sergeant mounted them and made for Dunearn Road. Almost at once the pair became the target for the rear-gunners of two Japanese bombers. De Mier was forced off the road; Smith, after charging through a hedge, found himself lying uninjured not far from his machine. They thought it best to continue on foot, and soon found troops of the 18th Division in position astride the road in front of the Hume Pipe Factory. A Japanese infantry gun was firing occasional bursts, but there was no other sign of enemy activity.

At this point Lieutenant de Mier picked up the carriers again, and the whole patrol passed through a position held by the 5/11th Sikhs on the Singapore Golf Course to reach the dense undergrowth of the catchment area. Heavy firing could now be heard from the direction of the racecourse, which enemy aircraft seemed to be attacking with bombs and machine guns. As the patrol drew near to the north-east slopes of Bukit Timah it became obvious that Japanese artillery were in action behind the hill. This was enough. The patrol returned to the Battalion, reporting to the headquarters of the 12th Indian Brigade on the way.

On this day an effort to recapture Bukit Timah village failed after fierce fighting with heavy loss on both sides. The naval base was finally abandoned, as much destruction as was possible having been carried out. A letter from General Yamashita, the Japanese commander, calling for surrender was dropped from the air—and ignored.

At dusk on 11th February the 2nd Gordons received orders to advance: they were to occupy a gap in the front on the right of the 22nd Australian Brigade between Racecourse Village and the railway. The move was made in darkness, with A Company as advanced guard, and all expected that at any moment they might clash with the Japanese. The only trouble, however, was finding the way across country into the right positions, and this was accomplished with difficulty. By dawn of the 12th B Company were holding the usual kind of perimeter position near the railway, with A Company about the hill feature called 115 on their right. D Company were behind B near Holland Road, and C Company at the Chin Haw High School.

General Gordon Bennett, commanding the 8th Australian Division, and also the Western Area of the island defence, had announced that this portion of the front—from Racecourse Village to Reformatory Road—was vital to the security of Singapore.

At dawn of the 12th enemy reconnaissance aircraft flew over unopposed. The Gordons sent out patrols to get into touch with the troops on their flanks and to locate the enemy; and one patrol went as far as Racecourse Village without meeting friend or foe.

The Battalion had their first sight of the Japanese about 9 a.m. when infantry moved into the valley between A and B Companies. The country in front consisted of long narrow depressions thickly covered with trees and long grass; and here and there were houses and huts still occupied by apathetic Malays. Thus there was ample cover for the advancing enemy, who could hardly be prevented from penetrating the front at some points; but the fire of the Gordons, who stoutly maintained an all-round defence, prevented a break-through, while fighting patrols were quick to engage parties of Japanese who appeared in rear of the position.

The intelligence officer, 2nd-Lieutenant V. I. D. Stewart, was sent to establish contact with the troops on the right, but could discover only a few isolated men of the Sherwood Foresters. From them he learnt that the Japanese had attacked with tanks down the Bukit Timah road, and had reached Racecourse Village. Here, and further to the right, our whole front had been pushed back.

On the left of the Gordons the 22nd Australian Brigade had been heavily engaged by greatly superior numbers but had held their own.

About noon Lieut.-Colonel Stitt was ordered to send a company with a section of carriers to the Bukit Timah road, where reinforcements seemed to be badly needed. C Company was chosen, their perimeter being taken over by D Company.

Captain Whitelaw's company were attacked from the air as they moved across to Dunearn Road. When they moved up the road towards Racecourse Village, with 2nd-Lieutenant Leckie's platoon as advanced guard, they found that a British artillery barrage in front of the village seemed to be checking any forward movement of the enemy.

Then two vehicles resembling armoured cars appeared between Leckie's platoon and company headquarters. In the leading vehicle, showing just above the rim of the manhole, the Gordons could see an Australian hat. Captain Whitelaw was suspicious, and passed the word for his men, who had taken cover in a roadside ditch, to be ready with automatics and grenades. The vehicles were now seen to be light tanks and, when the first one was about twenty yards away, a Japanese face was revealed beneath the Australian headgear. The Gordons opened fire but, having no anti-tank weapons, could do little more than kill the Japanese observing from the first tank. Opening with their machine guns and 2-pdrs.—fortunately without effect—both tanks drove on towards Singapore. The affair was over in a matter of two minutes.

The company moved back clear of the road, leaving some machine-gunners and a few men with grenades in the ditch. Then the tanks returned, and, after stopping to exchange fire, drove on in the direction of Bukit Timah. The Gordons had three men hit in this, their first, encounter with Japanese armour.

Japanese shells were falling on both sides of the road, but there was no sign of an enemy advance. Late in the afternoon C Company withdrew slowly to their old position, where they settled in about 6 p.m.

Half an hour later a Japanese truck suddenly appeared on Holland Road, and charged recklessly through B Company, who were so surprised that they let it pass without firing a shot. Further on Australian machine-guns opened, killing the crew, and setting the truck on fire. The resulting explosions of small arms ammunition finished the business and caused some alarm in the vicinity.

By this time General Percival had decided to establish a close perimeter defending the town, giving up the defences on the north-east, east, and south-east coasts of the island. This adoption of a kind of 'last ditch' defence was not altogether popular. Brigadier A. L. Varley, commanding the Australians, and Lieut.-Colonel Stitt both knew that their troops were still full of fight, and they were planning a counter-attack when orders came, through General Gordon Bennett, to withdraw to the chosen perimeter.

When night came the Japanese mortars opened a steady bombardment, and an infantry advance seemed probable. Patrols of the Gordons were active while routes of withdrawal were reconnoitred, and then the companies, in succession, made their way back to Tyersall. There was no question of a fighting retreat, for the Japanese showed no desire to come on, and all was accomplished without loss.

The Battalion had a short rest at Tyersall, but by dawn of Friday, 13th February, they had taken up their place in the perimeter: three companies forward of Farrar Road with their left on Holland Road; one company astride Farrar Road; Battalion headquarters close in rear. Together with the 2/26th Australian Battalion on their left, the Gordons were in a salient. On the right was a gap, then, further in rear, a mixed force of Indian troops—Dogras, Rajputs and Sikhs. Later the gap was filled by a company of Chinese at platoon strength, who were reinforced later by a platoon of men from the R.A.S.C.

On 13th February the Japanese intensified their air attacks upon the town of Singapore, which was also kept under artillery fire. Large numbers of Asiatics were killed or injured, the streets were blocked with débris, and much damage was done to the water system. The destruction of war material so that it should not fall into the hands of the invader was another sign that the end must be near. Reserves of ammunition still existed, but petrol was running short, and food would soon be a problem, for there were so many mouths to feed, and large supplies had been abandoned to the enemy. General Percival consulted with his commanders on the possibility of delivering a counter-stroke, and it was regretfully decided that to launch such an operation was not possible. There was still no intention to surrender.

For the Gordons and Australians the day was comparatively peaceful, for the Japanese seemed to have decided that attacks on this part of the perimeter were likely to yield no profit The enemy's artillery concentrated upon the area in rear of the Gordons; but one direct hit on a slit trench killed Lieutenant R. H. Irvine, his orderly, and Sergeant R. Mackinnon.

An unexpected diversion was the arrival of a group of Australians from the 2/30th Battalion near by with the request that they be taught how to patrol. This was a difficult and unwelcome task to undertake in the face of the enemy, the more so as the men proved to be confirmed individualists who appeared and disappeared at will.

On the left of the Australians the front extending to the coast was heavily attacked and, after a stout resistance, driven back. D Company of the Gordons were then ordered to move over behind the Australian left flank.

Orders had reached Lieut.-Colonel Stitt that one officer and fourteen other ranks, selected specialists, were to report to Keppel Harbour for evacuation. The naval authorities had announced that the night of the 13th/14th was the last night when it would be possible for ships to leave Singapore. To select the members of this party was not easy. Eventually the choice fell upon the quartermaster, Lieutenant W. E. Main; the orderly room Q.M.S.; the R.Q.M.S. and senior C.Q.M.S.; the senior sergeants in the signals, mortar, carrier, and pioneer platoons, and in the transport; the pipe-major and drum-major; and the four privates with the longest service.

The quartermaster did not leave on the ship with the others, for there was no room for him. He was able to embark later, and got safely away. The main party were never heard of again : one can only conclude that their ship was bombed and sunk, leaving few or no survivors.

Both Japanese and British artillery were active throughout the night, and on the morning of the 14th the enemy intensified his air attacks. The area of the Gordons' headquarters soon came under shell fire, and Regimental Sergeant-Major Milne was severely wounded in the back, a great loss to the Battalion. Private Thomson of the intelligence section was killed while trying to spot a Japanese mortar which had become a dangerous nuisance.

Otherwise the Gordons were not much troubled during the 14th. In the evening the British artillery caught some Japanese troops who were assembling in rear of Hill 100, and the Gordons were treated to the shrieks and yells of a discomfited enemy.

Away on the left, beyond the Australians, the Japanese again made progress, forcing back troops of the 1st Malaya Brigade despite their gallant resistance. Ground was lost, also, on the northern and north-eastern face of the perimeter. Singapore town was now in a worse plight than ever.

The night of 14th/15th February was reported by the Gordons as 'quiet', and in the morning little happened except the usual bombing and shelling of the back areas. At noon Lieut.-Colonel Stitt was summoned to a conference at Australian Headquarters in Tanglin barracks. General Gordon Bennett spoke of the breakdown of supplies and the shortage of water, and declared that not under any circumstances would he fight from house to house in Singapore. He told the assembled officers that General Percival had sent to ask for an armistice from 4 p.m., but that until definite orders to the contrary were received, fighting must continue with the utmost vigour.

While he was speaking Gordon Bennett sat unmoved by an open doorway in spite of a fierce bombing attack close at hand. At the end of the session he invited the commanding officer of the Gordons to have luncheon with him. Over this meal, which was as excellent as the British prospects were bad, he said how highly he valued the work of the Gordons, both on the island and in Johore.

In the morning General Percival had held his last conference. He was told that the water supply was unlikely to last more than twenty-four hours. In his opinion a strict defensive could not keep the Japanese out of Singapore, and once they succeeded in entering the town the fate of the population would be sealed. It was agreed that a counter-offensive was out of the question, so that the only course was to surrender.

Meanwhile the battle continued. The 1st Malaya Brigade were forced back from Alexandra barracks, which contained reserves of ammunition and stores; and unspeakable atrocities were committed by the Japanese at the Alexandra military hospital.

The Gordons remained in their position. Late in the afternoon the officer commanding a unit away on the right was seen to be displaying a white flag to enemy aircraft. He was promptly arrested by one of the Gordon patrols and taken to Brigade headquarters. Then, at half-past five, the Japanese began to shell the whole area, and the Battalion lost a number of men, killed or ounded.

General Gordon Bennett sent a message that all rumours of a 'cease fire' were false, and 2nd-Lieutenant Stewart conveyed this to the companies. Then he went over to the troops on the right and found that they had piled arms and hoisted white flags. They had heard that the cease fire had sounded at two o'clock in the afternoon, and told Stewart that they had been shelled and had suffered heavy loss after the aircraft had seen their sign of surrender. The white flags were now taken down.

After half an hour the Japanese bombardment ceased, and over the whole battlefield stole an uncanny silence. There was whisper of an all-out counter-attack, but the Gordons were slow to believe it. Suddenly were heard yells of triumph from the Japanese. This could mean only one thing ; and after a delay which seemed interminable arrived the order to cease fire and the news that an armistice had come into force at 8.30 p.m.

All was over, and the 2nd Gordons realised that high courage, devotion to duty, skill at arms, pride of Regiment, cannot always command success. It was the lesson which had been learnt by the 1st and the 5th Battalions on the Normandy coast twenty months before.

After the capitulation the 2nd Gordons waited for two days before they were moved to Changi. Located in and around the married quarters at Selarang, their old barracks, they found it possible to collect odds and ends of clothing and necessaries from the gymnasium, where kit had been stored before the Battalion had moved to Pengerantg. Looters had been busy, but some valuable items remained, and, at this stage, the Japanese guards took little interest in the activities of their prisoners.

Soon working parties had to be provided. One of these toiled at the docks, loading and unloading ships ; others constructed roads leading to the numerous shrines which the Japanese were building to commemorate their victory. These parties received increased rations and managed, also, to get hold of tinned food and naval chocolate and tobacco.

In October 1942 the bulk of the Battalion, with men of other units, were taken away to Siam, involving a railway journey of five days and nights with nearly thirty men crammed into each cattle truck. In Siam the base camp was at Chungkai, on the banks of the Mekong Nam Quenoi. All hands were now set to work on the construction of a portion of the Siam-Burma railway—the 'death railway'—and the sick rate and the death rate rose as jungle sores, dysentery, malaria, diphtheria and cholera took their toll. Scant sympathy for the sick was shown by the Japanese : anyone who could put foot to ground was forced to work. The Allied medical officers, with little equipment and meagre supplies, did all that was possible : operations were performed under almost unbelievable conditions.

Among those who died in Japanese hands were Captain J. G. Monro and Lieutenant V. I. D. Stewart.

The work went on. Bridges were built of unseasoned timber cut straight from the jungle. Lieut.-Colonel Stitt commanded a party of Gordons who worked on the embankments and bridges; others under Major R. G. Lees laid the sleepers and rails. Japanese eyes could not be everywhere, and opportunities were seized to sabotage the construction: bolts were left loose in laying the rails and red ants were allowed to ravage the woodwork.

As the workers moved forward further and further from the base camp rations grew more scanty and were supplemented by various edibles found in the jungle. Red Cross parcels were seldom seen, and the real life-saver was the duck egg. Originally plentiful in the base camp, the demand soon outstripped the supply; only by the courage and energy of one Boon Pong, a Siamese trader, was any sort of supply maintained. The efforts of this worthy must have saved many lives, and it is good to know that he was suitably rewarded after the War was over.

Neither mental nor physical torture—semi-starvation, 'beatings up', the absence of Home mail—broke the spirit of the 2nd Gordons who bore themselves in a way that compelled the respect of their captors. As, for a long time, officers and other ranks shared the same camps and conditions, the men did not lack the leadership they had relied upon in peace and war; and in the Highlander abode a tough pride—almost arrogance—which no indignity devised by an Asiatic could subdue. To many the religious training of their early years brought comfort and support: the opportunity to worship at divine service became a very precious thing.

Camp entertainments—musical and otherwise—were somehow organised, and were enjoyed even by the Japanese. News of the outside world was obtained through wireless sets, although the possession of one of these was regarded as a capital offence.

Escape was hardly to be considered, owing to the difficulties of the country and the tremendous distances involved. Siamese who might have acted as guides could not be relied on, and a good reward was offered for the apprehension of escaped prisoners. A few who attempted to get away were either recaptured or perished miserably in the jungle.

After the Siam-Burma railway was completed in the late summer of 1944—it never fulfilled its purpose—maintenance parties had plenty of work, for both permanent way and bridges developed defects, and were liable to be washed away in the heavy rains. About this time Allied bombing raids on railways in Siam brought hope of release to the prisoners, though some were killed and wounded when the target was the bridge at Temarkan.

Not all the prisoners remained in Siam. A large contingent was required in Japan, but the convoy in which these unfortunates sailed was attacked by Allied submarines, and the loss of life was heavy.

At the end of 1944 a move was made to separate officers and men, most of the former being sent to Kanburi, where conditions were better. The camp was enclosed by a double fence and a moat, the first attempt to keep prisoners within close bounds. Then, in May 1945, the officers were removed to a place north-west of Bangkok, and it was not long before the attitude of the Korean guards seemed to betoken a change in the state of affairs. At last came the announcement that the War was ended.

Soon it was possible for Gordon officers to set forth in lorries and locate the camps in which their men were held. And then deliverance: first the arrival of some of the Special Air Service by parachute, then the much needed supplies and medical stores dropped by Dakotas. Eventually came the flight to Rangoon in Dakotas, whose Canadian crews were kindness itself.

Plaque in Presbyterian Church, Singapore

THE PLATES

Imperial War Museum

General Wavell accompanied by Lieut.-Colonel W. J. Graham talks to men of the 2nd Gordons, Singapore, November 1941. *Left*: Lieutenant G. F. Moir-Byres.

100th (Gordon Highlanders) Anti-Tank Regiment R.A. demonstrate 6-pounder before H.R.H. The Duke of Gloucester, Beeston Park near Norwich. *Left to right*: Lieutenant C. Fraser, Captain A. M. Milne, Lieutenant O. E. G. J. Collard, Major S. F. Evans, A.D.C., Captain P. Burnett, Lieut.-Colonel R. W. F. Johnston, The Colonel-in-Chief, Major D. S. Mackay. On Gun: Sgt. G. Hobson and Gunner A. Gow.

Imperial War Museum

Imperial War Museum

The Prime Minister, accompanied by Lieut.-Colonel H. W. B. Saunders, inspects 5th/7th Gordons at Azzazia prior to moving up to the Alamein Defences. Second-Lieutenant W. G. Dey and Pioneer Platoon.

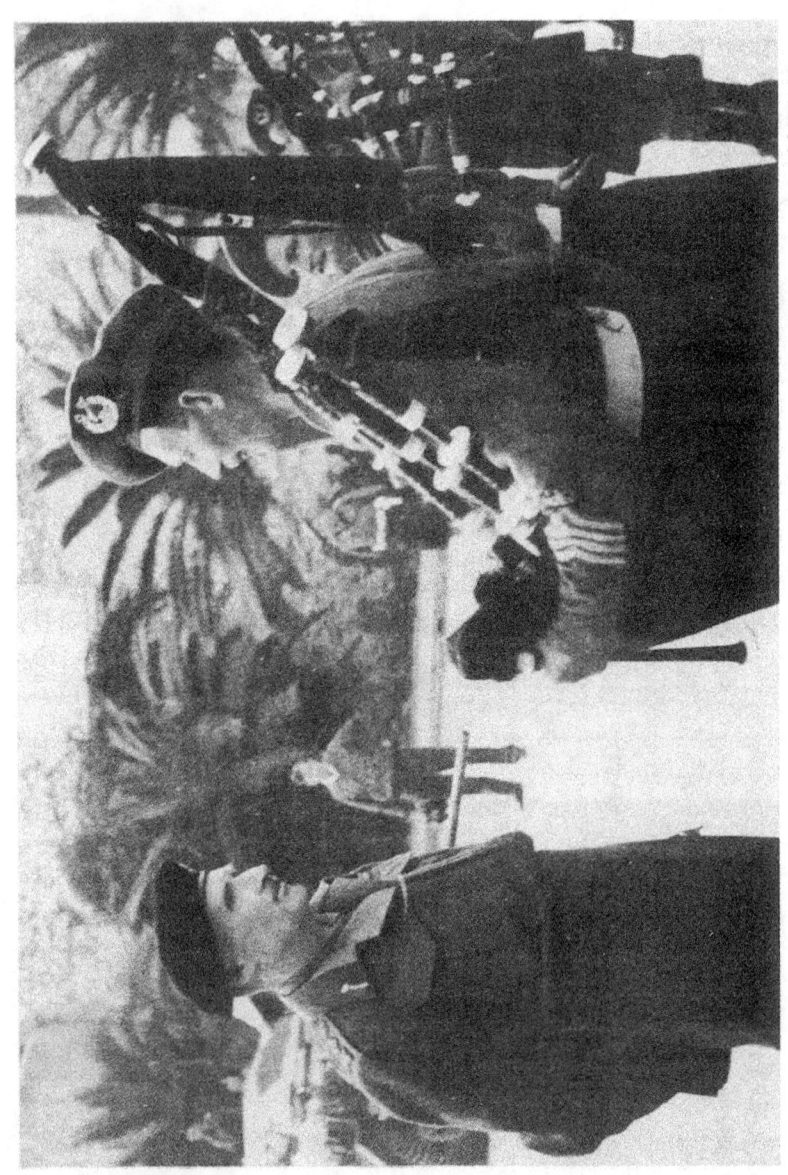

General Montgomery chats with Pipe-Major Anderson, 1st Gordons : Tripoli, February 1943.

Imperial War Museum

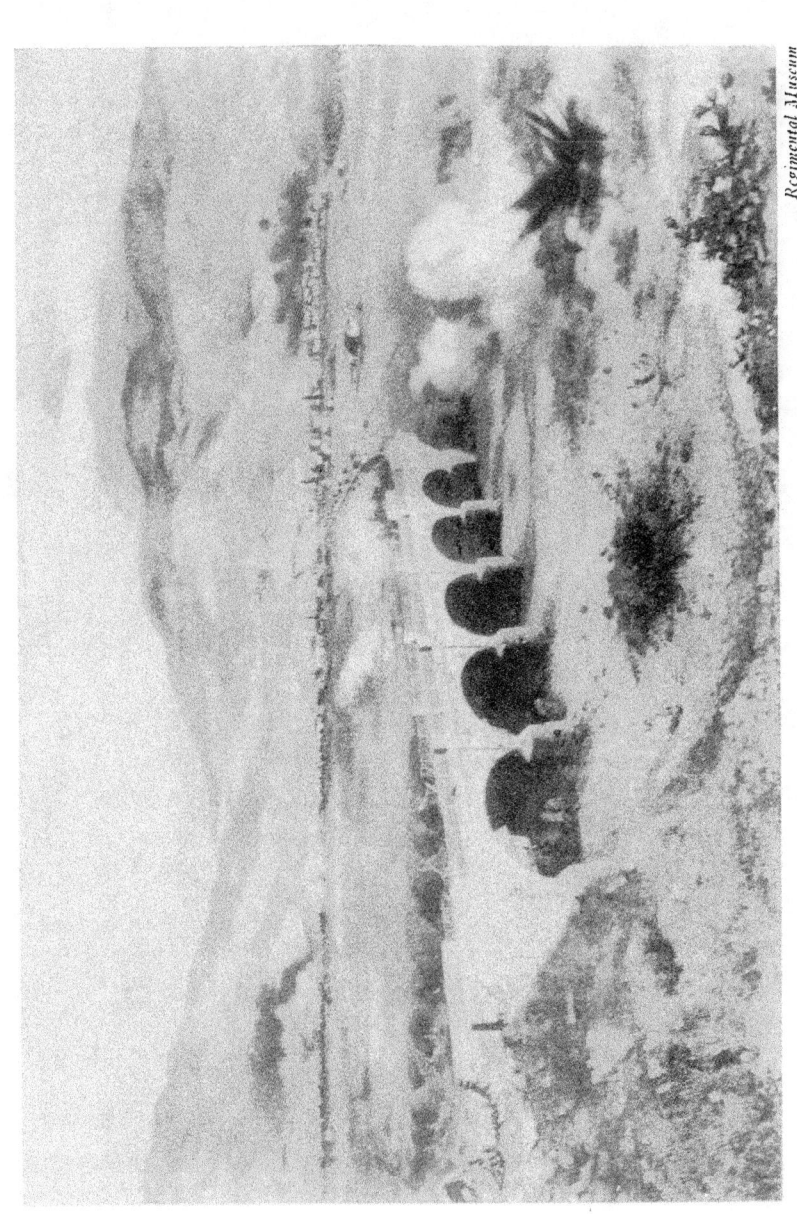

Regimental Museum

The Battle of Sferro, 18th-20th July, 1943. From the painting by I. G. M. Eadie, presented to 5th/7th Gordons by the people of Chalfont St. Giles.

6th Gordons near Marradi, September 1944.

Imperial War Museum

Current Affairs Ltd.

General Sir Ian Hamilton celebrates his 91st birthday with officers of the Regiment at his home, 1 Hyde Park Gardens, London, W.2., 16th January, 1944.

5th/7th Gordons in Kaatsheuvel, 30th October, 1944.

Imperial War Museum

5th/7th Gordons enter Germany: Reichswald, February 1945.

Buffaloes cross the Rhine, March 1945.

Imperial War Museum

Beyond the Rhine: 2nd Gordons on the floodbank, March 1945.

2nd Gordons in the woods beyond the Elbe, April 1945.

Imperial War Museum

General Sir Claude Auchinleck, Commander-in-Chief, India, reviews the 116th Regiment (Gordon Highlanders) R.A.C. at Bolarum, 1943.

A tank of the 116th Regiment (Gordon Highlanders) R.A.C. comes out of action near Taungtha, March 1945. Corporal J. Picken (Cults) in turret.

THE REGIMENT AT HOME

A few days after the evacuation of the British Expeditionary Force from Dunkirk at the beginning of June 1940 Italy entered the War. Before the end of the month France had fallen and the British forces which had continued the struggle in support of the last efforts of the French south of the Somme had been withdrawn through Cherbourg and the Brittany ports. Britain and the Commonwealth and Empire then stood alone against the Axis Powers and the Homeland faced the threat of invasion. In September and October the R.A.F., though tried to the utmost, defeated the air offensive which was to have been the first step towards a landing on our shores. The Battle of Britain was won.

Nevertheless the risk of invasion could not be discounted for many months, and the burden upon the Army was heavy. Our forces required to be re-armed, re-equipped, reorganised and trained, while coastal defences were rapidly developed and vulnerable points guarded. Assistance was needed on the land to maintain the Home food supply, and as soon as might be reinforcements must be sent to the Middle East and the Far East. In all these activities the Gordon Highlanders bore their full share, and eventually sent forth their battalions to nearly every theatre of war to tread the long road to victory.

Pride of place may here be given to the resurgent 1st and 5th/7th Gordons, since they were the first to go into battle again after Dunkirk. When they returned home from the Mediterranean at the end of 1943 their story belongs to the campaign in North-West Europe which ended with the downfall of Germany.

The 1st Gordons were re-constituted at Aberdeen before the end of June 1940, Lieut.-Colonel K. G. O'Morchoe assuming command. The six officers present were billeted in hotels; other ranks, numbering 107, were under canvas at the Depôt. Some were original 1st Gordons, reinforcements who had never reached the 51st Division, and had come back to England through Cherbourg after the fall of France.

In an air raid on the night of 30th June 200 incendiary bombs fell on Aberdeen, causing many fires, but the loss of life was small, and the Gordons reported no casualties.

Men continued to arrive, and by 3rd July the Battalion mustered seven officers and 354 other ranks. A few days later a move was made to Seaton Park, where all were in tents, and the arrival of men discharged from hospital brought the strength up to 430. Twenty-six officers had reported for duty.

Some training was done, but the 1st Gordons were now called upon to man posts in the Aberdeen defensive perimeter, Lieut.-Colonel O'Morchoe being appointed to command the southern sub-sector of these defences which were occupied by his own Battalion, the 10th Gordon Highlanders—a Home Defence battalion of whom more will be said hereafter—and one company of the 5th Black Watch. Two companies of the 1st Gordons moved to Balgownie camp in the middle of July.

The only other sign of hostile action had been a visit from a solitary German aircraft on 12th July. It was shot down, but caused a number of casualties in Aberdeen.

On 14th August the 1st Gordons were taken by bus to Mintlaw, where the woods provided good air-cover, but conditions were by no means comfortable. July had been very wet, and August came in cold and grey. The Battalion were now called upon to act as a mobile defence column, covering the coast from Buchanness to Aberdeen Bay.

This meant more action of a sort, the Battalion 'going flat out on anti-invasion duties', dashing in commandeered buses and lorries to Rattray Head and other points where their presence appeared to be urgently required. Alarms were frequent, but no invaders were seen.

By October the 1st Gordons had moved to Tarves, where their Colonel-in-Chief, accompanied by Sir James Burnett of Leys, saw them at work. On the 23rd the Battalion went into winter quarters at Inverurie, Aberdeenshire.

The ranks were filling up, and by the end of the month the Gordons mustered over a thousand officers and men. Training, which included boat handling in a river crossing exercise, had started in earnest; but after the turn of the year heavy snow persisted throughout January 1941. Normal outdoor activities were almost impossible: transport simply could not move. Having finished with coast defence tasks, the Battalion were anxious to press on with their preparation for active warfare, so the bad weather was frustrating in the extreme. In February came heavy rains, and a large-scale exercise planned for March was postponed owing to another heavy snowfall which blocked the roads. April was better, and much good work was done, but snow fell again in May.

Sir Alan Brooke, Commander-in-Chief Home Forces, who came to see their progress, commended the Gordons for what they had accomplished in such conditions. By this time the reconstituted 51st (Highland) Division had come into being, the three brigades bearing the old numbers. The 1st Gordons were in the 153rd Brigade, with what were now the 5th/7th Gordons and the 5th Black Watch.

On 25th June Lieut.-Colonel G. E. Malcolm assumed command of the 1st Gordons, who continued to train in Scotland, where the whole of the new Highland Division were located. The Battalion moved to Aden House camp, Mintlaw, in July, and in October arrived at Gordon Castle, Fochabers, Morayshire. On 17th October the commander of the Highland Division, Major-General D. N. Wimberley, inspected the Battalion, and expressed his satisfaction.

The winter again proved a trying one, snow interfering with training programmes. Some relaxation was possible, and in January 1942 the 1st Gordons won the Brigade Boxing Tournament and a Highland Dancing Competition. Many officers went away on specialised courses of instruction : laying and lifting mines, vehicle maintenance, camouflage, and mortars.

It was not until the winter had passed that the Highland Division left Scotland, the 1st Gordons going to Camberley in Surrey. On 22nd May Lieut.-Colonel H. Murray succeeded to the command of the Battalion. For the first time the commanding officer of the 1st Gordons came from outside the Regiment, but Lieut.-Colonel Murray, a Cameron Highlander but originally a Cameronian, could hardly have suited the Battalion better. Before the end of the month the Colonel of the Regiment paid another visit.

The 7th Gordons, recruited in 1939 as an offshoot of the 5th Battalion, took their place in the new 153rd Brigade of the new Highland Division as the 5th/7th Gordons.

The 7th Battalion mobilized at Banchory on 1st September, 1939 and, although numbers were satisfactory—over 600 of all ranks—and the men were of the right stamp, modern arms and equipment were 'in short supply'. On 13th September arrived one Bren carrier.

In October the men recruited in the Shetlands arrived and, a draft of 139 other ranks were sent to the 5th Battalion at Aldershot. At this time, of course, the original 51st (Highland) Division had not yet embarked for France.

Before the month was out the 7th Battalion were moved to Dunfermline in the Fife Sub-Area and then, in November, they departed for Orkney, concentrating at Kirkwall. Here their first task was a reconnaissance of possible landing places on the coast, for hostile raids were to be anticipated. From now on alarms and air raid warnings were frequent.

The island possessed few facilities for housing troops, and when the Divisional commander—the Battalion was at this time in the 9th Division, composed of Scottish units—paid a visit in January 1940 he was 'appalled by the living conditions'. Even so he ruled that the intake of recruits, mostly fresh from civil life, were to be trained and not employed in the working parties who were busy improving defences, unloading ships, and building huts.

So a winter of gales and snow and fog—and very hard work—was passed. In April 1940 Lieut.-Colonel D. W. Hunter-Blair, a Regular officer, succeeded Lieut.-Colonel J. N. Reid in command, and the Colonel of the Regiment, Sir James Burnett of Leys, came north to see the Battalion. In May the grave news from the Continent 'set all the men longing to get south and be trained for France'. It was sometimes hard for them to realise that although away in the north they were really 'in the war', for the Orkney defences protected the great naval base of Scapa Flow.

Modern equipment was slow to come by in Orkney. The Gordons record the arrival of five new Bren carriers in August 1940, 'three of them out of order'.

The summer of 1940 was not kind. One company lost their tents in a gale on 11th August. Then, during a cold and wet September the 9th Gordon Highlanders began to arrive in relief of the 7th Battalion, who reached Aberdeen on 20th October.

The 7th Gordons—now renamed 5th/7th Gordons—were joining the new 51st (Highland) Division, and took their place in the new 153rd Brigade. In wet weather the Battalion moved at once from Aberdeen to Ballater, and were soon receiving the equipment they needed. Brigade and divisional exercises occupied the next few months, although snow and frost were a handicap. In January 1941, Lieut.-Colonel H. W. B. Saunders, another Regular officer, succeeded Lieut.-Colonel Hunter-Blair in command.

In February the Battalion fired the Tommy gun (sub machine-gun) and the 2-inch mortar for the first time. This was a month of heavy rain with the river Dee in spate.

The 5th/7th Gordons went back to Aberdeen in March and, in better weather, worked on the coast defences. They carried out one exercise which came as a surprise, being hastily embarked on 9th April with rumours of a passage to Norway—or to Jugoslavia. And next day they were ordered ashore again.

The summer was devoted to hard training. In August the Colonel-in-Chief, the Duke of Gloucester, came to Aberdeen, and was present when the massed pipes and drums of the 1st, 5th/7th and the 8th Gordons and the Depôt played Retreat. In September the 51st Highland Division held their Highland Games.

In October the 5th/7th Battalion moved to Gordonstown, Elgin, for the winter. Guards were required for Lossiemouth aerodrome and, later, two companies manned certain vulnerable points at Fraserburgh. Some men were detailed to help the farmers on the land. In spite of these distractions individual and field training continued, one exercise consisting of an advance with machine guns and field guns firing live ammunition overhead. In January 1942 a heavy snowfall set the Battalion clearing the roads.

Having survived three implacable northern winters and become hardened and toughened thereby, the 5th/7th Gordons, with the whole of the Division, moved south to the Aldershot district in April. The Battalion occupied rather scattered billets at Camberley.

Both the 1st Gordons and the 5/7th Gordons now embarked upon the realistic training which was to put the final touches to the preparation of the Highland Division for modern war. Both Battalions ' stood in slit trenches while Churchill tanks drove over them '. They advanced in open order while machine guns fired overhead, and they practised co-operation with aircraft.

In May the 5th/7th Battalion received drafts amounting to 175 other ranks. They came from many regiments, London Irish, South Lancashire, Royal Scots and Glasgow Highlanders. It is regretfully observed that ' there were only 43 Scots among them '.

The whole Division now received tropical clothing, so it seemed that they were to go East to enter the War, but their precise destination was not divulged. At the end of May the transport drove to Southport for embarkation.

During these last days at home visitors included General Sir Bernard Paget, Commander-in-Chief Home Forces, and the Secretary of State for War. Then, on 1st June, came the King and Queen. The two Battalions of Gordons were among the troops who lined the road while their Majesties walked past, company commanders being presented as the Royal party came to them. And in the evening at Aldershot their Majesties were present when the massed drums and pipes of the Division played Retreat.

The 6th Gordon Highlanders, after landing in England from Dunkirk, were despatched to Rotherham, where they arrived on 2nd June 1940. Here the Battalion were reorganised, and gathered in stragglers who had arrived independently from France. Five days later the strength was twenty-two officers and 326 other ranks. Parties were detailed to help the Local Defence Volunteers (later Home Guard) to build road-blocks, a defensive measure against invasion ; but ' everyone was going on leave in turn '.

A draft of 150 men arrived from The Border Regiment, and forty-two came from the Depôt (now called Infantry Training Centre) at Aberdeen.

The Battalion moved to the Lincoln area, then to Woodhall Spa, and finally to Marsham-le-Fen in Lincolnshire on 28th June. At the end of the month the strength had risen to twenty-five officers and 840 other ranks, but although some progress had been made towards re-equipment, much remained to be done.

In July a newly formed 'tank hunting platoon' were ordered to have bicycles, but there were no bicycles. 'Rifles were the only weapons as yet.' However, the R.A.S.C. vehicles available were sufficient to move the whole Battalion on wheels; and it was announced that a motor-cycle platoon, part of Headquarters Company, were to have twenty-eight motor-cycles and four combinations. By the middle of August the Gordons were the proud possessors of twelve tommy guns.

A new battle drill was introduced in September, and special courses of instruction for platoon commanders were held.

The Honorary Colonel of the 6th Gordons, Sir George Abercromby, Bt., had launched an appeal for pipes and drums to replace those lost in France, and as a result eight sets of pipes and six side drums arrived. Sir George himself provided a bass drum.

In October an experimental mechanised company was formed, based on the carrier platoon, the motor-cycle platoon, and the mortar platoon.

On the 21st the 6th Gordons moved to winter quarters at Fulbeck. During their three months stay at Marsham the Battalion had done much to assist the Home Guard with their training, and this help was thankfully acknowledged.

The Gordons were still in the 2nd Brigade of the 1st Division who were clearly intended for more active service at no distant date. In November all men unfit for service overseas were transferred to Home units. Hard training by day and night continued during the winter of 1940-41; and in February, during a brigade exercise, a regrettable accident resulted in the deaths by drowning of a corporal and three privates.

In May the Battalion took over beach areas at Chapel St. Leonards, but returned to Fulbeck, where the Highlanders were very popular, in June. On 1st July Lieut.-Colonel Pirie was succeeded in command by Lieut.-Colonel J. Peddie, an old Gordon Territorial officer who came from the London Scottish.

August 1941 saw the Battalion in the Sherwood Forest training area, where the Royal Colonel-in-Chief came to see them at work. Autumn and winter were passed at Horncastle in Lincolnshire and Swaffham in Norfolk, and as the Gordons were called upon to assist the farmers, who were very short of labour, the training programme suffered.

In the spring of 1942 the Battalion lost a number of officers who were required for immediate service overseas. Training was pushed forward, and on 29th June came orders to mobilize. Drafts received a little later came from the London Scottish, the Liverpool Scottish and the King's Own Scottish Borderers.

Three new Bren carriers and four 2-pdr. anti-tank guns were received in July, and in August came two more anti-tank guns and enough bicycles to mount a rifle company.

Large drafts of the London Scottish arrived in September and the training of the anti-tank platoon received special attention; but there was no further word of departure to a theatre of war.

When the 6th Gordons shifted to King's Lynn in October 1942 useful training with tanks was carried out, and 'tank hunting' tactics were practised; but parties were still required to help on the land. Next came a move to the north, the Battalion arriving at Cumnock, Ayrshire, late in November. The companies were billeted in villages and settled down to training in wet and stormy weather. After a visit to Inverary for an exercise in combined operations, the Battalion went to Darvel in the middle of December.

The next four months were a time of training, with much speculation as to when orders to depart for active service would be received. At the end of the year—a Hogmanay dance for all ranks was held in the town hall at Darvel—instruction in the Vickers gun began, four of these weapons having been received; and in January two 6-pdr. anti-tank guns arrived.

Then, in February 1943 came a warning to prepare for embarkation. Before the end of the month the Gordons travelled to Gourock and were soon on shipboard—destination unknown.

The 8th Gordon Highlanders, sprung from the 4th Battalion at Aberdeen, started their separate existence on the first day of mobilization, 1st September 1939. They had plenty to do in the city, providing guards for foreign ships in the harbour and manning posts in the defensive perimeter. Nevertheless training as a machine-gun battalion soon started, although the Battalion were obliged to make shift with whatever kind of transport they could obtain.

In May 1940 the 8th Gordons became widely scattered, one company being sent to Shetland, one to Fife, and one to Kinloss. Headquarters and A Company remained in Aberdeen, but moved in mid-July to Craigellachie. Here, in August, Lieut.-Colonel Gordon departed to command the 10th (Home Defence) Battalion of the Regiment, Lieut.-Colonel R. W. F. Johnston succeeding him. The Gordon Highlanders never seemed to lack Territorial officers—not all of them young men—with the knowledge and capacity for training troops and leading them in action.

The new 51st (Highland) Division were now in existence, the 8th Gordons being the divisional machine-gun battalion, a company training with each brigade. All ranks were very keen machine-gunners, and their enthusiasm was not affected by the frost and snow which hampered their activities during the winter of 1940-41.

The Battalion, except for the company in Shetland who rejoined later, concentrated at Dufftown in Banffshire during August and moved to Huntly in December. Now the snow was a great handicap, especially on the range, and the Gordons were obliged to put in a lot of hard labour clearing the roads. A move to Kintilloch, near Perth, at the beginning of February 1941 brought even worse trials. On the range the snow obscured the targets, and the mechanism of the guns froze before they could be brought into action.

Spring and summer were spent at Huntly, drafts being received from machine-gun training centres. One feature of the training was the 'long carry' in which guns, ammunition, equipment and rations were man-handled in long marches across the hills. Only the very fit and hardy were capable of this performance, but very few men had to give up.

In other exercises the Gordons achieved distinction of a different sort. Once C Company were the 'enemy', dressed as Italians, covered with much grease paint, and speaking a language understood by none. On another occasion 'various officers and men incurred the anger of the opposing side by taking several senior officers prisoner, cutting wire, and damaging vehicles'. There was another time when the unlooked for enterprise of the Battalion annoyed the directing staff, 'but this was considered worth while'. It seems that 'many valuable lessons in night patrolling were learnt'.

Towards the end of August the first dial sights were received. 'They had been described and explained over many weary months.' And then, when the Gordons were almost fully equipped and their transport complete, the commanding officer announced that the War Office was about to disband them as a machine-gun battalion and reform them as an anti-tank regiment.

The Gordons had to start again from the beginning, learning a new weapon and new tactics. Training as gunners began as soon as the Battalion had moved to Buckie in October, with all ranks determined to excel in their new rôle. On the last day of the month the 8th (Machine-Gun) Battalion Gordon Highlanders became the 100th (Gordon Highlanders) Anti-Tank Regiment R.A. and the C.R.A. 51st (Highland) Division sent a message: 'Welcome to the Royal Artillery.'

But, 'once a Gordon aye a Gordon'.

In November, while the batteries were at Larkhill for training, the pipes and drums beat Retreat at Buckie.

Two awards for gallantry were announced in December: the M.B.E. to 2nd-Lieutenant B. D. Lowe and the B.E.M. to Sergeant Gill, both conferred for rescuing at considerable risk the pilot of a British aircraft which had crashed in flames.

In January 1942 it became known that the Regiment were to move to England. The news was received with mixed feelings, for officers and men had no wish to break the ties with the Highland Division; but, on the other hand, a move to the south might bring them a step nearer to active service. In any case, all regretted leaving Buckie, a happy station where they had received great hospitality.

Over icy roads the journey to Harwich began on 15th January 1942. The route was Perth, Dumfries, Catterick, Doncaster to East Dereham, outside Norwich. The whole Regiment arrived in good shape and were allotted a coast-defence rôle. They were now in the 76th Division.

Training continued, some of the later exercises including night work and river crossings. More equipment arrived, and by May two batteries were in possession of their complement of the latest 6-pdr. anti-tank gun with towing tractors.

The Regiment moved to Beeston in May and, while tactical training continued, the emphasis was on physical fitness. In some exercises only iron rations were allowed, but the Jocks voted them superior to ordinary rations.

The transfer of one complete battery (the old B Company) to the 53rd Field Regiment came as rather a blow, for all wanted to go to war together.

On 22nd June the Colonel of the Regiment paid a visit, and was entertained to dinner; of the officers present all but two were Gordon Highlanders, and the evening ended with the dancing of foursome and eightsome reels.

The Regiment had been complimented on its efficiency by both the Corps and the Divisional commanders. This was all very well, but now came a demand for drafts of trained men to go overseas so more of the 'old hands' departed. All ranks were beginnning to be impatient. They knew that their shooting was good, and were 'eager to be hitting enemy tanks'.

After a July spent in strenuous training, living hard and sleeping in the open in rainy weather, the Regiment were ordered, on 23rd August, to mobilize for service abroad.

This was welcome news, and a visit of the Commander-in-Chief Home Forces and the Secretary of State for War seemed in the nature of a farewell. Yet the autumn brought nothing but frustration. Embarkation was postponed several times, and the Regiment still languished under canvas in the rain. Early in November, however, a move to Southend provided comfortable billets in private houses—very welcome after six months in tents—and the unaccustomed luxuries of hot baths and frequent changes of clothes. It was arranged for the pipes and drums to play Retreat in Southend once a week.

The next move was not far—only to Leigh-on-Sea, where training and range facilities were limited. The Regiment were getting stale, but when Christmas drew near a tonic was provided by the start of embarkation leave. There was not long to wait now. On the night of 17th January, 1943, the pipes and drums played the Regiment to the station while anti-aircraft guns and searchlights came into action against German raiders flying over the Thames estuary.

After a night in the train the regiment reached Gourock and embarked. Their ship made slow progress down the Clyde as the convoy for the East assembled. They were off at last.

The 9th Gordon Highlanders (Strathbogie, Garioch and Strathdon Battalion), who owed their existence to the recruiting efforts of the 6th Gordons, moved from Keith to Huntly when mobilization began. Here, on 2nd September 1939, sixteen officers and 604 other ranks were present.

A guard was provided for a concentration camp at Banff, and an armed party held ready to assist the civil power in the event of an isolated hostile landing. But neither billets nor tents were available, and most of the men were dispersed to their homes until accommodation could be found for them.

The 9th Gordons were allotted to the 9th (Scottish) Division, in the 27th Brigade, commanded at that time by a well known Gordon Highlander, Brigadier G. T. Burney, but some time elapsed before the Battalion could be concentrated and equipped. Meanwhile some of the men were sent to help in the harvesting.

Seventy other ranks too young for service overseas were received from the 6th Gordons at the end of September. The 9th Gordons then assembled at Huntly, where bad weather interfered with training. And so many officers and non-commissioned officers were sent on courses of instruction that only elementary work could be done until they began to return.

The Battalion left for Alloa about the middle of October, and a month later arrived at Dunfermline, which was to be their winter station. The process of equipping the Gordons was a slow one. A solitary Bren carrier had been received in September; the issue

THE REGIMENT AT HOME

of rifles was not completed until the end of October; and steel helmets appeared in November.

Snow and epidemics of influenza proved a great handicap to training in the early weeks of 1940. Emergency arrangements were also in force to move the Battalion at short notice if the east coast of Scotland were invaded, and detachments were required at various ports to assist in the examination of neutral shipping. In the summer, however, it was possible to carry out mobile column exercises.

The Gordons ' moved to a flooded camp ' at Tarves in July. In August Lieut.-Colonel Murray Bissett was succeeded by Lieut.-Colonel A. D. Buchanan-Smith, who had commanded the 5th Gordons in France.

The 9th Division had now become the new 51st (Highland) Division, but the 9th Gordons were needed elsewhere. Early in September they sailed from Aberdeen to Orkney in relief of the 7th Battalion. The newcomers landed at Kirkwall on the 4th and took over the local defences and the protection of Halston aerodrome.

Training and improving the defences kept everyone busy throughout the autumn and winter. In January 1941 special carrying parties were needed to get rations through the snow to the more isolated posts. In the spring came a move to Tormiston Camp, where a full and varied training programme occupied the next six months. Combined operations by day and night and mobile exercises were practised, great emphasis being laid upon physical fitness.

Lieut.-Colonel G. H. Anderson succeeded Lieut.-Colonel Buchanan-Smith in command of the Battalion in July 1941. In August the Gordons provided a guard of honour when the King visited Halston aerodrome. Later in the month a small party paid a visit to H.M. battleship *Prince of Wales* in Scapa Flow.

The Gordons left Orkney in October for Alnwick, where they joined the 216th Brigade of the Northumberland Division, but in November they came under Newcastle Defences Command, and were told that they would soon depart for India. At the end of the year, however, came the depressing news that the Battalion, instead of going overseas, would be converted to another arm of the service.

Training continued in the vicinity of Newcastle, assault landings being practised on the Northumberland coast. In January 1942 the Gordons were again warned for India, and on 4th February a War Office order required the Battalion to be mobilized for service in a tropical climate by the end of the month. On 24th February all Bren carriers were handed over to the Ordnance, as no transport was to be taken overseas.

By 1st March the Gordons were ready to depart, but further disappointment awaited them. After moving on the 8th to Felton Park, north of Morpeth, they heard from Northern Command that they were unlikely to proceed overseas within the next two months.

Felton was an uncongenial place, described as 'lacking baths and drinking water', but intensive training continued. On 17th March came another change of command, Lieut.-Colonel Anderson giving place to Lieut.-Colonel J. N. F. Blackater of the 2nd Glasgow Highlanders.

The 9th Gordons were a hard, fit, well-trained battalion, ready to go anywhere, when, at last, in April 1942, they moved to a camp near Hexham to await embarkation. They left on 27th May for Glasgow, and boarded a large liner for their passage to the East.

The reconstituted 2nd Gordon Highlanders have their origin in the 50th Holding Battalion. Holding battalions consisted of recruits who were given basic training and then passed on, in drafts as required, to active units. The 50th was embodied in May 1940, the men coming from the Highland Infantry Training Centre, as the Depôt had become, and the Gordon company of No. 1 Holding Battalion.

This new Battalion was commanded by Lieut.-Colonel G. W. A. Alexander, a Regular officer, and assembled at Keith in June. Direct intakes during June and July brought the strength to twenty-one officers and 769 other ranks. Then, in September, the War Office decreed that all Holding battalions should become rifle battalions and train as such, and the 50th Holding Battalion became the 11th Gordon Highlanders.

On 14th October the 11th Gordons moved to Aberdeen and were quartered in the city. Unfit men were at once despatched to the 10th (Home Defence) Battalion. During the winter the 11th Battalion started their training programme, while manning part of the Aberdeen defences. The spring and summer of 1941 they spent in Northumberland, where they were responsible for a section of the coast defences. Lieut.-Colonel Alexander was obliged to go to hospital in July, and Lieut.-Colonel K. C. Davidson took command.

In September the 11th Gordons were sent to Orkney and settled down at Kirkwall and Tormiston as part of the 207th Brigade. They protected Skaebrae aerodrome, and provided a guard for Headquarters Orkney and Shetland Defences.

In January 1942 a German reprisal for our commando raid on Vaagsö and Maaloy was considered likely, so a party of Gordons reconnoitred possible landing places on the north-east coast. This was a hard winter, and not all men could stand it, but the sick were replaced by a large draft which arrived in March.

Lieut.-Colonel Davidson had departed in February to command a brigade, and he was succeeded by Lieut.-Colonel H. I. Bradshaw.

Milder weather in the spring enabled more training to be done, and when he paid a visit on 1st April Sir Bernard Paget, Commander-in-Chief Home Forces, found the Battalion in a very fair state of efficiency.

The curtain had rung down on the tragedy of Singapore in February 1942, and in May the War Office decided that the 11th Battalion should become a new 2nd Gordon Highlanders. The change of title, dating from the 28th of the month, was an inspiration to all ranks, who felt that their chance of active service overseas was increased thereby. But as yet there seemed no prospect of leaving Orkney.

Training proceeded throughout the spring and summer. In July the Colonel of the Regiment arrived by air and departed by boat after a three days visit. At the 207th Brigade athletic meeting the 2nd Gordons won the tug-of-war. In November the Battalion could muster two pipers and five drummers to play Retreat in Tormiston. The winter again proved a hard one.

In February 1943 the Battalion was reorganised as Headquarters company, support company, and three rifle companies. A fourth rifle company was added later. By this time the signallers were becoming familiar with radio communication.

A guard of honour was provided for the King when he visited Scapa Flow in March.

The 2nd Gordons moved in May to Hoy and South Ronaldshay to protect the Headquarters of Rear-Admiral Sir Lionel Wells, situated on Hoy island overlooking Scapa Flow.

The Battalion had been in Orkney nearly eighteen months when, in September 1943, they were moved south to Yorkshire. They were now in the 227th Brigade of the 15th (Scottish) Division and the rest of their story belongs to the victorious campaign in North-West Europe.

The 4th (Machine-Gun) Battalion of the Gordon Highlanders, who had done such good service in the Dunkirk campaign, were victims of subsequent re-organisations of the Army. They were never again permitted to enter the battle.

After landing at Dover early in June 1940 the Battalion were sent to various reception camps in south-east England; but they gradually assembled at Willsworthy camp, where re-equipment and re-organisation began. Nineteen officers and 466 other ranks were present, and on the 13th a draft of 161 men was received from an infantry training centre. Next day the 4th Gordons moved to Sheffield, where all were billeted in private houses. One hundred and fifty young men who had been evacuated from Guernsey were taken on the strength.

Early in July the Gordons joined the 54th Division as their machine-gun battalion, and took over defensive positions on the north-east coast from a point south of Berwick to the vicinity of Sunderland. A month later Lieut.-Colonel R. A. G. Taylor departed, the new commanding officer being Lieut.-Colonel A. Milne, who had long served in the Battalion.

At the end of August certain honours and awards won in the Dunkirk campaign were announced: the Military Cross to Captains W. A. Holmes and S. A. Wilson-Brown and Lieutenant and Quartermaster D. J. Palmer; the Distinguished Conduct Medal to Sergeant S. Lewis; and to Corporal McPhee, Lance-Corporal W. Morgan and Private F. Goodwin the Military Medal.

Winter quarters were at Bedlington, and training continued in very bad weather. In February 1941 a hundred men arrived from the machine-gun training centre at Gosport. The Battalion moved to the Cotswold country in the spring, the 54th Division now being in G.H.Q. reserve, and in addition to normal training, anti-invasion exercises towards the south coast were carried out. A visit to Bulford for a concentrated machine-gun course marked the end of the Campden period, for on returning from Salisbury Plain the Gordons packed up and moved to Chalfont St. Giles in Buckinghamshire. Exercises and tactical schemes were carried out with the local Command, and one big divisional operation lasting a week took place in Suffolk.

The Duke of Gloucester, Colonel-in-Chief, came to see the Gordons on 23rd October.

The Battalion knew themselves to be an efficient machine-gun unit, and hoped that the time when they would take the field again was not far off. Soon they were disillusioned. By War Office decree the 4th (Machine-Gun) Battalion Gordon Highlanders became the 92nd (Gordon Highlanders) Anti-Tank Regiment R.A. on 1st November 1941. The Regiment remained in the 54th Division.

Two weeks later the Gordons moved to Felixstowe to begin instruction in new weapons and new tactics. It was some time, however, before modern equipment was received, and training began with the old French '75' field gun. In January, however, the new gunners were able to examine the new Churchill tanks, and wanted the crews of this tank squadron to point out the most vulnerable parts of their charges. This the tank men were not disposed to do, being very proud of their Churchills; but combined training with tanks proved of great value to the Gordons.

The change over had been accepted by all ranks not only with a good grace, but with a resolve to excel in their new rôle. In essence, they were still Gordon Highlanders. Expert instruction was given the Regiment at Shoeburyness in February, and during the following months came plenty of range practice with the rather motley armament available. An influx of young gunners was not unexpected, and there was much coming and going of new officers.

It was not until November 1942 that the Regiment were fully equipped with 6-pdr. guns, and months were yet to elapse before the more deadly 17-pdr. was received. In January 1943 the three batteries were re-numbered, and in July a fourth battery was added, bringing the total armament up to sixty-four guns.

After a summer passed in assiduous training, the Gordon gunners found themselves, in November, lifting East Anglian beet and potatoes. All celebrated St. Andrew's Day and later Hogmanay in proper fashion. They regarded their labours on the land merely as an interlude before the sterner things to come, for they knew themselves to be an efficient, highly trained anti-tank regiment and were eager to take the field.

And then the preparations for the invasion of North-West Europe did the Gordon gunners an ill turn. The War Office decided that the infantry of the 54th Division were needed to provide 'beach battalions' for the landings in Normandy and the admirably trained division was accordingly broken up. The Gordons, much to their regret, passed from the 54th to become II Corps troops, but while in East Anglia they were posted to the 9th Armoured Division. Hopes of proceeding overseas revived.

The Regiment moved to Leyburn in Yorkshire early in 1944 and here some guns on self-propelled mountings were received. Two of the batteries were now tracked and two wheeled.

Soon the Regiment left for Wooler in Northumberland where they played a considerable part in 'Exercise Eagle', and when they came south to Leigh-on-Sea in April the vehicles are reported to have done the journey well, although the 30-cwt. portées were not powerful enough to tow the 17-pdr. guns.

D-Day came while the Regiment were at Leigh-on-Sea, and soon the manipulation of Britain's precious man-power again worked to the disadvantage of the Gordons. The 9th Armoured Division, instead of being held ready, were broken up to provide reinforcements for other armoured divisions; but the Gordons were told to be prepared to embark independently for France. This was hardly a promise, and if the announcement was received with some doubt such misgiving was soon justified.

Casualties among anti-tank regiments had been so heavy that all available reinforcements from training centres in the United

Kingdom were absorbed, and the Gordons were called upon to send a very large draft to Normandy. The depleted ranks were filled by untrained men and thus, by force of circumstance, the Gordons lost their operational status and became a training unit. It was not in this fashion that the officers and men of the old 4th Gordons would have wished to make their final contribution to the defeat of Germany; but duty must be done, and the heavy and rather unexciting work of a training regiment was faithfully performed until the end.

In August 500 other ranks arrived from light anti-aircraft regiments to be turned into anti-tank gunners; and after one month's instruction they were held ready as overseas reinforcements. All these men had seen service in France since D-Day. Also, many returned wounded were given a refresher course.

The Regiment spent the whole summer at Leigh-on-Sea, full use being made of the range at Foulness. Training was continued in Wiltshire later in the year, and then in Kent.

In April 1945 the Regiment had the honour of providing a battery—it was commanded by Major J. S. G. Munro—for duty with the Royal Guard at Sandringham.

The 10th Gordon Highlanders, a Home Defence battalion, was formed in Aberdeen in January 1941, and soon became nearly a thousand strong, organised in five companies. Detachments were sent to guard aerodromes and other vulnerable points—one even went to Shetland—but the Battalion remained part of the Aberdeen garrison. In June 1941 a machine gun of the 10th Gordons claimed a German bomber whose four occupants were killed when it was shot down.

At the end of the year the Battalion were re-numbered 30th. During the winter of 1941-2 defence duties were combined with such tasks as the clearance of snow.

In June 1942 Lieut.-Colonel J. H. McI. Gordon, who had been in command since the outset, was succeeded by Lieut.-Colonel G. W. A. Alexander. Numbers continued to grow, but in June 1943 the 30th Gordons were disbanded. The formation of three Independent Local Defence companies had already taken away some of the officers and men.

No. 1 I.L.D. Company was sent to Shetland. No. 2 Company contained men of various regiments, but most of them were Gordons; with headquarters in Fraserburgh, detachments were scattered over a considerable area, but in October a move to Shandon (Dumbartonshire) provided a month of dockers' work. Before the end of 1943 the Company had been moved to Cornwall. No. 3 Company remained in Aberdeen throughout its existence.

No. 1 (Shetlands) Independent Company of the Gordon Highlanders were formed on 15th February 1943 as part of the 228th Infantry Brigade (Shetland Garrison). The nucleus of the Company was drawn from the disbanded Shetland Defence Rifle Company—mostly Shetland-born men—and the first commander was Major D. Stewart of the Seaforth Highlanders. Major A. Paterson of the Gordons succeeded him in August.

The first duties of the Company consisted of guarding vulnerable points, manning watch posts, and the night patrolling of certain stretches of coast. Later the Company—which mustered four and then five platoons—took over defences on Stanley Hill, west of Lerwick and overlooking the town. Later still the unit formed a mobile column complete with adequate motor transport, wireless trucks, and medium machine guns. By steady training a high standard of efficiency was reached.

In July 1945 Major Paterson was succeeded in the command by Major A. H. W. Brebber, also a Gordon Highlander. By this time, of course, all threat to the islands had passed, but the Company were not disbanded until 1946.

VICTORY IN NORTH AFRICA
1942-43
EL ALAMEIN TO ENFIDAVILLE

Egypt

It was about the middle of June 1942, when the 1st and the 5th/7th Gordon Highlanders moved northward to the Mersey and the Clyde. The new 51st (Highland) Division were to embark for the East, but their precise destination had not yet been divulged. Everyone knew, however, that the Axis grip on the central Mediterranean prevented the passage of large troop convoys which were therefore committed to the long route round the Cape of Good Hope. The convoy left British waters on 21st June.

The monotony of the voyage, with physical training and lectures prominent in the routine, was broken by a call at Freetown for refuelling—there was no opportunity to go ashore—and an interlude at Capetown, reached on 18th July. Here, as the 1st Gordons thankfully record, the troops were landed to indulge in short route marches, and the men were given one free day to spend as they pleased. The next port of call was Aden, for refuelling only, and on 13th August the transports dropped anchor in the Gulf of Suez after a sea passage of 10,000 miles which had taken nearly eight uneventful weeks.

While the Highlanders had been on their way out from Home the tide of battle had turned against us in North Africa. On 27th May Rommel had attacked the Eighth Army at Gazala-Bir Hacheim and after weeks of struggle the Axis forces had recovered the whole of Cyrenaica. The Eighth Army had conducted a fighting withdrawal across the frontier into Egypt and now stood on the El Alamein position, presenting a front of forty miles from the sea to the Qattara depression, an impassable area of salt marsh. El Alamein was only about sixty miles from Alexandria. Rommel had attacked this position at the beginning of July, but could make no impression upon it, although fighting had continued for most of the month.

General Sir Bernard Montgomery had arrived in Egypt on 12th August and took command of the Eighth Army next day, the day that the 1st Gordons landed at Port Tewfik. The 5th/7th Battalion disembarked on the 14th.

Both Battalions were aware that all shipboard rumours could be disregarded and that their future lay with the Eighth Army. They were taken by train to Qassassin where the whole of the Division assembled. This camp, situated in a 'sun-baked piece of desert', some ninety miles north-east of Cairo, was a good one with running water and baths and a thriving N.A.A.F.I. establishment.

Officers and men were allowed a few days to shake down and to make the best of the heat and the sand and the flies; but by the 19th training in desert warfare was under way. Officers with experience of the Western Desert came to help and advise the Highlanders. There was much to learn. At the outset one great difficulty was lack of transport for, in the 153rd Brigade, only that of the 5th/7th Gordons was yet in sight.

On 22nd August Mr. Winston Churchill and the C.I.G.S., Sir Alan Brooke appeared on the scene. The Prime Minister inspected both Gordon battalions, and all officers, down to company commanders, were presented to him.

Four days later a move was made to Mena Camp on the Cairo-Fayum road. In this region the Division were allotted positions for the defence of the city, a responsibility which interfered somewhat with training. At the end of August the Eighth Army were heavily engaged in the Battle of Alam Halfa, and until Montgomery had foiled Rommel's attempt to break through to the Nile delta everyone was at two hours notice to man battle stations.

Training in desert warfare made progress. Companies had been practised in finding their way across sandy wastes where landmarks were few; battalions carried out movements in desert formation. The late arrival of the transport meant that many exercises had to be performed on foot, an unrealistic method when driving experience and discipline were of such importance. The few metalled roads were thronged with traffic and the desert tracks were apt to be confusing and not easy to identify upon the map; also, it was necessary to cultivate an eye for good going where no track existed.

On 10th September the Highland Division arrived in the Eighth Army operational area not far from El Hammam, and the work became more strenuous. The Gordon Highlander who had trained hard for nearly three years in England and Scotland was fast adapting himself to desert conditions. He dug one-man weapon pits in the sand and camouflaged them, judged distance in the unfamiliar light, conserved as a matter of routine his precious

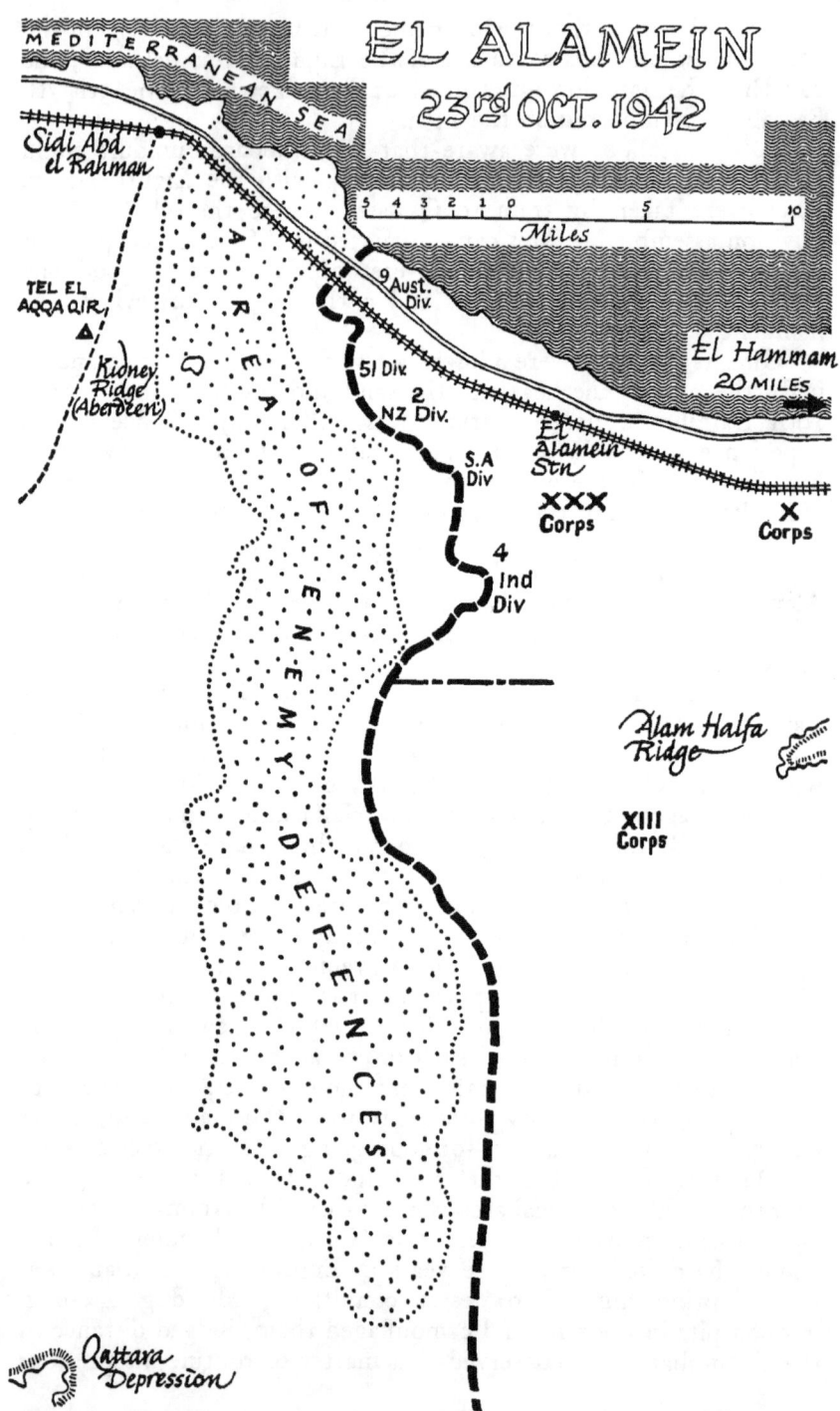

ration of water, learnt more about laying our mines and lifting those of the enemy, and began to move with certainty in an empty landscape by day and night.

Brigade and Divisional exercises were followed by a Corps exercise on 2nd October. On the 8th the 153rd Brigade took over for one week a sector of the XXX Corps defences west of El Alamein station, relieving the 152nd Brigade. The 1st Gordons on the left were in touch with the right of the South African Division. The 5th/7th Battalion were in reserve.

The 'line' consisted of a chain of forward defended localities protected by extensive minefields. Beyond were the enemy positions, three belts of similar defences extending to a depth of some four and a half miles.

Apart from an exchange of artillery fire little happened while the 1st Gordons were confronting the enemy. Two men were slightly wounded, and a German aircraft was brought down in the Battalion area. Patrols were sent out nightly. One from the 5th/7th Gordons, in reserve, came to grief and six men were lost; but their leader, Lieutenant Gould, was able to bring back some information of value.

Afterwards it transpired that the Germans had been able to learn nothing from the Highlanders they had captured: the prisoners did not appear to know how they had arrived in Egypt, the name of their commanding officer, or the names of any other commanders. They were rated as half-witted and handed over to the Italians who used more subtle methods. A hidden microphone was installed in the prisoners-of-war cage and the Gordons, talking among themselves, gave away information. But the information was out of date.

El Alamein

After relief on the night of 13th October training was resumed for a few days. Then the final preparations for the offensive were made, not the least important being an explanation to all ranks of what was required of them. The character and extent of the opposing defences were pretty well known, air photography having supplied much of the detail.

As Rommel's flanks could be accounted secure the only course was to mount a frontal attack, rather in the fashion of the First World War. The infantry were therefore committed to an advance through the enemy's minefields and to the capture of his defended localities in order to clear the way for our armour to go through and gain the open desert where manoeuvre was possible. The

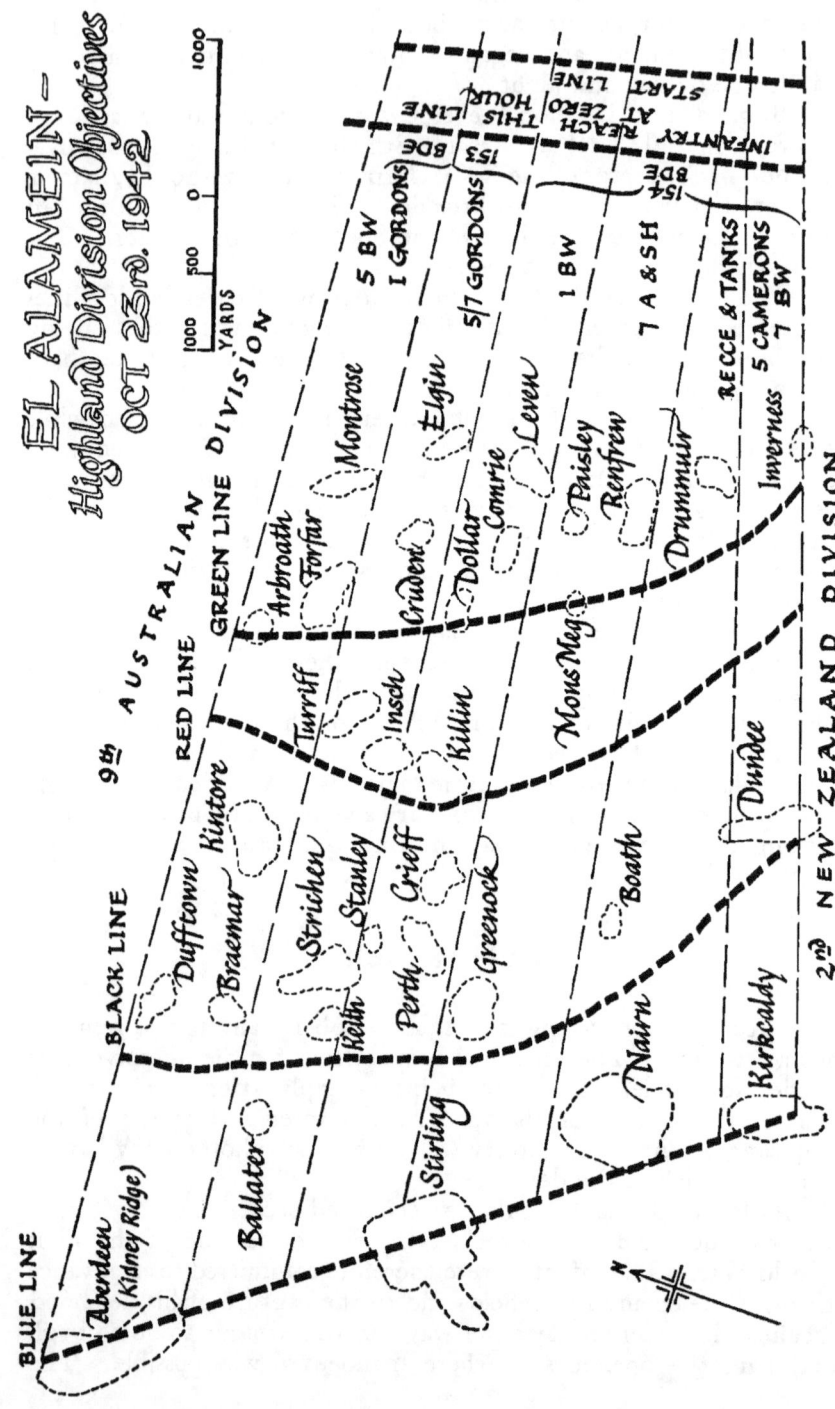

R.A.F. would make their maximum effort, first against the Axis communications and then the gun positions: our artillery, in addition to their counter-battery fire, would supply a lifting barrage to help the infantry forward.

On the front of the XXX Corps who were to strike the main blow the Highland Division were placed between the 9th Australian Division, forming the right of the offensive, and the 2nd New Zealand Division, with the 153rd Brigade next to the Australians. The Highlanders were certainly in good company.

The objectives were very plainly shown on the operation maps and the advance was to be by stages indicated by Green, Red, Black and Blue lines—nomenclature reminiscent of the First World War. Each of the enemy's defended localities was given the name of a town in the Home counties of the battalion who were to capture it.

In the 153rd Brigade the 5th Black Watch, on the right, were to go as far as the Red Line, about halfway towards the final objective. Then the 1st Gordons would come forward to complete the task. Next on the left the 5th/7th Gordons were to carry the attack through from start to finish.

The 5th/7th Battalion reached their assembly area beside the railway on the night of the 19th, and rested while digging parties went forward to prepare a position east of El Alamein station. Three nights later the companies moved up to occupy these slit trenches which had been partially covered in with corrugated iron and sacking. No unnecessary activity was allowed during day-light of the 23rd. Movement to and from the latrines was strictly controlled. No cooking was possible: the men ate a cold breakfast and a cold mid-day meal as they lay. A reserve of water had been placed in each trench, but no water was to be used for washing. No further supply could be expected until at least 24 hours after the attack went in. Flights of Allied aircraft passed overhead, and the hours of daylight dragged by. The cooks who arrived with a hot meal after dusk were very welcome.

At a quarter-past seven the 5th/7th Gordons began to wind in column along 'Sun Track', one of the lanes which had been cleared and taped through our own rearward minefields by the 152nd Brigade who held our forward defended localities 500 yards ahead. At 8.25 p.m. under a full moon the Gordons reached the start line and formed up in the desert 'box' formation they had practised: A and B Companies forward, C and D Companies in rear with Battalion headquarters in the centre.

Then came a fresh move forward, the intelligence section in front with a night-marching lamp as guide. Another party, with hurricane lamps, began to tape and light the route for the benefit of the battle transport following in rear. Each Gordon Highlander wore a white St. Andrew's cross on his back so that all might distinguish their friends.

At 9.40 p.m. the artillery of the Eighth Army—over a thousand guns—opened the bombardment in a storm of thunder and flame. The like had never yet been seen or heard in this war and to the Highlanders, as yet untried in battle, it was awe inspiring in the extreme.

The 5th/7th Gordons reached their position of readiness in ample time to advance at 10 p.m. when the infantry barrage came down. Once started, they went rather too fast and when they approached their first objective the barrage had not yet lifted. All lay down and waited, the enemy's defensive fire falling behind them. Ten minutes later they were able to go on, passing through a minefield and making for the localities called Elgin and Cruden. Few defenders were seen, for most of those who had survived the bombardment had fled; but A Company had to subdue a few spandaus (medium machine guns) which were still in action, and here Lieutenant J. Stewart was killed. At half-past eleven the Gordons were on the Green Line and made ready to continue their advance, but were forced to wait until the barrage lifted again. Under the fire of mortars and machine guns casualties, so far light, grew heavier. Parties of sappers who were cutting wire in front suffered severely.

At about midnight the Battalion were able to press on, but found themselves hampered by wire and a minefield. Some of the 5th Black Watch who had strayed too far to the left were mistaken for the enemy and the Gordons opened fire on them; but the mistake was realised before any damage was done. Despite the opposition of several spandau posts the two localities called Insch and Turriff were captured and A and B Companies reached the Red Line which represented an advance of 4,500 yards. On this line a halt of half an hour was prescribed before C and D Companies came through to deal with the remaining objectives. During the wait the enemy's mortar fire was heavy.

About 1 a.m. on 24th October C and D Companies took up the attack and covered nearly a thousand yards under shell fire. Then they were stopped by fire from a number of spandau posts— actually on the eastern edge of the Strichen locality—which lay directly in their path. Captain J. Sharp, with D Company, tried a flank movement to the left, hoping to find a position from which his Bren guns and mortars could cover C Company's attack. So D Company disappeared into the murk of smoke and dust. They were not seen again. It appears that they were caught by spandaus firing on fixed lines, for two days later Captain Sharp and

Lieutenant J. Jackson were found with many of their men lying dead in the middle of a minefield.

Meanwhile C Company, finding further progress impossible, dug in where they were, thankful for an early morning mist which gave them cover. Among other casualties they had lost Lieutenant R. Grieve. About 3.30 a.m. the battle transport reached Battalion headquarters, established in the neighbourhood of Insch. The transport, though shelled on the way up, had lost no vehicles although Lieutenant Gammie was hit. Some 3-inch mortars and machine guns were now sent forward to C Company.

In their preparations for battle the procedure of the 1st Gordons differed little from that of the 5th/7th Battalion; but as they had to follow the 5th Black Watch they entered the fight later. The 1st Gordons had a long march before they reached their ' holes in the ground ' where they passed the daylight hours of 23rd October, and were glad of a long rest. All were so well camouflaged that when Brigadier Graham paid them a visit he had great difficulty in finding them. At times, however, the Jocks showed a little too much interest in the bombing activities of the R.A.F. and ' had to be driven below '. A minor irritation was the non-arrival of hand grenades which were not delivered to the Battalion until after the cooks had come up to prepare the evening meal. Even then the grenades required to be cleaned of grease and primed.

The move forward began at 8.15 p.m. when C Company passed the starting point, a small bridge over the railway. A Company followed, then Battalion headquarters, B Company and one platoon of D Company. The rest of D Company were to advance with the tanks. The full moon was rising. Away on the right a column of Australians could be seen, and in front the 5th Black Watch were disappearing as they advanced to the initial assault. The column of the 1st Gordons wended their way through the forward gun positions, through our own line of defended localities and our minefields beyond. By half-past nine the Battalion were beginning to deploy in No Man's Land. They waited until the bombardment opened and, at length, when the 5th Black Watch were clear of the start line they moved up to it. The axis of advance was marked by a broad white tape with hurricane lamps at intervals. In continuing their progress the Gordons had to beware of treading too closely upon the heels of the Black Watch and it was necessary to call a halt about half-past ten. Then, at eleven o'clock, came a message from Major J. M. Hay who was with the Black Watch: that battalion had taken their first objectives and were going on.

The 1st Gordons now pushed ahead steadily, passing, on a two company front, well dispersed, through the first enemy minefield where our sappers were busy. The anti-tank mines were easily discernible in the hard ground but the smaller anti-personnel mines, said to be of Italian design, were more difficult to recognise. The Battalion went on through a second minefield and passed the localities named Montrose, Forfar and Arbroath which were now in the possession of the Black Watch.

The two leading companies of the Gordons were assembled about the Red Line from which their attack was to be launched, but Battalion calculations seemed to show that they were well in advance of the Red Line already. Then a heavy concentration of shell and mortar fire came down about three hundred yards ahead and some doubt prevailed as to whether this was defensive fire or our own barrage laid in front of the nearest objective, Kintore.

After a short delay the attack went in at about fifteen minutes past midnight, C Company on the left being directed upon Kintore, while A Company had orders to go straight on to Braemar and there establish contact with C Company. The Gordons pressed on through the smoke and dust which reduced visibility to about fifty yards. Kintore was taken and the two companies were soon lost to sight beyond. No further news came from them, for wireless had failed, and no runners got through.

Lieut.-Colonel Murray, on the Red Line with B Company and the platoon of D Company, was waiting for the arrival of D Company and the tanks. A burst of light automatic fire from the direction which C Company had taken caused him to send forward B Company to make good the ground. For over an hour an engagement ensued against an enemy difficult to locate, while a steady stream of wounded, mostly from C Company, trickled back. Among them was Captain G. A. Thompson, who died soon afterwards.

At about 2 a.m. on 24th October a squadron of the 50th R. Tank Regiment with D Company mounted on the tanks began to arrive on the Red Line. Soon the battle transport of the Gordons followed, and Lieut.-Colonel Murray proceeded to take further action. D Company and the tanks carried out a sweep over the ground already covered by B Company, and this was done with little loss. Then B and D Companies were set to advance straight through to the ultimate objective, Aberdeen, with the tanks on the left supporting D Company. Unfortunately this force ran into an unsuspected minefield and five tanks were blown up.

No gap through the minefield could be discovered. The time was nearly 4 a.m. and Aberdeen was still about 1,500 yards away, so there now seemed little prospect of reaching it and digging in before daylight came. Accordingly a withdrawal was made to the vicinity of Kintore where Battalion headquarters had been established. A position was organised for all round defence with the Battalion anti-tank guns, mortars and carriers and the two companies.

While the Highlanders dug with a will so that they should have effective cover when daylight came the commanding officer sent out a carrier patrol under Captain C. N. Barker to make contact with A and C Companies presumed to be in the vicinity of Braemar and Dufftown. The patrol could not find the forward companies, but discovered a gap in the minefield which had checked our tanks. Then the fire of anti-tank guns compelled a withdrawal.

To complete the story of the night the fortunes of the forward companies must now be followed, although nothing more was known of them at Battalion headquarters until much later. After leaving Kintore A and C Companies had fought their way on with great difficulty. Besides Captain Thompson C Company lost 2nd-Lieutenant W. Williamson, mortally wounded, and many more. Nevertheless they reached Braemar where they joined A Company. When the advance was resumed the Highlanders were impeded by wire and came under a deadly cross-fire. Captain H. H. Skivington, commanding C Company, fell. Captain McNeill would have taken over, but he had already been hit and soon afterwards was fatally wounded by the fragment of a mortar bomb. A Company now had only Lieutenant Ewen Frazer and one other officer left, C Company none but Lieutenant H. A. Gordon: but there was plenty of fight left in them. With bayonet and grenade they set to work systematically to capture every enemy post within reach and accounted for all but one. The cost was heavy for when daylight came the two companies could hardly muster sixty men between them.

Lieutenant Frazer was awarded the D.S.O. for his part in the night's work, and Lieutenant H. A. Gordon the Military Cross. Also to be remembered are Captain Skivington for his cool and gallant leadership and Corporal J. Scott, an outstanding section commander who was killed while bringing in prisoners.

When day came on 24th October our infantry were chiefly occupied in consolidating what they had won. They had bitten deeply into the Axis defences and now our armour came up and attempted to break through into the open desert. A tank battle continued nearly all day with losses on both sides and no definite result. Our armoured brigades were foiled chiefly by the enemy's anti-tank gun screen.

This battle was fought, as it were, over the heads of the infantry and neither the 1st nor the 5th/7th Gordons were heavily engaged by the enemy on this day. Though shelled and mortared, and sometimes under machine-gun fire, they were spectators of what, to them, was a new kind of warfare.

During the morning first Lance-Corporal Gordon and then Company Sergeant-Major Thomson arrived at Battalion headquarters of the 1st Gordons. They were both from C Company and described the happenings of the night. Lieut.-Colonel Murray promptly organised a column of carriers—one, for the transit of the wounded, flying a Red Cross flag—who were able to reach the forward companies with much needed supplies. The journey, forward and back, was comparatively easy.

The commanding officer wished to arrange artillery support for an attack on Aberdeen after nightfall but was told that this could not be provided. He visited the forward companies at and around Braemar and arranged their relief by B and D Companies in the evening with the intention of going for Aberdeen twenty-four hours later. At 6 p.m., however, he was informed that the Australians were attacking that same night and that the Division were ' very anxious ' that the Gordons should conform and occupy Aberdeen.

At such short notice all Lieut.-Colonel Murray could do was to carry out his relief as planned and then to push out battle patrols of B and D Companies towards Aberdeen. He went at once to these companies to explain what was required of them; but the tank battle had not yet died down and he was caught in a burst of shell fire and wounded in the wrist. The command devolved upon Major J. M. Hay.

At dusk B and D Companies relieved A and C around Braemar, the two last named being drawn into reserve as a composite company. Before this had been done the Brigadier arrived to urge further action. Consequently, about 4 a.m. on the 25th two platoons of D Company with a section of machine guns, the whole under Captain Paton's command, moved towards Aberdeen. Apart from some spandau fire this advance was unopposed, and Paton reached a position not far from the objective, making contact with some lorried infantry of the King's Royal Rifles (1st Armoured Division) who had suffered severely in their efforts to carry on the advance.

The 5th/7th Gordons had passed a more uneventful 24th October. They consolidated their positions at Insch and Turriff, and, in the late afternoon, discovered that the enemy no longer held Strichen in strength. Without much trouble Strichen was taken, together with a few prisoners.

On 25th October the tank battle broke out afresh, the enemy becoming more aggressive. Near Braemar D Company of the 1st Gordons were twice attacked by tanks. At 11 a.m. the German armour was halted about 200 yards from the foremost post of the Company, being severely punished by the anti-tank guns of the K.R.R.C. In the evening our Sherman tanks dealt with a determined advance made by their opposite numbers.

The 1st Gordons were under orders to occupy Aberdeen that night with the whole Battalion. About 5 p.m. Major Hay headed a reconnaissance party which went forward in three carriers, but the tank battle was flaring up again and a speedy return became necessary. Major J. M. Hay's carrier was blown up by a mine and he was severely injured, losing a leg. Command of the Battalion passed to Major J. E. G. Hay.

At about 9 p.m. B Company and a detachment of D Company, under Major Du Boulay, moved out silently to reinforce Captain Paton, thought to be at Aberdeen or in that locality. Unfortunately Major Du Boulay's force moved rather too far to the south; but the D Company platoons veered towards Paton's position which was actually north-east of Aberdeen. These platoons became engaged in a fire fight with German infantry and the noise of conflict enabled Paton to locate this reinforcement and draw it into his own area. He now had the whole of D Company with him.

In the meantime B Company, who formed the left of the advance, ran into heavy fire from machine guns posted in derelict tanks. A confused action ensued, and as he could make no headway and had lost touch with his D Company platoons Major Du Boulay decided to withdraw. When B Company reached Battalion headquarters about midnight, no news had been received from Paton. Thereupon Lieutenant W. M. MacFarlane volunteered to go forward and find D Company. With six men he carried up a supply of water, found the Company, and returned with details of Captain Paton's position. Nothing more could be done that night except to reorganise and prepare for a further effort.

The 5th/7th Gordons were under considerable shell fire for most of the 25th. On their left in the sector of the 154th Brigade the 2nd Seaforth (from the 152nd Brigade), who had relieved the 1st Black Watch, attacked with tanks and cleared most of the Stirling locality. This success disposed of the spandau post which had been annoying the left company of the Gordons.

For the time being the Battalion had nothing to do except to consolidate the positions where they lay.

The 26th October was a quieter day for the 1st Gordons. It was possible to send forward carriers, under the Red Cross, to remove the wounded of D Company from their position near Aberdeen. The Company were shelled and mortared at intervals, but Major Hay and the Brigadier were able to visit them about noon and planned to bring the whole Battalion forward to Aberdeen in daylight.

Captain Paton, however, pointed out that he was confronted by a concrete pill-box, several dug-in tanks and a number of anti-tank guns, besides machine guns. Eventually B Company under Captain Thom were sent up, but not before dusk. They took with them two mortars and four anti-tank guns.

About 2 a.m. on the morning of the 27th a mobile column of the Rifle Brigade came forward through the Gordons' position near Aberdeen and ' milled about ' for some three hours. So far as the Gordons could see these lorried infantry accomplished nothing and suffered rather severely from the enemy's anti-tank guns. At dawn, however, a battery of 6-pdrs. on armoured chassis—known as ' deacons '—appeared and the fire of these weapons induced the enemy in the Aberdeen area to surrender. About thirty prisoners were taken. The remainder of the 1st Gordons were now moved forward, and by the afternoon B Company and the combined A and C Company were in occupation of Aberdeen and in touch with D Company, who did not move. The night was quiet, except for bursts of spandau fire on fixed lines which caused a few casualties.

Major H. A. F. Fausset-Farquhar, who had arrived on the previous evening, took command of the 1st Gordons at 9 a.m. on 28th October. During the morning some readjustments were made at Aberdeen which embraced a kidney-shaped hill, the most prominent of the few landmarks in the vicinity. Two companies occupied the ridge forming the eastern edge of the hill and the remainder of the Battalion were concentrated in a shallow valley in rear.

The Gordons were now in touch with the 5th Camerons, the 152nd Brigade having relieved the Australians. The whole area was still under artillery and mortar fire, while machine guns and snipers caused some trouble. Lieutenant K. M. Craig was killed while going forward on reconnaissance.

While the infantry of the XXX Corps prepared against counter-attack the positions they had captured, elements of our armoured divisions still strove to extend the area of penetration. The 4th Royal Sussex, lorried infantry of the 1st Armoured Division, attacked on the left of the Gordons during the night of the 29th, but either lost direction or were unaware of the location of our forward positions. They opened fire on the Gordons, who lost several men killed or wounded, and a petrol truck went up in flames. As may be imagined, this contretemps caused the advance of the Royal Sussex to end in some confusion.

Soon afterwards the lorried infantry of the 1st Armoured Division put out and maintained a thin screen in front of the

153rd Brigade, whose defences were strengthened by many anti-tank guns of the 10th Armoured Division.

On the evening of 2nd November the 1st Gordons were relieved by South African troops and went back to an area near the Qattara track for a few days rest in reserve. A new phase of the offensive had already begun. At 1 a.m. on the 2nd an attack passing north of Aberdeen had been launched to open the way for the armour; further north the Australians were fighting their way forward to the coast.

During the last days of October the 5th/7th Gordons remained in their positions, exposed at times to desultory but well-aimed fire from 88-mm. anti-tank guns.

On the night of the 28th A and B Companies were ordered to cover the operations of the tank-recovery section of the 24th Armoured Brigade. This section had started late, and even when the Highlanders had made contact there was a lack of guides. The Gordon companies had moved at 8.30 p.m. but it was not until 2 a.m. on the 29th that they advanced south-westwards into the desert. About 1,200 yards were covered and a screen put out, but of the eight tanks located all but one had been burnt. The Gordons withdrew under heavy machine-gun fire, and all agreed that they had spent a very unprofitable night.

The Battalion did not move until 2nd November, when the whole of the 153rd Brigade were withdrawn, but the 5th/7th Gordons were then placed under the command of the 152nd Brigade. Orders and counter-orders followed, involving much movement and little rest: so far as officers and men were concerned all seemed to little purpose.

On the morning of 3rd November, while the Battalion waited in a state of expectancy, they were bombed by Stukas and Messerschmitts, but fortunately suffered little. Early in the afternoon Lieut.-Colonel Saunders received orders for an attack to be delivered south-westward across the Sidi Abd el Rahman track. Tanks were to take part.

The Gordons moved out at 3 p.m., faced with an approach march of three miles over mine-strewn ground to the start line. Zero hour was 6 p.m. but the 8th Royal Tank Regiment were rather late and only one squadron had arrived at the appointed time. Then a message was received from the 152nd Brigade: the enemy was withdrawing so no R.A.F. support or artillery barrage would be needed, but a smoke screen would be laid.

To the commanding officer it seemed that the quickest course was to send forward some of his Highlanders mounted on tanks while the rest of the Battalion followed at their best speed. The remainder of the 8th Tanks arrived while the men of B and C

Companies were climbing eagerly on to the leading tanks, and the whole tank and infantry attack went in. Then from front and from both flanks 88-mm. guns opened on our armour and spandau fire smote our infantry. The tanks carrying the Gordons forged ahead, but nearly all were hit and some were set on fire. Artillery support was sorely needed, but as none was forthcoming and the light was beginning to fade Lieut.-Colonel Saunders judged it best to call a halt.

B Company had no officer left, for Captain D. Greenhill Gardyne—his father and grandfather are well remembered in the Gordons as commanding officers and Regimental historians—and Lieutenant D. Harder were killed, Lieutenant C. P. Wormald mortally wounded, and Lieutenant J. W. Murray shot through the foot. In D Company Lieutenant A. Bruce was killed, and Lieutenant C. R. Rowan Robinson was severely wounded in a gallant attempt to bring in a wounded man. Also wounded were Lieutenant J. W. Ritchie, the intelligence officer, and Lieutenant J. C. Sanderson of the carrier platoon. Of other ranks fourteen were killed, including both company sergeant-majors, and forty-six wounded. Six tanks had been burnt out and eleven severely damaged.

As darkness fell the Gordons reorganised and dug in on the Sidi Abd el Rahman track south of Tel Aqqaqir; and during the night patrols found that the enemy had departed. In the early morning of the 4th, troops of the 4th Indian Division advanced through the Battalion, who were told that at first light our armour had reached the Daba track, meeting no resistance. Food came up to the Gordons and in the afternoon they moved forward to the Daba track and dug in again. Here they took the last flick of the enemy resistance for they were bombed from the air and lost seven men. Two portées and their two anti-tank guns were destroyed.

Actually the Axis forces were disintegrating and already in retreat. Montgomery's final thrust south of Tel el Aqqaqir, made on the night of 3rd November, had decided the issue. The battle of El Alamein was won.

On 25th November the 153rd Brigade concentrated at the aerodrome three miles south-east of El Daba, the 1st Gordons covering about twenty miles to get there. Next morning heavy rain flooded the place, but it was wonderful to see how quickly the R.A.F. overcame this trouble and got the aerodrome operational. The rain was of great benefit to Rommel, for the British armour sent by Montgomery to cut off the Axis forces retreating westward by the coast road was bogged down in the desert short of the Egyptian frontier and twenty-four vital hours were lost.

Nevertheless the pursuit of the Germans and Italians was pressed with all speed, although the Highland Division, for a time, had no part in it. The 1st Gordons moved on the 5th to an area five miles west of El Daba where they remained until the 15th, clearing up the battlefield—enemy guns, ammunition, equipment and documents were brought in—and doing a certain amount of training. The 5th/7th Battalion did likewise, and speak of the luxury of being able to clean up with water obtained from wells. So few officers were left that all the remaining subalterns were made temporary captains. Writing at this stage of the campaign Lieut.-Colonel Saunders deplores the loss of so many of his best officers and is thankful that of the 200 casualties among the other ranks 'a large number are very slightly wounded'.

On 9th November came the news that British and American forces had landed in Morocco and Algiers. It was heartening to know that the enemy was now to be assailed both from the east and the west, and a general feeling of optimism prevailed.

Both Gordon battalions moved on the 12th to Fuka, where they continued their salvage work and their preparations for battle. Conditions were none too comfortable, for the 1st Gordons remark that 'the flies and the fleas were terrific'. There was a church service and time was found for football.

On 14th November Major-General Wimberley, commanding the Highland Division, paid a graceful tribute to the Gordons. Writing to their Colonel-in-Chief he informed His Royal Highness that the two battalions of his Highland regiment serving in the Division had 'fought in the best traditions of their great past'. He continued: 'Actually as I write a well turned out Gordon Highlander guard in the kilt, with a piper playing "The Cock of the North", has mounted outside my caravan.'

Advance to El Agheila

Although the Highland Division began to move westward in the track of the pursuit on 15th November it was over a fortnight before the Gordons were again in contact with the enemy. The first stages from Fuka were covered on foot over desert tracks. On the 19th, however, enough transport was available to carry everyone and a great speed-up ensued. For instance, the 5th/7th Gordons did eighty-nine miles, halting for the night south of Sidi Barrani.

As the rain had made the desert tracks impassable the Brigade were obliged to turn north and follow the coast road next day, reaching the top of the escarpment by way of Halfaya Pass. So far

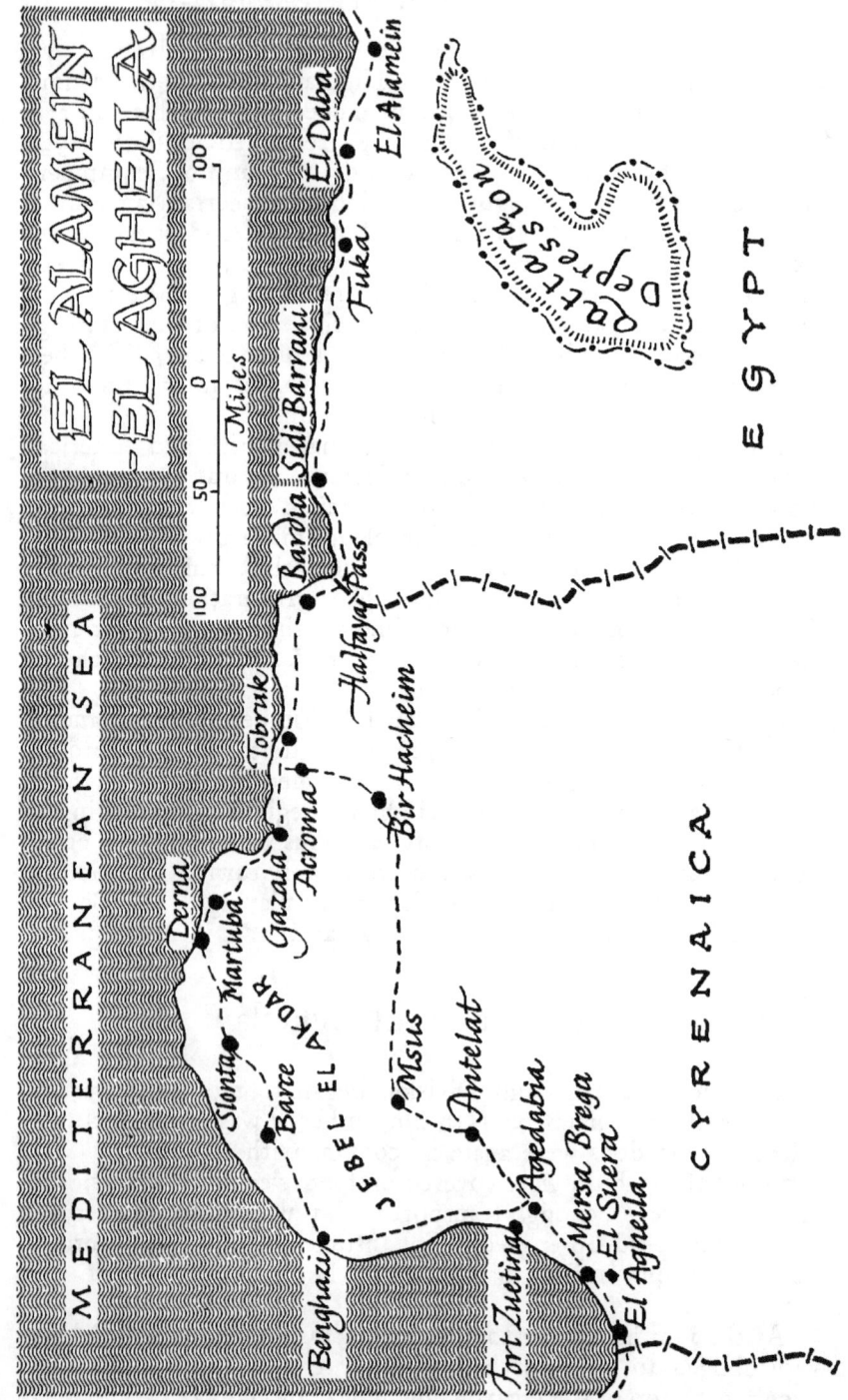

as they knew they were destined for Tobruk where the harbour needed to be opened for the reception of supplies by sea.

By the evening of the 20th the 5th/7th Gordons had crossed the Egyptian frontier and were well on the road to Bardia; on the 21st they reached the Tobruk area and camped further west at Acroma. Following the same route the 1st Gordons arrived near by on the 22nd. There had been many delays on the road for the press of traffic was tremendous. Supply columns as well as the vehicles of fighting troops were hastening westward.

The Gordon battalions spent two days near Tobruk, but were not required for work at the port. Instead, the 5th/7th Battalion were ordered to hurry on to Benghazi. They started on the 24th, driving along the coast road to Martuba (outside Derna) to reach Slonta next day. 'Very pleasant country' was the verdict of the Jocks; and Headquarters mess were able to feast on lamb as a change from bully beef. The only mishap was the loss of two trucks, blown up by mines planted at the roadside. On the 26th the way led down the deep inclines from the Jebel el Akdar, through Barce and the farmlands of the Italian colonists. For most of the journey wrecked trucks were a common sight: the enemy seemed to dispose of a prodigious number of mines.

Benghazi was reached at noon on the 27th, but the 5th/7th Battalion received orders to push on. So they drove another twenty miles, across desert land, before nightfall and next day came to Fort Zuetina, 'a wonderful Beau Geste fort', by the sea. Here the Gordons would have been content to linger, but on the 29th they moved on to an area some two miles south of Agedabia where they rejoined the Brigade.

In the meantime the main body of the 153rd Brigade had advanced across the desert. Starting on 25th November from the Tobruk area they drove in column southward to Bir Hacheim where the Free French had fought so gallantly six months before. A minefield compelled a detour, and the Brigade harboured for the night south-west of Bir Hacheim. Next day it was possible to drive westward in desert formation of four columns, the 1st Gordons being on the left. This the Battalion observes was 'well done', the standard of driving being very satisfactory. To preserve formation the vehicles in front maintained a steady speed of fifteen miles per hour, but those in rear were sometimes going at twice that rate in order to keep up.

The advance continued in the same fashion during the two following days. After halting on the evening of the 28th east of Msus the 1st Gordons sent out a party to reconnoitre a route past the aerodrome and over a deep wadi, one of the deep water-courses with steep banks so familiar in the North African scene. Speed was important, so at 3 a.m. on the 29th the Brigade started in single column to negotiate this difficult ground and all went well. They breakfasted in pouring rain some distance west of Msus and then moved on to Antelat, in desert formation wherever the absence of minefields permitted. After a long and tiring day the troops arrived south of Agedabia, the 1st Gordons coming in at ten at night, being near the tail of the single column in which the Brigade finished the march.

On 30th November General Montgomery appeared and talked to the commanding officers and company commanders of the Brigade. He lunched at the Brigade mess.

Next day began a move to the El Suera area completed by the morning of 3rd December. Battle positions were taken up with the 1st Gordons on the right and the 5th/7th on the left. This advance was not without incident so far as the 5th/7th were concerned. On their way forward on the night of the 1st the Battalion had failed to find any of the landmarks which had been evident during previous reconnaissance, and the commanding officer prudently called a halt to wait for daylight. About 3 a.m. next morning came a peremptory signal from the Brigade: 'Retrace your steps immediately.' The 5th/7th Gordons had bivouaced under the noses of the enemy.

The Highlanders were, indeed, again in contact, for there was some shelling in the area of the 1st Gordons and on the afternoon of the 4th seven aircraft delivered a machine-gun attack. Axis troops held posts nearly two miles ahead.

On the night of the 5th both Gordon battalions advanced to a ridge which gave better observation, and several days then passed with only patrol activity. The Brigade position overlooked El Suera village and the salt marshes northward towards the sea at Mersa Brega.

General Montgomery had rather expected Rommel to defend the 'bottle-neck' at El Agheila, the gateway to Cyrenaica from Tripolitania, but by 12th December it appeared evident that the enemy was thinning out his forces on this position. A reconnaissance in force was ordered by the Brigade, and this task was shared by the two Gordon battalions.

At 10 a.m. on the 12th the 1st Gordons sent forward D Company supported by a mortar section and a section of carriers. Heavy machine-gun fire greeted them, and it appeared that the enemy was still present in considerable numbers.

The 5th/7th Gordons employed a similar detachment, and when the enemy spandaus opened they were silenced by the Gordon mortars. One German prisoner was taken and was despatched to the rear with commendable promptitude, an over zealous non-commissioned officer using the commanding officer's jeep—that general utility 5-cwt. vehicle of American origin—for the purpose. Then a fairly large body of the enemy was seen advancing. At first it was thought that the Germans were coming in to surrender : actually it was a counter-attack made in numbers too great for D Company to take on. The Company withdrew under heavy fire with the loss of fifteen men, leaving behind Sergeant-Major D. Gairioch, who was too severely wounded to be moved.

The enemy withdrew during the night and on the morning of the 13th a general advance took place. The 5th/7th Gordons found their sergeant-major where they had left him, the enemy having taken his water and cigarettes. He had received no medical attention and died the same day.

Passing through the Axis defences the advance continued until the Brigade came to rest in a ' barren stretch of desert ' in the El Agheila area on 17th December, the 1st and 5th/7th Gordons having led the way. The 7th Armoured Division were now in front.

The battalions, being ' out of the line ', as the old phrase has it, started a period of training, special attention being paid to the instruction of junior leaders and specialists. Towards the end of the month exercises were carried out by night in co-operation with tanks to practise the assault against prepared positions protected by minefields.

To the 1st Gordons came news of honours and awards for El Alamein : to Captain W. M. MacFarlane the Military Cross ; to Sergeant Stephenson the D.C.M. ; and to Lance-Corporal Cable and Private Graham the Military Medal.

In the 5th/7th Battalion the Military Cross had been awarded to Captain McIntosh and Lieutenants Ritchie and Rowan Robinson; and three Military Medals were ' very well earned '.

There was opportunity to celebrate Christmas and Hogmanay, the troops faring not so badly in spite of the difficulties of supply. The 5th/7th Gordons enjoyed pork and Christmas pudding with a limited quantity of beer and an issue of rum. Football matches were played and the massed pipes and drums were heard at Brigade headquarters.

Buerat

The reason for the respite near El Agheila was the withdrawal of the enemy under threat of a turning movement from the south. Before the 153rd Brigade moved on, Rommel was preparing to stand at Buerat, some 220 miles further west.

Our attack on the Buerat position was delayed by reason of the supply situation—Benghazi was not yet fully opened as a port—but began on 15th January when the Highland Division went in astride the coast road. It was now General Montgomery's intention to drive straight through to Tripoli.

The advance of the 153rd Brigade started on 11th January. They moved along the coast by Marble Arch—the Mussolini monument now of so little significance—and Nofilia. In front were the 154th Brigade. By the evening of the 14th the 1st Gordons were close in rear of a wadi south of Buerat, and behind them came the 5th/7th Battalion.

The enemy appeared to be holding a long flat ridge behind an extensive minefield backed by a high apron wire fence. It was the task of the 1st Gordons to 'punch a hole' in this position on the night of the 15th so that the Highland Division could pass through and continue the advance.

As the minefield was to be breached in three places the attack was organised in three columns. The flank columns were each headed by two sappers followed by a platoon of Gordons, four scorpions (flail tanks which carried chains to flail the ground and explode the mines), a section of carriers with R.E. stores, and two 3-inch mortars of the Gordons, in that order. The centre column included no scorpions but was headed by a sub-section of sappers with Bangalore torpedoes. The 40th Royal Tank Regiment were in support and the initial advance, over about 2,000 yards of flat ground, would be covered by an artillery barrage. The guns and ammunition available were sufficient only for a one-battalion attack.

To mark the position of the start line Captain L. W. Millar of the 1st Gordons directed the building of cairns of stones. This he did in daylight and in full view of the enemy: and it is only fair to mention that the stones were carried up by men of the 5th Black Watch.

The columns moved up to the start line in brilliant moonlight, and were so early on the ground that they had to wait an hour before the barrage opened at 11.30 p.m. The companies of the 1st Gordons, closing up in rear, were played forward by their pipers.

It proved difficult to locate the forward edge of the minefield, and some sappers and Gordons came to grief on mines before the real work began. Enemy fire was not heavy, but in clearing the lanes through the minefield, which was nearly five hundred yards in depth, four scorpions were blown up. A Gordon mortar did good work, one round setting an enemy ammunition truck on fire after which a few more silenced an anti-tank gun which was said to have knocked out two of our scorpions. The sappers, as usual, worked gallantly and well, the apron wire was demolished by a scorpion, and at 2.40 a.m. the centre gap was reported clear. With very little delay C Company of the 1st Gordons came through and were followed by the rest of the Battalion; and before 5 a.m. the 5th/7th Battalion were entering the gap. On getting through they fanned out south-westward but found no enemy. He had made a swift retreat from his positions before the Highlanders could close.

Even so, the 1st Gordons reported 31 casualties, including two subalterns, Lieutenants Reekie and B. D. M. Rae, wounded.

During 16th and 17 January the other brigades of the Highland Division came through the 153rd Brigade. It was on the 17th that General Montgomery, feeling that progress was not fast enough, applied the spur to all troops and commanders. Tripoli was the goal. The success of the whole campaign depended upon a swift advance to Tripoli so that the port might be opened and the almost intolerable strain upon the communications of the Eighth Army relieved.

Tripoli

The Highland Division pressed on to Misurata and Homs, but the 153rd Brigade could only be ordered to 'follow as fast as possible', owing to the shortage of troop-carrying vehicles and the lack of petrol. Supplies of all kinds were running very short.

Both Gordon battalions moved about twelve miles on 17th January, and next day they managed another thirty miles. By the evening of the 19th the 5th/7th Battalion were outside Misurata. On this day, owing to lack of transport, the 1st Gordons did not move, being held in readiness to help the R.E. in road clearance. On the 21st, however, they were carried over 100 miles from their bivouac south-west of Churgia, passing south-east of Zliten to harbour in agricultural land two miles west of Homs. Part of the way lay through cultivation and the going, sometimes over plough, was very rough.

The Gordons expected to take part in an operation against the enemy's rearguard beyond Homs where heavy fighting had taken place; but the enemy faded away and the road seemed open for an advance upon Castel Verdi, not much more than twenty miles from Tripoli. This advance was to be made by 'Hammerforce', a column of tanks (one squadron of the 40th R. Tank Regiment), artillery, sappers, and machine guns with some infantry. The commander was Brigadier Richards of the 23rd Armoured Brigade. 'Hammerforce' was joined by D Company of the 1st

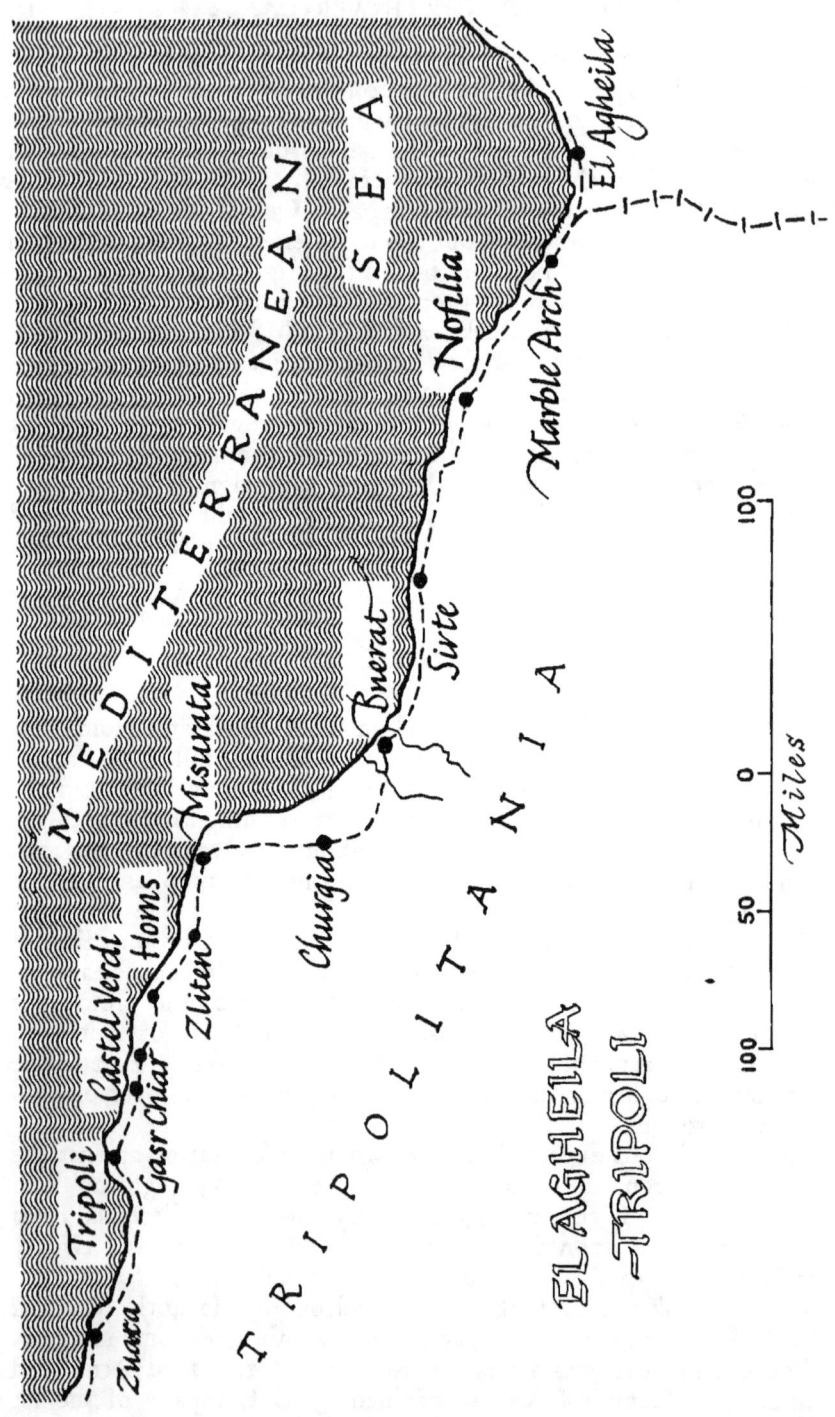

Gordons and, before action began, by the whole Battalion, D Company riding on the tanks, the other companies in troop-carriers. All Gordon transport was left behind.

A start was made at 10 p.m. on 21st January with orders to make good Castel Verdi by first light and clear the enemy from its immediate vicinity.

The road was not an easy one. In the first stretch called ' The Glen ' it led down from the hills to the coastal plain, and at the bottom of the declivity the way was barred by large craters in the road. As the road was blocked by the vehicles in front it was impossible to get the three rear companies of Gordons forward to help fill in the craters; so, rather than remain inactive, the Highlanders dismounted from their trucks and pushed ahead on foot for several miles. When the column was able to move again the Jocks were ordered to board any vehicle which could carry them, and by mounting tanks and even medium guns, some men soon reached the first demolition which proved to be a blown bridge over a deep and precipitous wadi. They set to work with a will, digging away the soft sides of the wadi, placing old rails horizontally across the sides, and binding them in with stone. By this time some of the Gordon vehicles had managed to get through the press and more men became available.

A second demolition, again a blown bridge, was reported a few miles further on, so all the leading vehicles carried Gordons forward to work on the obstacle, which was dealt with much in the same way. By now it was early morning and the Gordons were much dispersed, for nearly every vehicle in the column seemed to be carrying a few of them. Just to the west of Gasr Chiar a third demolition was tackled with undiminished energy, and as dawn was breaking ' Hammerforce ' entered Castel Verdi. C Company of the Gordons were detailed as garrison.

The local Fascist functionaries were lined up to receive Brigadier Richards and Lieut.-Colonel Fausset-Farquhar, and these worthies affirmed that the region was clear of Axis troops. ' Hammerforce ' then moved out westward in order to take up a defensive position in readiness for the main body of the 23rd Armoured Brigade to pass through. After two miles had been covered the forward troops came under machine-gun fire and mortar fire, which ceased when B and D Companies of the Gordons opened with their automatics. No enemy troops were seen, but the sound of explosions told of further demolitions on the road to Tripoli.

At Castel Verdi the 23rd Armoured Brigade passed through, but later in the day they reported a hold-up owing to demolitions and no possibility of by-passing them. So ' Hammerforce ' were needed again and moved on at 3.15 p.m. A and C Companies of the Gordons, riding on tanks, had orders to 'get to the harbour at Tripoli'.

When 'Hammerforce' came up with the Armoured Brigade they found that the enemy had mined the road and blown the bridges over two anti-tank ditches. While sappers lifted the mines Gordons, assisted by the tank crews, filled in the craters by shoring them up at the sides and bridging them with sleepers. Some of the timber was still burning. One last, smaller, crater was dealt with and the column moved on through the night while burning buildings, fired by the retreating enemy, lit up the scene.

At 5.30 a.m. on 23rd January 1943, the squadron of the 40th Royal Tank Regiment with A and C Companies of the 1st Gordon Highlanders riding on the tanks, entered the main square of Tripoli. These were very tired men, for they had been working harder than navvies, and most had had no sleep for the last forty-eight hours. And tanks are not constructed with a view to the comfort of outside passengers. But Tripoli was theirs. At 5 p.m. the Gordons pipes and drums played Retreat in the Piazza Italia.

No time was lost in painting a large Divisional sign upon one of the public buildings, the paint being supplied by the Divisional commander himself. He was very early on the scene. Major-General Wimberley was jealous of the prestige of his command, and took pride in every unit. It was characteristic of him, on the eve of one attack, to send this message to the 5th/7th Gordons: 'Slante Bydand—here's to the Cock of the North.'

The 5th/7th Gordons, near Misurata on 19th January, moved on past Zliten next day through cultivated country and clumps of palm trees, with grassy rolling hills on the landward side. They moved along the main road on the 21st to bivouac in an 'Arab infested area' among palm groves. This was a short trek and 'the Battalion had a washing day'. The 22nd brought them to the neighbourhood of Homs and on the morrow the curious and incurious alike inspected the excavations at the Roman city of Leptis Magna. The Battalion took the road for Tripoli at nine o'clock that night and a wearisome journey it was. The jam of battle traffic was bad enough, but the crowded column was held up at frequent intervals while demolition after demolition was made good. The Gordons spent the remaining hours of the night about two miles west of Homs.

Next morning they rejoined the slow procession and continued all day and well into the night. In the darkness at 2 a.m. on the 24th they reached the outskirts of Tripoli, having taken sixteen hours to cover the last fifty miles. Then came another wait. After the mid-day meal they moved into an orchard outside the city.

The fall of Tripoli marked the end of the Italian Colonial Empire in Africa and another stage in the victorious drive of our Eighth Army. The advance from El Alamein, over 1,400 miles, had been accomplished in exactly three months. Wherever the enemy had stood he had been attacked and forced to continue his retreat. Despite minefields and demolitions, sand storms and rain storms, shortage of water, petrol, ammunition and all supplies, the pursuit, though sometimes slackening, had never ceased.

Untried in battle before they attacked at El Alamein, the Highland Division were now war-hardened and desert-hardened. Of the two battalions of Gordon Highlanders their Brigadier (Brigadier D. A. H. Graham) wrote to the Colonel of the Regiment : ' All your lads are in excellent heart and ready to take on anything that may be before them. They are a grand lot.'

And it was proudly remembered that the 1st Gordon Highlanders were the first infantry to enter Tripoli. In honour of the event the pipe-major composed a march which was rehearsed by the pipe band without delay.

Tripoli possesses well laid out streets and fine buildings, but there is another side to the picture. The 5th/7th Battalion remark that ' Tripoli is not much : a few fly-blown shops selling razor blades and soap, and a moderately filthy Arab quarter.' Nevertheless the Jocks, who were located in and about a Government experimental farm, appreciated the unwonted luxury of fresh vegetables.

General Montgomery, who had entered Tripoli on the 23rd, established his headquarters a few miles outside the city. On 31st January he was present at a XXX Corps church parade and march past ; later in the day he addressed a great gathering of officers in a cinema, explaining his plans for a speedy advance into Tunisia.

But the great day of ceremonial was 4th February, when the Prime Minister, accompanied by Sir Alan Brooke, Generals Alexander and Montgomery, and Lieut.-General Sir Oliver Leese, the Corps commander, paid a visit to Tripoli. The Highland Division were very much in evidence, for their massed pipes and drums played throughout the affair, and a kilted contingent from every battalion were among the troops who marched past Mr. Churchill. The 5th/7th Gordons record their impressions of the scene in the Piazza Italia : the windows of the buildings round the square crowded with officers and men ; the streets below lined with tanks, armoured cars and gunners ; a naval contingent ' with remarkable beards ' ; a squad of nurses of Q.A.I.M.N.S. ; the saluting base flying the Union flag and festooned with signal flags ; and the central figure, Mr. Winston Churchill in the uniform of a commodore R.A.F. Conspicuous in the Service throng were the detectives in civilian clothes who attended the Prime Minister. When he drove away the crowds of Italians who had been 'herded into the background' by the military police, broke through the cordon and applauded with a loud clapping of hands.

Meanwhile the work of clearing Tripoli harbour and unloading supplies was proceeding apace, for Tripoli was to become a main base for the Eighth Army, dispensing with the long haul over the coastal road. The two Gordon battalions had started to supply dock labour as early as 26th January, and the work went on all round the clock. Probably the Highlanders performed no more important task during the Desert campaign. No-one could pretend that this was a congenial occupation for fighting men, but it was carried out with efficiency and good will. Here is a picture of the men at work supplied by Lieut.-Colonel Fausset-Farquhar commanding the 1st Gordons:

Last night we went to watch some of our men unloading stores in Tripoli harbour. It was a most inspiring sight, more like a " shot " from a Hollywood film than the dull routine of a fatigue. Tank landing craft had been moved up to an improvised quay which only that afternoon had been a pile of rubble, the result of enemy demolitions. The outline of the sturdy little ship stood out sharply against the tropical stars, the whole operation taking place beneath the towering walls of the old fort which governs Tripoli harbour.

In the bowels of the L.C.T. men, naked to the waist, their backs glistening with sweat, hoisted steel boxes filled with heavy shells on to roller run-ways. Gangs of men sent the boxes hurtling down the run-ways in a clattering rhythm to the waiting lorries. All was bright electric light inside the vessel, outside only a single arc lit the dark, and men and machines cast weird shadows as they moved across the beam.

In a remarkably short time the cargo was discharged and the men went back to their billets, singing as they marched through the silent streets of Tripoli.

Apart from work in the harbour the troops had anything but an easy time in Tripoli, and duties were frequently performed in heavy rain. The 5th/7th Gordons provided guards for the Fiat and Lancia motor works, a pumping station, a flour mill, a radio station, and a tank repair shop. In addition a certain amount of training was done. Relaxation was provided by performances of 'The Balmorals'—the Divisional concert party, which was really the child of Sergeant F. Barker, 5th/7th Gordons—and of the dancers of the 1st Gordons.

The 1st Gordons moved westward out of Tripoli on 4th February, but were still near the city. Three days later the 5th/7th Battalion took possession of an old Italian fort, about seven miles from Tripoli, and here they found an interesting assortment of guns and ammunition. In these new locations there was less harbour work and more training.

Tunisia

The port of Tripoli was now working well, and while the foremost divisions of the Eighth Army in the Tripoli area prepared again for battle the 7th Armoured Division pushed on westward with the 5th/7th Gordons under command.

On 11th January the commanding officer and the intelligence officer went forward to Pisida, the last village in Italian North Africa, to arrange the relief of a lorried infantry battalion of the 7th Armoured. German troops were reported to be on the Tunisian frontier holding a narrow belt of firm ground between the salt marshes and the sea. The whole landscape was barren and uninviting.

Next day the Gordons arrived at Pisida and prepared to regain close contact with the enemy. Patrols probed forward during the night, returning in the early hours to report that they had gone almost as far as the frontier, finding nothing but craters in the road and a number of dummy guns. At first light on the 13th a carrier patrol moved out, and A Company followed to fill in the nearest craters. One prisoner was sent back. He professed himself glad to be quit of the war, and said that there were no enemy this side of Ben Gardane.

The commanding officer, Major Barlow, Major Cochrane, R.A., Lieutenant McAndrew, a machine-gun officer and three other ranks had already gone forward. One party followed the main road where a man trod on a mine, the explosing killing the machine-gun officer and wounding Barlow and McAndrew. This was not the tale of the morning's disaster. Lieut.-Colonel Saunders and Major Cochrane were using a track some distance from the road when another mine explosion killed Cochrane and severely wounded the commanding officer.

The clearance of mines was now undertaken by the Royal Engineers and the 5th/7th Gordons continued their advance. Before nightfall their patrols had crossed into Tunisia and a pioneer had painted on a frontier building : 'First Across HD 92nd Bydand.'

Next day was to see the Battalion make their formal entry into Tunisia under the cameras of an Army film unit, so a certain amount of 'spit and polish' was necessary. It promised to be a good show. The morning was fine and, headed by the pipers playing 'The Cock o' the North', the Gordons swung proudly into French North Africa. But there was no picture, for the cameras had not used any film ; and so the companies were called upon to counter-march and come by for the second time, when all went well.

It was on this day that Lieut.-Colonel J. Sorel-Cameron, a Cameron Highlander, arrived to assume command.

The good Italian road ended at the frontier and on the bumpy track which led forward progress was impeded by craters and mines. By nightfall on the 14th the Gordons had covered ten miles. In moving into their position D Company encountered some trouble: they struck a minefield and lost a lance-corporal killed and two men wounded. The type of mine seemed to be new and not easy to detect.

Some diversion was created by the appearance of 'an incredibly dirty smelly Frenchman' who announced himself as chief of police for the area. The Germans, he said, had departed two days earlier and he promised to guide a carrier patrol next morning to a village on the left flank. The Frenchman also talked of the Mareth Line, said to have been partially dismantled by the French under Italian supervision after the fall of France.

This news was heard with some satisfaction. All were aware that the Mareth Line was the next important defensive position confronting the Eighth Army and that the Allied forces advancing from the west in Tunisia had suffered a check. Actually, the enemy had launched an offensive on 15th February and driven the U.S. II Corps on the right flank back towards Tebessa. There was now greater need than ever for the Eighth Army to press on and strike again.

The carriers of the 5th/7th Gordons, guided by their French friend, set out next morning to visit the village which lay south of the main track. The Battalion plodded on towards Ben Gardane, still impeded by mines and craters. The mines took their toll of the devoted sappers who lost six killed and seven wounded while lifting them. All day sounds of fighting were heard away to the left where the 7th Armoured Division seemed to be meeting with opposition due south of Ben Gardane. The firing died down towards evening and the night is described as 'peaceful'. By this time the Gordons were in sight of the town.

At 9 a.m. the next morning, the Battalion being about half a mile from Ben Gardane, the Brigadier arrived and indicated the positions to be taken up until the remainder of the Brigade arrived. The Gordons were to cover the tracks leading into the town.

There was no sign of the enemy, and in the afternoon a carrier patrol reconnoitred Zarzis, a prosperous little place still under military government with the tricolour flying from the prefecture. The Brigadier agreed that one company should be put into Zarzis next day.

The Zarzis column set out on the afternoon of the 17th, D Company being reinforced by machine guns, anti-tank guns, and some of the carriers. The passage through the salt marshes was by a much damaged causeway, a wet part, where the marsh met the estuary, proving particularly difficult. Zarzis was a pleasant little place. The detachment were greeted by a spruce little French captain who was very helpful, and D Company settled down in an olive grove overlooking the marshes. Soon came Arab vendors offering the inevitable eggs and chickens and the Highlanders 'looked like having a pleasant stay'.

On 18th February the remainder of the 153rd Brigade appeared at Ben Gardane and the 5th/7th Gordons were able to concentrate their rather scattered companies. Next day they began work on the repair of the causeway leading to Zarzis. Several huge craters containing water were filled in with stone carried from a considerable distance—heavy work indeed.

Just before dark an enemy aircraft flew low over D Company, who promptly opened fire with Bren gun and rifle. Such fusillades generally achieved nothing, but to the surprise of the Jocks the aircraft was brought down. The pilot disappeared and was never found. The machine, a Messerschmitt of a type not captured hitherto, was little damaged; and the Corps commander, Sir Oliver Leese, paid a special visit to congratulate the Gordons.

Mareth

Although his supply situation was not yet satisfactory, General Montgomery was pressing forward towards the Mareth Line. The 153rd Brigade moved east and north-east from Ben Gardane on 23rd February in order to gain contact with the enemy outposts, the 5th/7th Gordons being allotted a 'very safe looking place' behind Wadi Zessar which was very deep, with running water in the bottom. While they moved up Allied aircraft flew over to drop flares, and the bombing of the enemy continued all night.

Next morning the Gordons established an observation post on a flat hill 1,100 yards in front. There was a blanket-mist at 6.30 a.m. but later on the O.P. gave a good view of the Mareth Line nearly three and a half miles distant. The intervening ground seemed devoid of cover.

The task of the Highland Division was to push forward, passing north of Medenine, and establish a position within striking distance of the Mareth Line, between the Medenine-Mareth road and the coast. The 5th/7th Gordons made a slight advance on the night of the 24th and the 5th Black Watch, who were on the right, conformed to the movement. All was accomplished without incident.

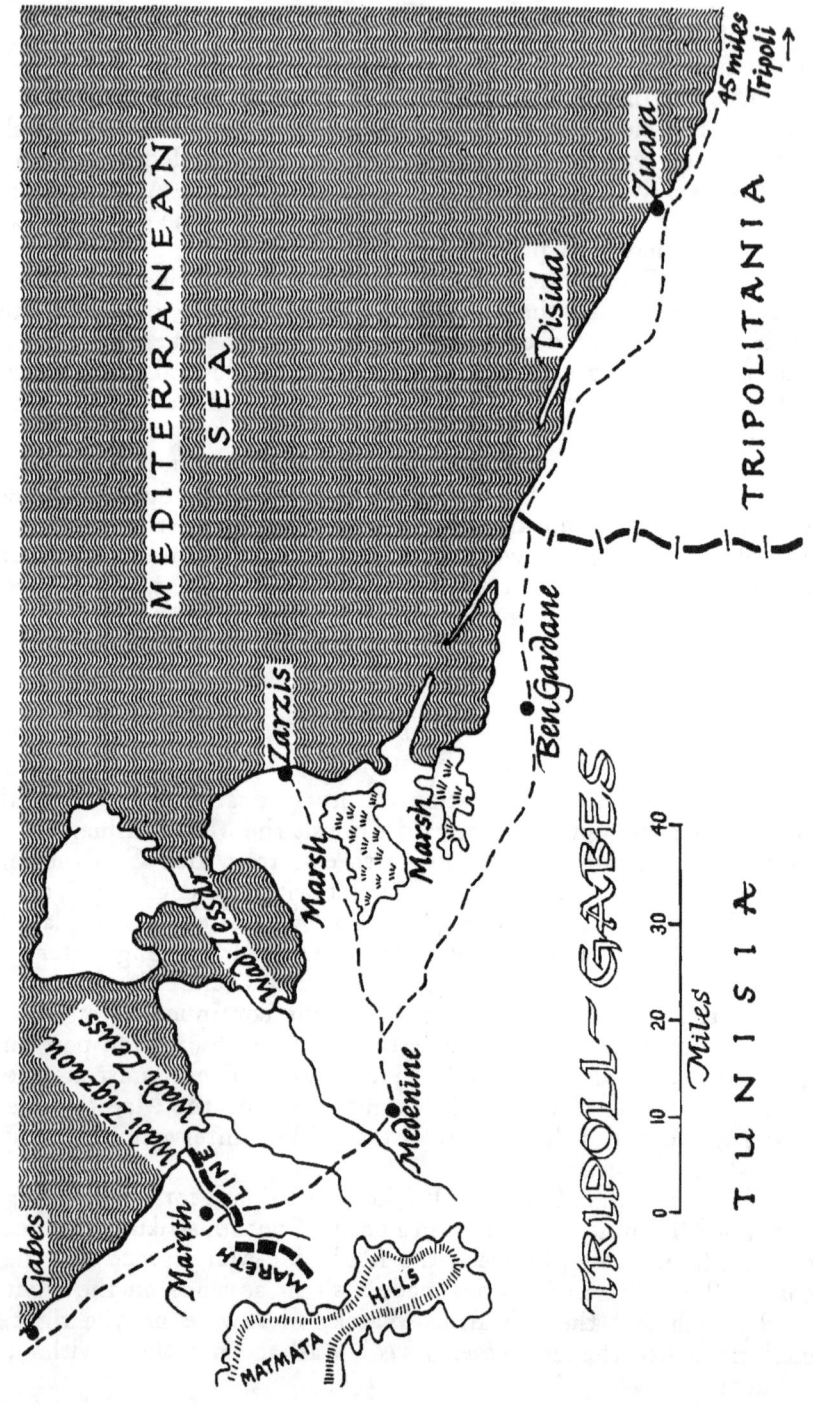

The next day passed quietly and at night the Gordons sent A Company to occupy the O.P. Patrols went on further and had trouble with mines which seemed to have been planted indiscriminately in this area. Lieutenant Nixon was wounded, and Lieutenant W. M. Grant, who took over, was also wounded; but he insisted on remaining with his men, and was killed a little later.

Accurate sniping by spandaus hampered movement during the daylight hours of the 26th and the enemy guns began to devote attention to the Battalion. One man was killed and Captain Yeomans and Lieutenant Forbes were wounded. Owing to mine casualties on patrol Lieut.-Colonel Sorel-Cameron refused to continue patrolling without the assistance of an R.E. mine-detector squad.

Quiet days followed and then, on the night of 1st March, the 5th/7th Gordons were relieved by one company and the carrier platoon of the 1st Battalion. The 153rd Brigade were now in position behind Wadi Zessar—which formed an excellent anti-tank obstacle—with infantry posts in front and a carrier screen patrolling towards Wadi Zeuss.

The 1st Gordons, who had left the Tripoli area and crossed into Tunisia on 17th February, moved as rear battalion of the Brigade, and were still in reserve when they halted east of Wadi Zessar on the 24th. It was not until the relief of the sister battalion on the night of 1st March that they renewed contact with the enemy. The 1st Gordons then put two companies west of Wadi Zessar, together with the carrier platoon and a mortar section.

On 2nd March there were signs of an impending enemy attack against Medenine, and at night the Gordons were ordered to withdraw their forward companies. The carriers and mortars remained in the outpost line. Next morning the carriers reported that the enemy were blowing mines along their front and in the afternoon tanks were seen 3,000 yards away moving south. Later hostile infantry advanced towards the carriers, who were then withdrawn. A night patrol taken out by Captain Ewen Frazer returned with nothing but machine-gun fire to report. On the 4th the carriers moved out again and came under mortar fire.

Certain honours and awards were announced on this day: the Military Cross to Captain L. W. Millar; the Distinguished Conduct Medal to Company Sergeant-Major Thomson; and the Military Medal to Corporal Irwin and Private Sheddon.

Bickering with the enemy continued on the 5th when the carriers received the fire of an anti-tank gun and the machine guns of the 1/7th Middlesex, supporting the carriers, did a little execution. The night was quiet, but after daylight on the 6th considerable enemy movement was seen; and after some hostile shelling two attempts of infantry to advance against the carriers were halted by fire.

This was the day when Rommel, as General Montgomery had anticipated, made his attack against Medenine. He lost much and gained nothing by this venture, in which his armoured divisions were badly battered. The Gordons were too far to the north to be directly engaged.

Early next morning in front of the 1st Gordons the enemy occupied a small hill known as Point 20 but withdrew when our machine guns opened. The carriers who were under mortar fire at times, had several arguments with enemy infantry: on one occasion, when 200 Germans and Italians advanced, the fire of the carriers accounted for about fifty of them. Before noon the enemy appeared to have had enough.

The 5th/7th Gordons in reserve had been out of things during these days. On the morning of 4th March, however, they were visited by the Divisional commander, the C.R.A. and the C.R.E. 'in a procession of jeeps', and were told to change their dispositions. Consequently they moved forward in the afternoon nearer to Wadi Zessar and settled down in a small branch wadi. Here they 'felt safe from anything but a direct hit or a visiting brass hat', and were at liberty to watch the fighter battles in the air above them.

The wadi had steep sandy sides falling 30 feet to a marshy bottom with a slow stream running through. The water was fresh and inviting and all ranks bathed, much to the inconvenience of the permanent inhabitants, frogs and water tortoises.

Then, on the evening of the 6th came orders for a southward move to join the 154th Brigade. The night was dark, and drizzling rain came on. Transport needed the guidance of a man walking in front with a torch. After passing through batteries in action to the southern flank of the Divisional front, the Gordons came to a halt at a wire fence enclosing a minefield.

Dawn found the Battalion facing the Matmata Hills and about a mile from the head of Wadi Zessar. The day, it is said, 'passed in peace': patrols had nothing to report, and the Jocks surveyed with interest a grassy plain strewn with the wrecks of Rommel's tanks. This interlude came to an end on the 8th when the 5th/7th Gordons, now following a well-lighted route, returned to their old position at Wadi Zessar. Here they remained undisturbed for two days.

The 1st Gordons, holding the left sector of the 153rd Brigade front, continued their patrol activity on the 8th and made ground as the enemy withdrew under shell and mortar fire. On the 9th the Brigade reached Wadi Zeuss. Next morning Captain E. F. Frazer, with Sergeant Grant and Private Duncan, went out in a carrier bearing a Red Cross flag to rescue two wounded artillery officers who had been blown up by a mine. This was done under a certain amount of mortar fire.

On the night of the 12th the 1st Gordons were relieved by a battalion of the Green Howards belonging to the 50th Division, who were taking over the seaward sector facing the Mareth Line. The whole of the 153rd Brigade were coming out to spend a few days in reserve about six miles back, so the 5th/7th Gordons were relieved likewise.

Being selected to head the next advance of the Brigade, the 5th/7th Gordons became busy on reconnaissance in the sector to the south of that which their Brigade had been holding. Here our forward posts were beyond Wadi Zeuss. Of the two crossings over the wadi one was an Italian-built bridge, the other a natural rock crossing used for centuries by camel caravans. Both required improvement. Company commanders reconnoitred forward routes and patrols endeavoured to locate enemy minefields, a difficult job as mines seemed to be in patches, ' all over the place '. Beyond these patches, however, a very deep minefield was located.

General Montgomery planned to deliver a frontal attack against the Mareth Line, which had been immensely strengthened by Italian labour under German supervision. This attack was confided to the 50th (Northumbrian) Division in the coastal sector. He intended also to outflank Rommel's position by an advance from the south round the Matmata Hills. It was the task of the Highlanders on the immediate left of the 50th Division to close up to the Mareth Line by destroying the enemy's covering positions on their front. This operation was preliminary to the main assault.

The 5th/7th Gordons had two rehearsals, one by day and one by night. An attack through a minefield against an enemy position was now rather in the nature of a set piece : first the artillery preparation, then the barrage to cover the advance, then the making of passages through the minefield, and, lastly, the infantry advance to the final objective. On this occasion reliance was again placed upon the scorpions to flail a way through the minefield.

The 5th/7th Gordons were carried forward in troop-carrying vehicles on the morning of 16th March, and, after a rest and a meal, moved up on foot in the evening. At 10 p.m. our artillery opened, machine guns firing from the flanks. In the van were a protective platoon supplied by the 1st Gordons, an R.E. party, and the scorpions. The routes to the two crossings over the wadi were well marked : beyond, taped and lighted paths showed the way.

On the left all started well. The scorpions negotiated without trouble the Italian bridge, and the leading machine swept a passage through the minefield to a depth of 300 yards—about half way. Then it broke down. The second scorpion broke down before reaching the gap, and it was left to the third, which arrived some time later, to drive the passage through. The time was now 3 a.m. and B Company of the 5th/7th Gordons, who had been waiting under some shell and mortar fire with what patience they could command, then moved forward. They walked on to their objective without hindrance, for the enemy had already gone.

On the right trouble began at the rocky causeway where the first scorpion crossed and the second stuck, holding up the third. The beginning of a gap was eventually made, but attracted the fire of three or four spandaus 'making life very unpleasant', as it was described. For a quarter of an hour before 3 a.m. our gunners fired smoke which blew back and reduced visibility to ten yards, certainly no help to the Highlanders. Captain B. C. A. Napier, commanding C Company, decided to take his men forward through the mines and wipe out the spandaus, but the venture started badly: Captain Douglas fouled the trip-wire of a mine and the explosion wounded him and three privates. As the spandaus were now silent, it was judged wiser to dig in and wait for daylight; meanwhile a patrol was sent forward to find a better route to the objective.

At 5 a.m. Lieut.-Colonel Sorel-Cameron set off to visit B Company who had been so successful. Nothing further was heard of him until half-an-hour later when he returned in his jeep, wounded. He and Captain W. G. Dey had been knocked out by the same mine. By this time C Company had advanced, finding in the enemy defences no living thing except a small white puppy.

Later on the 17th the Gordon patrols encountered heavy fire. While the Battalion were consolidating their position and the battle transport was coming up Major J. E. G. Hay arrived from the 1st Gordons to take command.

A company of the 1st Gordons had come forward and occupied an advanced position on the left flank of the 5th/7th Battalion. They encountered no opposition and at night they handed over to the 5th Black Watch. On the right the 5th/7th Gordons gained contact next morning with the left of the 50th (Northumbrian) Division, which lay astride the Medenine-Gabes road.

The whole sector of the 153rd Brigade was under shell fire on this day and the following days; and then, on the night of the 20th the 50th Division delivered their frontal attack against the Mareth Line. The struggle was prolonged and bitter. Despite the utmost endeavours of the Northumbrians, who did all that was humanly possible, the offensive failed to establish a bridge-head beyond the Mareth defences. After a German counter-attack on the 22nd, we were left with very small gains.

The 5th/7th Gordons, holding the right of the Brigade sector, were under considerable shell and machine-gun fire during these days, but lost very few men. On the night of the 24th the Battalion advanced some distance without opposition, but the 5th Black Watch, on the left, were not so successful. Next day the Black Watch were relieved by the 1st Gordons from reserve.

By now General Montgomery's 'left hook' in the south was succeeding, and the enemy was beginning to abandon the Mareth Line. Another defeat had been inflicted upon Rommel.

Patrols of both Gordon battalions were active on the 26th and 27th, drawing machine-gun fire and mortar fire. The 5th/7th Battalion lost Lieutenant Gilmour and a non-commissioned officer, both killed on the 27th. Next day carrier patrols discovered that the enemy was in full retreat.

Mareth to Sfax

The Highlanders were once more in pursuit. No limit was set to the advance of the 5th/7th Gordons, who headed the Brigade, but the ground was so bad for transport that the companies marched independently on foot. Mines were still the trouble. Two carriers were blown up with a loss of two killed and three, including Captain Best, wounded. A party returning from a rest camp lost two sergeants and a private wounded in the same way.

On the 28th the Battalion bivouaced north-west of the village of Mareth. The Mareth Line was an imposing sight, its blockhouses well sited and camouflaged, its communication trenches six feet deep, and an anti-tank ditch supplementing the formidable obstacle of the Wadi Zigzaou. Needless to say, the mine and wire defences were elaborate in the extreme.

Led by their carriers, the 1st Gordons had covered eleven miles on foot on this day.

On the 29th the Brigade continued the forward march with a section of Royal Engineers in front to attend to the mines. The route was bad, along rough tracks and sometimes across country, but generally following the direction of the Medenine-Gabes road. The 5th/7th Gordons, who reckoned that they had covered about twenty miles on this day, lost two men injured by mine explosion.

The Brigade bivouaced about five miles from Gabes, with the 5th/7th Gordons on the left, the 5th Black Watch on the right, and the 1st Gordons in rear. B Echelon which had come forward, and were five miles west of Wadi Zigzaou, rejoined next day.

Owing to the congestion of traffic on the main road the Brigade, although expecting to resume the advance, made no move on the 30th. Instead the battalions settled down for a rest, enjoying what the 5th/7th Gordons called a 'peace time routine'. The pipes and drums played Retreat and the footballs were brought out.

The other brigades of the Highland Division were now in front, and the 5th/7th Gordons lent two carrier sections to the 152nd Brigade for four days. They saw no action.

The immediate objective of the Eighth Army was now the port of Sfax, which General Montgomery had promised General Eisenhower—since January Supreme Commander of the Allied Forces in North Africa—to secure by or before 15th April. But beyond Gabes was another 'bottle neck' which afforded a strong defensive position. The 'Gabes Gap' extends south-westward for more than twelve miles from the coast to an area of lakes and marshes and is crossed by the formidable Wadi Akarit which is dominated on the landward side by the steep Roumana Hills.

The attack on the Gap was fixed for 6th April, and the 153rd Brigade were to provide a firm base for the assault of the other brigades of the Highland Division and support them by fire. On the right in the coastal sector were the 201st Guards Brigade; on the left of the Highlanders were the 50th Division.

The Gordon battalions came forward on 3rd April, the 1st Battalion passing through Gabes, and at night took over the front, the 1st on the right and the 5th/7th on the left, both very thin on the ground.

Next day the hostile artillery was fairly active, the 5th/7th Gordons losing three men and a carrier. At night many flares were seen and machine-gun fire was almost incessant, giving the 1st Gordons the impression that the enemy was 'very nervous'. Certainly he knew that an attack was coming. B Company of the 1st Battalion had advanced a little under cover of darkness and sent back twenty Italian prisoners.

The Gordon battalions continued to gain what ground they could during 5th April, trying to get, as the 5th/7th phrased it, 'right under the noses of the enemy' before the big attack went in. This was done under bursts of machine-gun fire and entailed some hard work: for instance, after dark, the 1st Gordons brought up their mortar ammunition by man-handling it across a wadi.

In the early hours of the 6th, while it was still dark, the assault upon the Gabes Gap was delivered, and bitter fighting continued all day. The Gordon battalions, who suffered some shelling, contributed mortar and machine-gun fire. They saw, with immense satisfaction nearly 700 prisoners—mostly Italian—pass back through their positions. By nightfall the enemy had had enough, and Rommel drew off his forces under cover of darkness. The way for a further advance of the Eighth Army was clear.

The 5th/7th Gordons were brought forward to the right of the 152nd Brigade, coming into position by first light on 7th April. Companies of the 1st Gordons also advanced.

It was on 7th April that the Eighth Army made contact with the U.S. II Corps on the Gabes-Gafsa road. The ring round the Axis forces in Tunisia was closed.

During the morning of the 7th the carriers of the 153rd Brigade were sent out to feel forward in front of the 23rd Armoured Brigade, and the part played by the carrier platoon of the 1st Gordons on this and succeeding days earned great praise from the commander of the armour.

The platoon crossed Wadi Akarit soon after ten o'clock on the morning of 7th April and moved across country towards the Gabes-Sfax road, five miles away. They rounded up about 250 Italians who were disarmed and sent back. About 3.30 p.m. the carriers gained fresh contact with the enemy, and immediately fanned out between the road and the sea. Advancing by a combination of fire and movement, the Gordons approached to within 400 yards of their antagonists, who suffered some loss. One wounded man was picked up. Soon afterwards rather severe shell and mortar fire compelled a withdrawal towards our tanks, and there was no further action that night.

At 5 a.m. the next morning the carriers went forward again. They had barely reached the position of the previous day when one carrier blew up on a mine. This brought the sappers on the scene, and when they had made a gap through an unmarked minefield the carriers pushed on. The next bout with the enemy occurred in the middle of the afternoon at Achichina. A report was sent back to the tanks who tried a turning movement which was greeted by shell and mortar fire, after which anti-tank guns opened and our armour was checked. The carriers took cover for the night in a wadi.

When the advance was resumed early on 9th April nothing was to be seen of any opponents. After crossing a wadi the carriers found a large crater in the main road. About breakfast time an enemy jeep came down the road and was ambushed, two Germans being captured. The Gordon carriers were now hard on the heels of the enemy and soon saw German light tanks and armoured cars about 500 yards ahead. These withdrew when ' our big brothers ', the tanks of the 23rd Armoured Brigade, came up. About noon movement was seen in woods some five miles south-west of Mahares.

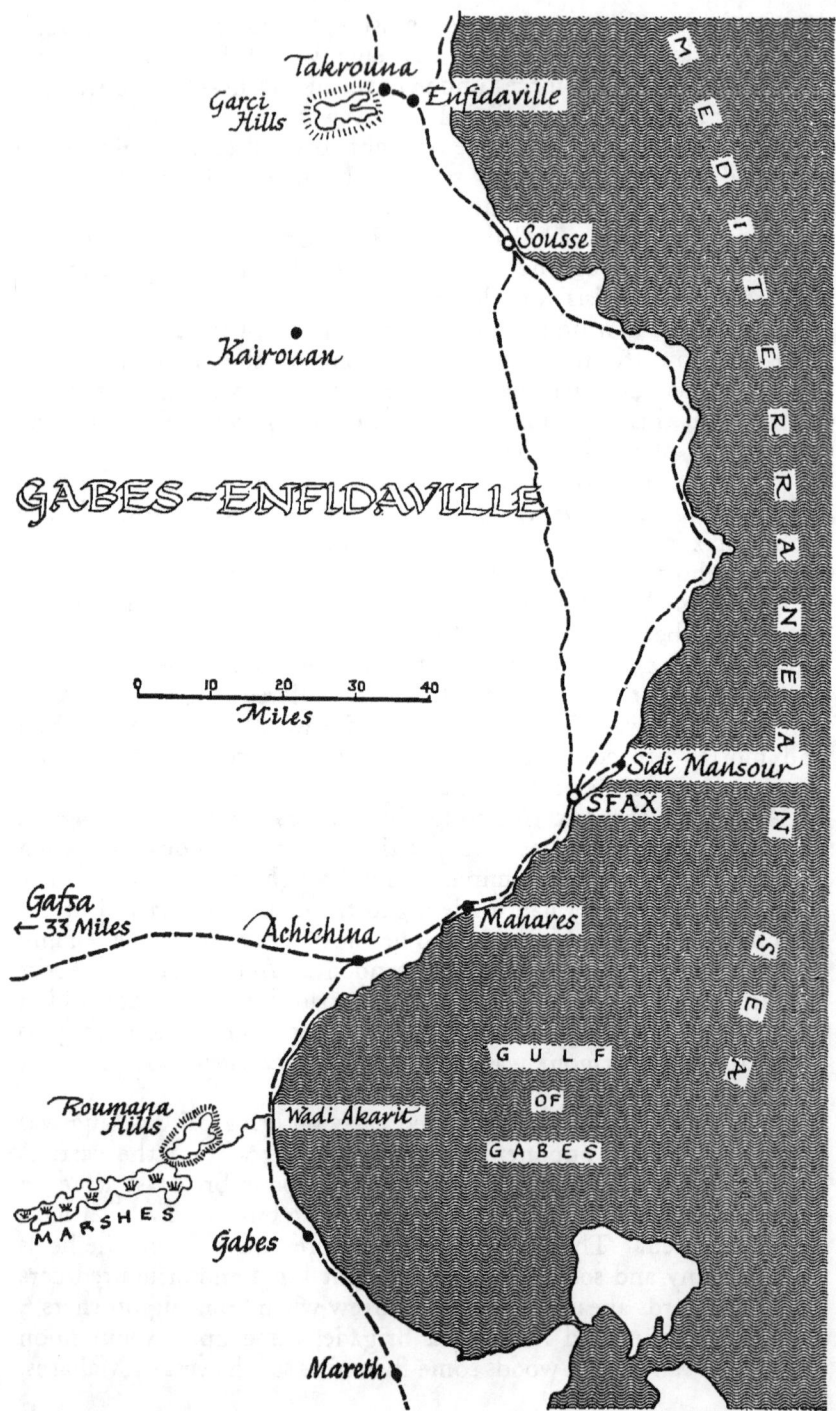

The carriers closed and started shooting at 200 yards, taking the enemy by surprise; but then the fire of anti-tank guns compelled a withdrawal. Our tanks tried a turning movement but the Germans did not stay, and the carriers took the lead again. The Gordons saw a number of Italians walking about the position which their Allies had abandoned, and opened fire on ' anything that moved '. These people disposed of, the carriers were able to enter Mahares about 1 p.m. after a few bursts from the Bren guns had brought out about twenty Italians running with their hands up. Mahares greeted the Gordons with enthusiasm, the French police being grateful for the rescue of some of their comrades who had been imprisoned by the Germans. But orders were received to push on faster.

About five miles beyond Mahares, between the railway and a wood—the railway follows the road along the coast—the carriers ran into trouble. Two were hit by 88-mm. shells, and the Brens could hardly prevail against anti-tank guns, spandaus and mortars. The Gordons were lucky to suffer no more than two killed and three wounded in this affair.

No more was done that day, and at night the carriers of the 1st Gordons were relieved by those of the 5th/7th Battalion. They had only five ' runners ' left.

Behind the carriers and the armour followed the infantry of the 153rd Brigade ready to deploy and attack should the need arise. The 1st Gordons, who started their advance on the night of the 7th, had taken to the main road on the 9th, and reached Mahares at 1 p.m. Further on they captured prisoners, guns and vehicles.

The 5th/7th Gordons who had collected much booty—rifles, ammunition, radio equipment, mortars and anti-tank weapons— together with nearly fifty prisoners on 7th April, were told that they were to be the road-makers of the Division on the way to Sfax. The Battalion, however, made an early start next morning. As they moved along the railway they passed many derelict guns and tanks : the only sign of the enemy was a little shell fire. When they halted in the dark at 10 p.m. they seemed to be right out of the picture. Patrols reported the main road to be pitted with craters and the Gordons filled in a huge one when they resumed their advance towards Mahares on the morning of the 9th. At night they leagured in rear of the 1st Gordons, about fifteen miles from Sfax. A large fire was seen in the direction of the town, and muffled explosions were thought to indicate the destruction of ammunition dumps.

The enemy, indeed, was in full retreat, and on 10th April the advance to Sfax was not contested. At the entrance to the town a bridge had been demolished and, until a suitable diversion could be provided further up the wadi, neither tanks nor carriers could get on. The marching troops could cross easily enough, and first to enter Sfax were A Company of the 1st Gordons, followed by the 5th/7th Battalion. From nine in the morning until late in the afternoon there was a continuous stream of troops and vehicles entering the town, and the people, obviously well pleased to be rid of the Germans and Italians, gave our men a rousing reception.

General Montgomery had promised to be in Sfax by 15th April, so he was better than his word; and now compliments are in order. The Commander of the Eighth Army, the Corps commander and the Divisional commander all expressed their satisfaction with what the troops had achieved; and Brigadier Richards wrote to Brigadier Graham in praise of the carriers, whose 'light cavalry' work during the advance from Wadi Akarit had been of such value to the 23rd Armoured Brigade.

Sfax, occupied by the 153rd Brigade, was in a terrible state. The bombing attacks of the R.A.F. had wrought great havoc, and the Germans had blown up much of what was still standing before they left. The water and drainage systems had suffered badly, and the 5th/7th Gordons who were quartered in the military barracks describe them as 'indescribably filthy and in utter chaos'. Perhaps the 1st Gordons, located in the public gardens, were a little better off; but the whole town, it was said, 'stank to high heaven'.

General Montgomery arrived on 11th April, and was greeted by the massed pipes and drums of the Brigade and the cheers of the population. In the afternoon the 1st Gordons played football.

Now was a great opportunity for cleaning up and smartening up, so the desert-worn Jocks soon looked different men. Sfax was an unhealthy spot, and on the 13th the Brigade moved some five miles out, leaving the 5th/7th Gordons behind to provide working parties in the harbour. The first ship arrived on this day, and the landing of supplies steadily proceeded.

On 17th April the 5th/7th Battalion moved to join the Brigade and settled down in an olive grove on the Sidi Mansour road opposite the 1st Gordons. Training was started in earnest, with a Divisional school to impart instruction in patrolling and minelaying, for the reinforcements lacked battle experience. On the 19th the 1st Gordons received a visit from their old commanding officer, Lieut.-Colonel H. Murray, who had been wounded at El Alamein. About this time he wrote to the Colonel of the Regiment: 'The men and officers have done all that I ever hoped they would do and more. . . . My one ambition is to get back and command them again.'

There was a good attendance of Gordons at the mobile cinema on the 20th when the El Alamein film ' Desert Victory ' was shown; but many of the Jocks were not impressed. Having experienced the real thing, they thought it ' a very feeble effort '.

Enfidaville

Many rumours were rife, and all ranks were wondering what would come next. At this time the Eighth Army had advanced northward, captured Sousse, and were now battering against the strong enemy position at Enfidaville between the sea and the hills. Enfidaville and Takrouna were captured on the 20th, but henceforward the main Allied effort was made by the First Army and the Americans and French, who were almost within striking distance of Tunis and Bizerta.

The 153rd Brigade moved on 21st April, driving first along the main Sfax-Sousse road, and then turning westward into the Garci Hills, west of Enfidaville. The front of the 5th Indian Brigade was to be taken over, and this promised to be a difficult business. Among ' a mass of large and small ridges, false crests and deep wadis ' it was not easy to locate and reach the points occupied by the forward companies. Commanding officers and their intelligence officers and company commanders spent the whole of the night of 21st/22nd in reconnaissance.

The Gordon battalions arrived by truck at the foothills after darkness had fallen on 22nd April, and carried out the relief during a thunderstorm. Mules were available to bring up ammunition and stores, but some of the steep slippery slopes were too much even for these sure-footed animals. Yet by dawn of the 23rd the 1st Gordons had taken over from the 4/6th Rajputana Rifles and the 5th/7th from the 1/9th Gurkhas. The positions, which required some adjustment when daylight came, were under spasmodic mortar fire.

Our own and the enemy's artillery were active at times, and some of the advanced posts of the 5th/7th Gordons, being on a forward slope, were unapproachable by day. On the night of the 25th the Battalion were pulled out to form a reserve, which meant a thinning out of the Brigade front. The 5th/7th marched back six miles before settling down for forty-eight hours rest ; then they moved over to the left and relieved Free French troops in the dark.

The new positions were the reverse of comfortable, for every movement seemed to attract fire. Major J. M. Glennie and Captain Angus were wounded by mortar bombs, and several men were killed or wounded on 29th April. On this day, too, C Company lost a corporal and a private, missing from patrol. At length, on the night of 5th May the Battalion moved out, leaving D Company to hold the fort until the French came in again. This was really a move to the reserve area for, after a march of three miles, the Gordons were picked up by transport and carried back another fourteen miles. They came to a very orderly well laid-out camp where baths were available; but all ranks wanted news of the war, and speculated as to what would happen to them next.

In the meantime the 1st Gordons were occupied in patrolling the wadis of the Garci range on their front, Captain Ewen Frazer and Lieutenant J. M. Robertson showing particular enterprise. On 29th April this rather dreary spell of position warfare was enlivened by the visit of members of a Chinese military mission. A few days later twenty shells from a 220-mm. gun fell near Battalion headquarters, but none of them exploded. On 3rd May the Battalion extended to the right, taking over the left of the 154th Brigade.

The Gordons were not content to leave the enemy in peace. Captain Frazer organised a succession of 'stonks' in which the fire of field guns, mortars and machine guns was concentrated upon selected spots; Lieutenant R. Bird located a heavy Breda machine-gun which seemed to be left unguarded, and this weapon was blown up later by a party under Major Du Boulay. Lieutenant W. Angus was wounded on 6th May.

On the night of 7th May, in the middle of a terrific thunderstorm, the whole Brigade were relieved by the French. The rain made two wadis impassable, and caused much delay, but the very wet 1st Gordons reached the reserve area before daylight of the 8th. The news had come that Tunis and Bizerta were occupied. Except for a few days to be spent in 'tidying up' the war in North Africa was over.

It is true to say that the men of the two Gordon battalions displayed no great enthusiasm over the victory. They had not been permitted to share in the final triumph, and their thoughts were now centred upon a long rest and, perhaps, Home leave. Some optimists even dwelt upon the likelihood that the whole Division would be sent Home; and when it was learnt that their next move would take them to somewhere on the Algerian coast this was felt to be a step in the right direction. Then orders for an early move were cancelled, courses for the instruction of specialists were started, and the regimental sergeant-major came into his own. However, difficulties caused by traffic congestion and supply problems were soon overcome, and by 12th May the Highland Division were en route for Algeria.

ALGIERS TO TUNIS

The Allied landings in Algeria and Morocco had taken place on 9th November 1942, but the advance to seize Tunis and Bizerta had failed. German reinforcements in considerable strength had reached these ports from Sicily and Italy with great promptitude: the British and Americans were hampered by the necessity to eliminate Vichy-French influence, by their long and difficult communications, and the lack of forward airfields. The enemy had reacted so strongly that in March 1943 the Allies, over thirty miles from Tunis, were still confronted by difficult mountainous country and a stout resistance.

The badly needed reinforcements for our First Army included the 1st Division, who had been held back in England until it was certain that they would not be urgently needed elsewhere. In the Division the 1st Brigade were replaced by the 24th Guards Brigade.

The 6th Gordon Highlanders, who left the Clyde at the end of February 1943, arrived at Algiers on 9th March, disembarking in the midst of an air raid which did them no harm. After a march of sixteen miles the Battalion went into billets in the Baraki area, 'occupying farms where all arrangements were primitive'. Although the eleven days voyage from Home had passed without incident so far as the companies were concerned, it was now learnt that the ship carrying the Gordon transport had been sunk. The whole of the Battalion stores, the drums and the sports kit were lost, but fortunately there was no loss of life.

On 19th March the Gordons left for Bône, and arrived there after an erratic train journey lasting three days. At Bône the men were able to bathe in the Mediterranean and rejoice in fine weather. Most of the lost vehicles and stores had been replaced and new carriers now arrived; but the Battalion still lacked 2-inch mortars and the base plates for their 3-inch mortars.

Soon came the time for action. The Gordons moved in motor transport to Teboursouk on the 24th, and on the night of the 25th relieved the 1st East Surrey in positions south-east of Medjez-el-Bab, overlooking the Goubellat plain.

The front occupied by the Battalion was in the right sector of a blunt salient divided by the wide valley of the Medjerda river, which runs through Medjez-el-Bab north-eastward to Tebourba and the sea. The Gordons lay west of the Medjez-el-Bab-Goubellat road, about two miles from the latter place. In front of them was a flat, treeless plain with scattered farmhouses held by the enemy as advanced posts which he sometimes left vacant during the day. There was no close contact, but patrols were active on both sides during the night. The Gordons found that unlocated

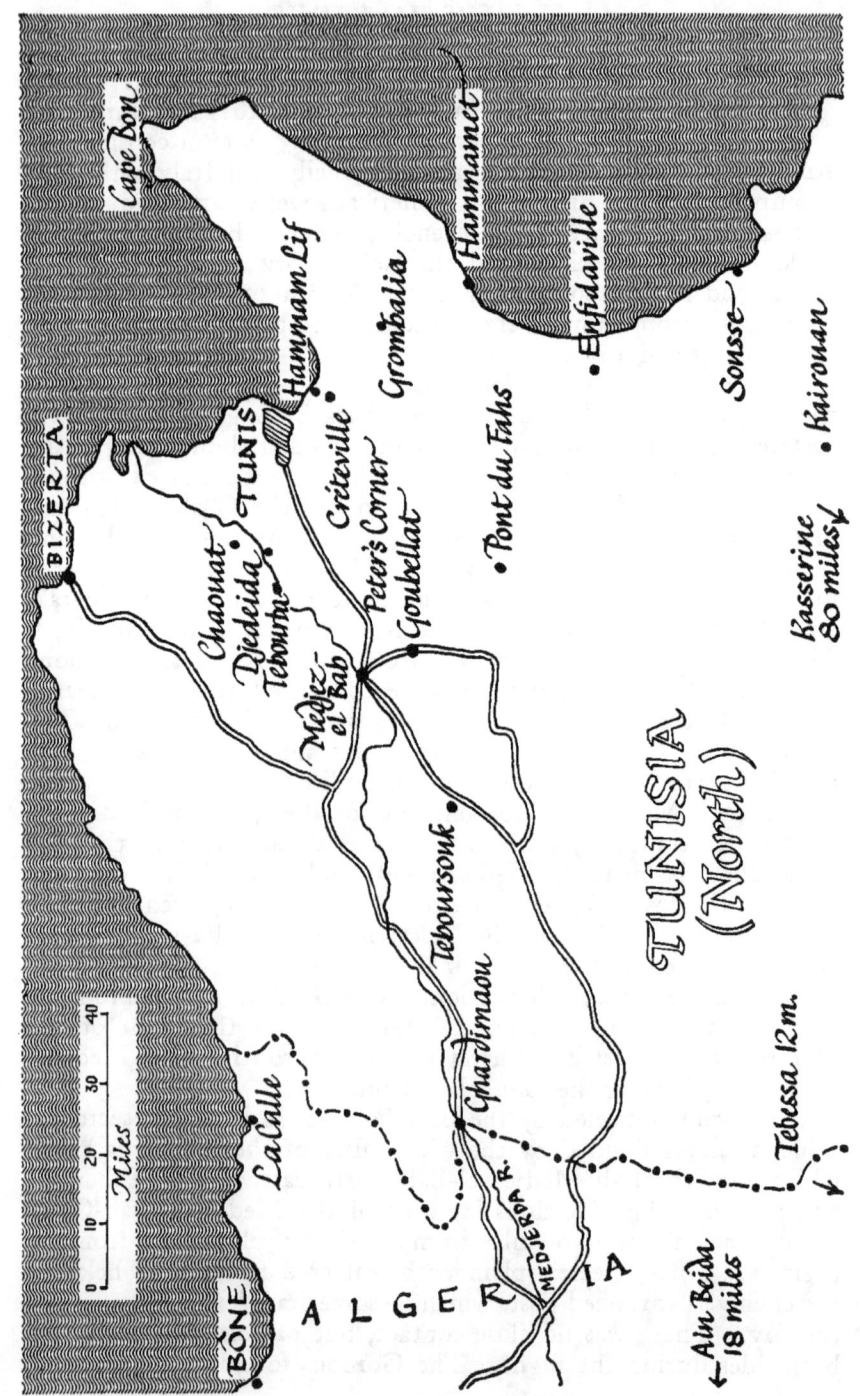

minefields compelled caution when moving in the dark, and by day activities were restricted, as the Germans possessed excellent observation from the hills beyond the plain. The artillery of friend and foe fired intermittently.

On 30th March a patrol of D Company came to grief, losing eight men.

With April the weather turned colder, bringing high winds and squalls of rain. Early in the month the Gordons received their 2-inch mortars, also eight ' projectors infantry anti-tank '—' Piats ' —to replace the ineffective Boys anti-tank rifle.

Affairs in Tunisia were progressing. On 7th April the Eighth Army linked up with the U.S. II Corps; on the 12th came the news that Montgomery was in Sousse. Also, preparations for a First Army offensive were in hand, and at night the front of the 1st Division became more active. In the early morning of the 19th the Gordons lost a small standing patrol which appears to have been taken by surprise and captured.

That same night the Battalion were relieved by the 2nd Bedfordshire and Hertfordshire, and moved to a concentration area near by in preparation for their part in the forthcoming attack.

The enemy anticipated our intentions by attacking on the night of the 20th. Part of the Hermann Goering Division supported by tanks—seventy were reported—advanced from the north-east across the Medjez-Tunis road and made some headway before they were repulsed. The Gordons remained alert in their slit trenches and lost nothing more than a night's rest; but on the following night about two platoons of Germans penetrated as far as the Battalion area. This calculated piece of impudence was suitably dealt with by B Company, who had one man wounded and killed two of the enemy.

The Gordons were to form the right of the 3rd Brigade which aimed at securing the cluster of hills called Gueriat el Atach. They were to safeguard the flank by capturing a hill known as Point 144, while the 2nd North Staffordshire in the centre and the 1st Loyals on the left went for the main objective.

On the night of the 22nd the Battalion moved up to the start line forward of the Medjez road, a harassing march in the darkness over a route congested by battle traffic. There was some confusion in forming up, but the companies, heavily laden with extra rations and carrying anti-personnel mines which proved an embarrassing burden, were sorted out in time to advance when the barrage, described as ' magnificent ', came down at 2 a.m. on 23rd April.

A Company on the right and B Company on the left led the way, with C and D Companies following. There was little opposition —a few Germans came running forward with their hands up—

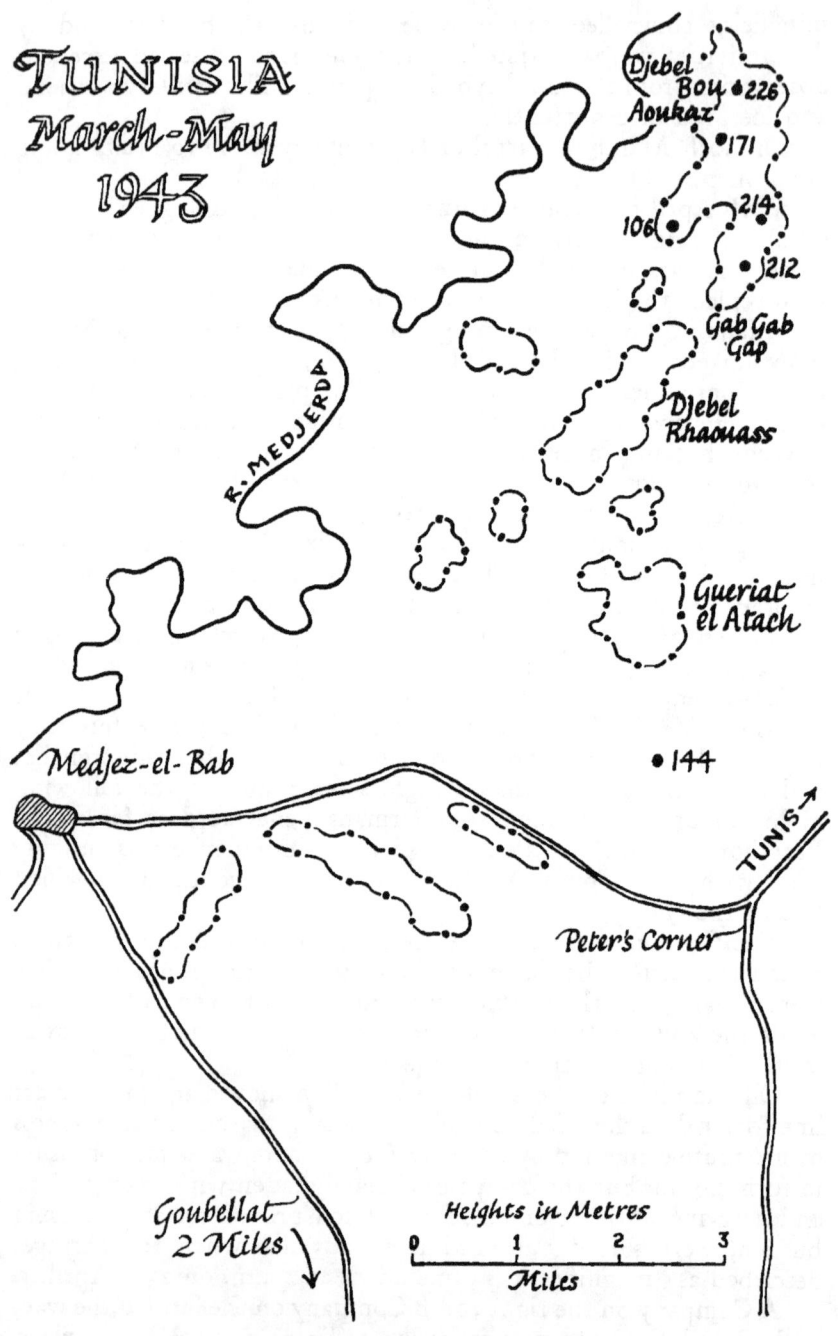

and before daylight the Gordons were in possession of Point 144 and another hill near by and had taken twenty prisoners. This was all done for the loss of twelve killed and wounded. Lieutenant R. D. Bain brought the carriers up promptly, so tools and reserve ammunition were soon at hand. A very welcome hot meal arrived soon after.

The companies were under shell and mortar fire all day on the 23rd. When German infantry and tanks advanced to counter-attack the fire of the Gordons discouraged them, although one or two determined attempts to close were made. Of these attempts A Company under Captain R. Rae bore the brunt, maintaining a most resolute defence. B Company, on the left, were so pounded by the German artillery that they were withdrawn for some distance early in the afternoon, but they held on in their new and more sheltered position.

Hostile fire slackened on the 24th and at night the other battalions of the Brigade, who had suffered severely in their partially successful efforts against Gueriat el Atach, were relieved by the 3rd Brigade. The Gordons remained in their position under 3rd Brigade command and saw the capture of Gueriat el Atach completed on the 25th.

In the meantime, on the night of the 24th, the 4th Division on the right of the Gordons had started their offensive against the strong enemy positions round the road junction known as Peter's Corner on the route to Tunis. The left of this attack came through the Gordon's area, and bitter fighting resulted. It was more important than ever that the Battalion should hold fast.

Hearing that two wounded men of the 4th Division were lying out in the midst of a minefield, the Gordons' medical officer, Captain G. M'Intosh, and Lieutenant Bain organised a stretcher party, and set out to the rescue. It was a hazardous undertaking, and four of the party, including the doctor, were seriously wounded by mine explosions. These casualties were tended by a gallant stretcher-bearer, Private R. M'Pherson, until he was mortally injured by another mine.

The Gordons were still under shell and mortar fire, and even received a visit from dive-bombers. On the 27th many of the enemy's shells failed to explode, causing some argument as to whether they were 'duds' or armour-piercing ammunition. Although the Battalion were very much in the front line, it was found possible to withdraw nearly everyone in turn to bathe in a wadi which contained running water, a very refreshing interlude since the days were hot although the nights were cool.

When on 28th April the Gordons were relieved by the 6th East Surrey they could pride themselves upon 'having held the right flank of the Division firm throughout a number of vicissitudes on the right and left '. Their losses had mounted to twenty killed and four officers and forty-seven other ranks wounded. The wounded included Lieutenant Stanley Martin, injured by a mine, and Lieutenant R. W. Smith.

On relief the Gordons moved into reserve behind Djebel Rhaouass, part of the rugged range of hills between the Tunis road and the Medjerda river, which terminated in Djebel Bou Aoukaz with a peak 700 feet high. Beyond Djebel Rhaouass was a break in the hills called the Gab Gab Gap through which tanks could move freely.

The Battalion arrived in their reserve position about one o'clock in the morning of 29th April and suffered another visit from dive-bombers as day was breaking. Fortunately the only loss was one petrol truck. There was no chance of a rest, for at 11 a.m. the Gordons were placed under command of the 24th Guards Brigade who, since the 27th, had been fighting their way forward towards Djebel Bou Aoukaz and now needed reinforcement.

The Guards had crossed the Gab Gab Gap, and the 1st Irish Guards had reached Point 212 and Point 214 on the eastern side of the ridge. Whether they were still there was uncertain—they were known to have suffered heavily—and two companies of the Gordons were now ordered to advance and make sure of these objectives.

Yet 29th April was a day of vexatious delays. A counter-attack by German armour penetrated the Gab Gab Gap from the east and, although this effort eventually came to nothing, it brought the 6th Gordons into a defensive position on Djebel Rhaouass where, with the Divisional reconnaissance regiment, they formed the centre of the Divisional front.

It was next morning that A and D Companies of the Battalion, under Major A. G. I. Fleming of D Company, came under the command of the 1st Irish Guards and advanced towards Points 212 and 214. They were taken forward in trucks as far as possible, but the dust clouds soon attracted hostile artillery fire, causing some casualties. As the precise location of the Irish Guards companies was unknown, no artillery or mortar fire could support the Gordons.

They deployed with D Company on the right and A Company on the left. Although there was half a mile of open country to cross under enemy observation few men were hit until the Highlanders began to climb the rocky boulder-strewn slopes of the ridge. Then machine-gun, mortar and small-arms fire threatened to break up the attack of D Company, but the section commanders pulled their men together, and the advance continued. Corporal Lamb, though wounded, indicated a machine-gun post which was ' flushed ' by Private O'Brien with a 2-inch mortar, the Germans being destroyed by Bren gun fire as they tried to escape.

Meanwhile A Company were in difficulties. Captain Rae, although badly wounded, continued to encourage his men until he collapsed; then Lieutenant N. Lawrie assumed command, but the company were now so reduced in numbers that they were ordered to withdraw through D Company and reorganise.

At Point 212 the Gordons found the Irish Guards—what was left of two companies—and Point 214 was then reached without much trouble. Here a position was established below the crest. The Guardsmen had almost run out of ammunition and water. Nearly all their carriers had been knocked out while endeavouring to bring up supplies.

Casualties in the Gordon companies amounted to forty killed and wounded and missing, besides Captain Rae, one of the pre-war officers. He had commanded the carrier platoon most ably during the Dunkirk campaign.

When darkness fell the Irish Guards were withdrawn and the Gordon carriers under Captain G. Donald and Lieutenant Bain brought up ammunition, food and water, not without loss from the enemy's mortar fire. All these supplies were more or less in bulk and to handle them up the mountain side in the darkness was a difficult and exhausting task.

The two companies were under almost continuous mortar fire and, during daylight, every incautious movement could be seen by the Germans on the highest ground of Djebel Bou Aoukaz. Owing to the rocky soil it was impossible to dig slit trenches more than 18 inches deep. The place was strewn with dead which could not be buried, and the days were scorching hot. Despite the nightly efforts of the carriers there was never enough water.

In these conditions Major Fleming's Highlanders passed the first two days of May. The remainder of the Battalion were having a comparatively peaceful time, having been withdrawn behind Djebel Rhaouass. They were even able to hold a church service in the open. Then, on the 3rd, they came into the battle.

B Company were sent up to reinforce the forward companies; C Company relieved the Guards at Point 171, about a mile northwest of Point 214; Battalion headquarters and the Headquarters Company moved to a hill between Djebel Rhaouass and the river. The whole of the Gordons were now under Battalion command.

On this day two deserters from the German I/962nd Regiment gave themselves up to A Company. They said that their whole company—about 200 strong—would 'come over if sent for'.

It was the enemy who renewed the struggle on 4th May. At 4.30 a.m., after heavy mortar fire, German infantry attacked

Point 212 and Point 214. The three forward companies of the Gordons, A, B and D, were equal to the occasion, although the enemy came on with great perseverance. D Company (now commanded by Captain J. S. Crewdson) repulsed one attack after an exchange of grenades, a burst of Tommy-gun fire completing the rout. Major Fleming—a first-rate company commander and the senior officer remaining of the old 'peace-time' 6th Gordons—was shot through the head while conducting the defence. Major R. L. H. Bridgman of B Company, who took his place, was hit almost immediately; and then Lieutenant Lawrie exercised command with great coolness and judgment until the engagement ended.

Meanwhile about twenty German tanks had come through the Gab Gab Gap and opened fire on the Gordons from the rear. The enemy infantry drew off about 6 a.m., but it was not until nearly eight o'clock that our anti-tank guns began to deal with the German armour. Nine of the tanks were hit before the remainder disappeared from view.

Lieutenant Lawrie was awarded the Military Cross. The fine leadership of Company Sergeant-Major Garioch, A Company, earned him an immediate commission. Lieutenant Fordyce was wounded but refused to leave until next day, when there seemed little more fighting to do. The stretcher bearers, as always, worked admirably with no thought of themselves.

The Gordon casualties, many of them suffered during the preliminary bombardment, amounted to thirty killed and wounded, besides the loss in officers.

And now the worst was over. On 5th May the Gordons held their front positions as a firm base while the 3rd Brigade, reaping where the Guards and Gordons had sown, attacked and captured the remainder of Djebel Bel Aoukaz. This was accomplished before dawn of the 6th, the day when the IX Corps launched their great attack, with Tunis as the objective of the armoured divisions. The Gordons, still under 24th Guards Brigade command, watched the start of this offensive from their vantage point in the hills, and German shell fire cost them six casualties.

On 7th May the Battalion were withdrawn to Point 144 and rejoined their own Brigade. There was little time to rest and reorganise, for at 7.45 p.m. orders were received to move in trucks at half-past eight. The destination of the Gordons was Djedeida on the Medjerda river, and their task was to assist in clearing enemy elements from the countryside.

The route, over badly marked tracks which did not correspond with the map, would have been difficult enough to follow by day: by night, driving without lights, it was clearly impossible, apart from the fact that heavy rain was fast turning the dust to mud. At 9.30 p.m. the Gordons climbed out of their trucks and went forward on foot. The march was probably the most unpleasant experience that the Battalion had so far endured. They plodded on in wet and bitter cold; and the men were wearing tropical clothing—khaki drill and shorts.

At nine o'clock next morning, having covered nearly twenty miles, the weary, cold and hungry Gordons approached the river. They halted for two hours and then came orders to cross the river and scour the country as far as Chaouat: one squadron of tanks would assist.

B and D Companies led the way, each with one platoon riding on tanks. Chaouat and nearby Si Abdallah were entered without a sign of opposition and two prisoners were brought in. B Company found a hospital containing 450 German patients, fifteen American, and one British. During the day about a hundred prisoners came through the Battalion area.

The Gordons found time to rest and wash, but they had to move again on the afternoon of the 9th, and next day the whole of the 1st Division were ordered to the region of Pont du Fahs. Orders and counter-orders followed. Moves were sudden and generally at the most inconvenient hours—often in the middle of the night. On the 12th the Gordons found that the tract of country they had been detailed to clear was being very well looked after by the 7th Rifle Brigade, to whom Germans and Italians were surrendering gladly. The fighting was over, for on this day the German Commander-in-Chief, Colonel-General von Arnim, made his formal capitulation.

Few of the enemy had contrived to escape to Europe, and the number of prisoners exceeded a quarter of a million, while vast quantities of weapons and equipment fell into the hands of the Allies. Victory in North Africa was complete.

TUNISIA—PANTELLERIA—TUNISIA
1943

On 14th May 1943, the 6th Gordons moved to the coast about four miles east of Hamman Lif. The countryside was bare, but the Jocks could indulge in sea bathing and there was little work to do. Church services were greatly appreciated by all ranks, and something of a holiday spirit prevailed.

At this time the Battalion were very weak in numbers, requiring 244 men to complete establishment and provide one-third of the prescribed first reinforcements.

The next move, on 19th May, was via Grombalia and Enfidaville to an area a little way east of Sousse, where the Gordons bivouaced in an olive grove. Next day Captains G. Donald and J. S. Crewdson and Lieutenant E. N. Grace, with twenty-five other ranks, represented the 6th Gordons at the Victory Parade in Tunis.

A draft of two officers and 175 arrived that evening. They were Highlanders, but came from the Black Watch. The Battalion were still short of six officers, but Lieut.-Colonel Peddie preferred to wait until he could get Highlanders—or at least Scotsmen—rather than accept Englishmen.

There were busy days ahead. On 26th May the Battalion began practice with infantry landing craft, embarking and disembarking. The commanding officer warned his company commanders that a new enterprise was in view: he could say no more than that, but it was obvious that the Gordons were intended to take part in some sort of assault landing from the sea. As training continued the men became adept in the use of scrambling nets to pass from landing ship to landing craft; the heavier work consisted in loading vehicles into another type of landing craft and getting them off again. One section per rifle company did Oerlikon training on 'flak ships'.

In the middle of these activities the Gordons found time to play a Free French team at football and beat them by nine goals to one.

On 5th June was announced the award of the Military Cross to Lieutenant G. Reynolds-Payne, and that of the Military Medal to Sergeant J. McConnachie, who had led a platoon with great courage and ability throughout the Tunis campaign, and to Private E. Brammer.

The plan for the capture of Pantelleria ('Operation Corkscrew') was divulged on 7th June.

As a first step in carrying their Mediterranean offensive into Europe the Allies were preparing for the invasion of Sicily, but before this could be launched there was work for the 1st Division. About fifty miles east of Cap Bon the volcanic island of Pantelleria, converted by the Italians into a fortress and air base, provided an excellent point of observation which could give the enemy ample warning of any Allied movement towards Sicily.[1] Also, it was reckoned that eighty fighter aircraft were based upon Pantelleria. Our aim was to occupy the island with the minimum of delay and the minimum expenditure of lives and material.

From 7th to 11th June Allied bombers attacked Pantelleria by day and night and our cruisers and destroyers bombarded the shore batteries near the harbour. The reply of the Italian gunners was feeble, but two calls to surrender were ignored.

Under cover of air and sea bombardment the 1st Division would make their landing. The 3rd Brigade were to go in first and establish a beach-head ; then the 2nd Brigade were to pass through, the Gordons following the 2nd North Staffordshire and making for Scirate.

The Gordons embarked on 10th June, B, C, and D Companies moving to Sfax, where they boarded the landing ships *Queen Emma* and *Princess Beatrix*. Battalion headquarters and A Company marched to the docks at Sousse, where Battalion headquarters embarked in the *Royal Ulsterman* and A Company in an infantry landing craft.

By 6 a.m. on the 11th the flotilla was passing Cape Bon. The morning was clear and the sea was calm. About half-past nine the first parties of Gordons were transferred from ship to landing craft and moved in towards Pantelleria, now visible about seven miles away. Soon the smoke and dust of the Allied bombardment almost blotted out the island. At noon the *Royal Ulsterman* relayed the signal ' No hindrance to landing of troops '. Forty minutes later all resistance was at an end.

About this time three Messerschmitts made a sudden attack upon the Headquarters ship, and their bombs, all ' near misses ', were a sharp reminder that anti-aircraft defence could not be neglected with impunity.

The landing of the Gordons proceeded smoothly during the afternoon, and by 3.45 p.m. the Battalion were assembled in the town of Pantelleria, which is at the north-western tip of the island. Three hours later they began to move on Scirate, using both the coast road leading south and an inland route.

Progress was slow, owing to the damage to the roads caused by the attentions of our bombers, and the Gordon vehicles could not

[1] See sketch on p. 221.

get very far. The Italian soldiery were eager to give themselves up, a whole battalion surrendering to D Company who also gathered in the commander of the coastal artillery.

At night the Gordons settled down at Scirate, having covered about four miles, and established a cage for prisoners of war. The wireless link with the Brigade was further back, as part of the coast road had been destroyed altogether by the bombardment and no vehicle could follow the troops.

The Battalion's only casualty on this day was a private soldier wounded by an Italian revolver while looking for booby traps. No-one else was hurt during the five days spent on the island.

On the morrow the Gordons were permitted to withdraw from Scirate so that they might be within easier reach of rations and water, but it was necessary to clear the coastal regions south of Scirate. The Gordon carriers were soon able to get supplies through by the inland route which ran past the airfield.

Near the little harbour of Porto di Scauri, about two miles from Scirate, the Gordons found a hospital with a staff twice as numerous as the patients; and in the harbour itself were two German landing-craft, laden with food and water, which appeared to have arrived just before the surrender.

The Gordons were ordered to prepare a mobile column as a precaution against ' any attempted hostile landing by sea or air ', and contributed some Bren gunners to reinforce the anti-aircraft defence at Pantelleria harbour. Opportunities were to be given for the men to rest and bathe in the sea, but many guards and patrols were required, and the enemy landing craft at Porto di Scauri needed to be unloaded.

The local people kept sending deputations to Lieut.-Colonel Peddie to say that they were starving. He had no authority and no facilities for collecting and distributing food, but he arranged for flour to be given to a local baker so that the Italians might obtain bread. No interpreters were available, so explanations were difficult until some of the Carabiniere were sent back to assist. Prisoners continued to come in with alacrity and, apart from the food question, the inhabitants seemed indifferent to the turn of events. They had suffered few casualties, for the many deep caves had provided excellent shelter from the Allied bombardment.

The Gordons left Pantelleria in landing craft on the evening of 16th June, the choppy sea making the return passage to Africa an uneasy one. Next morning they landed at Sousse and moved to their old camp where they were glad to welcome back two sergeants and seventeen others, recovered casualties of the Tunisian campaign.

One embarrassing result of the victory in North Africa was the enormous numbers of prisoners of war who required to be guarded and looked after until they could be shipped away. Some of these responsibilities now fell upon the 6th Gordons.

On 24th June the Battalion moved in R.A.S.C. transport through Enfidaville and Tunis to Ghardimaou, which was reached next day. Here the Gordons had not only to provide the guards and escorts, and transport for drawing rations, but also most of the administrative staff for a prisoners-of-war camp holding 10,000 men. Major J. L. Baucher of the Gordons was appointed camp commandant.

It was evident to all ranks that they were to have no part in the invasion of Sicily and, for the time at least, there seemed to be nothing ahead for them but a spell of monotonous 'non-operational' duties.

The prisoners at Ghardimaou were confined in a series of pens each enclosed by a triple Dannert wire obstacle, the whole surrounded by a fence of barbed wire. The Germans, who formed the great majority, gave little trouble, for they were firmly controlled by their own non-commissioned officers; but the Italians were more restive, and several made attempts to escape into the nearby olive groves, which afforded excellent cover. One man, in his break for liberty, was shot by a sentry.

These were unpleasant days for the Gordons. They were in bivouacs, the intense heat was trying in the extreme and conditions, generally, were primitive. Myriads of flies bred disease, and the sick rate mounted as malaria began to take its toll. Reveillé was now at 5 a.m., so that the troops might benefit from the cool of the early morning, for 'after ten o'clock it was too hot to do much'.

On and after 30th June, to the great relief of everyone, the prisoners were drafted away at the rate of over a thousand daily, and the final batch, mostly Czechs and Poles, departed on 4th July. Even then little training could be done by the Battalion, for numbers were short, owing to guard duties of various kinds and the despatch of leave parties to a rest camp at La Calle on the Algerian coast. This camp owed its existence to the initiative of the Gordons, who provided the staff to run it.

Two companies were sent to Tunis for escort duties which included guards for prisoners-of-war trains. Anti-paratroop patrols during the moonlight nights and various monotonous jobs in this 'lines of communication' area kept the rest of the Battalion busy, and all ranks were glad to leave Ghardimaou on 8th August.

The next location was about three miles north of Hammamet, where the Gordons settled down only 400 yards from the sea. On the 12th the two companies rejoined from Tunis, and training could begin in earnest. Two companies went away on the 21st to exercise with tanks for ten days.

On 4th September at a Divisional ceremonial parade the troops were inspected by General Eisenhower, who took the salute at the march past which followed. Another 'occasion' came ten days later, when the pipes and drums of the 6th Gordons, massed with those of the 1st Scots Guards and 1st Irish Guards from the 24th Guards Brigade, played Retreat.

Meanwhile great events had passed the 6th Gordons by. The fall of Mussolini became known on 25th July. On 17th August Allied troops were in Messina, and the conquest of Sicily was complete. On the morning of 3rd September our Eighth Army crossed the Straits of Messina and landed on the mainland of Italy. Six days later, after the surrender of Italy had been announced, came the Allied landing at Salerno. Italy, however, remained in the German grip, and the Allies were committed to a new and arduous campaign.

Now the training of the 6th Gordons seemed to assume a definite purpose, although there was no hint as to what the next task of the 1st Division would be. Many officers and non-commissioned officers of the Battalion attended special courses of instruction in mule pack transport, rock climbing, and mountain warfare. The Gordons, after being equipped with mule packs and 'man packs', left on 14th October for the mountain warfare training area near Grombalia. Work began in earnest a few days later, and continued into November. One exercise which included a mountain trek lasting from 9 a.m. till 3 p.m., with each man packing 25 lb. besides his weapons and ammunition, may well be remembered.

CONQUEST OF SICILY

1943

A New Venture

When the Highland Division moved from Tunisia to the Algerian coast regimental officers and men welcomed the change, but could only guess at the reason for it.

The journey was not without interest. The 5th/7th Gordons describe how, on 12th May, they drove 100 miles to Kasserine by way of the sacred city of Kairouan through hills 'more difficult than those at Gabes', and a countryside littered with wrecked tanks and guns. Kasserine was reached by two o'clock in the afternoon, there being little traffic on the roads and no delays. Next day, when over 130 miles were covered, the Algerian frontier was soon crossed and, after passing through Tebessa, a good run among the hills brought the Battalion to Ain Beida, where they harboured for the night. On the 14th they travelled a similar distance through a landscape 'more and more beautiful'; and on the 15th interest grew as the column passed through the Kerrata gorge, seven miles long with over-hanging cliffs on either side. This day brought the Highlanders to their destination, Djidjelli, standing high upon the cliffs about 150 miles east of the port of Algiers.

To the Gordon battalions the term 'combined operations' now acquired a real significance. Great emphasis was laid upon physical fitness: preliminary training included rock climbing by day and night, and swimming. The 1st Gordons' assault course provided practice in climbing ropes and negotiating wire obstacles. The 5th/7th say that 'for six weeks we jumped in and out of boats, ran up and down hills, carried enormous loads, bathed, drank wine and enjoyed odd days off', but this does not present the whole picture.

Lieut.-Colonel Fausset-Farquhar, with a training cadre of the 1st Gordons, had arrived at Djidjelli in advance, and the party had imbibed a deal of knowledge concerning combined operations. When the companies arrived, the commanding officer was able to explain in some detail what would be required of them, and mentioned the word 'invasion'. But he could not divulge where the landing was to be.

The Gordon battalions—in common with the whole Division —were making their first acquaintance with landing craft of various types, but chiefly with infantry landing craft (L.C.I.), which carried

200 men and their equipment, and the smaller assault landing craft (L.C.A.), which took one platoon ready for battle. To embark in and to disembark from these vessels, as well as to load and unload them, meant the practice of a routine which led up to tactical exercises starting with the passage from ship to shore and ending with the establishment of a beach-head.

As soon as the Divisional plan took shape, the 1st Gordons were detached from the 153rd Brigade to form, under 154th Brigade command, an independent battle group which included certain supporting arms—a battery of 3·7-inch howitzers, a detachment of sappers, a machine-gun company, and a platoon of 4·2-inch mortars.

Training continued by day and night and became increasingly strenuous. Hill climbing imposed a heavy strain on the mortar detachments and the signallers and others who carried the heavier loads. Battalion and brigade exercises were followed by a Divisional exercise wherein the troops were embarked at dusk and landed at first light next morning on a rocky shore through surf which drenched many to the skin.

Aerial photographs of the coast where the Division were to land were studied and sand models were used for tactical exercises; but the names of the physical features and the objectives were suppressed. The 'cover plan' to ensure secrecy included the attachment to the 1st Gordons of a Greek officer who 'recognised' the air photographs as part of the Greek coastline.

In the one day a week 'off' something of a holiday spirit prevailed among the Highlanders. Cinemas and performances by 'The Balmorals' and E.N.S.A. concert parties were well attended. Trucks conveyed Gordons on sight-seeing expeditions. The massed pipes and drums of the 153rd Brigade played in Djidjelli. A rest camp was opened at Constantine.

Towards the end of May Brigadier Graham left the Brigade to become G.O.C. 56th (London) Division. He took a regretful farewell of what he termed 'a happy family' after three years in command, and all were sorry to see him go. His successor proved to be Brigadier H. Murray, wounded at El Alamein while commanding the 1st Gordons, and the 1st Gordons were as glad to see him again as he was to see them. He paid his first visit to the 5th/7th Battalion on 4th June, an informal affair, but it is said that he made a 'pretty thorough inspection'. To officers and men he 'seemed to be a man of outstanding quality, both as a speaker and a leader'.

A draft of two officers and forty-nine other ranks—almost fresh from Home—had joined the 5th/7th Gordons on 1st June. They were Scots, but not Gordon Highlanders. On the 7th the Battalion received back two of their men who had been captured in the Garci Hills sector and released in Tunis after the capitulation. They reported that as prisoners of war they found the food bad, 'and the tea undrinkable'.

The 1st Gordons received a visit from Sir James Grigg, Secretary of State for War, accompanied by General Alexander, who was to command the Allied forces in the new campaign. And on 19th June the Battalion provided a Guard of Honour for the King at Algiers. His Majesty expressed his regret that he could not come further east to see the Highland Division.

For the Gordon battalions the move from Djidjelli began on 24th June, when advanced parties left for Sousse, a two days journey for the vehicles which went by road. The companies were taken by sea.

Inland the weather seemed cold, but it was hot enough at the concentration area about seven miles south-east of Sousse, where 'in blinding dust and dirt' the Highlanders began their final preparations. Nevertheless all were in good form, and presented a picture of physical fitness as they went about their camp duties stripped to the waist.

Where in Europe they were to land still remained a secret. On 30th June Major-General Wimberley sent a personal message to all ranks of the Highland Division: he said that they had not been present at 'the last surrender of their Desert adversaries' because they had already been selected to take part in another big enterprise, 'the invasion of Europe'. But the Divisional commander did not mention Sicily.

At the beginning of July the Gordons began to enter the assembly area where 'men and vehicles were fed, stage by stage, into the landing craft' The carriers, anti-tank guns, tanks, mountain guns, and essential stores were loaded first, all in their proper sequence, so that they should be in the right order for landing on the beaches.

On 1st July Brigadier Murray had delivered a lecture, described as very informative, to the 153rd Brigade. 'The only thing we don't know is where we are going.' In their assembly area the 5th/7th Gordons found themselves well looked after by the Welsh Guards, who were running the camp.

The movement of the 1st Gordons, under 154th Brigade command, was on rather different lines. On 4th July Brigadier Rennie addressed officers and men, outlining the special task of the 1st Gordons Group. Next day Battalion headquarters and Headquarters Company marched to Sousse harbour and embarked in two L.C.I.'s. The remainder of the Battalion stood fast.

To the 5th/7th Gordons embarkation meant a march of nearly ten miles with full packs in the blazing sun before boarding their

L.C.I.'s. The Battalion were split up, with their attached sappers and machine-gunners, between three of these craft.

On the afternoon of 5th July the assembly of landing craft gradually emerged from the harbour of Sousse and at sea joined the huge invasion convoy, an orderly expanse of shipping marshalled in six columns and escorted by a cruiser, two destroyers, and a number of motor launches.

No air cover was discernible, and the troops manned the ships' A.A. guns while Bren guns were made ready for action; but we were masters of the air as well as the sea. As the light faded three aircraft approached the convoy. They proved to be our own.

After an uneventful passage over a calm sea, the convoy arrived off Malta on the morning of the 6th, but it was late in the afternoon before every vessel had berthed in Valetta harbour. There was, of course, no thought of unloading the landing craft: the troops disembarked with their personal kits and weapons and were conveyed by transport to their camps.

The Maltese gave everyone a warm welcome: the 5th/7th Gordons say that they were 'treated like kings'. In their camp they found new blankets, new tents, and new cooking gear; and, as restrictions were few, the Jocks were able to explore the island freely. Malta was new ground to them, and the Battalion called the two days they spent there 'a glorious holiday'.

On 7th July General Montgomery visited each camp, calling the eager men around his car to compliment them upon their physical fitness and to remind them that they were among the chosen to carry the war into Europe: the quicker this was done and the victory gained, the sooner everybody would be back in their own homes. Once arrived in Malta, the officers had had no doubt concerning their objective, but after what General Montgomery said the general impression among all ranks was that ' Sicily might be the place '.

While at Malta the 5th/7th Gordons benefited from the Brigade decision to lighten the load of the soldier for the assault landings. A skeleton battle order was devised, packs to be dumped and only resumed when the beach-head had been won.

The Landing

Early on the morning of 9th July lorries were ready at all the camps to convey the troops back to their landing craft. Embarkation proceeded smoothly. Soon after mid-day the vessels began to leave, Pipe-Major Anderson playing those of the 1st Gordons out of Valetta harbour.

All were now aware that they were Sicily bound, and 'The Soldier's Guide to Sicily' was distributed. But in many a man the excitement and interest aroused were soon eclipsed by the mood of the fickle Mediterranean. As the light faded and the crowded flat-bottomed landing craft bucketed along against a head wind through rough grey-green seas, no remedy for sea-sickness seemed of much avail. Could any landing, however inhospitable the coast and however strong the opposition, prove worse than the misery of this passage?

To commanders and staffs the weather was a source of great anxiety for another reason. Once launched upon its way the expedition could hardly be recalled without admitting failure before the issue was joined; yet rough seas might make landings impossible or, at least, disorganise them to such an extent as to ruin the invasion plan.

As darkness fell the great convoy of sea-borne might was joined by the big ships bringing the 1st Gordon companies from Africa. The troops had moved by road from the Sousse area to Sfax on 7th July and embarked in the *Royal Scotsman, Royal Ulsterman* and *Queen Emma*, which carried assault landing craft slung out-board. After spending the next day in harbour the convoy sailed in time to make its rendezvous with the main invasion fleet.

The descent upon Sicily, the first big combined operation undertaken by the Allies, had been planned and re-planned, prepared in meticulous detail, and carefully rehearsed. In the Eighth Army the XIII Corps were to land south of Syracuse, with Syracuse and the anchorage at Augusta as their immediate objectives; the XXX Corps were to come in with the Highland Division astride Cape Passero, the south-eastern tip of the island, and the 1st Canadian Division on the left; the 231st (Malta) Brigade would link up the two Corps landings. The American Seventh Army were to land further west, and the Allies aimed to drive the enemy from Sicily by an advance converging upon Messina.

To secure Rada di Portopalo, with its beach named Amber Beach where supplies would eventually be landed, the Highland Division intended to attack it from flanks and rear. Amber Beach was considered so obvious a choice for an assault landing that its defences could be reckoned as particularly strong; but by choosing this difficult point, there would seem to be a greater chance of surprise. The 154th Brigade, coming ashore on the western flank, were to seize a ridge called by us Goal Ridge which lay nearly three miles inland and dominated Amber Beach. On the eastern flank the 1st Gordons Group were to land at Cape Passero and on the coast immediately to the north. They would form their own beach-head and secure the eastern end of Goal Ridge.

As the fleets neared the coast of Sicily the weather seemed a little kinder, but there was still a high sea running when the parent ships lowered their assault landing craft and the 1st Gordons climbed into them. This hazardous operation was performed without mishap, and the 1st Gordons Group set course for the waiting position some two miles south-east of Cape Passero, where

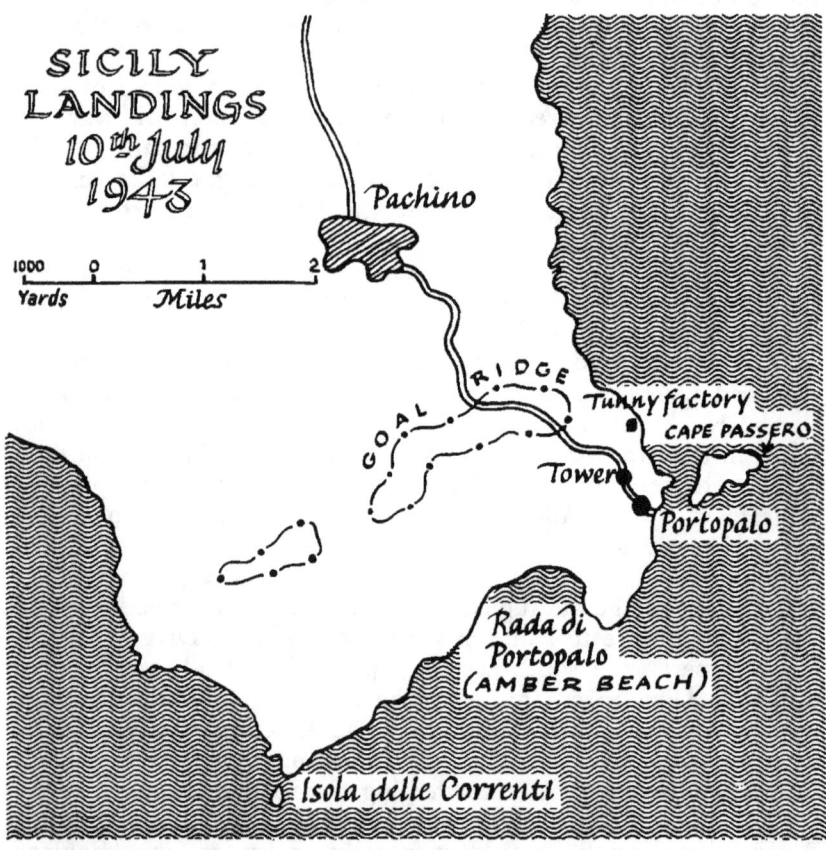

the landing craft took up their stations for the run in. There was no moon. At 2.45 a.m. on 10th July the start for the shore was made and as the vessels approached many enemy searchlights were directed skywards, perhaps in anticipation of attack from the air. The invaders were unseen, and soon the landmarks which had been studied so carefully on maps and air photographs became faintly discernible; and each craft seemed to be coming in to its appointed place.

The landing of the 1st Gordons on the rocky surf-bound shore of Sicily was a wet one, Major C. N. Barker, the 'unit landing officer', having to swim for it; but nothing damped the ardour of the Highlanders. Resistance was feeble in the extreme. On the right B Company touched down at the tunny factory at 3.45 a.m., and a very short encounter disposed of the Italian defenders, who were all killed or captured. In a building above the factory a Breda gun was taken after a little argument with grenade and bayonet, and B Company then proceeded to secure the Tower, a familiar landmark from seaward. Next on the left D Company had come in and occupied without trouble the fishing village of Portopalo. A Company had cleared up Cape Passero island after a scuffle, taking two prisoners.

Lieut.-Colonel Fausset-Farquhar established his headquarters under cover of a ledge behind the Tower, and was soon in communication with all his companies. He watched C Company come up from reserve to work forward towards the eastern end of Goal Ridge which looked down on Amber Beach and to the northward gave a view of the little town of Pachino.

Machine guns had been humped ashore, but day was breaking and the Gordons still awaited the arrival of the heavier supporting arms. Fortunately there were no signs of a counter-attack. Landing places for the tank landing craft proved hard to find, for the passages between the rocks were narrow, but the beach parties and the Royal Navy surmounted all difficulties. Almost the first arrival was a bull-dozer, which broke down a ten-foot bank and opened up an exit from the beach.

By 8 a.m. all the supporting arms of the 1st Gordons Group were on shore, the 3·7-inch howitzers were in position, and the tanks were starting for Goal Ridge.

C Company had made good progress. On their way forward an A.A. gun had opened on them, but was quickly silenced by the attack of one platoon. As the Gordons reached the top of the ridge the retreating enemy blew up an ammunition dump, and this marked the end of the affair. At 9 a.m. the ridge was completely in our hands, and two troops of tanks had taken up hull-down positions.

Back on the beaches willing Italians were helping to unload stores, and all the craft of the Group were cleared by ten o'clock. Lieut.-Colonel Fausset-Farquhar could be satisfied that his task had been completed with trifling loss.

D Company of the Gordons were now ordered to move along to the centre of Goal Ridge and reconnoitre a passage through a minefield down to Amber Beach. This was duly done.

At noon the carriers started off towards Pachino and, as they reached the outskirts of the town, they came under desultory fire which soon ceased. The carriers entered Pachino in company with a troop of Sherman tanks and the leading elements of the 5th Black Watch. Before anything more was done the 1st Gordons Group, whose landing had been entirely independent and self-supporting, was dissolved and the Battalion rejoined their own Brigade.

The 5th/7th Gordons were later in landing, the 153rd Brigade —two battalions—being kept as a floating reserve. The nature of their task depended upon the fortunes of the 154th Brigade who might require assistance in securing Goal Ridge: meanwhile the Gordons, tossing in their landing craft well out to sea, waited in the darkness while Brigadier Rennie's battalions went in to land, supported by a naval bombardment in which, for the first time, 'rocket ships' took part.

By 5 a.m. it was known that the landings were successful, and the craft carrying the 153rd Brigade began to close the coast. Not much more than an hour later the Gordons, who were the first to arrive, reached the shore and disembarked with surprising ease. Many men landed dry-shod, and few got wet above the knees. The Battalion found themselves in the vicinity of Isola delle Correnti with the companies well dispersed and under control. Prisoners were already assembled, one party of about seventy Italians being headed by an officer carrying a suitcase and accompanied by his dog.

Just beyond the beach was a field containing a crop of ripe tomatoes, which provided a welcome addition to haversack rations. Another discovery was that of a number of Italian uniforms which had been hurriedly buried, obviously by certain reluctant warriors who had decided to resume civilian status.

Then occurred an unfortunate accident which deprived the Gordons of their commanding officer. He was issuing orders to his 'operations group' when one officer let fall his machine-pistol: its accidental discharge wounded Lieut.-Colonel Hay in the thigh, and the state of mind of the unfortunate victim may be imagined. Major B. C. A. Napier, the next senior officer, assumed command of the Battalion.

Following reports that the left of the 154th Brigade needed assistance, the 5th/7th Gordons were ordered to reinforce that flank. Then it transpired that all was well on the left, and during the morning the Battalion concentrated under the western end of Goal Ridge.

In the meantime the 5th Black Watch had landed and had cleared the whole of the foreshore so that Amber Beach became available as the main landing place.

Advance Inland

By the early afternoon all was in train for the advance inland, so the 5th/7th Gordons moved north towards Pachino, in 'leaps and bounds'. Without incident they arrived at the air landing strip west of Pachino, and here two troops of Sherman tanks overtook them and passed through to the head of the column. Soon afterwards contact was made with the Canadians, who had landed further to the west.

When the head of the Battalion approached a cross-roads about a mile beyond Pachino firing broke out. It seemed that the 231st Brigade, who had landed on the east coast, were held up east of the Pachino-Noto road. Two companies of the Gordons were therefore deployed and advanced with the tanks to take the enemy in flank; but no enemy was encountered, and the Battalion halted about three miles north of Pachino. They bivouaced in a vineyard and found their first night on Sicilian soil cold and comfortless, for they had no blankets. The carriers and the transport were still somewhere in rear.

Near the patch of scrub dignified by the name of Battalion headquarters were found two American paratroopers who had landed a long way from their comrades, and had been lying up all day. The unfamiliar uniforms and the difference between the accents of Michigan and Buckie had made these worthies uncertain as to whether they had fallen among friends or foes, and so reluctant to declare themselves. As they were recovering from their first combat leap they 'did not feel so good', but were glad to be assured of an undisturbed night's rest after they had been regaled with tea and tomatoes.

The 1st Gordons had moved up through Pachino just before dark to spend the night in Brigade reserve just north of the town. Hostile aircraft were bombing the landing beaches on the east coast, less than three miles away, but the Battalion, with the exception of the sentries, slept soundly. Few had had any rest for the past thirty-six hours.

On Sunday, 11th July, the 153rd Brigade pressed on astride the Pachino-Noto road, with the 5th/7th Gordons and the 5th Black Watch still in the lead.

The Gordons, with their two troops of tanks, speak of a 'long and tiresome hike', sometimes across open country, taking all short cuts available, and along the roads where movement off them was difficult. For some of the distance Highlanders rode on the tanks. The Battalion had kept to the west of the main road, but came back to it in order to occupy, as a measure of precaution, a defensive

position at the bridge over the river Tellaro. Here A Company brought in twelve Italian prisoners and, later on, when some of the Gordons were washing at a stream, twenty-seven Italians, led by an officer, walked up to surrender. There was no sign of opposition, and every kind of transport, from D.U.K.W.s—2½-ton amphibious trucks—to horses and carts, all filled with troops, flowed forward over the bridge for the remainder of the day.

Still in Brigade reserve, the 1st Gordons had taken the road soon after dawn, passing through troops of the 231st Brigade. Water was short and the sun was hot, so to the Gordons, who were carrying full packs, any form of transport was welcome. A number of mules were commandeered for the later stages of the march, and the medical officer, whose stores were among the weightier loads, finished astride a recalcitrant mule to the admiration of all beholders.

The Battalion halted for a mid-day rest and a meal about half a mile behind the 5th/7th Gordons, in the vicinity of a peach grove which was duly appreciated. Then they received orders to pass through the rest of the Brigade and occupy the Montagna-Avola high ground beyond Avola.

The 1st Gordons were on the move again by 4 p.m., the transport problem being tackled by the impressment of two D.U.K.W.s which had come up with Divisional supplies, and a number of anti-tank gun portées. By using a shuttle service these vehicles helped all companies forward and cut down their marching time; otherwise the Battalion could hardly have reached their allotted positions before darkness fell.

B and C Companies were then about three miles forward of Avola on the Montagna di Avola heights, having been ferried up the steep mountain roads in D.U.K.W.s; A Company outside the town on the coast road; D Company astride the southern exits of the town. The carrier platoon with a party of sappers were sent ahead as far as the river Cassibile to safeguard a bridge which the enemy had prepared for demolition.

The advance had been so rapid that none of the usual troop-carrying vehicles were yet available. Consequently the leading troops were obliged to make use of whatever transport came to hand in order to save time; and the 1st Gordons had managed pretty well in this respect. As for the 5th/7th Battalion, Major Napier had been told to aim at the provision of one bicycle or mule per man, and the Jocks certainly rose to the occasion. Hand-carts and other contraptions were not despised, but more than 150 mules were collected; and when the Corps commander viewed the motley cavalcade he congratulated the Battalion on their animal management.

On this day, 11th July, both Gordon battalions had a glimpse of General Montgomery who, accompanied by Lord Louis Mountbatten—Chief of Combined Operations—beamed on them from the height of a D.U.K.W. in which he drove past. The news was good: the XIII Corps in Syracuse, the Canadians moving on Ragusa, and the U.S. Seventh Army doing well in the west.

The 1st Gordons did not move on 12th July except to send a carrier patrol north-westward as far as Canicattini, where they made contact with a company of the 5th/7th Battalion.

The 5th/7th were early astir on this day, for the 153rd Brigade had orders to relieve the 151st Brigade (50th Division) facing west on the high ground north-west of Cassibile. Following in rear of the 5th Black Watch the Gordons, who started at 6 a.m., had a long and dusty march which ended in a stiff climb. The relief was not easy, for only one road existed, but all was accomplished before the evening. While others rested, however, D Company were despatched to Canicattini Bagni, about five miles away to the north-west. Added to Major Glennie's command were a platoon of machine guns and a section of carriers, and the detachment entered the little town in the evening, to receive a warm welcome from the people. Major Glennie was appointed town major, so that order might be maintained.

On 12th July the Eighth Army 'bridge-head' extended from the vicinity of Augusta south-westward through Ragusta, were it linked up with the Americans. The advance was now to be northward near the coast, combined with a sweep north-westward further inland.

Vizzini—Sferro

The 1st Gordons moved next morning, their objective being Francofonte, almost due west of Augusta. Lieut.-Colonel Fausset-Farquhar took his company commanders forward on reconnaissance in advance of the Battalion, but the party was fired on and an artillery officer wounded. In the meantime orders had been changed: Francofonte was to be the objective of the 152nd Brigade. Brigadier Murray met the Gordons' main column near Monterosso Alno, and switched it to the road leading to Vizzini. Consequently the 1st Gordons spent the night about three miles south of that hill-top town, the leading companies, under spasmodic shell fire, having occupied a hill position as daylight was fading. In front of the Battalion were the 5th Black Watch.

During the day efforts to occupy Vizzini had been unsuccessful. The 231st Brigade approaching from Buccheri had been held up, and the 23rd Armoured Brigade were waiting to join the 153rd Brigade in order to press the advance northward.

Soon after dawn of the 14th the 1st Gordons received their orders. The advance upon Vizzini from the south was to begin at noon on a two-battalion front : 5th Black Watch on the left, 1st Gordons on the right. Actually the two battalions were to 'close in' on the town but not become involved in street fighting, because the 153rd Brigade were to be kept intact to take up the pursuit. If necessary the 231st Brigade would fight their way into Vizzini, thereby clearing the route for the further advance.

The day was the hottest experienced since the Highlanders landed in Sicily. Following five rounds per gun from the batteries of the 127th Field Regiment, the advance began over open country devoid of cover. Soon, however, the Gordons were scrambling up terraced hillsides among vines and almond trees, exposed to the fire of rifles and automatics. By a skilful combination of fire and movement and a bold approach which seems to have shaken the nerve of the defenders, the leading companies suffered very little loss : indeed D Company, who had one killed and three wounded by mortar fire while moving up to the start line, reported only one casualty thereafter. Well before darkness set in the Gordons had a good grip on their portion of Vizzini, with A Company at the cemetery on the right and D Company with a footing in the quarry below the large church called the 'cathedral'. Access to good spring water was a great boon after the heat and burden of the day.

As a precaution against snipers, C Company were moved up to put men on the roof of the cathedral, whence a large part of the town was under observation. On the vineyard slopes where Battalion headquarters were established, a complete Italian artillery unit made their surrender.

All this had been accomplished while out of communication with the Brigade, and Lieut.-Colonel Fausset-Farquhar saw no reason why he should not push his advantage further. However, it transpired that the Division who had heard nothing of the Gordons' progress, were ordering a bombardment of the eastern part of Vizzini. This bombardment was duly carried out and the Gordons took advantage of it. They formed up about 1 a.m. on the 15th and 'oiled forward' into the town without trouble. There was practically no fighting. Many hundred Germans surrendered, most of them belonging to the re-formed Hermann Goering Division who had fought in Tunis ; and under a railway bridge the anti-tank platoon under Captain W. R. MacMillan captured 500 Italians. A complete field hospital was discovered in a tunnel. Large quantities of foodstuffs were found in Vizzini, and these had to be placed under guard to prevent looting by the Sicilian population, who had a particular taste for chocolate.

So Vizzini passed into possession of the Highlanders, the western half of the town having fallen to the Black Watch. The Gordons, who had had Lieutenant K. Angus and a few men wounded, breakfasted in the piazza and then moved out northward to an area of farmland, where they rested and cleaned up.

The Vizzini episode may be rounded off by describing the advance of the 5th/7th Gordons. They came forward through Canicattini Bagni on 13th July behind the 152nd Brigade, who were making for Francofonte. By ferrying the companies and dumping stores there was enough transport available to bring the Battalion on without marching; but traffic congestion prevented more than two companies from reaching Buccheri before nightfall. The remainder of the Gordons reached this town at 2 a.m. on the 14th, but in the meantime D Company and the carrier platoon had been sent to clear the small hill towns of Ferla and Cassaro, some miles to the east of Buccheri. This was done without trouble, ninty-three prisoners of the Napoli Division, including a colonel and three other officers, being gathered in. The colonel was in a very emotional condition: first weeping in shame of surrender without a fight, and then smiling at the prospect of being out of the war.

Most of 14th July was spent by the 5th/7th Gordons 'sitting around waiting for word to move'. Much depended upon the occupation of Vizzini, but this was expected to happen by next morning. Later the Battalion were warned that on the morning of the 15th they would come under the command of Brigadier Richards, 23rd Armoured Brigade, for the advance on Miletello and Scordia. In the evening the Gordons moved up from Buccheri along the Vizzini road, the two leading company commanders making the acquaintance of the commander of the leading tank squadron.

On 15th July the 5th/7th Gordons went into action for the first time since they had landed in Sicily. They were ordered to move at 6.30 a.m. but the whole column made slow progress. The route lay through Vizzini. At ten o'clock when the leading tanks were only two miles beyond the town on the Miletello road two self-propelled guns, hidden in buildings beside the railway, opened fire. This was a surprise. The first two tanks were knocked out and a brisk fire fight ensued before the enemy guns were hit and destroyed. A Gordon carrier was badly damaged but no-one was hurt.

The road ahead was still under shell-fire when Brigadier Murray appeared. It was then decided to send A Company of the Gordons to clear the high ground commanding the road, and this was done by two in the afternoon when the shelling ceased. Nothing had been seen of the enemy, and the column made better progress.

Road demolitions about four miles outside Miletello were speedily made good by the sappers and the advance continued through the town and then on through Scordia. When a further eight miles had been covered the line of the river Gorna Lunga was reached and here the column halted for the night.

Miletello was in the wildest confusion when the Highlanders passed through. The inhabitants were looting a German quartermaster's stores, and people were staggering along the streets weighed down by all kinds of treasure trove. One old woman was seen to be bearing off two armfuls of football boots. As for Scordia, all three brigades of the Highland Division had converged upon the town, and the 5th/7th Gordons could not but add to the congestion.

The Battalion was given the task of holding three crossings over the Gorna Lunga. All three appeared to be free of the enemy, but a road bridge had been blown. At 7 a.m. on the 16th Lieutenant Brooks came back from C Company, who were at the wrecked road bridge to say that they were being heavily mortared and expected a counter-attack: also that Lieutenant Patterson and two sections had crossed the river unopposed to reconnoitre at 5 a.m. and had failed to return. A Company were sent forward to reinforce C Company, but the mortaring of the bridge position ceased before noon. C Company reported four men wounded and the machine-gun platoon (1/7th Middlesex) commander killed.

Two hours later three of Patterson's men returned and told their story. The patrol had gone a mile beyond the river. All was quiet, but when they started to return a German tank, two armoured cars and two motor cyclists appeared, opening fire at a hundred yards range. Patterson ordered his men to scatter to cover, but only the three who had hidden in a gully had managed to get away.

C Company were under mortar fire again in the evening before the Battalion were relieved by the 5th Camerons (152nd Brigade) and moved to join their own Brigade further west.

On the morning of the 15th the 153rd Brigade—less the 5th/7th Gordons—received orders to follow on to Scordia 'as opportunity offered'. At 5 p.m. the 1st Gordons joined the column, which was moving north by way of Militello, but then orders were changed. The Brigade were to halt when the head reached a road junction some three and a half miles south-east of Palagonia, which was being attacked from the west by the 1st Hampshire, detached from the 231st Brigade.

As the head of the long, close-packed column of vehicles moved downhill to the road junction and there came to a stop, a squadron of Messerschmitts appeared, and proceeded to shoot up the column with cannon and machine-gun fire. The Divisional commander and the Brigadier were bending over a map in the General's jeep: instantly both sprang for the roadside and took refuge in the ditch, the General arriving with the headphones of his wireless set still attached to him. By some miracle this fearsome and quite unexpected attack resulted in the loss of only two men wounded.

Soon afterwards heavy firing was heard from the direction of Palagonia, but little could be done before darkness fell. The 1st Gordons spent the night on the road some two miles east of the town, with the 5th Black Watch to their right rear.

At first light on 16th July Lieut.-Colonel Fausset-Farquhar received word that the mayor of Palagonia was ready to surrender the town 'to the good British'. Soon afterwards five Italian officers and sixty-five men arrived to give themselves up to D Company. At 9 a.m. the Gordons sent an advanced guard into Palagonia and the whole Battalion followed as soon as blown bridges and other demolitions allowed. The Jocks were received with acclamation, oranges and other fruits being showered on them; and the Battalion took the opportunity to make a few additions to the growing self-acquired 'establishment' of captured vehicles. Headquarters were set up under some orange trees on the outskirts of the town, and the companies occupied defensive positions.

In the evening the commanding officer was ordered to find a carrier patrol to move by moonlight *via* Ramacca and reach a bridge over the Dittaino river about a mile south-west of Sferro. This meant an incursion deep into enemy territory, and Lieut.-Colonel Fausset-Farquhar pointed out to the Brigadier the hazardous nature of the operation. But the patrol had to go. It was specially ordered by the Corps, who wished to know if the bridge were still standing, and required information concerning the enemy defences on the river line.

Captain J. Grant set off with his carriers at 10 p.m., crossed a bridge over the Monaci river three miles south of Ramacca, and started feeling his way up the mountain road towards the village. Then spandau fire opened and enemy movement was seen on either side of the road. The carrier crews dismounted and proceeded to stalk their antagonists, who soon disappeared. Further on an armoured fighting vehicle was discovered 'tucked in to the side of the road', and this also withdrew when the Gordons took to the hillside again. After another mile had been covered, however, the carriers came under heavy and accurate machine-gun and mortar fire: it was obvious that to push on was to court disaster and Captain Grant requested permission to retire. This was given at once, and the carriers returned.

The 16th July saw the 154th Brigade occupy Ramacca with comparative ease, and plans were made to penetrate northward into the Catania plain. Beyond Ramacca open undulating ground extended for over five miles, so a daylight operation was ruled out. When night came the 153rd Brigade and the 154th Brigade (right to left), each on a one-battalion front, were to advance in three bounds, the rear battalions coming through in succession as each objective was attained. There could be no artillery support as so little was known about the enemy's dispositions.

The 1st Gordons were to lead the 153rd Brigade. In the late afternoon the Battalion began to move forward in their transport, crossing the Monaci stream by a track diversion and concentrating in an area north of the blown bridge. B and C Companies had to be ferried up from Palagonia, and were in rear.

Orders were to secure the Catania road. Between five and six in the evening the Gordons began their advance with their carriers leading the way. At first the enemy made no sign, but when the carriers approached the Gorna Lunga river they drew artillery, mortar and machine-gun fire. Skilful manoeuvring brought them with little loss to the river bed, found to be dry. So the carriers crossed and deployed on the further side.

The two leading companies, A on the right and D on the left, had left their vehicles, deployed, and followed the carriers down to the river line, coming under shell and mortar fire as they did so. Their advance continued across the river, but on the further side they were held up for a short time by heavy machine-gun fire coming from the right flank. Captain P. J. Keogh, commanding A Company was hit, but a junior officer, 2nd-Lieutenant M. Morrison, restarted the advance and kept it going until the company were established along a slight rise beyond the Catania road. D Company, also, had arrived on the objective and the Gordons began to dig in by the light of burning haystacks. B and C Companies came forward in support, but were not engaged.

All was accomplished by 9 p.m. In the words of the Brigadier: 'The operation had been carried out extremely well and well up to time and made possible the success of the whole of the subsequent operations.'

Two hours later the 5th Black Watch began to come through. After overcoming some opposition they carried the advance

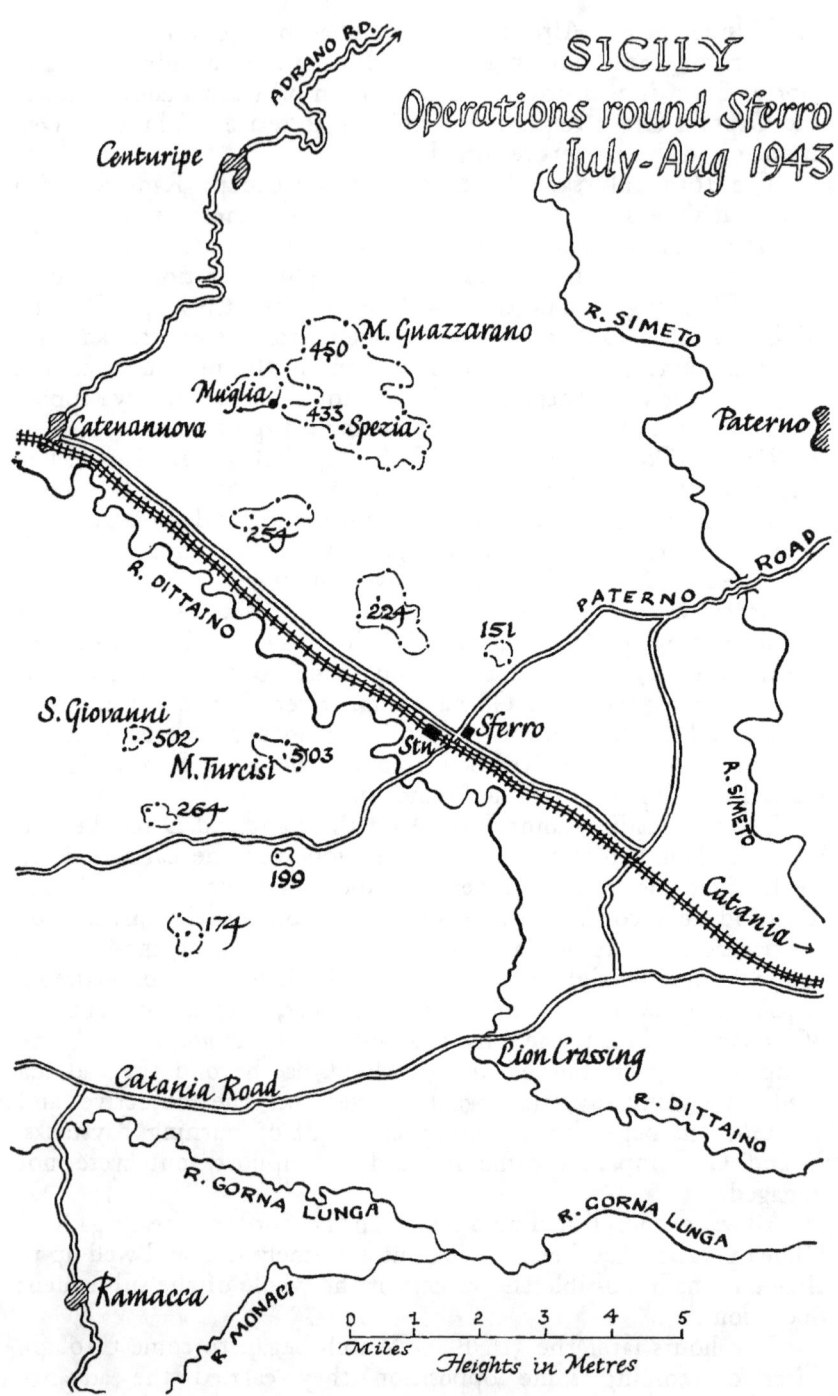

towards higher ground in the locality of what was known as Point 174. Then came the turn of the 5th/7th Gordons.

The companies were ready and waiting to advance long before they were required. It was not until 2 a.m. on the morning of the 18th that the Black Watch reported themselves as secure on their objective, but as soon as this was known Major Napier requested permission to move his Gordons, still in their transport vehicles, as far forward as the Black Watch position if not further.

The Brigadier, however, was averse to 'troops driving into battle in the darkness over ground they did not know'; but Major Napier was allowed to 'debus' his companies immediately in rear of the Black Watch. The Battalion formed up in the old Desert 'box formation' with the intelligence officer's lamp out in front to keep the direction right. When the advance started about 3 a.m. there was no sign of the enemy, but the commanding officer's jeep, which carried his wireless set, became stuck on a rock. Owing to this mishap the Battalion had no communication with the Brigade during the subsequent proceedings.

The way seemed very long and, after careful checking of the distance covered and the direction kept, it seemed obvious that the Black Watch had stopped some way short of their allotted position. However, the Gordons kept going, and when the leading companies appeared to be nearing their objective fire was opened on the right: the carriers were shooting up an Italian truck encountered upon the track they were using. There was no other alarm until, soon after first light, the advance was completed. The Battalion had reached the mountain region west of the Catania plain in the vicinity of Point 264. Monte Turcisi loomed large away to the north-east.

This thrust of the Gordons into hostile territory was attended by considerable risk, for they were beyond artillery support and had no knowledge of the enemy's strength and dispositions. Soon heavy fire opened from the foothills away on the left, where eight spandaus appeared to be in action. Then the Gordons showed that they 'knew their stuff': the mortars covered some skilful manoeuvring by C Company which resulted in the hoisting of the white flag at four machine-gun posts, while the rest of the opposition faded away. Thirty Germans of the Hermann Goering Division and two Italians were captured and six of the enemy lay dead. C Company had only three men wounded, despite their opponents' prodigal expenditure of ammunition.

During this affair the intelligence officer was mistaken for a foeman by the regimental sergeant-major, who assembled a number of servants and others to open fire on him. Fortunately the practice was bad, and the intelligence officer came into Battalion headquarters 'an uninjured if slightly irritable man'.

The intention had been to establish Battalion headquarters in a convenient culvert, but when it was found that a German light machine-gun appeared to be firing on a fixed line straight through the middle of the culvert, other arrangements were made in some haste.

It was difficult to determine the whereabouts of the Germans, but the mortars discovered some targets. The enterprising medical officer had been able to explore a farmhouse in front of the Gordons' position. At breakfast he announced, with great professional satisfaction, that he had been able to carry out an amputation with a carpenter's saw which he had found in the farmhouse. Presumably the German patient had also been discovered there.

About ten o'clock a German motor-cycle combination was driven down a hilly road towards A Company, but turned and managed to escape the fire of the anti-tank guns. An hour later a similar outfit—a very smart turn-out this—appeared on the same road and the anti-tank gunners got busy again, their solid shot bouncing off the rocks and the stone coping of the road. The Jocks roared with laughter as the driver strove to turn and escape, while the fat occupant of the side-car clung on desperately. Then this unhappy man was shot out as the machine was driven over the edge of the road, and the Battalion secured a very indignant prisoner and the mail which was in his charge. The medical officer inherited the motor-cycle and side-car, which served as a mobile regimental aid post for the remainder of the campaign.

Before noon the Brigadier arrived and expressed his satisfaction. For the remainder of the day the 5th/7th Gordons were under a certain amount of shell-fire, which did not worry them very much; but the enemy was still in possession of an eminence about two miles away up the Sferro road called officially Point 199 and by the Battalion 'The Pimples'.

For the most part 18th July was a day of waiting so far as the 1st Gordons were concerned, but their carriers were early in action. The 152nd Brigade had found it difficult to establish a bridge-head over the river Dittaino at the Catania road crossing —known as 'Lion Crossing'—and General Wimberley called upon the 1st Gordons to help by sending carriers and anti-tank guns.

These were despatched under the command of Captain J. Grant, who lost no time in crossing the bridge and fanning out his force beyond it to the distance of about a mile. With his carriers and guns disposed in excellent covering positions the infantry were able to cross the river and establish their bridge-head. Shortly afterwards Grant's forward carriers came under the fire of anti-tank guns and one carrier was knocked out, fortunately without loss to the crew. Their task completed, carriers and guns withdrew without further loss, and Captain Grant received the compliments of the Divisional commander.

The evening of 18th July saw the 153rd Brigade pressing their advance north-eastward to the Dittaino river in the general direction of Paterno in the foothills of Mount Etna.

The Black Watch were charged with the establishment of a bridge-head beyond Sferro, and with this accomplished the 1st Gordons were to come through and secure the hill called Point 151. Then it would be the turn of the 5th/7th Gordons: their objective was the line of the Simeto river another four and a half miles ahead. This was an ambitious programme, and success clearly depended upon the strength and character of the German resistance. The Italian forces could be regarded as a negligible quantity.

First it was necessary to clear the way by occupying the twin hills at Point 199. At about 6 p.m. the Divisional artillery brought down a heavy concentration on this position, setting fire to the stubble and a number of haystacks. In the light of the flames the Black Watch occupied the place well before midnight, the enemy having departed in some haste.

Without loss of time the Black Watch advanced upon Sferro, A and C Companies of the 5th/7th Gordons coming up to Point 199.

Now the troubles of the Brigade began. Although the Black Watch reached the river without much trouble, they were pinned down there by a very heavy bombardment. They could get no further. From Point 199 the watchers saw the whole area of Sferro village and railway station and the river bridge lit by fires and gun flashes, and tracer bullets criss-crossed at all angles. Tanks and armoured cars, as well as guns, mortars and spandaus, were disputing the advance, and it seemed obvious that the 5th/7th Gordons would never get a chance to reach the Simeto: indeed, one company of the Battalion had already been warned to stand by in case the Black Watch needed reinforcement, and D Company were sent forward in the early hours of the 19th.

The Gordon company were directed to the river bed at a point almost due south of Sferro in order to protect the right flank. The Dittaino, which pursues a sinuous course, contained little water at this season, but its banks are high and steep. Having made their defensive preparations, the Company could do little throughout the long burning hot day but take their share of the enemy bombardment, which our guns, though busy in retaliation, could not subdue. It was remarkable that the Gordons came off so lightly with only five men wounded. One of the casualties was Company Sergeant-Major Fraser.

During the night Major Napier had moved his headquarters to Point 199, near A and C Companies, B Company being left at a track junction south-west of Monte Turcisi to protect the axis of advance.

At 6 a.m. on the morning of the 19th a carrier patrol under Captain Sanderson pushed northward up this track to work round Monte St. Giovanni (Point 502) and see if the enemy held the hill. The patrol returned about five hours later having encountered none but civilians, and this information was passed on to a battalion of Royal Marines who were about to advance northward by this route. Then the Gordons were called upon to part with C Company, who were placed under the command first of the 23rd Armoured Brigade and then of the Royal Marines. The company did not go into action, but remained in reserve on the western slopes of Turcisi for some days.

Battalion headquarters had been heavily shelled, losing two officers. A carrier received a direct hit and Lieutenants M. Barr of the carrier platoon, and P. Macandrew commanding the mortars, who were sitting behind the vehicle, both received mortal wounds.

About 2 p.m. on the 19th Major Napier returned from Brigade with orders for a new attack. That night the 1st Gordons were to pass through the Black Watch, take Sferro village, and then send two companies on to Point 151 : under command would be A and B Companies of the 5th/7th Gordons, moving on the right of the road as far as the village.

The 1st Gordons had come forward on the previous night ready to take up the attack when the Sferro bridge-head had been established ; and, owing to the check in front of the village, the Battalion had spent the whole day lying on a sun-baked hillside, where they sought what shade was possible under corn stooks and vehicles. At 10 a.m., however, being warned of the operation planned for that night, Lieut.-Colonel Fausset-Farquhar took his company commanders forward to Point 199 to view the Sferro position. Owing to heavy shelling of the road down the forward slope towards the river bed—generally spoken of by the warriors from Africa as the wadi—it was impossible to approach nearer, and binoculars revealed little. Grass fires, burning railway wagons, and the smoke from bursting shells obscured the objectives.

When the light began to fail the commanding officer took his party forward in jeep and carrier to confer in the wadi with Lieut-Colonel Thomson of the Black Watch. Darkness had fallen before the 1st Gordon companies in their transport passed by Point 199. When half-way down the forward slope they left their vehicles and continued their advance on foot. On their right A and B Companies of the 5th/7th Gordons came forward in the same fashion.

Lieut.-Colonel Fausset-Farquhar found that to get into the wadi, where the Black Watch lay, scramble out on the further side and form up for the attack would take his leading companies longer than had been anticipated. Fortunately the commanding officer was able to get our bombardment postponed for thirty minutes in order to give his men more time. It was half an hour short of midnight when our guns opened on the road and railway and Sferro itself: five minutes later the attack went in, 1st Gordons and 5th/7th Gordons side by side.

The enemy's defensive fire caught the tail of the leading companies, and the rest were heavily shelled while crossing the wadi. All agreed that this was the fiercest bombardment they had ever endured.

Despite the shelling and considerable fire from rifles and automatics, B and C Companies of the 1st Gordons pressed on towards the railway over bare stubble fields. Soon the railway was reached and the Highlanders forced their way across the many sidings packed with goods wagons. Some of the wagons had been loaded with tar, and this was flowing over the permanent way in a molten mass. Neither these obstacles nor the enemy resistance prevented B and C Companies from reaching the road. They established themselves about 300 yards beyond it.

A and D Companies were following up. Captain W. M. MacFarlane, the new commander of A Company, was badly wounded and Lieutenant Morrison again proved himself a good leader of men. The railway station was cleared and Battalion headquarters established in the station yard; but when the commanding officer conferred by wireless with the Brigadier, it was agreed that the night was too far advanced for the attack to go through to Point 151.

Meanwhile A and B Companies of the 5th/7th Gordons, on the right of the road, had forced their way into Sferro village, which proved to be somewhat larger than expected. Confused fighting went on among the houses, and as the wireless sets with the companies were either hit or run down, no communication was possible either with the 1st Gordons or with Major Napier. Runners sent by the 1st Gordons had failed to reach the companies.

And then, as day was breaking, the Germans made a determined effort to turn the Gordons out of Sferro. An 88-mm. gun fired from one of the houses, seeking to demolish one building after another, while armoured cars began to shoot straight down the main street. Perhaps the 5th/7th Battalion have nothing finer to show than the performance of A and B Companies, who held on until the enemy tired of the struggle and withdrew. His going was hastened by the appearance of a troop of Sherman tanks, sent to the assistance of the Highlanders.

During this action Major Napier sent forward a truck of much needed ammunition. As the bridge over the river was known to have been mined, and was registered by the German artillery, his orders were that the vehicle should leave the main road well short of the bridge and make for Battalion headquarters in the wadi. There the ammunition was to be loaded into carriers who would take it forward into Sferro. To save precious time Captain J. W. Ritchie intervened. He stopped the truck before it left the main road, took the driver's place and, all alone, drove across the bridge under heavy shell-fire and so into Sferro. Having delivered the ammunition safely he walked back to Battalion headquarters.

A Company of the 1st Gordons had been held in readiness at the level crossing to counter-attack against the village should the necessity arise. B and C Companies of the Battalion had repulsed a counter-attack about 2 a.m. and had dug in by first light, although the ground was so hard that none of the trenches was more than two feet deep. The position extended in an arc from the railway station on the right to a gully about a mile to the north-west. Sappers had been hard at work clearing the mines around Sferro bridge, and later on the battle transport came forward ' at a spanking pace ', passing through heavy fire at the level crossing. The arrival of the vehicles ensured that by the time day broke the anti-tank guns were sited and food and reserve ammunition were available. A three-ton truck laden with water also got through to the 1st Gordons, and nothing could have been more welcome.

As soon as the decision was made to push the advance no further Major Napier was ordered to take over command of that portion of the bridge-head lying to the right of the road. He moved his headquarters to the wadi about a mile south of Sferro, near his own D Company. A and B Companies of the 5th/7th Gordons were now holding the further edge of the village, astride the Paterno road. The Battalion transport had arrived before daylight, and the companies were well prepared to hold what had been won.

In taking Sferro the casualties of A and B Companies had been light, although A lost Lieutenant H. Wallace, mortally wounded, and Lieutenant McCallum wounded. B Company had Lieutenant Oates wounded and Company Sergeant-Major Bell killed. Of other ranks in the two companies five were killed and five wounded.

During the daylight hours of the 20th the enemy maintained a steady bombardment of the bridge-head, hampering all movement. So far as could be ascertained the hostile infantry had retired towards Point 151, and in the afternoon, when the shelling slackened a little, the front companies of the 1st Gordons pushed forward a few hundred yards. On the left A Company occupied a farm house, found to be 'crammed with aeroplane stores and spare parts'. Battalion headquarters, now well protected by heavy sleepers, collected a valuable bag of wireless and field engineering equipment from wagons in the station sidings.

On this day the 1st Gordons lost their chaplain, the Rev. D. W. Rutherford, 'a shining example of what a padre should be'. He was wounded in the foot while visiting B Company.

The bridge-head sprang to activity at night when both Gordon battalions set to strengthening their positions with captured pickets and wire. The mortar platoon of the 1st Gordons carefully expended fifty rounds on an orchard, and the shoot was assumed to be effective, 'judging by what we got back next day'. Patrols explored some distance towards Point 151. The Black Watch were drawn back for a rest, leaving one company attached to the 5th/7th Gordons, whose C Company were still away.

Perhaps the most important event of this night was the arrival of a mail from Home.

The succeeding days were trying ones to all in the Sferro bridge-head. Owing to the heat, the flies, and the impossibility of moving in daylight without drawing fire, the 1st Gordons account this 'one of the least pleasant billets occupied since the Battalion came abroad'.

On the morning of 21st July the 1st Gordons suffered a particularly heavy bombardment which killed six men at C Company headquarters. Lieutenant Birrs of the anti-tank platoon was wounded. The 22nd was memorable for an anti-tank gun exploit. An enemy 88-mm. piece was located in a clump of cactus and disposed of, together with the gun detachment and ammunition, by two rounds from one of the Gordon 6-pdrs. On the night of the 23rd the Germans raided the Black Watch, who had relieved the 5th/7th Gordons in Sferro village, and attacked a wiring party belonging to C Company of the 1st Gordons, who lost a few men from the enemy's hand grenades before he was driven off. Next day it was found that he had left a light mortar behind him.

These raids would certainly have done more damage had it not been for the daring of Private Hyland of the 1st Gordons. 'Disguised as a stook' he had lain out all day 1,200 yards in front, and actually saw the raiding parties advance at dusk; and then he contrived to get back with his information.

The left flank of the bridge-head was open and the Gordons sent patrols nightly up the Catenanuova road. These patrols went out by truck and carrier as far as seemed prudent and then continued on foot. They found no enemy.

On the night of the 24th the 1st Gordons were relieved by the 5th Camerons (152nd Brigade) and withdrew to the area north of Ramacca for a brief rest. They took over from the Camerons again on the evening of the 26th, but this proved to be a short tour. Its chief incident was the bombardment of a farm by one of the 2-pdr. anti-tank guns which was taken forward to close range by a portée.

The 1st Gordons said farewell to the Sferro bridge-head on 29th July, being relieved before midnight by the 5th/7th Battalion. This day had seen a slackening of the enemy's fire, but about six o'clock in the evening a direct hit on the 1st Battalion's command post killed the intelligence officer, Captain L. W. Syme, his sergeant, and the signals exchange operator. Lieutenant S. A. Gillis, the signals officer, and two of his men were wounded.

The 5th/7th Gordons had been sharing the defence of the village with the 5th Black Watch. On the night of the 21st when the Gordons were relieved, they left D Company under Black Watch command; and when they came in again—with only three companies—forty-eight hours later, a company of the Black Watch remained in reserve. Before the relief was complete the Germans pushed a platoon out of a forward post in a cactus clump, and attempts to regain the place met with such heavy fire that the enemy was left in possession. Next day the cactus clump was heavily shelled and mortared, and Germans were seen running from it.

There had been a change in the command of the 5th/7th Gordons, Major R. W. M. de Winton arriving on 21st July to take over, temporarily, from Major Napier.

When the Black Watch came in again on the night of the 25th they kept A and B Companies of the Gordons. After the remainder of the Battalion reached their rest position near Point 264 C Company rejoined from their sojourn in the Monte Turcisi area. There was no shade in the vicinity of Point 264, so the Battalion continued to grill in the sun, but a church service proved 'a tonic to all who attended'. On the 27th a sudden long-range bombardment led to a hasty shifting of the camp. Then came the last turn of the Battalion in Sferro, with the relief of the 1st Gordons on the night of the 29th. After this had been accomplished D Company clashed with a German patrol over the possession of a farm.

The 30th July proved a peaceful day by Sferro standards, but a chance hit set an oil tanker ablaze and brought down mortar and field-gun fire while the Gordons were being relieved by the 2nd Inniskilling Fusiliers of the 5th Division.

During the relief one of our forward positions was promptly occupied by a German fighting patrol as a Gordon platoon withdrew from it. When the Brigadier came on the telephone to ask how the relief was progressing, he was told that all was going well except that one platoon area had been taken over by the Germans instead of by the Fusiliers. The Brigadier was not pleased, and curtly ordered the Gordons to 'get them out of it quick and give it to the right chaps'.

The Battalion moved back to reorganise in the reserve area. Since 16th July two officers and ten other ranks had been killed, and two officers and thirty-four others wounded; and two men were reported missing. Drafts received on the 23rd, 28th and 30th totalled seventy-nine 'mostly Gordons from hospital'.

There had been no chance of a spectacular success at Sferro, for the battle had developed into a defensive one owing to the re-grouping of the Eighth Army. General Montgomery had called off the attempt to drive the enemy from the Catania plain by direct attack from the south, and was staging an offensive further inland toward Centuripe and Adrano. His intention was then to pass north round Mount Etna and cut off the German forces near the coast. For the start of this movement Sferro was the pivot.

The Route to Messina

The Highland Division, relieved by the 5th Division at the end of July, had their part in the new offensive, but the 153rd Brigade were in reserve. The other brigades were to attack across the Sferro-Catenanuova road, and the objective of the 152nd Brigade, on the right, was the high ground of which Point 224 was a prominent feature.

The 1st Gordons were to support the 152nd Brigade, reinforcing them if need arose, and the Battalion moved to a position of readiness south of Monte Turcisi as darkness was falling on 31st July. Following a heavy bombardment, the attack went in a little before midnight, but for some hours it was not known if success had been achieved. As a precaution the Gordons were ordered forward, and at 5 a.m. on 1st August, in open formation they began to descend the northern slopes of Turcisi. They crossed the Dittaino and the main road and then came to a halt. It was now certain that the battle was going well, and the Battalion waited all day under intermittent shell fire. They had a good view of a tank action which ended in the defeat of the German armour.

Next morning the Gordons were ordered to stand by in readiness to move towards the village of Muglia. First a most distinguished party including the Divisional commander, the Brigadier and the commanding officer went forward to reconnoitre a new area of high ground looking across to Centuripe. Little was known about the enemy dispositions, but the party climbed and 'occupied' Monte Guazzarono without let or hindrance; and then a holding force consisting of A Company of the Gordons, a section of carriers, and a mortar detachment were sent up.

The remainder of the Battalion followed on the morning of the 3rd, and the Gordons sat down to admire a magnificent view of Centuripe and Etna. News came that the freshly landed 78th Division had captured Centuripe, and that the enemy was retreating on Adrano.

For a whole week the Battalion remained on Guazzarono, using the respite to overhaul and clean their weapons and to carry out some reorganization. And here B Echelon transport arrived from Africa, and was very welcome. During these days our aircraft could be seen bombing Adrano and Bronte and attacking gun positions and convoys. The Paterno area was lit by many fires.

The Gordons had received ample reinforcements of junior officers, for ten subalterns had joined since 24th July.

In the meantime the 5th/7th Gordons had waited all day behind the 154th Brigade on 1st August, and at 8 p.m. D Company and a carrier patrol were sent forward to exploit towards the Spezia feature, south-east of Muglia. They reached Point 254 and the remainder of the Battalion followed. At 6 a.m. on the 2nd one carrier was reported put out of action by a mine, and a few men wounded; but the enemy seemed to be retreating. The Gordons kept feeling forward with carriers and battle patrols and made no contact.

Later on the 2nd the Battalion moved nearer to Muglia, and on the 3rd on Muglia itself—a long climb very difficult for any kind of transport. On the hills near the village A and B Companies settled down with C Company in a farm further back. D Company were now in the rear.

Several days of waiting followed, a restful time though somewhat disturbed by orders and counter-orders. On the 5th Lieut.-Colonel J. E. G. Hay, wounded at the landing, returned to the command of the Battalion, displacing Lieut.-Colonel de Winton who went to Divisional headquarters.

The campaign in Sicily was moving to a victorious end. Centuripe had been captured on 3rd August, and Adrano fell on the 8th. The Highland Division were now transferred from the XXX Corps to the XIII Corps operating in the coastal strip, and the 153rd Brigade therefore moved eastward to the area between Etna and the sea. The Gordon battalions, driving by way of Paterno, through the foothills of Etna, had a rough journey over second-class roads and mule tracks.

The 1st Gordons moved up to Fleri[1] where, on the 12th, a reconnaissance party composed of the Brigadier, the commanding officer and others were spotted by the enemy and mortared. Lieut.-Colonel Fausset-Farquhar was slightly wounded above the eye but continued in command.

Next day the Gordons relieved a battalion of the Green Howards (13th Brigade) and pressed on with the pursuit, all available transport being used to ferry the companies forward to Milo. There was no fighting, but this was an enclosed country of terraced vineyards, so that movement off the road was hardly possible; and the road demolitions were truly formidable. In the course of little more than a mile five blown bridges were encountered. The leading companies proceeded on foot as best they could until a halt for the night was called.

To overcome transport difficulties called for an immense expenditure of physical effort. A carrying party of eight stalwart pioneers carried forward a wireless set and batteries on stretchers, and cable drums were manhandled down, across, and up the sides of 'wadis'. This, as it happened, availed nothing, for the 'earth return' circuit failed to work owing to the peculiar dryness of the lava soil. Pack mules were badly needed, and in their absence C Company carried forward by hand to the front companies rations, ammunition and signal equipment. Then, after midnight, thirty unfed mules arrived in lorries, and the animals seemed very glad to come to earth again. 'Once loaded there was hardly any holding them and they were sent forward with their Indian muleteers in small packets of two or three. Each packet was guided by a member of the intelligence section—and perhaps it says something for their training that when the mules returned at first light the muleteers were still walking while the guides rode.'

On 14th August the 1st Gordons entered Linguaglossa, the transport following as bridges were repaired and craters filled in. During the day about eighty Italians and one German had surrendered to the Battalion, who found Linguaglossa empty of the enemy, and the inhabitants glad to see them.

The 5th/7th Gordons, who had reached Zafferana Etna, began to move forward on the evening of the 14th. Progress through the demolitions was slow, but orders were to push on to Castiglioni that night; and so, after an evening meal, the Battalion moved through the 1st Gordons at Linguaglossa and tackled the cratered and mined roads which led up the hill to Castiglioni. The marching companies made their entry in bright moonlight at 1 a.m. on 15th August, but a blown railway bridge outside the town delayed the transport until next day.

[1] See map on page 196.

Castiglioni was empty, but on 15th August the mayor and the local police appeared and the people drifted back with tales of the atrocities committed by the Germans who had left twenty-four hours before the Gordons arrived. The Battalion spent a busy day. A bicycle patrol under Sergeant Findlay went northward to Francavilla, and Captain J. Stuart-Black's patrol, scouring further afield, made contact with American troops. This was not done without loss. Mine explosions killed Sergeant Findlay, as well as a number of Italian soldiers who had come in to surrender.

On 17th August American troops entered Messina, and next day General Montgomery, in a personal message, congratulated the Eighth Army upon the conquest of Sicily. On the 19th came a farewell order of the day from the Divisional commander. Major-General Wimberley had dined at 1st Gordons headquarters on the 16th, and he lunched with the 5th/7th Battalion on the 20th. He was a popular and inspiring commander who had early won the confidence of all who served under him.

The Gordon battalions settled down to a congenial routine. In Castiglioni the 5th/7th were particularly comfortable, with running water and electric light at their disposal and a cinema to enjoy. Italian soldiery, some in civilian clothes, continued to come in, all of them war weary. The needs of the inhabitants were soon relieved by an official food distribution; meanwhile, the Jocks had been only too willing to sacrifice half their rations so that the children should not go hungry. Life in the town soon revived, with the opening of shops and ice-cream bars, and 'vino of varying potency was to be had all at sixpence per mug'. We are told that 'the Sicilian women very cheerfully wash clothes'.

Both the 1st and the 5th/7th Gordons indulged in a general smartening up. As the 1st Battalion put it: 'The sight of well scrubbed equipment, guard mounting in kilts, sentry boxes, and the general turn out of all ranks brought back happy memories of soldiering in the so-called days of peace-time in the U.K.' The 5th/7th prided themselves upon their kilted guard at Battalion headquarters; and they sent one company to Lentini for guard duties at the Headquarters of the Eighth Army. Here they were seen by many distinguished persons, and fully upheld the reputation of the Regiment.

A number of honours and awards were announced at this time. In the 1st Gordons Lieut.-Colonel Fauesst-Farquhar received the D.S.O. and bar; Captain J. Grant a bar to his Military Cross; Major M. H. H. du Boulay, Captain Rutherford (the chaplain), Captain P. J. Keogh and Lieutenant R. Bird the Military Cross; Regimental Sergeant-Major Wright the M.B.E.; Sergeant J.

McKay, Corporals R. Taylor and J. Reaper and Privates J. Hyland and F. Lewis the Military Medal.

Of the 5th/7th Gordons, Major B. C. A. Napier received the Military Cross, Captain J. W. Ritchie, a bar to his Military Cross, and Company Sergeant-Major Bannerman, Corporal Robertson and Privates Burgess-Allan, Ritchie, Wilkie, Pearson, Ross and Brown the Military Medal. The two last named were stretcher bearers.

Before the end of August both Gordon battalions had made the acquaintance of their new Divisional commander, Major-General C. Bullen-Smith, parties had climbed Mount Etna, and a certain amount of training had been done. On the 26th the pipe bands of the 1st Gordons and 1st London Scottish, who were in the 168th Brigade of the 56th (London) Division, paid a visit to the 5th/7th Battalion in Castiglioni. Next day the three massed bands played Retreat and a party in the Battalion mess followed. The Brigadier was present, and fifty officers indulged in Highland dancing to the music provided by the three pipe-majors.

An unfortunate affair had increased the casualty list of the 5th/7th Gordons, fourteen men of D Company being wounded in an accident with a hand grenade.

At the beginning of September the 153rd Brigade moved into Messina, which involved a two days' journey over hill roads congested with traffic. A Company of the 5th/7th Gordons went at once to the dock area, where they took over guard and patrol duties. Other companies patrolled the coast. The intelligence sections of the Gordon battalions did observation duties in the lighthouse which was the nearest point in Sicily to the Italian mainland.

In the early morning of 3rd September the Allied bombardment opened and the invasion of Italy, in which the Highland Division were to have no part, began. For the next few days the lighthouse provided an excellent vantage point from which to view our bombers and fighters, wave after wave, passing over the Straits of Messina, and our ships and landing craft plying to and fro. There was no doubt that we had landed successfully on the mainland, and news of the collapse of Italy came on 8th September.

Lieut.-Colonel Fausset-Farquhar came back from short leave in Egypt on this day. While there he had visited infantry base depôts and other establishments, compiling a roll of 1st Gordons who were fit, with a view to asking for them to be returned to the Battalion.

By this time both 1st and 5th/7th Battalions had been withdrawn from Messina and were near S. Agata di Miletto on the north coast of Sicily. The parties at the lighthouse had been thankful to leave a place 'lousy with bugs and insects'.

Bathing parties were now very popular, and entertainment and good living were to be enjoyed. The Sicilians proved to be worthy opponents at football. As ever, the Gordons worked hard and played hard, and tactical training took a new turn: dispersal as practised in the Desert was 'out', and emphasis was placed upon camouflage. All ranks speculated upon what the future held. They knew that they were 'non-operational' so far as the Italian campaign was concerned, but expectations of an early return Home had been deprecated from on high.

The whole of the 5th/7th Gordons turned out on 13th September to quell a heath fire started by mortar shells. Equipment and weapons were saved from destruction at some risk and the carriers were called upon to push down trees. It was all 'very like a battle'.

On the 22nd the 1st Gordons moved to camp near Syracuse and the 5th/7th to a concentration area outside Augusta. Training continued and a Brigade assault-at-arms was held. With October came the rain, the first that the Gordons had seen in Sicily, and the 5th/7th were glad to leave their wet and muddy camp for billets in Augusta, part of the Battalion inhabiting an aircraft hangar.

On 'Alamein Day', 23rd October, the 153rd Brigade Highland Games were held in Syracuse stadium, and the gathering ended with the massed pipe bands playing Retreat. A commemoration service was held on the 24th.

The Highland Division were now definitely marked for Home: advanced parties were detailed, anti-tank guns, portées and carriers were handed in. And perhaps, at this closing stage, may be related the story of Donald the goose—or should it be gander?

Donald belonged to D Company of the 5th/7th Gordons, and had gone through the Sicilian campaign on the front seat of Major Glennie's jeep. When, at last, the Battalion were settled at Augusta and almost due to sail, it was decided to eat the bird at a farewell dinner. But Donald had other views. He disappeared and was never seen again.

In wet weather the final preparations to embark were made, and on 11th November the whole of the Brigade with a field ambulance and the Divisional R.E., left Augusta in the s.s. *Argentina*. After an uneventful and very comfortable voyage the convoy anchored off the Mersey on the 25th.

ITALY

1943-45

Farewell to Africa

It was near the end of the year when the 6th Gordons departed from Tunisia to set foot on the mainland of Europe. They moved to the locality of Créteville on 18th November. A few days later it became common knowledge that the 1st Division were about to leave Africa, but their destination remained a matter for conjecture. Then the Gordons were told that they would embark from Bizerta.

The heavy tentage was sent to Bizerta on 27th November and returned next day with the order that it was to be carried by the Battalion transport. As the Gordon vehicles had already been packed with stores and men, the situation was said to 'present some difficulties'. However, at the end of the month the whole Battalion was carried to Bizerta, most of them travelling in 3-ton trucks.

By 1st December two companies were embarked in transports. Changes in the shipping arrangements at the last moment caused difficulty and delay and, rightly or wrongly, the Gordons took a poor view of the methods of the American embarkation staff. Eventually it was decided that the remainder of the Battalion, with the 1st Loyals and a field regiment of artillery, would be put into landing craft and transferred at sea to the ship, the s.s. *Cuba*, before she docked. This procedure was calculated to save time.

Before midnight of 4th/5th December all troops were aboard their landing craft after two careless subalterns of the Gordons had 'stepped short and taken a ducking'. In the early morning of the 5th the transfer from landing craft to ship was safely accomplished, and by 8 a.m. the s.s. *Cuba* reached her berth and took on the remainder of her assignment.

The ship left Bizerta on the afternoon of the 5th and began a fairly smooth passage. Early on the 7th the troops sighted land, 'thought to be Italy'. Later in the day the Gordons disembarked at Taranto. A long and tedious railway journey up the Adriatic coast through Bari to Barletta and then inland to Canosa was accomplished by the evening of 9th December. Road transport then took them southward to Spinazzola, where the whole Battalion were assembled next day. The two companies who had been first to arrive were billeted in school buildings: the remainder were obliged to go under canvas 'in a newly harrowed field'.

The weather was much colder than Africa, and rain was setting in. The Gordons were told that no forward move was likely until the end of the month, but the companies were ordered to be dispersed for fear of air attack. The whole place threatened to become water-logged, so drains had to be dug, and altogether the Battalion existed in considerable discomfort. The inhabitants, who showed little desire to be friendly, were willing to wash clothes, 'but prices were very high'. It will be gathered that the Gordons' first impressions of Italy were by no means favourable.

All vehicles had arrived by 16th December, but the Battalion had brought from Africa only seven instead of twelve Carden Loyd carriers, so the transportation of anti-tank ammunition remained a problem.

The weather improved a little, and the companies were sent on route-marches which seemed to be the only possible form of activity. Although fairly happy, the men complained that there was 'no news from the front'. Indeed, no one had much idea of what was happening in Italy: 'all we know is that we are part of the Eighth Army'.

Actually, at this time, the Allied advance on Rome had slowed up before the thick belt of mountain defences, known as the 'Gustav Line' or 'Winter Line', which embraced strongly fortified Cassino.

The finer weather now permitted the Gordons to practise the laying and gapping of minefields, with the assistance of the 238th Field Company R.E. The pipes and drums played Retreat in Spinazzola, which certainly roused the Italians from their sullen indifference to the presence of the Jocks. And the companies enjoyed their special dinners at noon on Christmas Day.

Anzio

The Gordons had been warned of a possible move on 27th December, but on Boxing Day, very cold with intermittent rain, they were given two days respite owing to the bad weather. In the upshot it was not until the 31st that an advance party left, 'for an unknown destination'. Later in the day the Battalion were informed that previous plans—whatever they may have been—were cancelled: the 1st Division were moving to the region of Salerno, there to come under the Fifth Army. All divisional signs were to be removed from clothing and vehicles.

This news did nothing to check the celebration of Hogmanay, but New Year's Day was devoted to the striking of wet tents and packing up. At night the Gordons began a long drive through the Apennines which continued next day until they arrived near St. Lucia, in the Salerno area, on the afternoon of 2nd January. The 3-ton lorries had had trouble on the steep gradients and sharp turns, but all got through.

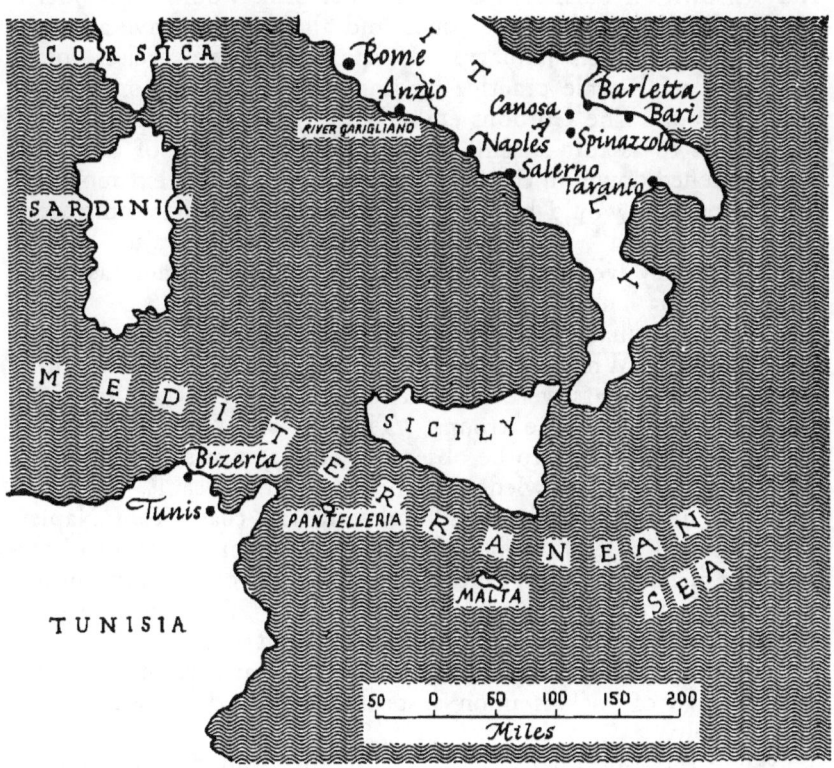

The companies were dispersed in farms. Next day the arrival of part of 'No 3 Beach Group' indicated that some sort of combined operation was in view. Training for such waited upon the arrival of a landing ship off the mouth of the Garigliano river. Parties of the 1st Reconnaissance Regiment and of a Royal Marine Commando were rationed by the Gordons, and a few days later some U.S. parachute troops paid a visit so that the Gordons could get to know them and recognise them readily in action.

From 9th January onward day and night practice with landing ships and landing craft went forward. Vehicles were waterproofed. General Lucas, commanding the U.S. VI Corps, came to view the preparations, and on 13th January, with due precautions to preserve secrecy, the plan was made known.

Under General Lucas, American and British forces were to make an assault landing at Anzio and threaten Rome, which was only thirty miles away, by an advance to the Alban hills. If all went well, the enemy's communications behind the Gustav Line would be cut, and the German armies defending the breadth of Italy thrown off balance. But the chief prize would be Rome.

The landing tables were issued and all administrative arrangements fixed by 15th January. After preliminary exercises something like a full-scale practice landing was carried out on beaches near Salerno. The Gordons embarked in a landing ship and were transferred to assault landing craft late on the night of the 18th. They touched down on the beaches soon after 2 a.m. next morning, and although it would be too much to say that 'everything went according to plan', the experience gained proved invaluable. All knew that they were now committed to a much sterner task than the Pantelleria landing.

On 21st January the heavy gear was stowed on the infantry landing craft. While the ships lay off the coast a little north of Naples Italian boats were allowed to circulate freely, selling fruit and other items to the troops. This, to the Gordons, seemed unwise if secrecy were to be observed, but as events were to show the enemy had no knowledge of the impending assault.

Anzio lies about a hundred miles up the coast from Naples. The approach to the landing places was made on the night of the 21st, the armada of over 250 ships and craft of all descriptions steaming in from the west over a calm sea. To ensure surprise there was no preliminary bombardment, but a little before the troops were due to touch down, one of our warships discharged a terrific salvo of rockets upon suspected enemy defences. There was no reply.

While the Gordons waited to leave their ship for the landing craft which were to take them ashore, spirits were high and the men sang lustily. Before midnight all had been transferred and were on their way. At 2.25 a.m. on 22nd January Battalion headquarters and A and C Companies touched down.

They came in about five miles north-west of the little town of Anzio, so the direction of the advance was north-eastward. A few mines were discovered, but there was no sign of any defensive position. Without fighting the companies pressed forward over rough uncultivated land covered with patches of scrub and clumps of bog oak. Soon the Gordons made contact with the 2nd North Staffordshire on the right, the two battalions being the first of the 1st Division to land.

One prisoner was taken in a farm and three Germans escaped in an armoured car, firing a machine gun as they sped away. By 6 a.m. B and C Companies, who had been landed by mistake more than half a mile further south, rejoined the Battalion.

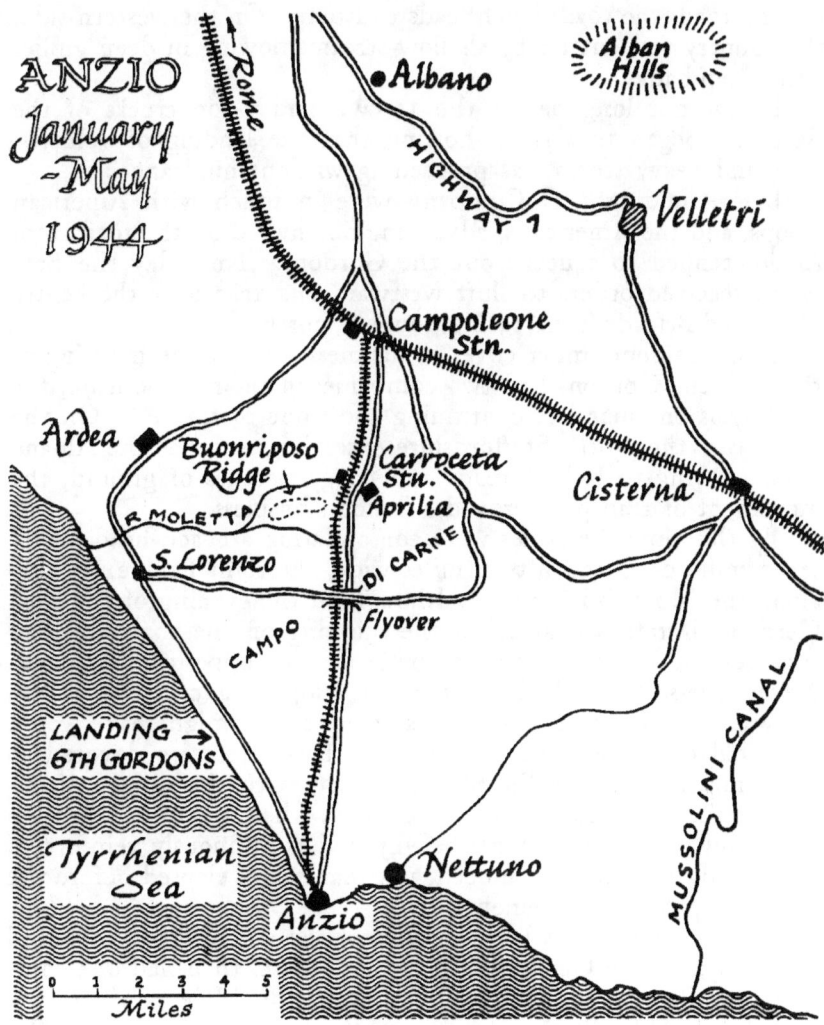

The Gordons moved forward to their first objective, patrols soon reporting that the final position they were to occupy was clear of the enemy. By eight o'clock it was known that the town and harbour of Anzio had been occupied without trouble, and that Nettuno was in American hands.

At 10 a.m. B and D Companies advanced to the region of Campo di Carne, the Gordons' position in the beach-head, and the remainder of the Battalion followed. With two companies forward, one in support and one in reserve, all dug in and prepared their fire plans. B and D Companies overlooked the Anzio-Albano road, the road which leads to Rome. On the western side, the country was cut up by shallow streams flowing in deep gullies with steep banks.

It was not long before the 15-cwt. and 3-ton trucks of the Battalion began to arrive, showing that the landing of vehicles, guns and heavy stores was proceeding without hindrance.

Before midnight D Company were in touch with American troops, and the Americans, advancing northward up the road from Anzio, tended to squeeze out the Gordons. Next day the Battalion received orders to shift westward and take over the centre of the 2nd Brigade front, facing, roughly, north.

This was done under cover of darkness, and by the morning of the 24th the Gordons had two companies in the new position, the 1st Loyals on their left continuing the front to the sea. On the right were the North Staffordshire extending as far as the Albano road. Owing to lack of roads and boggy patches of ground, the movement of transport proved a difficult business.

By this time the Allies were consolidating a beach-head nearly seven miles deep and fifteen miles wide, the right flank extending along the Mussolini Canal. Although on the evening of the 23rd German aircraft had attacked the shipping off the coast and had sunk several vessels, there was little sign of opposition on land. Nevertheless, the Allied commander adopted a cautious policy. He was reluctant to risk a rapid advance which might have won a spectacular success: instead the next few days were devoted to reorganization and to limited operations with the object of enlarging the beach-head. Unfortunately, when a general offensive was launched the Germans, heavily and continuously reinforced, were ready to meet it; indeed, not many days elapsed before the initiative passed to the enemy.

Twenty-four hours later the left of the 2nd Brigade advanced northward. The Gordons, still in the centre, then had one company on Buonriposo Ridge, overlooking the Moletta river, the remainder of the Battalion being south of the lateral road leading eastward from San Lorenzo.

When daylight came on 25th January it was discovered that a large tract of woodland, with almost impenetrable undergrowth, made communication with the Loyals on the left difficult to maintain. The Loyals had met some opposition during their advance, but only five of the enemy, two of them horsemen, were seen on the front of the Gordons. These Germans soon disappeared.

On this day in an attack northward up the Albano road the 24th Guards Brigade had established themselves in the Carroceto-Aprilia area after overcoming stout opposition. A German counter-attack with tanks was delivered on the 26th and repulsed by the Guards.

The Gordons had not been engaged, although they were in contact with German patrols beyond the Moletta river. On the 27th a hostile aircraft dropped a stick of bombs near Battalion headquarters, killing one man and wounding three; but there was some consolation later in the day to see three German bombers shot down by our fighters. The whole Battalion area was shelled on the 28th and A and C Companies suffered some casualties. C Company, the only one north of the San Lorenzo road, had a very trying time on the afternoon of the 29th when they suffered a heavy bombardment for two and a half hours. The western coast road was now under hostile shell fire and could only be used at night.

Another attack, preliminary to an Allied general offensive, was put in on 29th January when the Guards, after sharp fighting, cleared a start-line for the 3rd Brigade, who reached the railway embankment south of Campoleone, when the main attack was launched next day. They renewed their effort on the 31st but could make no further progress. Away to the east the Americans had delivered their attack towards Cisterna on 30th January, but after two days hard fighting could not reach the town.

The Allies now suspended offensive operations, and the 1st Division devoted their energies to organising the defence of the salient created by the advance up the Albano road.

On 30th January the Gordons had been informed that they were to be relieved at once by an American engineer unit, and could expect a few days rest. This relief was duly carried out, but as the Battalion marched back across country, Lieut.-Colonel Peddie was informed that he was to come under the command of the 24th Guards Brigade: the Gordons would relieve the 5th Grenadier Guards round the tobacco factory at Carroceto on the Albano road. This area included an estate, with shops and a cinema, where the employés of the factory had been housed.

The Gordons were carried forward in trucks and by 9 p.m. the whole Battalion were in position around the factory 'and under the fire of some very heavy guns'. Next day came another move, to take over from the 1st Scots Guards a position on the eastern side of the Albano road about half-way between Carroceto and Campoleone. This meant a return to their own 2nd Brigade.

The salient won by the 1st Division was about four miles deep and barely a mile and a half broad. The new position of the Gordons was on the eastern face. At the apex near Campoleone were the 3rd Brigade. On the right of, and south-east of, the Gordons, but not in close touch lay the Divisional reconnaissance regiment. Beyond the Albano road the position of the 1st Irish Guards on the western face of the salient lay along a ridge which overlooked the three forward companies of the Gordons.

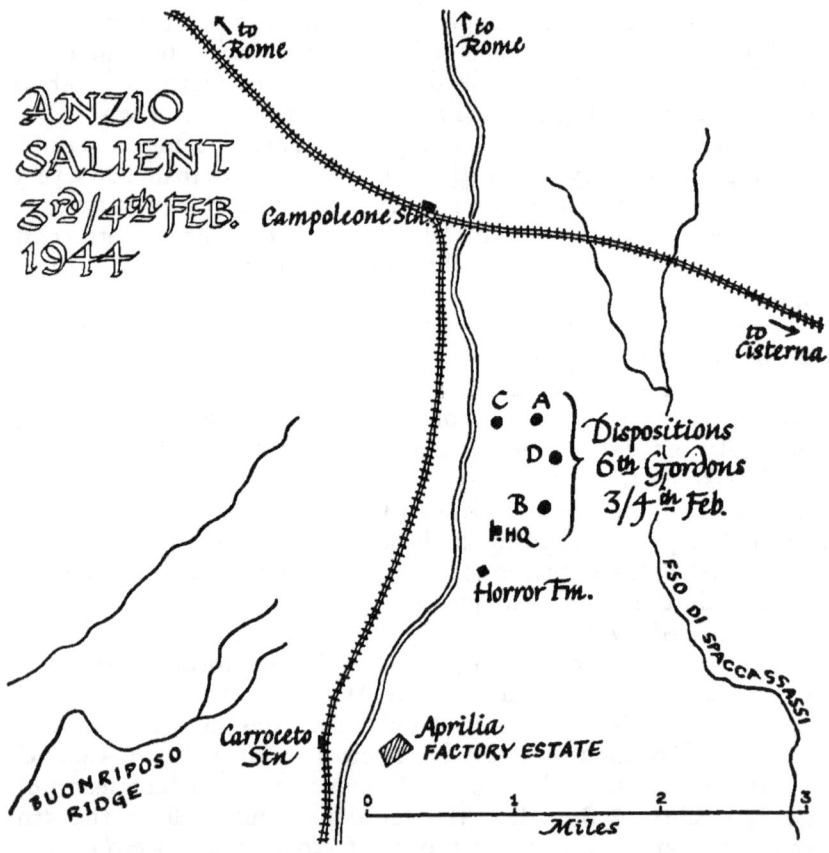

The Battalion were very thin on the ground and the companies too strung out for mutual support. There seemed little to prevent enemy penetration from the east, where numerous deep ditches and gullies provided convenient points of assembly and covered lines of approach. The Germans possessed good observation over the Battalion area both from the north and the east.

C Company, nearest the Albano road, and A Company occupied the forward positions, but D Company, about half a mile to the right rear of A, and B Company, about the same distance south of D Company, were equally liable to be attacked. Lieut.-Colonel Peddie therefore had no reserve.

There was no doubt that the Germans were preparing an offensive. Hitler had issued a special order: the Allied forces at Anzio must be driven back into the sea.

Although the German artillery and mortars were never silent for long, 1st February is described by the Gordons as 'a fairly peaceful day', but any movement in the area of A Company drew accurate fire. The next two days passed in much the same fashion and then, just before midnight on 3rd February, the Germans launched their attack against the Campoleone salient with the object of forcing their way through to the sea.

At 11.30 p.m. Battalion headquarters, situated some distance in rear of B Company and forward of some haystacks and buildings later known as Horror Farm, were heavily shelled for twenty minutes. Spasmodic shelling continued and our guns and mortars opened defensive fire. A little later B and D Companies each reported that German infantry had penetrated between them. It seems that this infiltration over-ran the position occupied by the Gordons' 3-inch mortars, but a prompt counter-attack made by Lieutenant J. W. S. Fordyce and his platoon drove the Germans off for a time. At 4.30 a.m. on the 4th a message was received from B Company to say that the enemy was digging in behind D Company.

It was evident that the companies must fight their own battle, seeing that Battalion had no reserve. Lieut.-Colonel Peddie therefore ordered them to hold their fire until they were directly attacked and then to let drive with everything they had. Meanwhile the machine guns of the carrier platoon fired by the light of the gun flashes at Germans advancing from the east.

The dawn of 4th February was overcast and drizzling rain began to fall. A squadron of the 46th R. Tank Regiment appeared at Battalion headquarters and went forward at 6.30 a.m. to help the companies in a counter-attack. Shortly afterwards reports were received from B and D Companies that the enemy were surrendering in large numbers. D Company were therefore ordered to advance behind the tanks.

At this time communication between Battalion and the companies was by wireless only. All lines had gone. Direct touch was possible with A, B and D, but as C Company could not be heard, direct orders to them were relayed through A Company.

About seven o'clock A Company reported six German tanks —believed to be Mark VI—deploying on their front. This was the last heard from A Company.

Meanwhile D Company had reported that our own tanks were 'doing a grand job of work', and that the enemy was surrendering freely. This was heartening news. It was not known until later that as the tanks continued their advance they came under such heavy fire that many were knocked out and all movement came to an end.

Next, D Company reported that A and C Companies were withdrawing. Lieut.-Colonel Peddie ordered D Company to contact these two companies and tell them to re-occupy their positions. Soon afterwards D Company went off the air.

About eighty German prisoners, all of them very anxious to reach safety, passed by Battalion headquarters, which were now under sustained shell fire.

Half a mile further forward B Company, under the able command of Captain R. L. H. Bridgeman, held on to their position, though they described themselves as 'thoroughly uncomfortable'. They seemed to be under fire from almost every direction, but were able to inflict considerable loss on the enemy, who also suffered from the fire of the carriers, who were further to the left.

Prisoners continued to make their way back, some without escorts, and the Gordons reckoned that about 200 had passed through.

After 8.30 a.m. the adjutant, Captain J. C. Williamson, went forward on foot in an attempt to find A and C Companies. He got well beyond B Company, only to discover that parts of the ridge to the west of the Albano road which dominated the Gordons' forward area were in the possession of the Germans. Heavy fire swept the ground ahead. It was useless to go on.

Two men eventually returned from D Company, and from A Company about twenty. C Company was a total loss.

We know now that a heavy barrage had been put down on the trenches of A Company before midnight of the 3rd/4th February, and that a strong enemy detachment had then advanced and dug in on the right rear of the company. About 6.20 a.m. on the morning of the 4th enemy tanks—seventeen, it was said, but the exact number is doubtful, and may have been less—appeared to the eastward and a combined infantry and tank attack soon threatened to over-run the position.

Lieutenant H. Garioch was ordered to make his way back to Battalion headquarters with a report, but he had not got far on his precarious mission before he was captured. Then a barrage came down and, in the confusion, he was able to break away. He returned to A Company and, soon after his arrival Major D. Hutcheon, the company commander, was killed by a burst of machine-gun fire.

C Company, after losing heavily, seem to have been overwhelmed by an infantry attack from the rear.

The outlook was grim. Although heavy loss had been inflicted on the Germans, the salient had become untenable, for the Anzio-Albano road was being swept by enemy fire. Now the pressing need was to extricate the 3rd Brigade, still in their positions south of Campoleone.

About 11.30 a.m. the Gordons—what was left of them—received word that the 1st London Scottish, belonging to a newly arrived brigade of the 56th Division, were coming through to counterattack. Needless to say, the Gordons did all they could to help their friends in their preparations; and in the afternoon, when the London Scots attacked with two squadrons of tanks, enough ground was gained to enable the 3rd Brigade to withdraw. After they had done so, and the London Scottish with their mission accomplished had pulled back, the Gordons could be taken out of the battle. Consisting of little more than B Company and Battalion headquarters, the Battalion assembled some three miles back, south of Carroceto. The day closed in showers of hail and sleet, heralding a night of bitter cold.

The Gordons counted seven killed and eighteen wounded, and ten officers and 319 other ranks missing. Four mortars and four anti-tank guns and the complete fighting equipment of three rifle companies had been destroyed or left on the field. Besides Major Hutcheon—a very gallant and capable soldier who had come from the 1st Battalion and had been adjutant before commanding A Company—Lieutenant J. M. Blandy was among the killed.

Other units had suffered severely, but although the Campoleone salient had been lost, the 1st Division had taken terrible toll of the enemy and prevented a break-through.

The story of the battle is not complete without mention of certain awards for fine leadership and personal prowess. Captain J. C. Williamson, the adjutant, and Lieutenant E. N. Grace, a platoon commander in B Company, received the Military Cross. Corporal G. Wilson, who knocked out a Tiger tank with his anti-tank gun; Corporal James Moir of B Company; and Private Mennim, a company runner, received the Military Medal. Lieutenant James Leckie, the signals officer; Sergeant John Thain (killed in action), Lance-Corporal James Agnew and Lance-Corporal A. Paterson, all of B Company, were mentioned in despatches; and to these names must be added that of Regimental Sergeant-Major James Underwood, who came through heavy fire to bring much needed ammunition by carrier to B Company.

A word may here be spared for the transport drivers of the Battalion, who in this action, and throughout the time spent in the Anzio beach-head unfailingly brought up rations and other supplies over rough tracks and cratered roads generally under heavy fire.

On 6th February the arrival of reinforcements—albeit with no battle experience for they were all fresh from Home—enabled a new C Company to be formed with Major E. J. Gordon in command. This draft was 'quite a large body of men', but there were not enough non-commissioned officers to form another company. The commanding officer had something to say regarding these reinforcements who came mostly from Lowland regiments 'with a smattering of Englishmen. A pity: you can't beat the Jock from the North-East as a soldier.'

So, as far as numbers were concerned, the Gordons remained a weak battalion. On the 7th Lieut.-Colonel Peddie took under command a 'beach defence company' of the Durham Light Infantry, who were armed only with rifles, and had never been in action.

The 1st Division had now to straighten their front and consolidate, paying particular attention to the Carroceto-Aprilia area on the Albano road. As there was little respite from artillery and mortar fire during the day the digging and the wiring and the laying of mines had all to be done at night.

On the evening of the 7th B Company were called upon to reinforce a squadron of the Reconnaissance regiment in the right sector of the Brigade front east of the Albano road. The company were ordered to fill a gap in the line, and they beat off by fire a German attack before they could reach their position; but owing to bright moonlight digging had to be delayed. Later, Major Bridgeman had to report the loss of a platoon commanded by Lieutenant N. R. Deboys. This platoon were sent to entrench a detached position where they arrived in the small hours of the morning. It was believed that under cover of a discharge of smoke our men were over-run by a sudden attack by a strong detachment of German infantry.

The remainder of B Company lay under such heavy shell-fire that a withdrawal was made to the shelter of some buildings where the daylight hours were passed. Only at night were the trenches manned. Major Bridgeman, an outstanding company commander, was soon afterwards awarded the Military Cross.

At 11 a.m. on the 8th the remainder of the Battalion were ordered to strengthen the front by coming in on the right of B Company. In rain and bitter cold the movement was made in the evening and when the new dispositions were completed this part of the line was a rather patched up affair. C Company were on the right of B and next on the right were the D.L.I. company who linked up with the 1st Loyals. On the left the 238th Field Company R.E., now placed under Lieut.-Colonel Peddie's command, filled a gap between B Company and the London Scottish. The whole sector was in the bend of the Spaccassassi stream where it turns east and south, and 'despite the appalling conditions the troops dug in well'.

Further away to the left, on and west of the Albano road, heavy fighting had begun on the night of the 7th and by the 10th the enemy, by his repeated assaults, had gained possession of Buonriposo Ridge, Carroceto railway station, and the Aprilia factory area.

The Gordons took no part in this struggle, but had enough to do to maintain themselves in the mud and cold under shell-fire which made all movement hazardous by day. Relief by American troops on the night of the 9th was very welcome. The whole Division were coming out and everyone looked forward to a few days rest.

For the Gordons there was little rest. They reached the reserve area at 5 a.m. on the 10th and were soon asleep; but at night they were called forward to complete the wiring and mining of a reserve position near the fly-over bridge. With short intervals for relief they toiled in the mud and the wet and the cold until 12th February. Then, at nightfall, they set out to relieve the Irish Guards in the line about two miles north of the fly-over bridge, west of the Albano road. Here they held a small sector under the command of the 3rd Brigade. C Company reinforced the 1st Duke of Wellington's further to the right.

The ground was broken by deep gullies which gave the enemy easy ways of approach, and movement during daylight usually brought down a storm of shell or mortar fire. The D.L.I. company, still attached to the Gordons, were the chief sufferers, and Private Hadden, a Gordon stretcher-bearer who was working for the company and had done much good service, won the Military Medal by his devotion in tending the wounded under heavy fire.

Defences were manned only at night, sentries and observers keeping watch by day, and in this fashion casualties were reduced to a minimum. Battalion headquarters were established in some 'magnificent caves'.

On the night of the 15th the Gordons were relieved by Americans, and withdrew into reserve, where C Company rejoined, having lost four wounded and three missing.

The Battalion's stay in the 'rest' area was an uneasy one, the whole of the Anzio beach-head being, as usual, under artillery fire; and the high-velocity shells which gave no warning of their approach were a severe trial. On the 17th Lieutenant J. Leckie, signals officer, was killed, and Lieutenant J. K. M. Methven, intelligence officer, was wounded.

The Germans were still attacking. On 16th February they had started a fresh drive down the Albano road, and by next day had gained some ground east of the road. In the afternoon the Gordons moved up to relieve the 1st Scots Guards near the fly-over bridge, Lieut.-Colonel Peddie now having only his own B and C Companies, for the D.L.I. company had departed.

The Gordons lay immediately west of the fly-over bridge, and when the Germans renewed their attacks on the 18th the Loyals, east of the bridge, were hotly engaged all day. B Company of the Gordons, their nearest neighbours, were heavily shelled and mortared, as the enemy artillery paid special attention to the prominent fly-over embankment. Yet no infantry attacks developed against the Battalion.

During the 19th the action continued in the same fashion, ground lost east of the bridge being regained by counter-attack. The Gordons had Lieutenant E. N. Grace wounded on this day, and at night an air attack struck B Echelon far in rear—only four miles north of Anzio—wounding Captains G. Reynolds-Payne and T. S. T. Tregallas and three others. Twenty-eight vehicles were damaged.

Hostile attacks died down on the 20th, although B Company were still under heavy fire and continued to be so during the night and the next day. On the evening of the 21st, however, it became possible to carry out a relief by putting in a newly-formed D Company.

Sufficient reinforcements had now arrived from Home to form this new rifle company. None of the new-comers had been in action, and non-commissioned officers and men were strangers to each other until they met in the beach-head. However, after a shaky start, D Company settled down fairly well to the grim business in hand.

They lost Lieutenant J. M'Masters, who had only just joined the Battalion, killed by shell-fire on the 22nd. A standing patrol came to grief early next morning when they lost four men wounded and ten missing; but nine of the missing men returned next day.

Even when the fighting died down, consolidation of the forward defences was not easy. Much of the ground was marshy and digging soon reached water level; and there was no material for the construction of breastworks after the out-moded fashion. Under the enemy's persistent bombardment the Gordons were fortunate to escape with comparatively few casualties.

The Battalion were relieved on the night of the 25th, except for D Company, who came out twenty-four hours later. In very wet weather the Gordons remained nearly five days in B Echelon area, the longest break they had had since they landed. They now discovered that, thanks to the enterprise of the 56th Division, the beach-head could provide such diversions as a concert, which was attended by practically all the Battalion. On the night of 29th February came a reminder that no region was safe from the attentions of the enemy: German bombers flew over and their attack killed three of B Company and wounded three. The commanding officer and others at Battalion headquarters had very narrow escapes.

At this time several new officers arrived, among them Captain G. J. Crawford of the Cape Town Highlanders, and this representative of an allied regiment received a hearty welcome. Captain Williamson took over D Company, Captain T. P. B. Nimmo succeeding him as adjutant. A Company was not reconstituted, so the Gordons could only take three rifle companies into action.

When on 2nd March the Battalion relieved the North Staffordshire on the front just east of the fly-over bridge, the Germans had given up all hope of driving the Allies into the sea, and were on the defensive. But excellent observation from the Alban hills enabled their artillery and mortars still to harass the whole Anzio area with great effect. Gradually our counter-battery work reduced the German fire, but the battalions of the 2nd Brigade near the fly-over bridge were in one of the worst sectors, and received more than their share of hostile bombardment.

Henceforward the usual routine was a spell in forward and reserve positions for two weeks or more, followed by five days ' rest '.

On 3rd April Lieutenant K. A. J. Ironside and one of his men were killed on patrol, but the German patrol leader who shot the officer was himself killed before he could make good his retreat.

Work on the defences became easier as the weather improved, and the spirits of all ranks rose as they saw signs of the Italian spring. When ' out of the line ' the Jocks could soon enjoy sea bathing and the entertainments provided for them. Towards the end of the month the pipes and drums of the Gordons played Retreat for the first time since landing at Anzio.

There were other patrol encounters, and on 29th April, while on their way up to take over one of the front positions, the Battalion came under shell-fire and were lucky to escape with only one killed and one wounded.

A reinforcement of fifty-eight other ranks arrived on 1st May. On the 12th, when the Battalion changed to khaki drill clothing, ' much relief was felt by one and all ', for the Italian sun was making serge battle-dress far too hot for comfort.

On the 18th Lieutenant A. S. McCallum was wounded by a mine while on patrol.

And then, on the 25th, when the Gordons moved from a front into a reserve position, the Anzio beach-head ceased to exist. Two days earlier the heavily reinforced Americans had opened an offensive in the region of Cisterna, and the advance on Rome had begun at last. Progress was slow, however, and the fighting was severe: it was not until 4th June—two days before D-Day in North-West Europe—that the VI Corps and the left of the main U.S. Fifth Army began to enter the city.

The time had come for the 1st Division to advance. Patrol activity was redoubled, and on 28th May the Gordons approached the Aprilia factory area, the transport making heavy weather among the craters of the Albano road. Next day the Battalion advanced along the railway bed between Ardea and Campoleone and dug in, as evening drew on, under spasmodic bursts of enemy fire. Eight casualties were suffered on this day. Patrols met some slight opposition when the advance was resumed on the morning of the 30th; later in the day the Gordons again dug in under shell and mortar fire. One who was present at this time has this to say of them.

> Today was a triumph for the Battalion; the men who had marched in the heat and the dust since 28th May with little rest impressed everyone with their cheerfulness and determination. For nearly the whole of the Battalion the last 48 hours had been a test of endurance after so long on the defensive in the beach-head. Although our artillery fire was short for a considerable time, officers, non-commissioned officers and men acted coolly throughout this very unpleasant period, thus saving many casualties.

One man was killed on this day and among the thirty-seven wounded were 2nd-Lieutenant G. R. Rose and Lieutenant J. W. Erskine. Sergeant G. Morton won the Military Medal for his coolness and leadership after his platoon commander had been wounded; the same award was made to a stretcher-bearer, Private William Pickard. The Gordons never lacked gallant stretcher-bearers.

On 1st June the Loyals, Gordons and North Staffordshire were on the line of the Ardea-Campoleone road. Enemy guns and mortars woke to life at intervals, and precautions were taken against counter-attack. The Gordons enjoyed the spectacle of our bombers, squadron after squadron, flying over to attack the discomfited enemy, and the roar of our artillery seemed to hold a triumphant note.

After dark on the 2nd, at considerable risk and inconvenience, the pioneer platoon laid a minefield in front of the Battalion position. Very early next morning the mines had to be very hastily taken up so that the 3rd Brigade could come through and continue the advance.

The Gordons moved again on 4th June, marching forward in great heat across country over dusty tracks. On the way came the news that the Allies were in Rome, and explosions were heard in the direction of the Tiber. The Battalion came to rest about ten miles south of the city and, after a hot meal, settled down to a peaceful night.

Now came an interval of real relaxation, with ample time for hot baths, the issue of clean clothing, and a general furbishing up. Parties of officers and men paid visits to Rome and mingled with the enthusiastic populace. On the 8th the pipers of the Gordons played through the city at the head of the 1st Duke of Wellington's, who formed the British contribution to the Allied occupation troops. The pipes were going very well, but the drums had proved difficult to keep going. At this time the Battalion could only muster a bass drum and three side drums.

The 150th anniversary of the raising of the Regiment—that is to say of the old 100th, soon renumbered 92nd, the first Gordon Highlanders—did not pass unregarded. A special issue of wine was arranged and the pipes and drums played Retreat in the evening. The B.B.C. had been at pains to arrange a special broadcast in commemoration, and for this the commanding officer and others of the 6th Gordons had supplied recordings: unfortunately reception of the broadcast by the Battalion was ruined by atmospherics.

The Gordons moved to a new area west of the Alban hills on 17th June, and here training began in earnest, but there were films and concert parties to beguile the leisure hours.

Lieut.-Colonel J. Peddie, having completed three years in command, left the Battalion on 23rd June, to the regret of all ranks. He had brought them through the Tunisia campaign, the Pantelleria excursion, and the trials and troubles of Anzio, and his good service was shortly afterwards rewarded by the D.S.O. His successor was Lieut.-Colonel J. B. Clapham, another Gordon Territorial officer, who had served in the London Scottish.

From the 5th to 14th July the Battalion trained for mountain warfare by day and night in the Alban hills, then returned to their former camp to exercise with tanks and practise river crossings on the Tiber. There were two ceremonial occasions: one a special church parade when the Divisional commander presented medal ribbons, the other an informal visit of inspection by King George VI, His Majesty receiving a rousing welcome.

Florence and the Apennines

The next move of the Gordons, made on 1st August, was via Rome to Foligno, but on the 6th the Battalion was despatched very hurriedly to a forward concentration area at Figline, fifteen miles south-east of Florence.

Here training continued, but it soon became time to renew acquaintance with the enemy. On the 10th the Gordons were carried forward in trucks to take over a reserve position south-east of Florence, B Company, coming under command of the Loyals and occupying some high ground further forward. They suffered five casualties from shell-fire before they rejoined the Battalion two days later.

At this time the Allies had closed up to the Arno, and plans had been made for the 1st Division to cross east of Florence; but it was not yet certain that the Germans intended to defend the river line. Then, as it became evident that the enemy was on the point of withdrawing into the mountains north of the Arno, the 1st Division were ordered to 'take over' Florence. Meanwhile the Gordons had been patrolling across the river and had had five men wounded by shell-fire while doing so.

On 16th August the Battalion were carried in trucks to Florence. The start was made in the early morning and as no lights were allowed it was a difficult journey. Five men of D Company were injured when one 3-tonner overturned. During the afternoon of the same day the Gordons crossed the river and took over the western portion of the city from the 3/15th Punjab Regiment (8th Indian Division).

German snipers and mortar and machine-gun detachments still lurked in the northern parts of Florence and were inclined to be aggressive. The days spent in the city were a new experience for the Gordons, whose fighting patrols were obliged to conduct their operations in the midst of an under-fed and panic stricken, if not unfriendly populace. On the 17th a party of about fifty Germans attempted to exterminate a Gordon anti-tank detachment and, although they failed, the gun had to be extricated next day with the help of Italian partisans.

This was the Gordons' first acquaintance with the partisans, whom they found brave but irresponsible and, very often, foolhardy.

Life had its contrasts, for men would come back from the shelled and mortared area in the north of the city to mount a smart guard at Brigade headquarters, and the pipe band played

Retreat in the Piazza Signora in the presence of thousands of interested spectators. The feeding of the people, many of them refugees from the countryside, became so pressing a necessity that the Gordons, like the other battalions in the Brigade, set up a food distribution centre.

Slowly the Germans withdrew. On 25th August the Gordon patrols pushed as far as the Rifredi area in the northern outskirts of Florence. There were a few stubborn encounters, and Lieutenant J. C. Napier was taken prisoner on the 29th whilst on reconnaissance. Two days later 2nd-Lieutenand P. H. Bunton was wounded.

When, on 3rd September, the whole Brigade advanced from Florence, with the Gordons on the left, the enemy were no longer disputing the way. The Battalion entered the foothills and were soon contending with wet weather and steep mountain tracks; and the shortage of mule transport became a handicap where the supply of the forward companies was concerned. There was no clash with the Germans, but a 3-ton truck ran over a mine, causing ten casualties.

By 8th September, impeded only by the hard going and the rain and mist which made it difficult to keep direction, the Battalion had traversed the peaks of Poggio del Giro and Monte Rotondo to reach Monte Montello, nearly 3,000 feet above the plain. Next day, being by then well over six miles north of Florence and west of Route 65—the road to Bologna—the Gordons were relieved by American troops.

Driving down from the mountains, the Gordons found Florence a more attractive city than when they had left it. There were films to see, and a boxing exhibition by Joe Louis, former heavyweight champion of the world, was a great attraction. The Battalion moved forward again on 15th September, to the vicinity of Borgo San Lorenzo, a place which they were to know well. The Italian summer had not quite departed and the journey was a hot and dusty one.

The Allied advance into the Apennines was well under way, the objective of the U.S. Fifth Army being Bologna and the plain of the Po, beyond the city. The Germans, however, had still to be driven from the chain of mountain defences known as the Gothic Line. The U.S. II Corps were using the main Florence-Bologna road, 'Route 65', whilst the 1st Division (in the British XIII Corps, which was at this time in the Fifth Army) opened the road through Palazzuolo which led to Faenza. This road, called 'Arrow Route', was not much more than a hard-surfaced track leading through deep gorges, very narrow in places, and dominated by the mountains on either hand. To advance astride Arrow

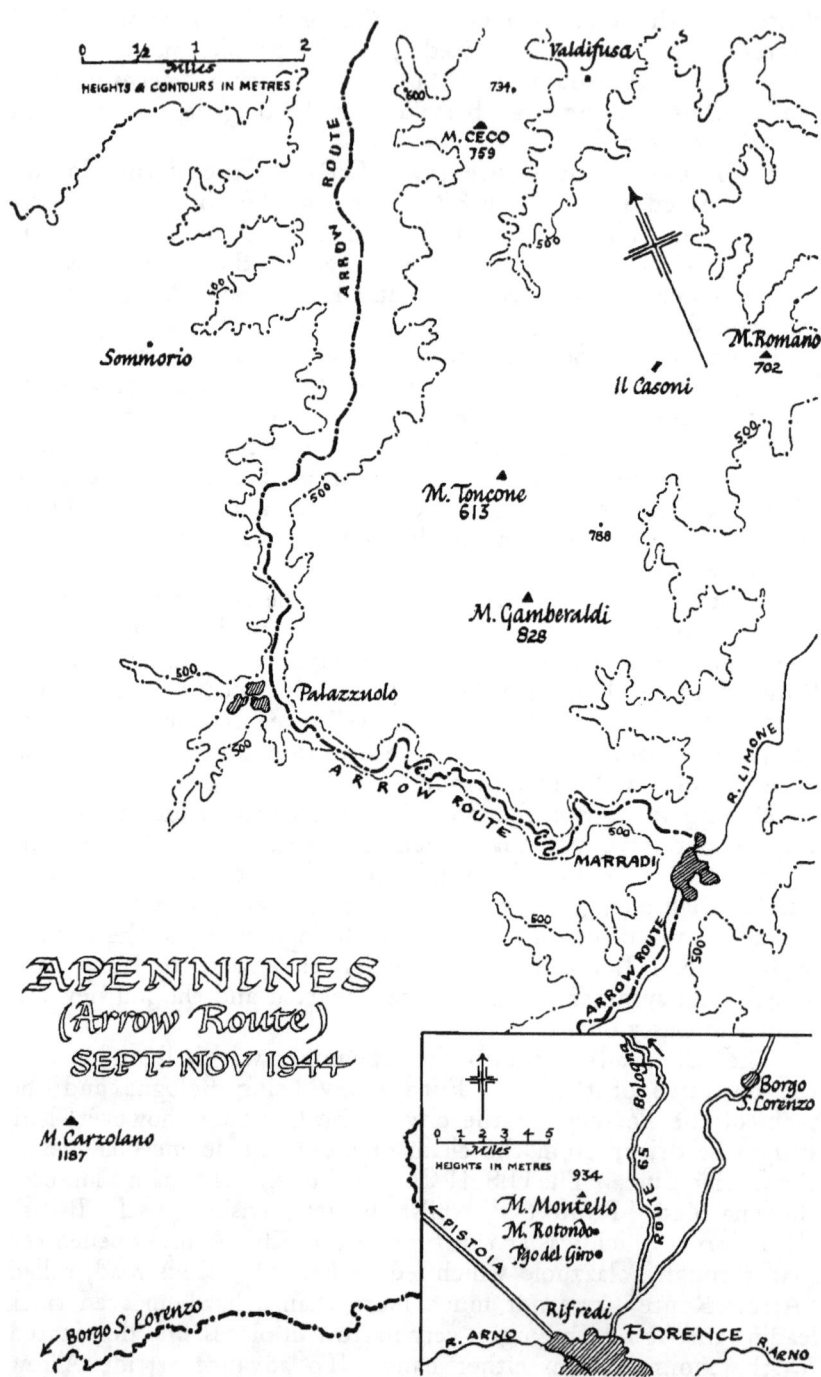

Route meant slow and arduous progress over a wearisome succession of ridges and mountain tops, clearing a stubborn enemy from his frequent vantage points on the way. This was no country for tanks, and the lack of gun positions prevented effective artillery support except on rare occasions. For the most part the infantry had to depend upon their own weapons and their physical endurance; and a battalion could not fight as a battalion. Success depended upon a series of company and platoon actions where subordinate commanders, down to section commanders, had to prove their worth.

By 21st September the 1st Division had broken into the Gothic Line and had secured key points where Arrow Route crossed some of the highest summits of the Apennines. But there was still much to do.

The Gordons had come forward after picking up mule transport and man-pack equipment at Borgo San Lorenzo. On the 20th, advancing through the mountains well to the north of the road, they took part in a concentric attack on Monte Carzolano, coming in across the high ground from the west. Three companies were committed, and although they met no enemy, the mist was so thick that they were obliged to halt when short of their objectives.

After a day's rest the Battalion advanced through the mountains south of Palazzuolo and on the 25th crossed the Palazzuolo-Marradi road. A few men were wounded and three prisoners were taken on the way.

In front was the commanding height of Monte Gamberaldi, which had already withstood two attacks. Now it was the turn of the Gordons. Major L. B. Smith's A Company moved forward on the afternoon of the 26th and attacked at 6 p.m. after our artillery and mortars had fired for half an hour. The narrow approach only permitted the deployment of one platoon, so Lieutenant J. W. Waddell's led the way, followed by the other two platoons in succession. Mortar fire could not stop them, but when they came to the foot of the last steep ascent they were taken in enfilade by machine-gun fire. Even then Waddell's men pressed forward until they were brought to a halt by the fire of automatics and showers of hand grenades.

Major Smith ordered the platoon to dig in where they were. Casualties were not heavy, but included Lieutenant H. R. McIntyre who was killed. In the early hours of next morning A Company were withdrawn.

27th September was a day of inaction spent near Palazzuolo in pouring rain, but the Gordons were ordered to try again for Gamberaldi on the morrow. The Divisional plan was for a wide flanking movement which would end in an attack from the north, but, whether the plan was understood by the Battalion or not, the Highlanders found a shorter way up from the west, a route which hitherto had been considered impossible. This was D Company's affair. In cold driving rain and thick mist they scrambled up the steep slippery slopes to find the enemy had departed. The weather had become the chief enemy. After occupying Gamberaldi and Point 788 some distance to the north-east, the Company were almost driven from their gains by a violent storm of wind and rain.

Major J. C. Williamson, the company commander, withdrew most of his men to a ruined farmhouse which offered some shelter. The prospect was dismal in the extreme. All were hungry, for D Company had travelled light, depending for supplies upon the mule transport which had not arrived. A dump of potatoes, found at the farm, was soon disposed of. It was the only fare.

The storm abated next morning and the forward positions were re-occupied. Guides had been sent back for the mule transport which arrived in the afternoon. At the same time was received a radio message from Battalion headquarters: D Company would continue to advance north-eastward and seize Il Casone, some two miles away. This was a nice task for men who were tired, wet, cold and still hungry.

The most had to be made of the little daylight left. Fortunately Sergeant J. Miller of C Company had already patrolled to some purpose: besides capturing two Germans he had learnt a good deal about the lie of the land. D Company were therefore able to push on at a fair pace, and by 6 p.m. had reached a position overlooking Il Casone. The attack went in about nightfall.

Lieutenant W. M'Hardy's platoon led the way, and the Germans were almost taken by surprise; but a spandau opened before the crest was reached and a fire fight ensued in the dark. Gordon automatics and a 2-inch mortar quelled the opposition and the Germans fled, leaving three dead behind. As soon as the hill was won, the victors were obliged to dig for their lives under a hail of high explosive while Lieutenant C. Black's platoon came through to clear some farm buildings on the forward slope, killing two of the enemy. The casualties of D Company had been surprisingly light.

By dawn of the 30th Major Williamson had made his dispositions for the day. He left none of his men forward of the crest, which had been prepared for defence and was held by two sections; the remainder of D Company were withdrawn to take what rest was possible and, of course, to 'brew up'. Some of the 'over thirties' were utterly worn out by the strain of the past two days, and fourteen men were sent back to find the regimental aid post.

It was ascertained that the farm buildings on the forward slope were now in possession of some of the 2nd Royal Scots (66th Brigade), who had come in from the north-west.

Major Williamson was out of touch with the Battalion, but about 8 a.m. Major L. B. Smith arrived with A Company, bringing orders for a further advance eastward against Monte Romano.

It was a depleted D Company who started on this new venture. The advance had only made a little ground when it came under accurate and heavy machine-gun fire; and, although Lieutenant M'Millan's platoon, who led the way, tried hard to get on, there was nothing to do but to extricate them and accept the check. Meanwhile A Company had probed forward with patrols with no better fortune. They lost Lieutenant J. Waddell, killed, and a number of men.

On 1st October the whole Battalion were withdrawn, and in the afternoon arrived back in Borgo San Lorenzo rest area, where they went into billets. The Gordons had every reason to be satisfied with their achievement during the last week of September. They had had a gruelling time, but had done much to loosen up the whole German defence east and north-east of Palazzuolo.

At Borgo San Lorenzo the Battalion reorganised. C Company were dissolved in order to reinforce the other rifle companies, the surplus men forming a 'fire support company' attached to the carrier platoon.

The Gordons moved into the mountains again on 6th October, taking over positions west of Monte Toncone, where they protected the right flank of the 1st Division, who were fighting for Monte Ceco. The relief was carried out in appalling weather, which probably accounted for the inactivity of the enemy. And the pitiless rain continued: slit trenches filled with water, mountain tracks became so slippery with mud as to become almost impassable by man or mule, and there was nothing on these bleak mountain-sides which the troops could use for shelter.

Apart from some patrol activity and 'a little shelling', this part of the front was quiet. The chief enemies of the Gordons were the wet and the cold.

The Battalion were relieved by the 1/5th Mahrattas (8th Indian Division) on the 13th and moved to the west of Arrow Route where, in the Sommorio area, they remained until 17th October.

By this time the 1st Division had captured the formidable Monte Ceco, and the height called Point 734 to the north-east of it. On 17th October A and B Companies of the Gordons relieved the 1st Hertfordshire (66th Brigade) on Ceco itself. The German guns and mortars were active, but seemed to do little harm.

Next day A Company sent out a platoon to relieve a platoon of the Hertfordshire on Spicco, north-west of Ceco, and on the 19th a patrol of the Company who approached Point 600 on the next ridge to the north drew shell-fire and sighted some Germans. In the evening A Company made several attempts to occupy Point 600, but no impression could be made upon the defence, the German mortar fire being very heavy. Similar activities continued without much result. On the 21st Lieutenant E. A. Lees was wounded by a shell.

Next day the Gordons were relieved by troops of the 66th Brigade, and went back to Borgo San Lorenzo, where another reorganisation took place. Owing to lack of reinforcements, the war establishment of all battalions in the 1st Division was reduced by five officers and 108 other ranks.

On 29th October the Battalion moved up to relieve the 2nd Royal Scots on Ceco and in Valdifusa, a village in the valley north-east of the mountain peaks. Hostile artillery and mortars were active in spite of the persistent heavy rain, but patrols made no contact with the enemy.

The Fifth Army offensive towards Bologna had now come to a standstill by reason of the weather, the state of communications, the shortage of ammunition, and the exhaustion of the troops. In order that the Americans should have the opportunity to build up reserves and reorganise for future operations, it became necessary for our troops to take over some of their responsibilities, and so the 1st Division were ordered to relieve our Allies in the Monte Grande sector.

This sector lay north-west of the region in which the 1st Division had been operating, but was east of Route 65. Monte Grande, captured by the Americans after prolonged and bitter fighting, marked the limit of their penetration and had created a not easily defended salient. From the heights Bologna was visible, and also the low-lying country in the valley of the Po.

The change over meant a difficult cross-country move for the 1st Division, for lateral communications were extremely bad, and those roads which were available proved to be in a terrible state.

The Gordons were relieved on Ceco and at Valdifusa by their old acquaintances the 1/5th Mahrattas on the night of 1st November, but it was not until a late hour on the 5th that they completed the take-over from the Americans in the Monte Calde-raro area, north of Monte Grande. Battalion headquarters came under mortar fire whilst moving up, and losses during the relief amounted to Lieutenant J. Holmes and six other ranks wounded.

Dry and frosty weather now set in. As the forward positions were under enemy observation no mules were allowed beyond Battalion headquarters, a restriction which called for regular carrying parties and added to the difficulties of supply.

Battalion headquarters were heavily shelled and mortared on 8th November, one man being killed and nine wounded; next day the whole of the Battalion area was kept under steady bombardment. In D Company's position a church spire used as an observation post was brought down by two direct hits. No casualties were caused, but one platoon which occupied the cellars beneath by day were buried for a time and badly shaken up; and much equipment was destroyed.

Patrols were active, but soon all movement was hampered by heavy mist and few Germans were seen. There were two dry, cold and sunny days before the Gordons were relieved by a battalion of the 3rd Brigade on the 12th. Our artillery had taken advantage of the improved visibility to carry out a special shoot against the German mortar positions.

A return to the hot baths, clean clothing and cinemas of the Borgo San Lorenzo rest area was very welcome; so, also, was the issue of such winter equipment as sleeping bags and string vests.

On 18th November the Gordons relieved the 11th Lancashire Fusiliers (66th Brigade) in the Frassineto-Monte Cerere sector on the eastern side of the salient. Now the sunny weather seemed to stir both friend and foe to activity. Patrol met patrol, and B Company lost six men from mortar bombardments. Battalion headquarters area received five 9-inch shells during the morning of the 21st, but no harm was done.

Some German movement was seen on the 22nd, and the Battalion mortars took advantage of the target, but A Company lost Lieutenant G. R. Rose, M.M., killed by mortar fire, on this day. By the 27th mist and heavy rain enveloped the mountains. On 2nd December a fighting patrol reached a point overlooking a German post, and fired all they had into it. A solitary spandau replied. The following day was remarkable for a heavy bombardment of Frassineto which, rather surprisingly, caused no casualties. Before midnight on the 3rd the Gordons were relieved by the 11th Argyll and Sutherland Highlanders, and withdrew to Borgo San Lorenzo, where leave to Florence was permitted so far as transport allowed.

When the Gordons came forward again on the 9th to take over the Castellero sector, they found the enemy in a rather aggressive mood. On the 10th Major D. Shepherd, R.A., a fine officer and a good friend whose battery had given the Gordons admirable support ever since the landing of Anzio, was ambushed and captured by an audacious German patrol not far from Battalion headquarters. He died as a prisoner-of-war. Next day the rear platoon of B Company were attacked from the east by a strong patrol and reported an officer and two men missing. The whole of B Company area was heavily mortared, and on the 13th the enemy reinforced his bombardment by a self-propelled gun.

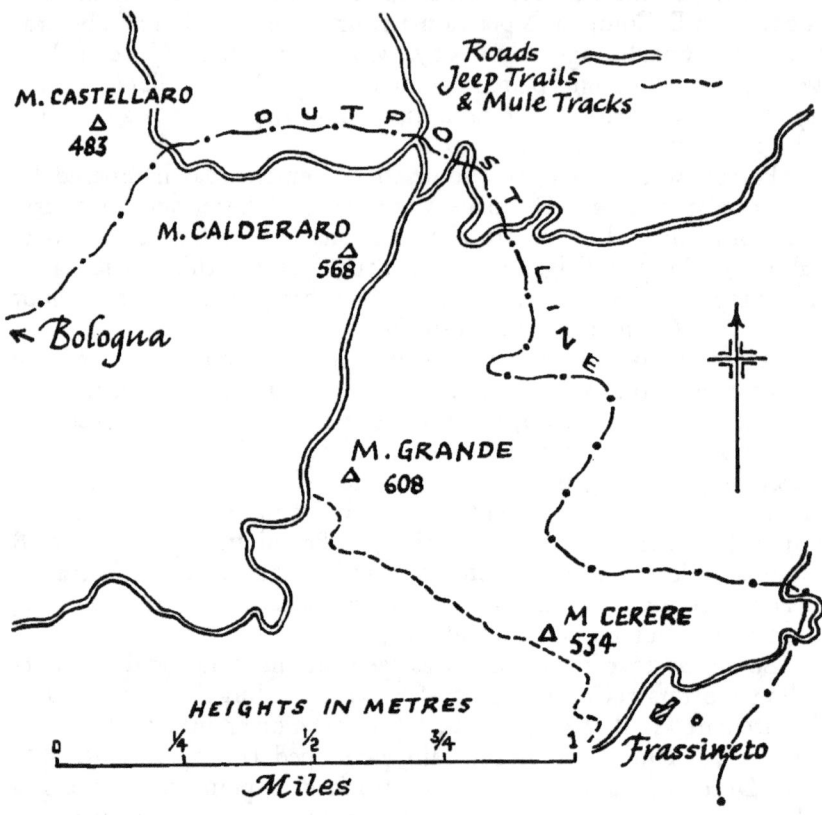

This was promptly destroyed by our artillery. On the 15th Battalion headquarters received a special concentration of fire and three men in a listening post of A Company were killed by a direct hit on their trench. This was altogether an unlucky tour for the Battalion. A platoon of A Company were cleaning grenades when one exploded, wounding an officer and nine others; the artillery observation officer was mortally wounded when a mortar bomb hit a house; and a strong fighting patrol failed to surprise a German post in a building and were obliged to withdraw under fire.

After relief by the Loyals on the 21st came another spell at Borgo San Lorenzo, where seasonable supplies were not yet available and Christmas was merely a time to luxuriate in hot baths and clean clothes. The Gordons took over the Monte Grande sector on

29th December and saw the Germans celebrate the passing of the Old Year by firing tracer bullets and signal lights into the air. This display seemed to extend for three or four miles behind the enemy's front positions.

The German mortars continued to be active and when, on the night of 3rd January 1945, the Gordons were relieved by the Loyals again, Lieutenant E. W. Cessford was wounded.

At Borgo San Lorenzo life took on a specially attractive aspect, for there was entertainment at the Divisional theatre, and it was easier to arrange transport for taking parties to Florence. On the 6th the officers sat down to a combined Christmas and New Year dinner. On the 8th the sergeants feasted in Florence. And then the Gordons began to pack up, for their time in the mountains was over; and it cannot be said that anyone was sorry.

From the time that the Gordons had left the Arno in September they had had their fill of mountain warfare in autumn and in winter. It had been a great ordeal. The soldier, heavily laden with weapons, ammunition, tools and rations, was called upon to make his way along slippery tracks and to climb steep mountain sides in order to get to grips with his enemy. In the small actions which ensued, sometimes only patrol or platoon affairs, no spectacular success could be achieved. In every kind of advance progress was slow, and the utmost effort appeared to be unrewarding. Even when the Battalion reverted to the defensive round Monte Grande their lot was ceaseless vigilance in mud and rain and frost and snow with only the bare necessities of life to sustain them. Conditions were, indeed, hard, ' but ', as their commanding officer could truly say, ' not hard enough to beat the Gordons '.

The work of the stretcher-bearers was, as it had always been, above reproach; but there were not enough of them. The Gordons were grateful to the reinforcement of gunners who did splendid work in the long and difficult carries from the aid posts.

Rations, ammunition and supplies of all kinds were sent forward in jeeps and then, as the tracks grew more difficult, on mules before being handed over to carrying parties for delivery to the forward positions. The mules and their Indian attendants were an indispensable part of the system of supply as the Gordons were quick to appreciate. And mule stretchers were sometimes employed for the conveyance of the wounded. The mule may not be everybody's friend, but who can gainsay his worth in mountain warfare?

The total battle casualties of the 6th Gordons from their arrival on the Arno until their departure from the Monte Grande sector were three officers and twenty-six other ranks killed, five officers and 111 wounded, and two officers and twenty-six missing.

The Gordons were not to see the final victory in Italy. On 9th January 1945 they left Borgo San Lorenzo for Garibaldi Barracks in Perugia where, although some training was done and packing up for a sea passage continued, there was time to pick a Battalion football team and to start on its career a Gordon concert party.

The train journey to Taranto began on the 17th, and by the 21st the Battalion were assembled at a transit camp near the port. On the 24th they embarked for Palestine on the s.s. *Duchess of Richmond*, which docked at Haifa on the 27th.

Palestine had been under British administration since Allenby's campaign of 1917 and was included in Middle East Command. The Gordons, now removed from a theatre of active operations, could only speculate as to what their future would be.

They were conveyed southward at once to a training camp some twelve miles from Gaza. This seemed a pleasant spot in warm and sunny weather, but there was plenty of work to do. Ranges were constructed and a training programme was soon under way. In view of the disturbed state of the country a warning was issued that all arms must be carefully guarded.

During the following months the Gordons pursued a course of training which included exercises with tanks, and instruction in bridging. There was plenty of football, and in April the Battalion almost swept the board at the Brigade rifle meeting. Leave was open to Cairo and to the United Kingdom. Peace seemed in the air. On St. George's Day the pipes and drums played before Lord Gort, V.C., High Commissioner for Palestine. Victory in Europe was celebrated on 8th May by a thanksgiving service and a sports meeting. The pipe band played in Jerusalem. Next day was a holiday, and a special dinner was served to all ranks.

The pipe band had been kept going with some difficulty. In July, after a welcome reinforcement had been received, the Gordons could muster twelve pipers and eight drummers.

On 21st May Lieut.-Colonel J. B. Clapham handed over command to Lieut.-Colonel P. J. Johnstone, a Seaforth Highlander.

The Gordons travelled north to the Lebanon on 25th June. Whilst in camp at Insiriye they practised river crossings on the Litani, and leave parties were able to visit Beirut.

About this time news was received of the award of a United States decoration—the Silver Star—to Lance-Corporal J. Agnew for gallantry at Anzio.

On 4th July the Battalion went to Damascus, where they took over internal security duties, the Arabs being restive under French administration. There were, however, no 'incidents' and before the end of the month the Gordons had moved out to train with tanks around Jebel Mazar. By 10th August they had left Syria and were back in camp near Gaza again, able to resume their normal routine.

The surrender of Japan on the 14th seemed to herald no change in the fortunes of the Battalion. As the new commanding officer wrote early in June, 'We are almost back to peace-time conditions here'. So far as officers and men could gather, there seemed no intention of bringing the Gordons home.

The award of the M.B.E. to Captain C. G. Munro, M.M., quartermaster of the 6th Gordons since 1936, pleased everyone. In 1914, when a lad of seventeen, he had joined the 5th Gordon Highlanders and, as a Regular soldier, he served between the two wars in the 1st Gordons His work as quartermaster in France and Belgium, Tunisia and Italy, in all conditions, was outstanding: as far as was humanly possible he ensured that the Battalion 'went short of nothing'.

VICTORY IN NORTH-WEST EUROPE
1944-45

Preparation

The liberation of North-west Europe had, in some manner, to be accomplished in the course of encompassing the final defeat of Germany. After Dunkirk we knew that we must some day 'go back' if victory were to be won; and before the end of 1941 a British plan for an assault landing on the coast of France had been prepared. But the time was not yet. Even when the United States entered the war Allied commitments in the Mediterranean and further East delayed the building up of the necessary resources in men and material. Planning, however, continued until at last the Allies evolved the tremendous project for a campaign in the West which, by establishing the much talked of 'Second Front', would assist the Russian offensive from the East. So, in 1944, the British and American armies landed on the coast of Normandy.

Late in November 1943 the ships bringing the 51st (Highland) Division from Sicily entered the Clyde and the Mersey. The two battalions of Gordon Highlanders (the 1st and the 5th/7th) were glad indeed at the prospect of seeing Home again. They travelled south after they landed, but leave to Scotland was opened before the Highlanders settled down to work.

All ranks knew that they had returned from Sicily to prepare for a fresh campaign in Europe, and the Gordons began their training in Buckinghamshire, the 1st Battalion at Stoke Poges and the 5th/7th in the villages of Chalfont St. Peter and Chalfont St. Giles.

On 19th December Lieut.-Colonel A. H. F. Fausset-Farquhar relinquished command of the 1st Gordons, and was succeeded by Lieut.-Colonel J. D. C. Anderson, another Gordon Highlander.

Before the end of the year deficiencies were made good, new equipment began to arrive, and both battalions practised themselves with new weapons in new tactics. The 5th/7th Gordons remark that in January 1944 they made the acquaintance of the Sten gun, 'considered better than the American Tommy gun'.

Despite the hard work and winter weather, the Gordons found life in southern England congenial enough. They were among hospitable and friendly people who could not have been better hosts. The children of the district presented each man of the Highland Division with a five-shilling savings stamp ' as a token of pride and gratitude ', and the 5th/7th Battalion responded with the gift of their week's chocolate ration—very much appreciated by the children for in those days the supply of sweets was small and severely rationed.

In January both battalions moved in turn to a district near Worksop for a week's training with the tank battalions of the 4th Coldstream and the 3rd Scots Guards. The Highlanders were much impressed by the Churchill tanks. They rode in them and learned to work with them, fraternising happily and usefully with the tank crews.

On 16th January, Sir Ian Hamilton's 91st birthday, the concert party band of the 5th/7th played at a party at the General's house in London, where many Gordon officers and their wives came to dance. A few days later the Duke of Gloucester and Sir James Burnett of Leys visited both battalions and saw them at work.

February was marked by a visit from General Montgomery and, later, came General Eisenhower, accompanied by General Montgomery and Air Chief Marshal Sir A. Tedder, Deputy Supreme Commander. When the King arrived on the 28th a number of his estate workers from Ballater, who were serving in the 5th/7th Battalion, were presented to His Majesty.

Training continued, some instruction being given by films. All ranks were expected to attain a high standard of physical fitness, and companies were practised in forced marches of ten miles covered in two hours. Bridging, river crossings, gas and intelligence duties, sniping, mine lifting and laying, and patrolling merged into tactical exercises carried out both by day and night. Anti-tank platoons fired their new 6-pdr. on the range at Foulness in Essex. Practice attacks with the support of flame throwers and mortars were carried out on the field-firing range near Harlington.

At the end of March the 1st Gordons moved to Long Melford in Suffolk, and a few days later the 5th/7th left the Chalfonts for Halstead. In these localities training grounds were hard to find, and for a time the rifle companies of the Gordons concentrated upon map reading and route marches. Both battalions, however, were able to send detachments in succession to the East End of London, where they practised street-fighting in the bombed devastated areas of Limehouse. During May some training with landing craft was done at Felixstowe.

On 16th May both the 1st and the 5th/7th Gordons moved to

their 'marshalling' areas, that of the 1st Battalion being at Orsett and Snaresbrook Park. The 5th/7th occupied the flat country along the Tilbury-Southend road. There was nothing much to do now in the way of training but officers and men kept fit by route marches, runs, and physical exercises. Cinemas and variety shows helped to keep boredom at bay.

Lieut.-Colonel Anderson left the 1st Gordons on 22nd May, owing to ill-health: he had never completely recovered from an attack of pneumonia after the Dunkirk evacuation. Lieut.-Colonel W. A. Stevenson, a Cameron Highlander, was the new commanding officer.

On the night of 25th May the camps were 'sealed': that is to say that in the interests of secrecy they were enclosed by wire, and only senior officers were permitted to pass in and out. Now began the final period of preparation, and surely no British soldiers had ever gone forth to war so elaborately furnished and equipped.

Each man received 'anti-louse' shirt and underclothes, ration pack, emergency ration, Tommy cooker, and water steriliser; also, for the voyage, lifebelt, anti-seasick chewing gum, 'vomit bags', and waders. There was a final check up of equipment, arms and ammunition and everyone was paid 200 French francs. Those who had English money to get rid of were able to resort to N.A.A.F.I.

By 30th May commanding officers, who had attended a conference called by General Montgomery, were in a position to pass on some information to their company commanders, but the men still did not know where they would go or when they would start. Actually the Highland Division, though not taking part in the initial assault landing, were to be one of the 'follow up' divisions landing later on 'D-Day'. Once ashore the rôle of the Highlanders would be determined by the course of events.

General Dempsey, commanding the Second Army, made a tour of the area on 2nd June. This was the last night that the 1st and 5th/7th Gordon Highlanders were to spend on English soil.

The 2nd Gordon Highlanders come into the picture when the 227th Brigade (10th H.L.I., 2nd Gordons and 2nd Argyll and Sutherland Highlanders) move south from the Orkneys in September 1943 to join the 15th (Scottish) Division which, by this time, had definitely been selected to fight in France.

The Gordons were in camp at Fimber, near Sledmere, when they took part in the realistic 'Exercise Blackcock' which lasted six days and included the breaching of a minefield to make way for the armour and the crossing of the river Derwent to establish a bridge-head. Although carried out in very cold and wet weather, the exercise provided some valuable experience, but led to a change in command of the 2nd Gordons. Lieut.-Colonel H. I. Bradshaw suffered a severe injury to his ankle and gave place to Lieut.-Colonel E. C. Colville.

The Battalion moved to Otley in October and, with the remainder of the 15th Division, continued training in Yorkshire. Street-fighting practice was carried out in one of the parts of Hull devastated by enemy bombing, and despite the wintry weather, which doubtless assisted the hardening process of all ranks, much other valuable work as done. In February the senior officers made the acquaintance of Lieut.-General Sir Richard O'Connor, commanding the VIII Corps, under whom they were to serve in Normandy; and General Montgomery came to inspect the 227th Brigade and address the troops. March was memorable for the visit of the King and Queen and Princess Elizabeth, the Royal party driving through the camp to watch demonstrations of waterproofing vehicles and bridging and to see flame-throwers in action.

One activity not wholly unconnected with preparation for war was the Divisional school for young pipers, Pipe-Major Nichol of the 2nd Gordons imparting instruction.

At the end of March came a short spell of training with the 4th Grenadier Guards Tank Battalion at Welbeck Abbey; and on the 31st the Gordons were much gratified by a visit from Mr. Winston Churchill.

The next move came in mid-April. At Muntham Court Estate, near Findon in Sussex, training included exercises wherein the Battalion were 'shot over' by 25-pdrs. and machine guns. The commanding officers of the Brigade were presented to General Eisenhower who, on 25th May, inspected the battalions and made a complimentary speech. The Supreme Commander, it is said, ' made a great impression on the Jocks '.

On 31st May the Divisional commander, Major-General G. H. A. MacMillan, addressed the Battalion for fifteen minutes, saying that this was probably the last the Gordons would see of him before they met ' on the other side '.

A night exercise under a full moon was held on 5th June, and next day news of the successful landings on the Normandy coast was broadcast. Finishing touches were made to all preparations, but the time for action was not yet. The advance parties of the 15th Division went to London on 8th and 9th June; it was not until the 14th that the Gordons moved to their marshalling area near Haywards Heath.

They had had no battle experience, this re-born 2nd Battalion of the Regiment, but they were of the right stuff and had trained hard and well in all weathers: they were ready now to prove themselves in actual combat.

The Triangle and Colombelles

The 1st and the 5th/7th Gordons landed on D Day after the 'Western Wall' had been breached and the leading divisions had started their advance inland from the coast. To the 5th/7th Gordons belongs the distinction of being the first battalion of the new Highland Division to set foot in France.

The 5th/7th Gordons moved to Tilbury Docks on 3rd June and embarked in infantry landing craft which joined a vast assembly of shipping down river off Southend. To those who had been at the Sicily landing the cramped space which forbade much movement and the prospect of an uneasy sea passage struck a familiar note.

Though due to sail at 8 a.m. on 4th June the craft remained at anchor, for the wind had risen and the weather promised ill. A start was made, however, at nine next morning and, as rough seas were to be expected outside the Thames estuary, each man was given a special sea-sick remedy, ' two pills containing a strong drug as used on drunks '.

In well escorted convoy, with bigger ships following, the landing craft proceeded at slow speed and were off Dover in the afternoon of 5th June. Maps and final instructions were now unsealed by the officer commanding troops on each craft, and the plan was explained to the men : the Battalion were to land on a beach in Normandy. During the night—a sleepless one for many—the convoy passed slowly down Channel. When off the Isle of Wight the course was changed to southward, the ships rolling in a 'medium' sea. This, 6th June, was D-Day.

The coast of Normandy came in sight and, lying off shore, a great mass of shipping was seen : liners, flak (anti-aircraft) ships, landing ships and craft of every kind, floating piers, and an impressive display of naval might.

As the Gordons came in slowly—there was some delay in finding the right beach—all on shore seemed quiet. Near the water's edge could be seen some forlorn vehicles which had been inadequately water-proofed. There was a little indiscriminate shelling, and a few fugitive attempts of enemy aircraft to bomb the new arrivals ; but there was no sound of small-arms fire. The sea-side villages showed signs of the tremendous pounding they had received ; the beach obstacles looked less formidable than had been expected.

The actual landing, which began at Courseulles on the afternoon of the 6th, took a long time, for the tide was not at its full and there was a considerable swell. Nearly all the Battalion got soaked in getting ashore from the landing craft, for most of the officers and men were obliged to jump into four feet of water. One man was swept under a neighbouring vessel and drowned; a few others required treatment at a nearby aid post before they could rejoin the Battalion.

Each man carried a pick and shovel and a small pack, his whole kit, with weapons and ammunition, weighing some 70 lb. The Piat 'projector infantry anti-tank'—was the heaviest weapon taken along, for the transport had yet to arrive; and the only link with Brigade headquarters, when it should be established, was one wireless set ferried ashore on an improvised raft.

There was only one exit from the beach, for mines had yet to be cleared from the dunes and from the marshland beyond; and the defile was congested by vehicles of the 3rd Canadian Division, one of the leading formations in the assault landing. However, by 8 p.m. the Gordons were all ashore and moving in detachments to Banville, four miles inland, where they concentrated for the night. And the night was a cold and miserable one, broken by occasional bursts of anti-aircraft fire.

The experiences of the 1st Gordons in their embarkation from Tilbury and passage to the Normandy coast did not differ much from those of their brethren of the 5th/7th. The 1st Battalion started to land near Courseulles rather later on 6th June, and had the same difficulties in getting ashore. The commanding officer, intent on leading the way, dropped into five feet of water, having, it is said, 'a most unpleasant time'. Late at night the 1st Gordons reached the concentration area at Banville.

All three battalions of the 153rd Brigade landed on 6th June, but as their own Brigade headquarters had not yet arrived, the Highlanders found themselves at the disposal of the 3rd Canadian Division, in whose area they were. The Canadians had penetrated inland to a maximum depth of seven miles, but the countryside was by no means clear of the enemy.

On the 7th the 1st Gordons moved forward to Colombiers-sur-Seulles. Here they found the former headquarters of a Panzer Grenadier battalion whose transport had been left behind and proved a gift to the Highlanders, still without their own vehicles. As to stores and equipment, 'some deficiencies were made up at the expense of the *Wehrmacht*'; also, documents of considerable importance were found. In the evening the Battalion moved to a new position as a 'back-stop' to the 7th Canadian Brigade. A day of inaction followed.

Meanwhile the 5th/7th Gordons had been ordered to Ste. Croix-sur-Mer, where about a score of prisoners were collected. Having as yet no transport of their own, the Battalion were glad to

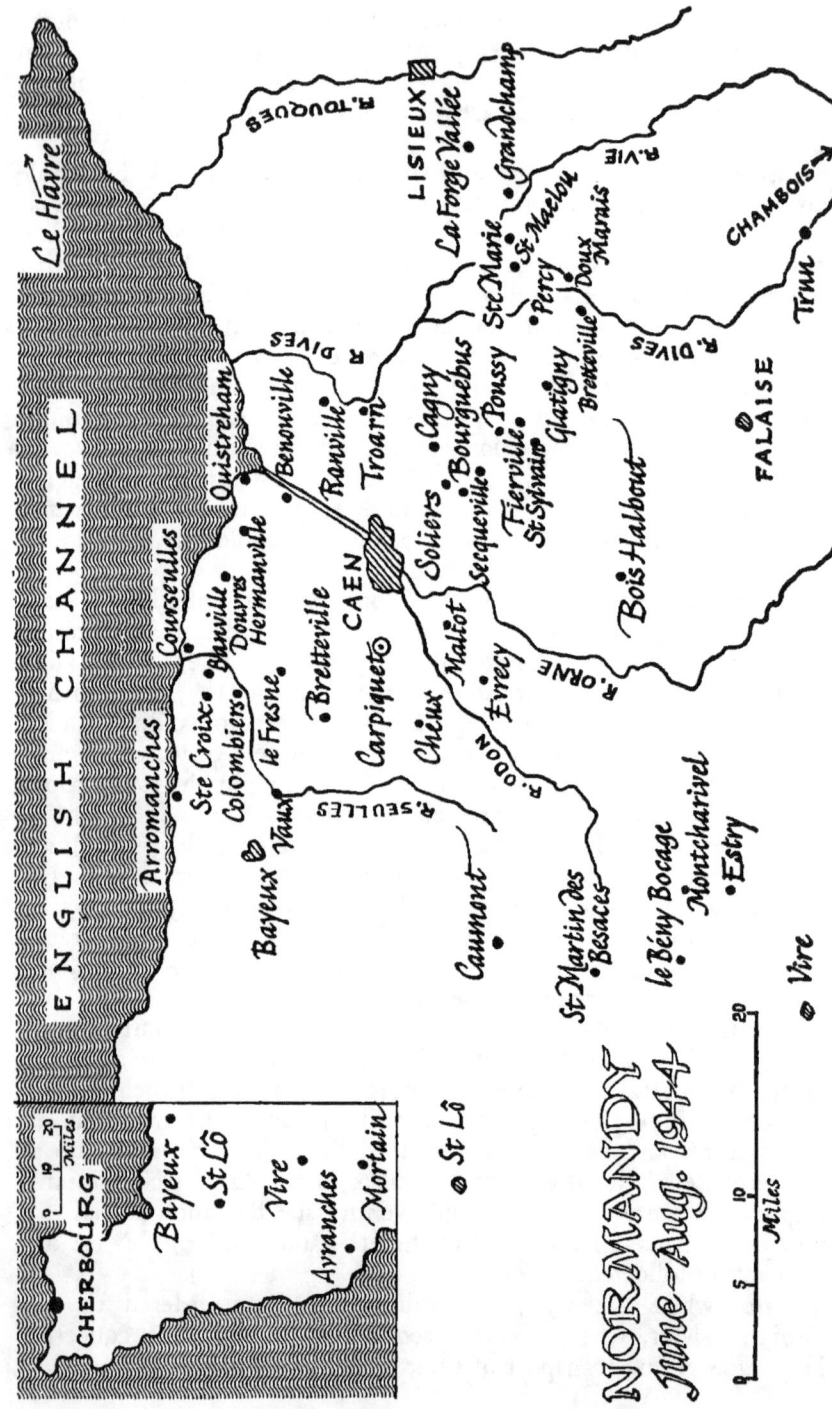

harness two farm stallions to G.S. limbers which had been discovered; and a donkey and cart were sent to the beach to fetch the blankets. The village people, of whom only some proved friendly, were surprised to see Highlanders instead of Russians, for 'Red Menace' propaganda had been rife in this district. Later on the 7th the Battalion went forward to le Fresne Camilly, and here the transport began to arrive. Next day saw the anti-tank guns of the Gordons in position, but although some tank encounters appeared to be taking place away to the right, the Highlanders were not involved.

The Brigade commander and the seconds-in-command of battalions had embarked at Portsmouth on 5th June and were timed to arrive in Normandy early on the 6th ready to receive the troops as they came ashore. Unfortunately their tank landing ship was delayed by the heavy swell when off the coast, so that their transhipment to a smaller craft did not take place until 7th June. The Brigadier got into touch with his battalions late in the afternoon of that day, and the transport began to arrive about the same time.

In the early morning of the 9th the 1st Gordons received a warning order and moved at 9.30 a.m. to the Benouville area to guard the bridges over the Ouistreham-Caen canal and the river Orne. Here was the eastern flank of the Normandy beach-head where the 6th Airborne Division had been dropped and now, reinforced by the 1st Commando Brigade, held the small bridgehead over the river and canal. The Airborne front was described as 'fluid'.

By the afternoon the 1st Gordons were in position. At seven in the evening, after some heavy shelling, several parties of men from other units hurried back over the bridges. It was a false alarm, and, to restore confidence, Lieut.-Colonel Stevenson and the company piper headed a dignified march of C Company, in threes, over one of the bridges. It was a disturbed day and night, for the *Luftwaffe* seemed to be able to attack the area at will.

The 5th/7th Gordons had been moved, on 9th June, to a position south of Hermanville, where they relieved a battalion of the 3rd Division and came under shell-fire for the first time. Captain H. Best, and three others, were wounded.

On 10th June the 153rd Brigade received orders to attack east of the Orne. Accordingly, the 5th/7th Gordons were carried eastward in transport and crossed the river and canal bridges in the evening. Some delay was caused by an air attack which did no damage.

As darkness fell the Battalion moved in single file through the woods, and in the early hours of next morning concentrated north of the junction of the Escoville and Bréville roads, south-east of Escoville, in the western part of Bois de Bavent. They were now 'in the middle of the 8th Parachute Battalion'. Their orders were to attack Touffreville, over a mile to the south, beyond the woods.

The 1st Gordons had followed on. After spending the night 'sleeping in a field', they moved at 5 a.m. on the 11th to relieve some of our parachute troops who were occupying the brickworks north-east of Touffreville. These brickworks provided a good observation post from which enemy movement along the Troarn-Caen road could be seen.

Our paratroopers had been in and out of Touffreville, but did not know if it were now occupied by the enemy. When the 5th/7th Gordons advanced on the evening of 11th June, they found no-one in the village except a few snipers. The Highlanders settled down for the night, having lost Lieutenant P. W. Brand and thirteen other ranks wounded. Bursts of spandau fire were frequent, and German patrols seemed to be prowling about in the darkness.

Enemy attacks, which started about 5 a.m. on the 12th, took the form of large-scale infiltrations. B and C Companies, in front and on the left, were drawn back to better defensive positions, but no-one knew where the Germans would appear next. 'Every company was surrounded at times which didn't worry them much.' Battalion headquarters, on the road beside an orchard in rear of Touffreville, were suddenly assailed by a strong detachment of Germans with a spandau, but the commanding officer inspired the defence by voice and example and the enemy was driven off with loss.

For his handling of the Battalion on this rather critical day Lieut.-Colonel J. E. G. Hay received the D.S.O.; and Provost-Sergeant McPherson, who did wonders with his Bren gun, was awarded the Military Medal.

Sergeant Aitkenhead of B Company was taken prisoner, but his captors made the mistake of leaving him with a single guard. The sergeant killed this man with a knife he had kept concealed, and, after hiding in a cornfield and in a farm, sometimes under British artillery fire, he managed to rejoin the Battalion. The first Highlander he met greeted him with 'Is that you Sergeant Aitkenhead? Aye, I ken't they could never kill *you*.'

The Germans drew off about noon and did not renew their attacks; and the 5th/7th Gordons could feel that they had more than held their own against good Panzer Grenadier troops. The Battalion had lost Lieutenant A. McIntosh, wounded, and of other ranks, three killed, twenty wounded, and four missing. Though very tired, the men were in good heart, the more so as they had received a Home mail on this day.

As for the 1st Gordons, they had no part in this affair, though they held one company ready to counter-attack in case of need. Some casualties were suffered from shell-fire, and the observation post at the brickworks was hit by a mortar bomb which wounded four men.

A German attack in the early morning of the 13th was regarded by the 5th/7th Gordons as of 'not much importance'. They were confident that they could hold on to Touffreville, and felt disgusted when ordered to withdraw later in the day. An attack on the right had failed, so that the Battalion—and the 1st Gordons too—were in a dangerous salient. It had therefore been decided to shorten and readjust the front, so both Gordon battalions were brought back in the evening.

They had been under fairly heavy fire for most of the day, the 5th/7th losing two officers and fifteen others, including Regimental Sergeant-Major A. Michie, wounded. The casualties of the 1st Gordons included Captain N. Peters and Lieutenants G. Duthie and G. C. Forbes, all wounded.

Before dawn of the 14th the 5th/7th Gordons were settled astride the Bréville road in the woods east of Escoville, with A Company forward near the apex of the triangle where the Bréville and Escoville roads meet. Further west, the Germans in Bois de Bavent were not far away.

On the right of the 5th/7th Battalion the 1st Gordons were dug in along hedgerows and under trees nearer Escoville.

The day was comparatively quiet, with some shell and mortar fire, but the 1st Gordons lost Lieutenant J. E. J. Gallup and a number of others wounded. Their patrols, who went as far as Butte de la Hogue, found the Touffreville brickworks and Escoville unoccupied by the enemy. The 15th June was another uneventful day, but on the 16th came the expected enemy attack, delivered in considerable force and with great persistence.

After a heavy mortar and artillery bombardment, German tanks and infantry advanced at 4.20 a.m. from the south-east across the front of A and D Companies of the 1st Gordons, making for Escoville. Our artillery opened with great effect and the enemy faltered, but he passed some troops into Escoville and the Gordons feared that an attack might develop from the village round their right rear. They made ready to meet this threat while our artillery fire broke up an advance of tanks and infantry against A and D Companies; but there was a slight infiltration between B Company and A Company of the 5th/7th Gordons near the apex of the triangle. Then, at 8.50 a.m., a storm of shell and mortar fire fell upon the whole area held by the 1st Gordons, a bombardment obviously intended to cover the retirement

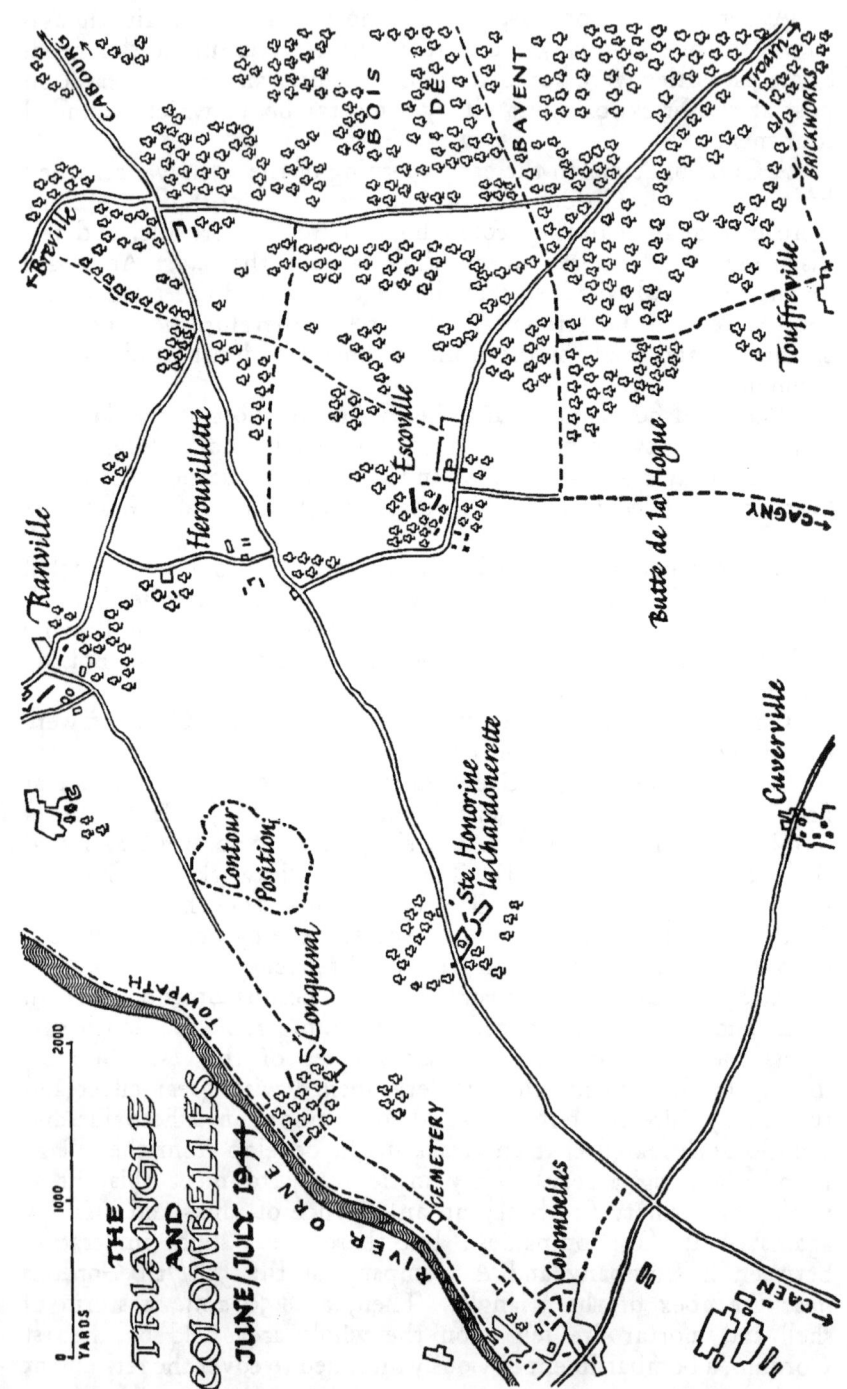

of the Germans from Escoville. As they retreated A and D Companies and the mortar platoon took ample toll of them.

The fight was not yet over. It was evident that the 5th/7th Gordons were heavily engaged in the triangle, and at 7.30 p.m. tanks were seen advancing from that region up the road to Escoville. The 1st Gordons were still under shell and mortar fire, and about an hour later German infantry took the same road and, turning north, began to shoot up Battalion headquarters. Confused fighting among the trees and hedgerows followed, and one platoon of C Company was over-run. Towards midnight Battalion headquarters managed to fight the Germans off and reach the area of D Company, and by this time the enemy effort had spent itself. The 1st Gordons were able to re-establish their positions without much trouble.

The 5th/7th Gordons, strung out along both sides of the Bréville road, had endured intense mortar fire which started at 4.25 a.m. and lasted for half an hour. The Germans then filtered forward through the woods. Major Muir's A Company in the apex were shelled and machine-gunned without respite until the enemy's attack came in. One of our forward anti-tank guns was captured and recaptured; a platoon was twice driven from its position and twice regained it; the Royal Artillery 17-pdr. anti-tank guns, attached to the Battalion, knocked out a self-propelled gun and a Mark IV tank. This was, indeed, A Company's battle, and when at last Major Muir fell back with his survivors towards Battalion headquarters he had held up the German onslaught for nearly twelve hours.

But the enemy was now in possession of the apex, and at 5.30 p.m. tanks, supported by infantry, advanced up the Bréville road. The tank commander could be seen urging on the infantry, who came forward through the trees. One 17-pdr. anti-tank gun fired without effect, and was soon knocked out. Then Lance-Sergeant Fraser came into action with one of the Gordon 6-pdrs. Thirty shells were pumped in and three tanks in succession were hit and burst into flames, 'a most encouraging sight'. This was enough, and the German infantry faded away. Later Brigadier Murray came up to congratulate each member of the anti-tank detachment.

The casualties of the 5th/7th Gordons, mostly in A Company, amounted to seven killed; Lieutenant J. W. Marsh, and twenty-three others wounded; and Lieutenants F. Stewart and T. McN. Scott and thirty-eight other ranks missing. Corporal Foster and a stretcher-bearer, who went out to bring in wounded, were deliberately fired on and killed.

The 1st Battalion were much more unfortunate as regards casualties to officers. Major D. C. Thom was killed; Captain

J. G. M. Birrs (who rejoined from hospital a few days later) and Lieutenants J. Martin, J. T. Maclaren, G. Gilmour and W. Reid were wounded. Lieutenant Gilmour, on loan from the Canadian Army, and described by his commanding officer as a 'damned good little chap', died of his wounds.

Now came a few days of comparative calm, for the enemy's bombardment abated and his few attempts at infiltration were suitably dealt with by the Gordons. A number of snipers were rounded up in workmanlike fashion.

Captain M. C. Gall, M.C., commanding the carrier platoon of the 5th/7th Gordons, was injured in an accident on 18th June. He had landed in Normandy only a few days before.

When the Brigade were withdrawn on 21st June the 1st Gordons went back to a 'rest area' at Ranville, which was so far removed from the attentions of the enemy as to permit of short route marches and drill.

The 5th/7th Battalion could hardly be said to have left the front line, for when they were relieved by the 7th Black Watch (154th Brigade) on the 19th they occupied Herouvillette with one company in an outpost at Escoville, 'that unpleasant little village'. However, Herouvillette provided an opportunity for 'wine hunting and the collection of fresh vegetables'.

On the Chardonerette road was discovered a 'secret weapon': a small radio-controlled vehicle which could be sent forward to lay a charge of 500 lb. of high explosive. On its return journey it paid out a wire by which the charge could be fired. As this little wonder was the first of its kind to be captured intact, the Royal Engineers were very glad to receive it.

Nearly everyone was in some sort of billet at Herouvillette so, although defences had to be manned and patrols sent out, life was not uncomfortable. A Divisional rest camp, to which ten men per battalion could go in succession, was opened on 26th June.

Two days later signals tuned in to a German radio station whence the voice of Lieutenant Stewart of the 5th/7th Gordons—reported missing on the 16th—was heard assuring his wife that he was 'safe' in German hands.

By 1st July the 1st Gordons were in Longueval with B Company forward in Chardonerette under command of the 5th Seaforth (152nd Brigade). The Battalion were ordered to lay an anti-tank minefield between the two villages, which seemed to show that no offensive action was contemplated in this locality. Captain D. L. Urquhart was wounded on 5th July, but during these days few casualties were suffered.

On the 8th the I Corps attacked Caen, which was captured after two days of hard fighting. On the 9th the 1st Gordons carried out a raid on the factory area of Colombelles, still unsubdued. This enterprise had the support of three field regiments and one medium regiment of artillery. A Company advanced along the tow-path from Longueval to form a firm base for the raiding party, twelve men of C Company, under Captain Gilchrist. The raiders entered a factory building and found it empty, but captured three Germans near by: when all withdrew under a barrage of heavy mortars, retaliation on Battalion headquarters was severe. Next day the Germans kept the whole of the Longueval area under artillery and mortar fire.

Preparations were now being made for a night attack by the 153rd Brigade on the village of Colombelles, with the 1st Gordons on the right and the 5th Black Watch on the left. The 7th Black Watch (placed under Brigade command) were then to go through and secure the factory area, where the sappers would destroy the tall chimneys used by the enemy as observation posts. The whole force would then be withdrawn.

This attack, with tremendous artillery support, was launched at 1 a.m. on 11th July. The Gordons had set A and B Companies to lead the way, but A Company, who followed the tow-path along the river, were soon out of touch with the rest of the advance. B Company cleared the first few houses of Colombelles and then came under the fire of heavy machine-guns and mortars. Major R. Andrews and Lieutenant C. Brown were wounded, and Lieutenant G. I. Robertson, who took over command, began to draw off the very weakened company to reorganise at the cemetery. The time was about 3.45 a.m.

Much earlier, soon after 2 a.m., D Company had been sent up with orders to avoid B Company's battle by keeping clear of the houses and pushing forward further to the left. They were checked by intensive mortar fire, and the commanding officer eventually ordered both B and D Companies to reorganise at the cemetery and await the arrival of tanks, which would support them in a fresh effort.

Encouraging reports had come in from A Company who, after clearing a number of buildings, announced that they were on their objective. Lieut.-Colonel Stevenson at once ordered C Company from reserve to take the tow-path route and assist A Company to clear and consolidate the south-western portion of Colombelles.

Then came a report that the sappers were having difficulty in clearing the tow-path for the passage of vehicles. B and D Companies were now under such heavy mortar fire in the vicinity of the cemetery that they were ordered back to their old positions in Longueval.

The success of the operation seemed very much in doubt. Before 5 a.m., however, C Company got in touch with A Company and the mopping up of the south-west corner of Colombelles seemed to be going well. Less than an hour later the tow-path was reported clear and the much needed battle transport of the two companies began to go through. Shortly afterwards, about 6 a.m., Lieut.-Colonel Stevenson was hit in the leg by a mortar bomb splinter and Major Hon. H. C. H.-T. Cumming Bruce (later to become Lord Thurlow), took over command. He was a Seaforth Highlander. At this time B and D Companies were still reorganising in Longueval with the prospect of delivering a fresh attack.

At seven o'clock the very venturesome chaplain of the Gordons returned from the German lines where he had been held prisoner for three hours. He said that 'the enemy appeared to be retreating'.

This was far from the truth. On the left the 5th Black Watch had seized their objective in the north-east portion of Colombelles, but at 7.30 a.m. they reported a counter-attack by German armour. It seemed that they were being 'badly shot up by Tiger tanks', and the Brigadier, deeming their position untenable, decided to bring them back. Further, he ordered a general withdrawal, and this was accomplished under a smoke screen which did not prevent some losses from the German bombardment.

When at 8.10 a.m. A and C Companies of the Gordons were ordered to withdraw they were very reluctant to do so, for they had made themselves masters of most of Colombelles, and were quite prepared to hold what they had gained. They were not permitted to do so. Leaving the 7th Black Watch, who had not been engaged, to 'hold the fort', the whole of the Battalion assembled in Longueval and then moved back to Ranville.

Besides the officers already mentioned, Lieutenant D. A. McColl had been wounded and Lieutenants H. W. Glennie and R. B. Anderson were missing. Lieutenant Anderson had been captured in Colombelles after being wounded, and was liberated when the Americans occupied Rennes on 4th August.

At Ranville the 1st Gordons were now under long-range artillery fire which damaged some of their vehicles. The carriers and one platoon were called upon to relieve the 1st Black Watch (154th Brigade) in Escoville, and at night the garrison of the village was increased by one Gordon company. When, on 15th July, the Battalion crossed the Orne and withdrew into reserve not far from Douvres, a platoon remained in Escoville to conceal from the enemy the fact that the Highlanders had been relieved by troops of another division.

It is now time to follow the fortunes of the 5th/7th Gordons who, on 30th June, had moved westward from Herouvillette to take over a position on a slight rise of ground in open country nearer Longueval. This, called the 'contour position', overlooked Chardonerette—the full name is Ste. Honorine la Chardonerette —and was 'no worse than any other place', although the forward companies were shelled at times.

Here let it be recorded that Private Whitehead of the Battalion had already been in Caen. He came over with a reinforcement on 11th June and, by some mischance, was mixed up with the Canadian R.E., who made use of him. Twenty-four hours later he was captured while on patrol in a minefield and confined in an upper room of a house in Caen. While the Germans were carousing in their billet downstairs he escaped by means of the window and made his way through the patrols of foe and friend to reach the British lines. He now rejoined the Battalion.

The following days were remarkable for the very wet weather, but the Highlanders had learned to endure the rain, and were more concerned by their move to Chardonerette, which had acquired an evil reputation as an 'unsavoury place'. This happened on 7th July, and next day the start of our attack on Caen brought down some extra shelling on the Gordons' position, Lieutenant B. G. Walters being killed. He had joined the Battalion as signals officer only a few days earlier.

In the Colombelles attack on the night of 10th/11th July the 5th/7th Gordons were not engaged, but they acted as a firm base for the operation. During the withdrawal on the morning of the 11th they came under heavy shell-fire which killed four men and wounded Captain Stewart Black, Lieutenant Bonar, and fifteen others. This shelling continued next day, when Lieutenant J. W. Murray was wounded.

The Gordons were glad to leave Chardonerette for the 'contour position' in the evening. Next day they moved back to Herouvillette, which was more peaceful and offered a better chance of sleep; and on the 15th, like their brethren of the 1st Battalion, they withdrew into reserve. In the open country near Douvres 'the companies spread out desert-fashion'.

Since they had crossed the Orne on the night of 10th June, the two battalions of Gordon Highlanders had been engaged without respite in the defence of the eastern flank of the Normandy beach head, the bastion which it was vital to hold secure while the offensive battle developed further to the west. To all ranks it was a new experience. Those who had fought in the Western Desert found that there was no chance here of taking part in an offensive on the grand scale, no opportunity to achieve a spectacular success. Fighting at short range in woods and around villages called for a new technique—sometimes akin to 'gangster' methods—and was variously voted 'rather a novelty' and 'a tricky business'. But the Gordons, in common with the rest of the Highland Division, had probably given a highly trained, aggressive, and more numerous enemy a worse time than they had themselves experienced.

Casualties in each of the two battalions amounted to about 250 of all ranks, the great majority of them wounded. The 1st Gordons felt the loss of Lieut.-Colonel Stevenson, a born leader who, at a crisis, would handle a Bren gun with the best. In both the 1st and the 5th/7th the number of officers lost was a matter of great concern, for to replace them it was difficult to ensure the posting of Gordons or, indeed, any Highlander. Also drafts which arrived to fill up the ranks often consisted of Englishmen; but these new arrivals soon acquired a pride of Regiment which, in itself, was a compliment to the Gordons.

Odon Battlefront

Rather more than a week after the 1st and 5th/7th Gordon Highlanders appeared east of the Orne the 2nd Gordons arrived from England.

The advanced parties of all battalions of the 15th Division had reached London on 8th and 9th June and left for France without undue delay. Apart from a slight collision with another ship when off Courseulles, the passage was uneventful.

The 2nd Gordons left Findon on 14th June for a marshalling area near Hayward's Heath, and on the 18th they embarked at Newhaven for Normandy in infantry landing craft. They left England on a beautiful evening to the sound of the pipes and the cheers of many spectators: there was no need for secrecy now for all the world knew that the Allies had landed in France.

One craft carried half the Gordons and half the 2nd Argyll and Sutherland Highlanders under Lieut.-Colonel Colville's command; another, took the other halves of the two battalions commanded by Lieut.-Colonel Tweedie of the Argyll. This was evidence of careful planning, for if one of the transports were sunk neither battalion would become a total loss.

Out in the Channel rising seas betokened trouble, and after an uncomfortable night the Gordons spent the next day tossing about some distance off the French coast. It was too rough to land until the afternoon of the 20th. Then one of the 'Mulberry' pre-fabricated harbours was used, the approach to the shore being by way of a breakwater formed of concrete-filled vessels and steel and concrete jetties which had been towed across from England. Then the Gordons had to walk half-a-mile along pontoons to the beaches near Arromanches. Once ashore they marched in detachments six miles to their bivouac area at Vaux-sur-Seulle, 'halting on the way for a cup of tea'.

These proceedings were conducted in peace and all ranks were surprised to see how little damaged by war the countryside appeared.

The Gordons dug their slit trenches and waited for their transport to arrive. Their first night on French soil was enlivened by a German bomber which crashed in flames about one hundred yards from one of the companies.

In daytime there was no interference from the *Luftwaffe*, but every night single aircraft came over to drop a few bombs and were greeted by the fire—some of it very erratic—from vessels lying off the beaches.

Not so uneventful was the passage of the Gordons' transport. The vehicles reached the Greyhound Stadium at West Ham on 14th June, and were on the quayside at Tilbury next day; but the ship which was to take them to France had not arrived. While waiting some of the Gordons saw the first of the famous—or infamous—'V' (flying) bombs fall on London, a number of them in the docks area. However, loading was completed on the 17th and after darkness had fallen the ship left in convoy for France.

Those on board had their first glimpse of the Normandy coast on the morning of the 19th when the worst June gale for fifty years had begun to rage. Landing was impossible until the gale abated: and in the upshot Allied operations were delayed for several days. It was not until the 23rd that the weather moderated sufficiently for the landing of stores, ammunition and transport to be resumed.

When, on this day, the ship carrying the Gordons' transport approached the beaches they were seen to be strewn with wrecked and damaged landing craft and other vessels. On the afternoon of the 24th the last of the Gordons' vehicles was transhipped; and then a deep hole in the sea-bed caused the first vehicle off the ramp to be submerged instead of entering the shallows. A halt was called, and, owing to the weariness of the landing craft crew, a high tide was lost before operations were resumed. However, on the 25th the whole of the transport gained the shore through three feet of water at Courseulles, and was able to join the Battalion that same day.

The 2nd Gordons had had three days of inaction in which to gather impressions of the French people. All ranks had heard much of the sufferings of France under the Occupation, also many tales of the French 'Resistance'; but these Normans seemed unimpressed by the turn of events. Some of the women had married German soldiers, and there was a general air of caution

—a reluctance to accept the presence of the invaders as a change for the better. 'The Boche had said that he would be back in three weeks.' A Gordon officer who wanted the use of a barn for his men was told by the farmer that it could not be permitted as the farm was the property of the Third Reich. Food was abundant and it seemed that in Normandy the German behaviour had been 'correct'.

As soon as the assembly of the 2nd Gordons was complete the time for action came. The biggest attack yet made from the Allied beach-head was about to be launched, and the objective was Caen. An advance from the north would be combined with a thrust further west to cross the Odon and Orne rivers, swinging south-eastward to cut off Caen from the south. This offensive had been delayed by the gale which had interrupted the disembarkation of material. Now it was to open on 26th June.

Late on the 25th the 2nd Gordons moved up behind the battle front. The 15th Division attack was to start from a line south of Bretteville l'Orgueilleuse—a village on the Caen-Bayeux road—the 44th and 46th Brigades having as objective a ridge running south of Cheux. It was the task of the 227th Brigade to pass through and secure the crossings of the Odon: this done the way would be clear for the advance of the British armour.

An optimistic picture was painted for the infantry: they would receive the strongest of air and artillery support and need not expect to encounter a very stout resistance. As some remarked, 'It sounded good'.

Early in the morning of the 26th the 2nd Gordons took an uncomfortable breakfast in a wet, cold wood. Then a march of three miles brought them to their forming-up place in a little valley north of Cheux. Tanks were there to support the advance, and the thunder of our artillery was reassuring; no enemy aircraft were in evidence and no enemy bombardment opened. Little could be seen in front, for the country was undulating with thick hedges, farmsteads, copses, orchards, and fields of standing corn.

It was a miserable morning. Drizzling rain had set in and visibility was so low that the promised air support—the planned attacks of our bombers—had been called off. After a long wait the Gordons moved off in a hail storm.

Progress was slow, with frequent halts, for the brigades in front were meeting with obstinate resistance. It was late in the afternoon when the Battalion entered newly-captured Cheux. Scattered shots in and around the battered village provoked the cry of 'snipers', and caused a certain amount of irresponsible firing. After some little trouble the companies emerged on the south side of Cheux, reformed, and resumed their advance.

The Gordons were to take Colleville and the adjoining village of Tourville. On their right the 10th H.L.I. had Grainville-sur-Odon as their objective.

A and B Companies who led the way found themselves hotly engaged from the outset. The Germans had sited their anti-tank guns and machine guns behind high hedges with here and there a dug-in tank; and they did not seem to have suffered overmuch from our artillery bombardment. Met by a withering fire the Gordons struggled on in the fading light. It is to the infinite credit of B Company that they got through to Colleville. A Company were more unfortunate: they were caught in the middle of an open cornfield by mortar fire which inflicted considerable loss and caused great confusion.

The remainder of the Battalion had lost touch with the forward companies who were, indeed, cut off, for the Germans had come in behind them. When darkness fell C and D Companies with Battalion headquarters were only about one mile south of Cheux, and here the transport, who had found Cheux jammed with battle traffic, managed to arrive. Lieut.-Colonel Colville organised a perimeter position close to the road and the Gordons, cold and wet through, spent the night digging in.

It was an unhappy night for half the Battalion were missing; all ranks knew that although they had taken fairly heavy punishment very little had been gained; and in the darkness and confusion of the battlefield it was impossible to determine the whereabouts of friend or foe. Apart from random bursts of machine-gun fire there was, however, little sign of enemy action, and parties were sent out to search for wounded along the hedges and ditches. The work of Captain McPhail, the medical officer, and his stretcher-bearers won the admiration of all.

By dawn of the 27th the Gordons were well dug in, so that when by one of those unhappy chances of war they were shelled for a time by our own artillery they suffered no casualties. Nevertheless this gratuitous bombardment was a nerve-racking experience which the Battalion could well have done without.

During the night parties of A Company had drifted back; and early on the 27th Major Hutchinson brought in B Company who had, as we know, reached Colleville. There they had remained for several hours on the outskirts of the village before slowly withdrawing in fair order from their isolated position.

Then the 2nd Argyll and Sutherland Highlanders came through. It was their task to establish a bridge-head over the Odon at Tourmauville, and they were able to walk into Colleville without much trouble. Evidently the thrust at the village by B Company of the Gordons on the previous evening had not been without effect.

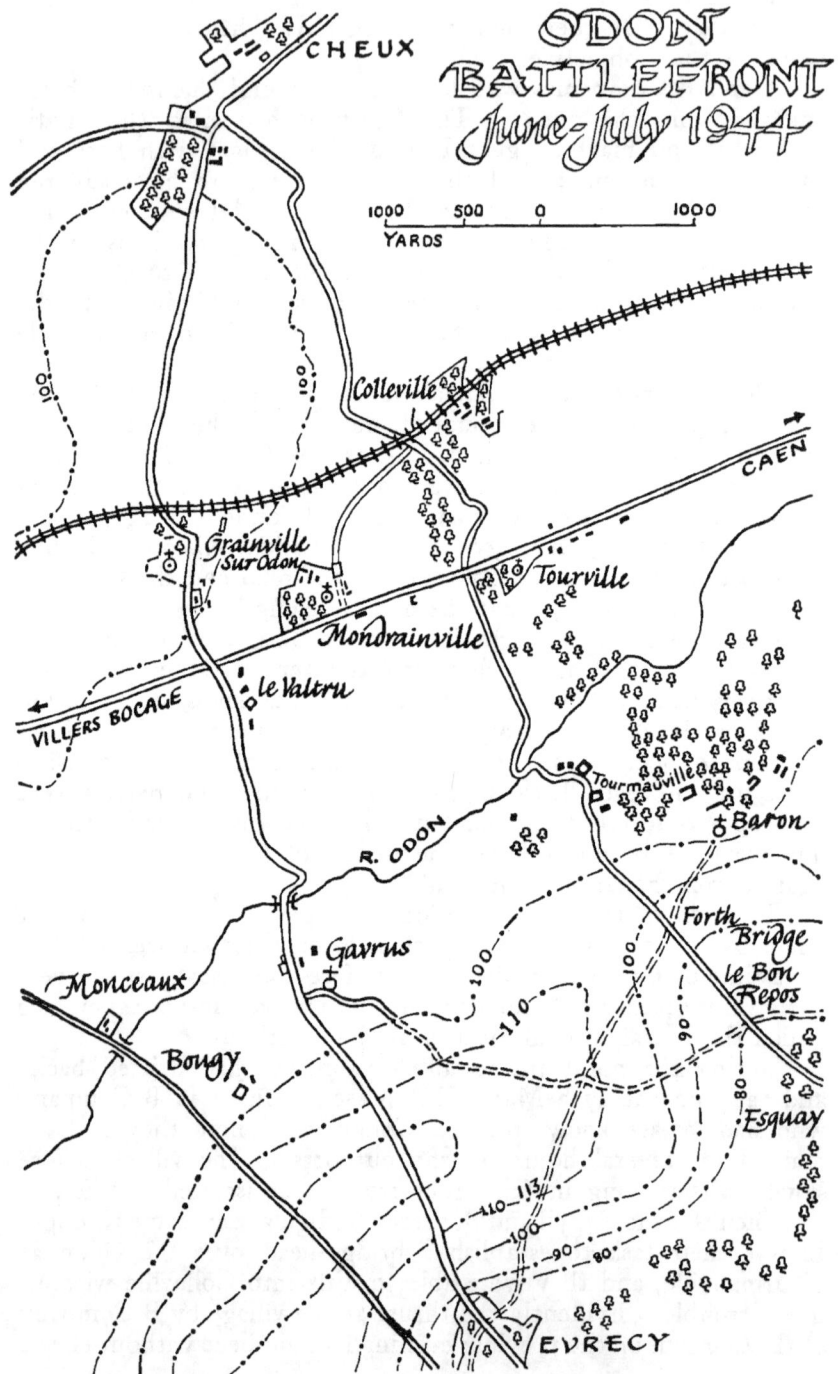

The Argyll continued their advance and the Gordons moved into Colleville where an outbreak of 'sniper fever' called for the suppression of several indiscriminate fusillades. Passing through Mondrainville the Argyll were now at Tourmauville on the Odon and about to cross the river.

In Colleville the Gordons were not left altogether in peace. Battalion headquarters, established in an orchard, came under the fire of the German *Nebelwerfer*—' Moaning Minnies' to the Jocks —the multiple barrelled mortars discharging bombs with air-ducts down their sides which produced a screaming noise during flight. All hastily sought their slit trenches, and the total damage amounted to a few men wounded and two motorcycles set on fire.

Later in the day the 2nd Glasgow Highlanders (46th Brigade) came up to take over from the Gordons who moved forward to Tourville—on the main Caen-Villers Bocage road—their final objective of the previous day.

There was trouble in Tourville. A German tank beyond the village was firing straight down the street and had hit several of of our tanks. German mortar fire added to the confusion and many of our vehicles were wrecked. It was some time before the Gordons could get clear and occupy some orchards on the south side of Tourville.

Here they settled down for the night which was enlivened at intervals by the rather random shooting of Tiger tanks. Every German tank was assumed to be a 'Tiger'.

On the next day, the 28th, the Gordons were undisturbed except for a few mortar bombs while the British armour passed through to cross the Odon at Tourmauville. The front, however, was far from 'firm', and the 15th Division were holding a salient about three miles long, and not much more than a mile wide; and the only line of supply was the road which ran through the bottle-neck of Cheux. The Argyll and Sutherland Highlanders, however, moved up stream and established a bridge-head at Gavrus.

The Germans counter-attacked strongly on 29th June and fierce fighting ensued on the western face of the salient at Grainville and le Valtru. At Gavrus the Argyll defended their bridgehead. Late in the day the Gordons were ordered to leave Tourville and move back to Colleville, there to be in readiness to counterattack should the 9th Cameronians, who were stoutly defending Grainville, be forced out of the village.

When the Gordons began to take the road for Colleville one of the carriers shed a track and the halted column became a target for the enemy mortars which wounded a number of men. Colleville was reached about 1 a.m. on the 30th and positions were taken up near the railway crossing. The Battalion were under intermittent mortar fire for the remainder of the night.

About this time the commanding officer and the second-in-command of the 10th H.L.I. were wounded, and the Gordons had to part with Major J. R. Sinclair who was called upon to command the H.L.I. He did not rejoin until 2nd July.

On the night of 29th June orders were issued for the withdrawal of the British armour across the Odon, and arrangements were made for the relief of the 15th Division. At first the Gordons knew nothing of these plans, for on the morning of the 30th the Battalion were released from their counter-attack role and ordered forward across the river at Tourmauville: they were to hold a bridge-head at Monceaux, about one mile upstream from Gavrus.

The Gordons passed through Tourville and when on the steeply sloping road which leads down to the Odon the leading companies came under heavy bombardment from the German artillery beyond the river. Further advance was out of the question, and cover was sought in ditches and in a small wood. An hour and a half later, when the British artillery had silenced the enemy guns, came orders to return to Tourville.

So the Battalion found themselves back in their old haunt among the orchards where they were obliged to remain inactive under a hail of fire. The German artillery and mortars seemed to be concentrating on Tourville, and the Gordons were obliged to sit still and take their losses. News that they were to be relieved was hailed with thankfulness, but it was not until the night of the 2nd July that they were able to hand over to a battalion of the 53rd (Welsh) Division.

Fortunately the Gordons succeeded in pulling out of Tourville in the dark without attracting the enemy's attention. Seven hours later they arrived in Bretteville l'Orgeuilleuse. All were very tired and, although the village was in the centre of the gun area, their sleep was sound despite the thunder of artillery.

A week had elapsed since the Battalion entered their first battle. Majors H. T. Aitchison and D. W. I. Souter, Captain J. A. A. Wishart, and Lieutenants A. B. Kiddie and D. H. Niven had been killed and eight other officers wounded. Of other ranks 254 were killed, wounded, or missing. Regimental Sergeant-Major Black was among the fallen.

It is true to say that this offensive, known as 'Operation Epsom', had not accomplished all that had been hoped of it, but the basic aim had been achieved. Between 26th June and 2nd July our Second Army had closely engaged a complete Panzer division, elements of six or seven others—all seasoned troops—and other formations beside. And while so much of the German strength had been drawn on to the British front, held there and hammered there, the Americans under much less pressure had forged ahead in their preparations to break out from the west. On 26th June they had captured Cherbourg.

The 2nd Gordons had found war, in the words of Montgomery, 'a rough and dirty business' and this was no surprise. If any of them were inclined to feel that in their first venture they had not accomplished much they could take heart from the message of the VIII Corps commander Lieut.-General Sir Richard O'Connor who praised the fighting qualities of the 15th Division. The divisional commander, Major-General G. H. A. MacMillan added his word of pride in what his troops had achieved, and writing to the Colonel of the Regiment on 5th July the commanding officer said:

> The battalion is out of the line and having a well earned rest. Our first introduction to battle has been a very hard test: we had a week of hell from the multiple mortars. . . . The one thing we can say is the battalion did all they were told to do . . . the Jocks behaved in their usual grand way. . . .

At Bretteville the 2nd Gordons re-equipped and reorganised, but, owing to their losses, they were obliged to reduce from four to three rifle companies. B Company was now commanded by Captain H. T. Slight; C by Major C. H. Hutchinson; and D by Major R. M. M. Tindall. Before, however, the Battalion went into battle again enough reinforcements had arrived for A Company to be reconstituted under Major Duke who came to the Gordons from the West Yorkshire Regiment.

Although the village was partly in ruins and very nearly deserted, many of the inhabitants began to drift back and some of the shops opened again. Like so many of the Normans the people were inclined to be cautious if not suspicious in their attitude to their 'liberators', but they thawed visibly when the pipes and drums of the Gordons played in the evenings.

The Battalion were called upon to enter the battle again on the evening of 14th July. By this time we were in Caen and had captured Carpiquet and its airfield; further to the south-west we were across the Odon. On this part of the front a fresh offensive was about to be launched, directed by the XII Corps. In the centre the 15th (Scottish) Division were to secure the line Bougy-Evrecy, with the left directed upon Maizet about two miles south-east of Evrecy.

Having reached Verson, about two miles east of Tourville, on the Caen road, by a night march the Gordons remained there until the afternoon of the 15th when they crossed the Odon and came to Baron. Their orders were to deliver a silent night attack to secure the high ground above Evrecy, and in the orchards around Baron they waited under a hail of shells and mortar bombs. An ammunition truck was hit and exploded, and just before the leading companies moved a pioneer truck went up: altogether a disconcerting prelude to the business of the night.

Forming up on the start line was accomplished in 'artificial moonlight', achieved by directing searchlights on clouds so that the reflection illumined the whole area. This was the first occasion on which the device was used.

The 2nd Glasgow Highlanders, whom the 227th Brigade had under command, started the ball. At 9.30 p.m. they advanced from their position north of Baron and, after hard fighting, dug in on the high ground above the village of Esquay which lies in a hollow. As events were to show, this effort was not sufficient to secure the left flank of the Gordons.

At about 11 p.m. the Gordons moved forward to the attack. They had left their carriers and anti-tank guns in Baron so that they could advance quickly and noiselessly. C and D Companies, commanded respectively by Majors Hutchinson and Tindall, were in front. The country was unreconnoitred and seemed 'a jumble of slopes' but the artificial moonlight made it easy to follow the marked lanes which led through our own minefield. The companies kept astride the track leading from Baron to Evrecy and went on with scarcely a check, gathering in a number of prisoners on their way. They reached their objective—the track from le Bon Repos to Gavrus where it crosses the ridge between Odon and Orne— and started to dig in.

It was the task of A and B Companies to come through and carry the advance to the high ground about Point 113 which overlooks Evrecy. With this accomplished the H.L.I. and the Argyll and Sutherland would come up to attack Evrecy itself and the Ferme de Mondeville on a ridge to the south-east of the village.

Then came bad news. Brigadier R. Mackintosh-Walker, who was at advanced Brigade headquarters in Baron, had been killed by a direct hit on the scout-car he was using. Lieut.-Colonel Colville was hurriedly summoned to take command of the 227th Brigade and Major J. R. Sinclair came up to lead the Gordons.

Major Sinclair knew that C and D Companies were on their objective, but found that A and B Companies who were to go through and carry on the advance were in serious trouble. They had only covered a short distance when, while crossing open ground, they had come under accurate machine-gun fire from the left flank. Casualties were heavy and, in considerable confusion, the advance petered out.

All that could be done was to reorganise the companies and set them to dig in. Major Sinclair established his headquarters close in rear. Soon he received a message from the Brigade forbidding any further attempt to advance; but the ground gained was to be held.

Dawn of the 16th revealed a very unpleasant situation. A and B Companies with Battalion headquarters were on an exposed ridge just south of 'Forth Bridge', the name given to the point where the Baron-Evrecy track crosses the Esquay-Tourmauville road. Several hundred yards further forward, isolated from the rest of the Battalion, were C and D Companies holding on to their objective.

After more than a dozen German fighters had flown over the Gordons, attacking with machine-gun fire which did little damage, the enemy artillery and mortars began a steady bombardment which continued all day.

C and D Companies in their isolated position were soon actively engaged. Their left flank was open: somewhere away on the right were the 6th King's Own Scottish Borderers of the 44th Brigade, but the Gordons were not in touch with them. The two companies beat off several counter-attacks with the aid of a battery of the 131st Field Regiment commanded by Major G. Campbell who was—and was often to be—a great comfort and support. In these encounters a number of Germans who had sought cover rather than retreat under our artillery fire were rounded up. Some of these worthies, on their way to surrender, became the target for their own 'moaning Minnies', to the grim satisfaction of the Jocks. By 1.30 p.m. thirty-five prisoners had been reported, together with the capture of a considerable quantity of German equipment and 'a marked map of some importance'. The medical officer, Captain A. N. McPhail, with his stretcher-bearers was doing devoted work among the wounded.

Even before daylight Major Sinclair and his adjutant, Captain K. J. Irvine, had attempted to get to C and D Companies, but each of their carriers lost a track in their efforts to do so. Beyond the Forth Bridge the ground was under fire from a high-velocity gun and several machine guns near le Bon Repos, and these changed their positions frequently and were difficult to locate. Attempts made in the course of the morning to send up to the forward companies two of the anti-tank 6-pdrs. also failed, no towing vehicle being left undamaged.

Early in the afternoon Major Sinclair received a message from Major Tindall, commanding C Company, to say that German tanks were approaching from the direction of le Bon Repos. Then the battalion commander saw five Mark IV tanks who seemed to be making straight for his headquarters; and the leading tank was only 150 yards away. The German armour opened fire on

B Company, killing Captain H. T. Slight, the company commander, but the enemy seemed quite unaware of the proximity of Battalion headquarters and of Captain Parish's anti-tank guns which, fortunately as it now turned out, he had been unable to get forward. Few men of the anti-tank platoon were left, but Parish and his sergeant man-handled one of the guns into position and opened fire. In succession all five tanks were hit and burst into flames; and of the Germans who baled out a few managed to escape but most were accounted for by B Company.

For the rest of the day our artillery prevented the Germans from pressing C and D Companies too hard, and Gordon patrols were able to drive off several groups of enemy infantry. In one unpleasant incident some Germans displayed a white flag from the turret of a disabled tank and then shot the Gordon corporal who went forward to take the surrender. That this was deliberate treachery is open to doubt, for shots may have been fired by our own men who had not seen the flag. The Highlanders on the spot held their own opinion.

In the evening the two company commanders were able to get back to Battalion headquarters for a conference and to receive fresh orders. At midnight the Gordons were to come under 44th Brigade command, the Argyll and the H.L.I. having already been taken out of the battle: their advance had been checked by heavy fire before deployment was possible. Furthermore the 158th Brigade (53rd Division) were to pass through the Gordons that night and renew the attack upon Evrecy; and after the Welshmen had advanced the Gordons could expect to be relieved. As other means of communication were unreliable Major Sinclair told the commanders of C and D Companies that when the time came he would send a message by runner with orders to withdraw.

As darkness fell there gathered a heavy mist which assumed the character of a thick fog when the enemy released smoke along the front of his positions. The Welsh battalions passed through C and D Companies of the Gordons about 11.30 p.m. and disappeared into the murk. So far as could be judged they seemed to be going well.

No order to withdraw reached C and D Companies, but runners might easily have lost their way in the confusion and the fog. After consultation the two company commanders decided that as the 158th Brigade had gone through they were justified in assuming that the time had come to rejoin the rest of the Battalion. So they brought their companies back.

When they appeared in the very early hours of the morning Major Sinclair could not but view their arrival with relief. He now had the whole Battalion under his hand, and C and D Companies were set to dig themselves in as soon as it was light enough to see. Meanwhile Major Sinclair had ordered the anti-tank guns back to Baron, but the passage through the minefield in the fog and darkness had proved difficult in the extreme. Two guns were abandoned till daylight came; one section was brought up again to Battalion headquarters.

Unfortunately the attack of the 158th Brigade had failed to get home, and soon after dawn the Welshmen were withdrawn through the Gordons about Forth Bridge.

All day on 17th July the Battalion, still in the forefront of the battle, remained under the intermittent fire of artillery and mortars, but the German counter-attacks ceased. In the evening enemy fighters and bombers attacked our forward communications, picking out their targets by the light of flares, our anti-aircraft guns replied with vigour, and then a squadron of our Typhoons flew over to set Evrecy ablaze.

At 9.30 p.m. the Welsh brigade again passed through to press the attack on Evrecy, but after heavy fighting they were again obliged to break off the action and withdraw.

Relief for the Gordons was now, however, at hand. On 18th July, after an uneventful morning, the 7th Welch arrived to take over and Major Sinclair was able to bring the Battalion out of action without much interference from the enemy.

The Gordons marched back to a large farm and orchard not far from Grainville-sur-Odon. As this place had been previously occupied by troops there was little digging to be done except to bury the many dead cows which lay around.

In this, their second action, the Battalion had lost one officer killed and three wounded, and of other ranks eleven killed, 107 wounded and seven missing. A draft of reinforcements was very welcome, particularly as the men came from the London Scottish.

Major Sinclair was confirmed in his appointment as battalion commander, and for the part they had played in the action Major Tindall and Captain Parish were awarded the Military Cross.

Once again there were many in the Gordons who felt that they had achieved no great success: in the confusion of battle it had been difficult for the regimental officer and private soldier to see the pattern of victory. It may have seemed to them that they had done little more than hang on grimly to their meagre gains amid storms of artillery and mortar fire; yet after the fighting which ended west of Caen on 18th July General Montgomery was able to express his satisfaction, for three Panzer divisions had been brought to battle and held there to the great benefit of the American operations further west. The master plan was working out.

The Gordons were glad of a few days respite, but a heavy downpour of rain on 21st July caused them considerable discomfort. Two days later came a change of scene, but it is now time to return to the 1st and the 5th/7th Battalions east of the Orne.

East of the Orne

On 18th July the VIII Corps—now comprising three armoured divisions—struck southward over the ground which the Highland Division had defended for many weeks. This advance reached the neighbourhood of Bourguebus, some four miles south-east of Caen and came to a standstill in rain and mud.

In the wake of this offensive the Gordons moved forward, the 5th/7th Battalion to their old haunt of Herouvillette, losing Lieutenant Boyd and seven others wounded by air attack on the way. Herouvillette, more shattered than ever, was rather well regarded by the Highlanders. 'Most of us have our own pet washerwomen here now.'

Under heavy rain and occasional shell fire the 5th/7th Gordons remained in the village until 22nd July. On the 21st Lieut.-Colonel J. E. G. Hay became lost to the Battalion: he was wounded in the head when his car was hit by a shell. Next day under the command of Major M. Lindsay who had come from the 1st Battalion, the Gordons advanced in 'company blocks' along muddy roads and through a jumble of traffic to relieve armoured troops near Cagny. They found the country 'bleak and uninteresting', the weather still 'filthy'.

At 'stand to' on 24th July Captain J. C. Thom, the medical officer, was found to have been killed by a direct hit on his slit trench during the night. The pipe-major played 'Lochaber No More' when they buried him, for 'he was a true Gordon at heart'.

On the 25th the 5th/7th were relieved and returned to Herouvillette which still remained a target for German long-range guns. Captain D. R. Dawson and nine other ranks were wounded here, and Lieutenant J. K. Seth was killed.

The Battalion were withdrawn altogether for a week on 29th July, moving back across the Orne to camp in a cornfield south of Douvres where they were no longer under fire. They had plenty of time for rest and cleaning up, and drill, physical training, football and visits to the cinema completed the daily round.

On 31st July Lieut.-Colonel H. A. C. Blair-Imrie assumed command. He came from the Black Watch.

The 1st Gordons had come forward on the night of 18th July to the Ranville area where they were under air attack and Captain

A. H. Gilchrist was wounded. On the 22nd they took over part of the front near Cagny as the 5th/7th were doing. Two platoons were set to dig night positions near the Lisieux road north-west of Cagny and by day the front was covered by observation posts and by carriers—afterwards replaced by Bren gun detachments—on the line of the Cagny-Caen road.

There was no fighting, and officers and men had ample opportunity to examine abandoned German weapons and equipment which lay around in great profusion. On the 25th the 1st Gordons moved back to the Ranville area where, on 29th July, they received a visit from the new commander of the Highland Division, Major-General T. G. Rennie. After order and counter-order the Battalion moved back on this day to the reserve area near Douvres where a week of relaxation and general tuning up was very welcome.

South from Caumont : Estry

The American 'break out' east and west of St. Lô had been fixed for 19th July, the day after our Second Army launched its offensive east and south of Caen. Bad weather caused a postponement : it was necessary to wait until conditons were favourable for the great bomber strike which was to pave the way for the advance of our Allies. Meanwhile it was arranged to free the division holding the extreme left of the American front and the 15th (Scottish) Division were selected to do so.

Accordingly, on 23rd July, the 227th Brigade moved fifteen miles to the west, the 2nd Gordons to a reserve position about two miles north of Caumont. The 10th H.L.I. were in Caumont itself and the Argyll in and about la Repas further east.

Relieving American troops was a new experience. The men of the 2nd Regiment, 5th U.S. Division, were of fine physique, well trained, and admirably equipped. Their rations seemed particularly good and their welfare service elaborate. Moreover they were an open-handed lot, for it is mentioned that they 'were not particular about what they left behind'.

This was the real bocage country, undulating, close, and intricate, with deep winding lanes, thick hedges, orchards, woods and copses, and patches of grazing land. There had been little fighting in this region, and the German 326th Division were some distance away. The peace of the countryside was broken by occasional shell-fire, but the Gordons appreciated their new environment where milk and butter could be had in plenty and eggs were not hard to come by.

On the 24th enemy aircraft attacked an anti-tank gun and a jeep of the Gordons on the road near Caumont. One man was killed and the seven wounded included Captain Parish, who remained at duty.

There was ample opportunity for Gordon patrols to work forward between Caumont and la Repas. A sharp encounter on the 27th resulted in a patrol under Lieutenant McIntyre accounting for three Germans, but one of his men was killed and two wounded.

On 25th July the American First Army had, at last, been able to launch their offensive, and by the 30th American armoured forces reached Avranches. Our Second Army had received at short notice orders from General Montgomery to attack on this day, the main thrust to be on the right in the sector extending to Caumont.

The 15th Division were to advance southward from Caumont towards the hills in the region of le Bény Bocage, nearly ten miles away. First in action would be the 227th Brigade, the 2nd Gordons and the 9th Cameronians (attached from the 46th Brigade) being given the task of clearing the ground up to the start line from which the main attack was to be launched. The Cameronians had to secure the hamlet called Sept Vents; the objective of the 2nd Gordons was Lutain Wood which crowned a rise about a mile down the valley from Caumont.

The Gordons were in good fettle and pleased to have the support of part of the 6th Guards Tank Brigade with whom they had trained in England. A squadron of the 4th Grenadier Battalion of Churchills were allotted to the Highlanders, together with a troop of 'flail' tanks to deal with minefields and one of Crocodile tanks, the flame-throwers.

It was still dark on the morning of the 30th when the Gordons formed up behind the Caumont ridge where they were joined by their tanks. The attack went in at 6.55 a.m., A and B Companies, each attended by a troop of Churchills, passing over the crest of the ridge and moving down into the valley astride the Caumont-Cahagnes road.

Lutain Wood was flanked on the lower ground by orchards which almost adjoined it. A Company went for the western orchard, B Company for that on the east. Despite the enemy's rifle and machine-gun fire both companies, with help from the tanks, secured their objectives without much trouble. B Company had the tougher task for they encountered anti-personnel mines, and anti-tank mines were found along the edge of the road. A carrier towing one of the anti-tank 6-pdrs. was blown up and among the wounded was the company commander, Captain E. R. MacDonald who had joined the Battalion only a few days before.

The task of clearing the whole place of mines proved too much for the pioneer platoon, so the Brigade were asked to send up sappers.

D Company, following in rear of B Company cleared the houses of Lieu Mondant on the left of the road. Then, with C Company from reserve, they advanced upon the final objective, Lutain Wood.

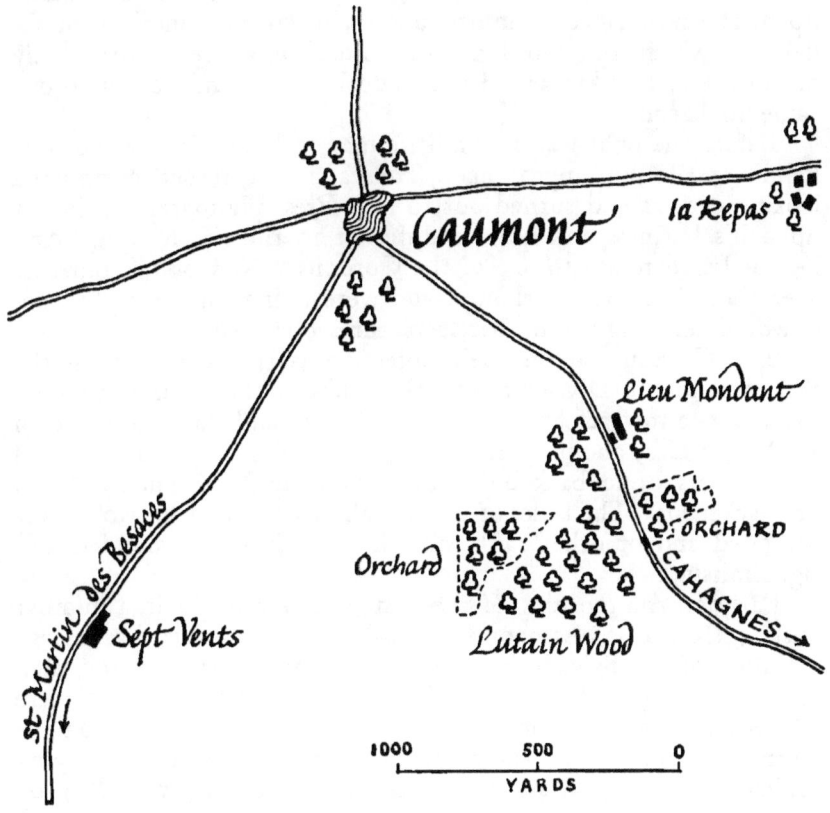

In approaching the wood the Crocodiles came into action, flaming the thick hedges on the northern slopes; but a high bank prevented the machines from reaching the edge of the wood itself. Nevertheless the flames shook the nerve of the defenders who began to withdraw through the wood with the Gordons pressing them hard. One section of D. Company killed two officers and ten men who were holding a post on the far side of the wood.

In such fashion the Gordons took Lutain Wood. It had been well organised for defence, with camouflaged machine-gun posts and dug-outs, and could have been a harder nut to crack had the enemy been in the mind for a stout resistance. Now he opened intense mortar fire, the high bursts of the bombs among the branches of the trees making the place almost untenable. So three companies of the Gordons dug in round the wood and clear of it, with D Company on the northern side in reserve. B Company on the left had to look to their flank, for the 43rd Division had made little progress towards Cahagnes.

Battalion headquarters, coming forward along a track leading up to the wood, had stumbled upon a forgotten American minefield of which the Gordons were quite unaware. Fortunately one of the flail tanks was at hand to deal with the mines and no-one came to harm.

Before the fight was over a little man in blue raincoat and steel helmet made his appearance. He carried a rather antiquated looking camera and turned out to be a Press photographer, intent upon his business and quite indifferent to the risk he ran. And he was heard to say to one of the Gordons, ' Now point your rifle over there and look as though you were doing something!' So, it would seem, are some battle pictures obtained.

The Gordons sat on their objective as the remainder of the Brigade and the Division, with the tanks of the Guards, took up the advance towards St. Martin des Besaces and Point 309, known as Quarry Hill, about a mile east of the village. Several batches of prisoners came back by Lutain Wood and the enemy's shell fire slackened. The losses of the Battalion amounted to two officers wounded and of other ranks nine killed, fifty-two wounded and eight missing.

Early on the morning of the 31st patrols brought in a number of stray Germans. At noon the Gordons moved forward as reserve battalion of the Brigade in a general advance southward and then south-eastward, a heartening sign, indeed. Attack orders were received by the Battalion and then cancelled. Eventually, on the morning of 2nd August the companies climbed into troop-carrying vehicles and, with tanks of the Scots Guards, led the 227th Brigade column through St. Martin des Besaces and on to the foot of a hill called Point 244 near le Bény Bocage. The going—over ditches and high banks—was too rough for half-tracked vehicles and wheeled transport, so C Company on foot followed two troops of tanks which gave the hill the full treatment with their Besa guns only to find no enemy there.

Now came two days rest. The inhabitants of a nearby farm regaled the grateful Gordons with fruit and vegetables from their garden, but these people could afford to be generous. Later it was learnt that they were refugees who had only taken possession of the place a few days before.

The Battalion discovered a great store of German equipment, together with documents of some importance to our Intelligence.

On the morning of 5th August the advance was resumed, the Gordons, with a squadron of Scots Guards tanks, moving eastward to Montcharivel. B Company were then sent forward to Au

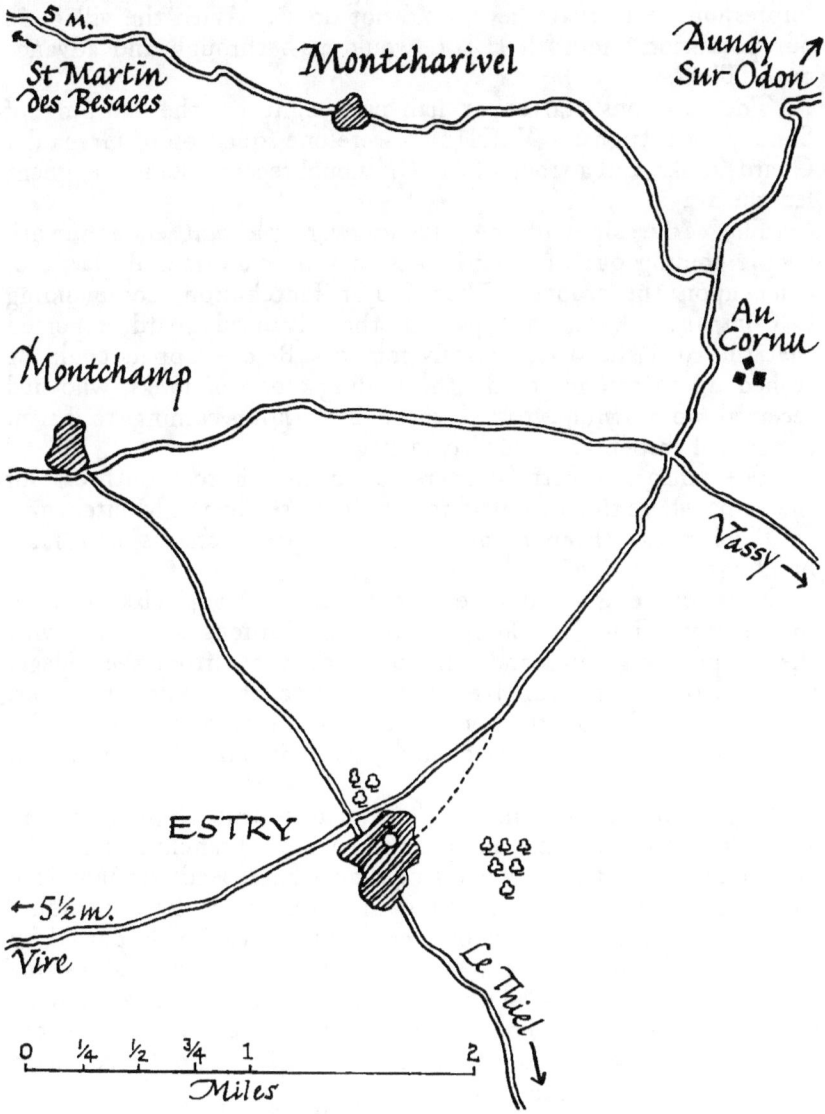

Cornu as advanced guard to the rest of the Battalion who came under shell fire as they moved forward. B Company drove off some Germans after reaching the cross-roads south of Au Cornu, but when the Battalion closed up the enemy's shelling and mortaring

became very heavy and caused some casualties. Among the killed was Lieutenant Fairhurst.

At night orders were received to occupy Estry on the morrow. No-one knew if the Germans meant to defend Estry, the general impression being that they would not do so. With the village in our possession the 10th H.L.I. would pass through and advance on le Thiel.

The Gordons started at half-past eight on the morning of Sunday, 6th August. With them were one squadron of Grenadier Guards tanks, and a troop of the Divisional reconnaissance regiment led the way.

The early stages of the advance were pleasant enough, with people coming out of their houses to press flowers and glasses of cider upon the troops. Then Major Hutchinson, commanding C Company who formed part of the advanced guard, reported that the road ahead was heavily mined. Before sappers could be rushed up to attend to this the leading troop of tanks, who had received no warning, passed through without coming to harm, a merciful dispensation of Providence.

The village of Estry clusters round the church south-east of the point where the main road to Vire is crossed by the Montchamp-le Thiel road. Round the cross-roads are orchards and farm buildings.

Near the cross-roads the reconnaissance troop clashed with the enemy. Then C Company of the Gordons advanced with their supporting tanks and, although under fire from the village, managed to install themselves at the cross-roads. When, however, they swung left to attack Estry they were at once checked by the hail of fire from machine guns, anti-tank weapons, and mortars.

Lieut.-Colonel Sinclair then decided to send in B Company with two troops of tanks along a track which, branching from the main road about three-quarters of a mile back, leads straight into the village. This attack failed with considerable loss, including several tanks, under the fire of every kind of weapon supported by artillery which opened at a very effective range. Fire also came from a small copse east of the village. Estry, in fact, was a little fortress: among the houses, walls and hedges were well-sited heavy machine-guns and mortars, cunningly camouflaged, with anti-tank guns and dug-in tanks.

The main body of the Gordons, still on the road, as well as the 10th H.L.I. who were following in rear, were now under heavy shell-fire and suffered accordingly. The tank squadron commander was killed and four of his officers wounded; and eleven tanks had been hit, several of them being on fire and blazing furiously. A

Churchill could not stand up to a direct hit from an 88-mm. gun. It was clear that no more could be expected from our armour.

Lieut.-Colonel Sinclair, who had a troop of self-propelled guns at his disposal, now used two of them to support a turning movement by A Company who endeavoured to work round to the north-west side of Estry. D Company with the other two guns were sent to try a similar advance from the east, going fairly wide in order to clear the copse. It was hoped that the guns would knock out some of the German tanks.

Both these efforts failed. A Company found great difficulty in negotiating the high banks which divided the fields and a tremendous hail of mortar bombs greeted their every movement. D Company were stopped mainly by the fire of hidden machine-guns.

Lieut.-Colonel Russell Morgan, commanding the H.L.I., had come forward to confer with Lieut.-Colonel Sinclair. There was only an hour or two of daylight left. It was arranged that C Company of the Gordons should be withdrawn from the cross-roads and that our medium artillery should be asked for a special bombardment of Estry. After this preparation the H.L.I. were to go in with their squadron of Scots Guards tanks behind a field artillery barrage; and when they had won through to the far side of the village the Gordons would come forward to do what mopping up was needed.

The Gordons dug in some distance short of the cross-roads, and after our medium artillery had fired their preparation the H.L.I. attacked with their tanks about 7.20 p.m. All was in vain. The German defence was still too strong and, after doing their utmost, the H.L.I. were obliged to withdraw.

The two battalions dug in for the night in a ' tight box ' N.N.E. of the cross-roads, a combined command headquarters being set up in an orchard.

One solitary item of success can be recorded. The troop commander of the self-propelled guns had managed to locate the exact position of a German tank near Estry church and knocked it out after firing several rounds.

This was a bad day for the 227th Brigade, for the attack of the Argyll along the road to Vassy had also been checked. The Brigade had clashed with the German troops fighting desperately on the western side of the Falaise ' pocket ' while the enemy counter-thrust was delivered on a front between Mortain and Vire towards Avranches.

The Gordons and the H.L.I. spent an uneasy night under considerable shell-fire. Orders from the Brigade to renew the attack next day were received with considerable misgiving, but these orders were cancelled later.

All day upon the 7th the troops had to endure a short-range bombardment from guns and mortars. A direct hit on the regimental aid post killed most of the Gordon stretcher-bearers; carriers bringing up supplies along the road from Au Cornu ran the gauntlet of heavy mortar-fire on every trip they made. Our mortars hit back by plastering the defences round Estry church. An attempt was made to deal with a tank which came forward at intervals to a bend in the road leading to Estry and fired a round at the cross-roads; but the Piat party who tried to get into position were checked by machine-gun fire.

During the morning the Brigadier arrived and there was talk of a fresh attack with the assistance of Crocodiles and converted Churchill tanks which discharged a large petard capable of blasting concrete defences. Late in the afternoon, however, the remaining Guards tanks pulled back amid a hail of mortar fire, and then came orders for the withdrawal of the two battalions.

This took place on the 8th when the German fire had slackened. The Gordons moved to a hamlet a few miles east of Montchamp. Estry had been their greatest ordeal since they landed in Normandy; and here perhaps it may be mentioned that on 8th August an attack against the village delivered by the 44th Brigade advancing astride the road from Montchamp had no success. The Germans departed from Estry in their own good time.

Hot shower-baths, clean clothes and a few days rest in good summer weather—fine summer days in 1944 were rare—did much to restore the spirits of the Gordons. Their losses had been heavy. Between 5th and 8th August one officer was killed and seven wounded; of other ranks twenty-one were killed, 146 wounded and twenty-two missing. It was again necessary to reduce the Battalion to three rifle companies, A, C and D.

Pursuit to the Seine

When the 1st Gordons and the 5th/7th Gordons returned to the battle it was to take the offensive and to continue in action until they had done their part in driving the Germans back over the Seine. The 51st Division, now under the command of the II Canadian Corps, came up to participate in the thrust down the Falaise road, but before the Canadians entered Falaise on 16th August the Highlanders had been directed eastward, still under Canadian command, and were on the road to Lisieux.

On the night of 6th August the 1st Gordons moved forward to Grentheville, west of Cagny, and made their preparations for an attack which was to be preceded by ' a vast bombing and shelling'.

The 5th/7th, who had received some reinforcements—two officers and forty-four other ranks of the Duke of Wellington's Regiment—came up to Soliers where they were practically in the battle-front for they were obliged to move back on the 7th out of the way of the air strike which was to precede the offensive. Captain H. Best was wounded on this day.

The Canadian Corps attack went in about midnight on 7th/8th August, the 154th Brigade advancing east of the Falaise road. They made good progress against a rather obstinate resistance which soon involved the 152nd Brigade who followed up; and it was not long before the 153rd Brigade, who had provided the 'firm base' were called into action.

The 1st Gordons moved forward, first in trucks and then on their feet, to Garcelles Secqueville. After an artillery bombardment they attacked Secqueville la Campagne at 5 p.m. with C Company on the right and A Company on the left. In an hour and a half the two companies were in full possession of the village, and B Company were then sent to clear, with the assistance of Crocodiles, a wood on the north-western side. By 8 p.m. this also was accomplished and carrier patrols continued the advance. Two officers and ninety other Germans were captured and the Gordon casualties were light; but Lieutenant G. Mitchell was severely wounded, his injured arm being amputated by some rather dreadful surgery with a jack knife.

Next day a patrol led by the commanding officer collected a German gun of the self-propelled variety which had been abandoned in a wood.

On 10th August the 1st Gordons took over St. Sylvain from the Poles who had captured it, a difficult and untidy relief as pockets of Germans still infested the place. By our standards the movements of our Allies were, to say the least, erratic. Contact was made with the 5th Black Watch on the western side of the village, and the 154th Brigade passed through next day to take up the advance.

The 5th/7th Gordons had come forward on the evening of the 8th, putting two companies into Poussy, which lies to the north of St. Sylvain, next morning. This was an uncomfortable position on a forward slope and every movement drew shell-fire. The afternoon was spent in determining whether certain 'things in front' were tanks or dummy tanks. They proved to be dummies. The Battalion were relieved by the 5th Seaforth (152nd Brigade) in the evening, having lost their signals officer, Captain J. G. Sinclair, who was wounded. By 11th August the 5th/7th were back among the battery positions near the Falaise road, but still under shell-fire.

Brigadier H. Murray bade farewell to both battalions of Gordons on the 12th. He was leaving for Italy. For the time being Lieut.-Colonel Hon. H. C. H.-T. Cumming-Bruce assumed command of the 153rd Brigade and Major M. Lindsay that of the 1st Gordons.

After sitting still under shell-fire for another whole day the 5th/7th Gordons came forward on 14th August towards St. Sylvain which they found to be still a target for the German artillery and mortars. They were ordered to secure a wooded ridge south-east of the village and the attack, delivered in splendid style, was completely successful. Unfortunately the loss in officers was heavy, for Major Glennie, Captain Inglis, and Lieutenants Aston, Taylor, Birse and Scott were all wounded. Of other ranks eight were killed and thirty-nine wounded.

Sergeant Birley of D. Company proved a tower of strength in this engagement. After his company commander and the other officers were wounded and nearly half the men had become casualties he took command as to the manner born. As usual the stretcher-bearers performed admirably, Private Hutchinson being singled out for special mention.

One quiet day followed. Then the Battalion moved forward to Percy en Auge and prepared to settle down for the night. Before they could do so they were ordered into transport vehicles and drove off in pitch darkness to secure St. Maclou, beyond the river Dives. The road, a rough track, was difficult to follow and 'no-one thought that we should arrive in the right place'; but C and D Companies who led the way performed the miracle. They 'landed dead on their objective', a ridge commanding the little town, and the Germans, who were taken by surprise, either surrendered or fled. Most of the fighting was done by the battle transport under Major C. F. Irvine. When dawn of the 17th came they found themselves surrounded by Germans, but Irvine's party, 'a motley crowd of anti-tank gunners, mortar-men and other individuals', promptly attacked the enemy and routed him.

No Germans remained in St. Maclou. The Gordons had taken the place for the loss of the signals sergeant, killed, and four men wounded. Captain Jamieson, the intelligence officer, found an observation post, killed the telephone operator, and got through on the line to a German headquarters. In creditable German, albeit with an Edinburgh accent, he announced that the 'English swine' had arrived and demanded surrender. Chuckles were heard, then a Teuton voice of authority; the demand was repeated—and the rest was silence.

Leaving the people of St. Maclou to greet their liberators with flowers, cider, and bottles of wine, one may now return to the 1st Gordons at St. Sylvain.

They had bad luck on 14th August when they lost thirteen trucks of the fifteen which comprised their battle transport, owing to a mistake in an Allied bombing strike. Late in the day, when the 5th/7th Gordons came up to attack south-east of St. Sylvain A Company of the 1st Gordons went forward to occupy Fierville.

This village was reported clear of the enemy, but the carrier platoon had a skirmish outside it, and two carriers were blown up in a minefield. A Company dug in on high ground near by.

During the night Allied aircraft bombed the Fierville area but fortunately did little harm. At 5 a.m. on the 15th platoons from B and D Companies did some clearing up, and in the evening the Battalion advanced from St. Sylvain. When they halted at Glatigny to dig in for the night they were caught by a shower of bombs from German aircraft, D Company losing Lieutenant E. D. Glass, a Canadian officer and two others killed and Lieutenant D. Howarth and twenty men wounded. Howarth, who came from the Rifle Brigade, was a great fighting man : in the Colombelles attack he had killed many Germans with his revolver.

On the 16th the 1st Gordons reached Percy en Auge, arriving late after the 5th/7th had left. A further advance towards the river Dives found the bridges blown and the enemy in position on the eastern bank. The leading companies were heavily shelled and all but two of the supporting tanks became bogged ; so for the night the Battalion remained around Percy en Auge. They were in brigade reserve.

The 1st Gordons crossed the Dives next morning at Bretteville where the 154th Brigade had established a bridge-head. Now the advance was north-eastward, and the objective the high ground round Ste. Marie-aux-Anglais. The Battalion attacked at 11 a.m. with three companies up, and they found the opposition stiffen as they forged ahead. C Company on the right were on open ground and were obliged to by-pass the village of Doux Marais. By late afternoon, however, two companies were established on the high ground with one company on each flank below them. Spandau patrols were wandering about and the position seemed an unsatisfactory one. Accordingly, for the night, the Gordons occupied a defensive perimeter with every man allotted a firing position and Battalion headquarters holding the rear.

Lieutenant J. J. Gallop and 2nd-Lieutenants R. G. Cowan and R. T. Foster were wounded on this day.

On 18th August the Gordons sent patrols forward to the river Vie, a tributary of the Dives. These patrols came under heavy fire when they tried to cross the open ground which led down to the river bank opposite Grandchamp.

The passage of the Vie was to occupy all three battalions of the 153rd Brigade. At St. Maclou the 5th/7th Gordons had received a reinforcement of one officer and sixty-four other ranks of the South Staffordshire Regiment and were reorganising. They had been told 'No move on the 18th', but were roused out at half-an-hour's notice with orders to attack Grandchamp that night. They were expected to establish a bridge-head on the far bank of the river, and to put a partially destroyed bridge into condition to take infantry.

This meant another unpleasant night advance in the wet, but, although heavily shelled as they neared the river, the Gordons made their crossing and started work on the bridge, though always under fire. By about midnight it was possible for the 5th Black Watch to pass over and attack the ridge beyond Grandchamp. They were ordered to secure it before dawn.

German resistance was spasmodic and the Gordons had taken a number of prisoners in Grandchamp. Their own casualties were light, but included Lieut.-Colonel Blair-Imrie who was killed while up with the forward companies. It was sad to lose so fine a commanding officer who had won the respect and admiration of all ranks during the short time he had been with them.

The Black Watch reached their objective but were hard put to it to maintain themselves. After daylight came on 19th August transport which approached the river was heavily shelled, and the road beyond Grandchamp was under machine-gun fire. Clearly, the 1st Gordons were needed.

So the 1st Gordons, favoured by a thick mist, crossed the river about 8 a.m. On emerging from Grandchamp they became hotly engaged in the orchards at the foot of the slope which led up to their objective, that part of the ridge called 'Ben Lomond'. It was not until mid-afternoon that the Battalion were firmly established on the left of the Black Watch.

During the advance Major J. Grant, who had commanded the carriers with so much distinction in Africa and Sicily and had done equally well as a company commander in France, was killed. He came from Aberdeen and was one of the keenest and best of Gordon Territorial officers.

The enemy's resistance was melting away and the morrow was devoted to clearing up. C Company of the 5th/7th Gordons, with a number of tanks, did good work in shooting along hedges where they flushed a number of Germans who were still in hiding. A complete new company of the East Lancashire Regiment now arrived and was placed under the command of Captain Henderson. Even so, the 5th/7th Battalion could only muster three rifle companies.

The 5th/7th had lost their commanding officer and Captain Jamieson and Lieutenant Wisley had been wounded; but other casualties amounted to no more than twenty. The 1st Battalion, besides Major Grant, had Captain J. B. Stewart, the anti-tank officer, and 2nd-Lieutenant Needs killed and Captain T. G. M. Birrs wounded.

Headquarters of the 5th/7th Gordons which had been established in the château at Grandchamp were shelled out of the place, but at night 'certain people sneaked back unofficially to sleep dry and warm', while the companies lay out, 'making the best of the filthy weather'. The rain never ceased for long.

Patrols of the 1st Gordons had been very active, and on the 21st the Battalion moved forward, meeting with no resistance, to dig in at La Forge Vallée for the night. Here they found a stud farm and training establishment whose English manager, having hidden his horses at neighbouring farms, was living underground.

The next objective of the 153rd Brigade was Lisieux, and the 5th/7th Gordons, now under the command of Major M. H. du Boulay, were in the van. They were ordered to establish a bridgehead on the river Touques, which runs through the town, so that the sappers could throw two bridges in place of the one which had been wrecked.

Entry into the near side of Lisieux on 22nd August was undisputed. The Brigadier and his intelligence officer drove in, followed by Major du Boulay and the officer commanding the attached tanks; then came a company of Gordons and a tank squadron.

The Gordons pressed forward and were soon across the river. In the houses on the further side, however, S.S. troops offered a determined resistance and progress was slow. It was here that Private Redican proved his worth. His platoon were in an awkward position and at a critical moment he opened covering fire with his Bren gun, keeping it in action after being wounded in both legs. He was recommended for the Victoria Cross and eventually received the Distinguished Conduct Medal.

Eventually the Battalion, all very tired men, won their way forward as far as the central square and barricaded themselves for the night. Much remained to do, for the Germans had to be driven from the eastern part of the town and from the high ground beyond. During the night Major du Boulay received orders to go on and finish the business, but he pointed out to the Brigade that this was too much to expect of his battalion alone.

The 1st Gordons, now very weak in numbers, were therefore called upon. At 8.30 a.m. on 23rd August B and C Companies received orders to help clear the houses and to 'sit astride the Lisieux-Paris road'. They found their task a hard one. By ten o'clock C Company were pinned down by the fire of automatics with no chance of getting on. B Company, striving uphill through the orchards on the south-east of the town, suffered from the fire of well hidden spandaus, and two tanks, moving in support, were knocked out by 'bazookas', the German equivalent of our Piats, whose real name was *Panzerfauste*. In any case, the slopes were too steep for tanks to give effective fire support.

Meanwhile the forward company of the 5th/7th Gordons—the new D Company under Captain Henderson—had done very well and made fair progress, but Henderson was badly wounded.

It was not until four in the afternoon that this 'tiring and unpleasant little battle' came to an end with the advance of a brigade of the 7th Armoured Division. The appearance of tanks in force seems to have taken the heart out of the enemy and Lisieux was clear of him when evening fell. The 1st Gordons then dug a perimeter position on the high ground south-east of the town. Men from the mortar and carrier platoons, the pipe band and the pioneers, strengthened the rifle companies, and a small reinforcement of one officer and twenty-three other ranks which arrived at 8 p.m. was at once formed into a platoon and put in to the perimeter. The night was a very wet one.

On 24th August the 5th/7th Gordons, most of whom had enjoyed a good night's rest in dry billets, were moved outside Lisieux to the neighbourhood of a nunnery, departing reluctantly from the only little bit of comfort they had known for some weeks. It was on this day that Lieut.-Colonel G. D. Renny, a King's Own Scottish Borderer, arrived to take command of the Battalion.

At Lisieux, as in other places, strict orders were in force against looting, but these were always difficult to enforce where ownerless livestock abounded. Private 'Joker' Watt, a jeep driver of the 5th/7th Gordons was busy plucking a hen when a senior officer—not of the Battalion—appeared and said sternly : 'You know very well that you are liable to be shot if you're caught with that bird.' 'Weel sir,' replied Private Watt, 'we're liable to be shot anyway, so it makes nae difference.'

The pipe band of the 5th/7th played Retreat outside the nunnery on the 26th, and the mother superior presented the pipers with a dozen bottles of cider.

Both the 1st and the 5th/7th Gordons were receiving reinforcements of Englishmen and not of their own people; but no representations to higher authority had any effect. However, the new arrivals settled down happily, their fighting qualities were never in doubt, and it was gratifying to see the pride they took in being of the Regiment. Some were very disappointed at not being able to don the kilt.

The loss in officers continued to be heavy and embarrassing. Lisieux had cost the 1st Gordons Lieutenant A. P. Donald killed and Major M. B. Reekie, Captain D. R. Reid and 2nd-Lieutenants F. G. Hopkins and H. G. Beardwell wounded.

Lieut.-Colonel Hon. H. C. H.-T. Cumming-Bruce returned on 24th August, the new Brigadier having arrived. He was none other than Lieut.-Colonel Sinclair from the 2nd Battalion.

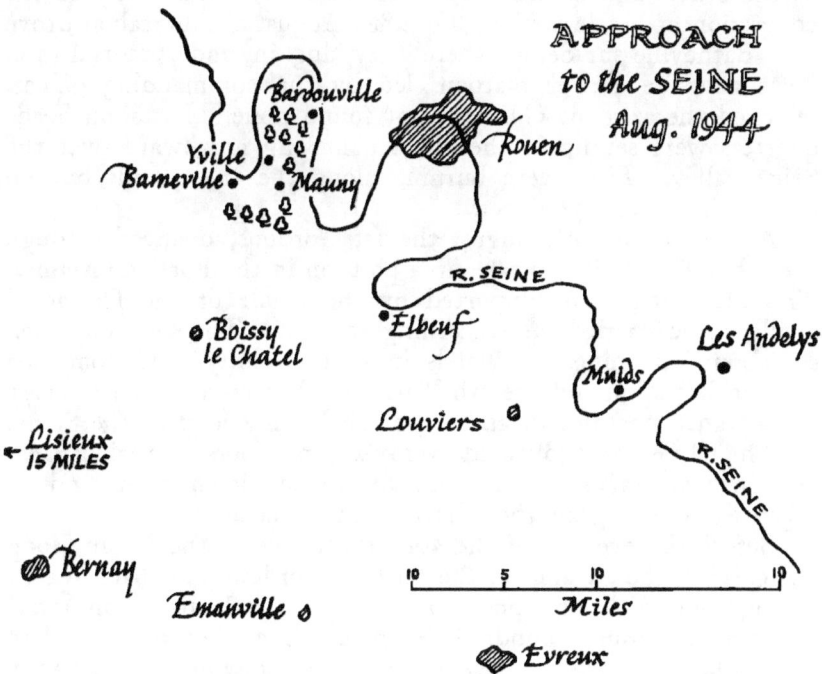

It was not long now before the 5th/7th Gordons reached the Seine. They moved on the 27th to Boissy le Chatel and next day were ordered to attack towards Yville. Before the Battalion lay orchards and a thick belt of trees, but to reach them the advance was over open ground. A Company, who led the way, were checked by fire and the whole Battalion area came under mortar bombardment. This was regarded as 'rather a sticky day'. At night A Company were withdrawn and the 5th/7th formed a perimeter.

On the morrow the action was renewed, C and D Companies managing to reach the top of a ridge whence they could look down upon the village of Yville. The gradient was adjudged to be too steep for tanks, so carriers which mounted flame-throwers plunged down to the attack, and by evening the château and the village were in the hands of the Gordons. The château had been a German headquarters but its owner was still in residence and proved a courteous host.

The day's success had cost little, but among the wounded was Captain Brand. A large reinforcement of three officers and 106 other ranks arrived, a very welcome addition to the strength.

The 1st Gordons had been longer on the road, partly owing to the orders and counter-orders they received and partly to the congestion of battle traffic. On 28th August the Battalion drove into Barneville-sur-Seine where they dug in under mortar fire. Next day the carrier platoon, led by the commanding officer, searched the area for Germans but found none. Battalion headquarters were set up in the château looking northward over the Seine valley. Fires were burning along the river roads but no enemy movement was seen.

At 1 a.m. on 30th August the 1st Gordons advanced through the 5th/7th at Yville to take up a position in the Forêt de Mauny. This movement was supported by the whole of the Divisional artillery and carried out according to plan. The Gordons then set about searching the woods in their vicinity. At noon the 5th/7th Battalion and the 5th Black Watch came through to carry the advance northward, and clear the Mauny loop of the Seine.

The 1st Gordons collected twenty-one prisoners ' of various races and nationalities ' on this day and then settled down to refit and reorganise, receiving another draft of reinforcements.

Before the evening of the 30th the whole of the Mauny loop was cleared, the advance of the 5th/7th Gordons and Black Watch having met with no opposition. The 5th/7th Battalion made prisoners of about a hundred Germans whom they discovered in various hiding places. They moved to Bardouville and ' a happy afternoon was spent watching the Jocks pounding about the roads on captured German horses '.

On 31st August the massed pipers of the Highland Division played Retreat at Divisional headquarters.

It has been said often enough that our Second Army was able to reach and cross the Seine against only slight resistance. With the bloody battles of Normandy in mind this may stand; but we have seen that two battalions of the Gordon Highlanders, in their advance to the Seine, were obliged to fight a series of nagging little actions against the German rearguards. Another battalion of the Regiment, the 2nd Gordons who started in the wake of the advance, fought their battle in the actual passage of the Seine.

The 2nd Gordons moved on the evening of 12th August, going northward away from the sounds of battle to the village of

St. Pierre Tarantaine. Here they welcomed a reinforcement of three officers from the London Scottish.

At this time the fighting in Normandy was drawing to its victorious end: the German counter-thrust towards Avranches had brought the enemy nothing but disaster and the gap between the American First Army near Argentan and the Canadians, still north of Falaise, was closing.

Now the 15th Division passed from the VIII Corps to the XII Corps and on 14th August the 2nd Gordons travelled eastward through Caumont and Carpiquet to the 'horrible country about Caen'. They found Maltot 'a filthy place where a very savage battle must have raged', if they were to judge by the amount of German equipment which littered the ground and the number of still unburied German dead.

News of the Allied landings in the south of France was received on the 15th.

The Battalion were glad to leave Maltot three days later when they moved south to the vicinity of Bois Halbout. Here company route marches and platoon exercises were carried out; a mobile cinema provided entertainment; and on the 20th a 'vicious air raid' on the Brigade area saw the Gordons escape with no loss. Next day a heavy rainstorm made every one uncomfortable.

On 22nd August the 2nd Gordons parted with their commanding officer, Lieut.-Colonel Sinclair leaving to command the 153rd Brigade of the Highland Division. His temporary successor was the second-in-command, Major R. Henderson, a Seaforth Highlander who had joined the Battalion at Otley.

Events were moving quickly. The Falaise 'pocket' had been sealed by the junction of the Allied forces at Chambois, fifteen miles south-east of Falaise, on 19th August; the broken remnants of the German Seventh Army were in full retreat; and the Allies, facing eastward, were taking up the pursuit to the Seine. Indeed on the 21st the Americans had crossed the Seine both above and below Paris which was entered on the 24th.

Next day the 2nd Gordons moved forward. The first part of their journey lay across the Falaise 'killing ground'. At the sides of the cratered roads were hundreds of destroyed or damaged tanks and trucks and other vehicles; and all about lay dead horses and dead Germans. In the hot sun the stench was almost intolerable and the Gordons were glad to leave behind them what had once been the town of Falaise.

Their route lay through Trun and then north-eastward and on the 23rd they would have reached Bernay had not the roads been congested by Canadian and French transport. It was good to get into clean, open country with men and women harvesting

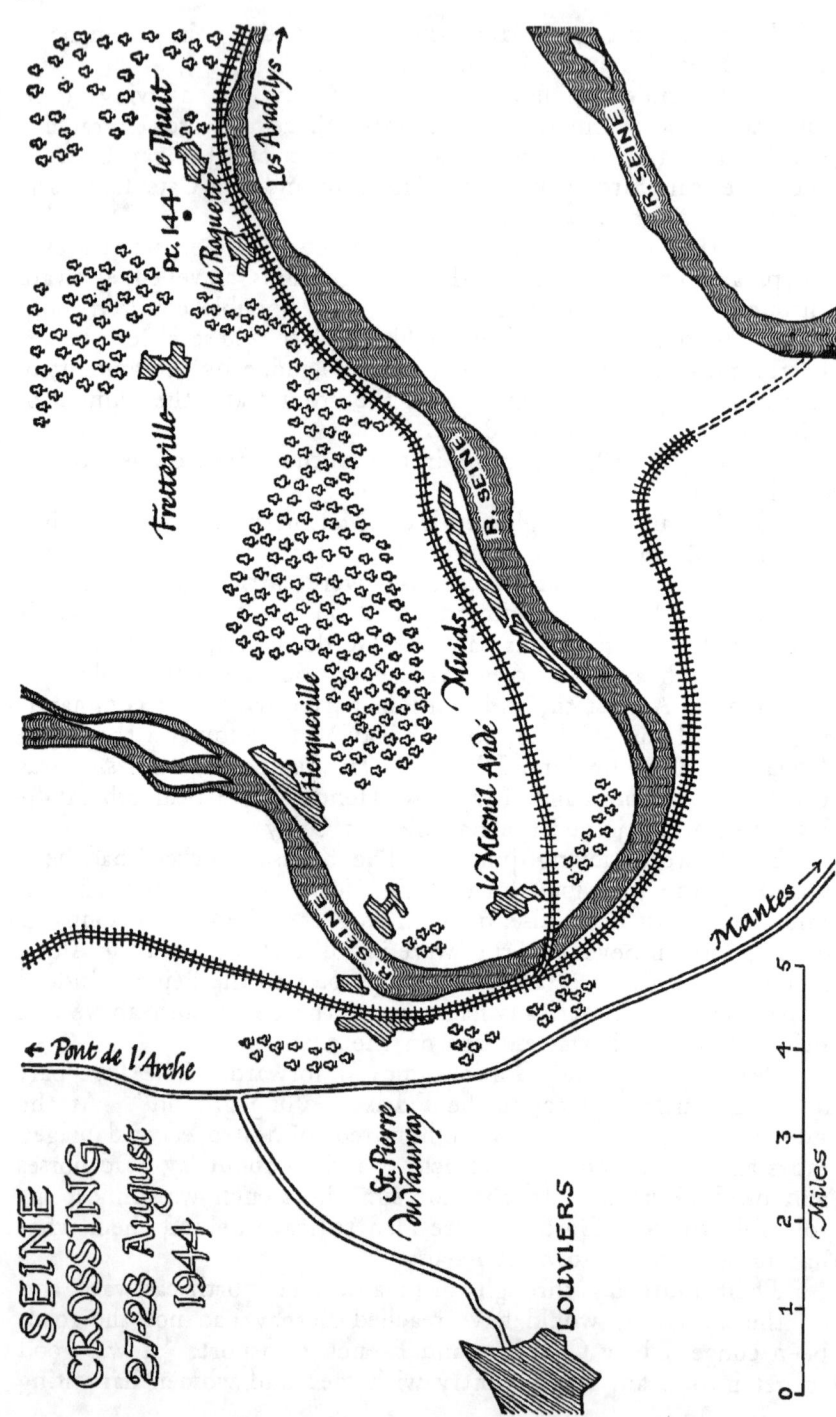

and the villagers pressing fruit and flowers upon the Jocks as the trucks went by.

On 25th August the Gordons took up defensive positions in the Emanville area, but left at three o'clock next morning to reach Louviers which lies in a hollow some five miles from the Seine. The Battalion occupied the western and the H.L.I. the eastern part of the town, and a watch was kept on roads and bridges. No enemy was seen.

The 227th Brigade pressed forward to the Seine on the morning of the 27th. At 9 a.m. the 2nd Gordons halted in a wood overlooking the river which they had orders to cross that evening.

Half a mile away, and nearly 400 feet below, the river curved towards them to form a blunt salient enclosing flat country with woods beyond. The point of passage was to be just south of the damaged railway-bridge near the small village of le Mesnil Andé.

The Germans were in no condition to conduct an organised defence of the Seine, but it did not follow that a passage at any point would be undisputed. For the Gordons all seemed to promise well. D Company carried their assault boats down the slope, over the railway track and across the open ground to the water's edge. There was no sign of movement on the further bank, nothing to indicate the presence of the enemy.

The assault boats with which the Gordons had been provided possessed out-board motors, but fitting them seems to have been a hurried job for none of the engines could be started up. So the engines were jettisoned on the river bank and the Highlanders prepared to paddle themselves across the river. Four boats pushed off, each boat containing twelve men.

The river here is about 300 yards wide, and more than half the passage was accomplished in silence. Then German machine-guns opened upon the defenceless little craft. Only one reached the further bank where its surviving occupants were captured.

Now the German fire was concentrated upon the remainder of D Company who were waiting to cross. The carrier platoon came into action in reply to the spandaus, but men began to fall fast. Lieutenant D. M. Fairlie stripped and plunged into the water, pulling several men to safety. One Gordon swam out, pushing a boat containing three dead men, to rescue some of his fellows who were marooned on a bastion of the bridge. And an angry company sergeant-major wounded in the arm, turned on his way to the aid post to shake his one good fist at the invisible Germans and shout ' I'll be back ye bastards! I'll be back!'

The commanding officer and the adjutant were on the river bank, directing the withdrawal of D Company who had few officers left. It was noticeable that the Germans forbore to fire on the stretcher-bearers as they toiled with their burdens up the steep slope from the river.

Fortunately the Gordons now received orders to stand fast and not to try again. Grievous loss, mostly in D Company, had been suffered: Major R. M. M. Tindall, the company commander, mortally wounded; Captain D. Spence, second-in-command and one time pipe-major in the Gordons, Lieutenant Aitken and thirty-seven other ranks killed; Lieutenant Lamont and forty-six others wounded; and three men missing.

After darkness had fallen the Gordons were taken in the amphibious vehicles called DUKW's two miles down stream to St. Pierre du Vauvray where the 10th H.L.I. had been fortunate enough to cross the Seine without opposition. The Battalion made the passage in power-driven boats and found that there was still work to be done. As the adjutant describes it: 'the night was spent walking round the big loop of the Seine in a thunder-storm, liberating small villages.' Thus le Mesnil Andé was cleared and Muids, the prisoners taken being 'mostly of the SS type', left behind in small bodies to delay the Allied advance.

When day broke on 28th August the Gordons advanced along the bank of the river from Muids and by nightfall had reached a hill known as Point 144. Then arrived an order to send a company to Fretteville where the Germans were proving troublesome. C Company found that Fretteville was more than one company could manage, as they were withdrawn to Point 144 where the Battalion concentrated. At night mortar fire caused a few casualties. Next day the transport arrived in pouring rain.

On the 30th came a welcome move to the small villages of le Thuit and la Roquette, more comfortable quarters, and the Battalion received a much needed reinforcement which consisted of a complete company of Lancashire Fusiliers. It was no more than ten weeks since the 2nd Gordons had landed in Normandy, but comparatively few of those who had then crossed the Channel now remained.

The new commanding officer, Lieut.-Colonel R. W. M. de Winton, arrived on 31st August.

On 1st September the pipes and drums played at le Thuit, and next day many Gordon officers attended the Divisional commander's party in the château at Herqueville belonging to M. Renault of automobile fame. On this festive occasion eightsome reels were danced.

Honours and awards were announced on 2nd September: the Military Cross to Major R. M. M. Tindall and Major A. W. Parish, the Military Medal to Sergeants J. Atherton and C. Harris, Lance-Corporal A. McConnell and Private J. McLean.

St. Valéry : Le Havre

On 26th August General Montgomery's orders included the following sentence. 'All Scotland will be grateful if the Commander, Canadian Army, can arrange that the Highland Division should capture St. Valéry.'

Little time was lost in doing so. Both the 1st and the 5th/7th Gordons were on the move before daylight of 2nd September, passing through Rouen where the traffic congestion was very great. This was a peaceful drive, and the 1st Battalion, covering seventy-seven miles in nine hours, arrived at Veules-les-Roses at 2.15 p.m. The 5th/7th went to Ielon. The Divisional commander placed each Brigade (152nd and 153rd) more or less in the positions occupied by the brigade which bore the same number in 1940; the old 1st Gordons had then been under 152nd Brigade command.

The Highlanders received a wonderful reception from the inhabitants who held in affectionate remembrance the prowess in arms of those of the old 51st Division who had fought their last fight at St. Valéry. The celebrations of the 1st Gordons at Veules-les-Roses on Sunday, 3rd September, may be taken as typical of the scenes in and around St. Valéry on this day, the fifth anniversary of the outbreak of the war.

At 10.30 a.m. a Battalion memorial service was held; at noon the commanding officer paid a visit of ceremony to the mayor; a 3 p.m. a dance for all ranks began in the village hall; and then followed an address by the commanding officer to the mayor and citizens of Veules-les-Roses. In the evening the pipes and drums played Retreat in the village, and the officers dined at the Hôtel de France.

At 4 p.m. the massed pipes and drums of the Division had played Retreat at Major-General Rennie's headquarters set up at Cailleville where Major-General Fortune's headquarters had been in 1940.

So the new battalions of the new Highland Division paid tribute to their predecessors; and Scotland could take comfort and pride in their triumphant appearance on the scene of the tragedy of 1940.

On 4th September the Highland Division moved to an area south-east of Étretât. The Division were now in the I Corps, and had their part to play in the reduction of Le Havre. First came a few days of relaxation. The 5th/7th Gordons mention shopping expeditions to Etretât and Fécamp, and an ENSA (Entertainment National Service Association) concert party whose bright particular star was Miss Gertrude Lawrence. At Fécamp the monks at the Benedictine abbey sold their liqueur freely at a reasonable price, and the town provided the most enthusiastic welcome so far encountered.

The town and port of Le Havre were heavily fortified on both the coastal and the landward sides. Isolated as they were by the Allied advance through Normandy the garrison might or might not be prepared to offer a stout resistance, but the I Corps left nothing to chance. Bomber Command of the R.A.F., two battleships and a monitor were to attend to the 'softening up' process. The artillery bombardment employed four field and four medium regiments and one heavy regiment; and the two assault divisions (49th and 51st) would have the support of heavy machine-guns and tanks of many types.

The attack was to go in from the Montivilliers area, north-east of Le Havre, with the Highland Division on the right and the 49th Division on the left. The latter were to open the ball by securing the high ground west of the Lezarde river which flows down into the estuary of the Seine. This done the Highlanders were to break through the German defences north of the Forêt de Montgeon and clear an axis of advance through the forest and so into Le Havre.

Heavy rain interfered with our bomber strike which extended over several days. At length, on the evening of the 10th, the 49th Division attacked and at a minute after midnight (11th September), when their neighbours had reported success, the Highlanders followed suit.

The 152nd Brigade moved first, their objectives being certain strong points north-east and north of the Forêt de Montgeon, and an anti-tank ditch which covered extensive minefields protecting the village of Fontaine-la-Mallet. All went well, and it was not long before flail tanks and R.E. tanks were tearing gaps through the minefields.

Leading the 153rd Brigade the 1st Gordons moved off at 3.55 a.m., but at 5 a.m. they were held up by a traffic block in the minefield gap east of Fontaine-la-Mallet. As the Gordons' battle transport could not get through the rifle companies went on alone.

B Company under Major MacMillan were in front, and by 7 a.m. they had cleared Fontaine-la-Mallet, now a mass of rubble, taking eighty prisoners. They pushed on as far as the railway bridge north-east of the forest, and here they were checked for a time by shell-fire and the fire of spandaus. Major Robertson's A Company came down the main road through Fontaine-la-Mallet and turned westward up the slope and into the forest, clearing out snipers and capturing four field-guns and two anti-tank guns. About one hundred Germans surrendered, and soon the whole of the northern part of the forest was in possession of the Gordons.

Although some groups of Germans resisted stubbornly, most of the enemy seemed to have little stomach for this fight. When, at 1.30 p.m., A and C Companies advanced against the German gun positions beyond the forest they were met by a display of white flags and the total of prisoners rose to 400.

While the Battalion were preparing to settle down for the night they received orders to advance before dawn next morning and clear up an area 1,200 yards broad extending down to the coast on the northern side of Le Havre. This was done without much trouble, another two hundred Germans being gathered in. Much valuable equipment and considerable stores of food were found in the coastal defences.

When the Gordons, whose casualties during the two days amounted to three killed and eleven wounded, moved back to Villainville on 14th September the commanding officer received the following message from Major-General Rennie:

> A note to congratulate you and your Battalion on their showing in the Havre battle. Your Battalion, more than any other, was responsible for starting the disruption of the Le Havre defences, and your quick exploitation of that opportunity must have saved a lot of casualties and a lot of tiresome sticky fighting for I Corps. Well done!

The 5th/7th Gordons, reserve battalion of the Brigade, did not move forward until after mid-day on 11th September. In the evening they passed through the 5th Black Watch who had followed in the wake of the 1st Gordons, and entered Le Havre, some of the men marching, some carried on tanks. They met no organised resistance, but A Company, with whom were a squadron of tanks, became separated from the Battalion and had a brush with a pill-box. Now and then our tanks fired a round or two, and one brought down a church steeple, dislodging some snipers.

When darkness fell the 5th/7th Gordons rested in an area of shattered streets not far from Fort Ste. Addresse which was still in enemy hands. Casualties for the day amounted to a despatch rider, injured by a fall from his machine. Although some of the French people expressed delight at the turn of events, others displayed resentment at the lives lost and the damage done by our air attacks. Nearly everyone claimed to belong to the ' Resistance ', and there was a clamour for instant vengeance upon a number of *collaborateurs*.

Next day Fort Ste. Addresse became the centre of interest. The commanding officer called it 'a model for toy forts'. It possessed a double moat—dry, but a formidable tank obstacle—turrets, bastions and gun emplacements, and its sheer walls rose to a height of nearly fifty feet.

All the morning the Battalion mortars and anti-tank guns bombarded the fort. To storm it would not be so easy. Major L. I. G. McLean's D Company, who possessed no such equipment as scaling ladders, were ordered to make the attempt with the support of all varieties of tanks after a preparation by the Divisional artillery. Many senior officers of the Division gathered at points of vantage to watch the proceedings which were to begin at 4 p.m.

Before that hour a terrific explosion shook the solid walls of the fort and caused a breach in them: the garrison had blown up one of their naval guns. Entry now would be so much the easier, but as zero hour approached the Germans fired three green Véry lights and then put out white flags. Had they delayed a little longer the battle would have been on, for a field battery had already been ordered to start ranging on the fort. This order was cancelled just in time.

In all fairness one must now mention a claim to the capture of the fort laid by the Chief Officer for Civil Affairs, I Corps. Quite unknown to the Gordons, he is said to have approached the place from the opposite side and peacefully persuaded the enemy to capitulate.

Seven officers and 242 other ranks were taken in Fort Ste. Addresse, but the surrender of the garrison became insignificant in the face of a more important issue. The Germans had destroyed much material of value, but a vast store of wines and spirits—accounts differ as to whether the Bollinger was '34 or '37—remained intact. The Gordons and the members of the French Resistance were quick to realise this: so also were other units in the vicinity. It is to the credit of the 5th/7th Gordons that order was so soon restored, although the popping of the champagne corks was said to be 'as loud as the preliminary bombardment'. And with the Gordons in possession one officer, who had failed to pass the sentries, lamented that it was harder to get in to the fort than when the Germans held the place.

Next day the 5th/7th discovered a German ordnance store 'filled with everything from a double bed to a tin opener', and organised parties collected many items described as 'necessary for the good of the Battalion'. Snipers were reported to be busy, but they proved to be members of the French Resistance cleaning their rifles.

The whole of the 153rd Brigade went back to the Villainville area near Etretât on 14th September, and on the 16th the massed pipes and drums played Retreat in the town. A large, admiring crowd gathered, and the officers and the pipe bands took wine in the Town Hall with the local dignitaries, the mayor making a speech of welcome.

Both the 1st and the 5th/7th Gordons now had a chance for training and for a general smartening up, the 1st Battalion contriving to mount a full guard in the kilt for the first time since landing in Normandy. Both battalions continued to be pleased with the fighting quality of their English reinforcements, but would, of course have preferred to see the return of their own men. The fact that sick and wounded Gordons, when fit again for active service, could rarely get back to their units remained a very sore point.

On 22nd September the officers of the 5th/7th Gordons entertained to dinner the Divisional commander, the Brigadier, and the commanding officers of the 1st Gordons and the 5th Black Watch. The spoils of Fort Ste. Addresse made this a notable occasion.

While the Highland Division near Etretât ' waited to re-enter the war ', the 154th Brigade were called away to take over the investment of Dunkirk; and in that vicinity they recovered two drums of the 6th Gordon Highlanders which had been left behind in 1940.

Into Holland

The 2nd Gordons moved away from the Seine on 3rd September, for the 15th Division were beginning to follow in the track of the Allied armies who had swept forward through France and Belgium. At la Tronquay the performance of the pipe band captured the hearts of the girls, much to the confusion of Pipe-Major Nichol on whom they lavished their caresses. After crossing the Somme on 5th September came a halt, no vehicles being available to carry the Gordons on; but they left for Courtrai on the 8th, passing near Arras and Vimy Ridge and through the mining districts of Lens and Loos where the people ' watched them without a smile '.

Belgium made a more favourable impression than France had done. The country seemed neater and tidier, the inhabitants more friendly, and comfortable quarters easier to obtain. After crossing the frontier near Mouscron—it was still only half-past nine in the morning—the Battalion made for Nazareth, some eight miles south-west of Ghent. In this area, northward of Kerkhove—Bossuyt, which the Brigade had orders to sweep clear of Germans, few of the enemy were to be found.

The Gordons left Nazareth on the 11th. They moved up to the Albert Canal and on the 13th they reached Meerhout.

The advance from the Seine of the 21st Army Group had been swift and easy. Brussels was liberated and Antwerp, although the clearing of the Scheldt estuary and the opening of the port was to prove a formidable task. East of Antwerp the numerous waterways of northern Belgium had checked our armoured forces in their forward drive and the difficulties of transport and supply from the far distant Normandy beaches were not easy to surmount. In the meantime the German armies were reorganising in preparation for an obstinate defence of the approaches to the Fatherland. On 13th September, when the Gordons arrived at Meerhout the 15th Division, now in the XII Corps had taken over the Albert Canal bridge-head near Gheel and the other battalions of the 227th Brigade were already in action. The fighting on this day left the 2nd Argyll dug in on the southern side of the Schelde-Maas canal, and the 10th H.L.I. in possession of Moll.

At this time the canal, a little short of the Dutch frontier, marked the limit of our advance and General Montgomery was about to launch 'Operation Market Garden' the drive which was intended to cross the Rhine, outflank the Siegfried Line on the north, and open the way to the North German plain. The plan has been described as 'laying a carpet of airborne troops' across the water obstacles which barred the way, the ground forces (XXX Corps) to link up by advancing along a single road through Eindhoven, Grave and Nijmegen to Arnhem, beyond the lower Rhine.

The 15th Division had no part in 'Market Garden' which opened on 17th September; but their operations were important seeing that the XII Corps were to come up on the left of the XXX Corps and widen the narrow corridor of penetration.

On 15th September the Gordons made a reconnaissance for a surprise crossing of the Schelde-Maas Canal west of Donck. The crossing began in the small hours of the 16th, C Company providing the assault platoon which was commanded by Lieutenant K. Brownlee-Lamont. All wore sandbags over their boots to deaden noise and carried the minimum of equipment in order that they might move easily and in silence. A taping party which led the way marked out the forward route—a distance of three miles—and a platoon of A Company brought up planks.

A backwater had first to be crossed, and this was done soon after 6 a.m. with the help of the planks laid across barges and covered by a carpet of sacks. Local bargees helped in this work.

Progress was soon held up by a machine-gun firing on fixed lines from a nearby lock, but as dawn broke the remainder of C Company, followed by B Company and D Company, with the carrier platoon on foot, made the crossing. But then the whole advance was pinned down between backwater and canal by heavy and accurate fire.

In the meantime A Company had attempted to cross the canal west of the lock in assault boats, but were stopped by machine-gun and rifle fire from the far bank. The commanding officer came up and decided that as the whole Battalion were already committed it was useless to persist. Certainly there had been no surprise. A withdrawal then took place leaving Major Duke's A Company in position near the canal bank with a section of carriers in support.

This venture had cost the Gordons Lieutenant Brownlee-Lamont and two other ranks killed and Major Follett, Captain McIntyre and nineteen others wounded.

The Battalion moved back that same day to Achterbosch and on Sunday, 17th September, to Kievermont. The 227th Brigade were now taking over the bridge-head at Aart, about three miles north of Gheel. During the 17th reconnaissance parties of the Gordons visited the bridge-head where two battalions of the 44th Brigade, due for relief, were repulsing a counter-attack.

On 18th September the Battalion sent three carriers to help get away the wounded of the Argyll who had taken over part of the Aart bridge-head on the previous evening. The Gordons moved up through Gheel to complete the relief that same night. The primitive cable-ferry had been badly damaged, so the companies crossed the canal in assault boats at hourly intervals and by 4 a.m. next morning completed the relief of the 6th King's Own Scottish Borderers.

The bridge-head had so shrunk under counter-attack that it now consisted of only the village street with the houses on either hand, the Argyll occupying one side and the Gordons the other. For two days the two battalions sat under a brisk bombardment, beating off a number of counter-attacks by their fire, ' all very unpleasant ' as the Gordons observed. They pulled out in the early morning of 20th September, the Gordons having come off lightly with about twenty casualties.

The operations of the 15th Division had occupied sufficient German forces to enable the 53rd Division to cross the canal further east at Lommel, and the Scots also were now to cross at Lommel, and continue their advance into Holland.

On 22nd September the Gordons crossed the Schelde-Maas Canal and the Dutch frontier. Next day they reached the northern outskirts of Eindhoven which had been captured by the XXX Corps on 18th September. The Battalion found themselves at the factory of a very well-known English radio firm whose employés spoke English and made the Highlanders very welcome.

At this stage the commanding officer disbanded B Company, preferring to have three strong rifle companies rather than four weak ones.

In their operations to widen the 'Market Garden' corridor and to give the XXX Corps flank protection the 15th Division had now established a bridge-head over the Wilhelmina Canal at Best, and on 25th September the Gordons went into battle again. Their task was to break out of the bridge-head and secure a firm base north of the canal and west of the railway, so that the H.L.I. and Argyll could form up for an attack on Naastbest.

The Gordons crossed the canal by a temporary bridge and at 10 a.m. emerged on to desolate heathland which afforded no cover. C and D Companies were in front, with A in reserve. The Germans were well dug in among railway trucks and held a cement factory upon which the rockets of our Typhoons appeared to have had little effect. Machine-gun fire soon began to take heavy toll of the Gordons whose leading platoons had no chance. It was impossible to drive the attack home, and after a trying and very depressing day the Battalion were withdrawn under cover of darkness.

Captain R. G. Hogg and Lieutenant G. E. Beaton had been killed; Major G. H. Hutchinson, Lieutenants G. C. McDonald and T. A. S. Johnson were wounded; Lieutenant Fairlie was missing. Other ranks lost nine killed, forty-seven wounded and fifty-five missing.

Some Germans, however, had had more than enough of war. Fifty-four of them, displaying white flags, came out of a wood to give themselves up to the Gordons; and more than half of them were killed by the fire of their own people.

The Gordons were on the western side of the Nijmegen corridor, and on the 26th they took over a reserve position from U.S. airborne troops. Next morning they relieved the 8th Royal Scots on the edge of a wood near Steenweg which was in enemy hands. Here the Gordons lived for a week in slit trenches while the rain came pouring down.

The 27th September was remarkable for an attack by our Typhoons, followed by a propaganda broadcast to induce the Germans to surrender. Next day the Typhoon treatment was repeated but the whole enterprise had no visible effect so far as the Gordons could judge.

The Gordons lost Captain A. W. Grendon and four other ranks wounded by shell-fire on the 27th. As the Brigade were holding a wide front, constant patrolling by day and night was necessary, and in those affairs two men were killed, two wounded and five missing. On the other hand a number of men reported missing on 25th September managed to find their way back. As the days passed the enemy showed a disposition to give ground, and was certainly very much on the defensive.

The last day of the month saw the arrival of a reinforcing draft which included five badly needed officers.

Now the 2nd Gordons, whose experience of campaigning in Holland had been by no means happy, were glad to hear that relief was at hand: and that, too, by the Highland Division. Here was a chance to meet old friends and, on 2nd October, Brigadier Colville commanding the 227th Brigade brought to the Battalion command post Brigadier Sinclair (153rd Brigade) and a number of officers of the 1st and the 5th/7th Gordons. The adjutant of the 2nd Battalion, Captain K. J. Irvine, and the second-in-command of the 5th/7th, Major C. F. Irvine, were brothers.

The relief of the 2nd Gordons was carried out next day, but by the 5th Camerons of the 152nd Brigade. The Gordons moved across the gradually expanding corridor to the eastern side. At Deurne they found themselves about two miles distant from a canal held by the enemy with 'just a few American armoured cars in between'. The Americans said that German patrols came up to the edge of the town at night, but 'not to worry'.

Billets at Deurne were comfortable, and for the first time since landing in Normandy the 2nd Gordons found it possible to run a central officers' mess. More reinforcements were received and a thorough reorganisation of the Battalion was carried out.

On 6th October the Divisional pipe band—massed pipes and drums of all battalions—gave a first performance on the Continent at Helmond, both Corps and Divisional commanders being present. Next day the massed pipe bands of the 1st, 2nd and 5th/7th Gordon Highlanders were able to play Retreat, for the Gordon battalions of the Highland Division were not so far away.

Hockey and football were played by the 2nd Gordons at Deurne and the Battalion were 'worried by a number of Dutch civilians who wanted to join the British Army'.

Certain honours and awards were announced on 13th October: the Military Cross to Captain A. N. MacPhail, the medical officer, and to Lieutenant J. H. Hitchcock, attached from the Canadian Army; and the Military Medal to Lance-Sergeant J. McGregor. To these may be added the D.S.O. of Brigadier J. R. Sinclair, former commander of the Battalion.

With the advent of the Highland Division the 1st and the 5th/7th Gordons now claim attention. The 153rd Brigade, who arrived first, left Normandy on 28th September and came up through Amiens and Cambrai, crossing into Belgium on the 30th. Both

Gordon battalions were impressed by the hearty welcome they received from the Belgians, and Brussels and Antwerp 'looked more prosperous and gay than London'. The Flemish dialect, it seems, 'sounded absurdly like broad Scots'.

They had entered Holland on 1st October and began to take over front positions from units of the 15th Division in daylight without delay. Until the relief was completed on the 3rd all three battalions of the Gordons, 1st, 5th/7th and 2nd, were holding the front alongside each other, a situation only once to be repeated —after the crossing of the Rhine.

The 5th/7th Gordons had said farewell to Major du Boulay who departed for a three months lecture tour in the U.S.A.

The 153rd Brigade now had the 5th Black Watch on the right, the 5th/7th Gordons in the centre and the 1st Gordons on the left, their positions lying between St. Oedenrode on the Dommel— a tributary of the river Maas, the French Meuse—and Fratershof.

The next fortnight is described by the 5th/7th Gordons as 'a quiet spell in the line', with mutual shelling and mortaring and some patrol activity. The period was looked upon as a Godsend, for many of the reinforcements had no battle experience and needed a gradual initiation. Only one rifle platoon commander had been in action before ; B Company had been made up with drivers from the R.A.S.C. and men of the R.A.M.C.

At Eindhoven had been opened a Divisional leave camp where men could get twenty-four hours rest, a bath, and clean clothes ; and on 17th October the first party went for a four days spell at a rest camp in Antwerp.

The 1st Gordons enlivened existence by a number of raids. A minor affair on the morning of 3rd October was followed by a more ambitious enterprise on the evening of the same day when artillery, mortars, Piats and A Company were employed. Six Germans were killed and one captured, but Captain C. R. Clay was wounded and two mortar men injured. An affray with grenades took place on the 7th and on the 8th B Company killed four of a German raiding party.

Later in the month the 1st Gordons reconstituted their D Company, under Captain R. W. Petrie, by drawing upon the other rifle companies, the carrier platoon providing Bren gun detachments.

Battles of the Maas

So far the operations on and beyond the Dutch frontier in which the Gordons had taken part were for the purpose of widening the Nijmegen corridor. Now a bigger offensive was impending.

Its object was to clear the Germans from the whole area south of the Maas, the XII Corps advancing westward from the general line Oss-Veghel-St. Oedenrode to link up with the right of the Canadian Army who were operating north-west of Antwerp.

In the 'Battles of the Maas', all three battalions of the Gordon Highlanders were engaged.

On 19th October the 5th/7th Gordons were relieved at short notice by the 2nd Gordons—of whom more hereafter—and the 1st Battalion by the 10th H.L.I. When the 1st and the 5th/7th reached their concentration areas on 22nd October the weather had cleared and the mud was beginning to dry.

The 'silent' attack of the 153rd Brigade was to be almost due north, and the 5th/7th Gordons were charged with the capture of Weibosch. On their left the 5th Black Watch had Schijndel as their objective. Zero hour was midnight, 22nd/23rd October.

The 5th/7th Gordons put C Company (Captain Brayley) and B Company (Major Gammie) in front. Advancing straight up the main road they were to clear the ground up to the edge of the village which would be dealt with by the other companies.

C Company headquarters came into action with grenades against the enemy's bazookas. B Company walked through a small minefield; and one platoon, led by Sergeant Stevens, stormed a strongly held post with great *éclat*. A and D Companies went through and took the village, together with thirty-five prisoners, the whole affair costing the Battalion two killed and eighteen wounded.

There was little left for the 1st Gordons to do, for Schijndel had been cleared by the 5th Black Watch. By noon the Battalion had arrived in Schijndel and proceeded to round up about two dozen German paratroopers.

23rd October was the anniversary of Alamein, and to mark the occasion, the 1st Gordons enjoyed a special ration of rum.

Now the advance was swinging north-westward and westward, the 5th/7th Gordons being directed upon Esch in the early morning of the 24th. They moved, for the first time, in Kangaroos— Sherman tanks stripped down to carry infantry—behind a squadron of tanks, and D Company, who led the Battalion, came under shell and mortar fire as they neared the village. There was the river Dommel to cross but the bridge was blown and the Germans appeared to have good observation from the further bank. A river crossing, 'as silent as possible', was now to be made in assault boats east of the village, the Gordons being required to establish a bridge-head while bridging operations proceeded. The crossing started at 7.30 p.m. on the 24th and was conducted without much trouble, for the German positions on the further bank were

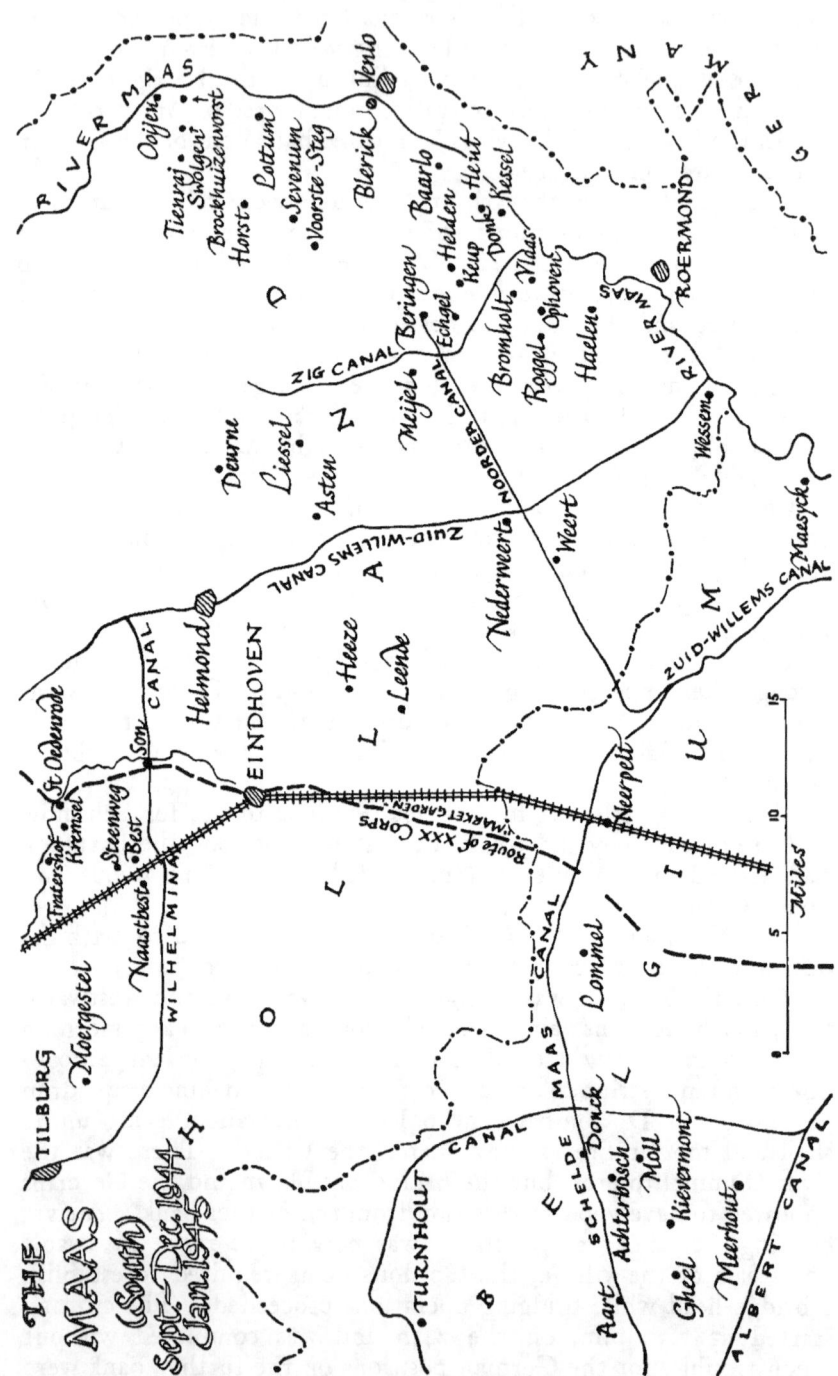

unoccupied, and the Battalion lost only one man killed and nine wounded. During the night, however, shell-fire interrupted work on the bridges.

About dawn of the 25th, in thick fog, the Germans began to attack the bridge-head. C Company (Captain Brayley) on the left drove off a detachment about eighty strong after 'quite a struggle' in which many Germans were killed and twenty-four prisoners taken including their commander, 'a cocksure young Nazi'. A Company (Major Muir) managed to surprise a patrol, after which the rest of this German company arose from a ditch and came forward to surrender. Then the company commander and his servant rode in on bicycles, being quite unaware of the turn of events. This German officer had been in the habit of spending his nights with a woman in a neighbouring village, so had missed the early morning battle. Altogether the 5th/7th Gordons took over seventy prisoners on this day. Their own casualties amounted to one killed and twenty-two wounded.

On the morrow, when bridging had been completed the 7th Armoured Division passed through.

The 27th brought the Battalion a very welcome visitor in the person of Lieut.-Colonel Howard Kerr, equerry to the Duke of Gloucester. His Royal Highness had asked him to visit one of the Gordon battalions to see how they fared. This cold and foggy day saw the 5th/7th moving forward behind the armour. No enemy was seen.

The 1st Gordons had moved to St. Michiels Gestel on 24th October and next day advanced south-westward sending infantry and carrier patrols to explore the Boxtel area. They found no enemy. At night the Battalion formed up to attack in the direction of Oisterwijk.

This affair began unfortunately. In the early hours of the 26th Lieutenant G. J. Heath was wounded by shrapnel; then Major B. D. M. Rae, commanding C. Company, Lieutenant G. M. Gray and Sergeant Honour, a platoon commander, were all wounded by machine-gun fire from houses and out-buildings. The company also lost five other ranks killed and five wounded.

When, however, A and C Companies attacked these buildings at 6.45 a.m. on the 27th with artillery and tank support they had their revenge. The tank shells smashed the houses and brought out twenty-five Germans covered with dust and plaster who were only too glad to surrender. In less than an hour success was complete.

Major A. Lumsden succeeded Major Rae in command of C Company, handing over the adjutantcy to Captain D. W. Martin.

On 27th October the 1st Gordons drove by way of Haaren to

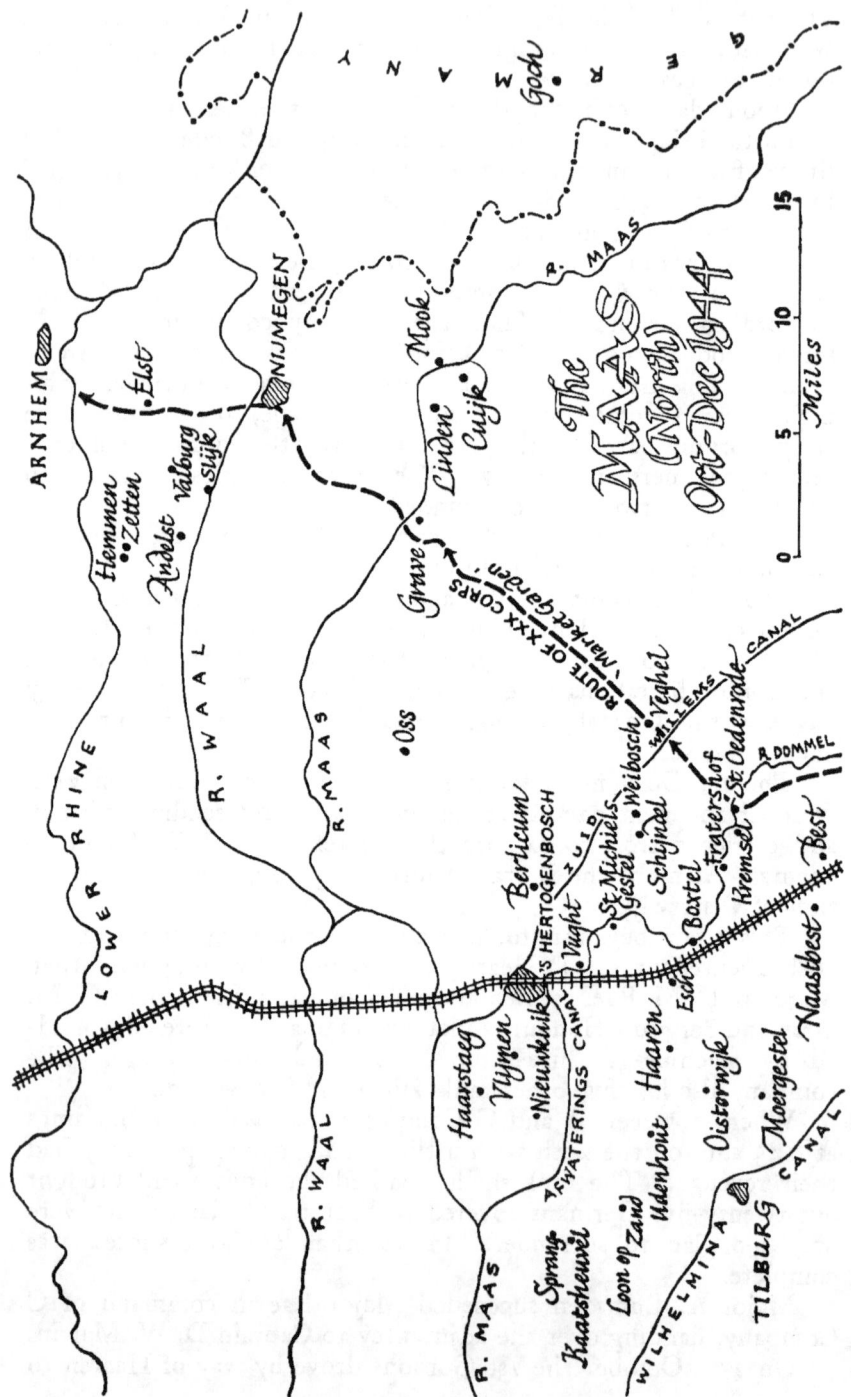

Oisterwijk. The advance of the 153rd Brigade was now northwestward towards Loon op Zand which the Battalion approached by vehicle and march on the evening of 28th October. D Company and the tanks encountered little oppostion except spandau fire, but a carrier patrol discovered a Tiger tank in time to avoid action with it. A Company helped the Black Watch to advance through the village against a very feeble resistance. The commanding officer of the Gordons tapped on a window and attracted the glance of a frightened German : seven of the enemy then came out to surrender.

Loon op Zand was shelled and mortared during the night, and early on the 29th the Gordons' command post was hit. Among the thirteen casualties was Captain Martin, the new adjutant, wounded.

The 5th/7th Gordons were now coming up. They passed through the 1st Battalion on the morning of the 29th and pressed forward on the left of the Black Watch along tracks in a wooded area west of the main road. Kaatsheuvel was the objective, and after the village had been shelled fiercely for ten minutes A and C Companies went in at two in the afternoon. More than thirty prisoners were taken, and the only active opposition came from a few snipers.

The Battalion found a warm welcome and comfortable billets in Kaatsheuvel. Hereabouts the enemy seemed in some confusion, for a ration truck drove, all unsuspecting, into the village and four more Germans were added to the bag. And not until 11 p.m. did the enemy discover that the Gordons were using electric light which he controlled. Thereafter darkness set in.

The 1st Gordons came forward to continue the advance and reached Sprang without opposition on 30th October. In the afternoon that enterprising spirit Major Lindsay made a reconnaissance in a carrier. He reached the Maas and saw about thirty Germans rowing laboriously across the river ; but he had left his Bren gun in the carrier some distance back so had to let them depart in peace.

Among five prisoners taken by the 1st Gordons on this day was one who proudly displayed a summons to return from the battle in order to take over the duties of *Reichsbreeder* in a district of Berlin. Such measures were not unknown among our chief enemy in the First World War.

On the last day of the month the 1st Battalion were relieved by a battalion of the 53rd Division and moved to 's Hertogenbosch which had been captured by the 53rd Division a few days earlier. ' The companies were located in that part of the city which had been most destroyed.' Next day Major Lindsay was injured by driving on to a mine while conducting a reconnaissance. He came back from hospital a few days later.

The 5th/7th Gordons had taken over a position from the 53rd Division at Orten, a little north of 's Hertogenbosch on 31st October. Here they were on a narrow causeway leading across flooded country to the river Maas.

In this quarter one task remained for the 153rd Brigade. It was to force the passage of the Afwaterings Canal west of 's Hertogenbosch in company with the 152nd Brigade on the left.

The 5th/7th Gordons relieved the Divisional reconnaissance regiment on the south bank of the canal while the 1st Battalion moved back to practice on the Wilhelmina Canal with their assault boats. All was ready by the morning of 4th November and the attack went in about four o'clock in the afternoon, the 5th Black Watch on the right and the 1st Gordons on the left.

The assault companies of the Gordons, whose objective was the western end of Nieuwkuik, were all across the canal in about half-an-hour. Casualties were few, for the flame-throwing 'Crocodile' tanks had a salutary effect upon the enemy who yielded prisoners of many different units. Nieuwkuik was in flames and the church a ruin.

At 9.30 p.m. the 5th/7th Gordons were ordered across the canal to assemble south-west of Nieuwkuik. By the time they had done so Captain P. J. W. Brand was slightly wounded and two other ranks killed and eight wounded. When the advance began D Company had some trouble at a railway crossing, but the Battalion were in Vlijmen soon after dawn of the 5th. The only obstacles were road blocks, mines and booby-traps, and Lieutenant G. L. Taylor, the intelligence officer, was blown up in his jeep by a mine and badly wounded. The pioneer platoon had a busy morning helping the sappers to lift mines. The Germans had disappeared completely and the only additional casualties reported were five wounded.

The 1st Gordons remained in Nieuwkuik. The Black Watch had advanced to Haarstaeg. Vigorous patrolling in this area seemed to show that no Germans remained south of the Maas: in fact, by 6th November the Highland Division had performed their share of the operation which brought the Second Army up to the river line in touch with the Canadian Army on the west.

On this day the 153rd Brigade were relieved by troops of the 7th Armoured Division and both battalions of Gordons withdrew to Vught.

When, on 19th October, the 227th Brigade moved across from the Deurne area and relieved the 152nd and 153rd Brigades it was to hold a defensive line while the Highland Division prepared for their offensive. The 2nd Gordons took over from the 5th/7th Battalion at Kremsel, near St. Oedenrode, where the programme consisted of night patrolling in the woods and harassing fire by our gunners. After the 153rd Brigade had launched their successful attack on Schijndel during the night of the 22nd/23rd it became evident that the Germans had withdrawn on the front of the 227th Brigade further south, and by the evening of the 24th the Brigade had advanced to the line of the Boxtel-Best railway.

The time had come for the 15th Division to begin their drive for Tilburg, so the Gordons proceeded to clear the woods on their front, a tricky progress through thick undergrowth and along paths which were mined. But the Germans had departed, and the whole 15th Division now seemed to be converging on Tilburg.

On 26th October the Gordons were in Moergestel. The further advance of the 227th Brigade was slowed by traffic congestion and a broken bridge, but the Battalion, on tanks and in Kangaroos, entered Tilburg soon after 5 p.m. A few snipers were found, but the greatest obstacle to movement was the cheering crowd of Dutch people who blocked the roads.

The Gordons—and not only the Gordons—could not but be thankful that Tilburg had been yielded without a fight, for its numerous waterways and bridges were ideal for defence.

Lieut.-Colonel de Winton was very anxious for a few days respite so that he might get the Battalion into better fighting trim; but although the Gordons had finished their part in the westward drive they were to have no opportunity for reorganization, and no chance of comfortable billets and a good clean up.

Along the eastern side of the Nijmegen salient the Germans had counter-attacked to some purpose. On 28th October they drove the Americans out of Meijel. Next day they recaptured Liessel and pressed forward for six miles up the Meijel-Asten road, and not until the 30th was their advance brought to a standstill.

The 227th Brigade being sent eastward in all haste by direct order of the Corps commander, the 2nd Gordons found themselves on 29th October in ' a horribly boggy area near Asten '. At dusk the whole Brigade moved south towards Meijel, and when they dug in the Battalion were between the H.L.I. and a wood to the south of Liessel. American troops withdrew through this position, and a number of Dutch people were evacuated. The Germans seemed to have in action heavier artillery than usual.

On the 30th a strong German patrol captured a farm held by C Company of the Gordons who lost five killed and two wounded. Later in the day, with tank assistance, the farm was retaken and twenty-one Germans, including an officer, were made prisoner.

On 1st November three Germans 'in poor condition' gave themselves up: they said that their company had suffered heavy losses. Lieutenant Griffiths and two sergeants were killed on this day.

Next morning, by a series of company advances supported by tanks, the Battalion gained ground without fighting, the H.L.I. keeping pace on the right. On the 4th it was clear that the Germans had started a general withdrawal, as usual leaving mines behind them.

The 6th Royal Scots Fusiliers (44th Brigade) relieved the Gordons on the 5th, and as the billets at Asten were considered 'unsuitable' the Battalion went to Helmond. For the next ten days short spells forward near Liessel alternated with short rests at Helmond. Some relaxation was possible here: on the 12th the Battalion actually gave a 'tea dance'.

In this flat country all movement in the forward area was by night in order to provide no targets for the enemy's mortar fire. Otherwise the Germans were quite inactive, but they had planted their mines very freely.

The next task of our Second Army was to drive the enemy eastward over the Maas. As the Highland Division were required for this offensive the 1st and 5th/7th Gordons did not stay long in their excellent billets at Vught.

Vught concentration camp made a sobering impression upon those officers and men of the 5th/7th Gordons who visited the place on 7th November. They saw a room with no windows, twelve feet square, in which sixty-seven women had been locked for twenty-four hours.

Next day the 5th/7th moved to Leende, away to the southeast of Eindhoven. The weather was vile with heavy rain, but good billets were found 'and the cafés were selling beer'. Orders were then received for an assault crossing of the Nederweert-Wessem Canal, an operation which required much preparation and rehearsal.

The 1st Gordons, whose pipes and drums had been often heard in Vught with great effect moved to the vicinity of Heeze where the pipers played Reveillé in the streets 'but not loud enough to wake the Brigadier'.

In wet weather both battalions practised with their assault boats which were to be brought to the bank of the canal before being opened up. Routes were reconnoitred for the advance of the carriers, tanks, Crocodiles and the amphibian vehicles called Buffaloes. The assembly, east of Weert, was accomplished in good order, although the deep mud proved a great trial to all vehicles.

It was fine but bitterly cold when the attack went in at 4 p.m. on 14th November, the 1st Gordons on the right and the 5th/7th on the left. A smoke barrage blew back across the canal but, despite the prevailing murk which made it difficult for the companies to keep direction, all went well.

The assault seems to have been a complete surprise. One prisoner, captured by the 1st Gordons, said that someone who had foretold an attack had been reprimanded for 'alarmist and anti-Nazi talk'. There is no doubt that the Germans were dazed by the fury of our supporting fire and very much shaken by the flame-belching Crocodiles. The sodden ground was our chief trouble for it slowed down the advance of B and C Companies of the 1st Gordons who found it impossible to dig when they reached their objective.

In the course of the action the 1st Gordons lost Lieutenants A. Chappell, E. S. Brown and R. E. C. Barbrooke, wounded by bullet or grenade, and of other ranks ten killed and twenty-two wounded.

The 5th/7th Gordons had used Major Gammie's B Company as a 'boating party' to manage the assault craft and see the other companies across the canal. This job was done supremely well, the Battalion making the passage quickly and with practically no loss. One platoon of A Company engaged a German platoon, killing nine and capturing twelve at the cost of four men wounded, Sergeant Molyneux being prominent in this affair. Altogether the Battalion reckoned to have disposed of nearly forty Germans, killed or wounded, and took as many prisoners; their own losses amounted to Lieutenant D. A. Vick and eight men wounded.

This action gave the 5th/7th some unsought publicity, for a B.B.C. correspondent transmitted a direct commentary of the proceedings; also, an article appeared in the American magazine *Life*, written by its representative who was likewise near at hand.

Later in the evening the 5th Black Watch passed through the Gordon battalions who were then out of touch with the enemy. On the 16th the 1st Gordons, advancing in Kangaroos with tank support, reached Roggel. Here the Dutch inhabitants said that the Germans had left early that morning after destroying the church and attempting to destroy a bridge. The Battalion drove on eastward, B. Company going to Vlaas. D Company sent a carrier patrol to the Zig Canal where Lieutenant C. E. Morley was killed by machine-gun fire while trying to cross at a lock. German shell-fire was rather heavy on this day.

Meanwhile the 5th/7th Gordons occupied without opposition the scattered hamlets of Ophoven and Bromholt.

On the night of the 17th the Brigade made the passage of the Zig Canal with the 1st Gordons on the right and the Black Watch on the left. B and D Companies of the Gordons advanced at 9 p.m. and the support of the Crocodiles is described as invaluable. Well hammered by our artillery the Germans offered little resistance, and about forty prisoners were gathered in. During the remainder of the night the enemy shelled the bridging sites on the canal.

Early next morning the 5th/7th Gordons took up the advance and were able to occupy unopposed the villages of Keup and Echgel. The German artillery was still active—Lieutenant H. F. McCormick was wounded by shell-fire—and the pioneers had to tackle a large minefield.

On the 20th the Battalion approached the Maas not far from Kessel. The afternoon and night were very wet and mines were still a nuisance, the pioneer officer, Lieutenant B. W. Fuller, being badly wounded by one while on reconnaissance. The companies were very tired when they advanced on Donk and Heut next day, and at the start an unsuspected belt of mines caused trouble. Captain J. S. Black was wounded by one of them. In the early afternoon progress was checked by fire, but the arrival of a squadron of tanks induced the Germans to depart from Donk in some haste. The Gordons entered the village before 5 p.m. their total loss amounting to less than a dozen of all ranks. Next day they occupied Heut and arrived on the banks of the Maas.

The German frontier, defended by the Siegfried Line lay a little beyond the river. In almost ceaseless rain, with forward routes impassable except by the lighter tracked vehicles, the Battalion spent a miserable time until relieved by troops of the 53rd Division on 24th November. That day was spent in getting the transport out of the mud.

The 1st Gordons, who were literally 'stuck in the mud', remained in their position forward of the Zig Canal until they also were relieved on 24th November. The Highland Division, moving north, were now to take over part of the Nijmegen bridge-head.

The experiences of the 2nd Gordons in the eastward advance to the Maas differed little from those of their brethren. The 227th Brigade, holding a defensive position facing Meijel, made their first move on 16th November when the 10th H.L.I. occupied the village which the Germans had abandoned without fighting. The Gordons came up to fill a gap between the H.L.I. and the left of the Highland Division, but were withdrawn to Helmond next day to prepare for a major action.

The Battalion drove forward through Meijel—what was left of it—on 20th November. Then, on foot, they advanced to Beringen where they passed through the H.L.I. and took the road for Sevenum. After covering a mile D Company, who were supported by tanks of the Scots Guards, drew accurate fire from woods and farms. The tanks went ahead to attack the buildings at close range, but three of the Churchills were hit when 88-mm. guns opened fire. At night the Gordons halted three miles forward of Beringen. Ahead of them the Germans were burning farms and villages as they withdrew, and a pitiful stream of refugees appeared through the mud and the rain. Forty-three prisoners had been collected and the Gordons counted thirteen of their men wounded.

Next morning the carrier platoon led the advance, but road-blocks, craters and blown bridges made progress slow and kept the sappers busy. The Gordons and the tanks did well to struggle through the mud and rain as far as Voorste-Steg. Sevenum, now a heap of rubble, was reached on the 22nd. The only casualty was Lieutenant Stewart, wounded by shell fire.

The Gordons, now rear battalion of the Brigade, were at Horst on the 23rd, and here they halted, owing to difficulties of supply. The rain had not ceased and the mud was worse than ever. On 25th November the Brigade advanced on Tienraj. The Battalion reached Swolgen before nightfall in time to see the Germans departing, and next day they arrived on the banks of the Maas. C Company encountered some slight resistance at Brockhuizenvorst where they occupied the south side of the village with A Company on the north side. D Company were at Ooijen.

On the further bank the Germans seemed active, and a ferry continued working until it was put out of action by our artillery. There was some trouble on the 27th with a German post further south in the direction of Lottum, and the day proved a harassing one for tired men employed in lifting mines, work which could not be done in the dark.

Late on the night of the 28th the Gordons were relieved by troops of the 11th Armoured Division and retired to the now familiar area of Asten. A draft of fifty-five reinforcements arrived on 30th November.

A week at Asten was followed by a return to the river line, this time further to the south at Kessel. All forward positions were overlooked by the enemy, so the companies sheltered in the farms by day and occupied the river bank at night. At night, too, the Germans indulged in the rather daring practice of sending out patrols in boats. One patrol was caught, after their boat had been sunk, and the captives explained that they had been sent out as a punishment for complaining about their rations.

The normal life of Kessel went on, for the stolid inhabitants seemed quite indifferent to this kind of warfare on their threshold.

Lieut.-Colonel de Winton now decided to reform B Company,

as the Battalion seemed strong enough to conform to normal establishment. The latest reinforcement had arrived on 12th December: twenty-one men from the Royal Inniskilling Fusiliers.

The Gordons were relieved by the H.L.I. on Christmas Eve and stayed for five days in a small village near Helden before taking over the left sector of the Brigade front at Baarlo on the Maas. Here the same conditions prevailed, but Battalion headquarters were in an imposing castle with *tout confort modern*, belonging to a Dutch baron. This castle was about half a mile from the river, and Germany was a short two miles away.

Now the weather was fine with hard frost, and outside a convent down the road nuns and Jocks skated together. With the New Year—Hogmanay was celebrated in the baron's champagne—Home leave was opened.

Most of January 1945 was spent by the Gordons in alternate tours of duty in the Kessel and Blerick (opposite Venlo) sectors on the Maas, the Helden locality being the reserve area.

Nijmegen Salient

The Nijmegen salient represented our furthest northward advance. On the left bank of the lower Rhine we held a dubious tract of country between the Rhine and the Waal known as 'The Island', and late in November 1944 part of this sector became the responsibility of the 51st Division.

On the 25th, having driven up from the south, the 1st and the 5th/7th Gordons debussed at Nijmegen and marched over the imposing bridge to relieve troops of the U.S. 101st Airborne Division. The 5th/7th went in on the right, and the 1st Battalion on the left.

The Waal was in flood and still rising, and if the Germans destroyed the dykes further up-stream the Island would be almost submerged and quite untenable. This contingency had been foreseen and an evacuation scheme, appropriately called 'Operation Noah', had been prepared.

This flat polder region between the two rivers was a land of many dykes, and roads which were really causeways. However, good billets were to be found in a number of large farms and small villages. In the 'front-line' villages, and in the reserve positions at places like Andelst and Valburg, the troops lived very well. 'Even the people in the front line had a satisfactory St. Andrew's Night.' Nijmegen was still a town containing a numerous civilian population who pursued their avocations without worrying much about the occasional artillery bombardment.

On 27th November Lieut.-Colonel J. A. Grant-Peterkin

was posted to command the 1st Gordons, Lieut.-Colonel Hon. H. C. H.-T. Cumming-Bruce having been given a brigade (the 44th) in the 15th (Scottish) Division. The new commanding officer, a Cameron Highlander, arrived on the 29th. In his first letter to the Colonel of the Regiment he voiced the old complaint that wounded and sick Gordon Highlanders seldom found their way back to their old battalions when fit for action again. 'It was sad to see the ranks filled up with English.'

The end of November was remarkable for some clear sunny days and the 30th for the disturbance of the peace by a German patrol which attacked the carrier platoon of the 5th/7th Gordons. The platoon billet was set alight by bazooka fire, and three of our men were wounded.

On 1st December a private of the 11th Parachute Battalion who had evaded capture since the Arnhem battle reached the forward positions of the 1st Gordons. Needless to say both he and a member of the Dutch Resistance who accompanied him received a warm welcome.

Next day came the news that the Germans had blown a gap in the dykes east of Elst and 'Operation Noah' had to be put in hand without delay. The waters rose steadily and it was sad to see cows and other animals who were beyond rescue left to drown. All civilians were evacuated at once, the Burgomaster of Hemmen paying a farewell visit to the 1st Gordons. The Battalion moved out on 4th December, transport using Nijmegen bridge while the rifle companies crossed the Waal south of Andelst in assault boats provided by the Canadian Royal Engineers.

The 5th/7th Gordons, though nearest to the rising floods, were the last battalion to go. They went on 6th and 7th December, some of the men wading for a considerable distance. Rafts were used, and the signal exchange was brought out by a DUKW. There was little transport left with the Battalion when, in heavy rain, it reached the Waal and crossed by ferry at Slijk.

Both the Gordon battalions were carried back to the Veghel area, south-east of 's Hertogenbosch. Here, although the weather was cold and wet and the first snow fell, all were glad of the opportunity to re-fit and to indulge in a thorough clean-up. The fitters and armourers were soon busy on vehicles and weapons. Short leave was taken to Eindhoven, Antwerp and Brussels, and the chaplain of the 1st Gordons opened a recreation club at the Royal Hotel in 's Hertogenbosch.

Contingents of both the 1st and the 5th/7th Battalions attended a service held by the Moderator of the Church of Scotland at Veghel on 14th December. At Veghel on this day the pipe band of the 5th/7th Gordons played Retreat.

To facilitate training some change of location was made, the 1st Gordons moving to Berlicum, east of 's Hertogenbosch.

The Field-Marshal held an investiture at St. Michiels Gestel on the 15th when the following officers and other ranks of the 1st Gordons received ribbons : Major J. M. Robertson and Captain D. R. Reid, Military Cross ; Company Sergeant-Major W. Jaffray, Sergeant Ison, and Corporals Cunningham and Hardy, Military Medal. In the 5th/7th Gordons the awards were : Majors C. F. Irvine, W. A. Muir, R. G. K. Evens, and L. I. G. G. M. Maclean, Military Cross ; Sergeant Longan, M.M., Distinguished Conduct Medal ; Sergeants A. Watt and J. Fraser, Lance-Corporal H. Rees and Private A. McKenzie, Military Medal.

Ardennes

The Hitler counter-offensive, launched on 16th December 1944, brought about a serious crisis. Advancing through the wooded hills of the Ardennes in ice and snow and fog the Germans aimed for Antwerp and Brussels. Theirs was a desperate bid for 'decisive victory in the West', and in achieving this they would 'cut off the British Army from its bases of supply and so force it to evacuate the Continent'.

The battle, which lasted a full month, was an American battle, though controlled with marked success by Field-Marshal Montgomery. Our own XXX Corps (which included the Highland Division) were moved south primarily to safeguard the line of the Meuse—known in Holland as the Maas ; and in the upshot all the Highlanders were called upon to do was to chase the German rearguards—an exercise of which they had had experience enough in Holland.

The 1st and the 5th/7th Gordons left their training grounds near 's Hertogenbosch on 20th December, knowing nothing of their destination. Both battalions reached the vicinity of Louvain late on the 21st over roads congested with traffic among which was seen 'a very very long queue of parked tank-transporters'.

Next day the Gordons crossed the Meuse and concentrated east of Maastricht, the Highland Division being now in reserve to the U.S. Ninth Army. Billets were good, all were told that no immediate move was to be expected, and preparations were made, accordingly, to celebrate Christmas and the New Year. Beer for the 5th/7th Gordons arrived from Brussels on Christmas morning.

Soon after mid-day came a warning to pack up at once in readiness to take the road again. So the Christmas dinner became a hurried affair, for in the afternoon began a journey to villages south of Liége where celebrations were resumed. The Highland Division, now on the threshold of the Ardennes, became reserve to the U.S. First Army.

Some of the V1's (pilot-less aircraft bombs) which seemed to be intended for Liége, fell in the Brigade area, wounding one of the 1st Gordons: otherwise there was nothing to prevent the two Battalions settling down to training. The pipe band of the 5th/7th Gordons gave much pleasure to the occupants of a children's home.

On 29th December Lieut.-Colonel Renny who had been selected to command the 9th Brigade was succeeded in the 5th/7th by Major C. F. Irvine. Colonel Renny left with mutual good wishes. He had been 'very proud and happy' to be with the Gordons, and said that the 5th/7th Battalion 'had the best company commanders in the Division and a fine lot of sergeants'.

Reconnaissance to the south was made, the weather being cold and frosty. Hogmanay went off as well as could be expected considering the flying bombs, the curfew imposed on all troops, and 'a shortage of liquor'. On 1st January came another move, this time to the neighbourhood of Ciney, the journey being complicated by the large scale movement of American forces and by the icy roads which obliged the tracked vehicles to move across country for most of the way. The Division now returned to the command of the XXX Corps.

Training was continued until the two battalions moved to a district a little north of Marche on 5th January. The news that they would 'stay here for some time' was received with considerable scepticism. Major Maclean of the 5th/7th Gordons at once set about organising a boar hunt, but although this sporting event attracted a distinguished company no boars attended it!

Orders to attack southward were received on the 7th. Although the country appeared to be less mountainous and arctic than expected, the conditions involved some special preparation. Companies began to construct sledges of corrugated iron to carry their blankets and greatcoats; and as this was to be a cross-country business and all tracks were snow-bound, jeeps and weasels—the latter with broader tracks than our carriers—were to be the only vehicles employed with the infantry.

The Brigade's advance along the slopes of the Ourthe valley was led by the 1st Gordons commanded by Major Lindsay, seeing that Lieut.-Colonel Grant-Peterkin was on leave.

The companies were scattered over a considerable area, the roads between them ice-bound and congested by battle traffic, the telephone 'out'. No one was more surprised than the commanding officer to see all the company columns arrive in the assembly area in the right order at 6 a.m. on 9th January. Here, close to the hamlet of Verdenne, the 1st Gordons breakfasted ' by the artificial moon of searchlights ' before beginning their climb by what was little more than a hill-path through the woods.

Those who hauled the sledges had a gruelling time before a small plateau was reached an hour and a half later when the wintry sun had risen. Then a way had to be found over the fields where, in places, the snow lay too deep for the vehicles. The next ridge brought the Gordons in sight of a valley with another wooded ridge—their objective.

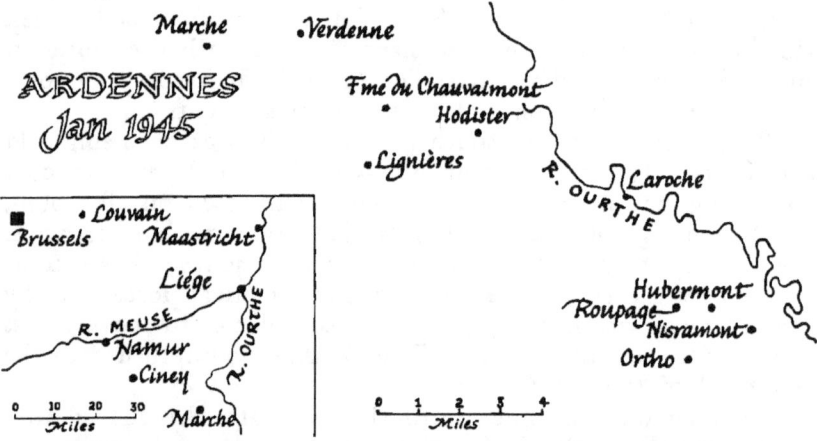

Half way down the near slope was the Ferme du Chauvaimont, soon occupied by A Company. The regimental aid post, travelling in jeeps, then moved in. Meanwhile two rifle companies crossed the valley and breasted the ridge where they found that mines and booby traps across the paths made progress very slow. They met no Germans. As the remaining company and Battalion headquarters crossed the valley they came under shell fire which was particularly heavy in the area of the farm. Here the ' well beloved doctor ' of the Gordons, Captain ' Bert ' Brown was killed—the only casualty of the day.

The Battalion dug in—a task which proved easier than expected and helped to keep everybody warm until the arrival of hot food some time later. The supporting tanks did good work in towing vehicles across the valley and up the hill, for the deep snow below and the icy ascent proved too much for the jeeps.

With the 1st Gordons firmly established on the ridge we may turn to the 5th/7th Battalion who had followed the 1st Gordons to Verdenne and moved forward in their wake about 10 a.m. They experienced the same difficulties with the snow and ice, but were able to pass through the 1st Battalion in the afternoon, led by the pioneer platoon and a bulldozer to clear a way through the snow. The 5th/7th were making for Hodister and encountered little opposition on the way. There were, of course, mines; and a number of self-propelled guns opened fire but were soon quelled by our artillery. Hodister was reached as darkness fell, and occupied without fighting. D Company, holding high ground west of the village, were obliged to spend the bitterly cold night in the open. The Battalion remained for the next two days in Hodister.

The 1st Gordons received orders late on the night of the 9th to secure Ligniéres, a small village about three miles away to the south-west. Next morning they advanced across country, but progress was delayed by tree-blocks, and to deal with the mines so well hidden in the snow the sappers decided that the only way was to 'pull them off'. The explosions soon brought down shell fire, but the advance continued: the Gordons entered Ligniéres at one end as a German artillery observation post departed from the other, the occupation of the village being unopposed 'apart from a little shell fire from our enemies and mortar fire from our friends'. Contact was made with troops of the 6th Airborne Division who were advancing from the west.

On 12th January the 5th/7th Battalion were carried forward in trucks towards the shattered village of Laroche. The column was halted for hours in the cold just north of Laroche under occasional artillery fire which killed Lieutenant H. D. McKibbin and three other ranks, wounded several, and destroyed a truck. In the evening the Gordons moved into Laroche which had been cleared by the 154th Brigade. At night, it is recorded, the temperature was 35 below zero. At 3 a.m. next morning the Battalion advanced on foot to Roupage, entered without fighting. Three prisoners were taken here. Then on for another two miles southward to Ortho where Lieutenant J. Paterson took in a patrol and returned with four prisoners, reporting the village clear. The Battalion moved in before dark.

On the 14th the Divisional reconnaissance regiment, who were clearing up south of Ortho, requested and received assistance from the Gordons in rounding up fifty-four Germans.

The 1st Gordons had been advancing further east. They had orders to occupy Nisramont on 13th January so came forward through Laroche and continued towards Hubermont which had been attacked by the 5th Black Watch. The Black Watch were undoubtedly there, and one of their companies could be seen at a cross-roads a little beyond the village. Major Lindsay, in a jeep with his intelligence officer, followed by the tank squadron commander in a scout car, drove down the village street where they surprised two German half-tracked vehicles and a scout car. The complete 'O' Group of the Gordons arrived in time to join in the skirmish which followed. When all was over the German scout car, with five casualties, remained in the hands of the Gordons; but Lieutenant D. C. Scott-Moncreiff, the intelligence officer, was wounded.

While the 5th Black Watch were consolidating in Hubermont the whole of the 1st Gordons came over the crest of the hill and down into the village. Then the Germans opened artillery and mortar fire. The tanks which were following the Battalion became the target of Panthers in action hull down 2,000 yards away on the opposite ridge, and in a few minutes three Shermans and one self-propelled gun were knocked out. There was no cover beyond the village so further advance was delayed until nightfall. Meanwhile the 1st Gordons spent an uncomfortable day in Hubermont under shell and mortar fire, losing about twenty men. Every vehicle coming over the crest in rear of the village was shot at by the Panthers, and it was not until 6.30 p.m. that a hot meal reached the Gordons. After this had been despatched A and B Companies advanced across country to Nisramont, and heard the enemy departing as they approached. The Gordons occupied the village that night and next day, the 14th, patrols explored as far as the river Ourthe, taking eight prisoners.

On 16th January at Houffalize, some seven miles east of Nisramont, the U.S. Third Army from the south joined hands with the U.S. First Army attacking from the north and the Ardennes battle was won. It had provided two battalions of the Regiment with a new experience, and these actions against German rearguards 'over snow-covered hills and valleys of great beauty' proved, in the opinion of at least one Gordon officer, 'a pleasant change from the mud of Holland'. But the 1st and the 5th/7th Gordons were now to return to the mud of Holland; and before them, and before the 2nd Gordons also, lay the bitterest fighting since the great battles in Normandy.

Rhineland Battle

The Allies had closed up to the Maas, and the Field-Marshal's plan for the next offensive had long been ready: the German forces between the Maas and the Rhine were to be driven back over the Rhine. This was 'Operation Veritable'. When it was successfully accomplished—and the Field-Marshal had no doubt of that—all would be in train for the crossing of the Rhine and the advance into Germany, isolating the great industrial district of the Ruhr.

The Canadian First Army, thrusting south-eastward from the Nijmegen salient, would have our XXX Corps under command, and in that corps were both the 15th (Scottish) and 51st (Highland) Divisions. From the south in the Roer sector a converging attack north-eastward was to be made by the U.S. Ninth Army; but, as it happened, this part of the offensive could not be launched until over a fortnight later.

No time was lost in bringing the 51st Division northward from the Ardennes. The 1st Gordons and the 5th/7th Gordons both moved on 18th January and were accommodated, on arrival, at Turnhout where there was a great congestion of troops. Some relaxation was now possible, and on 20th January the 5th/7th Gordons gave a dance for the nursing sisters of the Canadian hospital at Turnhout. The two Gordon battalions moved to the Tilburg district on the 23rd and the next fortnight was devoted to training and preparation for 'Operation Veritable'. General Horrocks commanding the XXX Corps paid a visit on the 29th and talked to all company commanders.

The 51st Division, forming the right of the Corps, were to open the road Mook-Gennep-Hekkens-Goch, the Corps axis of advance; but before the 153rd Brigade came into action it was necessary to secure the south-western corner of the Reichswald forest which was almost enclosed by the defences of the northern end of the Siegfried Line. For this operation the 5th/7th Gordons came under the command of the 154th Brigade who would be the first to enter the fight.

Accordingly the 5th/7th Battalion concentrated with the 154th Brigade not far from Linden on 29th January. Quarters were cramped and it was fortunate that 'everyone had a roof', for snow had fallen and the cold was bitter.

Thick fog hindered reconnaissance on the last day of the month and then, in the late afternoon came a rapid thaw. This was all to the bad for now there would be little firm ground on which armoured forces could manoeuvre: in fact, mud and water were to handicap all movement, slowing the progress of the fighting troops and complicating the problem of supply.

On 6th February the 5th/7th Gordons went into billets at Cuijk on the banks of the Maas. Next day the 1st Battalion moved up to Linden. Briefing had been very thorough and everyone knew what he had to do.

Our bombers struck on the night of the 7th, raining death and destruction from the air. At 5 a.m. next morning, more than

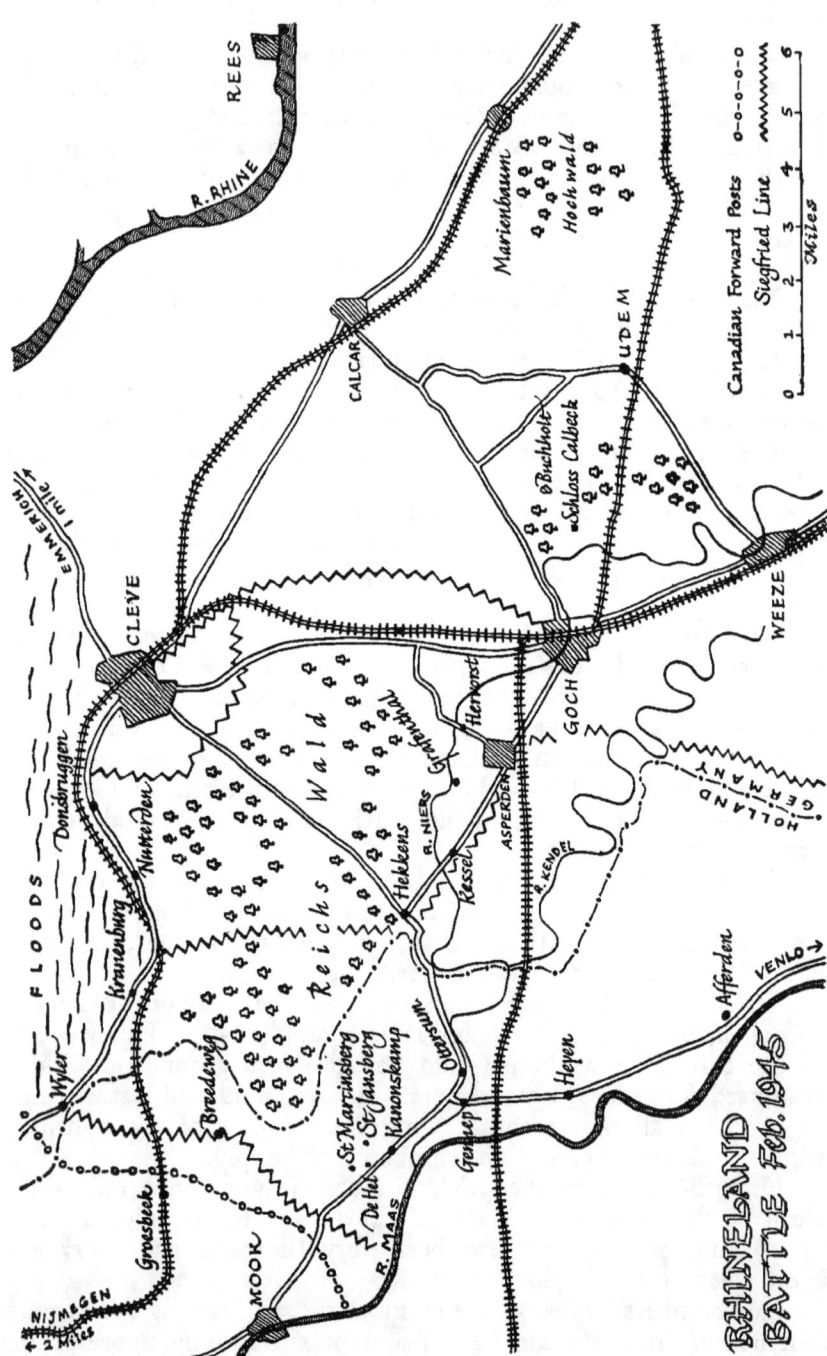

1,300 guns of all types and calibres began their bombardment. The infantry were due to advance at half-past ten.

The 5th/7th Gordons had an early breakfast before moving into their concentration area. Being in reserve to the 154th Brigade they had to wait until the two Black Watch battalions (7th and 1st) had captured Breedeweg and reached the edge of the forest. In the afternoon the Gordons went through to gain a hold of the high ground.

The air and ground bombardment had wrought havoc with the Siegfried Line, and the Battalion pressed on over smashed trenches and pill-boxes and fallen trees. Before nightfall C Company were on their objective. A Company went on into the forest, but the leading platoon, after engaging some enemy posts at close quarters, could make no headway. D Company, who had lost their commander, Major Maclean, wounded, and were now led by Major R. G. K. Evens (second in-command of the Battalion), were then sent to work round the enemy's left flank. The opposition soon melted away, and a B Company patrol under Lieutenant Paterson were able to reconnoitre the high ground which was the Battalion's final objective. About midnight B Company moved forward and occupied the position. All had been accomplished for the loss of thirty men killed and wounded.

In the course of an attempt to reorganise the Battalion, C Company, in the darkness and confusion, found themselves at a cross-roads in the middle of an enemy relief. As they afterwards described it, ' several hundred Germans were milling round in the area of the main track '. Though heavily outnumbered the company attacked at once and some of the Germans broke away; but they left many dead, and over 150 prisoners were captured by the Gordons who had only one man wounded.

This success appears to have loosened up the whole front of attack, for at 8 a.m. on the 9th the 152nd Brigade were able to push through and probe deeper into the Reichswald along one of the main tracks. The 5th/7th Gordons settled down to a meal, their first since breakfast of the previous day; and under some shell and mortar fire they enjoyed twenty-four hours rest.

The 1st Gordons crossed the Maas at Mook and reached their assembly area about 1 p.m. on 8th February. They were led by Major Lindsay for Brigadier Sinclair was in hospital, and Lieut.-Colonel Grant-Peterkin, after returning on 22nd January, had gone to command the Brigade. Now came a wait. As both 154th and 153rd Brigades were obliged to use the same route the latter were held back until the 154th had gained their objectives.

When, at last, the 153rd Brigade advanced the 5th Black Watch led the way and soon captured their portion of high ground in the forest. They reported, however, that the forest tracks were impassable for vehicles owing to the trenches, road-blocks, and fallen trees. Incidentally the Gordons had reduced their transport to a minimum in anticipation of difficulties; but they retained a weasel carrying 500 tins of self-heating soup, a notable example of good house-keeping in the field.

Rather than become entangled in the forest Major Lindsay set two companies of the Gordons, who had not been able to get going before dark, to work forward outside the edge of the Reichswald. In this way the whole Battalion were skilfully manoeuvred into a position near St. Jansberg. Tanks coming forward in support, however, had become bogged down. 'The mud had to be seen to be believed—ruts over two feet deep were common.'

The first task of the 1st Gordons was to clear the whole area between the Reichswald and the line of 'forward defended localities', held by the Canadians, which formed the southern end of the Nijmegen bridge-head. This involved a fanning out movement to north and west, and as the Battalion were not established in the St. Jansberg area until after midnight nothing more could be done with advantage until next morning.

The early hours of the 9th were devoted to getting a meal to the troops, for no vehicle had yet been able to reach them. Now the tanks came to the rescue, for they not only pulled jeeps out of the mud but carried forward a cooked breakfast for two companies of the Gordons.

Operations were resumed at 9 a.m. B Company and the carrier platoon mopped up St. Martinsberg and the German positions to the north and north-east of the hamlet taking fifty prisoners and meeting no opposition. D Company, advancing westward, were held up by fire, Lieutenant W. G. Fraser, commanding the leading platoon, being killed. This check necessitated some readjustment of the company positions to allow of an artillery preparation. After the gunners had done their job D Company advanced again, supported by a troop of tanks, and completed their task successfully. They sent back a dozen prisoners.

Later C and D Companies advanced southward against the hamlet of De Hel and a copse lying east of it. This effort enjoyed artillery and mortar assistance and went off well, although C Company had one sharp encounter which cost them ten killed and wounded. By this time the Battalion had captured over 250 Germans.

Now in mid-afternoon came a report that the 5th Black Watch, advancing southward from the Reichswald, had reached the Mook-Gennep road at Kanonskamp; but until the Gordons had cleaned up the enemy strong-points astride the main road in front of the Canadians the Corps axis of advance could not be opened.

The task was A Company's, but their attack from the north-east, assisted by tanks shooting from a position north of St. Martinsberg, was checked. They had come under the fire of well-sited spandaus and were hampered by mines. The Canadians put down mortar fire on the German positions, but still A Company could not get on. B Company, however, advancing between A Company and Battalion headquarters now established at De Hel, had cleared a wood by a bayonet charge.

Major Lindsay now prepared a night attack up the Mook road in order to take the German posts in rear. With himself in command, D Company went forward at 6.30 p.m. Just as the leading platoon passed the start line they were ambushed and the platoon commander Lieutenant J. A. MacPherson, was wounded in the leg by a stick grenade; yet the Gordons 'appeared to be quicker on the draw' and six Germans fell dead. Progress was difficult in the dark, but the first German position was taken and twenty prisoners were made. Further on the enemy appeared to be strongly entrenched round some buildings on a ridge to the north of the road. After two minutes rapid fire from every weapon which could be brought to bear the Gordons rushed in from the rear, well away from the road upon which the enemy's attention was fixed. All was soon over. Quite a number of Germans were killed and the prisoners amounted to seventy-one. Unfortunately the company commander, Major D. R. Reid, and 2nd-Lieutenant A. R. Porter were both injured by mines between the German and the Canadian posts.

The Gordons being now very close to the positions held by the Cameron Highlanders of Canada, the pipers of the two parties provided recognition signals. The Gordons, of course, played 'The Cock o' the North' and the Canadian Camerons responded with 'Piobaireachd Dhomhnuill'.

This last affair had cost the Gordons nine killed and seventeen wounded. Since entering the battle they had slain many Germans and had captured more than 350.

Next morning, 10th February, more Germans straggled in to surrender. The sappers had now cleared the Mook-Gennep road sufficiently for the Gordon vehicles to come up, and the Battalion were told that they might count upon thirty-six hours rest.

And now the 5th/7th Gordons come into the picture again. On the morning of the 10th they rejoined their own Brigade and moved at 10 a.m. with orders to clear the main road as far as Gennep. They approached Gennep without trouble, but before A Company could cross the river Niers the Germans blew the bridge which led into the little town. The leading platoon of Gordons were pinned down by spandau fire from buildings beyond the river, so our artillery put down a smoke-screen to cover the withdrawal of the platoon, but the whole business took an hour.

Meanwhile a patrol had turned up the Hekkens road and reported that there were no Germans in the neighbouring village of Ottersum. So C Company passed through A Company at the road junction and pressed on towards Ottersum. This road afforded no cover and was under machine-gun fire from Gennep, so C Company found themselves obliged to wait for the arrival of the tanks, and they entered the village behind the armour. After dark the remainder of the Battalion closed up, and all next day was spent in or near Ottersum, while the 1st Gordons were heavily engaged in Gennep.

On the night of 10th/11th February the 5th Black Watch had crossed the river Niers—now swollen by flood water to a width of sixty yards—in assault boats, and when day broke had two rifle companies in Gennep. The 1st Gordons came forward during the morning of the 11th. At 1 p.m. B Company (Major G. Morrison) and C Company (Major A. Lumsden) crossed the river by boat, the other rifle companies following two hours later. A communication trench, dug by the Germans along the riverside, provided a convenient means of approach to that part of Gennep held by the Black Watch.

The 1st Gordons now had to do their part in clearing the Germans from the place. The northern portion was under shell-fire; further back snipers and spandaus fired from the houses. Major Lindsay's plan was to clear the houses on either side of the main street as far as the level crossing; then to strike outwards and clear the whole area north of the railway before advancing further.

C Company led off about 3.30 p.m. and fought their way through the buildings on the west side of the street, occupying a factory of three storeys which provided a good field of fire across the railway. B Company followed on closely, dashed across the main street under cover of a smoke screen, and worked forward along the east side. The Gordons had learnt by experience the best method of street-fighting: it was to work by way of the back gardens from house to house, tackling one side of a street at a time.

As soon as C and B Companies had made some progress A Company (Major D. A. V. Aldridge) and D Company (Major R. F. Davies) came forward. Patrols reported that in the western part of Gennep the Germans had retreated over the railway line, but in the eastern part they were holding on at fairly close quarters. C Company in their factory, were the target for a bazooka sited about 100 yards beyond the railway.

A halt was called when darkness fell. Lieutenant P. B. Ayres had been wounded, and Captain E. J. Frary, the signals officer, had gone forward on reconnaissance, taken a wrong turning, and fallen into German hands.

Next morning, 12th February, a platoon of C Company occupied a factory beyond the railway and a company of the Black Watch cleared the station buildings. The 1st Gordons were then able to form up along the railway on either side of the level crossing in order to attack the high ground about a mile south of Gennep. On the left the 5th/7th Gordons prepared to capture the remaining features which overlooked the little town.

The 5th/7th Gordons had waited in Ottersum while the sappers, much impeded by hostile shell-fire, were throwing a bridge across the Niers. When the bridge was completed about 11 a.m. on the 12th a stream of tanks and other fighting vehicles began to pour across into Gennep. The Battalion followed.

A heavy barrage preceded the attack of the two Gordon battalions which went in at 2.30 p.m. The leading companies of the 1st Gordons, A and D, were protected from enemy observation by a smoke-screen which made it difficult to observe their progress. The smoke also bothered the tanks which were moving in support, but neither company had much difficulty in securing their objective. Captain F. G. Hopkins, second-in-command of D Company, was injured by a mine and Major Davies, the company commander, was wounded in the hand. He carried on for the rest of the day.

B and C Companies now came through. B Company, supported by tanks, charged with the bayonet a sandy ridge where thirty Germans were killed, and the advance only ended as daylight faded and heavy rain fell. By this time C Company had reached the near end of the hamlet called Heyen, where a spandau was firing from the ruined church.

The day had been a pretty satisfactory one for the 1st Gordons, considering that communication with the companies had been difficult owing to break-downs of the wireless sets, and that much inconvenience was caused by the delay in clearing the main road forward from Gennep. At the level crossing the road was blocked by railway trucks and mined, and southwards for 500 yards felled trees stopped the way. The sappers who did the clearance had been troubled by spandau fire, and the Gordons sent their carrier platoon under Captain M. Morrison to deal with this nuisance.

The 5th/7th Gordons who attacked on the left of the 1st Battalion made little of their part in the day's work. First they drove the Germans out of the eastern part of Gennep where Major J. I. Gammie, commanding B. Company, was wounded;

thereafter they advanced almost step by step with their brethren of the 1st Gordons. By nightfall they were digging in on their objectives, having lost thirty-one killed and wounded.

On the front of the 1st Gordons the night of the 12th/13th was remarkable for the behaviour of a German patrol who fired a phosphorus grenade into a house and set fire to the thatch. As our men came tumbling out a spandau opened fire, but caused no casualties. One German, afterwards found to be an officer, stood in the road and shouted 'Come out you English swine!' He was shot by Lieutenant Bickell's servant.

Next day Battalion headquarters were established in Heyen, the whole position was reorganised, and a machine-gun platoon and a troop of 17-pdr. anti-tank guns arrived. Patrols discovered Germans entrenched about 500 yards south of Heyen.

At about 4 p.m. an enemy self-propelled gun began firing from the woods to the south-east of the 1st Gordons, and a second gun soon joined in. Our artillery opened, and Captain N. L. Smith, commanding the anti-tank platoon of the Gordons, managed to get one of his 6-pdrs. into action against the nearest German gun. It was not easy to hit, but Captain Smith gave up only when his own gun was knocked out and he had received a shell splinter through his bonnet.

Following this, came a determined advance of German infantry up the main road in the dusk, an unexpected visitation. Some of the enemy got into the 'Kasteel', 200 yards from Battalion headquarters which the dismounted carrier platoon were called upon to protect, but B Company bore the brunt of this affair. In retrospect it was considered that the German attack 'never really amounted to much, but there was a great deal of noise'. Major Morrison's B Company certainly got in some good shooting and the mortar platoon fired many rounds.

Lieutenant J. McRae was wounded on this day.

The 5th/7th Gordons, after a wet and very uncomfortable night, were shelled and mortared and annoyed, also, by snipers on 13th February. D Company sent an urgent call for tank support about 4 p.m. as a German attack seemed imminent. Our artillery opened and the tanks arrived very promptly, only to find that the Germans had disappeared.

Now the two Gordon battalions lost touch with the Germans for a few days, as the 153rd Brigade were giving place to troops of the 52nd (Lowland) Division, and a Guards brigade.

On 17th February the 1st Gordons sent two companies back into Gennep so that the whole Battalion should be under cover. The Gennep-Heyen operations had cost four men killed and thirty wounded; and only seventeen effective officers were left.

As for the 5th/7th Gordons, they watched the 32nd Guards Brigade pass through on the afternoon of 14th February, an impressive and dignified procession of fighting men and battle vehicles, forming a 'picture-book display' which rather impressed the Jocks. After spending two nights in billets in Gennep the Battalion began to move forward in the wake of the advance.

The 2nd Gordons had entered the battle on the northern side of the Reichswald, and at this time were in Cleve.

When, during the last days of January, the 15th (Scottish) Division were relieved on the Maas the 2nd Gordons moved north to Turnhout to begin a short but intensive course of training. In particular they practised the penetration of minefields and the assault of pill-boxes and anti-tank defences.

In the afternoon of 5th February the Battalion began the drive up to Nijmegen which they did not reach until 3 a.m. on the 6th. The roads were bad and packed with troops and vehicles.

The first task of the 15th Division was to breach the Siegfried Line north of the Reichswald and capture the high ground overlooking Cleve. Of the 227th Brigade, the Gordons would be the last battalion to come into action.

At 7 a.m. on 8th February the rifle companies left Nijmegen on foot, passing by muddy tracks through our gun positions where the enormous deployment of artillery was in full blast. The day was spent by the Gordons in a small wood near Groesbeek; the night was one of 'fires, flashes and explosions'. On the right front the 53rd Division were fighting their way through the Reichswald; on the left the Canadians, in amphibious tanks were clearing villages in the flooded region between Nijmegen on the Waal and Emmerich on the Rhine.

About midnight the Gordons moved to their forming-up place at Kranenburg. The rifle companies and carriers found a fairly easy route. The battle transport encountered many difficulties: first two abandoned 3-ton lorries, one with its engine running, blocking the road; then two lines of trenches dug across the road; then a minefield; and finally a road-block of felled trees.

All this meant delay. It was not until dawn of the 9th that the Gordons passed through the 10th H.L.I. in what remained of Kranenburg and, with tanks of the Scots Guards, attacked the Siegfried Line.

They were in Germany now, but the assault of the frontier defences of the Fatherland proved something of an anti-climax. The formidable anti-tank ditch was spanned by a bridge which had not been blown, and Germans, with no fight left in them, surrendered freely. As the Gordons advanced along the road to

Nutterden they saw why the enemy's resistance had crumpled. Our fearsome bombardment had devastated the whole countryside: German gunners had left their batteries to take refuge in deep concrete shelters and emerged only to give themselves up. On this day the Battalion collected 135 prisoners.

Nutterden was reached and occupied in the afternoon and all seemed well. About eight in the evening, however, the Gordons suffered a nasty blow. The Battalion command post received a direct hit from a shell which killed Major A. W. Parish, Lieutenant Salter and nine other ranks and wounded Captain J. H. Thompson and four others.

Next day the Battalion pushed forward along the main road to Cleve, hampered by numerous road-blocks. At nightfall they reached Donsbruggen where they gained contact with troops of the 3rd Canadian Division. The place was simply a heap of ruins between the woods on one side and flood water on the other.

On 11th February the Gordons were ordered into Cleve, so resumed their advance. On the way they cleared the high wooded ground on their right with the help of the Scots Guards tanks, and by late afternoon were occupying their allotted portion of the historic city.

Behind the Gordons the floods were rising, and long stretches of the line of communication were under water. In Kranenburg the streets were flooded to the depth of four or five feet.

The Gordons, who handed over part of their area to the Canadians, spent six depressing days amid the ruins of Cleve. German aircraft came over occasionally and dropped a few bombs, but the *Luftwaffe* were no longer an effective force.

We return now to the Highland Division, for the 1st and the 5th/7th Gordons were about to go into action again. Their objective was Goch, a road and rail centre of importance and a strong bastion of the Siegfried Line. Already the other brigades of the Division had reached the south-east corner of the Reichswald and were across the river Niers at Kessel, Hervorst, and Asperden, but Goch was to be the target of a converging attack in which troops of other divisions were taking part. The 43rd Division probed the north-eastern defences of the town on the 17th; next day the 44th Brigade (15th Division) attacked in this quarter, and by the evening of the 19th this brigade had cleared the northern part of Goch down to the river Niers.

The 153rd Brigade, attacking from the north-west, had orders to take that part of Goch which lies south of the river. First the Black Watch were to advance as far as the main square; then the 5th/7th Gordons would continue the attack as far as the railway on the south-eastern edge; and, finally, the 1st Gordons would turn southward and complete the clearance of the town.

On the morning of 19th February the two Gordon battalions, in troop-carrying vehicles, arrived east of Kessel. The 5th/7th Battalion were first on the scene and Lieut.-Colonel Irvine went into Goch soon after day broke to find that the Black Watch had

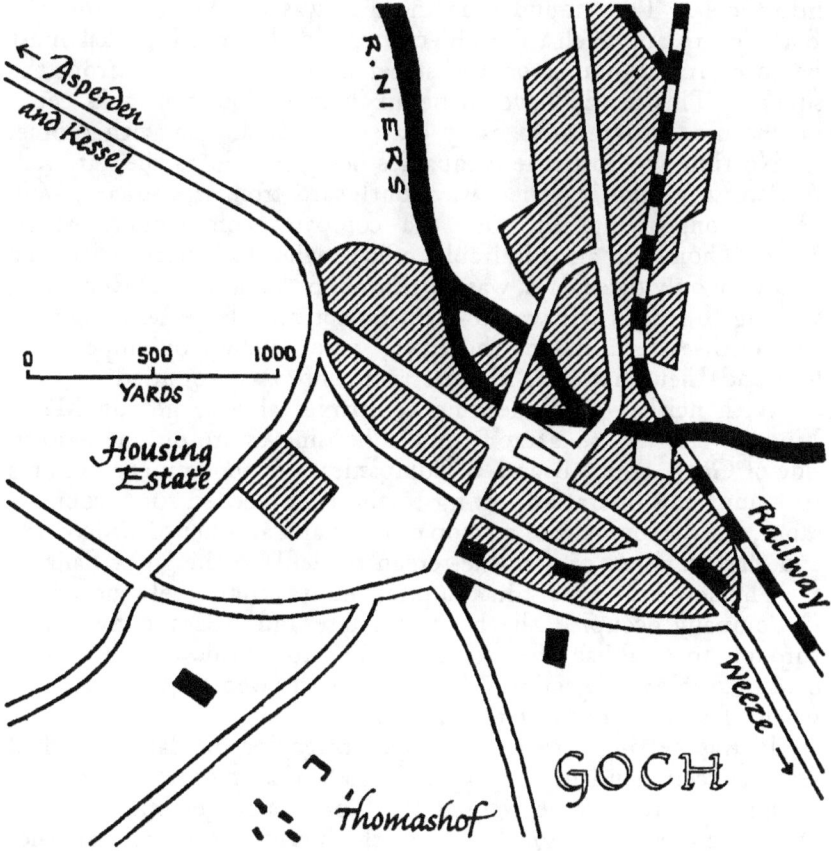

encountered little opposition to their entry in the small hours of the morning and had taken a number of prisoners. The commanding officer soon brought his leading company up, but it was not long before everyone realised that nothing more was to be gained without blood and toil

The start-line for the 5th/7th Gordons' attack was named as the main square which was supposed to be clear of the enemy; actually the leading company were hotly engaged before they got so far. The Germans were shelling 'our end' of the town and the Battalion were committed to a day of hard fighting in their endeavours to dislodge the enemy from ruined buildings and rubble heaps. By dark three rifle companies were involved in the struggle, the fourth company being used as a 'stop line' to prevent the infiltration of hostile snipers and patrols.

The 1st Gordons waited at the assembly area east of Kessel while Major Lindsay and his company commanders went forward into Goch. They found that the way was not yet open for the Battalion to approach their objectives, and that the first task must be to clear the houses on the street leading southward from the square. This would have to be an infantry job, for tanks could not be used in streets so badly cratered and blocked with rubble.

No time was lost, the companies being sent in as they arrived. A Company, fighting their way southward from the square, were very strongly opposed, and the company commander, Major A. J. Thomson, an admirable officer who had been with the Battalion only three days, was shot through the head. D Company, striving to force their way to their objective, a large building near the south-eastern end of the town, were held up by snipers and lost 2nd-Lieutenant H. E. Harrison who was wounded.

With neither of his leading companies able to get on Major Lindsay resolved to attack from a housing estate on the eastern side of Goch, using B and C Companies. It took ninety minutes to mount this operation, owing to the time needed for reconnaissance, the deployment of a troop of tanks and another of Crocodiles, and the provision of a smoke-screen to defilade the right flank.

The new assault went in at 4 p.m. and was completely successful. C Company occupied the housing estate and B Company passed through to establish themselves at the cross-roads in the middle of the original objective. One Crocodile went up on a mine when the cross-roads were reached.

It was getting late in the day. Brigadier Sinclair, who had resumed command of the 153rd Brigade that morning, now told Major Lindsay that he wanted the Gordons to get one company on to the cross-roads south-west of the housing estate and another into the large group of farm buildings called Thomashof about half-a-mile south of Goch : all this to be done without delay. Major Lindsay promised that this venture should start before first light next morning; in the meantime he ordered A and D Companies to get as much rest as possible, sheltering in cellars from the hostile shell and mortar fire which never ceased. A Company had only two officers left, and one platoon was commanded by a corporal.

The Divisional reconnaissance regiment had reported that D Company's objective, the cross-roads, seemed clear of the enemy.

Nothing was known of Thomashof, but during the night a patrol of B Company secured some houses in front of A Company.

The attack went in at 5.45 a.m. on 20th February when it was still dark, and D Company occupied the cross-roads without opposition. A Company were not so fortunate.

Our medium guns had been ordered to shell both objectives, but artillery fire was heavy on the road to Thomashof, impeding the advance of A Company who emerged from the streets south of the square in Goch. Major Lindsay therefore held A Company back while he took a bearing by the sound of the guns which were firing. They seemed to be ours but the echoes were deceiving and it was soon established that the German artillery had put down defensive fire.

A Company then pushed on. Their advance led them across open fields for part of the way. The light was sufficient to distinguish a man at fifty yards distance when the two leading platoons and company headquarters entered the nearest barns and cowsheds of Thomashof. The other platoon, with orders to clear the main farm building, met with disaster—perhaps through mistaking Germans for our own men in the dim light. The body of the platoon commander, Lieutenant C. C. Howitt, was found near the building next day.

In the meantime Major Lindsay, who was exercising personal command of the operation, had visited the rest of the company and found them firing and being fired on at close range. After consulting Captain Kyle, the company commander, he came back —all other means of communication having failed—with the intention of sending forward another company and enlisting the help of tanks. It seemed that A Company had taken on far too much.

B Company now prepared to reinforce A Company, but as no tanks were immediately available their advance was delayed. When they pushed forward from the left of D Company they took a row of houses and eighty prisoners. Over open ground swept by fire further progress was difficult, but B Company persevered and reached the farm buildings at Thomashof to find the Germans gone.

Before this a few stragglers from A Company had come in. They said that the whole company had been over-run; and a stretcher-bearer who had been captured and escaped later in the day reported that a strong German counter-attack had overwhelmed our men after a struggle. Many Gordon dead were found at Thomashof, and it seems that most of those taken prisoner were wounded. Captain Kyle was among the missing. The failure of communications at an early stage in the operations had much to do with this disaster to A Company.

Lieut.-Colonel Grant-Peterkin had now returned from the Brigade to resume command.

B and D Companies holding the forward positions south and south-west of Goch were intensively shelled and mortared during 21st February and the whole town was kept under heavy fire. A direct hit on a command post killed a platoon commander, Lieutenant I. Edgar. Our own guns and mortars did their best to subdue the German bombardment, but seemed to have little effect; and a strike of American bombers was partly misdirected and caused casualties to the troops in Goch.

In the evening the 3-inch mortars of the Gordons fired smoke in order to screen from spandau fire the ambulances going forward to remove the wounded of B Company. The Battalion lost heavily in subalterns on this day for Lieutenants I. T. P. Ventris, J. B. Coupar, J. G. Schofield and J. E. J. Gallop and 2nd-Lieutenant J. A. MacPherson were all wounded.

The German fire hardly slackened on the 22nd, and at night the 1st Gordons were relieved by the 5th/7th and concentrated in Goch. Lieutenant R. W. G. MacPherson, wounded, had to be added to the long list of officer casualties.

We left the 5th/7th Gordons fighting their way forward through the south-eastern part of Goch in the gathering darkness of 19th February. The struggle continued all night and all next day, but little progress was made. The assistance of tanks and flame-throwers, which could not get forward through the choked and cratered streets, would have been invaluable.

During the morning of the 21st the Germans began to withdraw and the Battalion were able to occupy their portion of Goch. They found that the excellent German cellars gave good protection against the heavy German shelling which ensued. Later in the day troops of the Lowland Division began to come through. The Gordons remained in the town, still under such heavy shell-fire that 'open-air life was very unhealthy'. Two vehicles were lost by direct hits.

When, in the evening of the 22nd, the Battalion relieved the 1st Gordons in the Thomashof area the hostile bombardment was still so heavy that the two forward companies could be supplied only by night.

Next day Lieut.-Colonel Irvine went home on leave, and command of the 5th/7th Gordons devolved upon Major R. G. K. Evens.

There was still another task for the Highland Division. They were to cross the river Kendel, a tributary of the Niers, and open a further stretch of the Mook-Gennep-Venlo road, an operation which meant crossing from Germany back into Holland.

The 5th/7th Gordons were involved, but not very deeply. The advance passed through the Battalion on 25th February and next day they were ordered to attack through the 5th Black Watch. On the night of the 26th and on the 27th the Gordons made steady progress, crossing the Kendel by an improvised bridge to the left of the 152nd Brigade. They met with little opposition, and when they were relieved by a battalion of the Lowland Division in the evening of the 27th they withdrew to Goch.

Neither the 5th/7th nor the 1st Gordons had any further part to play in the Battle of the Rhineland.

The capture of Goch had cost the 1st Gordons three officers killed, seven wounded, and one missing ; and of other ranks twenty-one killed, fifty-nine wounded and forty-eight missing. Their total casualties in the Battle of the Rhineland amounted to twenty officers and 183 others.

Before the end of the month drafts amounting to ten officers and 230 other ranks joined the 1st Gordons in Goch. A Company were reconstituted under the command of Captain Davis.

Major M. A. Lindsay and Major G. Morrison were awarded the D.S.O. for their good services in the battle, and Major A. Lumsden received the Military Cross. These honours were very gratifying, but the non-commissioned officers and men seemed to get little in the way of reward and Lieut.-Colonel Grant-Peterkin was not slow in raising the matter—it was a real grievance—with higher authority.

In the Rhineland battle the 5th/7th Gordons had suffered less than the 1st Battalion. They counted seven officers wounded and 126 casualties amongst other ranks, the great majority being wounded.

The first week of March, which brought colder weather with some snow, was spent by the 1st Gordons in Goch and by the 5th/7th a little further back in Hervorst. To this period belongs the following tale.

The headquarters of one company of the 5th/7th was established in a cottage, and the company piper was ordered to dig a latrine in the garden. It was not long before he reappeared in very mellow mood, clutching an armful of bottles. He had begun to unearth a cache of spirits and liqueurs. Willing hands soon completed the excavation, bringing to light six sizeable cases which provided the wherewithal for a generous company commander's hospitality. From this time forth the piper was ever ready to dig a latrine, no matter where the company might be.

The 2nd Gordons were heavily engaged a little further east while the battle for Goch proceeded.

They moved forward from Cleve on 19th February in readiness to attack next day, the objectives of the 227th Brigade lying beyond the Goch-Calcar road. After the leading battalions had secured a line which included the straggling village of Buchholt, the Gordons were to pass through and clear the woods round Schloss Calbeck as far as the Goch-Udem railway. They were to have the help of a squadron of Coldstream tanks and a half-squadron of Crocodiles.

The first objectives having been taken, the Gordon attack went in at 12.30 p.m. on 20th February. D and C Companies who led the way dismounted from their Kangaroos before entering the woods where they struggled forward along tracks deep in mud and rides intersected by wide ditches and blocked by fallen trees. The tanks became bogged, but a few got forward later, after tank bridges had been laid.

Most of the Germans encountered 'seemed a half-hearted lot', and by two in the afternoon D Company were in possession of the Schloss, with seventy prisoners. Our artillery had wrought considerable damage, but Battalion headquarters found the cellars quite habitable. By nightfall the Gordons had taken all their objectives and the number of prisoners had increased to 108.

At 1 a.m. on 21st February A Company advanced beyond the railway to secure a bridge-head over the nearby canal. They were supported by the 131st Field Regiment R.A., but the Germans, young parachute troops who were well trained but had never had a chance to 'drop', fought fiercely. A Company, bringing back two prisoners, were obliged to withdraw, but they retained command of the approaches to the bridge. They had lost fifteen, including Lieutenant Paterson, wounded.

Nothing further was attempted on the 21st until 8 p.m. when the 6th R. Scots Fusiliers (attached from the 44th Brigade) came through A Company of the Gordons and endeavoured to extend our foothold south of the railway. A fierce fight developed beyond the canal bridge, the Germans being now in considerable force, and the Fusiliers were checked.

They tried again at seven next morning and, after a struggle, managed to dig in round the cross-roads south of the canal bridge where they remained under heavy shell and mortar fire. The German reaction had grown much stronger.

It was the responsibility of the Gordons to keep open the main axis of our advance: the road through the woods by Schloss Calbeck and down to the canal bridge beyond the railway. All day on the 22nd the enemy deluged the woods with shells and mortar bombs. Outside the Schloss a salvo set four Bren carriers ablaze, one loaded with Bangalore torpedoes, and the resulting explosion nearly destroyed the cellar where Battalion headquarters were housed. There were many narrow escapes.

The Germans had filtered back into the woods north of the railway and fighting continued. In the afternoon C Company attempted to clear the enemy from a group of buildings and managed to inflict some loss, besides capturing fifteen prisoners. Major T. A. Gloster, commanding the company, was killed by a shell splinter.

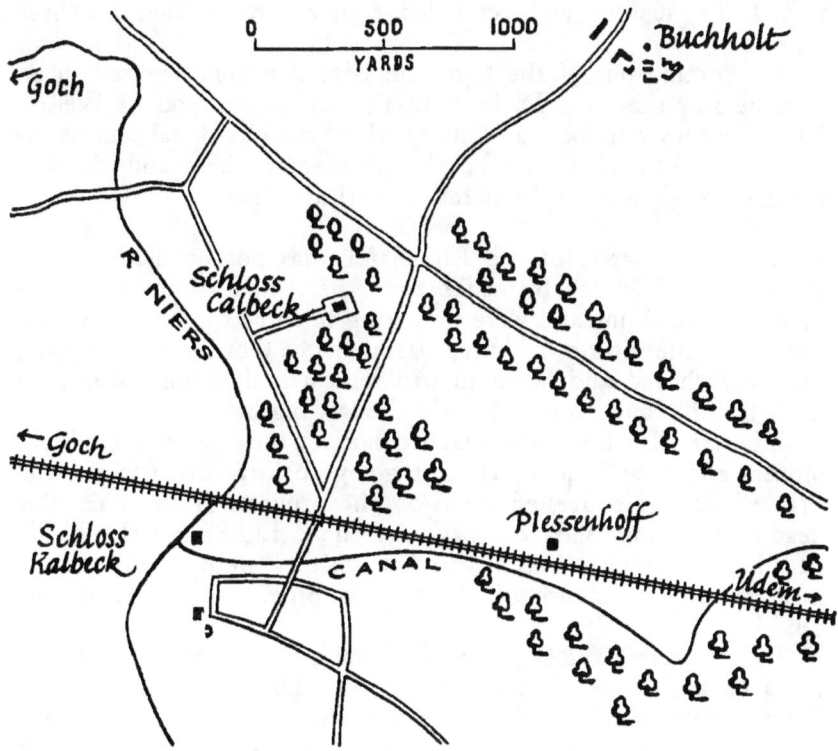

Later, the 46th Brigade came through to extend our gains south of the railway and canal, and in the evening B Company of the Gordons, attacked and captured the small hamlet called Plessenhoff. Lieutenants Harvey and MacFarlane were wounded in this affair.

On the morning of the 23rd a company of the Gordons, assisted by tanks of the Scots Guards, drove the Germans from Schloss Kalbeck which lies south of the railway on the canal near its junction with the river Niers. The remainder of the Battalion repulsed a determined counter-attack with considerable loss to the enemy who left many dead behind him. Lieutenant Hornsby was wounded on this day.

Meanwhile the 44th Brigade had passed through and the task of the Gordons was almost ended. They were relieved by a battalion of the 3rd Division on the evening of the 24th after nearly five days of confused fighting and pandemonium. In addition to carrying their objectives they had served the Division well by marking out routes of advance, evacuating wounded, and passing back prisoners. Besides the officer casualties already mentioned, they had lost eighteen killed, eighty-five wounded and three missing.

On coming out of the fight the Battalion concentrated in an area behind the 53rd Division in the neighbourhood of Weeze. Next day they were back at Tilburg where the Divisional commander, Major-General C. M. Barber, inspected them and thanked them for their work in 'Operation Veritable'.

This, the Battle of the Rhineland, was not concluded until the middle of March by which time the Allied armies had lined up along the Rhine and were preparing to force the passage of the river. In the interim all three battalions of Gordon Highlanders, 1st, 5th/7th and 2nd, were able to relax a little before beginning their training and preparation for the last big battle.

The 4th March was a special occasion for the Highland Division, officers and men from every unit going to Grafenthal where the Prime Minister addressed them on the progress of the war. He headed a distinguished company for the C.I.G.S. and the Field-Marshal were with him; and the visitors were treated to an impressive performance of the massed pipes and drums of the Division.

On 7th March the Highland Division moved to an area between Maesyck and Neerpelt and, as the 15th Division were no great distance away—the 2nd Gordons had arrived at the mining town of Eynsden in Belgium—the opportunity was taken on 13th March for a reunion of all three battalions. The headquarters of the 1st Gordons were at Haelen and, acting as hosts, they welcomed big parties of officers and men from the 5th/7th and the 2nd Battalions. In a football match the combined strength of the 1st and the 5th/7th proved too much for the 2nd Gordons who lost by six goals to two; officers entertained officers; other ranks sat down to tea together; and the massed pipes and drums of the three battalions played Retreat. Later, in the mess of the 5th/7th Gordons reels were danced with great abandon.

Passage of the Rhine

On 9th March the Field-Marshal had addressed to his troops a message in which he said ' The 21st Army Group will now cross the Rhine '. Plans and preparations were well in hand for the crossing which was to be on a twenty-five mile front between Rheinberg and Emmerich. Regimental interest centres upon the stretch of river between Wolffskath and Rees where three battalions of Gordon Highlanders were to go into action almost side by side.

Training for a river crossing was carried out on the Maas, near Maesyck, by night and by day, using the bullet and splinter proof amphibious conveyance called a Buffalo. A Buffalo could carry thirty men or eight men and a small vehicle. The 1st and the 5th/7th Gordons found rehearsals a harassing business for their efforts were hampered by the German mines which had not yet been removed from the banks of the river and by thick mist which was search-light proof. During one Brigade exercise by night at least seven Buffaloes were milling about in the Maas with all sense of direction lost.

So now to the passage of the Rhine. Our military and air resources were assembled in full panoply. A host of aircraft, a tremendous mass of artillery, airborne troops, every conceivable device of military engineering, a great array of tanks of all types, amphibious craft by the hundred : all were employed to put our troops on to the further bank of the Rhine swiftly and at the smallest possible cost. Even so, hard fighting was to be expected ; but all knew that this was to be the crowning effort of the campaign and should bring about the final defeat of the German armies.

Perhaps pride of place in the story should be given to the 5th/7th Gordons, since they were the first battalion of the Regiment to cross the Rhine.

On 21st March the 5th/7th moved up to their concentration area at Marienbaum which was hidden from enemy observation by the huge smoke screen put down to mask the deployment of our divisions. The companies went into camouflaged bivouacs. Next day the commanding officer and the company commanders found that they could see something of the country beyond the Rhine, but observation was hindered by the smoke. In the evening a change of wind made breathing uncomfortable, and in some cases respirators were worn for a time. A few German shells fell in the bivouac area, and a number of men were wounded.

The weather was ideal. At 5 p.m. on 23rd March the XXX Corps opened counter-battery fire and the 5th/7th Gordons moved

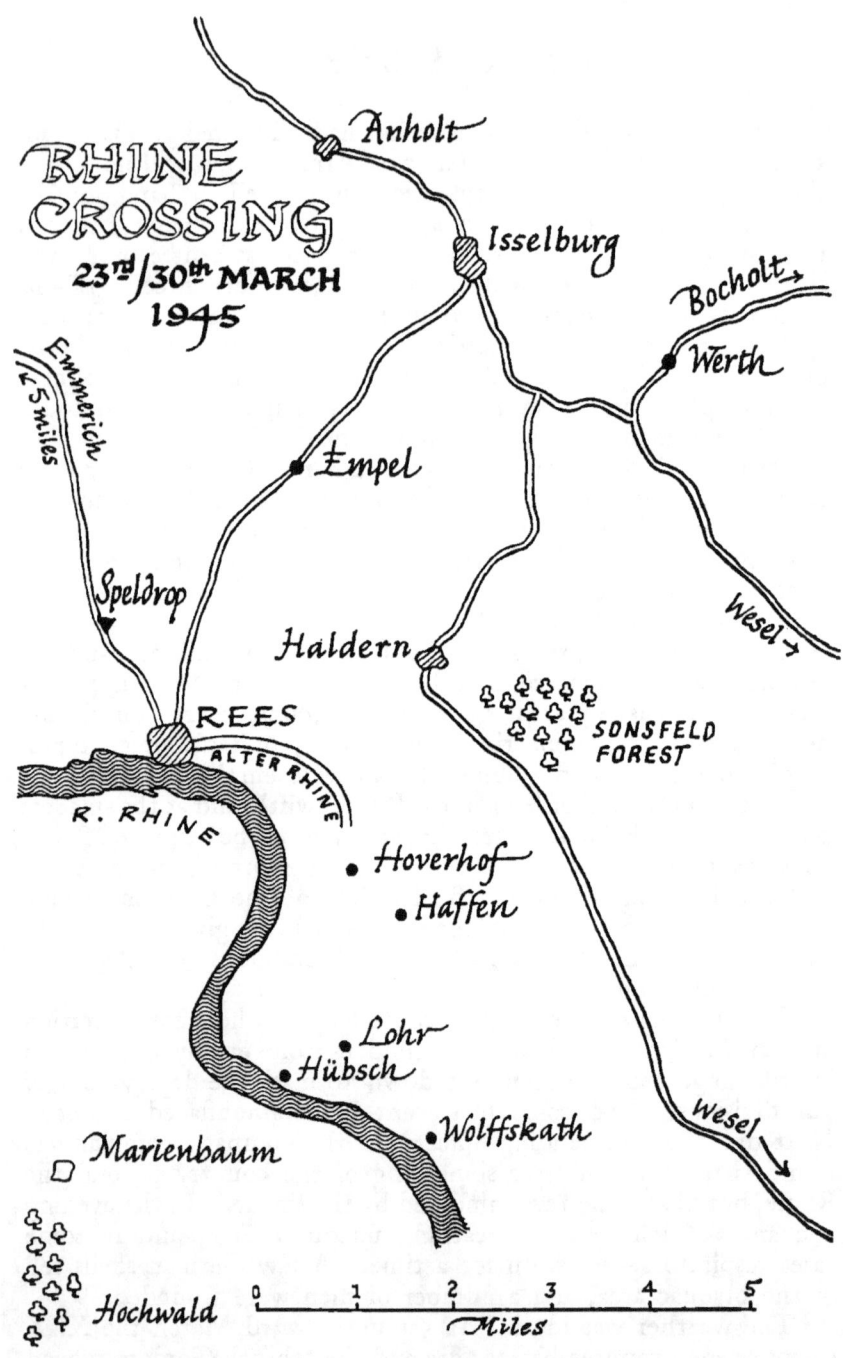

forward to their marshalling area. Our bombardment rose to a deafening crescendo which was augmented when the engines of the 'herds' of Buffaloes were started up. At 7 p.m. the first of these amphibians with their freight of expectant Highlanders rumbled off along the well-marked routes to the river. Two hours later those carrying B and C Companies of the Gordons entered the water. Without mishap or check of any kind the passage was made, and it only seemed a matter of minutes before the Gordons were ashore on the eastern bank of the Rhine.

In front of the Battalion lay a stretch of flat, open farmland. Beyond it, about a mile away, was a kind of backwater called the Alter Rhine, enclosing what was known as the 'Island'. This tract had to be cleared by the Gordons.

B Company, on the right, secured one farm within forty minutes of landing, a number of Germans being killed and forty taken. C Company made for the Alter Rhine to cross it and clear the further bank; but they found that the only bridge had been blown. As they approached they were received by heavy fire from the enemy beyond the stream. This was the first check. Meanwhile D Company had arrived and taken another farm without opposition, and still another was captured, with fifteen Germans, by a platoon led by 2nd-Lieutenant Stephen.

When day broke on 24th March the Gordons were certainly in possession of the Island, but they spent an uneasy time upon it. From the higher ground beyond the Alter Rhine German snipers and machine-gunners commanded the whole expanse of open land: all movement outside the various farm buildings drew fire.

During the afternoon orders were received from the Brigade to carry the Alter Rhine by night assault. All communication being by radio, this operation could not be undertaken in a hurry. 'It took two hours to arrange a smoke screen.' However, by 11 p.m. the carrier platoon had brought up the assault boats; and then zero hour was postponed owing to difficulties about artillery support. It was 1.15 a.m. on the 25th before the leading platoon of A Company got into their assault boats and almost at once they were greeted by intense machine-gun fire, the bright moonlight helping the defence. Captain A. R. McIntosh, commanding the company, was wounded and the assault failed. Before daylight came A Company were extricated and reorganised by Lieutenant Fisher, but the check had to be accepted.

Later on the 25th Major Evens went back across the Rhine for a conference at Brigade headquarters. Eventually it was decided that the 5th Black Watch, reported to be in the eastern part of Rees, should work eastward and clear the far bank of the Alter Rhine in front of the Gordons.

That night the Black Watch and the 1st Gordons—of whom much more hereafter—almost completed the capture of Rees, and when the 5th/7th Battalion began to cross the Alter Rhine about midnight they were not opposed. They advanced further, clearing the enemy from some farm buildings, and by daylight of the 26th they had gone as far as required and called a halt.

The 5th/7th Gordons had come off more lightly than might have been expected. Since leaving the western bank of the Rhine they had lost one officer wounded and of other ranks seven killed, thirty-five wounded, and one missing.

The 1st Gordons have left us the following description of the conditions under which they crossed the Rhine :

> On either side flat grass fields slowly dip down to the river where the banks are shingle. The river looked all the 450 yards it was, the current however being not very terrible. The buffaloes slowly crawled away over the fields, then dipped down into the water, became water-borne, and then one had the feeling of floating down out of control, yet each buffalo churned without difficulty out of Germany's greatest barrier and at the right place by the green flickering light. Once aground the buffaloes with vehicles took one 200 yards inland, those with troops deposited their load on the green fields, now baked hard by the recent fine weather, at the water's edge ; two bunds each about ten feet high stood up against the sky line, otherwise the flatness was unbroken. The night of the crossing was as perfect as it could be—warm, still, and with a three-quarter moon ; the normal peace, however, was shattered for the whole night and succeeding three days by a gun-fire which out-Alameined Alamein and out-Veritabled Veritable.

The 1st Gordons were to follow the 5th Black Watch in the Buffaloes when these returned from taking the Black Watch across the river. As we know, the 5th/7th Gordons had landed east of Rees. The Black Watch were to block the approaches to the town from the north-east and north ; the 1st Gordons were to attack Rees itself from the west.

So far as the 1st Battalion were concerned everything promised well. Thanks were showered upon the 1st Royal Ulster Rifles who held this sector of the near bank of the Rhine, for the Ulstermen not only dug slit trenches for the Gordons just behind the loading area but provided a special 'brew up' so that every man received a mug of tea well laced with rum before embarking.

Then came a delay. The first Buffaloes which returned from landing the Black Watch were not ready for the Gordons, for these craft found it difficult to get back out of the river on to the bank which was faced with stone. In attempting to land many of them damaged their tracks, and it was deemed quicker to bring along the Buffaloes which had already carried the 5th/7th Gordons across further up-stream. This check meant that the 1st Gordons could not start to attack Rees until 1 a.m. on 24th March and the respite must have been of value to the enemy. The Battalion were without their fighting vehicles which had to take their turn for embarkation and did not rejoin until the early afternoon of the 24th.

First into battle were Major Petrie's D Company who had accompanied the Black Watch for the purpose of securing a group of farm buildings which were to be used as a concentration area for the Battalion. Also with the Black Watch were a composite party under Major Rae: their task was to lift mines, lay out assembly lines, and guide the companies forward as they landed.

D Company lost no time in securing the farm buildings; but the Germans set fire to the place by means of incendiary bombs, and the company had to move away clear of the blaze. When the other companies came ashore they encountered a certain amount of shell and mortar fire and Captain K. J. R. MacDonald, the intelligence officer, was wounded.

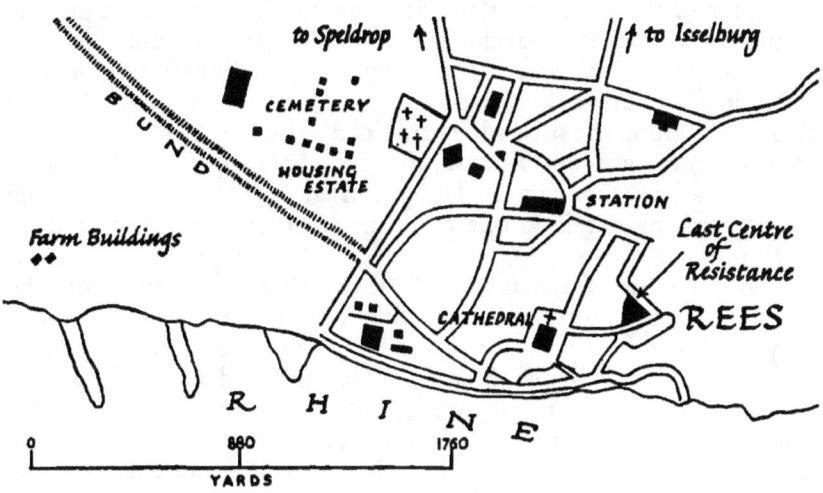

Major Morrison's B Company led the advance on Rees. Under cover of an artillery concentration and a smoke-screen they covered an open expanse of grass and cleared a bund which extended inland. Beyond, in a small housing estate, the Germans fought with some determination, but at 7 a.m. the company reported their task completed: they had reached the Rees-Speldrop road and turning right, had established themselves at the cemetery. They had taken seventy prisoners and were now in a position to safeguard the flank of C Company (Major Lumsden) who were to fight their way into the town.

C Company, following up, had turned right after crossing the aforesaid bund and their advance soon brought them under the fire of snipers and machine guns not easy to locate. Rees was in a state of ruin and chaos. Houses were shattered, streets blocked by craters and rubble; and the defenders—two battalions of fanatical fighters belonging to a parachute division—used to advantage tunnelled ways of which the Gordons knew nothing.

However, by 10 a.m. C Company had made good progress, and D Company, relieved by A Company, had entered the town by working forward along the river bank. They were able to link up with C Company, and then, handing over again to A Company, fought their way further along the river side. Meanwhile Major Lumsden had taken C Company forward to clear the northern part of Rees and link up with B Company.

All this was done by noon in the face of a dogged resistance. 'Prisoners and enemy dead confirmed that we were slowly destroying parts of the 8th Parachute Division.'

Lieut.-Colonel Grant-Peterkin took counsel with his company commanders and then decided that A Company should clear the centre of the town, working through C Company and then back towards D Company. First reconnaissance was necessary; and then, at 4 p.m. the Brigadier ordained that the clearing of Rees must continue without a pause, throughout the night if the operation should take so long. He promised that the Black Watch would assist by detailing one company to attack the railway station at 11 p.m.

To drive the Germans from their remaining hold upon the ruins of Rees seemed an impossible business in the dark. The commanding officer therefore asked if he might postpone operations until half an hour before first light which would allow the troops time for some badly needed rest. The delay could not be sanctioned, however, for the Corps commander was making the clearance of Rees a matter of 'the highest priority': until it was done the bridging operations which would enable our armour to cross the Rhine were held up.

It was now discovered that the Black Watch did not intend to attack the station direct, but were making a wide encircling movement which promised no speedy support to the Gordons. Lieut.-Colonel Grant-Peterkin eventually decided to resume the attack at midnight so that his men might be able to get a meal before they went in.

A Company—reconstituted after Thomashof—advanced as already planned and a concerted movement began. It might well have been that the Germans were beginning to lose heart, for the progress of the Gordons in pitch darkness through rubble heaps, round craters, and amongst ruins which harboured spandau and bazooka posts was quicker than was to be expected. At any rate, ' by first light we had placed ourselves ready to carry out in daylight a rapid clearing operation from an excellent firm base which it was hoped would finally finish off the town '.

The commanding officer was now asked to estimate when the river front would be cleared and also when the whole of Rees would be captured. He reckoned 11.30 a.m. for the river front and from 2 to 3 p.m. for the whole town. In the first particular he was better than his word for sappers were able to begin work on a bridge by 10.30 a.m. The complete clearance of Rees, however, was delayed by the fanatical resistance of the Germans in the ' last ditch '.

At 7 a.m. on the 25th D Company captured a strong point in the ruins of the cathedral. This success enabled B Company to complete the clearance of the river-bank region. Meanwhile A Company crossed the main street and took over the buildings—what was left of them—facing the cathedral. They were held up for a time by the fire of the Black Watch who were now closing in from the east upon the railway station.

Here one must salute the prowess of a gun detachment belonging to the 454th Mountain Battery under Captain McNair. No task and no hazard seemed too great for these gunners who brought their 3.7-inch howitzer into action at point-blank range from the ground, from rubble heaps, and even from an upstairs room, generally under enemy fire. This was McNair's first time in action: to the admiring Jocks he appeared to be a veteran warrior who gloried in the zest of battle.

Battalion headquarters had moved up into Rees after breakfast, and during the morning a burst of German shell-fire wounded Lieut.-Colonel Grant-Peterkin. Thenceforward Major Lindsay controlled the operations which were nearing their successful end. The Germans had now been driven back into a small corner on the eastern edge of Rees, and here they still resisted stoutly. In their attempt to close the Gordons lost Lieutenant V. M. Halleron killed, 2nd-Lieutenant A. K. MacDonald mortally wounded, and 2nd-Lieutenant P. G. Burrell wounded. Then, as darkness fell and fresh dispositions to renew the attack were being made the Germans melted away, most of them to surrender to the Black Watch.

The 1st Gordons had done well, and more than well. In the ranks were many young soldiers of nineteen and twenty in action for the first time: their spirit and tenacity during more than forty-eight hours of battle was above all praise. Besides the officers already mentioned the Battalion had lost Lieutenants A. Rodger, attached from the Canadian Army, and L. Titterton and 2nd-Lieutenant

A. R. Porter killed and Lieutenant C. M. Gray wounded. Of other ranks thirteen were killed and fifty-one wounded.

General Horrocks, commanding the XXX Corps, came to Rees to congratulate the 1st Gordons. So also did Major-General G. H. MacMillan, now commanding the Highland Division: on the morning of 24th March Major-General Rennie had been killed by a mortar bomb to the great regret of all who knew him.

Lieut.-Colonel Grant-Peterkin, who was able to rejoin the Battalion after a few days had again to deplore the high rate of wastage in officers and in senior non-commissioned officers; and he revived the old plaint of the difficulty in getting Gordons as Battalion reinforcements.

The 2nd Gordons crossed the Rhine further up-stream, the 227th Brigade being on the extreme left of the 15th Division who formed the left of the XII Corps. The Battalion assembled on the eastern edge of Hochwald after a long night drive, and rested for the whole of the 23rd.

On the right the 10th H.L.I. were to cross the Rhine in Buffaloes opposite the village of Wolffskath; the 2nd Argyll, on the left, were directed upon Hübsch. The Gordons had to wait upon events, but No. 16 platoon of D Company were lent to the H.L.I. and so became the first of the Battalion to cross the river. Lieutenant A. A. Cameron, the platoon commander, was slightly wounded soon after he disembarked.

It was about 11.30 p.m. on 23rd March when the Gordons marched forward to the place where they were to pick up their assault boats. Here, at a bund—the dyke built to contain the winter flood-water—some 300 yards from the river they waited while our tremendous bombardment rent the air.

Generally speaking all was going well, but the Argyll had had a difficult landing and needed reinforcement. A Company of the Gordons who had expected to join the H.L.I. were therefore diverted down-stream for 1,200 yards so as to come in opposite Hübsch. They started about 6.15 a.m. on the 24th. On the way across the river their boats ran the gauntlet of fire from the far bank and from enemy posts in Lohr. Lieutenant R. A. Patrick and three others were killed and ten men were wounded, some of the boats were sunk or drifted away: nevertheless, A Company joined the Argyll in Hübsch.

Later in the morning the remainder of the Battalion crossed to reinforce the Argyll. There were some minor troubles. The boat conveying the commanding officer and the adjutant ran out of petrol in mid-stream and was paddled until the sapper in charge produced a reserve tin.

Lohr had been captured before the main body of the Gordons arrived. In the afternoon they formed up south-west of Haffen which was still in German hands, and now A Company suffered further misfortune. They came under a sudden burst of mortar fire and lost their three remaining officers, Captain G. W. L. Smith, Lieutenant W. I. M. Ankers and Lieutenant W. McIntyre, all wounded.

The next task was to capture Haffen which the artillery did not shell as some of our tanks were, erroneously, reported to be entering the village from the east. At about half-past five B and C Companies of the Gordons attacked from the western side and cleared the place, taking seventy-one prisoners, mostly of the 18th Parachute Regiment. Lieutenant S. W. Telfer was wounded while this was being done.

D Company, following in support, were able to make contact with the 5th/7th Gordons of the Highland Division, and next day they relieved some forward posts of the Argyll and captured a German post at Hoverhof, sending back four prisoners.

On 26th March the 2nd Gordons occupied several farms and a number of prisoners drifted in, but 'there seemed to be a lull in the proceedings'. Then, on the 28th, the Battalion were relieved by troops of the Divisional reconnaissance regiment and taken swiftly northward to form the left of a new attack. This was to be delivered against Sonsfeld Forest beyond the Wesel-Haldern road.

The operation was a full-dress affair of its kind with four battalions up and two squadrons of the reconnaissance regiment on the left, supporting the Gordons with fire. D and C Companies who led were each attended by a Crocodile and an anti-tank gun. Our shells could be seen bursting ahead, sending up fountains where they fell in flood water. There was no sign of the enemy, only white flags sticking out of chimneys and windows of the houses along the road. The road, however, was mined and cratered, and the wood bestrewn with mines and booby traps. The Battalion had no casualties until, when the wood was almost cleared, Captain J. W. Buchanan, Lieutenant W. Tasker and four men of D Company were blown up. Mr. Tasker died of his injuries.

The Gordons consolidated on high ground which overlooked the eastern edge of Sonsfeld Forest; but next day companies were moved into billets in order to provide the men with as much comfort as possible. The arrival of four new subalterns with nearly sixty reinforcements was very welcome.

Officers and men now began to meet some of the German population. One belligerent young woman said that the war would not end until the last Nazi soldier was killed; she was told that we were killing off Nazi soldiers with that purpose in view.

On 2nd April the commanding officer and the adjutant visited the 5th/7th Gordons who were at Isselburg, nearly five miles north of Haldern. For the moment the 2nd Gordons knew nothing of their future movements.

After the capture of Rees, the next objective of the Highland Division was Isselburg.

The 1st Gordons concentrated in a wood near Empel on the afternoon of the 27th. Not far ahead an autobahn, crossing the main road, was under construction and its high banks provided an excellent defensive position. A and B Companies moved up on either side of the main road and deployed south of the autobahn. This was done without much trouble despite mines on the edge of the road, which held up the supporting tanks, and some spandau fire.

The attack across the autobahn was launched at 11 p.m. that night, C Company being followed by D Company who advanced a further 500 yards and occupied a factory area. Hostile action was confined to intensive shelling and mortaring, thirty-two prisoners of the 15th Panzer Grenadier Regiment having shown no desire to fight. Major B. D. M. Rose and Lieutenant N. M. Rowbotham were slightly wounded but remained at duty.

There was no fighting next day when D Company took possession of Königshof to afford flank protection to the troops advancing on the left of the Highland Division. Two other villages were occupied, and in this area the 1st Gordons remained inactive for a week.

The 5th/7th Gordons spent a quiet day on 26th March when a few German deserters came in and also a number of Russians and Poles who had been doing forced labour on nearby farms. The Battalion were still in touch with patrols of the 2nd Gordons.

On the evening of 27th March the 5th/7th moved forward on the right of the 1st Battalion and took a farm without opposition. The 5th Black Watch passed through at nightfall. Shelling and mortaring had killed two men and wounded five.

Pressing on next morning the 5th/7th Gordons occupied without trouble the area south of Isselburg. They cleared the main road into the town and the region towards Werth, German shell-fire accounting for another seven casualties.

The Battalion were placed under the command of the 152nd Brigade, who had already occupied Isselburg, on 29th March. After passing through the town the Gordons relieved the 2nd Seaforth and began to clear the woods on either side of the Anholt road. They met with no active resistance, but a bridge was found to be heavily mined and the supporting tanks became bogged when they tried a detour. By noon the prescribed advance was completed, and when a halt was called small groups of Germans came in to surrender, D Company collecting seventy prisoners in half-an-hour.

At night the Battalion welcomed back Lieut.-Colonel Irvine, rejoining from leave and subsequent sick leave.

The Guards Armoured Division took up the running on 30th March and the Gordons remained in the vicinity of Anholt until, on 5th April, the 153rd Brigade moved north over the Dutch frontier to Enschede, a pleasant town where both Gordon battalions found comfortable billets.

The Drive Through Germany

The Rhine had been crossed, the bridges built, and our armies well established beyond the river. Now the great forward drive through Germany could begin, to crush on its way such remnants of the German Army as still refused to accept defeat.

The 15th Division, in the XII Corps, were to advance to the Elbe, their ultimate destination Lubeck, so this was the path followed by the 2nd Gordons. Leaving the Sonsfeld Forest area on 4th April, the Battalion were carried to Emsdetten, nearly seventy miles away, in order to take part in the advance on Osnabrück.

At 9.30 p.m. orders were issued for a sweep of the high wooded ground in the Lengerich vicinity. The carriers of the Gordons, with one carrier section of the Argyll, were to do this, C and D Companies moving close in rear. A start was made at a quarter to eight next morning but traffic congestion on the road caused considerable delay. However, the advance went on peacefully enough, a few suspects being gathered in. The Gordons caught a local *Gauleiter* and made him dress up in his smartest uniform before sending him back to Battalion headquarters, ' an extremely resentful German '.

At this stage ' displaced persons '—refugees of many nations who had broken out of the German concentration camps—were streaming westward, and these destitute folk became a decided embarrassment to the advancing troops who had no means of keeping them in order or affording them much help.

The Gordons passed through badly damaged Osnabrück on the 6th and the carriers reached Weghorn. Next day the rifle companies got in, having picked up seventeen members of the *Hitler Jugend* on their way.

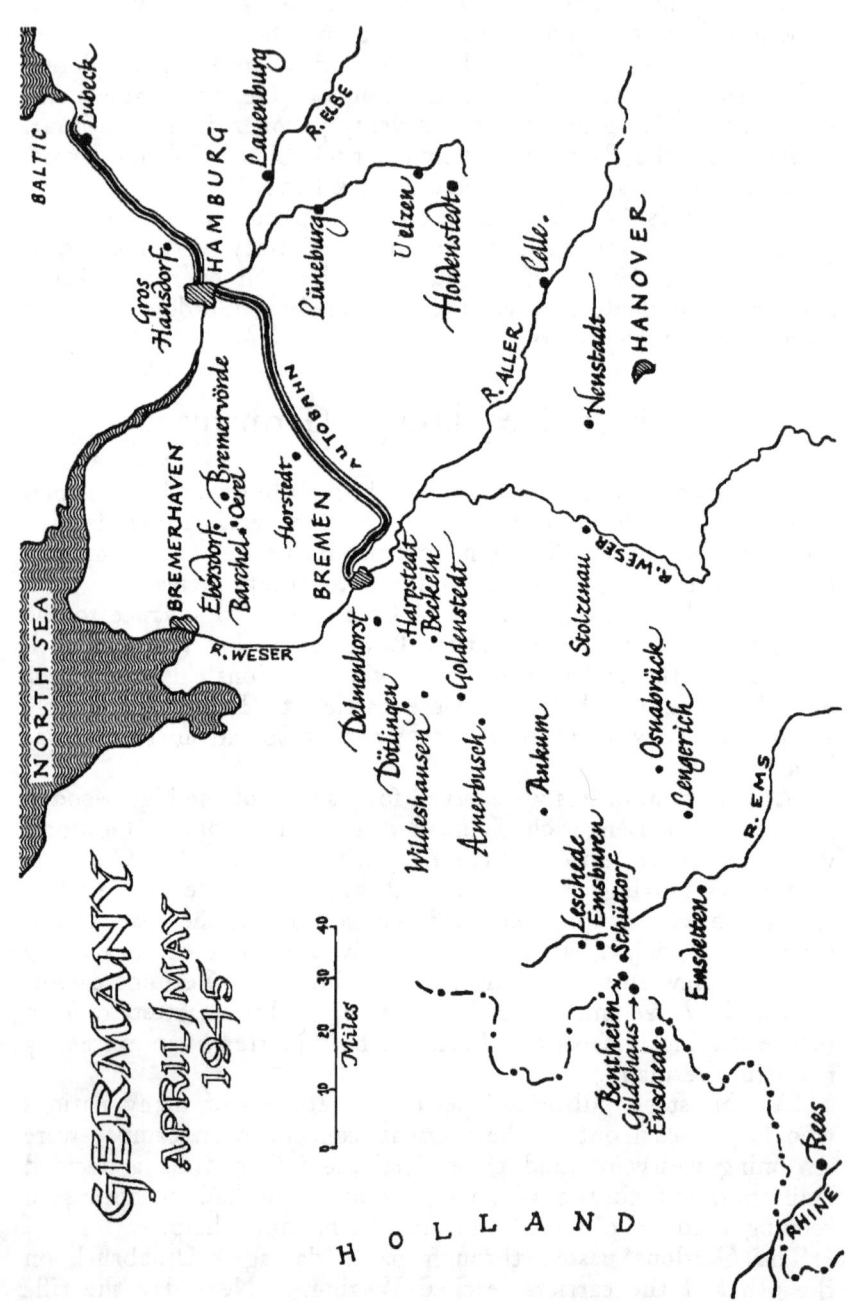

At Weghorn the Gordons acquired some of the spoils of war. There was a huge store of stationery in this village and the orderly room stocks were replenished; also, a considerable supply of hock and cherry brandy was found at Stolzenau near by, providing the wherewithal to entertain those good friends of the Gordons, the Scots Guards tank squadron.

The 227th Brigade were now half-way between Osnabrück and Celle which was all of fifty miles further on. When in the early morning of the 10th the Gordons led the advance D and C Companies rode on the tanks and the other companies followed in trucks. The march was delayed by demolitions and broken bridges. Later on D Company clashed with a detachment of the enemy who were covering the site of a blown bridge, but these recalcitrants were 'wiped out' early in the afternoon. Then the column was delayed while the sappers threw a 'scissors' bridge.

Such encounters continued to hamper the advance. One necessary detour took the column over a moorland track past an aerodrome 'beautifully camouflaged as heather'. Fifteen more prisoners were gathered in.

At 1 a.m. on 12th April it was found that the bridges over the canal south-west of Celle had not been effectively destroyed. D Company were therefore able to get a patrol into the town, and then it became a matter of securing bridges over the river Aller which runs through Celle. There were Germans about, and Lieutenant Jeffrey's platoon had two skirmishes in the centre of the town with the staff of the local Gas School.

The H.L.I. were coming through to take up the advance, but the many broken bridges still prevented an easy passage of Celle, although the Germans had ceased to defend it. A troop of Scots Guards tanks with a platoon of Gordons aboard hurried off to Alten Celle—two miles upstream—where two bridges, one over the Aller and one over the canal, were still intact. But they were rickety wooden affairs; and, when Gordons, Argyll and tanks followed up, the canal bridge collapsed, causing a big traffic block and a long delay.

On 13th April the Brigade moved from Celle upon Uelzen with the H.L.I. leading and the Gordons now in rear. The column was seven miles in length and the road was much damaged by craters and other demolitions so speed was out of the question. Two big detours through forest land were necessary, and at night the Brigade halted at Holdenstedt, some distance short of Uelzen. A score of prisoners had been collected during the day.

At 1 a.m. on the 14th the H.L.I. were sent forward 'at a cracking pace' towards Uelzen, but they were heavily attacked as they attempted to drive into the place. Uelzen was not to be rushed, and after brisk fighting on the outskirts of the town the H.L.I. had to accept a check. The Brigade then planned a night assault for the early hours of the 15th.

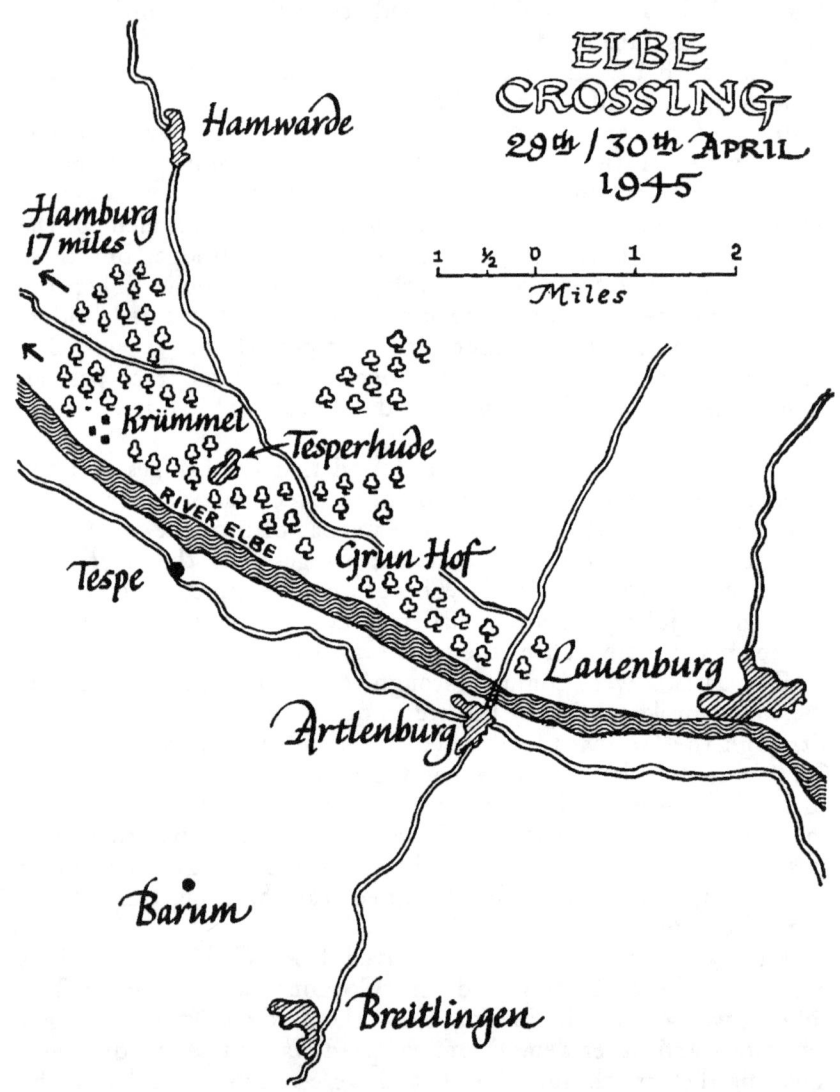

The Gordons were given the task of going straight in along the main road while the H.L.I. worked through the suburbs on the left. D Company of the Gordons crossed the railway line about 12.30 a.m. and at once came under heavy fire from buildings on front and flank. Self-propelled guns and anti-tank weapons opened on the Churchills of the Scots Guards and put several of them out of action. Seeing that he was making no headway against the houses and gardens so resolutely defended Major Grose, commanding D Company, tried a flanking movement on the left but with no better result. Eventually he was obliged to fall back on B Company some 300 yards in rear.

These two Gordon companies remained on the outskirts of Uelzen all day upon the 15th. Further to the left the H.L.I. had been able to do no better. After darkness fell troops of the 46th Brigade took over and the Gordons were withdrawn two miles to the south where, in the little village of Borne they passed two days of very welcome rest.

In the meantime Uelzen was most fiercely assailed by the R.A.F. and battered by our artillery; and after this treatment the place fell to the 46th Brigade.

Now began the final stages of the advance to the Elbe. The Gordons left Borne at 6 a.m. on 18th April, being lifted on tanks and on the transport of an artillery regiment, there being no other vehicles available. They passed through Uelzen, which was still burning, and after two long and tedious marches reached Barum which is about two miles short of the Elbe. The railway bridge leading across the river at Lauenburg had been blown, but there were still Germans on the near bank.

Next day, 20th April, D Company cleared the small village of Tespe with the capture of seven prisoners ' and no shooting '.

After days of heavy showers the weather was fine again, and this was pleasant unspoiled country. 'Our' bank of the Elbe, low and marshy, was overlooked by the bluffs on the opposite side. The river was about 300 yards wide and the current was estimated at about one-and-a-half knots. The factory at Krummel appeared to be still working and was occasionally visited by a train which emerged from a tunnel in Tesperhude. On 26th April our artillery shelled the train which was seen no more.

Preparations for the passage of the Elbe were now in full swing and the 15th Division were to lead. After the initial crossing the 227th Brigade would follow the 44th Brigade and play their part in expanding the bridge-head north-westward. 'The day' was to be 29th April.

The 2nd Gordons moved at 2.30 a.m. and breakfasted at Breitlingen two hours later. They crossed the Elbe at Artlenburg in storm boats, with their carriers and jeeps in Buffaloes, between nine and ten in the morning. The exit from the further bank of the river was through a ravine, and here as at their forming-up place, they were under considerable shell-fire.

Operating on the extreme left flank of the Division, the task of the Battalion was to advance north-westward along the main road which runs through the pine forest called the Grün Hof, parallel to and about a mile distant from the river. The village of Tesperhude, three miles away, was to be secured.

Before they had got very far the Gordons encountered two road-blocks, whereupon they took to the woods, leaving a party to clear these obstacles with sapper assistance. Opposition was not great and snipers—'every Jerry with a rifle was a sniper'—and 'bazooka parties' were expertly rounded up as the Gordons forged ahead. Before half-past five all objectives were reported taken, the prisoners numbering six officers and 205 other ranks. A few obstinate fellows who had refused to surrender had met their fate bravely.

The Battalion had lost six killed and twenty-five wounded, including that most gallant and popular artillery officer Major Gordon Campbell whose battery had been in support of the Gordons since Normandy. He was hit in the thigh by a sniper's bullet.

Still busy in well doing, the Battalion cleared the Krummel factory area during the night, gathering in two German officers and 116 other ranks. The 30th April was spent in clearing up along the river bank, and here were captured two 'frog men' whose mission, it seemed, had been to blow up the bridges we were throwing across the Elbe. The Germans were still shelling the bridges and ferries, and they managed to destroy three vehicles belonging to the Gordons: a ration lorry and a pioneer lorry and a half-track carrying medical supplies.

The carrier platoon had been sent northward to investigate Hamwarde, but although they brought back thirty prisoners they reported that the Germans were still holding the village. In the afternoon the Gordons were carried to Hamwarde on the tanks of the Grenadier Guards to find that the place had been secured by the Divisional reconnaissance regiment.

Next day, 1st May, B Company and a troop of tanks explored the woods round Hamwarde and collected forty-three prisoners. At night the Brigade were given orders for an eastward advance, the Gordons to be in reserve. Everyone knew that the Germans could not go on much longer, and the news of Hitler's death was hailed as a sign that the end had come.

In the meantime the Gordons' transport, parked near the north bank of the Elbe, had received a reminder that the war was not yet over. German shell-fire damaged the cooking gear and started a blaze among some R.E. lorries, packed with explosives, which were near by. The quartermaster of the Gordons, Captain W. G. Lewis, drove several trucks in succession out of this inferno at great personal risk, and for this gallant service he received the Military Cross.

On 2nd May the 227th Brigade started for Hamburg, and the 2nd Gordons enjoyed a slow, peaceful advance along country roads. Peace was, indeed, in the air for on this day Brigadier Colville handed over command of the Brigade to Lieut.-Colonel de Winton while he attended a conference with a member of Field-Marshal von Busch's staff concerning surrender. Such a portentious matter could, of course, be settled only at the most exalted level, but it was now obvious that the German commanders were anxious to capitulate.

At night came news of the German surrender in Italy.

By this time the Gordons had reached a village with the imposing name of Kroppelshagen-Fahrendorf where two shells landed. These were the last shots fired, so far as the Battalion were concerned.

On 3rd May a 'local truce' came into effect at Hamburg. The Gordons moved forward through lovely forest country, and on the 4th reached Gros Hansdorf, a few miles away on the north-eastern side of the city.

It was on this day, at Lüneburg Heath, that Field-Marshal Montgomery received, on behalf of General Eisenhower, Supreme Commander, the unconditional surrender of all German forces in Holland, north-west Germany, Schleswig-Holstein and Denmark. Hostilities were to cease at 8 a.m. on 5th May.

The war in North-West Europe was over.

The advance to final victory of the 1st and the 5th/7th Gordons must now be recorded. In the XXX Corps the Highland Division were directed towards Bremen, and the 153rd Brigade moved forward from Enschede on 5th April, the 1st Gordons to Gildehaus and the 5th/7th to Bentheim.

In clearing the axis of advance as far forward as the western bank of the Ems the 5th/7th Gordons were to lead the way. By the afternoon of the 6th bridges had been constructed over the stream at Schüttorf where the Battalion passed through the 5th Black Watch and made for Emsburen.

The Gordons moved in a mixed assortment of transport, the two leading companies riding on flail tanks, the remainder 'on anything that could be borrowed from other battalions'. Progress was slow. Fire came from front and flank and there were many craters in the road. As darkness fell one company took up a position on the edge of Emsburen in readiness for a night assault. On this day casualties amounted to fourteen, all but one of them wounded.

Emsburen was occupied by the Gordons during the night without a shot being fired, and the 5th/7th spent the next few days in the town. A church service was held, and the commanding officer conferred with his company commanders on the question of retaining captured enemy vehicles, for the Battalion was short of its establishment of transport. Throughout the Allied armies all movement was now on tracks, half-tracks or wheels and there was little time or opportunity for maintenance and repair.

Following their sister battalion on 6th April the 1st Gordons advanced east of the main road, dislodging with hand grenades some Germans found in a village. Further ground was covered in company 'jumps' without opposition, although one jeep was lost on a mine. Eventually Leschede was occupied by B Company and A Company passed through to reach the western bank of the river Ems. The road bridge was blown, and patrols reported Germans in the woods beyond the far bank.

The 1st Gordons were halted at Leschede for four days and in pleasant surroundings there was time for fishing and football. A match with the 5th/7th Battalion, who were at Emsburen, ended in defeat.

On 12th April both Gordon battalions moved forward to Ankum and next day the 1st Battalion took over from the 5th Camerons (152nd Brigade) at Goldenstedt. They advanced again on the 14th and were then required to clear the villages of Hoskensburg and Brettorf. Little oppositon was expected.

B Company pressed forward on the 15th and drove some Germans from a cross-roads; D Company went on along the main road and had their own little skirmish; and then C Company, continuing the advance, came under heavy fire. Meanwhile A Company had occupied Hoskensburg after quelling some resistance. All objectives had been taken in spite of the fire of some extremely well handled self-propelled guns. Lieutenant W. J. Hewitt lost his life in a mine explosion on this day.

The 5th/7th Gordons, from Ankum, reached Amerbusch on 13th April. Billets were bad, 'the area being full of gunners'. Although they were some distance behind the advance the Battalion were called upon to send out patrols, as Germans were reported in the surrounding countryside. Next day came a move to Wildeshausen, relieving a battalion of the 3rd Division, and here patrols got into touch with the 1st Gordons on the right and the 152nd Brigade on the left.

A carrier patrol were fired on, and German artillery began to shell the far edge of Wildeshausen a few of the Gordons being hit. At night A Company (Major W. A. Muir) were ordered to fill in a crater in the road and clear some houses near by. This was to be a silent attack with our guns on call.

A Company were met by spandau and rifle fire, guns and mortars soon joining in. 'Artificial moonlight' was employed to no purpose for it revealed all our movements, so that a flank attack by A Company could hardly get under way. The company held on while a bulldozer was brought forward to fill in the crater, and this was done under shell-fire. The work was completed by dawn of the 15th when tanks were ordered up.

At 8.30 a.m. flail tanks—one troop acting as ordinary tanks—came into action to help the Gordons; and in the ensuing *mêlée* many Germans were killed and a number captured. By 11 a.m. all resistance had ceased in and beyond Wildeshausen, and other troops passed through to carry on the advance. In this affair the Gordons were lucky to lose only ten men.

On 16th April the Battalion were told 'No move today'. Then in the middle of the morning came orders to capture the village of Dötlingen with the assistance of one troop of tanks and two of Crocodiles.

The carrier platoon led the advance and gained some ground. Then, after a twenty-minute artillery concentration starting at 2.30 p.m., the leading rifle company of the Gordons with tanks in attendance moved through the carrier platoon and entered Dötlingen as the Germans fled on bicycles from the other end of the place.

During the night, the Gordons being in comfortable possession of Dötlingen, a patrol of about twenty-six Germans under an officer were bold enough to approach the village. They were shot up by D Company who killed the officer and some others and took two prisoners. The remainder made good their escape.

On 17th April a wood, reported to contain some of the enemy was shelled by our artillery and two Germans came in to surrender. By the evening the 5th/7th Gordons had handed over to a battalion of the 43rd Division and were soon picked up by transport and carried to billets at Beckeln. The journey was made in a thunderstorm with great hailstones, and everyone got wet to the skin.

Lieutenant G. Gordon was killed by a shell splinter on this day and three men were wounded.

The 1st Gordons had moved from the Hockensburg area on 17th April, coming up east of Wildeshausen on the road to Harpstedt. Delmenhorst was the next objective of importance and, contrary to expectation, it was yielded without a fight, owing it seems, to the large number of German wounded in the town's many hospitals. When the 153rd Brigade moved in on 20th April the 1st Gordons took up a position covering the roads leading into the town from the north-east. During the next few days their patrols brought in many prisoners and deserters.

Delmenhorst had been left intact with the water and light services functioning as usual, so our troops enjoyed an unexpected degree of comfort; but the 5th/7th Gordons found the Germans rather active beyond the north-western limits of the town.

The Battalion left Beckeln, where a mobile bath unit, a Church of Scotland canteen and a visit from the Corps commander had been duly appreciated, on 20th April with orders to take part in an attack on Delmenhorst. As this proved unnecessary three rifle companies were passed into the western part of the town, while one company were sent forward in Kangaroos for over a mile to the north-west to guard a secret airfield at Heyenkamp until specialists could come and examine the place. The enemy opened shell and mortar fire which did little harm, and in the evening a patrol of the carrier platoon killed two Germans.

During the night the sound of horse and motor transport was heard, and the Gordons opened harassing fire. A rather venturesome German patrol lost two killed and a sergeant-major captured; but 'one man got away' as the Gordons regretfully reported.

On the 21st the Battalion were again under shell and mortar fire. Twelve prisoners were collected in the woods and, later, D Company gathered in another forty 'mainly due to the efforts of the forward observing officer who was with them'. The usual quota of civilians brought in for questioning included a young woman who was dubbed 'the bride of the Swastika'. She expressed her loathing of German officers.

Life on this side of Delmenhorst then became more peaceful. On 25th April, however, a Bren gunner fired two magazines into a German patrol of three men hung about the waist with grenades. 'The result was rather awful.'

About this time was announced the award of the Military Cross to Major J. I. Gammie and Lieutenant A. F. Manson.

This drive through Germany in pursuit of a defeated army was providing the Highlanders with a new experience. The German population seemed to be relieved by the arrival of the invaders who were themselves surprised at the comfort enjoyed by the people and by their air of well being. When shown the 'horror' photographs of the concentration camps the Germans expressed their complete ignorance of such happenings. It was difficult, perhaps, for the Highlanders to realise that they must not fraternise with these people who, for the most part, seemed quiet, placid folk; but it was remarked that 'the Jocks do enjoy turning all out of a house to acquire a comfortable billet'.

The whole Brigade were relieved on 27th April to concentrate beyond the river Weser. This meant a long and tiring drive for both Gordon battalions. Next day they moved again, the 1st

Gordons motoring up the Bremen-Hamburg autobahn. The 5th/7th Battalion had only five miles to go, but blown bridges compelled a detour of thirty miles. They advanced on Horstedt in the afternoon, only to find that all German troops had departed.

So April ended, and on 1st May at a quarter past ten at night the radio reported the death of Hitler in Berlin.

On this day the 1st Gordons moved to a position south-east of Bremervörde which was occupied by the 152nd Brigade that night. Oerel was reported to be strongly held by troops of the 15th Panzer Grenadier Division, old opponents of the Highlanders, and the Gordons were ordered to attack the place on the evening of the 2nd.

Tanks and Crocodiles were to assist, but the armour was held up by a traffic block; so, as the light was fading, Lieut.-Colonel Grant-Peterkin decided to attack without tanks. D Company led, and after an exchange of small-arms fire they established themselves in the village. Then, after darkness had fallen, B Company, followed by A Company, were ordered to push on to Barchel about a mile ahead. After covering about half a mile B Company were counter-attacked from front and flank; and although they drove the Germans off by fire they were obliged to spend the night concentrated about a farm in the midst of open fields.

Prisoners said that Barchel was held by two battalions of Panzer Grenadiers supported by self-propelled guns, so the commanding officer pulled B Company back into Oerel in order to mount a fresh attack with tank support. Later, on the morning of 3rd May, patrols reported that the enemy had left Barchel.

The 1st Gordons had fought their last fight of the campaign but it was galling to think that during the previous night a transport column had taken a wrong turning with the result that two carriers each with a 6-pdr. anti-tank gun in tow, had been captured by the enemy and one carrier knocked out by a *Panzerfaust*. However, the prisoners were recovered in Bremerhaven a few days later.

Since 17th April the 1st Gordons had lost three men killed, thirteen wounded, and nine missing.

During the last two days of April the 5th/7th Gordons had been at peace except for certain hostilities with our gunners over a matter of parking vehicles. They moved from the vicinity of Delmenhorst on 1st May and passed through Bremervörde next day. While the 1st Gordons were directed on Oerel, as we have seen, the 5th/7th prepared to advance north-westward on Ebersdorf. Reports were optimistic: everywhere the Germans were surrendering, with no fight left in them.

Nevertheless when the Battalion moved out towards Ebersdorf at 6 p.m. on the 2nd, the leading company being supported by a troop of tanks, they had to fight for each house along the road. The advance attracted the fire of a 'moaning Minnie' and some Russian heavy guns but these proved more noisy than harmful. Nearer the village, however, small-arms, mortars and a self-propelled gun opened fire straight down the road against our oncoming tanks. The light was fading; Germans in some force were seen on the high ground south-west of the village; and prisoners said that there were at least one regiment in Ebersdorf with a few tanks and a brigade headquarters.

When night came the leading company of Gordons were still 200 yards short of the village, and Lieut.-Colonel Irvine decided to put in a flank attack on the eastern side of Ebersdorf. Since our guns had silenced the 'moaning Minnie'—many people had seen it at close range and got its bearings—the road was now quiet and food could be brought forward without much trouble.

Soon after 2 a.m. on 3rd May our artillery shelled Ebersdorf for half an hour and then two companies of Gordons made a converging attack which, despite spandau fire, captured most of the place. When daylight came the enemy, with two self-propelled guns in action, held only the north-western part. Then ensued a duel between the German guns and ours of the same type, and the former were soon reduced to blazing wrecks. The fight was over.

The 154th Brigade now took up the advance and the activities of the Battalion were confined to clearing the country round Ebersdorf. Since starting their advance on the village they had killed many Germans and collected about 300 prisoners. Their own losses amounted to one officer slightly wounded and six other ranks of whom only one was killed. The 5th/7th Gordons were not called upon to go into action again.

The 2nd Gordons remained at Gros Hansdorf for a fortnight after the end of the war with Germany. On 9th May they were inspected and thanked for their good service by Major-General Barber, commanding the 15th Division. The main duty of the Battalion was to provide guards for the large prisoner of war camps in the vicinity. On the 19th the whole of the 227th Brigade moved to the Lubeck area, the Gordons and the H.L.I. being quartered in Lubeck.

Guards were now required for various factories, Red Cross food dumps, sugar barges, an ammunition train, a railway station, and an ordnance dump. Displaced persons remained a problem. On 27th May a riot of Russians and Poles in one of their camps was only quelled by a display of force—one platoon of Gordons and a carrier section.

In June an influx of refugees fleeing from Mecklenburg in the Russian zone to Schleswig-Holstein called for special guards on five bridges over the Elbe south of Lubeck.

The visit of General Dempsey, commanding the Second Army, in June was followed by that of Field-Marshal Montgomery in July to address all ranks of the 227th Brigade Group. On 6th July the 2nd Gordons sent a draft of ten officers and 104 other ranks to South-East Asia Command. The war with Japan was not yet over.

The 1st Gordons moved into Barchel on the day of the German surrender, and 5th May was devoted to 'rest and celebration'. The 5th/7th Battalion who were collecting German arms and ammunition round Ebersdorf celebrated with pipe music, and a dinner with Brigadier Sinclair as the principal guest. At Oerel, on the 6th, the two Battalions were addressed by the Divisional commander, and a church service was held. Then came a move to Bremerhaven.

Bremerhaven was entered and occupied on 8th May, all ranks finding comfortable billets in houses and flats. On 12th May the Highland Division held a victory parade, General Horrocks, commanding the XXX Corps, taking the salute. Both Gordon battalions managed a smart turn-out for this occasion, the 5th/7th taking special pride in the appearance of their ten carriers 'all freshly painted'.

Guards were required for the docks and warehouses to prevent looting by the masterless persons of many nations. A number of Germans, including four naval officers, were caught leaving the docks with what they could lay their hands upon. The area allotted to A Company of the 5th/7th Gordons included a food store filled with luxuries for provisioning submarines. Another complication was the presence in dock of the huge German liner *Europa* with 3,000 displaced persons, representing a dozen races, on board. The dock area was rather a problem in restoring law and order, for 'it took days to rid the place of women lying about by day and night'.

On 19th May came the ceremonial handing over of Bremerhaven to the U.S. 29th Division. The Highland guard of honour, wearing the kilt, was 100 strong—fifty from each of the Gordon battalions—commanded by Major B. D. M. Rae of the 1st Gordons. The massed drums and pipes of the Highland Division played 'Scotland the Brave' and the American brass band was remarkable for the antics of the drum-major, 'voted the highlight of the parade'.

The 1st Gordons then departed for Neustadt, north-west of Hanover, where they arrived on 25th May. On the 26th the 5th/7th Battalion reached the Stolzenau area, further west.

Among a number of ceremonial occasions was the 'Presentation of the Drum'. In May 1940 the 5th Gordon Highlanders had stored their drums in Metz before going south to the Somme; and one drum had been discovered by an officer of the U.S. Seventh Army at a barracks near Baumhelden. Lieut.-General A. M. Patch, the U.S. Army commander, decided that this drum should be restored, and invited a party of the 5th/7th Gordons to receive it.

Brigadier Sinclair represented the Regiment. The Battalion party consisted of Lieut.-Colonel Irvine, Captain D. A. Thom, 2nd-Lieutenant D. A. Craig, two warrant officers, six non-commissioned officers, and twenty-four privates; and, of course, the pipes and drums. The Gordons arrived at Augsburg on 5th June. On the 7th the drum was handed over with mutual military compliments before a very distinguished company on the Königsplatz in Munich. The drum itself had seen much service, being a gift to the 5th Battalion from Captain W. Stephen of Peterhead made before 1914.

One more change of command has to be recorded. On 7th June Lieut.-Colonel J. A. Grant-Peterkin left the 1st Gordons to command the 152nd Brigade and was succeeded by Lieut.-Colonel B. J. Maddon of the Black Watch.

More honours and awards were announced about this time. In the 1st Gordons Captain E. G. S. Traill was awarded the Military Cross for distinguished service at Thomashof, Sergeant J. Littlefair the Distinguished Conduct Medal, and Sergeant T. Townley the Military Medal. These non-commissioned officers were decorated for their gallantry at Gennep, Goch and Rees. Later came the award of the Military Medal to Regimental Sergeant-Major W. Pass and to Corporal A. Dale. Captain and Quartermaster J. M. G. Lindsay received the M.B.E.

Lieut.-Colonel de Winton who had commanded the 2nd Gordons since August 1944 received a bar to his D.S.O. The Battalion could also congratulate Privates Fawcett, Grosset and J. Smith on receiving the Military Medal.

All three battalions of Gordon Highlanders were anxious to restore the kilt to all ranks with as little delay as possible. At the close of hostilities the 5th/7th Gordons reckoned to have eighteen pipers on parade—'no other battalion can do better, if as well'— and were soon able to turn out the pipe band in proper sporrans, spats and hose. The 1st Battalion required more pipe kit sent out from home, and lamented the fact that their pipers were 'nearly all old soldiers and due for discharge'. In the 2nd Battalion Lieut.-Colonel de Winton had sent home for additional pipes and drums and 'certain regimental property'.

INDIA

1942-44

R.A.C. and Royal Artillery

The 9th Gordons little knew what was in store for them when they left the Clyde in convoy for the East on 1st June 1942. Passing through placid summer seas the ships reached Freetown and refuelled. There was no chance of going ashore, and 'the general appearance of this port was unfavourable'. Durban, however, proved different, for the welcome could not have been more hospitable : the Jocks were glad to stretch their legs on land and the pipes and drums were much in evidence. All ranks would have been glad to spend longer than a bare four days in Durban.

Resuming the voyage on 8th July the convoy steamed into Bombay sixteen days later, and the Battalion entrained at once for Sialkot. On the 27th, after they had settled down in cantonments, Lieut.-Colonel Blackater made the fateful anouncement : the 9th Gordon Highlanders were to become the 116th Regiment (Gordon Highlanders) Royal Armoured Corps.

This news was received with ' very mixed feelings ' but although a small number of men, regarded as ' unmechanisable ', were suffered to depart, the great majority were soon convinced that Gordons could fight as well in tanks as on foot ; and the new title showed that their identity would be preserved. Although Gordon Highlanders became ' troopers ' the pipe band continued to flourish and every effort was made to procure tartan flashes for all ranks. There was, however, another aspect of the transformation : a long period of training must now ensue before the Gordons could hope to go into action.

Obviously their enemy would be the Japanese. When the Regiment arrived in India the Japanese had occupied practically the whole of Burma, and India lay under threat of invasion. Nevertheless, despite his inadequate resources, General Wavell, Commander-in-Chief in India, was busy with plans for the re-conquest of Burma.

To convert the Gordons into an armoured unit was to prove a slow process owing to the almost complete lack of equipment. The commanding officer's visit to the District commander at Lahore produced a warm welcome but little else. Yet a start was made. Lieutenant J. F. McGillivray, the signal platoon commander, managed to produce over 200 operators, and the untiring efforts of Captain L. G. Linklater, the technical adjutant, provided the necessary drivers and mechanics. It was not until the Regiment had moved south to Secunderabad at the beginning of October that they began to receive Lee tanks and Grant tanks ' by driblets '. These made some kind of combined training possible, and all ranks put in some hard work. The hill station of Ootacamund was much appreciated at this time, and, needless to say, Hogmanay was celebrated in proper style.

By May 1943 the full establishment of fifty-two tanks had been achieved and the Regiment began to train as a regiment. Tank movements in and out of action by day and night over difficult ground where the scrub concealed large boulders required much practice, and the breaking of the monsoon proved a considerable handicap. Later came co-operation with aircraft and a Divisional exercise with infantry and artillery. The commanding officer wrote at this time : ' We are now beginning to look round for a suitable war where we can practise our new ideas and weapons.'

But the time was not yet. Towards the end of 1943 the Gordons were re-equipped with the heavier Sherman tanks, after having survived a shock. In October Lieut.-Colonel Blackater had been called to Delhi and informed that the Regiment were to be disbanded in order to provide men for Wingate's second long-range infiltration Chindit expedition. Fortunately the idea came to nothing. The higher authorities appear to have been persuaded that the Gordons were too good a unit to be broken up.

The Regiment were now in the 255th Tank Brigade of the 44th Indian Armoured Division, and at a Brigade sports meeting distinguished themselves by winning the tug-of-war against the Sikhs of Probyn's Horse.

Early in January 1944 came a move to Ranchi, the tanks going by rail and the transport by road. On the way a driving accident in a monsoon downpour caused the death of one trooper and severe injuries, resulting in the loss of a leg, to Captain J. F. McGillivray, an officer who could ill be spared. At Ranchi jungle training with infantry was the thing and among the knowledge acquired was ' the method of recovering tanks from bogs '.

While the Regiment were at Ranchi the Japanese invaded India. On 12th March began their powerful offensive across the frontier into Manipur state which isolated first Imphal and then Kohima and threatened the base and railhead of Dimapur, a vital point in the communications of the Allied forces (Northern Combat Area Command) in north Burma. Heavy fighting followed before Imphal and Kohima were relieved. At Kohima, as will be related presently, the 100th (Gordon Highlanders) L.A.A. and Anti-Tank Regiment R.A. fought with great distinction. Before the end of June the Dimapur-Kohima-Imphal road was reopened and preparations were in hand for a counter-offensive which was to re-conquer Burma. In this campaign the tanks of the Gordons, at long last, were to show their mettle.

When the Regiment left Ranchi for Assam in September 1944 they had been training in India for over two years, after nearly three years training at Home. No less than eighteen of the original officers had left, some through ill-health, some to take up staff appointments, some to be attached to other units. Lieutenant J. G. Duffus died in hospital while the Regiment were at Secunderabad; so also did Pipe-Major Coutts, 'a grand chap' who was a great loss.

The long road and rail journey to Assam brought the Regiment to Kanglatongbi, some twenty miles north of Imphal, where they camped amid 'rotting stores and rat infested trenches'. This place had been occupied for a time by the Japanese during their advance into India. Scrub typhus was prevalent and, as a precaution, all undergrowth round the bivouac area was burned. One trooper died of the disease.

Training continued, mostly in tank-infantry co-operation, and there was opportunity for gunnery practice. Unfortunately, in an accident on the field-firing range, a corporal and a trooper were killed.

While at Kanglatongbi the Regiment discovered the 8th Gordons, now the 100th (Gordon Highlanders) L.A.A. and Anti-Tank Regiment R.A. who were recuperating after the Kohima battle. They were located not far away and a party of officers, warrant officers and pipers climbed a slippery hillside to make contact. A bigger reunion was afterwards held in the log cabin mess at Kanglatongbi when Major-General Nicholson, commanding the 2nd Division, the commanding officers of the 1st Camerons and 2nd King's Own Scottish Borderers, and the High Commissioner for Australia were guests of the Gordons. As a memento of the meeting of the two Battalions—if they may still be so called—Lieut.-Colonel Blackater presented Lieut.-Colonel Campbell of the 8th Gordons with a quaich, one of two which he had had made by his attached Light Aid Detachment.

From Kanglatongbi 200 men of the Regiment made the long journey back to Calcutta, about 1,000 miles, to bring up transport vehicles for the Army.

On the night of 24th January 1943, the 8th Gordons—now the 100th (Gordon Highlanders) Anti-Tank Regiment R.A.—left the Clyde and began their voyage to the East. It was uneventful. On shipboard a full day's training with 6-pdr. firing practice and gun drill was the rule; all ranks did physical drill, and reserve pipers and drummers were rehearsed. Freetown, reached on 6th February, looked inviting but only a look was permitted. By request of the Commodore the Gordon pipes and drums played the departing convoy out of the roadstead, and on the 25th the ships arrived at Durban where Durban's traditional hospitality was to be enjoyed.

When at sea again it was realised that the Regiment were bound, not for the Middle East but for India. The convoy entered Bombay harbour on 17th March, the pipes and drums playing to show the world that anti-tank gunners could still be Gordon Highlanders.

In sweltering heat the Gordons travelled to Ahmednagar, and found the early stages of their service in India rather trying. But they were put on their mettle by finding themselves allotted to a British division of Regular troops—the 2nd Division who had been nine months in the country and were acclimatised, well-trained and fit.

Ranges and training grounds were prepared, all ranks going to work with a will, but the late arrival of transport proved rather a handicap. Vehicles were borrowed and for a time bullocks were used to tow the 6-pdrs.

The Regiment had embarked for India with three batteries, each of four troops, the batteries, formed of the old A, C and D Companies respectively, being numbered 168, 169 and 170. In April a new battery (numbered 321) was constituted by taking one troop from each of the existing batteries, so the new organisation was of four batteries each of three troops.

On 1st May the Regiment, with the rest of the 2nd Division, moved to the west coast of India some thirty miles north of Bombay for training in combined operations. At Aksa creek exercises were carried out with country craft, boats and kapok floats, the 6-pdr. guns being embarked and disembarked both by day and night. This led up to the employment of assault landing craft in tactical schemes, part of the Regiment acting as infantry.

Towards the end of the month the transport began to arrive—3-tonners and 15-cwt. trucks—and on 5th June the Gordons moved to Nira, 'a remote spot some fifty miles south-east of Poona', where the small rainfall made field work possible even in the monsoon. A good range kept the gunners in practice.

During this period the Regiment were attached to the 5th Brigade and made fast friends with the 1st Camerons. On many occasions the pipe bands of the Gordons and Camerons played together, and parties were held in the messes.

Anti-tank guns being considered a 'luxury' in the type of warfare for which the Division were training, the Regiment now received 3-inch mortars, the intention being to use the Gordons either as infantry with mortars or as anti-tank artillery. In October the Regiment provided an infantry demonstration company at a battle school.

A return to Ahmednagar was made on 28th October and the next thing was a Divisional amphibious exercise. As support group to the 5th Brigade the Gordons were organised on an infantry and mortar basis and embarked at Bombay in an infantry landing ship. The landing was made about 100 miles down the coast and proved a strenuous business. It was no light task to man-handle mortars and ammunition, using sally ports and scramble nets, from ship to assault landing craft.

The Gordons had settled down very well as an anti-tank and mortar regiment within the Division. They had not lost their identity. A kilted quarter-guard was provided at the Divisional commander's inspection; the pipes and drums played Retreat every Friday evening; and their own Regimental customs retained their place in the daily routine. But on returning to Ahmednagar towards the end of the year the Gordons suffered two blows.

The first was the loss of their commanding officer, Lieut.-Colonel R. W. F. Johnston, whose continued ill-health now compelled his departure. During his three years in command he had kept the Regiment at a high state of efficiency despite changes in organisation and armament, and enjoyed the confidence and respect of all ranks.

The second blow was a reorganisation that deprived the Regiment of two of their Gordon batteries. These were to be transferred to the 122nd (Royal Warwickshire Regiment) L.A.A. Regiment R.A. in exchange for the 401st and 525th light anti-aircraft batteries armed with Bofors guns. The Regiment would emerge as the 100th (Gordon Highlanders) L.A.A. and Anti-Tank Regiment R.A.

Permission to train two of the Gordon batteries as anti-aircraft gunners, and thus keep the Regiment intact, having been refused, the Gordons moved on 21st November to Kumbhargaon, in the Dhond region, where the exchange took place. The Regiment parted with the 168th (Major G. A. Rowton) and 321st (Major P. Burnett) Batteries who did not, however, lose their Gordon identity. A guarantee was given that they should keep their Balmoral bonnets and tartan flashes and wear the kilt for 'walking out'. And each battery retained a piper.

An exchange of seconds-in-command and regimental quartermaster-sergeants meant the loss of Major S. F. Evans—in command since Lieut.-Colonel Johnston's departure—and R.Q.M.S. Finlayson. Both had given valuable service ever since the raising of the 8th Gordon Highlanders in 1939.

Before and after the reorganisation, which dates from 1st December 1943, first the artillery commander of the XXXIII Corps and then the Divisional commander spoke to the Regiment on the necessity for the change. The reasons given were 'tactical policy and a conservation of man-power'.

On 5th December Lieut.-Colonel D. B. Anderson arrived to command. Although a Gunner, as was to be expected, he was also a Scotsman and not unknown to the old 8th Gordon Highlanders, having served previously in the 51st Division.

Training continued, both anti-tank and anti-aircraft gunners getting considerable shooting practice by day and night. Sappers gave instruction in the handling of mines and booby traps. These were strenuous days and the Christmas and Hogmanay break proved very welcome.

In January 1944 Lord Louis Mountbatten, Supreme Commander South-East Asia, visited the Gordons and explained to officers and men the reason why they had not yet been called upon to take the field: the proposed seaborne operation on the Arakan coast of Burma had been cancelled. All ranks were much impressed by Lord Louis. Other visitors during the month were the Divisional commander, Major-General J. M. L. Grover, and the commander of the XXXIII Corps, Lieut.-General M. G. N. Stopford.

Early in February training took a new turn when the 2nd Division moved into the Belgaum region to be practised in jungle warfare. This was the Gordon's first experience of living in the jungle and the men liked it, although malaria took its toll.

Late in March the call for action came. Mention has already been made of the Japanese invasion of India, of the powerful offensive which was launched on 12th March 1944, directed upon Dimapur and isolating Imphal and Kohima. The Regiment left Belgaum on the 21st, and at Visapur, near Ahmednagar, prepared to follow the 2nd Division to the scene of operations in Assam. The Divisional order of battle did not include the Gordons, but Major-General Grover made a special request for the Regiment.

The rail party left for Calcutta on 7th April, all ranks exhilarated by the prospect of getting to grips with the Japanese.

Kohima and After

The advance party of the Regiment reached Dimapur on 9th April, but the main body, coming by rail and road, did not all arrive until late in the month. On the 15th, however, the Gordons were able to muster an improvised infantry company—four officers and fifty other ranks—under Captain F. A. C. Noble to hold the southern approaches to the Nichugard Pass, on the Kohima road as it enters the Naga Hills eight miles south-east of Dimapur. Next day the Regiment's guns arrived.

On the 25th a road accident took heavy toll of the Gordons. A 15-cwt. truck plunged down over a cliff, killing Major J. H. Ogilvie and 2nd-Lieutenant Lidbury and injuring Captain A. M. Milne. One gunner and an Indian driver were killed and one gunner gravely injured.

The Regiment moved to the Zubza gun area (generally known as the 'Zubza Box'), about five miles from Kohima as the crow flies, on the 27th. Next day came another shock. A reconnaissance party had gone out after breakfast, and when six Japanese fighter-bombers swooped down the first bomb fell among the party with dire results. Major G. A. Burnett (commanding the 170th Battery) and Lieutenant J. J. Phillips were killed, Major D. I. S. Mackay (commanding the 169th Battery) mortally wounded, and the adjutant, Captain G. H. Campbell wounded. Nine other ranks were killed and fourteen wounded. The enemy aircraft were engaged by two troops of the 525th Battery and each troop claimed a hit. Later in the day Japanese field guns shelled the area and the 525th Battery lost four men.

For the next few days the two anti-tank batteries manned part of the Zubza perimeter where the guns of the 401st Battery were also located. The 525th L.A.A. Battery were in a forward position.

The infantry brigades of the 2nd Division were already fighting hard at Kohima. On the 20th they had helped to complete the relief of the scratch garrison who had held out for eleven days against great odds. The Japanese 31st Division, thrown upon the defensive, still held strong positions on the ridges through which wound the Dimapur-Kohima-Imphal road. A great effort was still needed to drive through and re-open the road; and the monsoon rains were due.

The Gordons were about to enter the fight not as a Regiment but by small gun detachments, sometimes of a single gun, sent up in close support of an infantry battalion. To the anti-aircraft batteries was confided the protection of forward areas and line of communication: this they did efficiently, their task diminishing as our mastery of the air grew more pronounced.

So the battle continued amid the jungle clad Naga hills with their hill-top villages. The enemy's defences behind the crests of wooded ridges and on the slopes of deep ravines were strong and well concealed. When the anti-tank guns and mortars of the Gordons came on the scene our infantry were at close quarters with the Japanese, in some cases almost intermingled. The rains soon made many of the hill tracks impassable and severely cramped the efforts of our tanks.

The names of the various objectives held by the Japanese from north of Naga Village to the Aradura ridge in the south—a distance of nearly four miles—are forgotten now but bore a grim significance at the time. On 2nd May Lieutenant Hall got a 6-pdr. of the

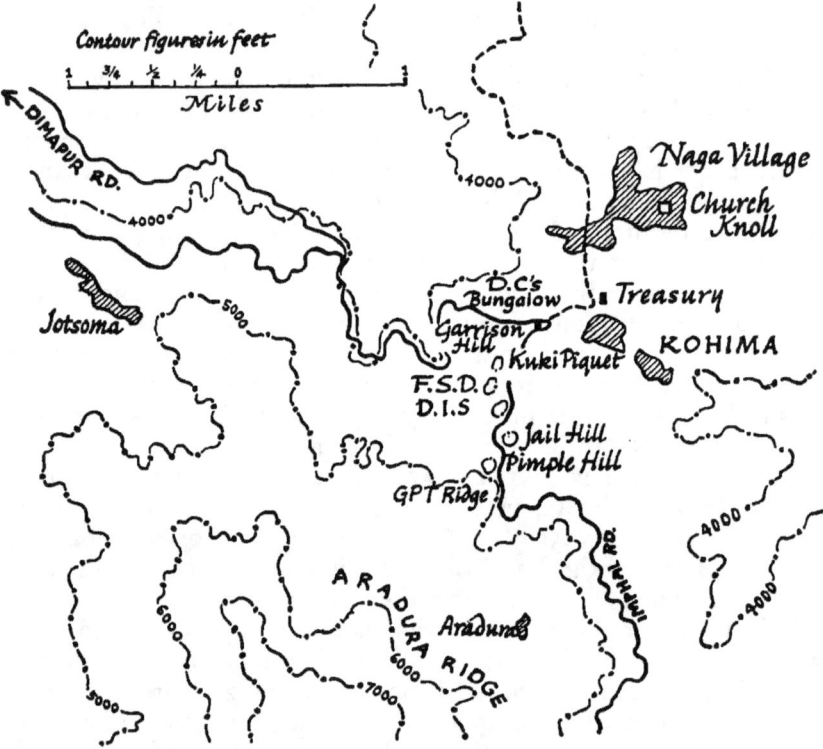

169th Battery up to Garrison Hill, the centre of the 2nd Division front, to engage the bunkers at Kuki Piquet. After being towed forward by a tank the gun was run up a ramp built by the infantry, fired a few destructive rounds, and was then run back under cover to escape the fire of Japanese snipers only 100 yards away. One Gordon gunner was killed and two wounded in this affair. At night the gun detachment acted as stretcher-bearers and next day the gun knocked out three bunkers.

A 3-inch mortar troop had been sent to the Jotsoma position to strengthen the defence of our flank against counter-attack from the south.

On 4th May the three brigades of the 2nd Division attacked against G.P.T. Ridge (where a general purposes transport company had been housed in peace-time), Garrison Hill, which was not yet wholly in our hands, Kuki Piquet and Naga Village; but success was small. Hall's gun destroyed six bunkers on or near Kuki Piquet and with armour-piercing shot knocked down a number of trees which hindered observation.

Two days later another gun on Garrison Hill fired on the ruins of the District Commissioner's bungalow and the bunkers in the tennis courts near it.

On 9th May the Gordons had four guns in action under Lieutenant I. B. Nicolson to assist a 4th Brigade attack at G.P.T. Ridge. This was a night operation. One gun was dismantled, man-handled piece by piece for half a mile up a steep and muddy slope, and then reassembled in the dark so as to ensure surprise.

Hard fighting continued throughout the 10th when the 33rd Brigade of the 7th Indian Division obtained a hold of Pimple Hill, the D.I.S. area (formerly the site of a daily issue store) and Jail Hill. One of Nicolson's guns was sited well forward in this vicinity and was run further forward still to deal with a fresh target. A gunner was wounded while this was being done, and snipers were so active that the gun was ordered out of action, its gun shields pitted with bullet marks. In this affair Gunner J. D. Satchell won the Military Medal for his efficient gun laying under constant and accurate enemy fire. On G.P.T. Ridge Lieutenant Hall had one gun man-handled under a smoke-screen to within fifty yards of a bunker. Two bunkers were engaged, but the gun detachment had to be withdrawn under a shower of Japanese grenades and the gun was protected by booby traps and light machine-guns firing on fixed lines.

The 13th May brought the 2nd Division some reward for they were able to occupy G.P.T. Ridge, F.S.D. Ridge (where a field supply depot had once stood) and Kuki Piquet, all evacuated by the Japanese. Next day Lieutenant J. Taylor brought two guns forward near Pimple Hill to a position commanding the Imphal road. Two more guns came up on the 15th.

The enemy had now been driven from his defences between G.P.T. Ridge and the Treasury area, but he still held on to Naga Village and, away to the south towards Imphal, the Aradura ridge.

Two of Captain G. H. Campbell's guns (170th Battery) were in action against the bunkers at Church Knoll on the 19th when the 5th Brigade launched an abortive attack against Naga Village; but the shoot was a good one, three bunkers being destroyed and two ammunition dumps sent up in flames.

Then for some days the fighting died down, but on the 27th

guns of the 169th Battery under Captain O. E. J. G. Collard in the G.P.T. area supported an attack, made in heavy rain, against the Aradura ridge. The gun-laying of the Gordons was particularly good and several bunkers were knocked out, but the infantry struggling up the slippery slopes were not able to close quickly enough. So the action ended in stalemate, and during the last days of May the 6-pdrs. of the Gordons fired on such targets as could be located. On the other flank Church Knoll had been captured: the Japanese were still in Naga Village.

The Zubza Box had been attacked by fighter-bombers on 14th March, but casualties were few, the A.A. fire of the 401st Battery proving very effective. Lieut.-Colonel Anderson, commanding at Zubza since 5th May, received orders on the 19th to convert the area into a transit camp capable of accommodating 1,500 troops. Regimental headquarters personnel and all other men available then started upon the task of making roads and erecting shelters.

On 1st June the 3-inch mortars of the 169th Battery were in action near Jail Hill and next day a 6-pdr. destroyed a bunker in Naga Village where the fighting ceased with the departure of the Japanese. Regimental headquarters moved from Zubza to Jotsoma on the 7th by which time the Japanese had abandoned the Aradura ridge and were in retreat from the Kohima battlefield.

The Regiment had been in action for over a month. With his batteries scattered over the battle area Lieut.-Colonel Anderson could exercise little control, so that the leadership of subordinate commanders, the standard of training, and the fighting spirit of all ranks, were well tested. The A.A. gunners proved themselves masters of their weapons: the anti-tank guns and the mortars brought great comfort and support to the infantry. Officers and men were entitled to be proud of the part they had played in the Battle of Kohima.

Now came the advance southward to open the Kohima-Imphal road. The 2nd Division led the way along the road itself and other columns operated in the difficult country on the flanks. Sharp fighting occurred with the Japanese rearguards, and the sappers had their hands full in clearing land-slides and road blocks and lifting mines.

On 11th June the 401st Battery were in action against ground targets and two days later the mortars of the 169th Battery registered on targets in the Viswema region where our leading troops had been checked before a strong enemy position. In the successful attack launched here on the 14th mortars and anti-aircraft guns alike fired on ground targets with good results. One troop of mortars fired 600 rounds in the course of ten hours.

The advance of the 2nd Division continued, and on 22nd June they met the 5th Division pushing up from Imphal. The Gordons saw no further action. Orders had been received for breaking up the A.A. batteries (401st and 525th) and, after some delay, this was carried out in July. The men were said to be required as infantry reinforcements, but the majority found themselves transferred to the 169th and 170th Batteries whose establishments were increased.

By the end of June the Regiment were concentrated near Karong on the Kohima-Imphal road. Little comfort was to be had while the monsoon rains continued: headquarters, established in a clearing between the jungle and the road, occupied a former Japanese divisional headquarters, but the majority of officers and men lived in tents and tarpaulin shelters. Perhaps it was as well that all were kept busy. The batteries embarked upon an intensive training programme with the mortar which was likely to be of more use than the 6-pdr. in the jungle fighting which, presumably, lay ahead. Troop and battery schemes were carried out and a range was available for field-firing exercises.

On 16th July Lieut.-Colonel D. B. Anderson, victim of recurrent malaria, was obliged to leave the Regiment for good. The new commanding officer arrived a few days later in the person of Lieut.-Colonel J. A. Campbell, a Gunner 'but at least of Scottish ancestry', who understood and encouraged the Gordon spirit. The Regiment were fortunate in their commanding officers.

Hard training and physical discomfort were rendered more bearable by the granting of leave, arrangements being made for twenty per cent. of the Regiment at a time to spend ten days in Calcutta, Darjeeling or Shillong. Regular church services were held and, thanks to the 2nd Division, a concert party and a mobile cinema provided much appreciated entertainment. A Regimental sports meeting proved a great success.

During July the last was seen of the anti-aircraft batteries and the Regiment, known henceforward as the 100th (Gordon Highlanders) Anti-Tank Regiment R.A., now consisted of the two Gordon anti-tank batteries (169th and 170th) each armed with 6-pdrs. and 3-inch mortars.

Visitors to the Regiment were many. Major-General C. G. G. Nicholson, new commander of the 2nd Division, came in July and in August General Sir William Slim, commander of the Fourteenth Army. At a guest night on 30th September the Divisional commander and the C.R.A. were entertained. Later came a call by a party, led by their commanding officer, of the old 9th Gordons, now the 116th Regiment (Gordon Highlanders) R.A.C. The old 9th Battalion were at Kanglatongbi, further down the road towards Imphal, and their representatives, as may be imagined, were received with acclamation. A return visit, made a few days later, belongs to the story of the 9th Gordons, seeing that they were the hosts.

At this time the Regiment could 'still turn out the mess pipers properly' and muster a number of pipers and drummers to parade with the massed pipes and drums of the 2nd Division. And there was a revival of Highland dancing among the Gordon officers.

VICTORY IN BURMA
1945

Operations on the Irrawaddy

Late in November the 100th (Gordon Highlanders) Anti-Tank Regiment R.A. moved forward to play their part in the liberation of Burma. By this time the Fourteenth Army had secured bridge-heads on the Chindwin and were preparing to break out into the open country of the central plain.

With the 2nd Division the Gordons came southward to Palel, thence to Tamu in the Kabaw valley and on to Yazagyo reached on 28th November. Here some road mending had to be done and a fairly long halt was called. The Christmas rations arrived on 17th December and the day was celebrated forthwith as there promised to be a busier and sterner time ahead. The 170th Battery (Major J. Duncan) moved with the 6th Brigade Group, spearhead of the Division, when the advance was resumed, orders being to cross the Chindwin and attack Pyingaing. The rest of the Regiment moved on the 18th, crossing the imposing Bailey bridge at Kalewa at night. As it happened the advance was rather a military promenade, for Pyingaing was entered unopposed on Christmas Day.

The next objective was the river Mu where the weir opposite Kabo controlled the irrigation of the Shwebo plain, and on the road to Ye-U the 170th Battery, with the 6th Brigade, brought their mortars into action on the 26th and 27th against Japanese rearguards. At least two enemy machine-guns were destroyed. The Battery were in Kaduma, about seventeen miles west of Kabo, on the last day of the year with one troop (two 6-pdrs. and two mortars) supporting the 1st. R. Welch Fusiliers at Kabo weir.

The Regiment moved up to the vicinity of Ye-U during the first days of January, the 2nd Division having secured the town and its airfields on the 2nd. Orders were then received for an advance on Shwebo, the 170th Battery being with the 4th Brigade and the 169th (Major A. M. Milne) with the 5th Brigade. The Japanese, however, evacuated Shwebo airport on the 9th, after having been attacked by the 19th Indian Division coming down from the north.

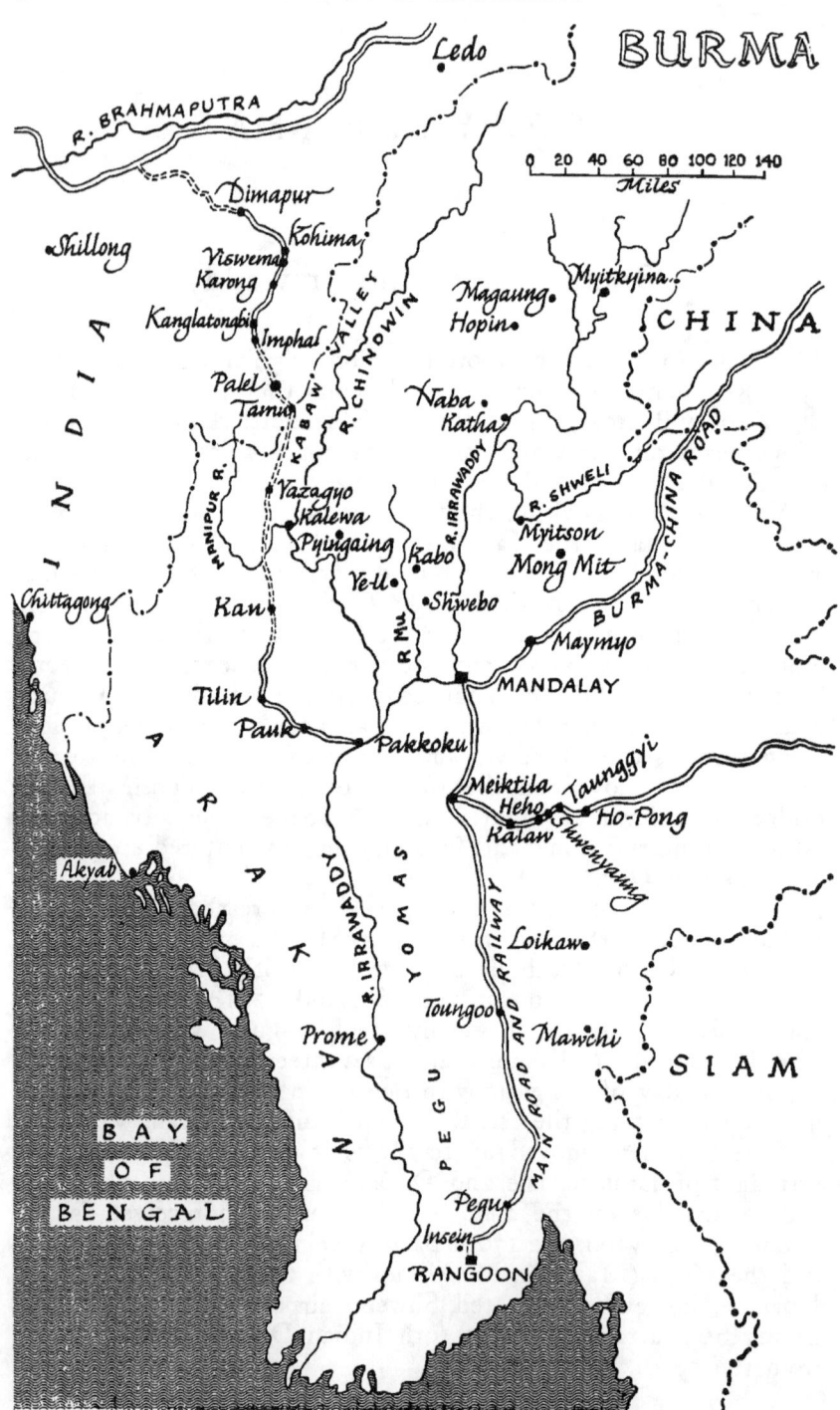

On the 10th the Gordon batteries sat in the outskirts of the town of Shwebo, with one troop of the 170th detached under command of the 2nd Reconnaissance Regiment in readiness for an advance towards Mandalay along the Shwebo road. A week later the Regiment received new and rather surprising orders.

The 6-pdrs. were to be parked and the two batteries (less one troop left with the 2nd Reconnaissance Regiment) organised as infantry. Their task would be to operate in the Mu river area as far south as the Irrawaddy 'to kill any Japanese retreating from the front of the 20th Indian Division advancing from the west'. In effect they were to protect the right flank of the 2nd Division who were pushing forward east of the river Mu towards the Irrawaddy. Throughout these orders the Regiment were designated ' 8th Gordons ', to the gratification of all ranks. They had been machine-gunners and anti-tank gunners and were keen to prove themselves as infantrymen; and they still retained some of their mortars, carried in jeeps.

The Regiment were now operating in open country, fertile enough after the monsoon but in some places covered with rock and scrub jungle. The hot weather had set in, and the Gordons who had been cold and wet often enough had now to get used to a blazing sun and tracks thick with dust.

Regimental headquarters were established at Sadaung but moved on 20th January to Dibeyingwe on the Mu, most of the men marching along tracks too bad for transport. On the previous day the 169th Battery (one troop on wheels with mortars and two troops of infantry) had arrived at a point about seven miles north of the confluence of the Mu and Irrawaddy. They lost no time in sending patrols along the Mu, laying ambushes at several likely crossing places. From this time forward it was found that the inhabitants of the numerous villages were friendly and gave what information they could concerning the movements of the Japanese. The latter seemed to have little knowledge of our dispositions, but before long it became obvious that they were by no means ready to retreat from the Irrawaddy river line.

On the 21st the 100th Brigade of the 20th Indian Division closed in from the west as far as the Mu so that the Gordons could now confine their activities to the eastern side of the river. Next day the intelligence officer made contact with the 4/10th Gurkhas at the remains of the railway bridge near Nyaungbinwun, and was played across the river by Gurkha pipers to the tune of ' The Cock o' the North '.

The 169th Battery now patrolled southward towards the Irrawaddy near Myinmu with the 170th doing likewise further east near Ngatayaw. Headquarters came forward to Legyi on the

22nd when the Gordons received the thanks of the Divisional commander for their work.

Typical of the Regiment's activities at this time was the investigation of Yawathitgyi, on the near bank of the Irrawaddy, by the 169th Battery on 24th January. Two sections, each of nine other ranks with one Bren gun were led by Captain F. A. C. Noble, and Captain A. Mackenzie-Smith commanded a mortar

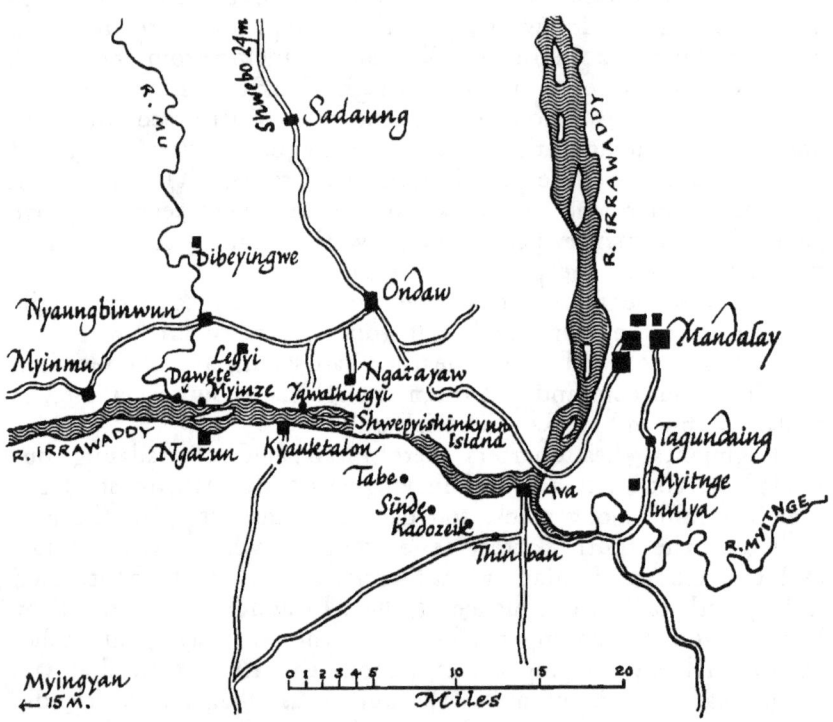

troop. As soon as the Gordons left their jeeps and deployed they were sniped at, and as they worked their way forward towards the village, which was surrounded by a thick belt of trees, a machine-gun opened on them. Then a mortar came into action. The Gordon mortars fired twenty rounds into a cotton mill and then covered the withdrawal of the patrol.

By this time the 2nd Division had occupied Ondaw and the 170th Battery supported the 1st Royal Scots (4th Brigade) as they set about opening the road to Yawathitgyi. Meanwhile the 169th Battery were busy further west. On 27th January one troop moved in towards Myinze but were caught by machine-gun fire at short range. The Japanese then brought a mortar and a grenade discharger into action, and the volume of fire was such that the troop were unable to withdraw until darkness fell. Their losses amounted to two killed, two wounded and seven missing.

At dawn of the 28th Lance-Sergeant Sutherland, who had been twice wounded, advanced with one gunner and reached the outskirts of the village. On his return he was able to report that the enemy had retreated across the Irrawaddy during the night. For his gallantry and enterprise he was awarded the Military Medal; Captain Mackenzie-Smith who on this and other occasions proved himself a particularly capable and fearless leader, received the Military Cross.

Gordon patrols continued to prowl about Yawathitgyi, and on the night of the 31st the 4th Brigade put in an attack against the village but could not secure the whole of it. The mortars of the 169th Battery were in action and silenced a Japanese field gun; the effect of their area shoots could not be observed.

For the first fortnight of February the Regiment were kept in reserve at Sadaung under the command of the C.R.A. Their infantry rôle was over. It was nearly time for the 2nd Division to make their crossing of the Irrawaddy, and for this operation the 169th Battery were to be attached to the 5th Brigade. The 170th took over the defence of Yawathitgyi which had been abandoned by the Japanese.

On the 22nd the 169th reconnoitred for mortar positions from which to support the passage of the river at Ngazun. Two days later they were ready at Dawete to cover with a smoke-screen the crossing of the 7th Worcestershire, the leading battalion. This was a night affair, and a hazardous one as the river was 1,500 yards wide with a 3-knot current. The first flight of assault boats came under heavy fire and many were sunk. However, an island in midstream was taken that night and a big concentration of artillery covered a fresh effort on the 25th. The 169th Battery were firing smoke shell all day and moved out of action with all their ammunition expended.

In the meantime the 170th Battery had carried out a mortar shoot against Kyauktalon, on the south bank opposite Yawathitgyi, and next day they fired on movement observed on Shwepyishinkyun island. By this time two brigades of the 2nd Division were across the Irrawaddy and the urgent need was to enlarge the bridgehead. For the time being the Gordons were out of the fight, but the commanding officer was anxious to get patrols across the river and to follow with the rest of the Regiment. Accordingly, both batteries trained with boats on the river Mu.

Kyauktalon was the next objective. On the morning of the 9th the 170th Battery fired sixty rounds harassing fire into the west end of the village. Plans were made to cross to Shwepyishinkyun island, sixty engineer personnel being attached to the Gordons to help with the boats and to clear mines and booby traps. The actual crossing was made on the night of the 10th, the noise of movement being drowned by the flight of aircraft. There was no opposition but Lieutenant A. D. Campbell was unfortunate enough to be wounded in a mine explosion. Next morning, Kyauktalon having been captured, the mortars engaged such targets as presented themselves in that region and before nightfall the whole Regiment were across the Irrawaddy.

The 2nd Division with their left on the river were now advancing eastward with the 20th Indian Division keeping pace on their right. Mandalay was to be the prize of the 19th Indian Division who were pushing down the left bank of the Irrawaddy from the north.

On the 14th two troops of the 169th Battery covered the right flank of the 2nd Dorsetshire (5th Brigade) who occupied Tabe unopposed. There was some resistance east of Sinde but Kadozeik was reached in the early morning of the 15th when the Gordons silenced some enemy mortars and a machine gun. Smoke bombs were used to set the village on fire and the advance continued.

The 170th Battery were with the 2nd Dorsetshire on the 18th when the infantry were near the south end of the Ava bridge at the confluence of the Irrawaddy and the Myitnge rivers. On the 20th, when the advance continued towards the Tagundaing road both 6-pdrs. and mortars had some good shooting. 'All ranks', we are told, 'were very pleased with themselves.'

On the 20th the 169th Battery were supporting the 4th Brigade who had troops at the village of Myitnge on the north bank of the river. The Gordon gunners fired 528 rounds before one troop crossed the Myitnge to gain contact with the 1/8th Lancashire Fusiliers. It was on this day that the 19th Indian Division, after heavy fighting, completed the capture of Mandalay.

Regimental headquarters were established at Inhlya on the 22nd and there was now time to look to the maintenance of vehicles. The 169th Battery were again in action next day, supporting an attack of the 1st R. Berkshire (6th Brigade) who were fighting in the loop of the Myitnge river. The guns and mortars fired their last rounds on the 24th when smoke was used to indicate targets to our aircraft.

All organised resistance round Mandalay now ceased and some relaxation was possible. On the 25th the first party of the Regiment went sight-seeing in Mandalay; a few days later sixty unfit cases—sufferers from boils, septic sores and similar ailments—were sent to the hill station of Maymyo; and on 29th March was held a swimming gala in which visitors from the 6th Brigade competed.

Now came another change in the fortunes of the Regiment. The 2nd Division, including the Gordons, were to be withdrawn to India, there to prepare for a fresh venture: as a follow-up division for the sea-borne expedition to Rangoon. So far as the Gordons were concerned the first step was to lend their vehicles to convey some of the infantry to an airfield near Myingyan. The passage to India would be by air.

To the Gordon armoured regiment at Kanglatongbi the war still seemed a long way off; but in the middle of December 1944 the Regiment began the long journey southward to enter the campaign which was not to cease until Burma was liberated and the Japanese armies decisively defeated in the field.

The Allied offensive was already well under way, for the troops of the Northern Combat Area Command were advancing southward from Ledo, and General Slim's Fourteenth Army had crossed the Chindwin and were directed upon Mandalay from the west. The IV Corps were to come in further south. After the 7th Indian Division, to whom the Gordons were attached, had secured a bridge-head over the Irrawaddy near Pakkoku the 17th Indian Division would pass through. Thrusting south-eastward their objective was Meiktila with its base establishments, depôts and airfields serving two Japanese armies fighting further north.

The Gordons started on 14th December, coming down through the Naga hills by Imphal to reach Palel about a week later. Here a 'magnificent Christmas dinner' was eaten, and on 27th December the Regiment crossed the Burma frontier and reached Witok, some twenty miles down the Kabaw valley from Tamu.

The celebration of Hogmanay owed something to the return of the Calcutta transport ferrying party who brought with them an ample supply of proof rum. This party also earned great praise for the excellent state of the vehicles they had conveyed and the speed with which they had carried out their mission.

The long trek towards the Irrawaddy continued, a secret advance of the IV Corps who aimed at a surprise crossing of the river. It was not an easy march, for time was all important and the troops were obliged to improve the jungle tracks as they went along and also to lay out airstrips. Supply by air transport was an essential of success.

On the way an order was issued for the removal of all badges, shoulder titles and flashes; and a 'bund buster' for attachment to the Sherman tanks was successfully tried out. Kan marked the centre of a particularly bad malarial region where the strictest precautions were enforced. So on to Tilin and Pauk. At Kan the tank transporters were left behind, being too unwieldy for the steep and awkward gradients. It was as much as the 3-tonners could do to get through, but the whole journey from Kanglatongbi to Pauk, 350 miles, was accomplished without the loss of a vehicle.

From Pauk the 7th Indian Division, with whom were the Gordons, led the way towards the Irrawaddy, and C Squadron were attached to the 114th Brigade for an attack against Kanhla, a village on the road leading to Pakkoku which lies on the edge of the river. The main portion of Kanhla, with its pagodas, stood on a bluff and reconnaissance showed that the best line of approach was from the north across a 'tankable' chaung, and from the north-east.

On 10th February Major P. W. Craig's C Squadron moved off at daybreak, each troop carrying a platoon of the 4/5th R. Gurkha Rifles. When the infantry 'de-bussed' about 8 a.m. only 400 yards from the nearest bunkers the tanks opened fire. The troop on the left, coming in from the north-east soon came under field-gun and mortar fire, but the work of destruction went on. Some Japanese fled from their bunkers and our infantry forged ahead through Kanhla, snipers being their chief trouble. Many of these were accounted for by machine-gun fire from the tanks but the mopping up and consolidation of the village occupied until the early afternoon when the tanks were withdrawn. A Brigade message to the Gordons ran: 'Well done! You seem to have had a good party.'

This was indeed the case. So far as could be ascertained twenty-two bunkers had been destroyed and the Japanese casualties were estimated at nearly 100. The Gordons lost one tank commander, killed by a shell splinter, and the Gurkhas reported thirty killed and wounded. Several tanks were hit but not damaged; one which threw a track was left with an infantry escort and recovered later.

In this action the Regiment secured their first battle trophy, a Samurai sword found in a bunker by No. 2 Troop.

Kanhla set the pattern of the fighting in the Irrawaddy area, for the country, mostly cultivated ground, was not difficult for tanks although certain hill features and deep chaungs sometimes hampered movement. The tanks usually advanced in depth so that bunkers over-run by the leaders could be tackled by the second echelon. Prompt indication of targets, a matter of first importance, presented some difficulty. The infantry had the better opportunity for observation and on one occasion at Kanhla a Gurkha was taken up by a tank to guide it into a position from which a troublesome target could be engaged. Japanese artillery fire, particularly when the guns could not be located, could be a considerable nuisance, and tanks were sometimes obliged to 'jink' in order to keep out of trouble.

Two troops of C squadron were in action again on the 12th when they worked with the 4/14th Punjab Regiment towards Pakkoku. No. 3 Troop drove straight through one village and destroyed a number of bunkers, trees were sprayed by the Brownings to bring down enemy snipers, and before noon the infantry had cleared the place. At 2 p.m. an attack against the next village went in, and, as the bunkers were hard to locate, the tanks plastered the whole gound with high explosive and machine-gun fire. This gave the infantry an easy passage and the tanks covered the consolidation before returning to harbour. Pakkoku was occupied without opposition on 15th February.

These operations served to distract the enemy's attention from the actual crossing of the Irrawaddy which was taking place a little further down stream at Nyaungu. Here the river was about 1,000 yards wide and the numerous sandbanks forced the assault boats to steer an oblique course.

In the early hours of the 14th one company of the 2nd South Lancashire made a silent crossing in boats and established themselves on the further bank. Then at first light the rest of the Battalion began to follow in outboard motor craft; with them were two tank officers of the Gordons, Captain J. Hughes and Lieutenant J. A. Lindsay-White. Aircraft roared overhead to drown the noise of the motors, but as the boats, in considerable disorder, approached the shore accurate machine-gun fire opened on them. Lindsay-White, ' a very promising young officer ', was killed and Hughes was an hour in the water after his boat was sunk; but he was rescued and brought back.

A fresh effort was made and our infantry soon began to cross the river and make their landings in considerable force. As soon as it was light enough to see they were covered by the fire of the tanks, B Squadron commanded by Major W. B. Gordon. No artillery ammunition was available so much depended upon the tank gunners who contributed some accurate shooting at 1,700 yards range, besides putting down a smoke screen. It was a very good performance, considering that the cliffs on the far side of the river were well above the level of the near bank.

Before darkness fell three battalions of infantry were across the Irrawaddy and six tanks of B Squadron had been ferried over on Bailey rafts. After what was described as a ' quiet night ' the rafts bearing the rest of the Squadron swept across to the landing bays at Nyaungu.

Two troops of Major Gordon's squadron were soon in action beyond the river. Nyaungu lies close to the ancient Burmese capital of Pagan and infantry and tanks were soon involved in a struggle among the catacombs excavated nearly 900 years before.

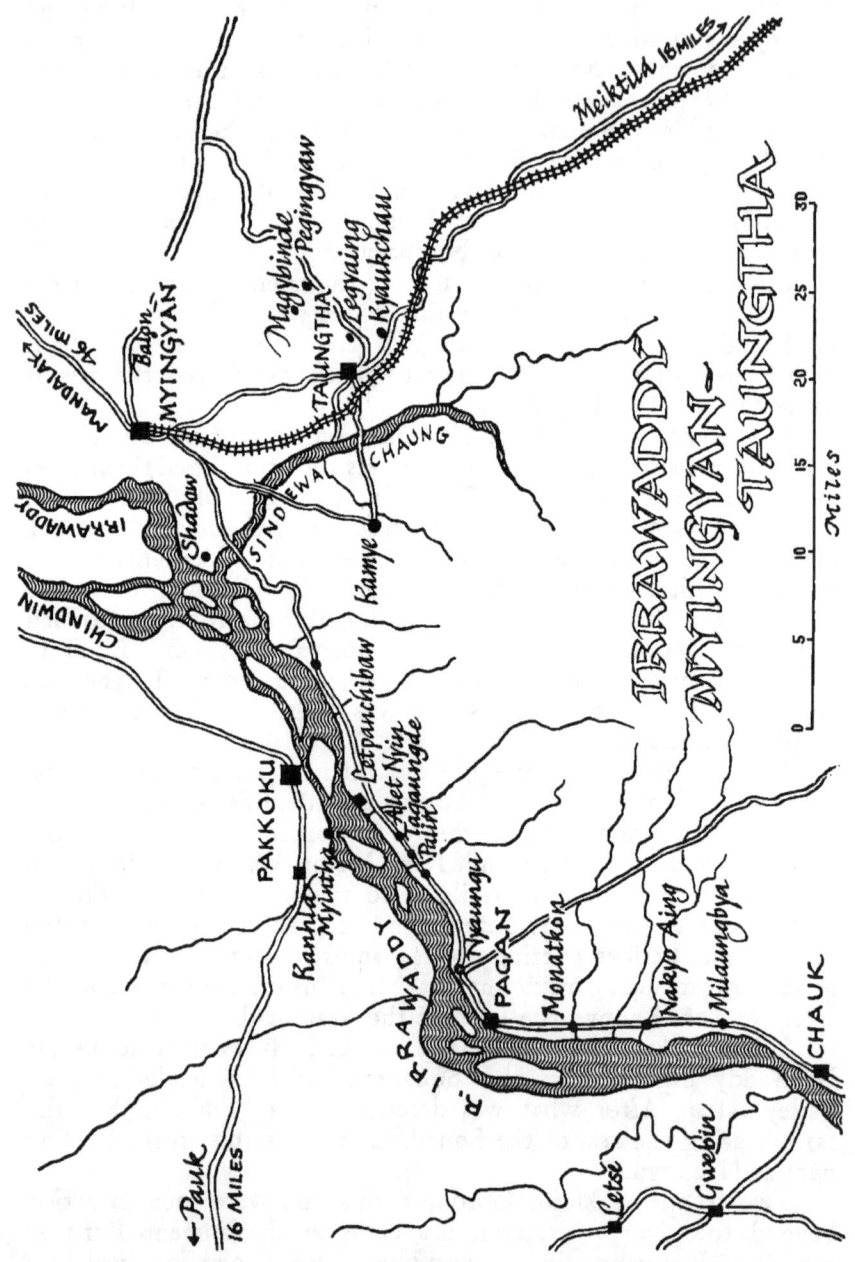

One troop passed round Pagan and reached the river below the town. Major Gordon's tank lost a track very early in the proceedings and the squadron commander thereafter exercised control from a jeep's radio. The driver of this very vulnerable vehicle with the radio operator ranged about with the greatest unconcern, although under fire for hours.

The operation continued on the 16th for some Japanese still lurked in the bowels of the earth while snipers were active even in Nyaungu. East of the place two troops of B Squadron worked with the infantry.

B Squadron were busy again on the 18th when one troop and a company of the 1/11th Sikhs attacked from Pagan towards a pagoda area on some high ground. Confused fighting followed and two jeeps were lost. Another troop were with a company of the 4/1st Gurkhas in an affair on the Palin road which ended successfully although the tanks were rather annoyed by fire from mortars which could not be located.

C Squadron were still operating on the right bank of the Irrawaddy. When Myintha was attacked and captured on 16th February Lieutenant H. Baker's troop appear to have had a most enjoyable time. They expended a lot of ammunition in shooting snipers out of trees, destroying the few brick buildings, and setting fire to bashaws, haystacks, hedges and an oil dump.

By the 18th the Squadron were back at Kanhla, but while moving to a new harbour the 'soft' vehicles were attacked by eight enemy aircraft. Two men were wounded and three vehicles were damaged.

When the island opposite Pakkoku was occupied on 20th February the infantry met no opposition and the tanks, in position ready to provide covering fire, were not needed.

C Squadron crossed the river on the 22nd and rejoined the Regiment to find that Major L. G. Linklater's A Squadron were now detached. On the 20th they had been ordered south to operate with the 28th East African Brigade in the direction of Gwebin.

On 21st February the 17th Indian Division began to advance through the bridge-head towards Meiktila; but there was still much to do in securing and extending the bridge-head, for the Japanese were beginning to counter-attack from the south.

An attack on Palin, when the 4/1st Gurkhas were 'shot in' by the tanks of B Squadron took place on 23rd February. The proceedings were opened by an air strike but this was made so early that an interval elapsed before the short artillery concentration came down. This bombardment, however, created enough dust and smoke to screen the tanks as they moved forward. They attacked from west and south and during the day an area of pagodas was cleared and the village itself secured with considerable loss to the Japanese. Of the seventeen tanks engaged one was damaged by a mine explosion.

Next day, the 24th, came the turn of C Squadron again. They were linked up with the 2nd King's Own Scottish Borderers of the 89th Brigade for an all Scottish attack southward beyond Pagan against Nakyo-Aing. Two companies of infantry went in on different sides each supported by a troop of tanks while another troop moved round to cover the escape route. At the start of the action, forty Japanese were caught retreating across the open and were mown down.

The fire of the tanks soon set the whole of the village ablaze, and No. 2 Troop drove into Nakyo-Aing before the flames had subsided, a rash proceeding which fortunately brought no evil consequences. It was Lieutenant H. Baker's troop who 'butchered the folk that flew'. Asked for a situation report Baker's exultant voice, interrupted by the sound of firing, was heard through the microphone: 'We are having a helluva party here! Bunkers all round us and Japs galore!' The tanks were giving chase to the foe, running down many who sought to escape.

Lieutenant W. J. Hendry left his tank under intense small-arms fire to rescue a wounded K.O.S.B. officer. With the help of his crew he placed the officer on the back of his tank and remained outside supporting him during the withdrawal to a medical aid post. Hendry was recommended for the Military Cross.

The Japanese heavy machine-guns were using armour-piercing bullets which penetrated half an inch of steel, and Hendry's tank received fifty hits on hull and turret. These did no harm, but No. 3 Troop had two tanks out of action with mechanical defects. C Squadron, were unanimous that in this affair they met the best equipped and hardest fighting Japanese in their whole experience.

On 25th February B Squadron went into action with the 1st Burma Rifles who passed through the 4/1st Gurkhas (both 33rd Brigade) and cleared the villages of Tagaungde and Alet-Nyin. Next day the 4/15th Punjab, advancing along the river road towards Letpanchibaw, were held up. A company of Gurkhas were therefore moved round to cut the road behind the Japanese while two troops of tanks joined the Punjabis and put in an armoured thrust. Shelling as heavy as it was unexpected caused the infantry to go to ground and the tanks to disperse, but eventually nine tanks tried an advance under cover south of the road where one tank threw a track. In the afternoon, however, the others were in action astride the road. At night they harboured in the Punjab 'box' and the stranded tank was brought in next day.

Two Japanese who had approached while the fitters were at work on it were disposed of by the fitters.

On the same day, the 26th, C Squadron were associated with a company of the 1/11th Sikhs in a visit to Monatkon which had been shelled and practically destroyed. No Japanese were found there, and in the afternoon tanks and infantry entered what remained of the next village. There was no fighting but two tanks of the squadron developed mechanical defects.

By this time the main offensive was making good progress towards Meiktila; but the troops of the 17th Indian Division had no easy passage along the main road, and fresh Japanese forces were beginning to close in behind them. The bridge-head now extended from a point about due east of Letse to the left bank of the Irrawaddy opposite Pakkoku.

C Squadron of the Gordons advanced out of the bridge-head on 3rd March working with a company of the 4/15th Punjab. Passing through Kamye the column reached a steep-sided watercourse called Sindewa Chaung where the road across the chaung was strewn with mines. The tanks made a detour and when they regained the road two tanks were hit repeatedly by anti-tank gun fire at less than thirty yards range. No damage was done, and Sergeant Cowie's tank, having spotted the flash, engaged and destroyed the gun as well as a heavy machine-gun sited near it. In this action a small village was set on fire and cleared of the enemy, although the tanks were rather worried by the Japanese artillery. The squadron finished with twelve runners, three tanks having broken down.

Two troops of C Squadron under Captain N. B. Smith, with another company of the 4/15th Punjab, advanced north-eastward towards Myingyan, the river port on the Irrawaddy, during the 5th. On this occasion Sergeant Stewart took on and destroyed an enemy field-gun at 600 yards, after his tank had received several hits. In the evening the Gordons lost an admirable troop commander when Lieutenant Hendry was killed by a mine explosion while on reconnaissance.

The most pressing need was for the 7th Indian Division to keep open their end of the road to Meiktila, and on 6th March C Squadron with a company of the 1st Burma Rifles advanced down the road and entered Taungtha, the opposition being feeble. Next day an attack upon a hill south-east of Taungtha was remarkable for the activity of the Japanese artillery. Tanks and infantry assaulted the hill from west and south, but although the tanks softened up the immediate opposition they could not subdue the enemy's shell fire. Eventually a withdrawal was ordered, one stranded tank being left behind temporarily under a guard of Bombay Grenadiers.

During the following days the tanks engaged several suspected observation posts and did some useful patrolling in this region. By 10th March the Regimental harbour had been moved forward to Kamye.

The Regiment had now been in action for a full month. All ranks had discovered that to spend hours in a closed tank under a blazing Burma sun was a very uncomfortable way of waging war, and 'battle exhaustion' took on a very real meaning. Nevertheless the Gordon tanks had done admirable work, nor did their efforts lack appreciation. The 1st Burma Rifles sent the Gordons a captured flag and the 4/1st Gurkhas presented a similar trophy; congratulations came from the 33rd Brigade, the 7th Indian Division, and the commander of the IV Corps.

That so many runners were kept in action speaks well for the Indian light aid detachment attached to the Gordons; and all had great confidence in the battle-scarred Shermans which stood up so well to rough usage and even to direct hits from field guns.

The pipes and drums had had two practices since the crossing of the Irrawaddy and ' it was hoped soon to play at the headquarters of the 7th Division '.

And now to follow the fortunes of A Squadron who had departed on 20th February to join the 28th East African Brigade. After driving through rough and unreconnoitred country the squadron arrived on the 22nd at Letse where supplies of P.O.L. (petrol, oil and lubricants) and ammunition were dropped from the air.

The Africans had carried out a deception plan opposite Chauk to cover the Irrawaddy crossing further north, and the Japanese reaction was so strong that the brigade had withdrawn some twelve miles after suffering rather heavy casualties. A Squadron of the Gordons were told that no gain of ground was expected, but the Japanese were to be held in check and kept under attack. The Somalis of the King's African Rifles, with whom the squadron were to work, had never trained or fought with tanks before, a distinct disadvantage.

The country was unsuited to armoured movement, and the only road the tanks could use was covered by the enemy's artillery and mortars. Nevertheless on 26th February a raid was carried out on a Japanese position known as 'The Springs', a ridge through which the road passed in a defile. Almost from the start the squadron and the infantry company with them came under mortar and machine-gun fire. No. 4 Troop worked towards The Springs from the north while No. 3, searching for a practicable way forward, skirted the ridge and came in from the rear through the defile to the surprise of friend and foe alike.

The fire of the tanks drove the Japanese from the forward slope of the ridge and killed many of them, but the African infantry found progress difficult. When they reached the crest of the ridge the tanks were fighting on the reverse slope where some of the Japanese endeavoured to close. Two of them who climbed on to a tank were shot by the Somalis firing from the crest of the ridge.

When the time for withdrawal came No. 3 Troop commander's tank became bogged and had to be towed out. The Japanese again tried to get to close quarters, but were driven off by the fire of the infantry and of the other tanks.

No. 1 Troop had the worst of it. Two Japanese climbed upon 2nd-Lieutenant R. Johnson's tank, throwing one grenade into the turret and another down the barrel of the 75-mm. gun. The tank caught fire, ran on, and crashed into a tree. One of the crew was shot as he emerged from the tank; the wounded driver was trapped; the co-driver, Trooper Gray, got clear and covered with a revolver the removal of 2nd-Lieutenant Johnson and the radio operator, both severely wounded.

These were the only casualties the squadron sustained. All tanks were in harbour by the early evening, after having brought back the African wounded. About eighty Japanese dead had been counted so the action could be reckoned a success.

Half the squadron moved out on 2nd March and shot up The Springs position but were shelled and mortared as they withdrew, two tanks being disabled by hits on their engines. These two were taken in tow and brought in.

On the 6th when another attack upon The Springs was made the fire of the enemy's anti-tank guns and mortars was very heavy, but the infantry got through to find the position deserted. Two tanks were hit and damaged in this affair. In the early hours of the 7th the Japanese took to the offensive and attacked the squadron harbour at Letse. Grenades thrown into the perimeter killed two of the Gordons.

A Squadron were now under orders to rejoin the Regiment and started to do so when daylight came. They arrived at Nyaungu on the 8th and reached Kamye on the 11th.

On 11th March an armoured sweep was carried out to clear two villages in the Taungtha area, C Squadron and a troop of the newly arrived A Squadron being accompanied by a detachment of the 4/1st Gurkhas. The whole operation was controlled by Lieut.-Colonel Blackater and went very well although some of the tanks came under short-range artillery fire in a pagoda area. The tanks destroyed an anti-tank gun and a field gun, sixty-three Japanese dead were counted, and three prisoners, two of whom died, were taken. These prisoners fell to the commanding officer who had conducted a small action of his own, killing a number of the enemy.

Two days later A and C Squadrons with companies of the 4/1st Gurkhas drove the Japanese from the hill near Taungtha, after rather confused fighting in which the enemy threw grenades and bricks at the Gurkhas. C Squadron took part in the capture of the hill while A Squadron, in clearing two villages near by, operated in jungle. One driver was wounded, three tanks were hit but not disabled; about forty Japanese were killed and two of their mortars taken.

On 16th March half of B Squadron and three troops of C Squadron were engaged in another sweep with the usual infantry contingent and for the first time met some of the Indian National Army, popularly known as ' Jiffs '. They were not nearly such doughty opponents as the Japanese who organised them, and quite a number were captured.

Myingyan, on the Irrawaddy, with road and railway communications and an airfield, was of importance. Once the place was in our hands supplies could be sent south river-borne. On the night of the 16th a platoon of the 4/15th Punjab advancing from the south were checked at the outlying village of Shadaw. Next morning A Squadron of the Gordons moved out to help. The tanks shot up many bunkers and in the afternoon provided covering fire for the passage of a chaung and a further advance.

But Myingyan was not to be easily taken. On the 18th half of C Squadron shelled the cotton mills which were then cleared by the infantry. On the 20th A and C Squadrons after moving eastward to locate and destroy enemy artillery were recalled to help in the capture of Myingyan. The tanks turned and attacked westward towards the railway line and by the end of the day the station was in our hands and only the area of the jail, further north remained to be cleared.

Fighting continued in the Shadaw-Myingyan region on the 21st, A Squadron and Regimental headquarters, with companies of the 4/15th Punjab, clearing out pockets of the enemy as they were discovered. On the morrow the jail was bombarded by tanks of C Squadron who shot a watch tower to pieces and made three breaches in the not very formidable walls. The rubble heaps blocked the passage of the tanks and the 4/1st Gurkhas got in only to find that the enemy had fled. Of more importance was the contact made at the airfield with the 7/2nd Punjab Regiment who had crossed the Irrawaddy in this vicinity.

On 23rd March the Regiment, less B Squadron of whom more presently, pushed forward from Myingyan along the Mandalay road, and next day tanks of A and C Squadrons made an almost circular sweep in this vicinity, shooting up the village of Balon which had been bombed from the air and was in flames.

At this time the Regiment was rather dispersed, for B Squadron had been operating near the Irrawaddy on the other flank. In probing south along the river towards Chauk on 8th March the squadron had found the twin villages of Milaungbya unoccupied. When, however, they paid another visit on the 18th the Japanese were there in considerable force. All the morning was spent in clearing the northern village, but tanks and infantry (4/5th Gurkhas) took heavy toll of the enemy: over a hundred dead were counted and five guns were knocked out. Our troops withdrew, but the whole place was found to be deserted two days later. An air strike seems to have been too much for the Japanese.

The Meiktila road in the vicinity of Taungtha was another, and most important, centre of activity and here two troops of C Squadron had been engaged. Attached to the 161st Brigade (of the 5th Indian Division now coming into the fight) the tanks, with a company of the 4th R. West Kent, had advanced down the Meiktila road from Taungtha on the 22nd and burnt Kyaukchau village. The clearing of mines kept a sapper detachment busy during this expedition, and two tanks were damaged by mine explosions.

On 26th March began operations to put an end to enemy opposition in the hilly country north and north-east of Taungtha. The whole region, very difficult for tanks, contained many Japanese gun positions.

From a point on the Myingyan-Taungtha road a column started to sweep along the eastern side of the hills, the spearhead being C Squadron of the Gordons and Regimental headquarters with one company of the 4/15th Punjab, the whole under Lieut.-Colonel Blackater's command.

After passing through two villages without opposition the tanks encountered bad ground and one of them became bogged. Accordingly the column moved to a higher level which brought both tanks and infantry under considerable shell fire. As C Squadron pushed on southward over difficult country seamed by deep chaungs they came within close range of the Japanese artillery. The two headquarters tanks had their own troubles, being trapped for a time in a steep-sided hollow. Meanwhile the squadron, by a most commendable display of dash and initiative, managed to destroy a 105-mm. gun and blow up an ammunition dump. Eventually a 'box' was formed for the night with the 4/15th Punjab near Magybinde.

None took harm from the efforts of the Japanese 'jitter parties' and next morning, the 27th, the advance continued. Magybinde was reached after a minefield had been cleared by Indian sappers and then the march was resumed. Soon the tanks were in action again and Lieutenant A. J. M. Simpson was wounded in the arm, but another 105-mm. gun was destroyed. After passing a deep chaung, keeping well away from the road which had been heavily mined, two parties of Japanese engaged in cooking were surprised and the column reached a pond on the outskirts of Legyaing. Here contact was made with a 161st Brigade column headed by tanks of the Gordons' A Squadron and Rajput infantry which had moved out eastward through Taungtha, clearing two villages on the way. In this vicinity confused fighting continued until another Japanese gun had been destroyed and the enemy fled.

There were still Japanese in Legyaing and here Corporal D. Morrison distinguished himself. A petrol stoppage brought his tank to a halt and when he climbed out to remedy the matter he engaged three Japanese in a bunker with his Sten gun and a grenade. Then rifle and automatic fire broke out on all sides, but Morrison organised his Bombay Grenadier escort and some of the 4/15th Punjab to give rather better than they received while, with his crew, he got the tank going again. He was awarded the Military Medal.

The tanks harboured for the night on the outskirts of Legyaing. Next morning the fighting in the pond area was renewed, but after C Squadron had destroyed two more Japanese guns the action ended in the final dispersion of the surviving enemy.

During the whole operation about seventy Japanese had been killed and practically every enemy gun engaged was destroyed. All had been accomplished for a trifling loss, and to the credit side could be added the destruction of a considerable quantity of food, stores and ammunition.

The Regiment now counted their total of Japanese killed as 1,166 with one prisoner of war. As we well know the Japanese preferred to die rather than surrender when escape proved impossible.

The last days of March provided a breathing space in which the Gordons could overhaul their equipment and vehicles. Officers and men were in good health although minor cuts and bruises often turned to septic sores. As regards their general well being they had not fared badly. Air transport of supplies had worked well, and towards the end of the month a limited quantity of stores arrived by road. Local barter had secured eggs, poultry, potatoes and tomatoes in exchange for bully beef and tinned fish, both very unappetizing in the great heat.

All ranks remembered with satisfaction that, although they were an armoured regiment, their pipes and drums, wearing the kilt, had played Retreat for their good friends the 4/5th Gurkhas.

Meiktila had been captured after four days of bitter fighting and at the beginning of April the Regiment moved there *via* Taungtha where the tanks were put on transporters.

To bathe in the lake at Meiktila was a joy and dhobies were much in demand. Reinforcements brought each squadron up to establishment, and parties of various infantry battalions came along to learn something of co-operation with armoured forces. On the 7th C Squadron moved out with an infantry company to clear two villages and killed a number of Japanese.

Towards Rangoon

And now comes the drive for Rangoon, 300 miles away to the south. Our aim was to enter the capital before the coming of the monsoon, reckoned to break about the middle of May, hindered movement and restricted supply by air. Two columns were to be employed: one following the Irrawaddy route and the other advancing down the main road and railway from Meiktila.

At Meiktila was assembled an armoured force to act as spearhead of the 5th Indian Division. This force included the Gordons, the 7th Cavalry (light tanks), one squadron of the 16th Cavalry (armoured cars), the 18th Field Regiment R.A., the 3/9th Jat Regiment, and one troop of a field squadron of engineers. The Gordons had with them as close escort a company of their old friends the 4/4th Bombay Grenadiers.

A start was made from Meiktila on 9th April and the armour halted that night some distance north of Pyawbwe which was finally wrested from the Japanese by the 17th Indian Division on the 11th. Along the road the Gordons saw many Japanese dead and managed to shoot a few stragglers who were striving to escape.

When the column reached Yamethin on the 11th all was quiet and some of the tanks opened up, their crews dismounting for a while. The march was resumed to a harbour five miles further on the way.

Meanwhile the Japanese had cut the road north of Yamethin and occupied the place. C Squadron of the Regiment soon found that something was wrong. They had harboured for the night at Pyawbwe and next day were to ensure a clear passage for the leading brigade group of the 5th Indian Division; but during the night a sudden sandstorm was followed by a thunderstorm and then, in the pitch darkness, firing broke out all round. The jeep carrying the fitters of the squadron was blown off the road by a shell and all three fitters killed.

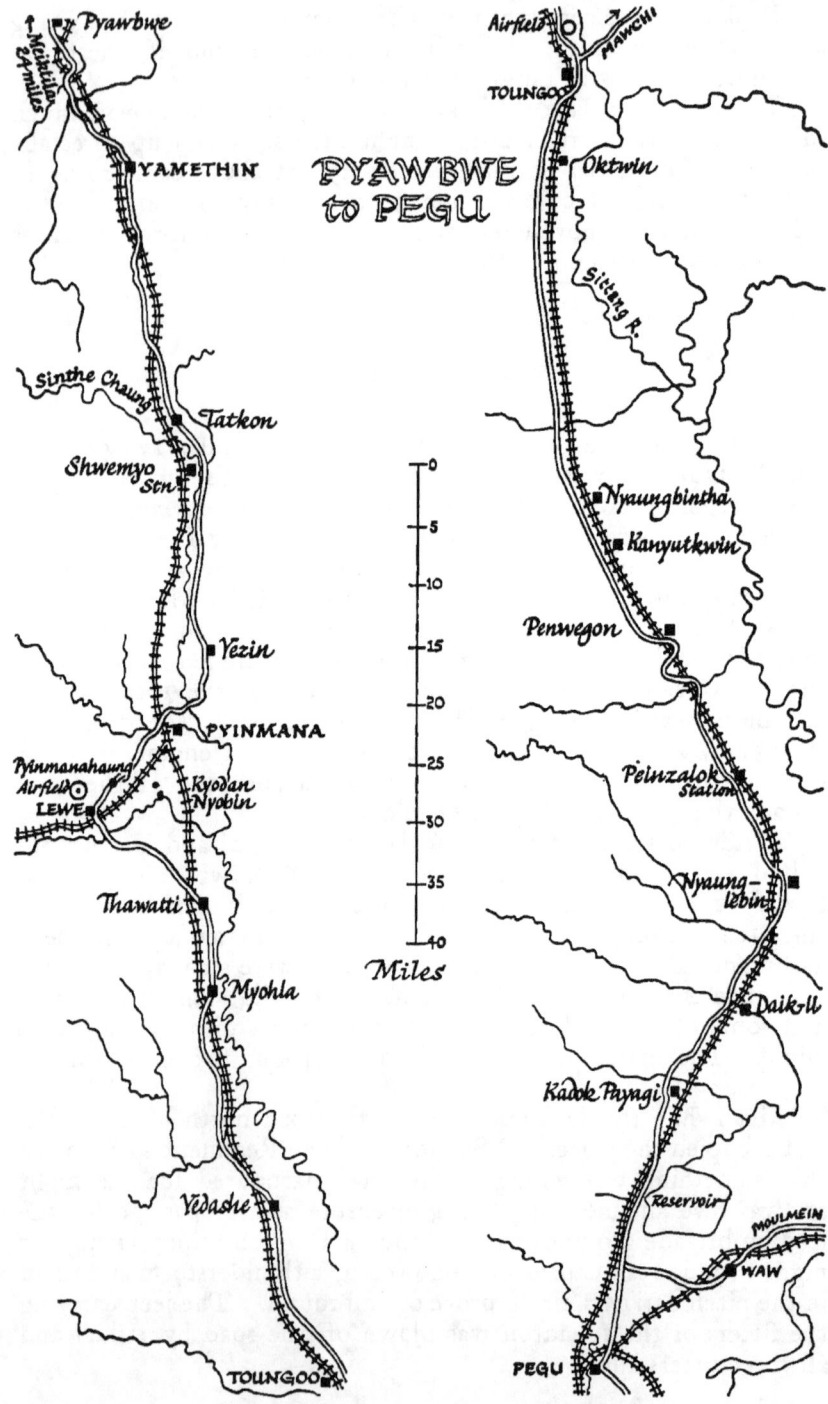

When the column of soft vehicles moved forward from Pyawbwe on the morning of the 12th four Japanese fighters flew in to attack and six petrol trucks were set ablaze. A halt had to be called before Yamethin was reached and another uneasy night was spent with many alarms and much indiscriminate firing.

On the afternoon of the 12th an unsuccessful attempt had been made to clear the enemy from Yamethin. C Squadron of the Gordons came forward with part of the 7th York and Lancaster, and half of A Squadron and two platoons of infantry were sent back by the armoured column. An attack from the north was delivered after an air strike and an artillery preparation, but the country on the outskirts of the town made tank action difficult. The infantry were checked and No. 4 Troop of C Squadron ran into trouble in the jungle.

Suicide parties of Japanese attacked with picric acid charges which they placed on the engine plates of the tanks. Lieutenant E. Holt's tank was completely burned out and one of the crew was killed; Holt and another were injured by blast and received burns. Trooper J. Lomas, the co-driver, was heavily sniped at but contrived to get some nearby infantry into a good fire position before going to the assistance of the wounded. He was awarded the Military Medal. Black smoke issued from Sergeant Cowie's tank but the crew remained inside until they were rescued by No. 2 Troop.

A tank of A Squadron became hopelessly bogged, and was destroyed by our own gun-fire.

At 5 p.m. a general withdrawal was ordered, the tanks carrying out many of the wounded, but another attack on Yamethin went in next day. C Squadron and a troop of A Squadron were engaged, and some progress was made, but the place was not completely cleared of Japanese until the 14th when the 123rd Brigade, leading the main body of the 5th Indian Division, took the matter in hand.

At noon on this day the armoured column resumed the advance but no part of the Regiment were in action. Tatkon was reached and at night transport was heard in motion away to the east. Actually, as the column advanced southward down the main road, the Japanese were also hurrying south along tracks and byways to the east and the west. They were hoping to stand and fight at Toungoo where reinforcements could be expected.

North of Shwemyo the road rounds a high bluff, and, being cut out of the hillside, allows no room for manoeuvre; so the column followed the railway line on the 15th. To take this route meant crossing Sinthe Chaung.

Two troops of A Squadron worked with the armoured cars east of Tatkon on this day; the other troops with a company of

Dogras, caught about 150 Japanese digging in at the railway bridge over Sinthe Chaung. About forty of the enemy were killed and the remainder fled to the shelter of nearby villages where the squadron commander called down an air strike upon them. B Squadron had little to do, and C Squadron, protecting the soft vehicles of the armoured column, accounted for a number of snipers. At night the Regiment harboured north of Sinthe Chaung.

Although Shwemyo, practically clear of Japanese, was reached on the 16th the column covered only four miles on this day, jungle country slowing down the advance which was also impeded by a chaung south of the railway station. Here a scissors bridge was laid by the sappers and B Squadron followed the armoured cars across. A Squadron were protecting the soft vehicles and killed a number of Japanese; C Squadron secured the eastern flank of the march and were also engaged. As the day wore on the enemy's artillery fire increased.

Next day B Squadron, still in front, passed through two villages, but thick jungle on either side of the road restricted the vision and the movement of the tanks. More infantry had to be sent up to deal with the enemy snipers and at night the armour harboured near Milestone 264—that distance from Rangoon. Abandoned dumps of stores and ammunition and a number of deserted machine-guns showed that the Japanese were being hustled back in satisfactory fashion; but the important factor was time.

Delay on the 18th was caused by the enemy blowing a bridge and defending the demolition. Here again was thick jungle country not easily negotiated by tanks and B Squadron could give little support to the infantry. All bridges were found to be mined but the Japanese, when seen and fired on, usually fled without argument. C Squadron did flank protection and A Squadron marched with the 255th Tank Brigade headquarters. Most of the Regiment harboured north of Yezin, but not before tanks of B Squadron, with some of the 7th Cavalry, had killed about forty Japanese in a sharp skirmish.

The task for the next day was to seize the Sinthe Chaung bridge north of Pyinmana (Milestone 240) and to capture the nearby airfield. C Squadron having 'pounded Yezin to bits', advanced over open country. The bridge over the chaung was mined, ready for demolition, but the Japanese sentry only awoke from sleep in time to make good his escape.

Pyinmana was too large a town to be tackled by an armoured column weak in infantry. The advance therefore by-passed the place and came in from the east to secure the airfields at Lewe, south-west of Pyinmana.

When the column moved west to gain the railway line the armoured cars reported sniping from the village of Kyodan and three Japanese tanks in the village of Pyinmanahaung.

A Squadron soon approached Kyodan, having encircled the neighbouring village of Nyobin. Sergeant W. Mathieson then took his tank through Kyodan, quite unsupported, and returned with valuable information concerning the strength of the enemy. As a result more infantry were brought up, and, after an artillery bombardment, an attack went in. Fighting continued until the fading light compelled a withdrawal: as was usual, the tanks brought out many of the wounded.

C Squadron's objective was the Japanese armour which they were very anxious to meet. After Pyinmanahaung had been shot up with much destruction of petrol dumps and other stores, a light tank and a 'tankette' both camouflaged, were discovered. These vehicles had the temerity to show fight and were accounted for by two rounds.

It seems that the Headquarters of the Japanese 33rd Army were shattered and dispersed on this day, the commander and his staff narrowly escaping capture. About 300 of the enemy were killed.

The column harboured for the night, a very dark one, astride the main road near Pyinmanahaung. At 5.15 next morning five Japanese trucks, all unsuspecting, drove in with their lights on from the north. At close range the fire of our Brownings 'got the lot'.

An early start was made on the 20th, the main line of advance being east of the main road; but B Squadron and Regimental headquarters headed west to secure Lewe airfield where a 'dropping zone' was soon laid out. Good progress was made against little opposition on this day and most of the Regiment harboured south of Thawatti. Before they did so about 150 Japanese were seen to be retreating southward down the bed of a small chaung and were fired upon by every weapon available. The slaughter was considerable. During this affray a party of Indian prisoners of war who had been enlisted in the Indian National Army came in to surrender. These were the first of many.

The armoured column were now making for Toungoo and expected to get there before the enemy could concentrate sufficient forces to hold the town. Mined bridges slowed down the advance on the 21st, but C Squadron killed twelve Japanese at Myohla and captured some staff cars. At Yedashe, where there was no resistance, many Japanese were caught in the open, and stores of sugar and rice were captured. Although the intention was to halt the armour after the airfields north of Toungoo had been seized Toungoo itself promised to fall an easy prey and fresh orders were issued accordingly.

On the 22nd C Squadron soon secured the airfields, one of which was ready for flying out casualties by 9 a.m. As Japanese were reported to be entering Toungoo from the east the Squadron were then ordered to guard the crossings over the Sittang river. This was done in conjunction with the 7th Cavalry.

The attack on the town concerned B Squadron who were committed to an advance through a jungle belt where tanks were at a disadvantage. One tank received four hits from armour-piercing shells which failed to penetrate, but another was not so fortunate, two of the crew being wounded, one of them fatally. This tank was abandoned but recovered afterwards in running order, although it had been in Japanese hands.

B Squadron felt that they were doing well enough and were disappointed to learn that they must withdraw while Toungoo was subjected to an air strike. Then the air strike was cancelled and a new attack arranged for the afternoon. Nearly the whole of the Regiment were to take part in this which began with an artillery bombardment and resulted in rather a walk over. By the evening Toungoo was ours and General Slim was swift in sending his thanks and congratulations to all concerned.

Now came a real opportunity for rest and maintenance, for the Gordons, located near the Toungoo airfields, were succeeded by the 9th Probyn's Horse as leading tank regiment in the advance on Rangoon. Actually there was little more to do, for sea-borne forces were approaching Rangoon and their leading brigade occupied the capital, which had been evacuated by the Japanese, on 3rd May. The war was not yet ended and the Gordons had still a part to play in it ; but at this stage they had the grim satisfaction of knowing that since entering Burma they had accounted for 1,600 Japanese.

On 26th April the Regiment moved southward in the wake of the advance and by 5th May had reached Pegu. B Squadron were then warned for mopping up operations with the 9th Brigade (5th Indian Division) and four sets of tracks were taken from the other squadrons to replace those too worn for further service. By this time track mileage throughout the Regiment averaged 1,200 miles and of this 800 miles had been during action.

B Squadron moved to Waw with their tanks carried on transporters during 8th and 9th May, but the boggy ground in this vicinity was no place for tanks. No. 1 Troop fired a few rounds, but the Squadron were back in Pegu on the 11th.

Five days later B Squadron went north to Daik-U. The Japanese still in the Pegu Yomas were expected to break eastward towards the Sittang river, and the tanks, with troops of the 48th Brigade, were, in the words of the squadron, ' to kill as many as possible '. Here again the nature of the country made effective tank action impossible and at Daik-U the squadron remained inactive until the end of the month.

On 17th May the remainder of the Regiment had moved down to Rangoon, being accommodated outside the city at Insein in the Rangoon Veterinary College. As the monsoon had broken all ranks were glad to find themselves in billets. The rains, however, restricted supply by air transport and, as preference had to be given to petrol, ammunition and such like, half rations were still the rule. Canteen supplies being suspended, a consignment of 4,000 cigarettes and parcels of such ' comforts ' as socks, toothpaste, soap and tea—all sent out by the Aberdeen Welfare Committee—were very welcome.

The award of the D.S.O. to the commanding officer, Lieut.-Colonel J. N. F. Blackater, became known on 18th May.

On the 23rd A Squadron moved north and by the 26th were back in Toungoo, the tanks travelling on transporters. The squadron were to work with Indian infantry of the 98th Brigade in operations towards Mawchi, in the Shan Hills, and one troop were speedily ferried across the Sittang. On the first day of action an advance was made through the jungle along a single narrow road, with the infantry fifty yards ahead. The tanks could see little and found few targets; one tank overturned and fell down a 25-foot slope, giving the crew a severe shaking. On this day, too, a trooper was killed through the accidental discharge of a Browning. The squadron were not in action again before the end of the month.

Regimental headquarters had left Rangoon on the 24th for Meiktila, whence the drive on Rangoon had started, and were decidedly better off than the squadrons who continued to operate as best they could despite the miseries and handicaps of the monsoon.

At the beginning of June Lieut.-Colonel Blackater left the Regiment, being ordered Home for a lecture tour in the United Kingdom. He did not return until 10th August and during his absence Major W. C. Dewar was in command.

The 255th Indian Tank Brigade were now leaving the IV Corps whose commander, Lieut.-General F. W. Messervy, sent a farewell message to all ranks of all units, thanking them for their good work.

On 3rd June a troop of A Squadron supported a company of the 1/15th Punjab in another advance along the Mawchi road which was found to be heavily mined. Stiff opposition was encountered, and when the order to withdraw was given smoke was required to screen the removal of the wounded. Sergeant Mathieson, who had done so well at Kyodan, won the Military Medal: he drove his tank forward over the heavily mined road so that he could fire his smoke shell at effective range.

Operations were resumed on the 8th when the 4/4th Gurkhas supplied the infantry and the tanks succeeded in destroying a number of bunkers, although observation was again difficult. On the 11th the enemy retreated at the sight of the tanks, but heavy rain soon put an end to operations on the Mawchi road. The whole of A Squadron were then concentrated in the sawmills area of Toungoo, and preparations were made to form a small mobile force of all arms, called 'Kris Column', under the command of Major F. J. R. Moir. A Squadron, less two troops, were included.

Half of B Squadron had been sent from Daik-U to Penwegon on 4th June, joining a mobile column formed by the 63rd Brigade. Reconnaissances were made both east and west from the main road, but no Japanese were seen. There was little the tanks could do, for movement off the roads was impossible, and the rest of the month passed in watchful inactivity.

C Squadron arrived at Meiktila on 3rd June and took over seven tanks from the 25th Dragoons. On the 7th half the squadron supported a 64th Brigade advance eastward along the road to Kalaw. Kalaw, however, was found empty of Japanese, and for the rest of the month the tanks remained in and about the town while the infantry patrolled to the south and the east.

In July the squadrons were still concerned with the expected Japanese break-through from the Pegu Yomas across the main road and the Sittang to the Shan hills. Yet C Squadron at Kalaw were first in action. On the morning of the 8th they reached Heho where a company of the 1/3rd Gurkhas forced the crossing of a deep chaung. Only one troop of tanks were able to leave the road, but their fire saw the infantry through. The squadron then moved to a new harbour at Shwenyaung. Later in the month no less than three attempts were made to push the advance towards Taunggyi, but the opposition was too strong.

On 3rd July the half of B Squadron at Daik-U were flooded out and moved to Penwegon. A week later two troops under Captain Hughes joined a mobile column ordered to operate as far as Kadok Payagi. There was a skirmish on the 16th, and on the 21st Captain Hughes with No. 3 Troop moved north of Kanyutkwin to bombard two villages. Here Lieutenant N. G. Findlay was mortally wounded. He had left his tank to prop up a telephone cable, and while doing so was struck by a shell splinter from a round fired by another tank. Meanwhile No. 1 Troop, working with a company of the 6/15th Punjab, accounted for over forty Japanese near Nyaungbintha.

Penwegon perimeter was attacked that same night, a hopeless and desperate venture which left thirty Japanese dead outside.

On the 23rd No. 2 Troop engaged some of the enemy south of Penwegon, and two days later a large number of Japanese were seen in the long grass about 2,000 yards north-east of the town. Three tanks, three armoured cars of the 16th Cavalry and a platoon of the 6/7th Rajputs opened on them and the slaughter was great. B Squadron had no opportunity for further action in July.

The tanks of A Squadron with Kris Force do not come into the picture till late in the month. Captured Japanese orders indicated a proposed break-through eastward over a distance of about seventy-five miles—between Nyaunglebin and Toungoo— and on 15th July Major Moir's column moved to Oktwin. He had under his command four tanks of A Squadron, two companies of the 5/10th Baluch—the Gordons seemed to be making the acquaintance of every regiment in the Indian Army—a mountain battery, a detachment of sappers, and a platoon of Sikh machine-gunners. Contact had been made with No. 136 Guerilla Force— commanded, as it happened, by a Gordon officer—who acted as an intelligence screen.

After several days of patrolling without much result the Japanese were encountered in fairly large numbers. The break-through eastward had begun. On the 21st nearly 300 of the enemy were seen entering a village called Le-aingzu, so the infantry, covered by the fire of the tanks and the mountain guns, advanced. The Baluch company, who had to cross open paddy fields two feet deep in water, made three attempts to get in, but each effort was checked by machine-gun fire; then an air strike caused great confusion among the enemy and provided the tank gunners with some good targets before the column withdrew.

The tanks were operating in the Oktwin area again on the 23rd when the guerilla force caught many Japanese drifting down the Sittang on rafts, but by the 25th the whole squadron were back in Toungoo. Infantry and artillery were still engaged, but further tank action in the water-logged countryside had to be ruled out.

The end was now very near. The Japanese having retreated from Taunggyi, tanks of C Squadron joined a company of the 1/3rd Gurkhas in an advance southward along the Ho-pong-Loikaw road. Three times the enemy retreated from good positions in the hills after the tanks had shelled him. The last occasion was on 9th August. Further operations were planned but were cancelled when, on the 14th, news was received that the war was over.

B Squadron who at this time were on their way northward to Meiktila, lament that, although they learnt the good tidings, they 'didn't have the necessary to celebrate the victory'.

Japan had capitulated on 14th August. It was not until 12th September that at Singapore Lord Louis Mountbatten formally received the surrender of all Japanese forces in the area of South-East Asia Command. By that time the Gordons were concentrating at Meiktila where they were soon to hand over their tanks to the 5th Horse and the 9th Horse of the Indian Army.

The Gordons were the last regiment of the Royal Armoured Corps to come out of action and also proved to be the British unit fighting furthest away from Home when the war came to an end. Their losses in killed, missing believed killed, and dead from other causes during the liberation of Burma amounted to four officers and twenty-one other ranks.

The Lost Batteries

When the 168th and 321st Batteries left the 100th (Gordon Highlanders) Anti-Tank Regiment R.A. to become part of the 122nd Regiment they were, officially, Gordon Highlanders no longer; but they remained very jealous of their origin, rather to the disapproval of the English portion of the Regiment. English reinforcements posted to the Gordon batteries 'seemed to have no ear for the pipes and no wish to learn'. To the end of the war the 168th and 321st Batteries considered themselves Gordons.

Like the 100th Regiment the 122nd had little chance to function as a regiment, and their changes in armament were much the same.

The Japanese offensive in Arakan, part of their general plan for the invasion of India, sent the 168th Battery to Chittagong early in March 1944. Their 6-pdrs. were left at Chittagong as the officers and men were required to reinforce the personnel of two field regiments of the 36th Division. This meant active service conditions but no close contact with the enemy; and for their work in digging emplacements, protecting observation posts, and laying signal lines they earned the thanks of the field gunners. On 5th May the Battery left for India and at Shillong began training with the 3-inch mortar. This was a pleasant interlude which lasted until October.

Meanwhile, in August, a composite troop of the 321st Battery (fifty strong with two 6-pdrs., Lieutenant K. W. Sanderson in command) had been flown into Myitkyina to join the advance southward of Northern Combat Area Command. Passing through Mogaung the troop caught up with the 36th Division and were attached to the 72nd Brigade. The guns were the only British artillery with N.C.A.C. and proved of great moral and material support to the infantry during the advance in heavy monsoon rains across flooded chaungs and through sodden jungle. At the end of the month the troop were at Hopin and took a month's well-earned rest.

The remainder of the 321st Battery were retained at Ledo to help with the air supply by sorting and packing stores, some men going in the Dakotas to the dropping zones where the packages were kicked out of the aircraft. These trips were sometimes under Japanese air attack.

When the advance southward towards the Irrawaddy was resumed in October the 168th Battery, flown into an airstrip near Mogaung, also took part. In December the remainder of the 122nd Regiment came forward from Ledo.

Christmas 1944 was spent by the 321st Battery in 36th Divisional headquarters box at Naba, Hogmanay at Katha on the Irrawaddy where the whole Regiment concentrated. The 168th Battery say that 'Christmas was celebrated by a joint sing-song with the Burmese locals, and a valiant effort was made to salute Hogmanay in cocoa.' The battery piper played in the New Year.

The Irrawaddy was crossed on rafts early in January 1945 and the advance continued towards the river Shweli. Resistance grew stiffer, and the mortars of the 168th Battery were frequently in action. On 1st February the forward guns of the 321st and the mortars of the 168th helped to cover an attempt to force a passage over the Shweli at Myitson, but the operation failed. The 168th Battery fired 1,350 rounds while the infantry withdrew.

A few days later a Japanese shell fell in the area of the 168th Battery, mortally wounding Major G. A. Rowton (an Aberdeen solicitor who had commanded the battery for three years) and killing Lieutenant R. A. D. Harman, Battery Sergeant-Major Webster, and seven others. The wounded numbered twenty, including Captain I. S. Gavin.

Captain J. R. Lawrence, also of Aberdeen, succeeded Major Rowton, and the Battery were again in action on 9th February when the Myitson crossing was successfully accomplished, the 6-pdrs. of the 321st destroying at short range many Japanese bunkers. For a time the bridge-head was held against strong Japanese pressure, then the advance continued and before the end of February the batteries were at Mong Mit.

They saw no further fighting. In May they were flown out from Meiktila to India where, in the Poona district, they began to receive new equipment.

INDIA

1945

On 2nd April the 100th (Gordon Highlanders) Anti-Tank Regiment R.A. left Inhlya for an airfield near Myingan. They were flown to Chittagong and on the 11th arrived at Bansbaria, some thirty miles north of Calcutta. This was a new camp, and the first task was to 'organise amenities'. By the end of the month the guns had arrived and stores and vehicles had been brought up to establishment. For the Rangoon expedition, however, the scale of transport was considerably reduced.

At the same time orders were received to form an additional battery to be numbered 401.

Training proceeded during the ensuing weeks. Football and swimming helped to fill the leisure hours and leave parties visited Calcutta. At a Regimental ball all units of the 2nd Division were represented. Then, on 26th May, Major-General Nicholson came to inform the Regiment that their long attachment to the 2nd Division had come to an end. The Gordons would be re-armed with self-propelled anti-tank guns, but were first to move to Ranchi.

All ranks were sorry to leave the 2nd Division. Their relations with both infantry and gunners had been cordial and mutually appreciative and the Divisional commander, in bidding them farewell, thanked them in glowing terms. The future was uncertain, but re-armament implied a further period of intensive training. There was little prospect of seeing Rangoon.

In the middle of June the Regiment left for Ranchi, but Lieut.-Colonel Campbell did not accompany them; he left for three months leave in South Africa and Major R. A. Cumberlege assumed command. At Piska, some distance from Ranchi, the Gordons found a 'practically virgin area' which required much work before it could be made into a habitable camp. As the monsoon had broken this was an unpleasant prospect, but a few weeks' toil worked wonders and even cricket and hockey grounds were prepared. And the Regiment had a football team again.

Training began in earnest with the arrival of twelve 57-mm. half-tracked guns, and soon the Gordons were firing the new weapons on the range. Six Valentine tanks became available for instruction in driving and maintenance.

When the war against Japan came to an end the Regiment were still at Ranchi. The victory was celebrated on 15th and 16th August, but to all ranks the last months had proved an anti-climax. They had been withdrawn from the battle when much was still to do; they had received large reinforcements who were gunners, not Gordons; and they were training with a new weapon for what purpose it was hard to tell. Yet, through all, the Gordon spirit prevailed, owing much to the sympathetic understanding of Gunner commanding officers. When the Regiment left the 2nd Division they could still muster a number of pipers.

Before the end of August Lieut.-Colonel Cumberlege departed for Home and Major A. M. Milne became the new commanding officer. He had joined the 8th Gordon Highlanders as a second-lieutenant when the Battalion were raised at the beginning of the War and had long commanded the 169th Battery.

EPILOGUE

So, in August 1945 the surrender of our enemy in the East followed that of our enemy in the West which had taken place three months before, and the Second World War was over.

On 20th August the Colonel-in-Chief of the Gordon Highlanders, at that time Governor-General of Australia, cabled from Canberra the following message to the Regiment:

> On the momentous occasion of the end of the War I send to all ranks of my Regiment my best congratulations for the out-standing work they have done during the past six years. By their devotion to duty and their courage they have made a wonderful contribution to the Victory which has been achieved. They have added splendid pages to their previous illustrious record. I am proud to be your Colonel-in-Chief.
>
> Henry.

The Gordons may well be content with this tribute from His Royal Highness. They had fought in three continents, first in the struggle against odds and then in the arduous campaigns which ended in the final triumph. The price they paid in all theatres of war was 2,400 killed or died of wounds.

The names of the fallen are preserved in the Books of Remembrance at Regimental Headquarters and at the Regimental Clubs in Aberdeen, Edinburgh and Glasgow.

When Peace came the 1st, 2nd and 5th/7th Battalions of the Gordon Highlanders were part of the Army of Occupation in Germany; the 6th Battalion were in Palestine; in India were the old 8th Battalion, the 100th (Gordon Highlanders) Anti-Tank Regiment R.A.; and the former 9th Gordons, the 116th Regiment (Gordon Highlanders) R.A.C. lay in central Burma.

At Home were the old 4th Gordons, the 92nd (Gordon Highlanders) Anti-Tank Regiment R.A.; three Local Defence companies who still contained a large proportion of Gordons; and No. 1 (Shetland) Independent Company who were still in being.

Demobilization was bound to be a complicated and a not altogether joyful business. Regulars, Territorials, National Service Men were all veterans now, a great number of them due for discharge. From the Regular battalions the old hands would disappear, giving place to what seemed a new generation. The coming of Peace ended another phase in the life of the Regiment who were now to face a changing world: but the old loyalties were strong as ever.

INDEX

Note.—The rank of an officer given in parenthesis is the highest attained during the period of the narrative. (Canada) denotes an officer attached from the Canadian Army.

cds = commands   m/d = mentioned in despatches

Aart bridge-head, 303
Abbeville, actions before, 68
Abercromby, Lieut.-Col. Sir G., Bt., cds. 6th Bn., 19, 118
Aberdeen, air raids on, 113, 114, 128
Aberdeen ladies, work of, 38
Aberdeen, Lord Provost of, 26, 27
Aberdeen, Marquess of, 26
Aberdeen Welfare Committee, 403
Adam, Lieut.-Col. R., cds. 5th/7th Bn., 19, 20
Afwaterings canal, passage of, 312
Agnew, Lce.-Cpl. J., m/d, 229; U.S. silver star, 246
Aitchison, Major H. T., 270
Aitken, Lieut. (2nd Bn.), 296
Aitkenhead, Sergt. (5th/7th Bn.), 256
Aldridge, Major D. A. V. 330
Alexander, Capt. D., 72
Alexander, Lieut.-Col. G. W. A., cds. 50th(H) Bn., 124; cds. 30th Bn., 128
Alexander, Major-Gen. (Field-Marshal) Hon. H.R.L.G., 25, 35, 42, 155, 189
Algiers, Allied landing in, 145, 173
Altham, Capt. E., R.A.M.C., 85
Anatolia, operations in, 6, 7, 8
Anderson, Lieut.-Col. D. B., cds. 100th Regt., 372, 376, 377
Anderson, Lieut.-Col. G. H., cds. 9th Bn., 123, 124
Anderson, Lieut.-Col. J. D. C., cds. 1st Bn., 248, 250
Anderson, Lieut. R. B., 262
Anderson, Pipe-Major (1st Bn.), 190
Andrews, Major R., 261
Angus, Capt. (5th/7th Bn.), 171
Angus, Lieut. K., 200
Angus, Lieut. W. 172
Ankers, Lieut. W. I. M., 351
Annand, Capt. D., 52
Anzio: preparations for, 220; landing at, 222; operations, 223
Apennines, operations in, 237
'Arkforce', 76
Arnim, Colonel-General Sixt von, 181
Arno, advance from river, 237
'Arrow Route' 237
Assche, action near, 50
Aston, Lieut (5th/7th Bn.), 286
Atherton, Sergt. J., M.M., 296
Aylmer, Capt. S., 71, 74
Ayres, Lieut. P. B., 331

Bain, Lieut. R. D., 177, 179
Baker, Lieut. H., 389, 390
Bannerman, C.S.-M. (5th/7th Bn.), M.M., 217
Barber, Major-Gen. C.M., cds. 15th Div., 342, 364
Barbrooke, Lieut. R. E. C., 315

Barchel, action at, 363
Barker, Capt. (Major) C. N., 139, 192
Barker, Sergt. F., 156
Barlow, Major (5th/7th Bn.), 157
Barr, Lieut. M., 208
Battle Honours, Second World War, 31
Baucher, Capt. (Major) J. L., 53, 185
Beardwell, 2nd.-Lieut. H. G., 291
Beaton, Lieut. G. E. 304
Belgian Army, capitulation of, 53
Bell, Lieut.-Col. F., cds. 1st Bn., 11, 12, ; cds. Depôt, 18
Bell, C.S.-M. (5th/7th Bn.), 210
Best, Capt. H., 165, 255, 285
Best, action near, 304
Bird, Lieut. R., 172; M.C., 216
Birley, Sergt. (5th/7th Bn.), 286
Birrs, Lieut. (Capt.) J. G. M., 211, 260, 289
Birse, Lieut. (5th/7th Bn.), 286
Bizerta, occupation of, 172
Black, Capt. J. S., 216, 263.
Blackater, Lieut.-Col. J. N. F., cds. 9th Bn., then 116th Regt., 124, 367, 368, 369, 393, 395, 403; D.S.O., 403
Black Sea, Army of, 3, 6
Blair-Imrie, Lieut.-Col. H. A. C., cds. 5th/7th Bn., 276; killed, 288
Black, R.S.-M. (2nd Bn.), 270
Blandy, Lieut. J. M., 229
Bonar, Lieut. (5th/7th Bn.), 263
Boon Pong, 111
Borthwick, Lce.-Cpl. (5th Bn.), 77
Boudet, Pierre, 82
Bradshaw, Major (Lieut.-Col.) H. I., 46; cds. 11th Bn. then 2nd Bn., 125, 250
Brand, Lieut. (Capt.) P. W., 256, 292, 312
Brayley, Capt. (5th/7th Bn.), 307, 309
Brebber, Major A. H. W., 129
Bridgeman, Capt. (Major), 180, 228, 230; M.C., 230
Britain, Battle of, 113
BRITISH ARMY—
 21st Army Group, 302, 305, 343
 First Army, 171, 173, 175
 Second Army, 278, 292, 312, 314
 Eighth Army, 130, 131, 155, 157, 158, 166, 167, 171, 175, 186, 191, 198, 213, 216, 220
 Fourteenth Army, 379, 385
 I Corps, 260, 298
 II Corps, 50, 56
 VIII Corps, 251, 276, 293
 IX Corps, 180
 XII Corps, 271, 293, 302, 307, 350, 353
 XIII Corps, 191, 198, 214, 237
 XXX Corps, 133, 135, 142, 191, 214, 302, 303, 304, 320, 321, 325, 343, 359
 Guards Armoured Division, 353
 1st Armoured Division, 67, 140, 142

BRITISH ARMY—continued
  1st Division, 25; France (1939-40), 34, 42;
    Dunkirk campaign, 49, 50, 118; Tunisia,
    173; Pantelleria, 185; to Italy, 219; Anzio,
    220, 222, 226, 230, 231, 234, 236; Apennines,
    237, 239, 241, 242; Recce. Regt., 221, 226,
    230
  2nd Division, 370, 372; Kohima, 375, 377;
    Irrawaddy, 379, 382, 383, 384; 385, 408;
    Recce. Regt., 381
  3rd Division, 47, 255, 342
  4th Division, 39, 47, 50, 51, 56, 177
  5th Division, 53, 56, 213
  6th Airborne Division, 255
  7th Armoured Division, 149, 157, 158, 290, 309,
    312
  9th Armoured Division, 127
  9th (Scottish) Division, 122; becomes new 51st
    Div., 116, 123
  10th Armoured Division, 143
  11th Armoured Division, 317
  15th (Scottish) Division, 125, 250, 251;
    Normandy, 264, 266, 269, 271, 277, 278,
    280, 293; 301, 302, 303; Holland, 304;
    battles of the Maas, 313, 316; Rhineland
    battle, 325, 333; Rhine crossing, 350;
    Germany, 353, 357, 358; Recce. Regt., 282,
    351, 358
  18th Division, 93, 101, 105
  36th Division, 406
  43rd Division, 280, 334, 361
  49th Division, 298
  50th (Northumbrian) Division, 53, 57, 163, 164,
    166
  51st (Highland) Division, 18, 28, 40; France
    (1940), 41, 42, 43, 44; Saar front, 58;
    south of the Somme, 65; withdrawal to
    St. Valéry, 75; St. Valéry and after, 79;
    the new division, 114, 115, 117; Egypt, 131;
    El Alamein, 135; El Alamein to Enfidaville,
    144; Algeria, 187; Sicily, 190; 248; Nor-
    mandy, 252, 255, 276, 284; St. Valéry and
    Le Havre, 297, 298; 301; Holland, 305;
    battles of the Maas, 307, 314; Nijmegen
    salient, 318; Ardennes, 320; Rhineland
    battle, 325, 334; Rhine crossing, 343, 352;
    Germany, 359, 365; Recce. Regt., 312, 323,
    336
  52nd (Lowland) Division, 332, 338
  53rd (Welsh) Division, 270, 303, 311, 312, 316,
    333
  54th Division, 126, 127
  56th (London) Division, 229, 233
  76th Division, 121
  78th Division, 214
  6th Guards Tank Brigade, 278
  32nd Guards Tank Brigade, 333
  1st Brigade, 173
  1st Commando Brigade, 255
  2nd Brigade, 25; France (1939-40), 34, 42, 43;
    Dunkirk campaign, 45, 48, 49, 53, 55; 118;
    Tunisia, 175, 177; Pantelleria, 183; Anzio,
    224, 225, 230; A/Tk. Coy., 38, 43, 48, 50,
    53, 54, 55
  3rd Brigade, 46, 177, 180, 183, 225, 226, 231,
    235
  4th Brigade, 375, 379, 383, 384

BRITISH ARMY—continued
  5th Brigade, 370, 371, 375, 379, 383
  6th Brigade, 379, 384
  13th Brigade, 56
  23rd Armoured Brigade, 153, 154, 167, 199, 208
  24th Armoured Brigade, 143
  24th Guards Brigade, 173, 178, 180, 225
  27th Brigade, 122
  44th Brigade, 266, 284, 303, 334, 342, 357
  46th Brigade, 266, 357
  66th Brigade, 241, 242
  143rd Brigade, 56
  151st Brigade, 57, 198
  152nd Brigade, 28, 68, 70, 75, 78, 133, 142, 143,
    198, 200, 206, 213, 285, 297, 298, 327, 352,
    360
  153rd Brigade, 18, 28, 40; France (1940),
    42, 43; Saar front, 59, 64, 65; south of
    the Somme, 63, 72; withdrawal to St. Valéry, 75;
    A/Tk. Coy., 82; the new brigade, 115;
    Egypt, 131; El Alamein, 135; 144, 145,
    147, 148; Buerat, 150; 151, 158, 159;
    Mareth, 161, 162, 164, 165; 166; Sfax, 170;
    Garci hills; 171, 188, 189, 190; Sicily landing,
    194; 195, 198; Vizzini, 199; 201; Sferro, 203,
    207, 208; 213, 217, 218; Normandy, 253, 255,
    261, 262; pursuit to the Seine, 285, 288, 289;
    St. Valéry and Le Havre, 297, 298; 300, 305;
    Holland, 306; battles of the Maas, 307, 312,
    315; Ardennes, 321; Rhineland battle,
    325, 327, 329, 332, 334, 336; Rhine crossing,
    345, 348; 353; Germany, 359, 362
  154th Brigade, 58, 59, 72, 75, 76, 150, 162, 172,
    188, 191, 203, 214, 285, 287, 301, 325, 327,
    364
  158th Brigade, 274, 275
  201st Guards Brigade, 166
  207th Brigade, 125
  216th Brigade, 123
  227th Brigade, 125, 250; Normandy, 266, 272,
    277, 278, 280, 283; pursuit to Seine, 295;
    302; Holland, 303, 304; battles of the Maas,
    312, 316; Rhineland battle, 333, 340;
    Rhine crossing, 350; Germany, 355, 357, 359,
    364, 365
  228th Brigade, 129
  231st (Malta) Brigade, 191, 195, 199

  5th Grenadier Guards, 225
  1st Scots Guards, 186, 225, 232
  1st Irish Guards, 178, 179, 186, 226, 231
  1st Royal Scots, 382
  2nd Royal Scots, 241, 242
  7th Royal Northumberland Fusiliers, 80
  7th Royal Norfolk (Pioneers), 79, 80
  2nd Bedfordshire and Herts, 175
  1/8th Lancashire Fusiliers, 384
  11th Lancashire Fusiliers, 243
  6th Royal Scots Fusiliers, 74, 314, 340
  2nd K.O. Scottish Borderers, 390
  6th K.O. Scottish Borderers, 303
  9th Cameronians, 269, 278
  2nd Royal Inniskilling Fusiliers, 212
  7th Worcestershire, 383
  1st East Surrey, 173
  6th East Surrey, 177

INDEX

BRITISH ARMY—*continued*
1st Duke of Wellington's, 231, 235
4th Royal Sussex, 142
1st Hampshire, 202
2nd Hampshire, 25
2nd South Lancashire, 387
2nd Dorsetshire, 384
7th Welch, 275
1st Black Watch, 11, 67, 68, 79, 141, 262, 327
4th Black Watch, 28, 61, 62, 73, 76
4th/5th Black Watch, 18
5th Black Watch, 114, 115, 135, 136, 137, 138, 150, 159, 164, 165, 194, 195, 198, 199, 200, 202, 203, 205, 207, 208, 209, 211, 212, 261, 262, 285, 288, 292, 299, 306, 307, 311, 312, 315, 323, 324, 327, 328, 330, 331, 334, 335, 339, 345, 346, 347, 348, 349, 352, 359
6th/7th Black Watch, 18
7th Black Watch, 261, 262, 327
1st Loyal Regt. (N. Lancs.), 25, 42, 46, 51, 52, 54, 55, 175, 224, 231, 234, 236, 244, 245
2nd Loyal Regt. (N. Lancs.), 96
1st Royal Berkshire, 384
1st Q.O. Royal West Kent, 17
4th Q.O. Royal West Kent, 395
1/7th Middlesex, 161, 201
2nd North Staffordshire, 25, 42, 46, 48, 51, 52, 53, 175, 183, 222, 224, 233, 234
1st Manchester, 100
7th York and Lancaster, 399
Durham L.I. Beach Defence Coy., 230, 231, 232
2nd Highland L.I., 11
10th Highland L.I., 267, 274, 277, 282, 283, 295, 296, 302, 307, 313, 314, 316, 318, 333, 350, 355, 356, 357, 364
2nd Glasgow Highlanders (H.L.I.), 269
2nd Seaforth Highlanders, 11, 70, 73, 79, 80, 82, 141, 352
4th Seaforth Highlanders, 68, 70, 79
5th Seaforth Highlanders, 285
1st Gordon Highlanders: Home service, 3, 24; Turkey and Thrace, 6, 8; Malta, 8, 9; Egypt, 10; India, 10; Palestine, 12; France (1939-40), 33, 42, 43, 44; Saar front, 59, 64; south of Somme, 67; actions before Abbeville, 67, 68, 70, 71; withdrawal to St. Valéry, 72, 73, 74, 76, 78; St. Valéry and after, 79, 81; the new battalion, 113; 117; Egypt (1942), 131, 133; El Alamein, 135, 137, 141; 144, 147, 148, 149; Buerat, 150; 151; Tripoli, 151, 155, 156; 161, 162, 164, 165, 166; carriers in action, 167; Sfax, 170; Garci hills, 171, 172; Algeria, 187, 188, 189; Sicily landing, 190, 191; 195, 197, 198; Vizzini, 198; 201; Sferro, 203, 206, 208, 210, 211, 212, 213, 215, 216, 217, 218; leave Sicily, 218; 248, 249, 250; Normandy, 251, 255, 256, 257, 259, 260, 261, 263, 276; pursuit to Seine, 284, 285, 286, 288, 289, 290, 291, 292; St. Valéry and Le Havre, 297, 298; 301; Holland, 306; battles of the Maas, 307, 309, 311, 312, 314, 315, 316; Nijmegen salient, 318, 319; 320; Ardennes, 320, 321, 323, 324; Rhineland battle, 325, 327, 330, 331, 332, 335, 336, 339, 342; Rhine crossing, 346, 352; Germany, 360, 361, 363, 365, 366

BRITISH ARMY—*continued*
1st Garrison Bn., Gordon Highlanders, 5
2nd Gordon Highlanders, 4; Home service, 4, 13; Gibraltar, 22; Singapore (1937-39), 22, 87; defence measures, 90, 91, 92, 93; Johore, 93; defence of Singapore, 101; capitulation and after, 110; the new battalion, 124, 125; 250; Normandy, 264, 277; pursuit to Seine, 292; 301, 302; Holland, 303; battles of the Maas, 313, 316; Rhineland battle, 333, 339; Rhine crossing, 350; Germany, 353, 364, 366
3rd (Spec. Res.) Bn. Gordon Highlanders, 4
Depôt Gordon Highlanders, 17, 26; becomes Highland I.T.C., 124
4th Gordon Highlanders, 5, 18, 19, 20, 27, 28; M/G bn., 28, 29, 38; France (1939), 39; Dunkirk campaign, 47, 50, 56; 125. *See also* 92nd (G.H.) A/Tk. Regt. R.A.
5th Gordon Highlanders, 5; amalgamated with 7th Bn., 18 new; 7th Bn. formed, 29; 40, 41; France (1940) 41, 43; Saar front, 61, 62; south of Somme, 67, 68; actions before Abbeville, 69, 71, 73; withdrawal to St. Valéry, 74, 75, 76, 77, 78; St. Valéry and after, 79, 80, 82
5th/7th Gordon Highlanders, 18, 27, 28; battalions divided, 29; the new battalion, 115, 116; 117; Egypt (1942), 131, 133; El Alamein, 135, 139, 141, 143; 145, 147, 148, 150, 151, 154; Tripoli, 155, 156, 157, 158, 159, 162; Mareth, 163, 165; 166, 169, 170; Garci hills, 171; Algeria, 188, 189, 190; Sicily landing, 194; 195, 197, 198, 200; Sferro, 201, 205, 214, 215; leave Sicily, 218; 248, 249; Normandy, 252, 253, 263, 264, 276; pursuit to the Seine, 284, 288, 289; St. Valéry and Le Havre, 297, 299; Holland, 306; battles of the Maas, 307, 311, 312, 314; Nijmegen salient, 318, 319; 330; Ardennes, 320, 322, 323, 324; Rhineland battle, 325, 329, 331, 332, 333; 342; Rhine crossing, 343; Germany, 359, 360, 362, 363, 365, 366
6th Gordon Highlanders, 5, 18, 19, 20, 27, 28, 29; France (1940), 41, 42, 43; Dunkirk campaign, 45, 48, 51, 52, 53; 117; Algeria, 173; Tunis campaign, 173; 182; Pantelleria, 183; 185; to Italy, 219; Anzio, 220; 235; Florence, 236; Apennines, 237; Palestine, 246; drums recovered, 301
7th Gordon Highlanders, 5, amalgamated with 5th Bn., 18; new battalion formed, 29; 115, 116; become 5th/7th Bn., 115, 116
8th Gordon Highlanders, formed as M/G bn., 29; 119. *See also* 100th (G.H.) A/Tk. Regt. R.A.
9th Gordon Highlanders, formed, 29; 122; India, 367. *See also* 116th Regt. (G.H.) R.A.C.
10th (Home Defence Bn.) Gordon Highlanders, 114, 128; renumbered 30th, 128
11th Gordon Highlanders, 124; becomes new 2nd Bn., 125
30th (Home Defence Bn.) Gordon Highlanders, 128
50th (Holding Bn.) Gordon Highlanders, 124

BRITISH ARMY—continued
No. 1 Shetland Independent Coy. (Gordon Highlanders), 128, 129
92nd (Gordon Highlanders) A/Tk. Regt. R.A., 126
100th (Gordon Highlanders) A/Tk. Regt. R.A., 120, 369; India, 370; reorganised, 371; Kohima, 373; 376; reorganised, 377; Irrawaddy operations, 379; 385, India, 408; re-equipped, 408
116th Regt. (Gordon Highlanders) R.A.C., equipment and training, 368; Burma, 385; operations Irrawaddy—Taungtha—Myingyan, 386, 389, 390, 391, 393, 395; operations Gwebin area, 389, 392; advance to Toungoo, 397; Rangoon, 403; operations Sittang valley, 403
1st Q.O. Cameron Highlanders, 370
2nd Q.O. Cameron Highlanders, 16, 17
4th Q.O. Cameron Highlanders, 70, 71, 73, 74, 79
5th Q.O. Cameron Highlanders, 142, 201, 212 305, 360
1st Royal Ulster Rifles, 346
1st Argyll and Sutherland Highlanders, 25
2nd Argyll and Sutherland Highlanders, 99, 100, 264, 267, 269, 274, 277, 302, 303, 350, 355
7th Argyll and Sutherland Highlanders, 72, 76
8th Argyll and Sutherland Highlanders, 72, 76
11th Argyll and Sutherland Highlanders, 243
7th Rifle Brigade, 181
1st Hertfordshire, 241, 242
1st Kensington, 64, 72
London Scottish, 16, 17
1st London Scottish, 217, 229, 231

8th Parachute Regt., 256

4th Grenadier Guards Tank Bn., 251, 278, 282
4th Coldstream Guards Tank Bn., 249
3rd Scots Guards Tank Bn., 249, 280, 283

5th Royal Inniskilling Dragoon Guards, 50
Royal Scots Greys, 20, 24
15th/19th King's Royal Hussars, 50
25th Dragoons, 404
1st Lothians and Border Horse, 76
8th Royal Tank Regt., 143
40th Royal Tank Regt., 150, 151, 154
46th Royal Tank Regt., 227
50th Royal Tank Regt., 138
116th Regt. R.A.C., see Gordon Highlanders

53rd Field Regt. R.A., 121
75th Field Regt. R.A., 74
127th Field Regt. R.A., 199
131st Field Regt. R.A., 273, 340
9th Coast Regt. R.A., 90
454th Mountain Bty. R.A., 349
14th A/Tk. Regt. R.A., 50
92nd A/Tk. Regt. See Gordon Highlanders
100th A./Tk. Regt. See Gordon Highlanders
122nd (R. Warwickshire) A./Tk. and L.A.A. Regt. R.A., 371, 406, 407
168th A./Tk. Bty. R.A., 371, 406

BRITISH ARMY—concluded
321st A./Tk. Bty. R.A., 371, 406
238th Field Coy. R.E., 220, 231

Royal Marines, 208
Royal Marine Commando, 221
B.B.C., 235, 315
Brooke, Lieut.-Gen. (Field-Marshal) Sir A., 39, 114, 131, 155, 342
Brooke, Lieut. B., 72
Brooks, Lieut. (5th/7th Bn.), 201
Brown, Capt. ' Bert ', R.A.M.C., 322
Brown, Lieut. C., 261
Brown, Lieut. E. S., 315
Brown, Lieut.-Col. P. W., cds. 2nd Bn., 5, 13; cds. Depôt, 17
Brown, Pte, (5th/7th Bn.), M.M. 217
Brownlee-Lamont, Lieut. K., 302, 303
Bruce, Lieut. A., 144
Bruce, Lieut.-Col. R., cds. 7th Bn., 18
Buchanan, Capt. J. W., 351
Buchanan-Smith, Lieut.-Col. A. D., cds. 5th/7th Bn., 27; cds. 5th Bn., 62; cds. 9th Bn., 123
Buerat, action near, 150
' Buffaloes ', 314, 343, 345, 346, 357
Bullen-Smith, Major-Gen. C., cds. 51st Div., 217
Bunton, 2nd-Lieut. P. H., 237
Burgess-Allen, Pte. (5th/7th Bn.), M.M., 217
Burn, Lieut.-Col. H.P., cds. 1st Bn., 9, 10; cds. Depôt, 17
Burnett, Lieut.-Col. J. L. G., cds. 2nd Bn., 14, 15. See also Burnett, Sir J.
Burnett, Sir J., of Leys, Bt., 15; Colonel of Regt., 30; visits Gordon battalions, 40, 114, 115, 116, 121, 249
Burnett, Capt. K. M., 92
Burnett, Major G. A., 373
Burnett, Major P., 371
Burney, Lieut.-Col. (Brigadier) G.T., cds. 2nd Bn., 17, 23; cds. 153rd Bde., 40, 41, 42, 58, 68, 72, 74, 77, 83; death of, 84; cds. 27th Bde. (1939), 122
Burrell, 2nd-Lieut. P.G., 349
Busch, Field-Marshal E. von, 359

Cable, Lce.-Cpl. (1st Bn.), M.M., 149
Caen, capture of, 260
Caithness, Earl of. See Sinclair, Major (Brigadier) J.R.
Cameron, Lieut. A. A., 350
Campbell, Lieut. A. D., 384
Campbell, 2nd-Lieut. D. I., 92
Campbell, Major G., R. A., 273, 358
Campbell, Capt. G. H., 373, 375
Campbell, Lieut.-Col. J. A. cds. 100th Regt. 369, 377, 408
Campbell, Major V., 82
Cape Passero landing, 192
Carr, Brigadier L., 25
Catania plain, advance into, 203
Cessford, Lieut. E. W., 245
Chamberlain, Rt. Hon. N., 26, 33
Chanak, 9
Chappell, Lieut. A., 315

INDEX

Cherbourg, capture of, 271
Chindit expedition, second, 368
Christie, Capt. H. L., 85
Christie, Major R. N., 63, 64
Churchill, Rt. Hon. W. S., 26, 45, 131, 155, 342
Churchill tanks, 117, 126, 278, 283, 317
Clapham, Lieut.-Col. J. B., cds. 6th Bn., 235, 246
Clark, Major (Lieut.-Col.) J., cds. 5th Bn., 64, 71, 73, 76, 77, 81, 83
Clay, Capt. C. R., 306
Cochrane, Major, R. A., 157
Codrington, H.M. destroyer, 55
Collard, Capt. O. E. J. G., 376
COLONIAL FORCES—
  28th East African Bde., 389, 392
  King's African Rifles, 392
  1st Malaya Bde., 90, 109
  2nd Malaya Bde., 89, 90, 92, 100, 101
  Malay Regt. 22
Colville, Lieut.-Col. (Brigadier) E. C., cds. 2nd Bn., 250, 264, 267, 271 ; cds. 227th Bde., 272, 284, 305, 359
Colville, Capt. F. J., 82
Comines canal, action on, 56
Compulsory Training Act, 28
Condé, General, 64
Congreve, General Sir. W., V.C., 10
Coupar, Lieut. J. B., 338
Coutts, Pipe-Major (116th Regt.), 369
'Cover plan' (Sicily), 188
Cowan, 2nd-Lieut. R. G., 287
Cowie, Sergt. (116th Regt.), 391, 399
Craig, 2nd-Lieut. D. A., 366
Craig, Lieut. K. M., 142
Craig, Major P. W., 386
Craufurd, Major A., 6
Crawford, Capt. G. J., Capetown Highrs., 233
Crewdson, Capt. J. S., 180, 182
Crichton, Capt. D., 85
Cumberlege, Major (Lieut.-Col.) R. A., cds. 100th Regt. 408, 409
Cumming-Bruce, Major (Brigadier) Hon. H. C. H.-T., cds. 1st Bn., 262 ; cds. 153rd Bde., 286, 289 ; cds. 1st Bn., 291, 297, 319
Cunningham, Cpl. (1st Bn.), M.M., 320
Crocodile tanks, 278, 279, 312, 314, 315, 316, 336, 340, 351, 361

Dale, Cpl. A., M.M., 366
Davidson, Lieut.-Col. K. C., cds. 11th Bn., 124, 125
Davies, Major R. F., 330, 331
Dawson, Capt. D. R., 276
Delmenhorst, situation at, 362
de Mier, Lieut. W., 104, 105
Dempsey, General Sir M., 250, 365
Dendre river, withdrawal from, 49
Denniston-Sword, Lieut. (1st Bn.), 70
'Desert Victory' film, 171
Destroyer Flotilla, 4th, 22
Dewar, Major W. C., cds. 116th Regt., 403
de Winton, Major (Lieut.-Col.) R. W. M., cds. 5th/7th Bn., 212, 214 ; cds. 2nd Bn., 296 304, 313, 317, 350, 359 ; D.S.O. and bar, 366
de Winton, Lieut. P., 85
Dey, Capt. W. G., 164

Diack, Capt. W., 68
Djebel Bou Aoukaz, action near, 178
Dill, Lieut.-Gen. Sir J., 42
DOMINION FORCES—
  Australia :
    8th Div., 90, 93, 105
    9th Div., 135
    22nd Bde., 99, 103, 105, 106
    27th Bde., 95, 96, 98, 99
    5th Bn. (Victorian Scottish), 21
    2/26th Bn., 96, 97, 98, 99, 107
    2/27th Bn., 96
    2/30th Bn., 98, 99, 108
  Canada :
    First Army, 307, 312, 325
    II Corps, 285, 293
    1st Div., 41, 191, 195, 198
    3rd Div., 253
    7th Bde., 253
    48th Highlanders, 21, 24, 41
    75th Toronto Scottish, 41
    Cameron Highlanders, 329
  New Zealand :
    2nd Div., 135
  South Africa :
    1st Div., 133, 143
    Capetown Highlanders, 21
Dommel, passage of river, 307
Donald, Lieut. A. P., 291
Donald, Capt. G., 179, 182
Donald the Goose, 218
Douglas, Capt. (5th/7th Bn.), 164
Dress, 11, 14, 15, 16, 19, 35, 41, 366, 371
Drums, recovery of : 2nd Bn., 16 ; 6th Bn., 301 ; 5th Bn., 366
du Boulay, Major M. H. H., 141, 172 ; cds. 5th/7th Bn., 289 ; 306 ; M.C., 216
Duffus, Lieut. J. G., 369
Duke, Major (2nd Bn.), 96, 97
Duke Major (2nd Bn.: from W. Yorks), 271, 303
Duncan, Major J., 379
Duncan, 2nd-Lieut. N., 64
Duncan, Pte. (1st Bn.), 163
Dunkirk, withdrawal to, 53, 56 ; operations in perimeter, 54, 57 ; evacuation from 55, 57
Dunlop, 2nd-Lieut. J. I. R., 38, 82
Durban hospitality, 367, 370
Dutch Army, capitulation of, 47
Duthie, Lieut. G., 257
Dyle, march to river, 45 ; operations on, 46, 48 ; withdrawal from, 48

Eagle, H.M. aircraft-carrier, 10
Ebersdorf, action at, 363
Edgar, Lieut. I., 338
Edward VII, H.M. King, 24, 30
Edward VIII, H.M. King, 24, 27
Egypt (1934), 10 ; (1936), 22
Eisenhower, General, 166, 186, 249, 251
El Alamein, battle of : plan, 133 ; objectives, 135 ; course of, 135
El Suera, affair near, 150
Elbe, passage of the, 357
Elsmie, Capt. (2nd Bn.) 96
E.N.S.A., 188, 297
Erskine, Lieut. J. W., 234

416   LIFE OF A REGIMENT

Escaut river, withdrawal from, 52
Esch, action near, 307
Estry, action at, 282
Europa, s.s., 365
Evans, Major S. F., 371
Evens, Major R. G. K., 327; cds. 5th/7th Bn., 338, 345; M.C., 320
'Exercise Blackcock', 250
'Exercise Eagle', 127
'Exercise Pack', 37
Exeter, H.M. cruiser, 22

Fagalde, General, 41
Fairlie, Lieut. D. M., 295, 304
Farquhar, Capt. (2nd Bn.), 96, 99, 100
Farquharson, 2nd Lieut. I. S., 48
Fausset-Farquhar, Major (Lieut.-Col.) H. A. F., cds. 1st Bn., 142, 153, 156, 187, 193, 198, 199, 202 208, 209, 213, 215, 217, 248; D.S.O. and bar, 216
Fawcett, Pte. (2nd Bn.), M.M., 366
Ferme du Chauvaimont, 322
Findlay, Lieut. N. G., 404
Findlay, Sergt. (5th/7th Bn.), 216
Finlayson, R.Q.M.S. (100th-122nd Regt.), 372
Fisher, Lieut. (5th/7th Bn.), 345
Fleming, Major A. G. I., 178, 179, 180
Florence, operations in, 236
Follett, Major (2nd Bn.), 303
Footballs, gift of, 39
Forbes, Lieut. (5th/7th Bn.), 161
Forbes, Lieut, G. C., 257
Forbes-Robertson, Lieut.-Col. J., V.C., cds. 2nd Bn., 15, 16, 21
Fordyce, Lieut. J. W. S., 180, 227
Fort Ste. Addresse, 299
'Forth Bridge', 273, 275
Fortune, Lieut.-Col., A. S., cds. 6th Bn., 20, 27
Fortune, Major-General V. M., cds. 51st Div., 39, 42, 45, 64, 72, 73, 74, 75, 76, 77, 78, 79, 81, 83, 84
Foster, 2nd-Lieut. R. T., 287
Foster, Cpl. (5th/7th Bn.), 259
Frary, Capt. E. J., 331
Fraser, Sergt. J., 259; M.M., 320
Fraser, C.S.-M. (5th/7th Bn.), 207
Fraser, 2nd Lieut. R., 43
Fraser, Lieut. W. G., 328
Frazer, Lieut. (Capt.) E. F., 139, 161, 163, 172; D.S.O., 139
FRENCH ARMY—
  First Army, 47, 48, 52
  Second Army, 65
  Third Army, 64
  Ninth Army, 47, 51, 61
  Tenth Army, 67, 75, 76
  IX Corps, 67, 75, 76
  2nd Armoured Div., 68
  31st Div., 68, 69, 71, 75
  40th Div., 75
  4th Dragoons, 38
  34th Regt., 59
  48th Regt., 44
Frobisher, H.M. cruiser, 16
Frontier civil duties, 32, 44
Fuller, Lieut. B. W., 316

Gairioch, S.-M. D., 149
Gall, Lieut. H. McR., 63, 74
Gall, Capt. M. C., 260
Galician piper, 12
Gallop, Lieut. J. E. J., 257, 287, 338
Gamelin, General, 34, 35, 52, 64
Gammie, Lieut. (Major) J. I., 137, 307, 315, 331; M.C., 362
Garci hills, operations in, 171
Garioch, Lieut. H., 228
Garioch, C.S.-M. (6th Bn.), 180
Greenhill Gardyne, Lieut.-Col. A. D., cds. 2nd Bn., 4, 5
Greenhill Gardyne, Capt. D., 144
Garland, Boy, 15
Gavin, Capt. I. S., 407
Geddes, Lieut.-Col. G. P., cds. 5th/7th Bn., 20, 27
Gennep, action at, 329
George V, H.M. King: inspects 4th Bn., 20; Silver Jubilee, 22, 24, 26, 27; death of, 24
George VI, H.M. King: Coronation, 23, 24, 27; 24, 25; visits troops, 39, 40, 117, 189, 235, 249, 251
GERMAN ARMY—
  Seventh Army, 291
  326th Div., 277
  Hermann Goering Div., 175, 199, 205
  8th Parachute Div., 348
  15th Panzer Grenadier Regt., 352
  18th Parachute Regt., 351
  I/962nd Regt., 179
Gibraltar, reunion at, 12, 22
Gilchrist, Capt. A. H., 261, 277
Gill, Sergt. (100th Regt.), B.E.M., 121
Gillis, Lieut. S. A., 212
Gilmour, Lieut. G. (Canada), 260
Gilmour, Lieut. (5th/7th Bn.), 165
Glass, Lieut. E. D. (Canada), 287
Glennie, Lieut. H. W., 262
Glennie, Major J. M. 171, 198, 218, 236
Gloster, Major. T. A., 341
Gloucester, H.R.H. the Duke of (Colonel-in-Chief): presents colours, 1st Bn.; 24; 30; visits Gordon units, 35, 39, 44, 114, 116, 118, 126, 249; his message to the Regt. (Aug. 1945), 410
Goch, capture of, 334
Goodwin, Pte. F., M.M., 126
Gordon, Major D. W., 70
Gordon, Major E. J., 230
Gordon, Lieut. G., 361
Gordon, Lieut. H. A., 139; M.C., 139
Gordon, Lieut.-Col. J. H. McI., cds. 4th Bn., 19, 20; cds. 8th Bn., 29; cds. 10th Bn., 119, 128
Gordon, Major W. B., 387, 389
Gordon, Lce.-Cpl. (1st Bn.), 140
Gordon Bennett, Major-Gen., 105, 107, 109
Gordon Highlanders Regimental Association, 21
Gordon Highlanders Club (Aberdeen), 21
Gorna Lunga river, 201
Gort, Lord, V.C., C-in-C. B.E.F., 35, 39, 48, 52, 53; High Commr., Palestine, 246
Gothic Line, 237
Gould, Lieut. (5th/7th Bn.), 133
Grace, Lieut. E. N., 232; M.C., 229
Graham, Brigadier (Major-Gen.) D. A. H. cds. 153rd Bde., 137, 140, 142, 155, 158, 188

INDEX

417

Graham, Major (Col.) W. J., cds. Depôt, 18, 26 ; cds. 2nd Bn., 23, 88, 89, 91
Graham, Pte. (1st Bn.), M.M., 149
Grandchamp (river Vie), action at, 288
Grant, Capt. (Major) J., 202, 206, 207 ; killed, 283 ; M.C. and bar, 216
Grant, Lieut. W. M., 161
Grant, Sergt. (1st Bn.), 163
Grant-Peterkin, Lieut.-Col. (Brigadier) J. A., cds. 1st Bn., 319 ; cds. 153rd Bde., 327 ; cds. 1st Bn., 338, 348, 349 ; wounded, 349 ; cds. 1st Bn., 350, 363, 366
Grant tanks, 368
Gray, Lieut. G. M., 309, 350
Gray, Tpr. (116th Regt.), 393
Grendon, Capt. A. W., 304
Grieve, Lieut. R., 137
Grigg, Sir. J., (S. of S. for War), 117, 189
Grose, Major (2nd Bn.), 357
Grosset, Pte. (2nd Bn.), M.M., 366
Grover, Major-Gen. J. M. L., cds. 2nd Div., 372
Groves, Lce.-Cpl. (1st Bn.), 72
Guerat el Atach, action near, 175
Guerilla Force No. 136, 405
Gustav Line, 220
Gwebin area, operations in, 389, 392

Hadden, Pte. (6th Bn.) M.M., 231
Haffen, capture of, 351
Hall, Lieut. (100th Regt.), 374, 375
Halleron, Lieut. V. M., 349
Hamilton, General Sir Ian S. M., 17, 21, 22, 26 ; relinquishes Colonelcy, 30 ; birthday party, 249
Hamilton, Lieut.-Col. J. M., cds. 1st Bn., 12, 25, 26
' Hammerforce ', 151
Harder, Lieut. D., 144
Hardy, Cpl. (1st Bn.) M.M., 320
Harington, General Sir C., 8, 22
Harman, Lieut. R. A. D., 407
Harris, Sergt. C., M.M., 226
Harrison, 2nd-Lieut. H. E., 336
Harvey, Lieut. (2nd Bn.), 341
Hay, Major (Lieut.-Col.) J. E. G., cds. 1st Bn., 141, 142 ; cds. 5th/7th Bn., 164 ; wounded, 194 ; cds. 5th/7th Bn., 214 ; wounded, 276 ; D.S.O., 256
Hay, Major (Lieut.-Col.) J. M., 137 ; cds. 1st Bn., 140 ; wounded, 141
Hay, 2nd-Lieut. P. B., 61, 80
Heath, Lieut. G. J., 309
Henderson, Lieut.-Col. R. L. J., cds. 4th Bn., 20, 27
Henderson, Major R. cds. 2nd Bn., 293, 295
Henderson, Capt. (5th/7th Bn.), 288, 290
Hendry, Lieut. W. J., 390, 391
Hewitt, Lieut. W. J., 360
Heyen, affair at, 332
' Highland Laddie ', 21
Hindenburg, President, 17
Hitchcock, Lieut. J. H. (Canada), M.C., 305
Hitler, Adolf, 17, 26, 33, 34, 227, 320 ; death known, 358, 363
Hitler Jugend, 353, 28
Hogg, Capt. R. G., 304

Holmes, Capt. W. A., 51 ; M.C., 126
Holmes, 2nd Lieut., 242
Holt, Lieut. E., 399
Honour, Sergt. (1st Bn.), 309
Hopkins, 2nd. Lieut. (Capt.), F. G., 291, 331
Hornsby, Lieut. (2nd. Bn.), 342
Horrocks, Lieut.-Gen. Sir B., 325, 348, 350, 365
Howard Kerr, Lieut.-Col., 309
Howarth, Lieut. D., 287
Howitt, Lieut. C. C., 337
Hubermont, affair at, 323
Hudson, Brigadier C. E., V.C., 25
Hughes, Capt. J., 387, 404
Hughes, 2nd-Lieut. (5th Bn.), 83
Hunter-Blair, Lieut.-Col. D. W., cds. 7th Bn., 116
Huntly, Marquess of, 26
Hutcheon, Lieut. (Major), 49, 228, 229
Hutchins, Major C. M. D., 72, 82
Hutchinson, Major C. H., 267, 271, 272, 282, 304
Hutchinson, Pte. (5th/7th Bn.), 286
Hyland, Pte. J., 211 ; M.M., 217

Ihler, General, 77, 81
India, 10 ; invasion of, 368
INDIAN ARMY—
 Fourteenth Army, 379, 385
 IV Corps, 385, 403
 XXXIII Corps, 372
 4th Division, 144
 5th Division, 395, 397
 7th Division, 375, 385, 386, 391
 17th Division, 385, 389, 391, 397
 19th Division, 384
 20th Division, 381, 384
 44th Armoured Division, 368
 5th Brigade, 171
 8th (Bareilly) Brigade, 11
 9th Brigade, 402
 12th Brigade, 87, 105
 22nd Brigade, 99
 33rd Brigade, 375
 48th Brigade, 403
 63rd Brigade, 404
 64th Brigade, 404
 98th Brigade, 403
 100th Brigade, 381
 114th Brigade, 386
 123rd Brigade, 399
 161st Brigade, 395, 396
 255th Tank Brigade, 368, 403
 5th Horse, 406
 7th Cavalry, 397, 400, 402
 9th Probyn's Horse, 368, 402, 406
 16th Cavalry, 397, 405
 1/2nd Punjab Regt., 23
 7/2nd Punjab Regt., 394
 4/4th Bombay Grenadiers, 391, 396, 397
 1/5th Mahratta L.I., 241, 242
 4/6th Rajputana Rifles, 171
 6/7th Rajput Regt., 405
 3/9th Jat Regt., 297
 5/10th Baluch Regt., 405
 1/11th Sikhs, 389, 391
 4/14th Punjab Regt., 387

INDIAN ARMY—concluded
1/15th Punjab Regt., 403
3/15th Punjab Regt., 235
4/15th Punjab Regt., 390, 391, 394, 395, 396
6/15th Punjab Regt., 405
2/17th Dogra Regt., 92, 100
24th Punjabis, 6
1st Burma Rifles, 390, 391, 392
4/1st Gurkha Rifles, 389, 390, 392, 393, 394
2nd Gurkha Rifles, 11
1/3rd Gurkha Rifles, 404, 405
4/4th Gurkha Rifles, 404
4/5th R. Gurkha Rifles, 386, 395, 396
1/9th Gurkha Rifles, 171
4/10th Gurkha Rifles, 381
1st Mysore Infantry, 93
Indian National Army (' Jiffs '), 394, 401
Inglis, Capt. (5th/7th Bn.), 286
Innes, Major (2nd Bn.), 96
Innes, 2nd-Lieut. D. A., 62
Ireland, 3, 4, 13, 15
Irrawaddy: passage west of Mandalay, 383; at Nyaungu, 386; operations south of river, 384; operations Nyaungu, area, 389, 390, 395
Ironside, General Sir E., C.I.G.S., 39
Ironside, Lieut. K. A. J., 233
Irvine, Major (Lieut.-Col.) C. F., 286, 305; cds. 5th/7th Bn., 321, 335, 338, 353, 364, 366; M.C., 320
Irvine, Capt. K. J., 273, 305
Irvine, Lieut. R. H., 108
Irwin, Cpl. (1st Bn.), M.M., 161
' Island ', Alter Rhine, 345
' Island ', Nijmegen, 318
Ison, Sergt. (1st Bn.), M.M., 320
Italy, German surrender in, 359

Jackson, Lieut. J., 137
Jacob, General Sir C., 10
Jaffray, C.S.-M. W., M.M., 320
Jamieson, Capt. (5th/7th Bn.), 286, 289
Japan, surrender of, 406
JAPANESE ARMY—
33rd Army, 401
31st Div., 373
Jeffrey, Lieut. (2nd Bn.), 355
' Jiffs ', 394
Johnson, Lieut. T. A. S., 304
Johnson, 2nd-Lieut. R., 393
Johnston, Lieut.-Col. R. W. F., cds. 8th Bn., 119; 100th Regt., 120, 371
Johnstone, Lieut.-Col. P. J., cds. 6th Bn., 246
Johore, operations in, 93

' Kangaroos ', 307, 313, 316, 340, 362
Kanglatongbi, reunion at, 369, 377
Keogh, Capt. P. J., 203; M.C., 216
Kiddie, Lieut. A. B., 270
Kilt, wearing of, 35, 41, 145, 155, 216, 301, 366
Knight, Pte. (1st Bn.), 72
Kohima, battle of, 373
' Kris Column ', 404, 405
Kroppelshagen-Fahrendorf, 359
Kyle, Capt. (1st Bn.), 337

Lamb, Cpl. (6th Bn.), 178
Land, help on the, 117, 119, 122, 127
Langham, 2nd-Lieut. M. S., 64
Lawrance, Capt. J. M., 89
Lawrence, Miss Gertrude, 299
Lawrence, Capt. J. R., 407
Lawrie, Capt. W. H., 63, 64, 80
Lawrie, Lieut. N., 179, 180; M.C., 180
Leal, R.S.-M. (1st Bn.), 72
le Brun, President, 37
Leckie, Lieut. J. 231; m/d., 229
Leckie, 2nd-Lieut. P.B., 103, 106
Ledingham, Lieut.-Col. J. L., cds. 6th Bn., 27, 42
Lee tanks, 368
Lees, Lieut. E. A., 242
Lees, Major R. G., 111
Leese, Lieut.-Gen. Sir O., 155, 159, 194
Le Havre, capture of, 298
le Mesnil Andé, action at, 295
Lewis, Pte. F., M.M., 217
Lewis, Sergt. S., D.C.M., 126
Lewis, Capt. and QrMr., W. G., 358; M.C., 359
Lidbury, 2nd-Lieut. (100th Regt.), 375
Lindsay, Capt. and QrMr. J. M. G., M.B.E., 366
Lindsay, Major M., cds. 5th/7th Bn., 277; cds. 1st Bn., 286; 311, 312; cds. 1st Bn., 321, 323, 327, 328, 329, 330, 336, 337, 349; D.S.O., 339
Lindsay-White, Lieut. J. A., 387
Linklater, Capt. (Major) L. G., 368, 389
' Lion Crossing ', 206
Lisieux, action at, 289
Littlefair, Sergt. J., D.C.M., 366
Local Defence Volunteers (Home Guard), 117
Lomas, Tpr. J., 399; M.M., 399
Longan, Sergt. (5th/7th Bn.), M.M.; D.C.M., 320
Louis, Joe, 237
Lowe, 2nd-Lieut. B. D., M.B.E., 121
Lubeck, occupation of, 364
Lucas, General 221, 222
Lüneburg Heath, German surrender at, 359
Lumsden, Major A., 309, 330, 347, 348; M.C., 339

Maas river, northern advance to, 307; eastward advance to, 314
Macandrew, Lieut. P., 208
McAndrew, Lieut., 157
McCallum, Lieut. (5th/7th Bn.), 210
McClintock, Major (Lieut.-Col.) S. R., 7; cds. 2nd Bn., 16, 17
McColl, Lieut. D. A., 262
McConnachie, Sergt. J., M.M., 182
McConnell, Lce.-Cpl. A., M.M., 296
McCormick, Lieut. H. F., 316
MacDonald, 2nd-Lieut. A. K., 349
MacDonald, Capt. E. R., 278
MacDonald, Capt. K. J. R., 347
McDonald, Lieut. G. C., 304
MacFarlane, Lieut. (2nd Bn.), 341
MacFarlane, Lieut. (Capt.) W. M., 141, 209; M.C., 149
McGillivray, Lieut. (Capt.) J. F., 368
McGregor, Lce.-Sergt. J., M.M., 305

INDEX

M'Hardy, Lieut. W., 240
McIntosh, Lieut. (Capt.) A. R., 256, 345
McIntosh, Capt. G., R.A.M.C., 177
McIntosh, Capt. (5th/7th Bn.), M.C., 149
Mackintosh-Walker, Brigadier R., 272
McIntyre, Lieut. H. R., 239
McIntyre, Lieut. W., 351
McIntyre, Lieut. (Capt.) (2nd Bn.), 278, 302
Mackay, Major D. I. S., 373
McKay, Sergt. J., M.M., 217
McKibbin, Lieut. H. D., 323
Mackinnon, Lieut.-Col. L., cds. 4th Bn., 18
Mackinnon, Sergt. R., 108
Mackenzie-Smith, Capt. A., 382; M.C., 383
McKenzie, Pte, A., M.M., 320
Maclaren, Lieut. J. T., 260
MacLean, Major L. I. G., 300, 321, 327; M.C., 320
McLean, Pte. J., M.M., 296
M'Masters, Lieut. J., 232
MacMillan, Major-Gen. G. H. A., cds. 15th Div., 251, 271; cds. 51st Div., 350, 365
MacMillan, Capt. (Major) W. R., 199, 298
M'Millan, Lieut. (6th Bn.), 241
McNeill, Capt. (1st Bn.), 139
McNair, Capt., R.A., 349
McPhail, Capt. A. N., R.A.M.C., 267, 273; M.C., 305
McPhee, Cpl. (4th Bn.), M.M., 126
MacPherson, Lieut. J. A., 329, 338
MacPherson, Lieut. R. W. G., 338
McPherson, Provost-Sergt. (5th/7th Bn.), M.M., 256
M'Pherson, Pte. R., 177
McRae, Lieut. J., 332
Macready, General Sir N., Bt., 13
Maddon, Lieut.-Col. B. J., cds. 1st Bn., 366
Maginot Line, 58
Main, Lieut. and QrMr., W. E., 108
Malaria, 185, 273, 385
Malaya, invasion of, 91; retreat in, 92
Malcolm, Major (Lieut.-Col.) G. E., 25; cds. 1st Bn., 115
Malta, 8, 9
Mandalay, capture of, 384
Manson, Lieut. A. F., M.C., 362
Mareth Line operations, 163
Marsh, Lieut. J. W., 259
Martin, Capt. D. W., 309, 311
Martin, Lieut. J., 260
Martin, Lieut. S., 178
Mathieson, Sergt. W., 401, 404; M.M., 404
Maxwell, Brigadier D. S., 95, 99
Meiktila, capture of, 397
Mennim, Pte. (6th Bn.) M.M., 229
Messervy, Lieut.-Gen. F. W. 403
Methven, Lieut. J. K. M., 232
Michie, R.S.-M. A., 257
Miletello, advance on, 200
Millar, Capt. L. W., 150; M.C., 161
Miller, Sergt. J., 240
Milne, Lieut.-Col. A., cds. 4th Bn., 126
Milne, Capt. (Lieut.-Col.) A. M., 375, 379; cds. 100th Regt., 409
Milne, R.S.M., A. W., 92, 108
Milne, Lieut.-Col. J., cds. 5th/7th Bn., 18, 19
Milne, Field-Marshal Sir G., 19

Milton, C.S.-M. (2nd Bn.), 100
Mitchell, Lieut. G., 285
Mitchell, Pte. (1st Bn.), 85
Moir, Major F. J. R., 404, 405
Moir, Cpl. J., M.M., 229
Moir-Byres, Capt. (2nd Bn.), 97
Molyneux, Sergt. (5th/7th Bn.), 315
Montgomery, General (Field-Marshal) Sir B., 131, 144, 148, 150, 151, 155, 159, 162, 163, 166, 170, 175, 190, 198, 213, 216, 249, 250, 251, 275, 278, 297, 302, 320, 324, 342, 343; accepts German surrender, 359; 365
Morgan, 2nd-Lieut. F. D., 51
Morgan, Lce.-Cpl. W., M.M., 126
Morley, Lieut. C. E., 315
Morrison, Corpl. D., 396; M.M., 396
Morrison, Major G., 330, 332, 347; D.S.O., 339
Morrison, Capt. M., 331
Morrison, 2nd-Lieut. M., 203, 209
Morrison, 2nd-Lieut. (5th Bn.), 63
Morton, Sergt. G., M.M., 234
Mountbatten, Lord Louis, 198, 372, 406
Mounted infantry (1st Bn.), 6, 7
Mu river operations, 381
Muir, Major W. A., 259, 309, 360; M.C., 320
'Mulberry' harbours, 264
Munich agreement, 26
Munro, Capt. and QrMr., C. G., M.M.; M.B.E., 247
Munro, Capt. J. G., 110
Munro, Major J. S. G., 128
Murray, Lieut.-Col. H. (Brigadier), cds. 1st Bn., 114, 138, 140; wounded, 140; 170; cds. 153rd Bde., 188, 189, 198, 201, 202, 203, 205, 206, 213, 217, 255, 259, 262, 286
Murray, Lieut. J. W., 144, 263
Murray, Major L. G., 38, 48, 49, 54, 55
Murray Bissett, Lieut.-Col. W. T., cds. 9th Bn., 29, 123
Mustafa Kemal (Kemal Ataturk), 6, 8

Napier, Capt. (Major) B. C. A., 164; cds. 5th/7th Bn., 194, 197, 205, 208, 209, 210; M.C., 217
Napier, Lieut. J. C., 237
Nederweert-Wessem canal, passage of, 314
Needs, 2nd-Lieut. (1st Bn.), 289
Neish, Major W., cds. Depôt, 17, 18
Neustadt, 365
Nichol, Pipe-Major (2nd Bn.), 251, 301
Nicholson, Major-Gen. C. G. G., cds. 2nd. Div., 369, 377, 408
Nicolson, Lieut. I. B. (100th Regt.), 375
Nimmo, Capt. T. P. B. 233
Niven, Lieut. D. H., 270
Nixon, Lieut. (5th/7th Bn.), 161
Noble, Capt. F. A. C., 373, 382
Norman, Major A. M. B., cds. Depôt, 26
North Russia Relief Force, 4
Northern Combat Area Command (Burma), 368, 385, 406, 407
Norway, operations in, 45

Oates, Lieut. (5th/7th Bn.), 210
O'Brien, Pte. (6th Bn.), 179
O'Connor, Lieut.-Gen. Sir R., 251, 271

Ogilvie, Major J. H., 373
Ogston, Lieut.-Col. C., cds. 1st Bn., 7, 9
O'Morchoe, Lieut.-Col. K. G., cds. 1st Bn., 113, 114
'Operation Corkscrew', 182
'Operation Epsom', 270
'Operation Market Garden', 302
'Operation Noah', 318, 319
'Operation Veritable', 324
Orkney and Shetland Defences, 124
Oisterwijk, affair near, 309

Paget, General Sir B., 117, 121
Palestine, (1934), 12; (1945), 246
Palmer, Lieut. and QrMr. D. J., M.C., 126
Pantelleria, occupation of, 183
Parish, Capt. (Major) A. W., 274, 278, 334; M.C., 275, 296
Pass, R.S.-M. W., M.M., 366
Patch, Lieut.-Gen. A. M., 366
Paterson, Major A., 129
Paterson, Lce.-Cpl. A., m/d, 229
Paterson, Lieut. J., 323, 327
Paterson, Lieut. (2nd Bn.), 340
Paton, Capt. (1st Bn.), 140, 141, 142
Patrick, Lieut. R. A., 350
Patterson, Lieut. (5th/7th Bn.), 201
Pearson, Pte. (5th/7th Bn.), M.M., 217
Peddie, Lieut.-Col. J., cds. 6th Bn., 118, 182, 184, 227, 230, 231, 235; D.S.O., 235
Penang Island, 92
Percival, Lieut.-Gen. A. E., 90, 93, 95, 99, 101, 107, 109
Peterkin, Lieut.-Col. C. D., cds. 4th Bn., 18, 19
Peterkin, Q.M.S. J., 103
Peters, Capt. N., 257
Petrie, Capt. (Major) R. W., 306, 347
Philip, Lieut.-Col. W., cds. 4th Bn., 27, 39
Phillips, Lieut. J. J., 371
Phillips, Admiral Sir Tom, 92
Picard, General, 37
Pickard, Pte. W., M.M., 234
Picton-Warlow, Major (Lieut.-Col.) I., cds. 1st Bn., 10, 11
'Probaireachd Dhomhnuill', 329
Pipe bands, state of, 15, 19, 43, 118, 125, 235, 246, 366, 367, 378, 392
Pirie, Lieut.-Col. P. T., cds. 6th Bn., 42, 46, 119
'Plan D,' 35, 37, 45
Plumer, Field-Marshal Lord, 10
Porter, 2nd-Lieut. A. R., 329, 350
Prince of Wales, H.M. battleship, 91, 92, 123
Princess Beatrix, landing ship, 183
Prisoners of War camps, 85, 86, 110, 112
Pyawbwe, capture of, 397
Promotion, slowness of, 17

Queen Emma, landing ship, 183, 191
Quaich, presentation of, 369

Rae, Lieut. (Major) B. D. M., 151, 309, 347, 365
Rae, Capt. R., 177, 179
Rations in Burma, 396, 403
Reaper, Cpl. J., M.M., 217

Redican, Pte. (5th/7th Bn.), D.C.M., 289
Reekie, Major M. B., 291
Reekie, Lieut. (1st Bn.), 151
Rees, capture of, 346
Rees, Lce.-Cpl. H., M.M., 320
Reichsbreeder, 311
Reichswald, action in, 327
Reid, Capt. (Major) D. R., 291, 329; M.C., 320
Reid, Lieut.-Col. J. N., cds. 7th Bn., 29, 116
Reid, Lieut. V., 48
Reid, Lieut. W., 260
Reinforcements, character of, 184, 188, 213, 230, 264, 275, 285, 288, 290, 296, 301, 305, 318, 319, 350
Rennie, Brigadier (Major-Gen.) T. G., cds. 154th Bde., 189; cds. 51st Div., 277, 297, 299; killed, 350
Renny, Lieut.-Col. (Brigadier) G. D., cds. 5th/7th Bn., 290, 321
Repulse, H.M. battle cruiser, 22, 81, 92
Rhine crossing, 345, 346, 350
Reynolds-Payne, Lieut. (Capt.) G., 232; M.C., 182
Richards, Brigadier G. W., 151, 153, 170, 200
Ritchie, Lieut. D., 74; M.C., 74
Ritchie, Lieut. (Capt.) J. W., 144, 210; M.C. 149 bar to M.C., 217
Ritchie, Pte. (5th/7th Bn.), M.M., 217
Rhodes, Lieut. (1st Bn.), 62; M.C., 62
Robertson, Lieut. G. I., 261
Robertson, Major J. M., 298; M.C., 320
Robertson, Major R. D., cds. Depôt, 18
Robertson, Cpl. (5th/7th Bn.), M.M., 217
Rodger, Lieut. A. (Canada), 349
Rome, occupation of, 235
Rommel, Field-Marshal E., 130, 131, 133, 144, 148, 149, 162
Roper-Caldbeck, Capt. G. R., 103
Rose, Major B. D. M., 352
Rose, 2nd-Lieut. G. R., M.M., 234, 243
Ross, Pte. (5th/7th Bn.), M.M., 217
Rowan-Hamilton, Brigadier G. B., 40
Rowan Robinson, Lieut. C. R., 144; M.C., 149
Rowbotham, Lieut. N. M., 352
Rowton, Major G. A., 371, 407
Royal Guard: Ballater, 5, 14, 24; Sandringham, 128
Royal Scotsman, landing ship, 191
Royal Tournament, 14, 15
Royal Ulsterman, landing ship, 183, 191
Russell, Lieut. J. A. P., 97
Russell Morgan, Lieut.-Col., 283
Rutherford, Rev. D. W., 211; M.C., 216

Saar front, German attacks on, 63, 63; Allied withdrawal on, 64
St. Valéry-en-Caux, withdrawal to, 77, actions round, 80; surrender at, 84; return to, 297
Salter, Lieut. (2nd Bn.), 334
Sanderson, Lieut. J. C., 144
Sanderson, Lieut. K. W., 406
Sanderson, Capt. (5th/7th Bn.), 208
Sandison, 2nd-Lieut. J. F., 103
Satchell, Gnr. J. D., M.M., 375

INDEX

Saunders, Lieut.-Col. H. W. B., cds. 5th/7th Bn., 116, 143, 144, 145; wounded, 157
Schelde—Maas canal, action on, 302
Schloss Calbeck, capture of, 340
Schofield, Lieut. J. G., 338
Scott, Cpl. J., 139
Scott, Lieut. T. McN., 259
Scott, Lieut. (5th/7th Bn.), 286
Scott-Moncreiff, Lieut. D. C., 324
Scott-Raeburn, 2nd-Lieut. (5th Bn.), 63
Scrub typhus, 369
Scutari, 8, 9
Seine, passage of, 295
Seth, Lieut. J. K., 276
Sfax, occupation of, 170
Sferro operations, 207
Shand, Lieut. H., 52
Shankley, Capt. (5th Bn.), 75, 83
Sharp, Capt. J., 136
Sheddon, Pte. (1st Bn.), M.M., 161
Shepherd, Major D., R.A., 243
Sherman tanks, 141, 194, 368, 392
Shropshire, H.M. cruiser, 22
Siam-Burma railway, 110, 111
Siegfried Line, 316, 325, 327, 334
Silver Jubilee (George V), 22, 24, 26, 27
Simpson, Lieut. A. J. M., 396
Simpson, Lieut.-Col. C. J., cds. 1st Bn., 3, 4, 7
Sinclair, Capt. J. G., 285
Sinclair, Major (Brigadier) J. R., cds. 10th H.L.I., 270; cds. 2nd Bn., 272, 273, 274, 275, 282, 283; cds. 153rd Bde., 291, 293, 301, 305, 327, 336, 365, 366; D.S.O., 305
Singapore (1937-39), 22; defence measures, 87; air raids on, 91, 93, 101, 103, 104, 107; invasion of island, 103; capitulation, 110
Sittang valley operations, 402
Skivington, Capt. H. H., 139
Slight, Capt. H. T., 271, 274
Slim, General Sir W., 377, 402
Smith, Capt. G. W. L., 351
Smith, Sergt. H., 104, 105
Smith, Pte. J., M.M., 366
Smith, Major L. B., 239, 241
Smith, Capt. N. B., 391
Smith, Capt. N. L., 332
Smith, Lieut. R. W., 178
Snowball, Capt. E. J. D., 38
Sonsfeld Forest, action at, 351
Sorel-Cameron, Lieut.-Col. J., cds. 5th/7th Bn., 158, 161; wounded, 164
Souter, Major D. W. I., 270
Spanish civil war, 22
Special Air Service, 112
Spence, Capt. D., 296
Stack, Sir Lee, 10
Stansfeld, Capt. J. de B., 37
Stephen, Capt. W., 366
Stephen, 2nd-Lieut. (5th/7th Bn.), 345
Stephenson, Sergt. (1st Bn.), D.C.M., 149
Steuart-Menzies, Lieut.-Col. R., cds. 6th Bn., 19, 20
Stevens, Sergt. (5th/7th Bn.), 307
Stevenson, Lieut.-Col. W. A., cds. 1st Bn., 250, 255, 261; wounded, 262; 264
Stewart, Major D., 129
Stewart, Lieut. F., 259, 260

Stewart, Lieut. J., 136
Stewart, Capt. J. B., 289
Stewart, Lieut. J. M., 6
Stewart, 2nd-Lieut. V. I. D., 106, 109, 110
Stewart, 2nd-Lieut. (2nd Bn.), 317
Stewart, Sergt. (116th Regt.), 391
Stitt, Major (Lieut.-Col.) J. H., 91; cds. 2nd Bn., 92, 95, 96, 98, 104, 106, 107, 108, 109, 111
Stolzenau, 355, 365
Stopford, Lieut.-Gen. M.G.N., 372
Strachan, Pltn. S.-M. (2nd Bn.), 98
Strike duty, 3, 13
Sutherland, Lce.-Sergt., 383; M.M., 383
Syme, Capt. L. W., 212

Tasker, Lieut. W., 351
Tattoo, 44
Taungtha-Myingyan, operations in area, 391, 393, 395
Taylor, Lieut. G. L., 286, 312
Taylor, Lieut. J., 375
Taylor, Cpl. R., M.M., 217
Taylor, Lieut.-Col. R. A. G., cds. 4th Bn., 39, 57, 126
Tedder, Air Chief Marshal Sir A., 249
Telfer, Lieut. S. W., 351
Territorial Army (1920), 5; to be doubled, 28
Territorial Force, 5
Thain, Sergt. J., m/d., 229
' The Balmorals ', 156, 188
' The Cock o' the North ', 21, 145, 157, 329, 381
' The Springs ', action at, 392
' The Tiger and Sphinx ', 20
Thom, Capt. D. A., 366
Thom, Capt. (Major) D. C., 142, 259
Thom, Capt. J. C., R.A.M.C., 276
Thom, 2nd-Lieut. (5th Bn.), 71
Thomashof, action at, 336
Thompson, Capt. G. A., 138, 139
Thompson, Capt. J. H., 334
Thomson, Major A. J., 336
Thomson, Lieut.-Col. (5th Black Watch), 208
Thomson, C.S.-M., (1st Bn.), 140; D.C.M., 161
Thomson, Pte. (2nd Bn.), 108
Thrace, operations in, 9
Toungoo, advance to, 397; action at, 401
Tilburg entered, 313
Tindall, Major R. M. M., 271, 272, 273, 296; M.C., 275, 296
Titterton, Lieut. L., 349
Townley, Sergt. T., M.M., 366
Traill, Capt. E. G. S., M.C., 366
Tregallas, Capt. T. S. T., 232
Tripartite Pact, 87
Tripoli: entered, 154; ceremonial at, 155; dock labour in, 156
Tunis, occupation of, 172; victory parade in, 182
Turkey and Thrace, 6, 8
Tweedie, Lieut.-Col. (2nd A. and S.H.), 264

Uelzen, action at, 355
Underwood, R.S.-M. J., 229
U.S. Army —
    First Army, 278, 293, 321, 324
    Third Army, 324

U.S. Army—*concluded*
  Fifth Army, 234, 237, 242
  Seventh Army, 191, 198, 366
  Ninth Army, 320, 325
  II Corps, 158, 167, 175, 237
  VI Corps, 221, 234
  5th Div., 277
  29th Div., 365
  101st Airborne Div., 318
  2nd Regt., 277
Urquhart, Capt. D. L., 260
Usher, Capt. (Colonel) C. M., 15 ; cds. Depôt, 18 ; cds. 1st Bn., 25, 34, 35, 37

' V ' (flying) bombs, 321
Varley, Brigadier A. L., 107
Ventris, Lieut. I. T. P., 338
Veules-les-Roses, evacuation from, 84 ; return to, 292
Vick, Lieut. D. A., 315
Vizzini, capture of, 199
Vught concentration camp, 314

Waddell, Pte. G., 7 ; R.H.S. medal, 7
Waddell, Lieut. J. W., 230, 241
Wadi Akarit, advance from, 167
Wallace, Lieut. H., 210
Wallace, Major J. F., 51
Walters, Lieut. B. G., 263
Watt, Sergt. A., M.M., 320
Watt, Pte. ' Joker ' (5th/7th Bn.), 290

Wauchope, General Sir A., 12
Wavell, General Sir A., 93, 101, 104, 367
Webster, B.S.-M. (168th Bty.), 407
Weibosch, capture of, 307,
West, invasion in the, 45
Weygand, General, 52, 64
Whitehead, Pte. (5th/7th Bn.), 263
Whitelaw, Capt. (2nd Bn.), 106
Wildeshausen, action at, 360
Wilkie, Pte. (5th/7th Bn.), M.M., 217
Williamson, Capt. (Major) J. C., 228, 233, 240, 241 ; M.C., 229
Williamson, 2nd-Lieut. W., 139
Wilson, Cpl. G., M.M., 229
Wilson-Brown, Capt. S. A., 57 ; M.C., 126
Wimberley, Major-Gen. D. N., cds. 51st Division, 115, 145, 154, 162, 189, 202, 206, 213, 216
Wishart, Capt. J. A. A., 270
Wisley, Lieut. (5th/7th Bn.), 289
Wood, 2nd-Lieut. J. A., 51
Wormald, Lieut. C. P., 144
Wright, Major (Lieut.-Col.) H., cds. 1st Bn., 37, 68, 69, 72, 74, 78, 79, 82
Wright, R.S.-M. (1st Bn.), M.B.E., 216

Yamashita, General, 105
Yamethin, action at, 397, 399
Yeomans, Capt. (5th/7th Bn.), 161

Zig canal, passage of, 315
' Zubza Box ', 373, 376

www.ingramcontent.com/pod-product-compliance
Lightning Source LLC
Chambersburg PA
CBHW061924220426
43662CB00012B/1796